SECOND EDITION

MW01115001

CONTEMPORARY
AMERICAN SOCIETY
AN INTRODUCTION TO THE SOCIAL SCIENCES

SECOND EDITION

CONTEMPORARY AMERICAN SOCIETY
AN INTRODUCTION TO THE SOCIAL SCIENCES

Willard W. Sloshberg
Mercer County College

William C. NesSmith
Florida Junior College at Jacksonville

WEST PUBLISHING COMPANY
St. Paul   New York   Los Angeles   San Francisco

PHOTO/ ILLUSTRATION CREDITS

Chapter 1   p. 4, Cary Wolinsky/Stock Boston; p. 9, Owen Franken/Stock Boston; p. 20, Library of Congress; p. 21, The Bettmann Archive.
Chapter 2   p. 36, by Baron Hugo VanLaWick © National Geographic Society; p. 40, Harry Nelson.
Chapter 3   p. 52, Wide World Photos; p. 54, Alma Blount; p. 55, Christopher S. Johnson/Stock Boston; p. 68, from "Teaching Language to an Ape," by Ann James Premack and David Premack, Scientific American, October 1972, p. 92. Copyright © 1972 by Scientific American, Inc. All rights reserved.
Chapter 4   p. 79, Michael Hayman/Stock Boston; p. 80, Michael Grecco/Stock Boston; p. 82, James Holland/Stock Boston; p. 85, James Holland/Stock Boston.
Chapter 5   p. 103, Library of Congress; p. 110, Frances M. Cox/Stock Boston; p. 112, The Bettmann Archive; p. 116, Martha Bates/Stock Boston.
Chapter 6   p. 131, *The Christian Science Monitor*; p. 135, James Holland/Stock Boston; p. 137, Hazel Hankin/Stock Boston; p. 142, Elizabeth Hamlin/Stock Boston; p. 145, UPI.
Chapter 7   p. 160, Stock Boston; p. 163, Donald Dietz/Stock Boston; p. 172, Ken Robert Buck/Stock Boston; p. 174, Ellis Herwig/Stock Boston.
Chapter 8   p. 194, Nancy Warnecke/*The Tennessean*; p. 198, published by permission of Transaction, Inc. from *Transaction*, Vol. 7, No. 12, p. 29, Copyright © 1970 by Transaction, Inc.; p. 204, Wide World Photos; p. 205, UPI.
Chapter 9   p. 219, Hazel Hankin; p. 220, Wide World Photos; p. 222, UPI, Bettmann; p. 225, Wide World Photos; p. 228, Owen Franken, Berlin Wall; p. 239, J. Berndt/Stock Boston.
Chapter 10   p. 249, Library of Congress; p. 250, Library of Congress; p. 259, Ellis Herwig/Stock Boston; p. 269, James L. Shaffer.
Chapter 11   p. 276, National Archives; p. 280, U.S. Department of Agriculture; p. 287, George W. Gardner/Stock Boston; p. 289, Rosemary Rank/Black Star.

Chapter 12   p. 303, Peter Southwick/Stock Boston; p. 311, William Koechling/Black Star; p. 316, James L. Shaffer; p. 318, James L. Shaffer.
Chapter 13   p. 331, Department of Agriculture; p. 333, The Bettmann Archive; p. 336, R. Norman Matheny/*The Christian Science Monitor*; p. 346, Gordon N. Converse/*The Christian Science Monitor*.
Chapter 14   p. 362, Stock Boston; p. 365, Wide World Photos; p. 372, Wide World Photos; p. 378, Wide World Photos.
Chapter 15   p. 389, The Bettmann Archive; p. 391, Wide World Photos; p. 398, George Malave/Stock Boston; p. 401, U.S. Department of Housing and Urban Development; p. 406, Wide World Photos.
Chapter 16   p. 413, Wide World Photos; p. 418, Culver Pictures; p. 423, Embassy of Israel; p. 428, Ellis Herwig/Stock Boston; p. 436, John Deere & Company.
Chapter 17   p. 444, Peter Menzel/Stock Boston; p. 452, The Bettmann Archive; p. 454, Wide World Photos; p. 460, Frank Hoffman/Black Star.
Chapter 18   p. 472, Federal Reserve Bank of Minneapolis; p. 474, Wide World Photos; p. 477, UPI.
Chapter 19   p. 495, U.S. Denver Mint; p. 498, Wide World Photos; p. 503, U.S. Department of Housing and Urban Development; p. 509, James L. Shaffer.
Chapter 20   p. 521, The Bettmann Archive; p. 524, Washington Post. Reprinted by permission of the D.C. Public Library; p. 530, The Bettmann Archive.
Chapter 21   p. 539, American Philosophical Society; p. 542, © West Publishing Company; p. 548, National Archives.
Chapter 22   p. 567, The Bettmann Archive; p. 570, Wide World Photos; p. 573, © Kathleen Foster/Black Star; p. 577, Library of Congress.
Chapter 23   p. 587, Library of Congress; p. 588, Library of Congress; p. 589, Gabor Demjen/Stock Boston; p. 595, Gale Zucker/Stock Boston.
Chapter 24   p. 609, Wide World Photos; p. 610, UPI; p. 611, UPI; p. 613, Wide World Photos; p. 617, Owen Franken/Stock Boston; p. 619, American Vietnam War Memorial Fund; p. 621, Wide World Photos.

COPYRIGHT © 1983 By WEST PUBLISHING CO.
COPYRIGHT © 1988 By WEST PUBLISHING CO.
50 W. Kellogg Boulevard
P.O. Box 64526
St. Paul, MN 55164–1003

Printed in the United States of America

LIBRARY OF CONGRESS
Library of Congress Cataloging-in-Publication Data

Sloshberg, Willard.
   Contemporary American Society: an introduction to social science
/ Willard Sloshberg, William NesSmith.—2nd ed.
      p.   cm.
   Includes bibliographies and index.
   1. Sociology. 2. United States—Social conditions—1980- 3. United States—Economic conditions—1981- 4. United States—Politics and government—1981-   I. NesSmith, William C. II. Title.
HM51.S59   1988   301'.0973–dc19   87–31029
ISBN 0–314–62483–X   CIP

1st Reprint—1988

Copy Editor: Gordon Andersen
Interior Design: Lucy Lesiak Design
Cover Design: Lois Stanfield
Cover: William Low/The Image Bank

WCN

To Maureen, Vanessa, Katherine, and my parents

WWS

To my old college friend and mentor, Ignatius J. Rielly

CONTENTS

CHAPTER 6

Social Interaction: In Groups and in Collective Behavior 129

CHAPTER 7

Social Stratification 155

CHAPTER 16

Economic Systems and Production   411

CHAPTER 17

Distribution of Product and Profit   443

CHAPTER 18

Government and Economics in the United States   467

CHAPTER 24

International Relations 605

APPENDIX

The Constitution of The United States of America 625

INDEX

643

PREFACE

A basic premise of this book is that the social sciences offer a perspective that is essential for anyone desiring a well-rounded education. American education is returning to fundamentals and should, in our view, include the social sciences as well as language and mathematics.

This book's goal is to provide students with the elements of the social science perspective. That goal has two parts: first, the book must offer that portion of social science knowledge expected of an educated person; the second part of this goal is that of transmitting to the student the attitude and thinking skills used in the social sciences. Exposure to the scientific attitude and an introduction to social science-related skills will, we feel, help the student interpret and evaluate the knowledge he or she is offered. We begin this effort in the first chapter by introducing the basic idea of science and social science. Then, each chapter introduces a skill that is reinforced in other chapters.

We strove to produce a book that was adaptable to the wide diversity of people teaching the Introduction to Social Science course. Teaching this course is indeed a demanding assignment for the many instructors who do not feel comfortable dealing with several disciplines, and this feeling is intensified when those instructors turn to a textbook to find it based on some particular approach with which they are not familiar or comfortable. Indeed, instructors may conclude that the theme of such a social sciences textbook forces unnecessary contortions in the subject matter. This textbook avoids imposing theoretical rigidity upon the introduction to social science. We do not present the disciplines through any "pet" theories, nor do we limit ourselves (and thus the student) to only one viewpoint. Rather, the approach of the book is one that can be adapted to any instructor's theoretical preference. We might say that the book offers the student nutritious and appealing food for thought and growth; the instructor is responsible for providing the additional, distinctive flavor of the material.

The organization of the book allows the instructor to use the material in either a one- or two-term course. The balance between the sociology-psychology-anthropology portion and the economics-political science part ensures a well-rounded introductory experience for the student, and as such divides easily for use in a two-term social science course. The moderate length of the chapters and the separateness of the Special Topics, which can be omitted, allow the book to be easily adapted to a one-term course. The instructor of a one-term course may also decide to delete some of the chapters and still offer a sound introduction to all of the social sciences.

The organization within each chapter is unique. Each chapter opens with a high-interest piece to engage the reader's interest. Next follows the basic chapter content complete with the skill building material. This is followed by a Special Topic which explores an issue—often controversial—related to the chapter. A short, speculative essay on the future pursuing a theme from the chapter is then presented to provoke students into considering the possibilities of change that they may well face in their lifetimes.

Each chapter also includes self-test questions and answers for student self-review, and suggestions for further reading. As important terms are introduced in the text, their definitions are provided in the margin. This is intended to help ensure that the student refers to the definition and thus builds his or her vocabulary. Also found in the margins are problems and questions aimed at reinforcing previously introduced social science skills. These not only refresh the student's memory of the skills, but also the skills relate to the various topics that comprise the social sciences.

This book was written *for the student*, with close attention paid to reading level. Reading level determines the accessibility of a book's content, and we believe that the social sciences are too important to be presented to the typical student on an inappropriate level.

A 30-part television series linked to the text is also available at moderate cost. The series has been tailored specifically to supplement the material contained in the text. Contact West Publishing Company for further information.

The improvements in this edition reflect the two basic goals of the revision project: (1) updating the material and (2) strengthening our use of theory, especially in the sociological chapters. Toward these ends, and in response to the helpful suggestions of our reviewers, we have added a new chapter and substantially rewritten others. More specifically, the introduction to scientific attitude in Chapter One has been given more focus and strength. Chapter Two reflects recent developments in anthropology. Chapter Four has been almost completely rewritten, with a new focus on the socialization process and attention given to theories of human development and sociobiology. The issues of increased teenage suicide, anorexia, and bulimia are also discussed. The treatment of group theory in Chapter Six has been strengthened. Chapter Seven contains more theoretical treatment of social stratification and more recent research is evident, especially in the section on social mobility. The description of U.S. minorities in Chapter Eight has been updated. The treatment of gender in Chapter Nine has been expanded, as well as the treatment of deviance theory. Updating in Chapters Ten and Eleven reflects the ongoing research on the family and the schools. Chapter Fourteen reviews current world population trends and environmental concerns, while Chapter Fifteen examines recent changes in city patterns and problems. Chapters Sixteen through Nineteen are an update of world economy, domestic economic trends, the fate of unions in America, and social consequences of recent economic patterns. The Political Science chapters and the new chapter on International Relations reflect current political events of the nation and the world.

All textbook authors are indebted to the scholars whose work is the essence of the textbooks we write. In addition to these people, we were assisted in more personal ways by friends and family members. Of course the support of our families was invaluable. We also wish to thank the reviewers who offered valuable suggestions and criticisms: Margaret Park, St. Louis Community College; John Flanagan, University of South Dakota; Joseph Rish, Marywood College; Peter Bearman, University of North Carolina, Chapel Hill; Donald Alexander, Prairie Street College; Quentin Newhouse, Howard University; Susan Cohan, Pensacola Junior College; Gene Minor, Atlanta Junior College; Stephanie Moussali, Pensacola Junior College; Drew Hurley, Santa Fe Community College; Norm Budow, Truman City College; Margaret Sielski, Pensacola Junior College; William Callam, Daytona Beach Community College; Bill Byrne, Olive Harvey College.

1 THE SOCIAL SCIENCE PERSPECTIVE

PREVIEW

Who Is Paul Kurtz?

A psychic predicts that Niagara Falls will collapse, causing a tour boat to sink and several people to die. Reporters from all over the nation show up for the disaster. Up steps Paul Kurtz, who with his twelve-year-old son takes a ride on the very boat that is expected to sink. Kurtz and his son return from their boat ride, giving Kurtz a chance to scoff at the psychic.

A statement is signed by 192 scientists, 19 of them Nobel laureates: "It is simply a mistake to imagine that the forces exerted by stars and planets at the moment of birth can in any way shape our futures." When this group of scientists was formed, its co-chair announced: "When a society ignores all objective standards of knowledge it opens the door to the possible development of ideological cults."[1] The person behind both these statements was Paul Kurtz.

A group calling itself the Committee for the Scientific Investigation of Claims of the Paranormal searches out and attacks such things as astrology and psychic predictions. Hard at work on that committee is Paul Kurtz.

Who is Paul Kurtz? He might be described as a professional skeptic who makes it his business to disprove such things as palm-reading and astrology. The important thing for us here is that Kurtz embodies one of the qualities of a good scientist: skepticism. He simply demands proof from mystics and psychics, whom he sees as dangers to society's frame of mind. With his skepticism, Kurtz represents the scientific viewpoint, as opposed to superstition and mysticism. With Kurtz and the attitude he embodies, we begin our introduction to social science, which is based on the belief that we can more effectively address personal and social problems with the scientific attitude than with tea leaves or star charts.

We have all heard of the "mad scientist" character. Take Professor X, who confesses, "I search for knowledge for its own sake. In plain English, what I do has no known practical value whatever. It's completely useless. Yet, there is a method to my madness."[2] This side of science, called basic or pure science, does exist, and from such cases we sometimes get the impression that science is simply a sophisticated game played by a few academic types. But even in his mad search for knowledge, Professor X, if he happens to be a social scientist, may well indirectly provide us with some answers that will help us choose the best school for our kids, vote for the right political platform, or choose the best neighborhood for our family. Such practical problems are the stuff at which applied science, in contrast to pure science, is more directly aimed. But whether it is pure or applied, science is not a useless game. Indeed, the main point of this book is that one of the most valuable sources of information we can use regarding our personal and social decisions is social science. Yes, we agree with Paul Kurtz in the chapter preview: Give us social science for answering many of our personal questions; give us science rather than psychics or readers of tea leaves.

SEARCHING FOR FACTS

We all need information to cope with our environment, information for making decisions, forming opinions, and solving problems. We often look for information that is factual. Facts are verified data that have been proven—so far—to be accurate descriptions of reality. A major reason we sometimes choose the wrong course of action is that we use facts that turn out to be false. Therefore, our search for facts must be careful and critical.

An example of "facts" perhaps turning out to be false involves the "Stone Age" Tasaday people on the Philippine island of Mindanao. The discovery of the Tasaday was announced in 1971, and was hailed as a wonderful opportunity to study humans unspoiled by contact with the rest of the world. The Tasaday were described as having lived in isolation from the rest of humankind for perhaps thousands of years. Recently, however, the revelation of the Tasaday as Stone Age people has been called a hoax, perpetrated by a Philippine government official in search of publicity.[3] It is alleged that the official induced local tribespeople to move into caves and to fake a "Stone Age" lifestyle. The "facts" about the Tasadays' lifestyle had been incorporated by many people into their thinking about human nature. Whether the Tasaday were authentic or not, this case shows the need to search carefully for factual information.

There are several sources of accurate information. Not all people use the same source, because people have differing needs and accept different kinds of evidence. Some trust common sense or intuition to give them answers about the world. This attitude involves an acceptance of what "feels" or "seems" to be true, and it can be dangerous, unless one's mind is somehow empowered to radiate truth. We can expect to get out of our minds not much more than what we put in.

We might instead base our search for facts only on what we observe: "I'll believe it only if I see it." The chapter preview described the "show me" attitude, but there are dangers in carrying it too far. For one thing, if we do indeed limit our knowledge to what we observe, we will deny ourselves a great deal of knowledge discovered by other people, some of which could be valuable. Few people would seriously limit themselves in this way; we must trust what some other people observe. There is another danger in relying only on our own observations or those of trusted friends: We may not always see clearly, or we may disagree with our friends about what we see. To be most effective, an observer must be disciplined, and for most people this takes special training.

Instead of relying on observations, we can go to experts, who base their statements on a large part of the existing knowledge on the topic. Many of us find it necessary to rely on experts, especially in those topics that are beyond our training, skills, or experience. Thus we often seek truth from professors, journalists, and others whom we expect to be knowledgeable within their fields. The danger is that authorities cannot always be trusted to be informed or sincere; nor do they always agree with each other. Further, it is not always easy to judge who is indeed an expert. And some experts offer views on topics out of their mastered fields—a chemist discussing the reasons for soaring divorce rates, for example. Still, to reject all experts would confine us to our own experiences, making us that much less able to cope with the world.

The source of factual knowledge on which this book is based is science. The aim of science is to give us more understanding of the observable world, the world within reach of our senses. One aim of this chapter is to describe the nature of science. Indeed, a basic assumption of the entire book is that we cannot ignore the value of science as a source of knowledge if we hope to be able to cope with the forces that challenge and threaten us in the world. The authors hope you will gain from this book such knowledge based on science.

There is, however, another source of knowledge to be aware of. For many people religion is an important source of truth, of knowledge. Religion deals not only with the observable world but also with knowledge beyond the reach of our senses. While science requires that we follow reason, religion at some point requires faith, a belief not just in our own powers but also in supernatural authority. In this way religion offers us knowledge in matters that lie beyond the reach of science. We will return to religion in a later chapter, but for now let's focus on science.

HOW SCIENCE WORKS

We quote Kai Erikson speaking of himself and his fellow sociologists: "We are then engaged in a haughty business, for we are declaring for all practical purposes that trained and thoughtful

A scientist searches for facts in the sensory, observable world.

observers can see in the conduct of fellow human beings something they are not aware of. . . ." [4] Social scientists, including sociologists, do aim to see in people's behaviors things which the people themselves do not see. For example, this "haughty business" can show us, as Erikson goes on to say, that we as workers are probably alienated—even though we may not be aware of it—"cut adrift from (our) natural moorings in the world as the result of unnatural, alien work arrangements." In other words, social science can help us put our finger on vague yet deep dissatisfactions, on the source of hopelessness or despair. Social science can help explain our lives to us. How does social science, or any kind of science, work?

Science is both a way of reaching understanding of the observable world and the results of that reaching. It is both a tool and a body of knowledge gained from the use of the tool. Most of this book presents some of that body in such a way that the knowledge will be of use to the reader. In this section, however, the book will offer a glimpse at science as a process, a method, a tool.

The Scientific Attitude

Science is not simply a search for facts; it is a very disciplined search. To be disciplined, and thus scientific, research must be founded on certain qualities. Otherwise, the results will be given little respect. While there is no official list of such qualities, there are several that help define the scientific attitude:

Science is logical. In making its statements about things, science presents arguments that are given convincing form through logic. Logic demands that any reasoning must follow certain rules. Insofar as the rules are followed, the argument is given weight, respect. Thus, conclusions of a logical argument cannot be ignored, even if they are unpleasant. Science uses this discipline of logic.

Science is skeptical. As shown in the chapter preview, the scientist will not accept any idea until it has been shown to be based on sufficient evidence. The scientist should be open to unproven, new ideas but should at first only consider, not accept, them. This attitude is quick to allow that something is possible, but slow to accept it as truth.

Science is empirical. This means that science is based on the world of experience and observation. It sometimes goes beyond this, using guesses and abstractions, but science limits its search to the knowable, sensory world. It is anchored in the concrete world.

Science is objective. Scientists try to prevent emotions and personal values from affecting what they observe. Their aim is to see the world as clearly as possible. This does not mean that scientists avoid all feelings; indeed, they may feel intense interest in the research at hand. But to be scientific, these feelings must not alter what is seen. This is the ideal; no one can be completely objective.

The total absence of feelings and of values might not be entirely desirable for a scientist. The scientist's personal values and feelings provide guidance as to the questions to be asked, the interpretations to be made, and the perceptions that are registered. A purely objective scientist, then, might be well trained for research but would lack guidance as to how to use that training. Philosophical biases and moral commitments offer guidance to the scientist and encourage the speculation that has provided the bases for much of human intellectual progress.

Besides these qualities, scientists should also have a quality people may not expect of them: humility. There are two reasons that scientists should be professionally humble. First, they must remember that the tools at their command can take them only so far. Their statements will often describe only what is usual or probable, not what is certain. While we can speak of the search for "truth," scientists must remember that truth is elusive, that humans can often only guess at it. What we might call truth is merely what our experience has led us to believe; scientists know that such beliefs can be destroyed by new experiences. Thus all statements of science could be prefaced with "As far as we know at this time. . . ." The second reason scientists are humble is that they can hope to make only a tiny contribution to the fund of human knowledge. If they are lucky, they will add a small link to the long chain of knowledge that has led humans to a world of greater comfort, longer life, and more opportunity. The contribution of each scientist is small, and they are indebted to the work of many others, but it is valuable and thus satisfying to the researcher.

Strategy and Tools

The goal of science is an increased understanding of the concrete world. The basic question of science is: What is going on, and why? Answering this question involves both describing and explaining things in the observable world. Because there are so many parts in that world, the task of science is clearly a formidable challenge.

The Strategy of Inference. The basic approach in dealing with the many parts of the concrete world involves inference, drawing a logical conclusion from given knowledge. Inference is the process by which scientists hope to find patterns or order among the pieces of the surrounding world. From specific facts, scientists make general statements about how those pieces are related and how other pieces may be related. For example, a scientist studying two hundred families discovers a pattern in the way spouses feel about each other that is related to the balance of power within their marriage. From these specific cases, the scientist might make a general statement about the relationship between the quality of a marriage and the balance of power in other, similar cases. This is one kind of inference: building a general statement from specific facts. It brings some order to the pieces of reality around us. With such order, our understanding is enhanced, which is the goal of science.

INFERENCE: Drawing a logical conclusion from given evidence or statements.

Tools. In trying to explain how the parts of the concrete world are related, science uses abstract tools. These tools are used to bring order to, or organize, what is observed.

CONCEPT: A symbol or label identifying classes of phenomena.

GENERALIZATION: A statement that describes the relationship among concepts.

HYPOTHESIS: An informed guess about the relationship of two or more concepts; an unsupported generalization.

THEORY: An explanation of the causal relationship of phenomena; more strongly supported than a hypothesis.

Concept. The most basic abstract tool is the concept. With this tool, scientists transcend what they perceive, going to what can be done with those perceptions. Concepts are labels that refer to specific classes of objects or their relationships. Many of the chapter titles of this book refer to social science concepts, such as culture, education, and power. Concepts are symbols that stand for related pieces of the world. They give scientists a vocabulary with which to describe and explain the world.

Generalization. From concepts one can build generalizations, which are statements that tie concepts together in meaningful ways. For example, we might want to make a generalization about the effect of power struggles on education. We might observe a sample of schools and determine how internal power struggles affect their functioning. From our conclusions we could make a generalization about what we expect in similar school situations. This tool thus enables us to reach out and give some order to a larger part of our surroundings. It is a product of inference. If a generalization poses only a possible or suspected relationship between two concepts—that is, if we did not yet observe or measure anything—it can be called a hypothesis.

A hypothesis is merely a guess, based on other, related knowledge. In our example above, we might hypothesize that the more decentralized the power is within a school, the higher the students' academic achievement will be. Further study would be needed before the hypothesis can be considered anything more than an unsupported generalization. Its value lies in the direction it gives to research efforts. (The hypothesis will be explored in the Skill Box in Chapter 9.)

Theory. Theories are built from related generalizations. A theory is an important tool for researchers. It links generalizations in a way that specifies one concept as a cause and another as the effect. In this way a theory can help us predict that one event will follow another. If such a cause-effect statement is based on strong enough evidence, it is considered a theory. If in our example we had found strong evidence that decentralized power in schools caused greater student achievement, we might have a theory. The goal of science is achieved to the extent that a theory explains how some of the world's pieces are related to one another; that is, the theory gives us some degree of understanding. Beyond that, a theory can generate more hypotheses. Each such step of science makes possible further steps.

Theories are of limited value, however. They can predict only that one or more concepts will probably—not certainly—cause something to occur. They can state that it is usual or typical for certain concepts to be related in a certain way, but rarely can the word "always" be used in these descriptions. Science aims to refine theories so that they allow fewer and fewer exceptions, making their predictions ever more accurate, though rarely perfect.

In summary, the strategy of science is building generalizations from concepts, and building theories from the generalizations. While theories explain how pieces of the world are related, they

SKILL BOX

Establishing Cause-Effect Relationships

The goal of science is to achieve greater understanding of the world, which requires that we discover the ways in which the world's parts are related to one another. Science is most interested in those relationships in which one thing causes another thing to happen. As science discovers much cause-effect relationships, it can offer us greater understanding of the working of the world's parts. The problem is that such relationships are difficult to establish. The difficulty lies in the need to control all factors that might influence or cause the result or effect.

Let us say we want to determine if smoking causes cancer. To prove a cause-effect relationship, we could compare the cancer rate of smokers with that of nonsmokers. Let's say the results looked like this:

	Cancer	No Cancer
Smokers	20%	80%
Nonsmokers	20%	80%

This would suggest that smoking makes no difference in one's chances of getting cancer.

If the results looked like this,

	Cancer	No Cancer
Smokers	80%	20%
Nonsmokers	20%	80%

It would appear that smoking is related to cancer. But some other factor not controlled in the study might be the actual cause of the smokers' high cancer rate. For example, it might be that the smokers in the study live in a different town than the nonsmokers. In that case, the smokers' high cancer rate may have been caused not by smoking but by the air or water in their town.

All possible causes must be controlled if a cause-effect relationship is to be firmly established. This control means that the influence of all other relevant factors must be eliminated. In our example this would require that the *only* difference between smokers and nonsmokers was the presence or absence of smoking in their lives. As much as possible, there must be no difference in the age, sex, racial composition, or other relevant variables regarding the two groups. The two groups' past and present nutrition, exercise habits, and physical environments must show no significant differences—and so on with other factors.

Scientists can take certain steps to help prevent such outside causes from influencing the results of their experiments. In social science, however, such steps would require a great deal of control over the lives of human subjects. In our example, the ideal research design would be to assign a large number of nonsmokers by chance to smoking and nonsmoking groups. Some people would thus have to agree to take up smoking if the flip of the coin decided it would be so. Then the two groups would be required to live the same life-style for the duration of the study. Thus the problems social scientists face in trying to establish cause-effect relationships are many.

are always in need of further refinement. The process of building and refining theory is demanding, but it can be exciting for those involved.

Steps in Scientific Research

So far we have explored the attitudes of science and the overall strategy of scientists, and we have seen that theory-building is the focus of science. Now we can move in closer for a look at how scientists gather evidence with which to build theories.

There is nothing official about the steps followed by researchers. It is debatable whether there is really *one* method—*the* scientific method. Still, people with the scientific attitude who pursue the goal of science would end up taking most of the steps described below. The basic method simply makes sense for solving problems, and it fits the plan and the outlook of the scientist. It can thus be seen as a natural outgrowth of the needs of science. It serves as a general guideline for researchers (though verifiable facts can also be produced in other ways).

Defining the Problem.   Researchers begin by precisely defining the problem to be solved, that is, defining exactly what they want to find out. The problem chosen should be one whose solution would be a useful addition to the existing fund of knowledge. Taking this first step requires much background study, often called a review of the literature. Scientists cannot know what questions need to be answered unless they are acquainted with the problem area. The researcher needs a thorough exploration of the work already done on the research topic. It may be that the problem has already been solved, or the topic sufficiently investigated. A review of the literature, in fact, can even be considered a separate step in the scientific method. Scientists can also benefit from such a review because a knowledge of related, established theories can give them direction in this regard. Let's say that such study leads a scientist to this problem: What is the effect of teachers' attitudes on the quality of a school?

With the problem defined, the scientist develops a possible answer to the research question. This is the hypothesis, a well-founded guess as to what the problem's solution will be. Making a guess sounds easy, but forming a good hypothesis is no simple matter. A hypothesis defines the limits of the research. It precisely defines the concepts so that the data collection will be controlled. It not only states what data are to be gathered, but also suggests how the data should be gathered. A hypothesis must be one that can be tested, that is, one that is within reach of the researcher. The rest of the steps in the research process are devoted to testing the hypothesis, so the hypothesis must be stated precisely. Our scientist forms this hypothesis: Schools with teachers who have high scores on (specified) personality tests and high ratings on attitude scales have larger gains than other schools in student (specified) achievement test scores over a year.

One step in the scientific process involves careful collection of data.

Research Design. The next step is to develop a research design that will effectively test the hypothesis. The hypothesis has indicated what data are to be collected. The researcher must now decide how to collect the data and how to analyze it. Which schools will be studied, and which teachers and students will be tested, by whom, and when? These decisions guide the construction of the research design. The major concern in designing this research plan is ensuring that the data collected will properly represent the kind of data required. Are these schools, teachers, and students typical of those we want to know about? The research design must also guard against contamination by unwanted data. Perhaps the students have already taken a similar version of the achievement test we want to give—won't this boost their scores? If misleading or inaccurate data are collected, they cannot be safely used as evidence to test the hypothesis.

Collection of Data. Now the data can be gathered in accordance with the research design. There are many ways of collecting data, depending on the subject matter and available tools. One scientist may gather data through interviews, another through a telescope. Whatever techniques or tools are used, care must be taken that only the right data are collected and that their collection in no way distorts the nature of the data. The data collected must faithfully represent the reality sought for study. In our study we collect test scores and ratings in a controlled way and from the right teachers and students.

Data Analysis. Once the data are gathered, they must be analyzed. In our study we want to compare school averages. Based on this analysis, the hypothesis can be accepted or rejected. The data will be used as evidence to test the accuracy of the proposed answer to the research question. In our example, we would want to know if the schools with high teacher scores and ratings have bigger increases in student achievement over the year.

Most social scientists use statistical tests to analyze their data. These tests tell the researcher the degree to which the collected facts can be trusted to represent the reality under study. Put another way, statistics are used to tell how probable it is that chance or outside factors were responsible for the results obtained. The tests give some degree of assurance that if many other observations were made the same results would be obtained.

Conclusion. The conclusion of the research is based on the statistical analysis. Did the schools' averages (on the achievement tests) differ more than we would expect them to differ simply by chance? If not, this means that the hypothesis is not supported by the data, and the scientist can redefine the problem, refine the hypothesis for further testing, or test a different hypothesis. If the data do support the hypothesis, the findings are then fitted in with existing knowledge.

Even though the research project appears to be finished when a conclusion is reached, the researcher's job is not finished. The scientist still must report his or her findings to other interested workers in the field, through written articles or in meetings with other scientists. And in such reporting the researcher is expected to suggest the implications of his or her conclusions for future research.

SOCIAL SCIENCE

Science is a demanding, rigorous process. From the process come valuable results, which are also called science, a body of knowledge. The body of knowledge constructed by science can be divided into two main parts: the natural sciences and the social sciences. The natural sciences are concerned with knowledge about the natural environment. Included in the natural sciences are the physical sciences, such as chemistry and physics, and the life sciences, such as botany and zoology. The other part of scientific knowledge is the social sciences. Their focus is the social environment of humans. Each of the social sciences studies some aspect of human relationships.

The Nature and Worth of Social Science

The body of human knowledge includes not only the natural sciences and the social sciences but also the humanities, or arts. Of course the three branches are not completely distinct, but the social sciences fit neatly between the other two. While social scientists maintain the scientific attitude, as do natural scientists, they also share concerns with people working in the humanities, such as human culture and values. The interest of the arts, what *ought to be,* clearly affects what *is* in the social world of humans.

In fact, the social sciences were born of one of the humanities, philosophy.

Though it has links with the arts, social science is still science. It is based on the objective, empirical, skeptical attitude of all scientists. It builds and tests theories (though some of the fields, such as economics, find this easier than do others). And social science aims to advance understanding of the observable world, even though the world it studies is not easy to observe or measure.

The social sciences face special difficulties in pursuing the goal and strategy of science. They are sometimes described as the "soft" sciences because their conclusions are not as firm as those of the natural sciences. They produce findings with too many exceptions. They are thus less useful in making predictions about their subject matter. Indeed, social scientists have more reason than natural scientists to be humble about their offerings.

One problem the social scientist has in being scientific is personal bias. The natural scientist also may find it hard to ignore personal feelings when researching things related to weapons, abortion, or gene control. But because the social scientist deals more directly with human concerns, questions of values are more likely to arise. In dealing with inequality, race, or human rights, for example, it is difficult to put aside one's feelings completely, as a scientist should. If research findings seem to point toward a conclusion one finds morally appalling, it is tempting to modify them, to make them "right" if not accurate. Scientists are expected to let the facts speak for themselves, but social scientists are more likely than other researchers to be faced with facts that challenge or threaten them personally. In such cases, bias can creep into the process and distort the results.

Social sciences are also sometimes considered to be not scientific because they are not often precise. While the natural sciences construct laws that can predict with great accuracy, the social sciences can rarely do that. This makes the social sciences seem in comparison less useful and more speculative.

Social science has problems in making precise predictions because of its subject matter: human relationships. It is difficult to predict what will happen among humans because each person is unique. This is less true among plants, animals, or chemicals. Because of the richness of human culture and the human brain, human behavior can be predicted only through statements of relatively low probabilities. Humans are also hard to study because of ethical concerns. To construct a strong theory to predict that one thing will cause another, it is necessary to control strictly the subjects under study. Our cultural values do not permit such control. For example, we cannot randomly choose one group of infants and deprive them of a loving home to see what the effects will be. While that sort of control is often possible in the natural sciences, social science must devise other research designs, which render weaker conclusions. Along with these reasons, social science deals with concepts that are not easily measured, such as social power, emotions, and self-image. If the object of study is not precisely measured, the research findings will be vague.

These explanations are not apologies. The social sciences are no less important because they may be less precise and less objective than the natural sciences. The challenges of social science are formidable, and the answers provided by social science more directly affect the quality of everyday human life.

The social sciences aim at increasing understanding of human relationships, from which we derive our most important rewards. The efforts made by social science cannot legitimately be criticized because this goal is elusive.

While natural science is often described as being more "scientific" and more objective than social science, natural science is not free from the effects of personal biases. For example, biological theories, especially since Darwin, have drawn upon the scientists' own views of how society should be. A sociologist, Howard Kaye, describes many of the important biologists since Darwin as "bio-philosophers," each one working from his own moral or metaphysical assumptions. According to Kaye, biologists "have not acted in the disinterested fashion of scientists....," but have instead been motivated by "philosophical commitments, social concerns, and mythological ambitions."[5] Kaye reminds us that "scientific knowledge remains that tentative product of passionately committed and socially constrained minds."[6] Indeed, the reader would do well to keep this point in mind: the body of both natural and social science is the product of humans, not of mechanically precise, detached, superhuman beings called scientists.

The Methods of Social Science

Within the social sciences, several research methods are used in following the basic strategy of science. Some fields lend themselves more readily to certain methods than others. Even within one field, one method may be more useful for one situation but not for another. This results in a variety of research methods in the social sciences. The methods used can be classified into four groups. The skills involved in these methods will be described more fully in the Social Science Skill boxes throughout this book.

Experiment. Most people think of experiments when they think of scientific research. Indeed, a good experiment most closely embodies the ideals of science: efficient, fruitful study of cause-effect relationships. Of all the methods, it involves the most control of the relevant factors. Because of this control, the experiment can yield the most reliable conclusions.

The experimenter's aim is to control all relevant variables. A variable is simply some part of the surroundings that varies over time, from one object or person to another, or from place to place. Examples are feelings, age, and income. The basic tactic is to try to hold all variables constant except for one, which is manipulated. If some other factor is then affected, the effect may be the result of the impact of the manipulated variable. That is, one factor may be causally related to the other, establishing a causal link.

Survey.   The survey is an important research method in the social sciences. It is useful for establishing relationships among variables and for spotting patterns from which to make generalizations. A major strength of the survey method is that it is quantitative; that is, it deals with measurable properties. The survey can produce large bodies of data ripe for statistical analysis. Such results are precise and manageable and can be compared to other results.

Not all social scientists find the survey method valuable. It can produce mountains of useless data if not properly directed. Also, it often limits the responses to restricted categories and may thus miss important data, in an effort to make the data manageable. For example, responses may be limited to "yes," "no," and "maybe." These choices may be insufficient for finding out the truth of the matter.

There are several ways to question a large number of people. A common way is through interviews. The face-to-face interview is expensive and requires training of the interviewers. Surveys through the mail can be cheaper, but these often suffer from a low response rate. Telephone surveys can cause certain kinds of people, such as those without telephones or those who work odd hours, to be neglected in the survey.

Observation.   While every scientist observes, the observation method is still distinct from the first two methods described. It is less structured than either the experiment or the survey. This method does not involve control of the variables, as the experiment does. Instead, the researcher reports what the environment offers, without trying to change the environment. And unlike the survey, observation is often not very standardized data-gathering. The data are not easily analyzed because this is a qualitative approach. That is, rather than numbers or measurements, this method more often produces statements of impressions and feelings. Because it is not standardized, this method can be flexible. Rather than following a highly structured procedure, the observer can change direction in order to track down valuable data. Although they can play it by ear to some extent, researchers must still maintain a disciplined perspective. This method is also different from others in that its success may depend on the researchers' relationships with the subjects. Rather than keeping their distance, researchers must often establish a relationship of trust with the people they study. This can yield great insight into the subjects, but the scientist may then find it difficult to remain objective.

Secondary Sources.   The social scientist does not always generate new knowledge, or primary data. Sometimes it is useful to use sources of secondary data, or data gathered by other people.

Sources of such data include other research findings in journals or books; private letters of famous people; newspapers; and government records such as the census. Secondary data are often easier to gather than new data. They also allow the researcher to study the past. Such data can be useful in making comparisons. For example, in comparing marriage in twelve cultures, researchers need not collect data from all twelve themselves if they can find previous studies that cover them all. This method simply makes use of data already available.

The Social Sciences— For Each Its Own Search

The search for greater understanding of human relationships requires that the social sciences cover a wide range of subjects, which in turn requires a division of labor. That is, the field must be divided into several sciences, each with its own specialized concerns.

While there are problems with this division of labor, there are benefits too. The division is not arbitrary, but it is artificial. It may give the student the impression that the various areas of knowledge are clearly distinct from one another, which is not the case. Still, it helps the student grasp the wide variety of topics. This division points up the importance of each topic, but some questions may fall into the cracks among the sciences. Because each science is specialized, the knowledge of any one field is less likely to be seen as related to that in others. While specialists can probe deeply into a confined topic, they may form a limited perspective about what broader questions might be asked. Despite its drawbacks, the division of labor in the social sciences makes the study of the human social world more manageable. We will use this division here to introduce the social sciences one by one.

Anthropology.   Anthropology is perhaps the broadest of all the social sciences. It studies humans as physical beings within their social contexts. This study often focuses on how humans and their ways of life vary and how humans adapt to their surroundings. The focus of anthropology could also be described as the varied responses created by humans as they adapt to their physical worlds. The breadth of this science makes it hard to define easily.

Anthropologists cover a wide range in their studies. They want to know about past as well as present adaptations of humans. As for the present, the scope of study extends to all parts of the world and to all kinds of peoples.

The study of humans from the viewpoint used by anthropologists has a long history. The ancient Greeks were concerned with the variations among the peoples they encountered. With the Renaissance came a renewed interest in the earthly nature of humans. This period also brought voyages to new lands, and the discoveries of new peoples and new ways of life sparked inquiry into the reasons for variations. By the start of the eighteenth century, scientists were also becoming interested in the various classes of living things and the place of humans in that scheme. From this came thoughts on the origins of humans, including the idea of evolution. From all this wandering and wondering in the last century grew studies of race, language, and other ways in which humans were seen to vary.

In this country, Franz Boas shifted the focus of anthropology away from grand theories to the collection of data on the primitive ways of life that were quickly disappearing. Under his direction, American anthropologists worked to preserve and record these parts of the human story.

Since World War II, anthropology has expanded and matured. Its focus now includes modern, urban societies. The theme of evolution has been revived. Methods have become more disciplined and less intuitive. Comparisons of different ways of life are now founded on a larger data base. The collection of data on specific cases no longer dominates the science as it once did; generalizing from these pieces is now once again seen as important too.

Because it has such a vast scope, anthropology is a varied science. It is divided into two main branches, physical and cultural, both of which are aimed at an understanding of how the human body relates to and adapts to the world.

Physical anthropology studies the human body as it varies among peoples today and as it has varied in the past. It seeks to explain these variations, especially as they relate to the human social world. There are several subfields of physical anthropology, each with special interests. One subfield attempts to trace human evolution. Another studies physical differences among human populations. One special area studies human skeletal material, while another studies differences among animals most closely related to humans, the primates.

Cultural anthropology studies the adaptations of peoples to their surroundings. These adaptations vary over time and from place to place and form the basis for cultural differences. Those of the past are studied by archaeologists, who dig in the earth for data. Ethnographers observe the life-styles of people today for their data, while ethnologists compare traits and cultures. There are many other areas of anthropological interest, including linguistics, musicology, religion, and medieval anthropology, as well as applied anthropology. Most anthropologists go to "the field," wherever their subjects live, in search of their data. From the many pieces of knowledge they collect there, the researchers try to form general statements that help explain what they observe.

Psychology. Though it is focused on the individual, psychology is closely linked to other social sciences. After all, human social relations are comprised of the behaviors of individuals. To delete psychology from the social sciences would be like studying a forest without understanding the trees.

The aim of psychology is to use the scientific approach to study human—and animal—behavior. This science, however, perhaps has the most problems in being scientific. Its goals require more than the other social sciences do—the manipulation of their human subjects. This, as we have seen, is hard to achieve when studying humans, for there are both ethical and practical problems in controlling humans in a research design. For example, there would be obvious problems in devising research to find out how pain affects infant learning. One alternative is to use animal studies, from which we can speculate about humans.

As in the other social sciences, psychology can be grouped into different specialties. Clinical psychologists deal with abnormal and problem behavior. Others research learning and perception. Some psychologists focus on the study of the brain in an attempt to help explain behavior. Others research how people grow and change over time, and may specialize in the behavior of one age-group, such as the aged. Some psychologists explore personality. Others specialize in school, industrial, or military psychology. Social psychologists study the person in a group setting. All these specialties have developed in only the past one hundred years.

In the nineteenth century, psychology emerged as a distinct science, growing from ancient musings about human nature. Following the lead of other developing sciences, psychology sought to use direct observation and experiment to gather empirical evidence. From this intention various theories and approaches developed. These will be described in Chapter 5.

Sociology. Several chapters of this book are sociologically oriented. A glance at the chapter titles will reveal that sociology deals with social structures and behaviors—in other words, what happens when two or more people get together. From this interaction flow social rules, problems, and patterns which govern humans and their groups.

The history of this social science has only recently become clear. The earliest peoples were interested in many of the subjects of modern sociology. The roots of this science reach far back into our history. Since the Renaissance, there have been efforts to bring order and discipline to the study of these subjects. Sociology became a distinct science in the eighteenth century when Auguste Comte gave it its name. Comte also helped the new area of study become a scientific one through his search for predictive patterns in human behavior.

Sociology became established in the United States in the last half of the nineteenth century. It entered the curricula of many colleges by the beginning of the 1900s, and flourished in several major universities, especially the University of Chicago. Today, like the other social sciences, sociology is offered in most colleges, as well as in some high schools.

Sociology contains many specialized areas of study. Some involve applying the science to such topics as crime, mental illness, and teaching. Some sociologists are theorists, others specialize in the methods used by researchers in their field. Some researchers focus on one part of the human social world, such as the schools, family, law, or religion. Others study population patterns and may specialize in urban or rural settings. Sociologists can also focus on the group or on a specific type of group. Related to this are the study of the group and the person and of the interplay among persons. Much work has also been done on the social layers into which many peoples divide themselves.

Geography.   The science of geography straddles the natural sciences and the social sciences. It studies oceans, mountains, plains, and other physical features of the earth. It also studies certain areas, how they differ, and how this affects humans. It deals with the types of settlements humans have built and how humans use their resources. All this is aimed at understanding how the physical world affects people's lives.

The topics of this science have long been of interest. Ancient scholars wondered about the size and shape of the world. Rulers and explorers were interested in the earth's pathways and resources. Mapmaking accompanied this intense concern with the concept of place.

Modern geography began during the nineteenth century, when theorists began to gather data to construct a view of the earth as a context for human life. From these efforts came the work of the determinists, who tried to show how geography affected human history. Other geographers, who believed that the determinists put too much emphasis on the environment as a cause of human behavior, demanded more empirical proof of such causal links. This is where today's geography is.

Geography has developed four approaches.[7] Some geographers focus on space, concerning themselves with its measurable aspects, such as distance and form. Others study a certain area in detail, including both physical and social aspects. A third approach studies the way humans use the land; here conservation is a key topic. A fourth approach can be called earth science, the study of the earth as a physical body, its seasons, life forms, and land forms.

Economics.   Economics is one of the most easily defined social sciences. The scope of economics is quite clearly limited: it deals with how humans produce and distribute the goods and services they need and want. This in turn involves the study of how humans choose to allocate their scarce resources. The economist tries to understand the process behind these human efforts and choices. From such study the science may help us get more of those things we seek.

The field of modern economics emerged only recently as a science in its own right. Its topics were studied in ancient times as part of ethics or politics, when the early Greeks raised the fundamental questions still pursued by economists today. Through the Middle Ages these questions were studied as concerns of moral philosophy. By the eighteenth century, the basic issues were more political, dealing largely with trade among nations and later with socialism.

Today economics has become a science. Its focus is no longer on what ought to be; instead, the main aim is to determine what is and what will be. In order to explain the present and predict the future, economists rely on the scientific method, including heavy use of statistics.

Political Science. Political science is the study of how humans govern themselves. It explores the processes and structures of governments. The aim of political science is to show us what is good or bad about a system and how it can be improved. Political science studies government so that government may better serve us.

Until the scientific attitude emerged, this field of study was based on value judgments rather than facts. Since the time of the ancient philosophers, humans have mused and argued about how people are governed and should be governed. Early thinking was often based on some accepted "truth." With the Renaissance, theorists began instead with facts and then proceeded toward general statements about what is true.

Political scientists do not agree on how much the methods of science should be used in their field. Some prefer to use logic and philosophy to form and to explore the value judgments on which they say politics are based. This traditional view has been challenged over the past few decades by those who want to base their conclusions on empirical data. These scientists use quantitative methods to analyze governments. They try to use the scientific method, as much as possible, the way it is used in the natural sciences. That is, they want to be empirical and objective and to avoid the value-laden traditional approach.

History. History is the scientific study of the past. The objective, skeptical frame of mind is of value to the historian as it is to other scientists. Historians proceed from a clearly defined problem in an orderly, logical way toward the research conclusion. They must judge carefully the data they find. They must be critical thinkers.

The benefits of history are not limited to an understanding of the past. An accurate description of the past—which is the historian's goal—can help us better interpret the present. With such enhanced perspective, we are more able to give proper value to the importance of today's events. Besides this, a knowledge of the past can help us describe where we want—or do not want—to go in the future.

SUMMARY

We need empirical data to deal more satisfactorily with our world. Science is one of the better sources of such data and is the one on which this book is based.

The attitude of scientists is logical, skeptical, empirical, and objective, and it should also be humble. The basic strategy of the scientist is inference, drawing conclusions from evidence or statements. The scientist's basic tools are the concept (a label for kinds of objects or relations), generalization (description of relations among concepts), and theory (explanation of a cause-effect relationship). The scientist follows a sequence of steps, or a method. First the problem must be clearly defined and a hypothesis (informed guess) formed. The research design, which determines what data are to be collected and how, is then constructed. After the data are collected, it is tested and analyzed; then a conclusion is drawn as to whether the hypothesis was supported.

The social sciences fit in between the natural sciences and the humanities. Though social science faces special difficulties not faced by natural science, it still has an important task: to help us understand our social world. To accomplish this task, social science uses several methods: the experiment, the survey, observation, and secondary sources.

The social sciences are divided into several disciplines. Anthropology studies humans as physical beings adapting to their environments. Physical anthropology focuses on the variations among humans' bodies today and throughout the past. Cultural anthropology centers on the varying ways people have adapted to their environments through culture. Psychology studies individual behavior from a variety of perspectives. Sociology studies human social life and also contains a number of subfields. Geography deals with the interaction of humans with their physical setting, studying how each affects the other. Economists study the production and distribution of goods and services. Political science studies how humans are governed. History is the scientific study of the past.

Now the reader should be ready to make use of this book. We have seen what the social sciences are and how they work. The remainder of the book will use them to explore our society. This approach, using all these sciences, will introduce social science as well as American society.

Because they are sciences and not arts, the social sciences offer results that we, can use to understand better and perhaps even control our social world. Each valid research finding is a tiny bit of fact. From these pieces, we can hope to construct a clearer and larger picture.

SPECIAL TOPIC

Portraits of Two Giants of Social Science

Social science is a body of knowledge created by people. These people are real, with dreams, faults, and problems large and small. Most of this book will describe what these people learned and wrote; but here you can have an intimate look at two of these people. This glimpse may provide a better feel for the sources of social-science knowledge, and show that social science is a living body of knowledge formed and shaken by humans whose lives have shaken our own.

Two of the biggest names in social science are Karl Marx and Sigmund Freud. The scope of this book allows only a limited treatment of their ideas, but here these giants' lives will be examined more closely.

KARL MARX (1818-1883)

No writer in social science has affected the lives of so many people as directly as Karl Marx. In his own time he had only a little power, but his ideas survived to imprint his name on millions of people. His fundamental ideas served as a basis for changing the lives of people who could not even understand what he wrote. Indeed, it was his ideas, not he personally, that changed the world's history.

It is easy to see why Karl Marx had a hard time leading or changing people's destinies personally. Though his conversation could be brilliant, he was not a pleasant person to be around. In fact, he was able to establish a closeness with few people. He could not sweep a crowd off their feet with his presence; he could not easily make personal allies; he could not often count on personal encounters to further his influence. Rather than friends, he sought people he could dominate. To most people he met, he was cranky, treacherous, and violent in temperament—not the kind to win friends and influence people. Even in his childhood, Karl was brilliant but unsociable. While he impressed adults, he had few friends his own age. He was a quiet, swarthy, black-eyed boy full of energy and ideas.

The world's most famous radical was born in Germany in 1818 to a middle-class Jewish family. Karl Marx had little reason to rebel. While he took riding and dancing lessons, and for a while was even something of a dandy,

Karl Marx. His ideas have had a profound effect on several social sciences, especially political science, economics, and sociology.

Karl's main interests were of the intellectual kind. He loved literature—Shakespeare was his favorite—and astonished people with his conversation. At this point in his life, it seems that he could have directed his energies toward the settled, comfortable life of a lawyer, like his father. But in high school Karl became a freethinking poet and an atheist. In college he became a radical.

In his first year at the university, at age seventeen, Karl was hardly a model student. In fact, he was scarcely a student at all. He rarely attended classes or did any schoolwork. Instead, he ran the streets, piled up debts, and was arrested for being drunk and disturbing the peace. He even fought a duel with pistols.

Having thus spent his first year in school, Karl returned home and became engaged to a girl four years older. Jenny was the daughter of a prestigious official, a friend of the family. She was a beauty, too, and much sought after. But she was, and would ever be, devoted to Karl.

Karl returned to school, but he soon also returned to his habit of missing classes. He joined a group of freethinkers who spent much of their time in beer cellars and cafés. They passed their days chatting, drinking, and criticizing the social order. Soon he was running short of money, as he would be for the next thirty years.

Karl's values began to take firm shape during his early twenties. At that time he saw all around him the terrible results of the early stages of the industrial revolution and of capitalism. The ideas of socialism—then also known as communism—contrasted sharply with the widespread poverty and exploitation of the time. But at first Marx found communism distasteful, probably because he did not much like "the people," who would be given power under that system.

In his mid-twenties, Marx took some important steps: He married Jenny and moved to Paris; he met Friedrich Engels; and he converted to communism. Engels, son of a businessman, had been leading a double life as a gentleman, while living as a worker with a working-class woman. Engels became an aide, never an equal, of Marx, though Marx would depend on Engels for money the rest of his life. (Marx never did make much of a living with his writing, and he never took another kind of job.)

Marx became convinced that one country or another in Europe was on the verge of a workers' rebellion, and he worked toward that goal. At the urging of Engels, Marx began work on a book that would spark the revolution. Meanwhile, he wrote in newspapers, attacking the social order. Marx and Engels also formed the first Communist Party. Karl viciously attacked any other socialists, whom he saw as dangerous rivals. His *Communist Manifesto* was an emotional appeal to recruit workers, who were not much interested in joining his party. He started front organizations to attract, and then convince, the workers. To achieve his goal, he used methods both devious and vicious. He would try nearly anything to give the workers their communism, even though few wanted it.

Because of his radical writing, Marx was pressured or forced to leave Paris, then Brussels, then Cologne. He went to London to await the coming revolution. In London, now in his thirties, Marx and his family lived in poverty. Three of his seven children died in childhood. He had no prospects, no connections, and no money. Thrown out of their flat, the family had to pawn all their goods to pay their debts. They had to move into a slum, but Marx went to the library to read every day for hours. He suffered from outbreaks of boils, liver trouble, headaches, and other problems. His hair turned gray, and he smoked a great deal. His very clothes were pawned, and he spent a few nights in jail on suspicion of pawning stolen silverware.

In his later years, Marx would gain some relief. His *Das Kapital* brought him some money.

Sigmund Freud's ideas fundamentally altered the way many sciences view human nature.

Engels had gone back into his family's business and set up a lifelong pension for Marx.

The man whose ideas would shake the world died in his sleep in 1883 at the age of sixty-five. Only a glimmer of the workers' movement he envisioned could be seen at that time. His ideas lived, however, and are influencing the lives of over a quarter of the world's current population. It is through social science that the important ideas of Marx are studied, explained, and expounded.

SIGMUND FREUD (1856–1939)

Sigmund Freud's life was not quite as dramatic as that of Marx, but it too shook the world of social science. Besides the importance of their ideas, the lives of Freud and Marx were alike in several ways.

Like Marx, Freud was also born to Jewish parents but never was religious. Also, Sigmund the boy was expected to be a genius. Both his parents saw Sigmund as a special child, and many of their hopes rested on their firstborn. This was especially true of his mother, who adored Sigmund and gave him his lifelong sense of being morally right and secure in his judgment. Even as a child, Sigmund, like Marx, hoped to be nothing short of a hero or a genius.

Sigmund's childhood appeared normal enough, though he later pointed to evidence of his early sexual longing for his mother and his jealousy of his father. But on the conscious level, Sigmund seemed to be simply a studious boy with loving, indulgent parents. Like Marx, young Freud read widely. He was usually at the head of his classes. In time he mastered several languages. He had a photographic memory, which helped the student a great deal. His biggest hobby would always be collecting books. His main exercise was walking and a little swimming.

One of the many contradictions in Freud was that he had high ambitions but always felt he needed a better brain. Also, he was not easily satisfied with his achievements, even as he strove for high goals. Indeed, he was always modest and quiet, though in control of his relationships with other people. He was kind but not always polite. With other people he could be impressive and attractive, but not until later in life could he be graceful in his manners.

When it came time for Freud to choose a career, he saw no clear path. He wanted to discover why humans behave as they do. How was he to tackle such a huge task? Darwin's current work lighted the way toward biology. To that end, Freud chose medicine. Like Marx, he put a high value on the need to be orderly and disciplined in his thinking, on being scientific.

At the age of seventeen Sigmund Freud entered the University of Vienna. He loaded himself down with more studies than were required. After all, he wanted to be more than just a doctor. He wanted to discover something basic about human behavior. While still a student, he produced some excellent research on nerve cells. He was selected to be a member of a community of scholars, so he could devote much of his time to his research.

Freud's father was a merchant whose business was not going well, so Sigmund had to think about supporting himself. Reluctantly, he decided to start practicing medicine. Research would have to take a back seat for a while.

Another event made Freud consider his financial future. He fell in love quickly and deeply. The object of this love was Martha Bernays, who was five years younger than Sigmund. As was true of the beloved of Karl Marx, Martha was a very attractive person with many ardent suitors. Freud has been portrayed as a very reserved man, but he was overwhelmed by his feelings for Martha.

For several years Freud suffered doubts and jealousy and demanded that he come first in Martha's life. He resented Martha's closeness to her brother and mother and devised tests of her loyalty to him and his family. He demanded that she identify herself with him and allow herself to be shaped by him. She refused to go that far, and in time he became impressed with her independence.

Eventually Sigmund became more assured of and comfortable with his love. The engagement lasted four and a half years, during which time the two wrote long letters daily, because they were separated for most of the time. The relationship settled into a deep love and respect. Freud's courting of Martha revealed the volcano of emotions in this man who would later help us understand our own feelings.

Sigmund was obsessed with his need to marry Martha. He worked to make his medical practice pay, but the wedding date remained beyond his reach until some wedding gifts made it possible. The couple established a marriage of great harmony, and they maintained a strong marriage throughout their life together.

Meanwhile, Freud had been doing some research in neurology, searching for a big discovery to win him fame—and the money to marry soon. He came upon the drug cocaine, which helped some of his patients, and he was impressed with the effects of the drug, using it to calm himself, relieve his depressions, and heighten his energy. He urged Martha, his friends, and his sisters to use it as well. In fact, Freud often promoted the medical use of cocaine. When the bad effects of the drug were revealed, he was accused of unleashing the third such evil on the world—the other two being alcohol and morphine.

During his early married years Freud enjoyed the fruits of his marriage and of his professional work. In his practice in neurology, he was able to intensify his study of human behavior. This led him into the beginnings of psychotherapy, in which a person's subconscious was searched for clues to mental problems. On the domestic front, Freud showed himself to be a warm and loving husband and father. For leisure, he played cards and chess, walked, and did some mountain climbing. He enjoyed a few close friends and stayed out of the professional limelight.

His health at this time was far from perfect, though it was much better than it would be later. He was bothered by sciatica, nasal and sinus problems, and indigestion. Also, migraine problems would lay him low from time to time, as they would for the rest of his life. His habit of smoking cigars (as many as twenty a day) did not help.

Freud's mental health was not perfect either. He suffered from extreme moodiness. Depressions and anxieties plagued him. He decided to apply to himself some of his insights gained from his work with his patients. With a great deal of effort and courage, Freud used self-analysis to delve into the reasons for his own problems. This was an amazing feat. The first person ever to look into his very core, his subconscious mind, did so with some knowledge of the frightening secrets he might find there. His main method was to study his own dreams as a window to his subconscious mind. One of his most important books, *The Interpretation of Dreams*, resulted from this effort.

His claim that even infants are sexual creatures shocked the people who read his works. His theories on the importance of sex in our behavior made him something of an outcast for a while. He was ignored at first, then denounced by scientists and others. His views on sexuality were seen as dangerous and disgusting. Just before World War I, the attacks became savage. People who followed his ideas were fired and censored. Some careers were ruined because of the violent emotions aroused by Freud's views.

More disturbing to Freud than those attacks were the arguments among the small band of men who practiced and promoted his ideas. The feuds among these men, and the defections of some of them from Freud, caused him sorrow. Six of the faithful followers formed "the Committee," which would support and fortify the master.

After World War I, Freud's work and name were becoming known all over the world and his ideas were gaining wider acceptance. Stu-

dents came from all over the world to Vienna in order to learn his technique. He enjoyed some success in promoting journals and societies for the advancement of psychotherapy.

Through all this fame, Freud remained unchanged personally. His manner was still quiet and dignified. To his several friends he was warm and kind—though so honest as to be less than gracious at times.

Against the love of his family and the respect of much of the world of science, Freud faced in 1923 a battle that he would endure for his last sixteen years. At the age of sixty-seven, cancer was found in his jaw. He would undergo thirty-three operations throughout his remaining years. The first major one removed his whole upper jaw. A special mouthpiece was needed to separate his mouth from his nasal cavity so he could eat and speak. He could do neither very well ever after, and the pain and discomfort were nearly constant. The continuing effort to improve the always poor fit of the mouthpiece never succeeded. Freud endured pain that was not constant but at times horrible. He did so with no complaining and no drugs. Painkilling drugs would cloud his mind, and he said he preferred the ability to speak and think to relief from the torment of his pain.

While Freud's health was declining, his psychotherapy movement was being crushed by Hitler. Freud was forced to leave Vienna for London in 1938. (His escape was made possible by friends in high places and involved President Franklin Roosevelt's aid.) In London, Freud was given a warm welcome. He was treated with great respect and acclaim but died in his sleep after only about a year in London.

This man of courage, genius, and quiet dignity had in his eighty-three years managed to shake the world of social science, as had its other giant, Karl Marx.

SELF-TEST QUESTIONS

1. On which of the following is the scientific attitude NOT based?
   a. subjectivity
   b. skepticism
   c. empiricism
   d. logic

Match numbers 2–5 to the descriptions on the right:

2. concept — a. description of the relationship among concepts
3. generalization — b. label that refers to classes of objects
4. hypothesis — c. informed guess; unsupported generalization
5. theory — d. explanation; supported generalization

6. The decision either to reject or to accept the hypothesis is made in which stage of scientific research? _____

7. True or false: Two problems faced by social scientists are personal bias and imprecision.

8. Which research method tries to control all relevant variables?
   a. experiment
   b. survey
   c. observation

9. Which social science focuses on the individual?
   a. anthropology
   b. sociology
   c. psychology
   d. economics

10. Which social science focuses on the production of goods?
   a. anthropology
   b. economics
   c. psychology
   d. sociology

ANSWERS TO SELF-TEST QUESTIONS

1. a	6. conclusion
2. b	7. true
3. a	8. a
4. c	9. c
5. d	10. b

NOTES

1. Duncan M. Anderson, "The Number One Skeptic and His Debunking Brigade," *Science Digest Special* (Spring 1980): 80–83, 118.
2. Mark Davidson, "Confessions of a Mad Scientist," *USA Today* 111 (September 1982): 32–33.
3. Sharon Begley and Debbie Seward, "Back from the Stone Age?" *Newsweek* (May 5, 1986): 69.
4. Kai Erikson, "On Work and Alienation," *American Sociological Review* 51 (February 1986): 6.
5. Howard L. Kaye, "The Uses and Abuses of Biology," *The Wilson Quarterly* 11 (1987): 90.
6. Ibid., p. 93.
7. William D. Pattison, "The Four Traditions of Geography," *Journal of Geography* 63 (May 1964): 211–16.

SUGGESTED READINGS

Babbie, Earl R. *The Practice of Social Research.* 4th ed. Belmont, Calif.: Wadsworth, 1986.

Batten, Thelma F. *Reasoning and Research: A Guide for Social Science Methods.* Boston: Little, Brown & Co. 1971.

Chase, Stuart. *The Proper Study of Mankind.* 2d ed. New York: Harper & Row, 1962.

Hoover, Kenneth R. *The Elements of Social Scientific Thinking.* New York: St. Martin's Press, 1976.

Reinharz, Shulamit. *On Becoming a Social Scientist.* New Brunswick, N.J.: Transaction Books, 1984.

Senn, Peter R. *Social Science and Its Methods.* Boston: Holbrook Press, 1971.

2 HUMAN EVOLUTION

PREVIEW

Excerpt from Report No. 179–206

Report No. 179–206,
pp. 297–34.
Filed by ReconPatrol 75A

... Degree of complexity below that of Specimen (IIG) 3a, one of the most numerous and fascinating of the planet's large mammals. Specimen 3a is a widely dispersed creature with numerous superficial variations. Erect, two-legged posture. Color, stereoscopic vision. Forelimbs have excellent grasping capability. Large skull and brain; much of brain's potential is underdeveloped. Hairless body except for a few patches of hair. Widespread use of artificial coverings for body. Often consumes liquids, smoke, and other nonnutritive substances even when no hunger or thirst is apparent.

Prefers to gather in high-density habitats where large, usually orderly crowds are common. Mating groups are fairly permanent, usually limited to one male and one female, who reside together with their immature offspring. The male prefers more than one female, but material limitations usually do not permit such arrangements. Mating season continues with few interruptions throughout solar cycle.

Highly unusual feature of 3a is marked hostility among populations. Aggressive acts, including invasion of territory and even large-scale destruction of life, are not uncommon. Even within some populations, violation of property and personal security is quite common. Such antisocial acts are sometimes perpetrated upon individuals living nearby, even among mating-group members. Along with aggression within populations, tremendous differences of power and material well-being exist among population segments.

Technology of 3a has moved into Stage II yet is still largely dependent on organic fuels and consumption of natural resources with little recycling. Large-scale abuse of physical environment. Transportation still limited to three dimensions. Communication limited to waves, beams, and pulsations of Level 4 particles. Manipulation of crude genetic structures barely beginning.

Specimen 3a presents excellent case of Cycle 2 body-structure change, with dependence on physical environment's pressures. Further study of this specimen's structural change through time is recommended.

The specimen that so fascinated the observer in the chapter pre-view does indeed deserve further study. Many of the specimen's unusual behavioral and social features will be explored in the chapters of this book; in this chapter we will focus on the develop-ment of the specimen's physical features. The process by which the specimen came to be what it is makes for intriguing study.

Indeed, this chapter should have special appeal for those who enjoy doing puzzles. This chapter's puzzle, human evolution, is a challenge because some pieces are missing; in fact, the picture itself is incomplete. Also, more pieces are being added all the time, and the puzzle may never be completed.

Why study evolution in a book that introduces the social sciences? For the same reason that we put down the foundation of a house before we put on the roof. The body and brain we have evolved are the basic structures upon which we have built our so-cial world. Our nervous system, our sensory equipment, our hor-mones, and other aspects of our body affect our social lives. Since present human biology is best explained by evolution, the topic is a logical one with which to begin a study of the social world.

In this chapter we will try to put together the puzzle of human evolution. The body of the chapter deals with the process of evolu-tion and its results with regard to the human lineage. Then the Special Topic deals with the racial variations found among hu-mans today.

THE EVOLUTION PROCESS

The reader who comes away from this section feeling that evolu-tion is just a scheme constructed by scientists has failed to see the beauty of evolution. This grand, elegant process is not a cold, academic construct. However it came into existence, the process of evolution is a thing of wonder to anyone who becomes familiar with it. Here only its outline is offered: how the theory developed, and how, through the interplay of genes and natural selection, the process works. We begin with the development of the theory.

A History of the Idea

Even when Charles Darwin's book, *On the Origin of Species*, appeared in 1859, the basic concept of gradual change through ac-cumulated improvements had been discussed for thousands of years. Some of the ancient Greeks and Romans had guessed at it, but as the Christian religion gained power in the Western world, any notion that contradicted the Bible was rejected. Not until the seventeenth and eighteenth centuries did free inquiry flourish again.

In the 1600s, some thinkers tried to explain the origins and variations of life forms in terms of evolution. The changing nature of life forms was recognized by many, some of whom suggested that species are not fixed but change over time. Though several people guessed that living forms change over time, no one knew how this happened. The interaction of the environment and life forms was also examined during this time. Scholars guessed that this interaction had something to do with the variety of life forms. No one had yet linked the guesses together; that is, no one had yet put all those speculations together into one grand theory.

Charles Darwin seems to have been the first person to put together these two pieces in the puzzle of evolution: change of life forms and the effect of the environment on those forms. In doing so, he explained *how* the change process works. (Note: Before he published his theory, Darwin learned that Alfred Russel Wallace had taken the same step toward solving the riddle. Moreover, there is some question as to how fairly Darwin treated Wallace.) [1] In 1859, Darwin published his book, and the notion of evolution was placed in full view. He and his theory were at first denounced, but gradually they were accepted by more and more scientists.

Even today, however, there are those who protest the teaching of evolution because, as they say, it contradicts the words of the Bible. Various religious groups have demanded, in the pulpit and the courts, that the biblical version of human origin (creationist theory) be presented as an alternative to evolution.

In Darwin's day, most of the criticism—and some of the praise—he received was not justified. Modern discoveries in several of the sciences have upheld Darwin's basic theory. Though he wrote before genes were generally understood, Darwin accurately pointed the way to a fuller understanding. But Darwin has also been praised for inventing the notion of evolution. As we have seen, the basic idea was already an old one. Darwin deserves much credit, however, for explaining *how* the process works.

How the Process Works

Darwin fitted together several major pieces of the puzzle. He offered some basic clues, the main one being that life forms are transformed over time through an accumulation of changes. The concept of natural selection, the big contribution of Darwin and Wallace, explains the way these changes accumulate. Later, when genes were discovered and studied, natural selection could be understood more fully. In fact, an understanding of genes and gene frequencies is essential for dealing with the theory of evolution.

EVOLUTION: The process by which a genetic population is transformed through an accumulation of genetic modifications.

GENE: A functioning section of DNA which directs cell growth of the organism.

CHROMOSOME: A structure found in the cells of animals and plants. Chromosomes are shaped like rods and arranged in pairs; on them the genes are arranged.

DNA (Deoxyribonucleic acid): A large molecule carrying the genetic code.

POPULATION: A group of interbreeding individuals.

Changes in Gene Frequencies Equals Evolution. The gene is where the action of evolution occurs. Genes are the basic pieces of the puzzle. In the cells of any animal or plant are pairs of chromosomes, which are comprised of genes. Genes are made of DNA, among other things. The arrangement of the DNA molecules determines what message each gene will send in the reproductive process. Along with the environment, this message, or code, determines the structural traits of the animal or plant.

The proportion in which the various genes occur in an inbreeding population is called the gene frequency. For example, a population might be comprised of 40 percent gene A, 25 percent gene B, and 35 percent gene C. Evolution occurs when gene frequency changes. That is, if a population's proportion of some gene grows or decreases, that population is evolving. But how do gene frequencies change?

How Gene Frequencies Change.   Now we are ready for another piece of the puzzle. Among humans, because each child receives chromosomes from two parents the child will not be exactly like either parent. The child's combination of the mother's genes and the father's genes will be unique, and the child will look at least a little different from the parents. But this difference between the two generations does not mean that the frequencies of the population's genes have changed. Instead, it merely shows that the existing genes have been reshuffled within the population. Such reshuffling leaves no chance for evolution to occur. To illustrate this, imagine a deck of cards in which there are thirteen cards in each of the four suits. The frequency or proportion of the cards is 13, 13, 13, 13. Every time the deck is dealt out, the proportions within the deck remain the same. There would be no change in the card frequency from one deal to the next, just as there would be no change in the gene frequency of a population from one generation to the next—unless there was some way to place new cards in the deck. To go beyond a mere reshuffling of the genes in a population, to allow for change in the gene frequency, three mechanisms operate: mutation, migration and mixing, and genetic drift.

GENE FREQUENCY: The percentages of various genes occurring in a particular population.

Mutation.   The kinds of genes passed from one generation to the next can change (and thus the gene frequency would change) through mutation. A mutation occurs when the DNA structure of a gene in egg or sperm is somehow altered. This alteration changes the code, or message, to be sent by the gene. If this new message is transmitted to the next generation, a mutation occurs. This is the starting point of all evolutionary change. The mutation is an important source of variation. The variation resulting from the combination in an offspring of the parents' genes is only a reshuffling of existing genetic codes, but mutations create new codes, new messages—and perhaps, over time, new gene frequencies.

MUTATION: An alteration in the DNA which creates a new genetic code.

Migration and mixing.   The gene frequency of a population can also change as a result of migration and mixing. This occurs when individuals from one population move to another. If they then add new genes to the population, its gene frequency changes. For example, if a few horses of Breed A long ago had migrated across some barrier to interbreed, or mix, with a population of Breed B horses, the gene frequency of B would be changed by that mixing.

Many human societies have rules requiring their members to seek mates outside their own group, thus bringing new genes from neighboring populations. The process is called gene flow. A flow of new genes into the home population may alter its gene frequency. For example, a red-haired population might begin to exchange many of their daughters for daughters from a nearby blonde

GENE FLOW: The movement of genes from one gene pool to another; the result of interbreeding.

GENETIC DRIFT: An event, involving a randomly selected sample, which causes a change in the gene frequency of a population.

population. The red-haired people may soon have a new frequency of the genes involved in hair color. Such migration (of the daughters) is a possible source of evolutionary change.

Genetic drift.   Genetic drift is another factor that can cause changes in gene frequencies. This is most likely to occur in small populations. For example, if by chance a group of individuals is removed from a small population, and those lost members comprised most of the carriers of a particular gene, the event will change the population's gene frequency noticeably. Likewise, a new group entering the population may, by chance, contain a higher proportion of certain genes and change the gene frequency. Either way, evolution has occurred in that population as a result of random sampling of the lost or entering group.

So far we have seen that new genes are made available to a population through mutation, migration and mixing, and genetic drift. But just because a new gene form is made available does not mean that the new form will become a relatively permanent part of the population's gene pool (the population's "deck of cards"). There must be some process that determines which genes are to become part of the gene pool. That process is called natural selection.

GENE POOL: The total repertory of genes in a population.

NATURAL SELECTION: The process by which the physical environment interacts with the gene frequencies of populations to increase the reproductive abilities of those populations.

Natural Selection.   When natural selection was added, the puzzle of evolution began to take shape. This was the major contribution of Darwin and Wallace. They saw that the natural environment can affect an organism's chances for surviving to the age of reproduction. This effect of the environment on the survival chances of genes is the essence of natural selection and the key to evolution, because if some genes tend to survive more than others, the gene frequency will be affected.

An excellent example of this selection process is the case of peppered moths near a city in England. Before the nineteenth century most of these moths were a speckled gray color, which helped the moths to blend in with lichen-covered tree trunks. The few dark-colored moths were at a disadvantage on these light-colored tree trunks, for the birds ate more of the dark moths than light ones because they stood out. The birds, part of the natural environment, kept the gene frequency slanted in favor of the light coloration. The environment later changed, however, and so did the gene frequency. In the last half of the nineteenth century, pollution from factories became part of the environment. The lichen was killed and the trees turned dark. Environmental pressure now was "selecting" darker coloration for the moths. Now it was the darker-colored moths that escaped the birds more often. The gene frequency changed to a higher proportion of genes for dark color. In the twentieth century, the air pollution was somewhat reduced and the gene frequency changed back toward the earlier proportions. The case of the peppered moths clearly illustrates how gene frequency responds to environmental pressures. This is natural selection in action.

The phrase "survival of the fittest" has sometimes been used in connection with natural selection. "Survival of the fit" is more accurate. The picture is not that of one surviving organism being clearly the "fittest" of all; all organisms that reproduce well are "fit." Over generations, such fitness will show up in the gene frequency. Genes that somehow give their carriers an edge for reproducing themselves will come to comprise a larger proportion of the population. The natural environment in this way "selects" the more fit genes, and the population's genetic makeup changes. This is evolution.

Notice that in this description there is no mention of man or other animals fighting with each other for survival. The important struggle is the struggle of each population with its environment. While each organism must adapt to its surroundings in order to reproduce itself, it is the total reproductive success of the population that matters. If too many members lose their struggles, the population may become extinct. This is especially critical when the environment is changing. For the population to survive, enough of its members must have or get genes (through mutation, genetic drift, or migration) that enhance reproductive success chances. The successful genes will be the ones most commonly reproduced, and this will change the gene frequency of the population. That is how nature pressures a population to change its gene frequency. Evolution is based on this pressure, this struggle to reproduce.

An all-too-familiar example of a population's struggle with the environment is that of the common cockroach. In the United States, pesticide companies find they must continually change their poison formulas because the cockroach populations continually adapt to the latest substances used. Only a few roaches out of a population need to be adaptive enough to tolerate the poison; they can then reproduce more of their own kind, who may eat the poison for breakfast. In fact, there is some fear that we have been breeding a "superroach." The past years of poisonings may have simply weeded out the "unfit" roaches, leaving only those able to tolerate the changing demands of their poisoned environment. It seems that the roach is winning the struggle with its environment.

Darwin saw the importance of the struggle of populations with their environments. From the writing of Thomas Malthus, who studied the interaction of populations and their environments, Darwin saw that each population has such a potential to reproduce that the surrounding resources could become severely taxed. Thus, in its effort to exploit the environment, one population competes with others for increasingly scarce resources. This image of a struggle is useful in understanding the reasons populations change. If the environment never changed, and if each population merely replaced itself rather than growing each generation, the struggle—and the changes it produces—would not be necessary.

New Views on the Process

As scientists have added new pieces to the puzzle of evolution, the picture has begun to look different. Today the "struggle for survival" is not emphasized as much as it was in Darwin's time. Instead of a competitive struggle among organisms, the focus today is on each population's reproductive success. Moreover, there is some debate among scientists today about whether a new life form emerges only because it is more fit than others. Mutation may produce a new form that survives even without being superior to the old form, as long as the mutation is not harmful—does not actually lessen reproductive success.

Another part of the modern picture of evolution is that "fitness" is relative. There is no fixed, absolute adaptation that can protect a population from extinction. One reason for this is that the environment is not fixed. Rather, it changes, and thus its demands on the organisms change. As the environment changes, it "selects" different genes. Of course, these genes may later become outmoded by new environmental demands.

Also, evolution is seen today as a process with a direction. As life forms have evolved to fill more and more of the available niches in the world, the forms have become more complex. Life forms with more specialized organs and greater systems of coordination have evolved. All life forms, plants and animals, evolved through the same basic process toward this complexity.

Today the debate continues over the pace of evolution.[2] Darwin believed that species evolve gradually, one small change at a time. Some theorists today point to examples of species appearing quite suddenly. In fact, this is seen in the stages leading up to humans. Each stage changed very little over its million or more years on earth. Then the next stage, quite different, appears suddenly. Such evidence suggests that evolution may proceed through sudden, rather than gradual, changes. This is just one more area in which evolution is still being argued today.

THE RESULTS OF THE PROCESS

So far in this chapter only part of the evolution puzzle has begun to take shape: the process. Let's work on another part of the picture: the results of the process.

Evidence of Evolution

All around us are the results of evolution. The plants and animals in our world present a beautiful array of life forms. Trying to bring some order to this overwhelming array, scientists have worked on the puzzle of evolution. In so doing, they have used two basic types of evidence: direct evidence and indirect evidence.

Indirect Evidence. Some of the indirect evidence supporting evolution is found in the study of embryos (animals in early stages of growth in the womb). Many examples of embryos at certain stages of growth exhibit features found in "older" members of the animal kingdom. For example, human embryos go through a stage in which gills are formed and then grow into more suitable structures. Tooth germs develop in certain whales, even though the adults, unlike their ancestors, have no need for teeth. These are but two of many cases in which reminders of the past put in a brief appearance in the very early growth of animals. Other indirect evidence of evolution is found in the functionless features found in some animals when they are mature. Humans have the appendix, which also no longer serves useful purpose. Such features seem to be leftovers from past structures.

Direct Evidence. Such indirect evidence is impressive to those who study it, but there is also direct evidence of evolution. Scientists have actually observed new life forms evolving in nature; moreover, new species have been produced in laboratories.

Fossils and skeletal materials. Most direct evidence, however, is based on the study of fossils. Fossils, the casts of previous life forms, allow scientists to construct a picture of structures as they evolved through time. Bones and teeth are more likely to survive over the ages than other body parts. From these hard parts, much can be guessed concerning the soft body parts of an animal.

Remains are dated in several ways. Relative dating tells us, for example, if one bone is older or younger than others. If one bone is found more deeply buried than others, it can usually be assumed to be older. Besides this and other relative dating methods, methods have been developed that indicate the absolute age of an item. These methods are based on the decay of certain radioactive substances found in fossil materials. The rate of decay is assumed to be constant, and it can be measured. By measuring the amount of decay, a good guess can be made about how long the substance has been decaying. These guesses give us valuable estimates of age. The substances used in such absolute dating include uranium 238, carbon 14, and argon 40. These names are attached to each method. Dates derived from these methods can read as, for example, 1500 B.P. (before present) $+ - 500$ years. This would indicate a date ranging from one to two thousand years ago. Instead of a day, year, or century, the date occupies one thousand years.

Genetics. More recently, the study of genetics has helped elaborate these fossil stories of the past. By comparing the chromosomes and DNA structures of different life forms, much has been learned about the past forms and how they were related to others. The study of protein structures has also been helpful in this way.

Our description of the evidence for evolution has been sketchy. The evidence becomes much more convincing if one digs into more specialized sources. For the time being, however, we will move on to the picture that emerges from the pieces of evidence available.

SKILL BOX

Inductive Reasoning

We can assume that the scientists who were discovering and studying evolution did not use wild guesses or undisciplined thinking—they used logic. Logical thinking—thinking that follows certain rules in its search for truth—is the basis of scientific investigation, but it can be of use to the lay person too. Logical thinking can help us make sound judgments; that is, it is useful in examining the value and truth of our own opinions and beliefs as well as those of other people. In addition, logical thinking helps us make sense of the world. It helps us to deal with confusing, puzzling ideas and to think through problems to reach a well-founded solution.

When we are thinking logically, we are probably using either of two approaches. One is deductive reasoning, which begins with generalities and forces from them logical conclusions concerning specific cases. Inductive reasoning, on the other hand, produces general statements from specific statements or cases. The two approaches flow in opposite directions, but both are logical in nature. Here we will explore inductive reasoning. Deduction will be given separate treatment in the next chapter.

Induction pulls together isolated observations and makes them add up. From the small pieces of our perceived world it produces a larger view, a general statement, a conclusion. In this way we can discover patterns and gain more understanding of the overall picture. From this broader perspective we can better predict and control the parts of our world.

To illustrate, imagine we were lost in a forest. It would be of little help to study each tree by itself. Instead, we would need a larger view of our circumstances, a knowledge of the nature of the forest. With inductive reasoning we could try to pull together our knowledge of the individual trees to build an understanding of the forest. If we knew, for example, that certain types of trees grew in low, boggy areas, or that others grew in dry, sandy soils, we could use such knowledge to guide ourselves to higher or lower elevations, and from one area in the forest to another.

Inductive reasoning follows a basic strategy as it moves from specifics to generalities. In a study of fossils, for example, we might begin with knowledge of Fossils X, Y, and Z. We reason inductively that what is true of those three fossils is also true of all other members of Fossil Category 9, to which X, Y, and Z belong. Let us say we then learn that X, Y, and Z are a million years older than was previously believed. From knowledge of these three cases, we draw a conclusion in the form of a general statement: *All* fossils of Category 9 are one million years older than previously thought. In this example we reasoned from three cases to the other cases in the category, from a specific level to a general level.

Conclusions from inductive reasoning are tentative because they are not logically demanding, that is, other conclusions are possible. One obvious alternate conclusion in our example is that X, Y, and Z are a distinct group of fossils and do not belong in Category 9. The less certain we are that X, Y, and Z are representative of Category 9, the more tentative our conclusion must be.

The Animal Kingdom

Because we focus on human beings in this chapter, we will limit our description to the animal world. A look at how animals are classified can help us understand human features. Here we will find our way through the maze of animal forms and locate our place. Our biological address or taxonomic description is as follows:

Kingdom.   Animalia is composed of living things with a limited growth period and the ability to move. Members of this kingdom consume other organisms and include all animals from amoebae to mammals.

Phylum Chordata.   This includes all creatures with an internal stiffened rod, like our spinal cord.

Subphylum Vertebrata.   All chordata with a segmented spinal column are included here.

Class Mammalia.   All mammals have features that include warm blood, hair, sweat glands, a heart with four chambers, a diaphragm for breathing, and mammary glands to feed milk to their young.

Subclass Eutheria.   This class of placental mammals brings forth their young after a full-term pregnancy, as opposed to egg-laying mammals and marsupials such as the kangaroo.

Order: Primates.   Primates are one of several types of placental mammals. Primates have such traits as hands that can grasp, two breasts on the chest, few offspring per birth, and long pregnancy and infancy periods. The tree shrew, lemur, and tarsier make up one suborder of primates. Humans are grouped instead with the monkeys and apes, all of which share good vision and a complete bony eye-socket.

Superfamily Hominoidea.   The hominoids include only the gibbon, orangutan, chimpanzee, and gorilla and are noted for their lack of a tail.

Family Hominidae.   Hominids include humans and their closest ancestors.

HOMINOID (hominoidea): The superfamily grouping that includes hominids, gibbons, orangutans, chimpanzees, and gorillas.

HOMINID (hominidae): Humans and their direct, nonape ancestors.

Working our way through all these animal forms, we have narrowed the structural features to those of humans. In each step we took toward humans, we discarded some nonhuman features. The further we went, the more closely the remaining forms resembled humans. In hominids we will see our most direct ancestors. They have many features similar to our own. By tracing the development of the hominids, we will see evolution at work.

From Apes to Hominids

At this point we will focus on the part of the evolutionary puzzle in which humans and their closest ancestors begin to emerge from the larger category of hominoids. The task of completing the puzzle becomes complex. We'll begin with the time frame involved, then work our way into a description of the creatures that seem to fit our puzzle.

Anthropologists still disagree about when the first hominids emerged. There are arguments over methods of analysis and over the significance of various early species.[3] The last few decades have seen a surge of relevant discoveries; yet, as the search for the first hominid has become more intense, much confusion remains. Much of the fossil evidence consists only of teeth and jawbones, limiting the conclusions that can be drawn. The point at which the hominids diverged from the great ape can only be guessed at, but a good estimate is that the first hominid appeared between 10 and 15 million years ago. Fragments have been found of creatures of that period which were clearly hominoid but had a suggestion of the hominid. Those creatures may have been not fully apes but direct ancestors of humans.

The First Hominid?   During the last 15 years, several dozen fossil finds have occurred regarding the emergence of hominids. Until recently, *Ramapithecus* was the mostly likely candidate for first hominid. Its teeth and jaws seemed to have been more humanlike than apelike. *Ramapithecus* may have been in the process of adapting to life in open areas, rather than forests where more apelike creatures lived. But newly discovered fossils have clouded the picture.

Some biochemists question the claim that the lines of humans and apes split as long as 15 million years ago. Scientists have compared such things as the blood proteins and DNA structures of humans and animals; if such materials have evolved at a constant rate, they may provide a way of figuring the time elapsed since life forms diverged. Indeed, if average rates of change over a large period of time are used, molecular genetic data can give us a rough evolutionary clock,[4] perhaps one more accurate than the clock given by fossils.[5] For example, if the differences in the blood proteins of two species are figured to have taken 10 million years to evolve, these two species must have diverged that long ago. This approach has yielded dates that conflict with the fossil evidence. Subsequent research has confirmed an earlier estimate that humans and African apes diverged only about 5 million years ago.[6] Before scientists can agree on the story of the earliest hominids, this gap between the evidence of fossils and other time clocks must be resolved.

As more fossil evidence is found, the picture becomes less clear. Between 10 and 15 million years ago, many hominoids appeared and then became extinct. Several hominoid lines may have been developing in a humanlike direction. If this were true, it would be even more difficult to identify the first hominid (the next part of our puzzle). The puzzle will probably not soon be pieced together.

Australopithecus.   If *Ramapithecus* is not proven to be the first hominid, the next oldest candidate would be *Australopithecus*. *Australopithecus* is more well known than *Ramapithecus*, perhaps because many more fossils of the genus have been found. *Australopithecus* seems to have been a fascinating mixture of apelike and humanlike features.

SPECIES: One or more populations of plants or animals capable of interbreeding and producing fertile offspring.

GENUS: Two or more species classified together because their biological traits make them more similar to one another than to other species.

While humans are the only species to depend on tool use, other species occasionally use tools. Here a chimp uses a stem as a tool with which to extract termites, a taste treat.

BIPEDAL: Naturally and usually walking on two legs.

In general appearance this creature was apelike in many ways. The huge jaws jutted forward. The low forehead sloped back to a flattened skull. The brows over the eyes were massive. Also, *Australopithecus* was rather small: adult males of some species weighed less than one hundred pounds.

However, there are important hominid traits held by *Australopithecus*. One is the brain. While the modern gorilla brain is about 500 cubic centimeters in volume, *Australopithecus'* displacement was about 600 cubic centimeters. The quality of this creature's brain was probably improved over his apelike canines. In fact, evidence suggests that the brain had developed so much several million years ago that language was possible. This implies that social behaviors, such as cooperation and planning, may have been part of the life-style of *Australopithecus*. The brain, then, clearly shows that the creature was more than an extinct ape.

The size of the teeth of *Australopithecus* shows a clear trend toward *Homo*. Likewise, the teeth were arranged in an arc rather than the square pattern of the apes. The shape of the teeth, notably the canines, is more human than ape. In these ways, the dentition of *Australopithecus* shows a clear step toward humans and away from apes. Indeed, it may be that the most characteristic feature of the *Australopithecus* genus is a trend toward increasingly efficient food-grinding jaws and teeth.[7]

Another divergence from apes is seen in the posture of *Australopithecus*. At around four million years ago, they were clearly bipedal—walking on two feet.[8] Bipedalism is not the apes' natural means of locomotion. Because *Australopithecus* was bipedal, it can surely take its place among the hominids.

Besides certain kinds of brain, teeth, and posture, another feature typical of hominids—and so probably of *Australopithecus*—is tool-making. Other animals have been seen to use tools: Wasps use pebbles as hammers; birds use twigs as probes; sea otters smash shellfish with stones; polar bears bash prey with blocks of ice. These and other cases show that tool use is found among nonhumans.

Among the apes, not only tool use but tool*making* has been observed. The best-known example of nonhominid toolmaking is the chimpanzee's termite stick.[9] The ape strips the twigs and leaves from a small branch, thus fashioning a stick that can be poked into a termite mound and withdrawn, bringing termites to be licked off. Chimps have also made sponges from leaves. These are just a few of the many examples of tool use and toolmaking that have forced us to qualify the statement long used by scientists that hominids are the only toolmaking animals. Now it seems more accurate to define hominids as the only beings that *depend* on toolmaking for their way of life. Indeed, some authorities have gone as far as to define hominids as "habitual toolmakers . . . distinct in this respect from all other primates." [10] Human beings are makers of patterned tools. One of a kind will look like others of the same kind, which indicates the transmission of knowledge and hence communication between individuals. This can be an indicator of culture, the learned, shared behavior that defines a population as "human." We can conclude, then, that the overall picture of the hominid line leads us to expect that *Australopithecus,* hominid in several important other ways, did make tools.

The Advent of Humans

Whence Sprang *Homo*?   Let's take stock of our human evolution puzzle pieces so far. We've seen that *Ramapithecus* may have been the earliest creature that was more humanlike than apelike—a hominid. *Australopithecus* clearly was a hominid and was more humanlike than was *Ramapithecus.* Whether or not it made tools, the teeth, brain, and posture of *Australopithecus* had become unlike those of other apes. The question concerning *Australopithecus* is, Was it an ancestor of humans or just a humanlike creature that became extinct?

Until the past decade, *Australopithecus* was believed to be part of the lineage of humans. The creature was seen as the man-ape stage of human development. Recent findings have strongly questioned this view. Anthropologists have not yet reached a general agreement on the question of what creature served as the transition from ape to human. Therefore we can say only that the transition occurred between about 4 million and 1½ million years ago.

Scientists offer several family trees concerning that period of 4 to 1½ million years ago. The old version claimed that of the several kinds—or species—of *Australopithecus,* one evolved into *Homo*—the same genus as modern humans. *Homo habilis* was a toolmaker with a more humanlike appearance than *Australopithecus.* The discovery of *Homo habilis* makes it less likely that *Australopithecus* was part of the human lineage. *Australopithecus* may have been just a hominid standing on the sideline, not evolving into *Homo* itself. In other words, some scientists believe *Australopithecus* became extinct rather than evolving further. We have introduced *Australopithecus* because it is also possible that this newly found *Homo habilis* sprang from some early species of *Australopithecus,* or that both evolved from some third, earlier form. The debate continues.

The identification of the creature that made the transition from ape to *Homo* will not be settled for years to come. Each important finding requires time to analyze. Scientists must figure out how to interpret the evidence. New discoveries can confuse the picture. At this time, we can say only that some species of *Australopithecus* may have been the ancestor of the earliest *Homo* species. There are many possible lineages, involving several species of *Australopithecus.* Figure 2–1 sums up the most common views. For the time being, we will have to leave this part of the puzzle incomplete. As we turn our attention to the next part of the evolutionary story, the picture comes into focus.

FIGURE 2-1

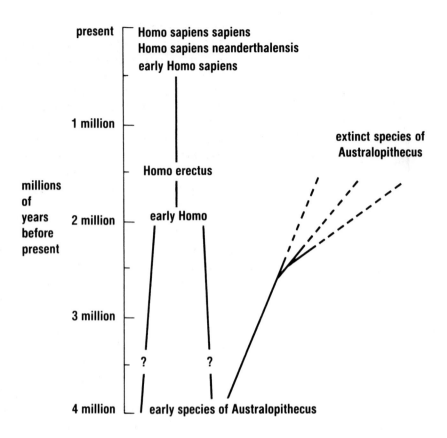

Homo Erectus. The lines of human development become clearer after *Australopithecus*. Between 1 million and 2 million years ago, a species had emerged that is easily grouped in the same genus as modern humans. *Homo erectus* was taller than *Australopithecus* and had a larger brain and a more advanced culture. While its skull was still long and low, the rest of the body was quite modern. Indeed, the 1984 discovery of a nearly complete *Homo erectus* skeleton in Kenya revealed that 1.6 million years ago creatures existed with skeletons—except for the skull—very nearly the same as ours today.[11]

Homo erectus was not confined to Africa, as was *Australopithecus.* Several racial types of this species have been found throughout the Old World. Remains have turned up in Java, China, Europe, and Africa. Some have been given nicknames, such as "Java Man" and "Peking Man." That this species was so widespread is proof of its success, much of which can be attributed to an improved brain and the culture this made possible.

The brain size of *Homo erectus* approached that of modern humans. While today's size is about 1,400 cubic centimeters, *Homo erectus* samples average about 1,000 cubic centimeters. That makes its brain nearly twice the size of that of *Australopithecus* and about 75 percent the size of the modern human brain. The

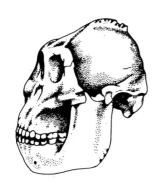

Australopithecus

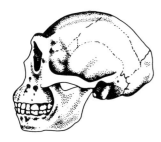

Homo erectus

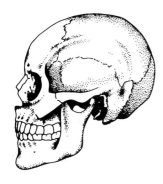

Homo sapiens

Here the development of the hominid skull is clear. Homo erectus has a larger brain cavity than Australopithecus but still lacks the high, rounded skull and flattened face of modern humans.

wide range of brain sizes among the *Homo erectus* samples—775 to 1,255 cubic centimeters—suggests a rapid expansion of the brain. This expansion may be linked to the increasing cultural complexity of the species, as evidenced by the presence of better tools and the use of fire and huts.

The tools made by *Homo erectus* are more refined than earlier tools. This is to be expected. Simple flaking techniques had been developed. Besides stone, both wood and bone were worked.

A dramatic event is the controlled use of fire. While it is unclear whether *Homo erectus* could make fire, there is evidence that it controlled fire for its own use. Hearths have been found, along with charred animal bones. Using fire could have extended the life span of *Homo erectus*; cooking meat helps to tenderize it, allowing older, toothless individuals to maintain a regular diet more easily. Fire also may have aided *Homo erectus* in hunting; grass fires could help stampede prey into ambushes. The use of fire also could have extended the activities of *Homo erectus* into the night, into dark caves, and into colder climates, such as northern Europe. In other words, with fire *Homo erectus* increased its chances for survival and extended its territory.

Besides making better tools and using fire, *Homo erectus* also seems to have made shelters. In southern France there is evidence that huts may have been built by this species 300,000 years ago, showing a big step toward control over the environment. *Homo erectus* was less likely than earlier species simply to take what it was given. We could expect that such industrious creatures would try to advance their life-style in nonmaterial ways.

Evidence suggests that Peking Man may have used ritual. This would be a cultural advance, but there is no concrete proof. The skulls of fellow Peking people seem to have been saved for use, perhaps only as drinking bowls but perhaps as trophies of victims or mementos of friends. Part of any ritual involving these skulls may well have included a gruesome feast. "Peking Man probably did eat the brains of his fellows . . . [but] the feast may have been a ritualistic one rather than mere gorging on human flesh." [12] Eating a brain may have been an attempt to obtain the powers of its owner or to maintain a link with relatives. Whatever the reason, the fact that the skulls were not simply smashed open suggests some ritual motive. Ritual is a human trait, and *Homo erectus* may have progressed in this respect.

Neanderthal Man. Now the picture of human evolution becomes even clearer. There emerged about 125,000 years ago the earliest forms of human beings, often called archaic humans. They have the same genus and species label as we have: *Homo sapiens.* However, we fully modern humans have the full label *Homo sapiens sapiens.* These early or archaic humans that emerged over a hundred thousand years ago are called *Homo sapiens neanderthalensis* by most scientists. The Neanderthal seems to have

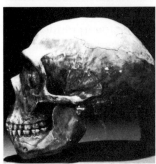

Neanderthal had a rather modern skeleton except for the skull, as seen in the long, low crown, the protruding mouth and jaws, and the heavy brows.

been the last stage before fully modern human beings appeared, though the two were for a time contemporaries. As we could expect, their structure and technology were a clear step beyond *Homo erectus* and toward *Homo sapiens sapiens.*

The Neanderthal was much like us in structure. Brain size was within the range of modern humans. From the neck down, this "caveman classic" was like us. Large brows, a big face, and a long, low, broad skull give the Neanderthals their "caveman" image.

These physical changes were accompanied by advances in technology. Refined flaking techniques produced blades and points as well as axes and scrapers. There is evidence that shelters were built. Of course, fire was used, as with earlier species. All this technology meant that Neanderthal was becoming more able to control the physical environment.

Besides their improved technology, these archaic humans may have made another dramatic advance in their life-style: the use of religion. While it is possible that *Homo erectus* engaged in rituals, it is likely that Neanderthal had religious rituals. The burial practices of the Neanderthals strongly suggest that there was a ritual concern with an afterlife. At one site, a ring of goat horns surrounds a child's grave; at another, a corpse was buried with flowers. Scientists also discovered what may have been a family burial site. And at several cave sites, the remains of bears were arranged in a way that suggested cult practice. Such evidence does not prove that the Neanderthals had developed religious rituals or beliefs, but it does strongly suggest it.

The exact role of these archaic humans in the development of *Homo sapiens sapiens* is unclear. It is likely that only some local populations evolved into full humans. The Neanderthal may have been a dead-end form that simply could not meet the demands of the environment and became extinct. Some have speculated that Neanderthal lost out in direct competition with the newcomer, *Homo sapiens sapiens,* or that Neanderthal mixed with *Homo sapiens sapiens.* While the fate of Neanderthal leads to some fascinating speculation, the important point here is that Neanderthal faded away as fully modern humans stepped into the picture.

Modern Humans. About 40,000 years ago, *Homo sapiens sapiens*—humans with the same basic anatomy as ours—appeared in several parts of the Old World. One of the first early specimens of this new species was found in a village of southern France called Cro-Magnon. The Cro-Magnon people and several other variations of the species were spread from Europe and Africa to Asia and Australia. Sometime in the past 40,000 years, probably by about 20,000 years ago, humans moved into the New World. For the first time, humans were then found on all the earth's continents except Antarctica.

While our puzzle now shows humans that were fully modern, it at the same time shows a way of life that is far from modern. We are nearly ready to shift our attention from physical evolution to the evolution of humans' ways of life: cultural evolution. In fact, the next chapter will focus on culture, which is more important to us now than the kind of body we have evolved. Thousands of years ago, with their hunting skills, improved tools, and cave art, the first modern humans began to build ways of life to fit the demands of their environments. Soon, however, the evolution of these life-styles began to outstrip the evolution of the human body. The remaining chapters of this book focus on the way of life created in our part of the world in our time.

HUMAN EVOLUTION TODAY AND TOMORROW

Our puzzle of human physical evolution is nearly complete. A picture of both the process and its results has emerged. Some of the pieces are still missing, and parts of the picture are still unclear, but we can now look at what science has offered us so far—and form hypotheses for the future. But at the same time we must note that the picture of human evolution is changing.

It is proper to view humans today as only the current stage in the evolution of the species. If we somehow survive another 100,000 years, what will we look like then? That will depend on the demands of the physical and cultural environments. To see how our species is changing now and will change in the future, we must examine the interplay of two factors that determine the direction of evolution: natural selection and environment.

Controlling the Environment

With our technology modern humans have become increasingly able to control a major factor in the evolution process: the environment. For other species, evolution is a matter of changing genes to adapt to surroundings, but humans adapt by changing their surroundings to fit their genes. In fact, humans are changing the earth so much that they are denying many other species the chance to exist. Recently, it was estimated that about 75 percent of the world's large mammals and 30 to 70 percent of its plant species would disappear by the year 2100 if the present pace of land development continues.[13]

Of course, we do not completely control the environment, nor would complete control mean that humans would evolve no further. Control only means that we can to some extent choose the changes that will be made in our environment. We will probably never be able to prevent change completely. As we change our environment, we create new selection pressures. These new pressures seem to change our gene frequencies; that is, affect our evolution. One such pressure we create is pollution. We have added new substances to our environment, some of which are suspected of causing mutations. Pollution may thus cause a higher mutation rate, thereby changing the gene frequency. And because most mutations are harmful, our pollution may be changing the gene frequency in a way we would not otherwise choose. The pollution example suggests that we need to be more conscious and careful of the choices we make in trying to control our environment. There is also cause for concern regarding our impact on the other factor in evolution: the selection process itself.

Controlling the Selection Process

In the past, natural selection has made sure that harmful mutant genes were reproduced at a very low rate, if at all. Today, rather than allowing nature to take its course, we choose to use technology to fight death. In our efforts to save the lives of people born with genes that carry physical and mental defects and diseases, we are allowing those genes to survive. This raises a moral question: Should we interfere in the selection process? On the one hand we might reason that the most humane course is to take the long view and do what will improve the chances of the species to survive, or even prosper. By allowing natural selection to "weed out" non-adaptive genes, we might strengthen future generations rather than invite increasing dependence on technological aids to keep afflicted individuals alive and functional. On the other hand, we must ask who is to decide which genes are harmful, which defects are not worth being rectified with technology and the attending financial costs. Who will decide which other humans must be sacrificed because they carry the "wrong" genes? By keeping people with "defective" genes alive, are we polluting our gene pool with weak genes or are we showing our fundamental human bonds with one another?

Perhaps the definition of fitness needs to be changed. After all, social functioning today depends less on physical "fitness" than on "mental fitness." Perhaps medical aids, instead of threatening our society's health by polluting our gene pool, are allowing more people with mental—and thus social—fitness to contribute to our society. Remember, fitness is a matter of surviving and reproducing within an existing environment. If that environment offers appropriate medical aid, the physically defective person can still enjoy success. An obvious problem with this viewpoint is that a large part of a population might become dependent on such artificial aids. Such dependence would make a society vulnerable to a drastic change in environment or a loss of the artificial aids.

Another issue concerning control of the selection process is how our population's gene frequency is affected by the differing birthrates among social classes. Generally, the lower the social class, the larger the family. If it could be shown that lower-class people have inferior genes, our population might be faced with a gradual decrease in our gene quality. But that is a very big "if." A clear link between social class and gene quality has yet to be found—indeed, none may ever be found. Social class seems to be determined more by social environment than by genes. Still, a few people would call for decreasing the propagation of the lower classes, an attempt that would involve direct control over the gene frequency of the society, as well as raise serious moral questions. Because the evidence points to no link between gene quality and social class, the higher birthrate among poor people seems to pose no danger to our gene pool.

Besides talking about tampering with selective pressures, humans are also coming close to directly manipulating genes. The future holds a real prospect of genetic engineering. That is, we may be able to substitute one gene form for another. This would prevent much suffering and heartbreak now caused by genetic defects. But how far will we go with this power? Will we choose our child's eye color and hair type? Moreover, will we be allowed to choose freely? Some talk of future population policies that might restrict the kinds of genes parents would be allowed to reproduce. Who will decide which genes are acceptable? The main problem with such programs is the cost in terms of freedom. How much freedom are we willing to give up for greater control of our genetic directions?

As we become more able to control our environment and the selection process, we also become more responsible for our actions. As humans gain more influence over their own evolution—and that of other species—they will be faced with decisions of vast importance. One task of social science is to offer humans a sound basis for those choices. We hope this book offers some help in making these decisions.

SUMMARY

Since the middle of the nineteenth century, humans have begun to understand their origins better. Darwin and Wallace unlocked the secret of evolution. Discoveries in genetics have thrown more light on the subject. We now see how the gene frequency of a population is affected by the demands of the environment. Genes that help a species reproduce tend to become more common in that species. As the gene frequency changes, evolution takes place.

In the past few decades, great progress has been made in piecing together the past of human evolution. As more fossils are found and genetics is more thoroughly explored, we become more certain about some parts of the story and remain confused about others. Still, a clear picture has emerged. The transition from lower forms to humans has been broadly outlined, but arguments will continue over the details.

The first hominid (direct, nonape ancestor of humans) was probably *Ramapithecus.* The next creature—and certainly a hominid—to appear was of the genus *Australopithecus.* This creature seems to have been the first to use tools. The genus *Homo* may have sprung from *Australopithecus.* From the early species of *Homo* evolved *Homo erectus,* who showed dramatic physical and cultural advances. The next stage was Neanderthal Man, archaic humans who showed further progress in body structures and culture. After them came *Homo sapiens sapiens*—modern humankind.

The principles of evolution still work today, but they are applied to a different situation. That is, humans are gaining greater control over both the environment and the selection process.

But scientists cannot predict the results of such control. In this case, as in others, power offers both promise and threat. It may be comforting to know that our genetic future will take a long time to arrive.

SPECIAL TOPIC

"Races": Variations Among Humans

No longer can one write about race in a textbook without having second thoughts about it. The concept of race has itself become unfashionable among some scientists. Indeed, most scientists contend that the term "race" is not appropriately applied to humans. It has been suggested that "race" be dropped and other terms used.

But, although race is considered by many scientists a technically incorrect term to use regarding humans, it is the term nonscientists use. (See how the Census Bureau deals with race: Figure 2–2.) Just as it would be absurd to say that the concept of race does not exist, it would be unwise to give the concept no exploration here. So we shall explore race, while noting that, according to many scientists, race is an imprecise term to use regarding humans. Perhaps now the reader wonders what all the fuss is about. Just what does race mean?

WHAT RACE IS AND IS NOT

A simple way to define race is to focus on the distinctive physical traits or subgroups in a species. A more accurate definition of race is that of a breeding population with a gene frequency distinct from those of other populations in the species. Thus we can view a race as a subspecies. This means that while one race can breed with others and produce fertile offspring, each race differs enough physically from the others to be distinct. Indeed, the reader would do well to keep in mind that whenever the word race is used in this discussion, we are discussing biological features of socially defined categories. We will stick with the term "race" because the reader can more easily connect this term with his/her real-life experience.

The physical differences among races are due to differences in gene frequencies. Today's scientific view of race is usually based on genes, rather than merely on outward appearances. This focus on genes does not make the concept any easier for nonscientists to deal with.

There are several reasons why many scientists also are uneasy dealing with race. It is an imprecise concept. One might ask, How different must two populations be to be considered distinct? Indeed, where does one draw the line between two groups within the same species? There is no clear answer, so there is no agreement about even such a basic question as the number of human races. Furthermore, there is often much confusion when we try to classify individuals according to race. If we speak of races in terms of different gene frequencies, we can only guess about any one person's race. That is, if we somehow determine that a per-

FIGURE 2–2
Resident Population, By Race and Spanish Origin: 1980

In the 1980 census, respondents were asked to identify their race by choosing from 15 groups listed in the questionnaire. No definition of race and no consideration of biological stock was used in this categorization. The figure shows the extent to which nationality and other social features are implicated in the common use of racial groupings. Note that while "Spanish origin" is not considered a racial category, "Filipino origin" is.

White	188,372,000
Black	26,495,000
American Indian	1,420,400
Chinese	806,000
Filipino	774,700
Japanese	701,000
Asian Indian	361,500
Korean	354,600
Vietnamese	261,700
All other races	6,999,200
Spanish origin	14,609,000

SOURCE: U.S. Bureau of the Census, *Statistical Abstract of the United States: 1986* (106th edition) Washington, D.C., 1985, p. 29, no. 32.

son has the genes found in high proportions in a certain race, we can only say that the person probably belongs in that race.

Because we cannot examine a person's genes directly, nonscientists commonly use physical traits to classify a person according to race. There are several problems with this approach too. First, most racial traits are matters of degree. That is, skin color, hair type, and other such features are not always clearly of one or another type. Also, what if a person has the hair of one race but the skin color of another? There are few pure racial types, unless we use only the most vague indicators. (In fact, many do use such vague indicators of race, which allows them to classify people any way they wish.) We are faced with the question of why some traits, and not others, are considered "pure." Purity seems to be a matter of gene frequency. Within a population, how large a proportion must a trait be to be considered the ideal or pure trait? Because of these problems, racial groupings are of limited value for classifying individuals. However, race is more useful in classifying populations, so it is still socially functional.

So what is race? Scientists in this area do not present one clear picture of what race is. Most views of race do include a breeding population with a common genetic heritage. Just how distinct the gene frequency must be to be considered a separate race is the basis of disagreement. It is easier to find agreement on what race is *not*.

Race is not a clear-cut category. Race is not based on language or nationality, even though we hear of the "Aryan race" or the "English race." Nor is race the same thing as religion, though we often hear of the "Jewish race." Race is thought to be many things that it is not. Therein lies many of our social problems with this biological concept.

Though we cannot easily define race, there are groups with different racial traits. Race does exist, but it is a vague concept. Perhaps it will become less vague with some knowledge of how races formed.

HOW RACES FORMED

Science cannot pinpoint just when or where the races began to form. It is likely that today's races diverged only after *Homo sapiens sapiens* had appeared. As the new species emerged, it migrated throughout the Old World. Different groups settled in different environments. If a group remained isolated in an environment that was different enough for a long enough time, different physical traits would evolve. Though science cannot tell us just where or when races formed, it can paint a clear picture of how it happened.

Isolation seems to be the key to the formation of races. Thousands of years ago, geographical barriers must have isolated groups of humans long enough for such groups to evolve slightly different traits. Each group would adapt to its own environment over time. With no other genes entering the gene pool—except for mutations—each isolated group would establish its own unique gene frequency. Each gene pool would, through natural selection, be shaped by the demands of the surrounding environment. The gene frequencies of such isolated groups would be slightly different from one another, roughly as different as the demands of their various environments. In this way, isolated groups evolved different adaptive, genetic packages—racial features—according to the demands of their environment.

Some racial features may be explained as adaptations to cold and heat.[14] Mammals living in cold places tend to have greater bulk and shorter limbs. This is a way of preserving body heat. A key to minimizing heat loss is reducing the area of exposed skin. A big body has a lower ratio of skin to bulk, and so retains more heat. Skin area is reduced also in short limbs, noses, ears, and so forth. A short, fat leg may produce as much heat as a long, thin leg, but the long leg exposes more skin to the air and thus loses more heat. In a cold climate, that heat loss can be dangerous. A long-limbed person is more likely to suffer and die from the cold than a person with a more compact body. Genes for long limbs, over time and in an isolated population, will thus tend to be reproduced at a low rate. A gene frequency being shaped by a cold climate will in this way be different from those of other populations. In a hot climate, long limbs would be selected. Racial distinctions may have come about in this way.

Not all adaptations to climate are visible—many are internal. Some racial groups have a mechanism that sends an increase of warming blood to cold hands. Another adaptation to cold is a high body metabolism; some racial groups burn calories at a high rate to keep warm. People with such internal "bonfires" can tolerate greater cold than other races.

Other racial groups have adapted to cold by other means. In one race, the limbs receive little heat during sleep, while the trunk stays warm. By an arrangement of the blood vessels in the limbs, the warmth of the outgoing blood of the arteries is transferred to the incoming, cooler blood of the veins. The trunk thus retains much of its heat. The limbs are cool, but the vital organs in the trunk are kept warm. People with this adaptation can sleep in the cold of the desert night without discomfort. In some cases, races have evolved different ways of dealing with the same kind of climate. Thus two cold-adapted races may differ in appearance. In such cases, each race found its own solution to cold. Other racial traits evolved in response to pressures from the environment other than cold or heat.

Skin color is the most dramatic racial feature, but the reasons for color differences are not well understood. On the one hand, dark skin is believed to offer protection from the harmful effects of sunlight. That is, a dark-skinned person is less likely to suffer from sunburn or skin cancer than a person with light-colored skin. We could thus expect dark races to have evolved in very sunny regions, where light skin would decrease survival chances. On the other hand, dark skin could cause problems. Skin is able to produce vitamin D from sunlight, but dark skin color can block out so much sunlight that too little vitamin D is produced by the body. This would lead to rickets, which could threaten survival. In addition, dark surfaces absorb more heat than lighter ones, so a dark-skinned person would be more likely to suffer from a high body temperature, which can put a dangerous strain on the body.

The adaptive value of skin colors is not yet clear. An environment may have weighed all the costs and benefits of skin colors and selected the color with the highest total advantage. Scientists have yet to discover the score sheets.

So far the formation of races looks like evolution of a limited scope. It is the same process of the environment selecting for specific

changes in the gene frequencies of populations. This seems to be how the earliest racial groups occurred, but over the past few hundred years, the few basic races have become blurred while newer groupings have emerged. These newer categories, if they can be called distinct races, seem to have resulted from genetic drift and migration and mixing, two processes which require further study here.

Earlier in this chapter we described how random genetic drift can cause the gene frequency of a population to change. Many years ago, when most human groups were small and isolated, a sampling "accident" that increased or decreased the frequency of a gene, regardless of the gene's adaptive value, could have a big impact on that group's gene frequency. Such a group, with its unique gene frequency, could be called a distinct race.

Also, as the isolation of racial groups has broken down, the migration and mixing of races has produced new gene frequencies. If people of Race A move to a new place and mix their genes with those of Race B people, the resulting gene frequency will probably be unique. Not all scientists would call this new group a race. As already noted, the boundary lines of races are not agreed upon. A race remains only what we say it is. Humankind lists the criteria to be demanded of any group.

This section has presented an overall picture of how races formed. Starting with isolated groups in different environments, natural selection worked to produce unique gene frequencies. Each environment selected for genes, perhaps obtained through mutation, which enhanced the survival of the population. From these early races, through genetic drift and through mixing, many unique gene frequencies have been formed. Scientists have not been able to agree on how many races exist, nor have they explained many racial variations. The process of race formation, like evolution itself, remains a wonder and something of a mystery. Though we have tried here to treat race as a biological phenomenon, it is used more commonly as a social category, with implications we will explore in Chapter 8.

SELF-TEST QUESTIONS

1. True or false: The idea of evolution was invented by Charles Darwin.

2. Found on each chromosome, made of DNA, it carries the reproductive code from one generation to the next:
   a. population
   b. race
   c. species
   d. gene

3. When the gene frequency of a population changes, _____ occurs.

4. New gene frequencies can result from:
   a. mutation
   b. migration and mixing
   c. genetic drift
   d. all of the above
   e. none of the above

5. Today the study of natural selection focuses on:
   a. survival of the fittest
   b. struggle or competition among organisms for survival
   c. adaptations of populations to their physical environments
   d. evolution toward the state of perfect fitness

6. Humans are included among:
   a. placental mammals
   b. primates
   c. hominoids
   d. hominids
   e. all of the above
   f. none of the above

7. True or false: Scientists have directly observed evolution in nature and in the laboratory.

8. The study of genetics, fossils, and embryos are all used to _____.

9. The oldest creature clearly labeled a hominid is:
   a. *Ramapithecus*
   b. *Australopithecus*
   c. *Homo erectus*
   d. Neanderthal

10. True or false: *Australopithecus* made, used, and depended on tools.

11. True or false: Experts agree that *Australopithecus* was the genus from which *Homo* sprang.

Match numbers 12–15 to the descriptions on the right:

12. *Australopithecus*   a. the first to spread over several continents

13. *Homo sapiens sapiens*   b. Cro-magnon

14. Neanderthal   c. the last stage before modern humans

15. *Homo erectus*   d. hominid, but not in same genus as us

16. Humans today are affecting their own evolution by:
    a. controlling mutations
    b. controlling the environment, and thus its selection pressures
    c. softening the natural selection process by saving some "defective" genes from early and natural death

ANSWERS TO SELF-TEST QUESTIONS

1. False. Darwin (and Wallace) explained *how* the idea worked; the idea itself had been discussed long before.
2. d
3. evolution
4. d
5. c
6. e
7. True
8. support the theory of evolution
9. b
10. True
11. False. Some experts argue that *Australopithecus* become extinct and that *Homo* evolved from some other path.
12. d
13. b
14. c
15. a
16. b and c

NOTES

1. John L. Brooks, *Just Before the Origin: Alfred Russel Wallace's Theory of Evolution* (New York: Columbia University Press, 1984).
2. John Gliedman, "Miracle Mutations," *Scientific Digest* 90 (February 1982): 90–92, 96.
3. Kathleen Reichs, ed. *Hominid Origins: Inquiries Past and Present* (Washington, D.C.: University Press of America, 1983).
4. Matthew Nitecki, ed. *Biochemical Aspects of Evolutionary Biology* (Chicago: University of Chicago Press, 1982).
5. Roger Lewin, "Molecules v. Morphology," *Science* 228 (May 3, 1985): 743–5.
6. Allan C. Wilson, "The Molecular Basis of Evolution," *Scientific American* 253 (October 1985): 164–73.
7. Yoel Rak, *The Australopithecine Face* (New York: Academic Press, 1983).
8. Kenneth Weaver, "The Search For Our Ancestors," *National Geographic* 168 (November 1985): 560–623.
9. Jane Goodall, "Chimpanzees of the Gombe Stream Reserves," in *Primate Behavior,* ed. Irven DeVore (New York: Holt, Rinehart & Winston, 1965): 425–73.
10. Harry Nelson and Robert Jurmain, 2nd ed., *Introduction to Physical Anthropology* (St. Paul: West Publishing, 1982): 352.
11. Richard Leakey and Alan Walker, "Homo Erectus Unearthed," *National Geographic* 168 (November 1985): 624–29.
12. Richard E. Leakey and Roger Lewin, *Origins* (New York: E. P. Dutton, 1977): 132.
13. *USA Today* 110 (February 1982): 15–16.
14. Carleton S. Coon, *The Origin of Races* (New York: Alfred Knopf, 1966).

SUGGESTED READINGS

Darwin, Charles. *On the Origin of Species.* New York: Mentor Books, 1958.

Eisley, Loren. *The Immense Journey.* New York: Random House, 1957.

Gould, Stephen Jay. *The Mismeasure of Man,* New York: W.W. Norton, 1981.

McKusick, Victor. *Human Genetics.* 2d ed. Englewood Cliffs, N.J.: Prentice-Hall, 1969.

Napier, John. *Monkeys Without Tails: The Story of Man's Evolution.* New York: Taplinger, 1976.

Stern, Curt. *Principles of Human Genetics.* 3d ed. San Francisco: W. H. Freeman, 1973.

Stone, Irving. *The Origin: A Biographical Novel of Charles Darwin,* New York: Doubleday, 1980.

3 CULTURE: THE ESSENTIAL HUMAN TOOL

Culture: Handle with Care

The story of the Ik of Central Africa shows how fragile culture is and how much we depend on culture to make us human.[1] Just after World War II, the Ik of Central Africa were forced to cease their migratory hunting and adopt a new way of life, farming and living in one place. Their major hunting ground had become a national park, off limits to the Ik hunters.

Such drastic changes would disrupt any culture, but the Ik adapted. They had been friendly, happy people, secure in their way of life. Even when they were forced to settle in one place, they maintained their basic values—but only as long as their basic needs were met. When starvation as a result of drought hit the Ik, it took only three generations for a way of life to develop that was shocking in its ugliness. Colin Turnbull, the anthropologist who studied the Ik, was shaken by what he found. The starvation of the Ik had caused them to become obsessed with food. "Even when lying down, their heads or their eyes were flicking back and forth to catch sight of some sign that would lead them to food, even if they were so full they could hardly walk."[2]

Turnbull found that the Ik rarely shared food; each person searched for his or her own food. Those who found food would gorge themselves before others found them. No one saved food because it would be stolen; the rule was to eat it, even if one's stomach was stuffed. In fact, Turnbull saw only one instance of a parent feeding a child over three years old. Family members would try to avoid sharing food with spouse or children.

At this point one might say, "I don't care if they *are* starving. Such selfishness just isn't natural. People just don't act like that." The speaker would thus be defining or redefining humanness in light of the Ik.

Family life for the Ik was reduced to its barest form. Rarely did parents spend time with children. After age three or four, children were put out of the house to live in gangs. Turnbull saw only one new marriage formed in his two years of observing the Ik. There was little love or affection between spouses. They rarely even helped each other find food.

Friendship and kinship are certainly seen as basic to human nature, but these starving people seem to disprove that. The Ik could not afford those luxuries. All but a few relationships among these people were based on each person's efforts to acquire food. The only friendships formed were temporary and fragile, and these were aimed at exploiting some food source. Kinship was not important; aged parents would be put out of the house when they could not feed themselves. In effect, each person was alone.

Such lack of affection causes us to doubt what is called "basic human goodness." The children showed not just meanness but also malice to one another and to helpless elderly people. Another person's suffering would be the cause of laughter for others. One mother was pleased when onlookers watched with delight as her child crawled up to a fire and was injured, causing laughter. Another mother was glad when her baby, whom she had left alone at a water hole, was carried off by a leopard; after all, she no longer had to feed and carry the infant.

"What kind of people are these?" we might ask about the Ik at this point. If we think for just a moment how quickly these people were reduced to their selfish, barely social state, we may ask, "What kind of people are we all?" This chapter cannot answer that question, but it will describe the basic nature of culture, which was crumbling for the Ik. Their story shows us the kind of fate that awaits a people whose cultural foundation is severely shaken. This foundation is not something we can take for granted.

CULTURE: The learned, integrated way of life of a people.

We can fly through the air at hundreds of miles an hour. We can command a tiny machine to handle huge amounts of data quickly. We can travel under rivers and through mountains. We can safely avoid many diseases and look forward to a long, comfortable life. We can do these things because of culture, the tool humans use to control, to some extent, our world. In this chapter we will explore some basic questions concerning this powerful tool of culture. First, we will determine what ingredients make up culture. Then we will look at culture from several angles. Next we will see how culture developed from its infancy to its current stage. Last, we will explore the basis of culture: language.

THE NATURE OF CULTURE

Let us put the concept of culture under the microscope, turning it over and over to view it from all angles. We can look at its insides and then back off and view it from a distance. A concept so basic to the world of humans deserves thorough study.

Just how does culture, the mighty human tool, affect our lives? A debate has been brewing recently. On the one hand, culture has generally been seen as a force which tells us toward what goals we should work. One culture's system of values, for example, may cause people to direct their energies toward personal glory in battle. Another might hold loyalty and cooperation as the measures of a person's success. And a culture such as ours makes economic success as the goal, as embodied in the wry slogan, "Whoever dies with the most toys, wins." Culture, in other words, affects us by selecting our life goals for us.

On the other hand, an alternative model of culture has been recently offered.[3] In this model, culture offers means rather than ends. Instead of setting our goals for us, culture is seen as providing us with a tool kit, an array of ways of regulating our conduct, of evaluating reality, of organizing our energies, and of interpreting our experiences.

Thus, we have two views of the cultural tool. In one, culture spotlights some goals rather than others, and directs our efforts. In the other view, culture offers us certain ways—rather than other ways—of working toward whatever goals we choose. In either view, culture clearly helps determine what we do with our lives.

What Is Culture Made Of?

In the past, Western scientists and laypeople alike used the concept of culture in a limited way. "Culture" was seen as something that made people refined and polished. Only *some* people had culture—those whose life-styles embraced such things as ballet and sculpture. Today, social scientists no longer use "culture" in this narrow, exclusive way. The term now includes anything having to do with human life-styles, including such things as bubble gum, ballet, comic books, and jogging.

There are a surprising number of elements in all cultures. Such elements, called cultural universals, have been listed by the anthropologist George Murdock and include age-grading, cleanliness-training, division of labor, family, fire-making, incest taboos, language, law, property rights, religious ritual, sexual restrictions, weather control, and so on.[4] Except for the basic forms of the nuclear family and incest taboos, such universals are not found in the same form in all cultures. General forms are adapted by each culture in specific ways. For example, weather control in one culture may take the specific form of prayers and offerings to gods; in another, weather control may involve advanced technology. Both of these forms of weather control are adapted to the whole fabric of each culture.

To achieve a fuller understanding of the vast array of cultural ingredients, we must go beyond universals to the study of all cultural elements. Such a study requires that we categorize the elements. One classification system describes cultural elements according to the size of their groupings. This system deals with traits, complexes, and institutions.

Skill Reinforcer 3-1*

How might inductive reasoning be of use concerning these universals? That is, where might induction lead us?

CULTURAL TRAIT: The smallest meaningful unit of a culture.

Traits. A cultural trait is the smallest part of a culture. It can be material or nonmaterial. A material trait has substance; it can be touched or seen. Nonmaterial traits have no substance. A book is a material trait, while the ideas found in the book are nonmaterial.

CULTURE COMPLEX: A grouping of related culture traits.

Complex. A culture complex consists of related traits grouped into a pattern. We organize some parts of our lives around culture complexes, which are made up of material traits, such as television cameras and receivers, and nonmaterial traits, such as program ratings, network policies, and governmental regulations.

INSTITUTION: A system of cultural elements organized around an established way of meeting a basic social need.

Institution. Cultural complexes can be grouped into institutions, which are the major pieces of a culture, the main building blocks of a way of life. Such large cultural patterns include many cultural traits. Any one institution includes all the cultural elements that are related to one broad social need. Each institution is a giant grouping of traits centered on one such need. For example, all religious beliefs, rituals, buildings, objects, and other related traits are part of the religious institution. This institution is the system of traits organized around the way a people relate to the supernatural. Other institutions are government, education, family, and economy. They all are organized ways of meeting basic social needs, huge groupings of cultural traits.

A subculture is a distinctive way of life existing within a larger culture.

Another system for classifying cultural elements is that developed by the anthropologist Ralph Linton.[5] By relating Linton's scheme to a concrete situation, we can explore the question of whether it would be better to live in a village culture or in a big city culture. Linton's system can be used to analyze the costs and benefits of such different ways of life. The system is composed of three classes of cultural elements: universals, specialties, and alternatives.

Universals are the values, habits, and beliefs shared by all sane, adult members of a social system. Examples are shared views on religion, money, or sex. Of course, the universals of one culture may be quite different, in kind and in number, from those in other cultures. In any one culture this core of shared beliefs and values is the basis of social harmony: The smaller the core, the more frictions that can arise. On the other hand, the larger the core, the more elements each person must accept and agree to. Agreement on basic values brings harmony, but it also demands great conformity. The cost of harmony is that the same big pill must be swallowed by every member; the cost of freedom is friction.

In other words, one's decision about whether to live in the village or the city would have to be based in part on how many of the village's widely shared values one would be willing to accept for the sake of harmony, or how much of the city's disharmony one would accept in order to be more free of the necessity to conform.

Specialties are knowledge and skills shared only by certain socially distinct categories of people. For example, distinct classes of people, such as women or welders, would possess skills that other members of the same social system would lack.

Specialties can be blamed for many of our social inequalities. People who possess highly valued skills will lead very different life-styles compared to other people. These specialties divide us into different social rankings, different social worlds. The fewer specialties a culture offers, the more equal the members will tend to be. There will be fewer bases for different life-styles.

As with universals, there is a cost for having either few or many specialties in a culture. With few specialties, there are not as many opportunities to find a satisfying outlet for one's productive talents. The city, for example, offers many more job opportunities than the village, but having many specialties contributes to unequal social rankings.

Alternatives, Linton's third class of cultural elements, are shared by some people, but not by all members of the system or even by members of distinct groups. They include tastes, interests, and viewpoints. For example, a bus driver and a doctor belong to different social groups, but both might share an alternative such as yoga, chess, or socialism.

In the example of city versus village life, the village, like cultures with many universals, has few specialties and alternatives. There would be harmony, but little opportunity or excitement. A city, like cultures with few universals, would have many specialties and alternatives; it would offer little harmony but more personal freedom. The village offers peace; the city offers freedom. Both have their costs.

Classifying the elements of a culture is not simple, because many cultures, including our own, are made up of various subcultures. Complex urban industrial systems have many subcultures. The United States has many groupings of people whose norms and values differ from the general culture; these people belong to subcultures.

SUBCULTURE: A cultural segment, differing from the general pattern, shared by a particular group within a society.

A subculture is the way of life shared by only one or a few segments of a social system. Members of a subculture feel a unity among themselves and identify with one another to some extent. Still, they share parts of the general culture too. Their subcultural identity may be based on social class, ethnicity, religion, or other factors. Thus we can speak of a middle-class black subculture or a rural Southern subculture in the United States. A person can belong to several subcultures at the same time. For example, one may be Jewish, black, and upper-middle-class.

Criminal identity can be a basis for subculture. Juvenile gangs or motorcycle groups can develop their own unique subcultures based on their shared attitudes toward certain laws. On such a basis, a subculture can develop its own mode of dress and speech and its own prestige system. In these ways, the life-styles of members of the subculture differ from those of the general culture. And if such groups reject some of the values of the mainstream, their life-style is a counterculture.

A subculture can also grow from a religious basis. For example, the Amish share not only their religious ideas but also distinctive beliefs regarding transportation, schooling, and dress.

As we saw in our discussion of Linton's specialties, occupation can also be the basis for different ways of life. The lives of a plumber and a professor will differ in many ways. Their views concerning government, education, and leisure, for example, are affected by their different job experiences. Though they may share many parts of the American culture, they differ in significant ways; they live in different subcultures.

Subcultures, then, are parts of cultures, much as individuals are parts of families. In fact, the grouping of subcultures within a culture is in several ways like a family. Usually the family's members work toward the same basic goals, though they have their own special interests too. They are distinct from one another yet are clearly similar in important ways. They share many values. They may argue about some issues, but they are likely to stand united in a crisis, because in the end they depend on one another. The family must adapt to the needs and desires of its members; or it may be destroyed. In all these ways, cultures and their subcultures are related as are families and their members.

Ways of Looking at Culture

Something as close to us as our way of life can be difficult to see clearly. Here are several arms-length views of culture, each offering a different perspective. The first view helps us see how good our culture is. The second view will show how fragile culture is. The third view explores how exclusively human culture is.

Is Our Culture Number One?

Ethnocentrism.   Other people may be "religious fanatics," but we are "true believers." Others are "pushy," but we are "assertive." Many people view other cultures in this distorted way. Ethnocentric people are culture bound, because they start from the premise that their own culture is the best, and will see anything foreign and different as inferior to their own. They use their own culture as the standard against which others are judged.

The ethnocentric viewpoint is found in all known societies and probably in every human group. Whether it be a nation, a church, or a school, the members are likely to view it as better than all others. Although ethnocentrism is in all human groups, it is not in every person. Some people can view their own groups more objectively. Others have an ethnocentric outlook in one area but not in another. Social scientists have yet to agree on what causes variation among people in this regard.

ETHNOCENTRISM: The view that one's culture is superior to others.

The ethnocentric viewpoint is unhealthy. It distorts our perceptions and gives us a dangerous foundation for decisions and opinions. It also closes our minds to anything different. Change from outside our group is likely to be resisted as some foolish foreign notion. The ideas of outside groups will be ignored or rejected, even if they might be valuable. This close-minded attitude brings to mind the tourist who refuses to appreciate any foreign ideas. By denying the value of other ways, such a person gains little from contact with other cultures except for a few photographs. In these ways, ethnocentrism can blind a group to valuable influences from outside.

Ethnocentrism can also have negative results for other people. If "we" are so right, and "they" are wrong, we might feel justified in changing them, even if they resist. A great many people have been killed, tortured, or enslaved by others who were convinced of their own rightness. Ethnocentrism can be dangerous for "them" as well as unhealthy for us.

Is there any value to the ethnocentric viewpoint? Indeed, the attitude of "our way is the best" can be helpful in several ways. By resisting outside ideas, ethnocentrism promotes stability. The culture is spared disruptions from outside sources that might hinder progress toward the group's goals. Disruptive ideas are easy to reject when the group strongly believes in its own values.

Ethnocentrism also gives group members something to believe in and work for. People who believe their group is superior to all others are more likely to work and sacrifice for the group's goals. We call this group loyalty "patriotism." Without such support, a group will not compete well with challengers, for instance, during

Ethnocentrism involves the belief that one's own culture, religion, or race is superior to others.

The belief that "our own way is best" can have negative or positive repercussions.

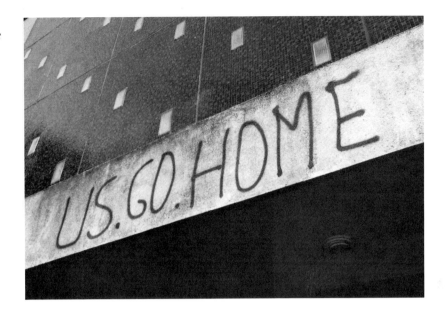

wartime. Such a belief serves to unite the members of a group and urges them to action. It boosts their morale because, after all, they feel they are on the best team.

While ethnocentrism can cause conflict among groups, it can create harmony and strength within groups. While a certain amount of ethnocentrism benefits a group, especially when it is threatened from the outside, too much ethnocentrism can get in the way of a group's progress.

Cultural Relativity. "That culture is rather different from our own, but it seems to work for those people." This statement illustrates the concept of cultural relativity, which can be seen as the opposite of the ethnocentric viewpoint. It is an open, tolerant, accepting outlook. Most social scientists try to use this perspective in viewing their own culture and other cultures.

CULTURAL RELATIVITY: The attitude that each culture and cultural element must be viewed in the context of how well it works for its people.

There are two basic parts to the cultural relativity perspective. First, all cultural pieces should be seen as parts of wholes. Second, all cultures should be respected to the extent that they meet the needs of their people.

From a culturally relativistic viewpoint, a cultural element is to be understood on the basis of how it fits into the cultural whole. It does not allow us to label some practice or belief as odd or wrong until we see how it fits into the cultural framework. We will usually find that the elements of a culture work together in a functional, sensible way. The relativistic perspective requires that we stand back and view the parts in relation to the whole. Imagine how hard it would be to study some animal using a magnifying glass, studying only a small part at any one time. Many of the parts would look absurd seen by themselves. We could understand neither the parts nor the whole from such a limited perspective.

The other part of cultural relativity is the attitude that all cultures are worthy of respect to the extent that they work for their people. Cultures are not judged or understood on how they fit the perspective of our *own* culture. The relativistic view requires that we free ourselves from the limits of our culture, that we forget to some extent what we have learned about what is right and wrong, pleasant and distasteful. Approaching a culture with such an open perspective allows us to see it more clearly.

The ethnocentric viewpoint is like studying a fish by comparing it to ourselves. From this point of view, the fish looks horribly deformed. In such a study, too, the fish would be placed in a human environment. As it lay gasping and wriggling helplessly, we would conclude it to be a poorly designed creature. The relativistic perspective would study the fish by exploring how well it functions in its proper, natural habitat. Only by viewing it in its own world could we fully understand the fish. In this way, the relativistic viewpoint can help us understand other cultures.

Cultural relativity does not require that we judge all cultures to be acceptable. It is helpful for understanding other cultures, but we need not try to avoid making any judgments at all. In fact, we are probably unable to avoid judging other cultures. Our judgments, however, can be based on a clearer understanding of cultures by using the tool of relativity.

Cultural relativity is based on a functional viewpoint, which means that a way of life is understood, and perhaps judged, on how well it functions to fulfill the needs and wishes of its people. For example, infanticide, the killing of infants, violates our values regarding human life. However, infanticide is practiced in some cultures as a way to improve the survival chances of the group as a whole. It controls population and helps ensure that the group's energies are invested wisely. Seen from this perspective of its function for the group, infanticide is easier for us to understand. We can thus base our judgment of infanticide on its functional value.

Of course, science has no business telling us what judgments to make. Instead, it can help us base our judgments on a better understanding of how a culture functions. Social science offers cultural relativity as a tool to help us in this way.

If we attempt to judge other cultures on how well they function, how should we evaluate this functioning? Certainly, a culture should meet the basic survival needs of its people. It must help the people be healthy, help them reproduce. It must also maintain the emotional health of the people; surely we cannot call a culture good if its people are always unhappy and depressed. Also, a culture should help its people realize their goals.

The description of the culture of the Ik in the chapter preview shows that not all cultures necessarily work well for their people. Many cultures are not able to adapt to the new demands and pressures created by the political and technological changes of today's world. The Ik are an example of failure to adapt to drastic changes.

Our own culture may be an example of a life-style that threatens its own survival. Surely other people are more contented and happy than us, though they may lack the comforts and the life expectancy offered by our way of life. Of course, the extent to which Americans can make full use of their culture varies with social class and other factors, but comparing our pressures and worries to the relaxed, peaceful lives of some technologically primitive groups helps remind us that our way of life does not function for us as well as it could.

Another issue arises when discussing cultural relativity: What if a culture functions well for its people but threatens or destroys others? We might say that the culture, or subculture, of Nazi Germany met the needs of those it accepted as members. The killing of millions of Jews could even be viewed as functional, as meeting the goals of the Nazi subculture, if the relativistic view was pushed to the extreme, but surely no one wants to carry the relativistic view to such lengths.

Not all cases of infanticide are clearly vital to the culture's survival. Female infanticide was common practice in northern India before the British declared it illegal in 1870. Even today, daughters suffer from so much neglect that the proportion of surviving males-to-females is abnormal. The reason for such intense preference for sons rather than daughters may lie in the manner of economic production in that part of India, dry-field plow cultivation requiring little female labor. This, plus inheritance rules, made parents see the birth of a daughter as an expensive misfortune, so in earlier times they killed her. Now the parents "lethally neglect" her.[6] Female infanticide may provide some usefulness relative to that culture's functioning, but how useful must it be to justify the practice?

Culture as a Jigsaw Puzzle.   Most people have played with a jigsaw puzzle and enjoyed fitting the pieces together. Another way of looking at culture is to see it as a shifting jigsaw puzzle. While the parts of a culture do not usually interlock as well as puzzle pieces, they do fit together to some extent. The elements of an established culture have been shaped over time to fit together. The parts of this cultural puzzle are integrated; they form a working, fairly cohesive whole. Each part has its place and its function.

These interlocking parts of the puzzle fit snugly when the pace of change is slow. The parts are able to adjust their shapes, and the culture's functioning is barely disrupted. When the pace of change is fast, however, a culture is constantly being disrupted. The parts do not have time to adjust. Their smooth interlocking is upset. This disruption is evident in many developing nations today. The modern world has severely shaken cultural puzzles. Large new pieces have been introduced into the puzzles, requiring drastic shifting and altering of the old pieces. For example, electric power, money, and birth control all require major changes in other parts of a culture. Also, as one new piece gains a place in the puzzle, other new pieces often follow.

SKILL BOX

Deductive Reasoning

The argument presented above regarding judging cultures shows an attempt at logical thinking. It begins with a problem (how are we to judge cultures?) and uses logic to reach a conclusion. The structure of the argument is:

1. If we will use cultural relativity to judge cultures, and
2. If cultural relativity bases its judgment on how well the culture works for its people,
3. Then we will judge cultures on the basis of how well they work for their people.

This is an example of deductive reasoning.

Deductive reasoning is one of two approaches to logical thinking. Inductive reasoning, which was discussed in the previous chapter, moves from specific data to general conclusions. Deductive reasoning is the flip side of that approach; it puts to use the general statements obtained through inductive reasoning by applying those statements to a particular case. Deductive reasoning helps us use what we have gained from inductive reasoning. Together the two approaches move us from specific data to general knowledge to solutions for specific problems.

DEDUCTIVE REASONING: That which moves from a general statement to a specific conclusion.

INDUCTIVE REASONING: That which begins with specific statements of pieces of information, then moves to a general conclusion.

Deductive reasoning is a form of logical argument that flows from an assumption toward a logically demanding conclusion. The reasoning begins with a general statement and from it deduces a conclusion for a specific case. It takes this form: "If this statement is true in general, then this conclusion must follow from it in this particular case." Used properly, such reasoning compels us to accept an argument's conclusion, presuming its assumptions are accurate.

SYLLOGISM: A form of deduction, composed of a major premise, a minor premise, and a conclusion.

The syllogism is the most common form of deductive reasoning. As in the argument above on judging cultures, it is constructed of two premises and a conclusion. A simple example of the syllogism is:

1. All cherries are red. (A general statement or assumption)
2. This is a cherry. (A particular case)
3. Therefore this is red. (A conclusion about that particular case)

The first statement in this example is called the major premise. It is a general statement and is the product of inductive reasoning, which is based on our previous experience or research concerning cherries. The syllogism assumes this statement is true, though it may not be, depending on the quality of the inductive reasoning it came from.

The second statement of the above syllogism is the minor premise. It states a particular case related to the first statement. In our example, the minor premise describes one specific cherry, which relates to "all cherries" mentioned in the major premise.

In a syllogism there must be a term that is mentioned in both premises. This ensures that those two statements overlap. Only if they relate to each other can some conclusion be drawn from the two statements. For example, we could draw no conclusion from these two statements: "Roses are red" and "This house is large."

The second statement would at least have to mention redness or roses for the syllogism to begin to work for us. The two premises must be linked by a common term.

The last statement of a syllogism is the conclusion. It is an inference drawn from the premises. The conclusion is valid if it follows inescapably from those premises.

The conclusion, and the whole argument, may be valid and logical, but it is inaccurate if the premises are false. For example, the following syllogism is valid, but it is untrue because it is based on a false assumption:

1. All apples are blue.
2. This is an apple.
3. So this is blue.

The syllogism is a valuable tool. It helps us construct compelling arguments and can be used to evaluate arguments. By putting an argument in the form of a syllogism, we can see whether it follows a logical path to a valid conclusion. If we also believe the truth of the premises, we can then accept the argument.

If a cultural puzzle is disrupted enough, it may be destroyed. The plight of the Ik showed this all too clearly. Many developing countries are fighting this disruption, trying to keep the pieces of their puzzles together. So many pieces may be replaced by new ones that the puzzle may lose its essential identity. The cultural puzzle is a fragile one; it can stand only so much change, and only so fast.

In South Korea, a dizzy pace of change requires that one cultural heritage be fitted into another. According to the ancient Confucian heritage, workers should be paid according to their age and social status. Yet, according to the invading western commercial practices, workers are paid according to responsibility or skill. The Hyundai Motor Company in South Korea decided to blend both eastern and western models. Workers with higher social status were paid more, but overtime work was awarded more to skilled workers. Thus, both eastern and western values are upheld, and the South Korean cultural puzzle is held intact despite very rapid change.[7]

Culture is Only Human.   All animals have a way of life, so might they not also have cultures? To answer this question we must delve more deeply into the meaning of culture, first by elaborating on our definition of culture as the way of life of a people. We have seen that culture is a way of life that has many integrated parts, like the pieces of a jig-saw puzzle. More important, culture is *learned.* Because of this, it can be modified, shared among all members of the group, and passed from one generation to the next. Thus we can define culture as a way of life that is learned, shared, and integrated.

Animals cannot rely on learning from one another. They depend instead on their genes to tell them how to survive. Even though the way of life of some social insects is highly organized, it is not learned. Bees and ants do not—cannot—learn from one another how to build their social system. They "learn" from their genes. In addition, because they cannot share much knowledge with one another, animals can effect little change in their way of life. If one animal discovers some improvement in its life-style, it cannot share this with its fellows. The group's way of life goes on unchanged.

Despite these handicaps, some animals have shown signs of culture. In a few instances, apes have learned a new life-style trait and shared it among the group members. This shows a glimmer of culture-building ability, but only a glimmer.

In such ways, apes have shown some capacity for culture, but they have not produced anything beyond the barest beginnings of a culture as it has been defined here. Thus it is still safe to refer to culture as a human product.

The Limits of Culture's Power.   Culture determines to a large extent the kind of person each of us becomes. Cultural expectations help shape our personalities, our values, our morals. Culture influences the kinds of foods we find delightful or disgusting. Culture influences what kind of clothing we wear. It influences how we make love, when, and how often. Culture influences our ideas regarding God and worship. Culture dictates what is beautiful and what is repulsive. Through culture we understand nature and ourselves. It is through culture that we decide why we live and die, how we should live, and how we should die.

Culture makes us human, enabling us to fulfill our potential as human beings rather than to live as grunting, snarling, ape-like brutes. With culture we can dominate other species as well as contemplate the nature and the destiny of our own. To appreciate the differences between ourselves and other species is to appreciate the power of culture to shape our humanness.

Is the power of culture unlimited? There are many views on this question, and they can be seen as arrayed on a spectrum between two extremes. On one hand, culture can be seen as completely beyond human control. (We will explore this view as espoused by Leslie White in Chapter 13.) On the other hand, we can be seen as autonomous, free-willed beings, able to decide what kind of persons we will become, affected by culture but not controlled by it. In this view we are seen as conscious of ourselves and of the forces acting on us, and we choose how we will react to those forces. While no one can offer empirical proof of a free will, the concept is widely accepted. After all, it makes us feel comfortable to believe that we control our lives, that we are not merely puppets manipulated by our culture.

Another view of culture's power involves a very controversial theory called sociobiology. Sociobiologists acknowledge that culture plays an important role in influencing human behavior, but

---

Skill Reinforcer 3-2

What conclusion can be deduced from these two statements?

1. Culture is a way of life that must be learned from previous generations.

2. Humans are the only creatures capable of learning a way of life from previous generations.

3. Then . . .

they contend that culture is restricted by biological forces. This new field, barely two decades old, has attracted some social scientists as well as biologists and zoologists. Since it was brought into the spotlight in a 1975 book by its major proponent, Edward O. Wilson, sociobiology has generated considerable controversy.

The basic thesis of sociobiology is that some human behaviors are genetically based, especially those behaviors related to reproduction. The label of sociobiology aptly captures the link claimed between social behaviors and their biological bases. According to sociobiologists, human *behaviors,* as well as the human *body,* are the products of millions of years of evolution. These behavioral features, like the physical features, evolved and have been passed on through generations because they helped humans survive. Behavior tendencies such as territoriality, dominance, and conformity are genetic predispositions which are regulated and modified by culture.[8] Even the universal restrictions on incest have been explained in terms of biology.[9] While most social scientists accept the idea that the physical structure of humans is determined by genes, few accept the idea that genes influence fundamental human behaviors.

Indeed, social scientists have attacked sociobiology on two major grounds. First, they say, it is based on evidence from animal studies. Sociobiologists offer intriguing explanations regarding *human* behavior, but no proof. While there is considerable agreement among social scientists that most animal behaviors are genetically based, few are willing to jump the chasm between these species and humans. The second widely-held objection is that in jumping from animal studies to humans, we ignore the uniquely human feature of culture. Social scientists believe that culture is the most important determining factor regarding human behavior. Some sociobiologists acknowledge culture's importance, but argue that the genes limit the kinds of behaviors that can be expected of humans. In other words, while cultures can vary a great deal in the directions in which they demand human behaviors be shaped, the genes determine the far boundaries of human behaviors. In this view, any culture would fight an uphill battle if it defied the natural inclination of human genes and demanded that men be passive and women aggressive and promiscuous.

Excluding the extremists in both camps, the core of the controversy between most social scientists and the sociobiologists is the *degree* to which genes influence human social behaviors. Some basic questions, then, are: How much of human nature is predetermined by genes? Also, how much can culture change or override any genetically based tendencies? Some scientists might admit to the possibility that some human behavior patterns are genetically influenced, but few would accept the argument of an individual explaining his/her unpleasant personality trait by claiming, "My genes make me do it."

We return to the question at hand: Is human behavior a matter of free will, of genetic control, or of culture? The answer of most social scientists lies between the two extremes of genetic control and complete freedom. Our will seems to be somewhat limited by the cultural environment, and by the values and norms which impinge on our decision making. But while we are not entirely free to choose our behaviors, not even the staunchest sociobiologist would claim that all our behaviors are controlled by our genes. In other words, we are not entirely free of culture's influence, and we may not be free of genetic influences on our behaviors, but for most social scientists, most human behavior is explained by the concept of culture.

THE FORMS OF CULTURE

Another way of exploring the concept of culture is to contrast various categories of cultures. By arranging cultures along a spectrum, we can better appreciate the possibilities of the concept. There are several ways to categorize cultures. For our purposes we choose the one based on the cultural evolutionary approach, not because it is accepted by all social scientists (it is not) but because it enables us to survey the spectrum of forms cultures can take. An example of that approach is Marshall Sahlins' categories of hunting and gathering groups, tribes, chiefdoms, and civilized states.[10] The evolutionist perspective employed by Sahlins assumes that more complex cultures (though not necessarily better ones) develop from simple cultures. While this perspective is accepted by many social scientists, one need not accept it to benefit from the panorama of cultural forms it offers.

Hunters and Gatherers

Perhaps for some of us, paradise is envisioned in terms of a small, peaceful, stable group of people sharing an intimate social life as they live in harmony with nature. The few surviving hunting and gathering bands of today have been pushed into the least desirable lands, but perhaps life was at its best when all humans shared this life-style in the finest land. This cultural form goes back as far as several million years ago, when hominids began using tools as hunting weapons. They had been gatherers of food for a long time, so with tools they became also hunters. For a long time before and after the appearance of Homo sapiens, hunting and gathering was the basis for human survival.

The technology of the first humans was quite simple. At first, they probably used only tools they found. Armed with an increasingly advanced technology, hunters and gatherers gradually improved their chances for survival.

Hunting and gathering keeps the people on the move. Their movements are directed by the seasons, and such groups may follow herds of game. Being on the move, the accumulation of wealth is neither easy nor sensible. Because possessions must be carried, they are kept to a minimum. Anyway, this level of technology produces no great wealth to accumulate. Thus, such groups are not divided into rich and poor.

The degree of social equality varies from one hunting and gathering society to another, as we might expect. That variation seems to be based at least partly on environmental opportunities.

The now-extinct Sek'nam of Tierra del Fuego, for example, could not farm or even gather much food from their freezing landscape.[11] Hunting was the main source of food, and hunting was men's work. Thus, men enjoyed more social power than women. In some settings, then, hunters and gatherers are somewhat male-dominated.

In addition, a group that hunts and gathers has no need for schools, for the skills required to live are simple and can be learned informally. And hunters do not need to know how to read or write.

The relatively high degree of social equality of hunters and gatherers is reflected in the family life of such groups. Relationships are relaxed and based on affection more than on production.

Because of the way they live off the land, hunting and gathering groups are likely to be small. They cannot concentrate their food sources, so each group needs plenty of room and therefore groups are widely dispersed. Because of their size and dispersion, hunting and gathering bands leave little mark on the environment, disrupting their surroundings only in small ways.

Tribes

A tribe is a loose grouping of bands. The special feature of this stage is that the groups no longer depend solely on hunting and gathering. They can control animals and, more important, plants enough to enjoy them as dependable sources of food energy.

Besides farming and herding, there are only a few differences between the cultures of tribes and hunting-gathering bands. Members of tribes, as in hunting-gathering bands, are ranked mostly by age, sex, and personal traits. In the tribe, however, it is more likely that some council will have special powers over the other tribe members. There may be a camp police group or special leaders, but such power groups are usually used only on special occasions.

Unlike the hunting-gathering stage, clans are important in the tribe. Members of the clans are related to one another by blood or by myth. One's clan membership is a major part of one's identity. At this stage, clans are ranked quite equally.

Chiefdoms

The differences between chiefdom cultures and tribe cultures are mostly matters of degree. The trends toward greater food production and more unequal social rankings are the biggest differences.

At the chiefdom level, a food surplus is common. The skills of the people enable them to exploit their surroundings in several ways. They may use specialty crops, fishing, floodwater farming, and hunting and gathering. Often people specialize in only one kind of production, such as hunting or fishing. With specialists, efficiency is enhanced. When people specialize in a skill or craft, they are likely to be ranked differently in the social system. If the skills of a person are very important, so is the person. With the advent of specialization, a new basis for social inequality is created.

Unequal social ranking is most visible in the leadership of the chiefdom stage. Leadership is no longer based on personal traits; no longer do group members choose their leader. Chiefs inherit

---

Skill Reinforcer 3-3

Using deductive reasoning, what conclusion can be drawn from these two statements?

1. Except for hunting and gathering bands, all cultures rely on farming.

2. This people's culture relies on no farming.

3. Then . . .

their status through their clans, which are unequally ranked. The chief may get a special house and special dress and even speak a special dialect. He may also demand to be carried about on his litter by another cultural development: the servant. Besides chiefs, servants, and highly ranked specialists, a system of nobles is set apart from the commoners. In the chiefdom, the social gap begins to open wide and separate the people into distinct unequal social rankings.

Religion at the chiefdom level supports this system of nobles and commoners. An organized system of full-time priests maintains temples and rituals. When a noble dies, goods and even humans may be sacrificed in elaborate rituals, and the grave may be set apart from those of the commoners. Through ritual murder of group members, the priesthood recognizes the special status of the chiefdom leaders.

The Early State
From the earlier, relatively simple, easygoing cultural forms, we now come to the stage of the early state, which features deadlines and commands for farm workers and incredible power for rulers. In fact, the world's earliest states arose on the productivity of the farm workers and the strength of the rulers of those societies. It was the productivity of the workers that produced the food surpluses that were transformed into social power by some members of the societies. The food surplus and unequal social power arose hand in hand.

Strong central leadership is needed before the state can exist. This need is easily seen in the rise of irrigation, on which the earliest states depended. Imagine all farmers trying to divert to their land as much of the water as they could; their efforts would be limited by neighbors' efforts to use the same water. Bickering would be common, and each farmer's system of dikes and canals would be less efficient than a larger-scale system. Those who gained the power to organize and regulate production would gain the power to rule. With rulers, the state could be born, as happened in Mesopotamia and Egypt, which serve as excellent historical examples of early states.

In the early state, social power was concentrated. Kings could lead lives of luxury. Part of their wealth was used to maintain armies—another cultural development. Backed by soldiers, a king could exert total power over the other members of the system. The people of these early states were also subjects to their religion. The priests, along with the kings, controlled the people. Religion was a tool of the state.

Education was another tool. The world's first schools were formed in the early states. The schools' function was to support the state by training people who could write and read. With a complex system of government and trade, the state needed written records and laws, and the schools met this need.

The food production of the early state soon improved to the point where the group could release many workers from farming chores. Workers could specialize and improve their crafts on a full-time basis. As the early states flourished, technology boomed.

Advances in technology resulted in even better food production. They also included better means of transporting the food, so the huge food surpluses could reach and support large numbers of people. From such advances in agriculture and transportation, the city arose.

The Modern State

The industrial nation-state is in clear contrast to the culture of the early state. In fact, the modern state is in several ways more similar to the hunting and gathering bands than the early states. The family life of modern states is much more like that of the band than that of the early state; there is more affection than discipline, and the atmosphere is relaxed and warm rather than cold and formal. Functionalists today would say that religion serves the needs of the person first, the social system second, unlike the early states' religion. (Marxists claim that religion is still another tool for the oppression of the masses.) Though we are firmly plugged into the modern state's system, we demand a great deal of personal freedom and leisure, as the hunters-gatherers had.

On the other hand, the nation-state is more urban than any culture before it. Also, members of the state are ranked in a more complex yet fluid social system and are also more likely than ever before to be well integrated into the system. The nation-state is increasingly able to adapt to its surroundings and to transform energy for its use, more so than any other cultural stage reached so far.

SUMMARY

The concept of culture has evolved from being limited to the artistic and refined parts of human living to including all the human-made parts of our way of life. This way of life is constructed of traits (the smallest units) and complexes (groups of related traits) and institutions (giant groupings of traits centered on a basic human need). All cultures have some of these ingredients, because humans the world over have produced similar solutions to social problems. The elements of culture can also be grouped according to how widely they are shared. Universals are shared by all participants of a culture. Specialties and alternatives are shared within more limited segments. Within the larger culture there may be a subculture, a way of life shared by only some of the people.

The concept of culture can be viewed from several perspectives. The view that "our group's way is the best way" is called ethnocentrism. Cultural relativity judges a culture according to how well it meets the people's needs. However it is judged, culture can be seen as a fragile puzzle of interlocked pieces which only humans can construct.

Cultures can be put into categories, the simplest being hunting and gathering, which comes close to achieving social equality. Tribes have some simple farming, but the chiefdom goes a step further and produces a food surplus through production specialists. With this comes more social inequality. Greater technology and greater control of the people through kings and priests result in the evolution of great city-based states. The industrialized states of today developed from the earliest forms of states.

SPECIAL TOPIC

Language: The Key to Culture

Earlier in this chapter we concluded that only humans create culture to any important degree. One reason for this is that even if an animal learns some valuable new behavior, it cannot easily share this with its fellows. If animals were able to communicate ideas among themselves and to the next generation, they might be able to integrate new traits into their way of life more easily. With language, animals might come closer to creating cultures.

Language is the key to culture. Here we will define language, then imagine building a culture without it. Then we will explore the question of whether animals use language.

WHAT IS LANGUAGE?

One part of the controversy surrounding the study of language today is the fact that language is difficult to define. Just what is required of communication that it may be called language? Language may be defined as a system of communication based on the use of symbols in grammatically ordered sentences. Thus, the two basic features of language are symbols and grammar.

Words Versus Growls: Symbols and Signals

The primary basis of language is the use of words, or symbols. This sets language apart from other forms of communication. In order to define language more clearly, it is useful to distinguish between symbols and signals.

Symbol. A symbol is a stimulus—a sound or gesture—with no meaning in itself, to which meaning must be assigned and then shared. The sounds we make when we speak have no meaning to someone who has not learned the meanings we have attached to them. We have learned in our culture that the symbols on this page have certain meanings. For example, the symbol "page" has no meaning in itself. We have assigned meaning to it. Further, we can change its assigned meaning if we wish. We can also create new symbols for new meanings with which we must deal. Thus the meaning attached to a symbol is learned and flexible, not inherent or fixed.

Signals. Signals are sounds and gestures that have built-in meaning for their users. For example, when a bird sings, other birds know the meaning of this signal without having to learn it. The users of a signal do not need to agree among themselves about its meaning: the meaning is naturally clear to them.

Most messages are sent with signals. Animals use singing, growling, chirping, roaring, and other sounds to warn and attract others. Baboons display their huge canine teeth to threaten one another. Dogs and other animals raise their hackles to intimidate; some apes pound their chests. Animals also use gestures to attract mates. Dances, feather displays, and other signals convey mating intentions.

Humans also use signals. We use whistles, cries, and other such stimuli. The signal of a smile, for example, has the same meaning to all humans, no matter what language they speak. Some of our communication seems to be based on universal signals, not learned.

Though we use signals, most of our messages are conveyed by means of symbols. These symbols are mostly words, but some of our gestures could be considered symbols. Many gestures and expressions are learned and thus are symbols. Especially in the Mediterranean region, many hand gestures have been assigned very specific meanings. For example, in some countries, to offer one's left hand in friendship would be interpreted as a highly offensive gesture, because there the left hand is used in place of toilet tissue, and is considered "unclean." Thus gestures can have meanings that are assigned and flexible and that are therefore symbols.

The Words Must Fit Together

The second basic feature of language is that the symbols are arranged in some grammatical order, usually a sentence. A sentence is a grouping of symbols, or words. The arrangement of the words is based on principles of correct usage, or grammar. The use of sentences can greatly enhance messages; complex ideas can be expressed accurately. With the sentence, the symbol can be used to its fullest extent, and language is produced.

CULTURE WITHOUT LANGUAGE?

If humans lacked language, could they build cultures? A good way to explore this question is to imagine how the earliest builders of culture could have managed without language. This places us a few million years back in time. We will imagine that somehow hominids, the direct non-ape ancestors of humans, had evolved with all their talents and traits except language. What sort of problems would they have faced in building a culture?

Tied to the Concrete and the Present

Without symbols, the hominids would not be able to convey abstract ideas or deal with the past or future. The use of symbols frees one to speak about anything and in any tense; there are no restrictions on topics one can discuss. Without language, the hominids would be in this way limited.

Present Tense. Without symbols the group could not speak to one another about the past or the future. Little of the knowledge gained from the past could be conveyed to the next generation. For example, how does one tell a child how to foretell and prepare for a flood if the child has never seen a flood? Also, without symbols there could be little discussion about the future. This would prevent much planning. Without planning, the survival chances of the group would be greatly reduced.

Concrete. Without symbols the hominids could not deal with abstract ideas. They could not distinguish between what is real and what is imagined, what happened and what might happen. They could not speculate. They could not discuss ideals or morals.

Without abstract ideas there would be little social order. In fact, it is difficult to imagine social life even existing without language (or, like the animals, instincts) to establish order. It would be hard to establish rules without symbols. How would the hominids know what rules they were agreeing on? A rule could be created by force, but not by agreement. Clubs and fists, not arguments, would be used in disputes. The social order would be based on fear and force.

Learning Only from One's Own Experience

Learning would be limited to imitation if the hominids had no language. An adult could prepare a child for only a few tasks or events by using signals. One hominid could not teach another to anticipate or to wonder. Most of the knowledge and wisdom gained by one hominid would remain locked inside him and die with him. Many inventions and discoveries would never be transmitted beyond one individual, one group, or one generation. The group's storehouse of knowledge would never grow very large, as each new generation would have to learn not from the elders' experience but from their own experience.

In all, the way of life of hominids would never have developed far without language. They would have remained mired in what might be a brutish and boring social life. The group would lack goals, ideals, and morals. Their knowledge base would grow very slowly, and there would be little improvement over time. The hominids' culture would still be in its most primitive form. Without language, hominids might never have become humans.

WHO HAS LANGUAGE?

Who among our ancestors had language? That is, when did language develop? And do any animals today have language? These questions are not easily answered.

How About Those "Cavemen"?

The first question is a matter of debate that may never be resolved. Since spoken language leaves no direct clues, scientists can only guess which hominids could speak in symbols. (Written language was not invented until about five thousand years ago.)

When did language begin? One theory is that life in the trees called for a fairly accurate signal system but that when apes of long ago left the trees their dangerous new surroundings demanded a more complex system of communication.[12] Thus, perhaps the Australopithecine "ape men" used language because their way of life on the ground required it. Some parts of their life-style suggest this. They lived in groups and probably hunted big game animals. Rules and plans are needed for these behaviors, and both require language. According to this line of reasoning, language developed with *Australopithecus* about three million years ago.

Other researchers contend that articulate speech was not possible until archaic *Homo sapiens* developed a new, lower larynx, or voice box, about 300,000 to 400,000 years ago.[13] Only when the larynx is situated further below the mouth, lower in the throat, can speech be relatively clear and rapid. With such rapid speech, which is based on syllables rather than merely individual sounds, we can use long sentences and thus more complex thought. Another scientist claims that archaic humans were not yet able to utter or process anything but the simplest, crudest messages.[14] There is still considerable controversy as to when articulate speech evolved.

Language Among Animals?

A controversial question today is whether animals have language. Animals do send some fairly complex messages. Though one animal may not agree with another's message, it rarely seems to misunderstand the message. Is this language?

Bees are a striking example of complex communication by a nonhuman species. When a scout bee discovers a source of pollen, it returns to the hive and, using a dance, describes to the worker bees what it found.[15] This dance informs the other bees about the distance and direction to the pollen source.[16] The amount of pollen the scout brings back tells the bees how many workers are needed to exploit the pollen source. While this is impressive communication, it is limited to the topic of pollen. More important, it is an instinctive, not learned, system of communication.

Thus it is with other animal communication systems. Though they may be accurate and efficient, those systems do not use symbols— unless they have human help. Throughout the twentieth century there have been attempts to teach animals to "speak." Horses, dogs, and other animals have been studied. A parrot has been trained to use vocal labels for several dozen objects.[17] Over the years, researchers have tried and failed to teach apes to use oral language; apes probably lack the proper throat and mouth structures to vocalize words.

In the last two decades, researchers have reported success in teaching apes to use nonvocal symbols. Apes have been taught to use the American sign language, geometric shapes, and other means to convey messages with symbols.

Some say that even though apes can use symbols it does not mean they can employ language.[18] Remember, language is based not

Sarah the chimp learned to read symbolic messages and respond appropriately.

only on symbols but also on sentences. There is some doubt that the apes can construct sentences based on rules of grammar. That is, apes may simply imitate human trainers without creating their own sentences.

It may be a long time before scientists agree on this question. The issue is complex and there are many other points argued by the scientists involved.[19] Most of these issues relate to the basic question of whether apes can use symbols in logical, meaningful sentences. For now, we can say that apes can be taught by humans to use symbols. Scientists have yet to agree on whether this use of symbols can be called language.

It has been suggested that the ability of humans to build and use language is based on a genetic program.[20] That is, our language may be shaped by a "bioprogram," which clearly allows many variations but still shows up in any child's first efforts to speak. If such a genetic program could be proven to exist, we might reason that the animals' potential for developing a language, even with human help, is clearly limited by their lack of a bioprogram for it.

Even if apes can use language, that would hardly put them on a level with humans. The apes still depend on humans for their training. Also, the level at which apes use these symbols is still quite basic. Their "speaking" is usually compared to that of a human child, not an adult. Even if it is proven that humans are not the only creatures with language, human abilities are still far beyond those of all other creatures on earth. Because of our superb language talents, humans can be said to be in the world of animals, but of an entirely distinct realm.

SELF-TEST QUESTIONS

1. Which best describes the current view of culture?
   a. refined, artistic pursuits
   b. learned, integrated way of life
   c. an enduring group of people
   d. civilization

2. The smallest meaningful unit of a culture is a _____ .

3. A large grouping of cultural traits based on a fundamental human need is _____ .

4. In Linton's scheme, a culture with many universals will have:
   a. many specialties and alternatives
   b. few specialties or alternatives

5. A way of life shared by only one part of a society is a _____ .

6. "Our way is superior to all other ways" illustrates _____ .

7. _____ is an attitude that judges a cultural element on the basis of how it works for its people.

8. True or false: Some animals have shown signs of culture-building.

Match numbers 9–12 to the descriptions on the right:

9. hunting and gathering band   a. cities

10. tribe   b. no farming

11. chiefdom   c. barely developed farming

12. state   d. food surplus but no cities

13. Sociobiologists claim that:
    a. culture determines human behavior completely
    b. human physical features are culturally determined
    c. some human behaviors are influenced by genes
    d. biology should rule society

ANSWERS TO SELF-TEST QUESTIONS

1. b
2. trait
3. institution
4. b
5. subculture
6. ethnocentrism
7. cultural relativity

8. true
9. b
10. c
11. d
12. a
13. c

ANSWERS TO SKILL REINFORCERS

3–1. From these data, gathered from many cultures, induction could be used to build a general statement about the nature of humans. Examples of such generalizations are found in the two paragraphs following Skills Reinforcer No. 1.

3–2. Conclusion: Only humans can have a culture. From a generalization about culture, we can draw a logical conclusion about a particular creature: humans.

3–3. Conclusion: This is a hunting and gathering culture. We can apply general knowledge to this particular culture and identify it through logical thinking.

NOTES

1. See Colin Turnbull, *The Mountain People* (New York: Simon & Schuster, 1972).
2. Ibid., p. 98.
3. Ann Swidler, "Culture in Action: Symbols and Strategies," *American Sociological Review* 51 (April 1986): 273–86.
4. George Peter Murdock, "The Common Denominator of Culture," in *The Science of Man in the World Crisis,* ed. Ralph Linton (New York: Columbia University Press, 1945).
5. Ralph Linton, *The Study of Man,* student ed. (New York: Appleton-Century-Crofts, 1936): 272–74.
6. Barbara D. Miller, *The Endangered Sex* (Ithaca, New York: Cornell University Press, 1981).
7. Kyu Han Bae and William Form, "Payment Strategy in South Korea's Advanced Economic Sector," *American Sociological Review* 51 (February 1986): 120–31.
8. Joseph Lopreato, *Human Nature and Biocultural Evolution* (Boston: Allen and Unwin, 1984).
9. Joseph Shepher, *Incest: A Biosocial View* (New York: Academic Press, 1983).
10. Marshall D. Sahlins, "Evolution: Specific and General," in *Theory in Anthropology: A Sourcebook,* ed. Robert Manners and David Kaplan (Chicago: Aldine Publishing, 1968): 229–41.
11. Anne Chapman, *Drama and Power in a Hunting Society* (New York: Cambridge University Press, 1983).
12. Dean Falk, "Language, Handedness, and Primate Brains: Did *Australopithecus* Sign?" *American Anthropologist* 82 (March 1980): 72–78.
13. Robert Finn, "Origins of Speech," *Science Digest* (August 1985): 53–54, 64.
14. Philip Lieberman, *The Biology and Evolution of Language* (Cambridge: Harvard University Press, 1984).
15. Karl Von Frisch, *Bees: Their Vision, Chemical Senses, and Language* (Ithaca, N.Y.: Cornell University Press, 1950).
16. J. Gould, M. Henerey, and M. C. MacLeod, "Communication of Direction by the Honey Bee," *Science* 169 (1970): 544–54.
17. Jake Page, "Call Me Ishmael," *Science 82* 3 (March 1982): 88–89.
18. H. S. Terrace, "How Nim Chimpsky Changed My Mind," *Psychology Today* 13 (November 1979): 65–76.
19. Jean L. Marx, "Ape-Language Controversy Flares Up," *Science* 207 (March 1980): 1330–33.
20. Derek Bickerton, *Roots of Language* (Ann Arbor: Karoma Publishers, 1982).

SUGGESTED READINGS

Benedict, Ruth. *Patterns of Culture.* Boston: Houghton Mifflin Co., 1934.

Kluckhohn, Clyde. *Culture and Behavior.* New York: The Free Press, 1962.

Nance, John. *The Gentle Tasaday.* New York: Harcourt Brace Jovanovich, 1975.

Service, Elman R. *Profiles in Ethnology.* New York: Harper & Row, 1963.

Williams, Robin M., Jr. *American Society: A Sociological Interpretation.* New York: Alfred Knofph, 1960.

Wilson, Edward O. *On Human Nature.* Cambridge, Mass.: Harvard University Press, 1978.

Yankelovich, Daniel. *New Rules.* New York: Random House, 1981.

4 HUMAN DEVELOPMENT AND SOCIALIZATION

PREVIEW

Genetic Engineering

Genetic engineering may well have an impact on human personality development in the near future. Advances in molecular or genetic biology have proceeded at a tremendous pace in recent years. One striking example of this pace is the fact that scientists have already established a method of controlling evolution. For many years breeders of dogs have used selection techniques to shape the physical and behavioral traits of the various subspecies of dogs. Now, certain genes have been implanted in mouse embryos, which successfully matured and transmitted the genes to the next generation. It is imaginable that this method will enable scientists to insert "personality tendency" genes in animal species. In fact, genetic engineering may be used to produce entirely new species.

What does this manipulation have to do with human behavior? The possibilities of genetic experiments with humans are as intriguing as they are frightening. If the genes that are suspected of directing some human behaviors can be identified and isolated, experimenters could manipulate those genes. It is safe to assume that most social scientists would expect no genetic determinants to be found for human behaviors in such experiments. However, if the improbable occurred, the manipulation of personalities would become possible. Applications of that technology to behavioral problems, such as in criminals, and to intellectual development, as in the mass production of geniuses, would become feasible.

At the very least, advances in genetic engineering may result in gene therapy for a few genetically-based disorders, including physical, mental, and perhaps even a few behavioral problems. Gene manipulation may also eventually enable scientists—and parents—to control or select particular hormone levels for children. Insofar as hormones influence human personalities, genetic engineering may well have its impact regarding such personality traits as aggression, extraversion, and frustration tolerance.

The human baby seems designed to arouse our affection and attract our attention. It is such a helpless creature, obviously needing our protection, our care. But from that innocent infant can develop a brutal, vicious adult. The transformation of a blameless baby into possibly a murderous adult is infinitely more interesting than the development of caterpillar into butterfly. While the butterfly's story is one of biological factors, the human story has two sides. Human development is a story of not only biological factors but critical, very influential social interaction with other humans. Here we outline the growth and development of the human, and explore both the biological and the social determinants of the human personality. The personality is the individual's typical behavior patterns in interacting with the environment; it defines the individual as a unique member of the species.

PERSONALITY: The traits, forms of behavioral adjustment, that characterize the individual in relation to others in the environment.

HUMAN GROWTH

The growth of a butterfly larva into a butterfly is marked by clear stages, and each butterfly seems to be quite similar in its structure and its behaviors to those of others of its kind. Human growth is more subtle and complex. Rather than a series of dramatic, distinctly separate stages, human growth is a relatively smooth, gradual process. Here we look at that general process, beginning with conception; later we will look at how the process produces such a great variety of personalities.

Prenatal Development

CONCEPTION: The moment of fertilization of an ovum by a sperm.

Our physical structure and, to some extent, our temperament are affected by sheer luck, by the chance combination of two sets of genes. Our first moment of worldly existence—conception—is the most important moment of our life. Much of what we are and will be is based on the luck of that moment. Here we explore the many ways in which that luck affects a human's growth and development.

The human is created through matching two halves of typical cells from its mother and its father. The regular cell structure of any person contains two strings of chromosomes. These strings hold the pattern for an individual's development. The patterns are contained in genes, located on the strings of chromosomes. When we describe a person with blue eyes, curly hair, a big nose, or any of the many physical features that we do or do not notice, we are speaking of traits inherited from one's genetic parents. The typical cell in every person's body contains two such parallel strings of chromosomes. The special cell associated with reproduction has only one string, or half the genetic pattern, for an individual.

OVUM: The female reproductive cell; also, the fertilized organism until the time at which it attaches itself to the uterus in the human being, which occurs during the second week following conception.

The sperm of the male and the ovum, or egg, of the female each contain half the genetic pattern of the people who are to be a child's parents. When the sperm combines with or fertilizes the egg, a zygote is created. A zygote is a fertilized egg. The contributions of both parents transmit patterns of growth and development to their child. A child receives half its genetic material from its mother and half from its father.

ZYGOTE: A fertilized egg formed by union of sperm and ovum.

In other than purely physical areas there are strong indications that a child's intellectual and behavioral potentials are largely inherited. Because it generally contains only half of a parent's traits, the new cell (the zygote) is unique and unlike any possessed by the father or the mother. After its creation, this cell contains all the genetic material necessary for the development of the individual. As this cell divides and duplicates itself, the child's development begins.

The zygote, or fertilized egg, which contains equal amounts of genetic material from both parents, begins to grow almost immediately after conception. All divisions typical of the normal body cells mark the growth. Division results in duplication of the original cell as opposed to the splitting in half of the sexual cell. (Such splitting would create a cell of only 50 percent of the genetic material.) As the zygote reproduces itself during the first two weeks of pregnancy, it creates a hollow sphere of multiple cells. This stage is referred to as the germinal, or ovum, stage.

EMBRYO: An early stage in the development of an organism, from the third to eighth week after conception in the human.

MALFORMATION: A faulty, irregular, or abnormal formation.

The second prenatal period is called the embryonic stage and lasts from the third to eighth week of pregnancy. During this stage the primitive structure, which will become a human baby, rapidly develops. The embryo is a delicate structure and is easily affected, resulting in malformation in the child. Malformation can be traced to the actions of gene defects and other factors. If the defects are based on genes, they are called congenital defects. At this time little can be done either to predict or correct them. In recent years some operations have been performed on unborn children to correct apparent defects, but these attempts are of minor importance in the total picture.

CONGENITAL DEFECTS: Genetic defects that developed in the prenatal environment.

In addition to the congenital defects, viral infections can affect the embryo. If a pregnant woman develops German measles (rubella) during the embryonic period, the chances of damage to the embryo are as high as 60 percent. To a great degree the type of resulting deformity is linked to the time of infection in relation to the age of the embryo. Some abnormalities that can result are deafness, eye defects, and congenital heart disease. Women can avoid such prenatal dangers through immunization that prevents rubella (German measles) infection. The injection must be given before conception, however, because the results would be similar to an actual case of German measles.

The importance of prenatal care for the unborn child cannot be understated. Unfortunately, many women, whether through ignorance, laziness, or lack of access, seek little or no prenatal care during the course of their pregnancies.

The major prenatal period is the fetal stage. During this stage the unborn child begins to develop sexual organs, teeth, fingernails, and hair. A variety of conditions during the prenatal period may affect the development of the unborn child.

Maternal nutrition has an extremely important effect upon the unborn child. The child can get nourishment only from the mother, because it is dependent upon the mother's bloodstream

PLACENTA: The organ that serves as the structure through which nourishment for the fetus is sent and wastes are removed.

through the placenta for all such supplies. The mother's diet should be controlled carefully to provide enough proteins, fats, and carbohydrates. The diet must supply adequate nutrition both for herself and for her unborn child.

Certain vitamins, such as B_6, D, E, and K, are needed to ensure a child's healthy development. Research shows that during pregnancy, a diet low in protein may result in a loss of a very large portion of the child's mental potential. This can never be recovered. Also, poor diet during pregnancy can be related to a higher rate of newborn deaths, stillbirths, spontaneous abortions, and premature births. Another maternal health condition that may affect the unborn child is endocrine disorder, which can transmit glandular imbalance, infectious diseases, and extreme weight gain.

ENDOCRINE: Relating to any gland-produced secretion carried by the bloodstream to other parts of the body whose functions it controls.

Expectant mothers should not take drugs during pregnancy. Sometimes even drugs ordered by physicians have had nightmarish results. Not too many years ago a large number of pregnant women were given a drug named Thalidomide, which affected the unborn children and resulted in the formation of small, useless limbs. Children reacting to Thalidomide were born with no arms, no hands, hands at above the elbow, and no fingers or only a few; legs and feet were similarly affected.

Drug addiction has also been responsible for a large number of infant deaths. Until hospitals became aware of the effect of a mother's drug addiction on the child, many babies died of withdrawal symptoms. The typical experience at first bewildered concerned medical staff. A normal baby would first develop symptoms unexpected in a child and then die. When this was connected to the mother's drug addiction, hospital personnel took steps to test the woman and maintain the child as an addict on an ever-reduced supply of the addictive drug. The child was born as an addict. A further· problem for the newborn addict has been the discovery that in babies methadone causes a more severe addiction than heroin. The widespread use of methadone in drug-control programs complicates motherhood further.

Smoking during pregnancy has been linked to premature births. Heavy smokers have been found to have more premature births than nonsmokers.

Birth and Infancy

By the time of birth, the developing child's basic physical potentials have been set. From this point on, the social influences on the personality begin to outweigh the physical ones. More and more, the actions of the people around the child begin to mold his or her own actions. Here we look at the effects of the birth and of the first two years after.

The birthing experience itself is dangerous to the child. Premature births result in infants with skulls not yet well formed. Another serious problem associated with births is the possibility of anoxia (lack of oxygen). Lack of oxygen causes brain damage, which may result in death, apathy, intellectual deficiency, and motor retardation. The use of forceps to aid delivery, or anesthetics given the mother, may damage the infant. If a mother suffers from gonorrhea, passing through the vagina can blind the child. In recent years a procedure in effect in most states requires cleansing the infant's eyes directly upon birth.

The birth experience can also be a joyous, rewarding event for the parents and an easier time for the infant. Over the past decade, "prepared childbirth" has become more popular in the United States. Many parents prepare for the birth by going to what are known as Lamaze classes. There they learn how the father can be present and the mother conscious during this momentous event. The birth can take place in the home, in the hospital delivery room, or perhaps in a "birthing room" in a hospital or birth clinic. Wherever the birth occurs, the Lamaze method reduces the need for drugs during birth, to the benefit of mother and infant. The parents may even choose "quiet birth"—also called the Leboyer method, after its inventor. This method uses dim lights, soft music, and the delivery of the infant into a warm, womblike bath. The Lamaze and Leboyer methods both aim at a gentler, more comfortable birth experience.

When a child is born, it enters a stage called infancy, where it will remain for a period of about two years. During this period, physical growth in all areas is rapid. The nervous system, immature at birth, continues to develop.

During infancy the human's need for physical care begins to be eclipsed by the need for social nurturing, for being loved and taught. While the infant has been described as a pulsating sponge, he or she actually is able at a very early age to respond to and to appreciate social stimuli. The kind of person the infant will eventually become depends greatly on his or her experiences with other people.

Childhood and Adolescence

The preschool years are marked by a form of "parallel play." In this activity children play side by side but independently. The conversation and activity of these children have nothing to do with their playmates. In a sense they are playing as individuals in a crowd.

During this period a preschool child will tend to act out roles, or parts played by people in particular social positions. In the beginning the roles are mostly domestic in nature, the child taking the part of father, mother, sister, or brother. It is interesting that the sex of the child or the role played makes no difference to the child. A boy will as easily play the mother as the father, and a girl will play the role of the father as easily as the mother. There is no need at this point for the child to identify with the role played.

By the age of three, hair length and mode of dress indicate gender identification. The child slowly becomes aware of the physical difference between the sexes. Sexually defined behavior expectations in our society have yet to be impressed upon the child.

The rules of behavior for each sex are in effect patterns of social expectations of the manner in which a member of a sex group will act. Small children must be taught how to act according to what their culture expects of their sex. The psychological term for this learning process is sex-typing.

Extensive experiments with young primates indicate that all the differences between boys' and girls' behavior are not learned. Young male primates are far more aggressive than females. The conclusions of these experiments are not clear. For many years scientists will argue about the amounts of learned and inborn sexual behavior built into a person's personality structure.

At school age, a child becomes more independent and less egocentric. Independence allows the child to associate with his or her peer group, breaking down the closeness with the family. A reduction of egocentrism permits the child to join in group activities as opposed to playing alone, even in a group. The center of the child's world expands beyond the home and family.

Adolescence can be divided into two major portions, but the division is not based on age. The first is physical adolescence, that period from the spurt of prepubertal growth to full adult maturity. During this stage the development and growth from child to adult occurs. Next is psychological adolescence, which is determined by culture.

Different societies interpret psychological adolescence differently. Often within the same society, levels and classes may differ on what adolescence is. The social or economic stress of a particular time may require a person's earlier or later maturity. In our own society the individuals of the middle and upper classes tend toward a longer period of adolescence; they are apt to go to school longer and to marry later.

Adolescence in most Western societies is a time when peer-group relationships are most important. It begins with a sex-linked group, and it may continue well into physical adulthood. Each of us has passed through a period of extensive group friendships during adolescence. Often these groups shrink when mate-searching begins in earnest. Such a pattern is typical of many nonhuman, mammalian groups. Mating is serious business with most mammals, and the human mammal is no exception. In human beings the period of peer-group importance sees a sharp decrease in the number of family-oriented pastimes. The adolescent tries to spend as little time as possible at home and usually avoids family functions like the plague.

The adolescent focuses on the search for identity. Beliefs and values assume an importance that is missing in other age-groups. A story about a French prime minister illustrates the age-old adolescent tendency toward activism. The prime minister's secretary burst into his office one day with the news that the prime minister's son had joined the Communist Party. The prime minister said, "If he had not joined the party by the time he was twenty-two, I would have disowned him. If he is still a member at twenty-five, I'll disown him then."

PEER GROUP: A group of equals in a particular social situation.

EGOCENTRIC: Viewing everything in relation to oneself: self-centered.

PREPUBERTAL: Describes the time before the state of physical development when sexual reproduction first becomes possible.

SKILL BOX

> ## Measuring Central Tendency: Mean, Mode, and Median
>
> Numbers arranged in a meaningful way are called statistics. The job of statistical analysis is to use a number to summarize the meaning of the set of numbers. One way to do this is to search for some central tendency of the statistics.
>
> There are three kinds of central tendencies: mean, mode, and median. The mean is the average. To find the average of a set of measures, add them together, then divide that sum by the number of measures in the set. The mode is the number that occurs most often in a set of numbers. The median is the middle number of a set of numbers.
>
> To illustrate, we will use this set:
>
> $$10, 9, 6, 5, 4, 3, 3, 3, 2$$
>
> The mean of this set is 45 divided by 9, which equals 5. The number that occurs most frequently is 3: the mode. The median is the number above and below which half the numbers fall. Here it is 4.
>
> The mean is the most important measure of central tendency. It is the foundation of most other statistical tools. It is more stable than the median, which means that it is less easily affected by the addition of new numbers to the set. Still, the median can sometimes be useful in reflecting the tendency of a set of scores that includes some extremely high or low numbers; that is when you want something more responsive than the stable average. The mode is not often used.

In idealistic movements of our own nation the most fervent members are often the youngest. Youthful membership is neither good nor bad, just expected. In certain periods of their development, people need to be devoted, committed, and identified with a cause or a project. While not all our adolescents are involved in such movements, the devotion helps to ease the identity crises of the young. An alternative to these movements is the serious questioning of lifetime goals. What am I aiming for? What will I be? What will I do for the rest of my life?

While identity is very important to the adolescent, so are popularity and acceptance. The adolescent is very much tied to a concept of conformity. The dress and life pattern of the peer group are such that the individual must conform or be an outcast. The peer group is often seen as acting in a different or unique manner. Often the very uniqueness sought results in conformity to a set pattern.

We have now followed the outline of human development from conception to physical maturity, which occurs in the late teens. That story was a general one, however, and tells us little about why each individual has his/her own unique personality. Remember that the personality process has two sides, the biological and the social. We deal with the biological side first.

BIOLOGY AND PERSONALITY

The fruit of the young human's growth is the creation of a unique personality. This personality we might call the blossom of human growth; as it develops it will be the fulfillment of the human potential for a unique selfhood. All the factors that determine just what an individual's personality will be can be put into two categories, which have been labeled nature and nurture. The nature category includes all influences based on our biological or genetic features. In other words, a person may be said to have been "born that way," at least to some extent. Nurture refers to the care and attention the individual receives from the people around him or her. Nurture comes from the social environment, the people surrounding the individual. Our development as human beings, then, is partly controlled by our nature and partly by our nurture. Here we explore the nature side of personality first.

Our Basic Biological Package

The human infant can be seen as a lump of clay, ready for molding into some particular shape. The infant's biological equipment is the basic material from which will develop a human with a unique, integrated system of behaviors—a personality. First, to behave in a manner that could be called typically human, one requires the human nervous system, complete with nerve cells, synapses, spinal cord, brain, and so forth. The most important quality of the human brain is the capacity for language. Language enables humans to imagine, to plan, and to learn. Because socialization is essentially a learning process, it requires the capacity for language. Without this capacity, human development as we know it could not proceed. While bipedal (two-footed) posture and our sensory capacities, such as stereoscopic and color vision, are part of the normal biological package, these features are not essential. A human born without the capacity for vision or for walking, for example, can develop a human personality, but without an adequate nervous system, the person will perhaps look human but not behave or respond in a recognizably human manner.

The endocrine glands, such as the pituitary and the adrenal glands, are also an important part of the human biological equipment. These glands prompt the moods, sexual behaviors, and emotional responses typical of humans.

Another important part of the biological package of humans is the capacity for a relatively long life. The longevity potential of humans allows a full development of other human potentials, such as intellectual achievement, judgment, and love. If humans commonly died before the age of ten years, as do many creatures, we could not take full advantage of our capacities. Starting with little personality at birth, we need several decades for our personality to bear fruit.

One of the most important features of human biology with regard to personality development is the freedom we have in responding to our environment. The behavior of most creatures is

INSTINCT: An unlearned, complex, species-wide, automatic response to environmental stimuli.

determined by instincts. An instinct is an unlearned, complex, species-wide, automatic response to environmental stimuli. The instinct allows no freedom, no flexibility; no robin can decide to construct a new type of nest—or no nest at all.

Instead of instincts, the human biological package includes drives and reflexes. Reflexes, such as the dilation of the pupil of the eye, are simple, automatic reactions. Reflexes have little influence on human development. A drive is an internal tension that prompts us to satisfy some physiological need. Humans have drives involving hunger, thirst, sex, and self-preservation. These and other drives create discomfort within us, building up to the point that we are likely to act in some way to satisfy our internal urgings and needs. Drives are helpful in that they communicate to us our bodies' needs. However, we can ignore these messages. This is the crucial difference between the instincts that control the lives of animals and the drives that motivate humans. An instinct is a command; a drive is a suggestion or urging. While we feel an urge to eat or drink or have sex, we can refuse the urge. If we choose to respond to the urge, we can do so in virtually any manner.

Biological Particulars

Normal humans are all born with the same basic package of universal biological features, the foundation of a human personality. Why then does each human have a unique personality? There are two explanations for our unique behavior tendencies and patterns. First, people around us act as shaping forces, which we will deal with later in this chapter. Second, there is a biological side to the explanation. Except for identical twins, humans are born with different biological capacities and features beyond the basic universal requirements. Each of us has biological features unique to us that we can call particular rather than universal. Many of these particulars have no impact on our personality development, but those that do can be categorized as external and internal.

Our biological features that are visible to others can affect our personalities because of the way people react to those features. Our overall body size and shape, facial features, and qualities of the skin and hair can all influence the way people respond to us. These responses are greatly influenced by cultural preferences and tastes. For example, the tall, thin female will be pitied in one place and time, admired in another. On the other hand, in any culture the six-foot-nine, 260–lb. male is not as likely to be shy as is a diminutive male. It is partly from these reactions of other people to our physical features that our sense of self forms. From our self-image flow personality traits, from jolliness to dourness, brashness to shyness.

The facial expressions of infants seem to be a significant physical feature affecting the way people respond to them. One study found a significant difference in the facial expressions of male and female infants.[1] The females' faces typically showed more interest, perhaps an early indication of the greater sociability that girls

The individual faces the world with her own set of biological particulars.

Our physical features can have some influence on our personality.

generally exhibit later. The facial expressions of the male babies, on the other hand, made them seem "less interested in and receptive toward others than females, and perhaps less inviting and approachable."

Along the same line, premature infants receive more attention and affection from their mothers, according to one study. Mothers seem to respond to the greater needs of the premature infants, as suggested by the fact that the difference in the care given to such infants and that given to otherwise similar infants decreased as the premature babies developed.[2] It seems that an individual's particular physical needs influence the attention and care received. Similarly, hyperactive children elicited different responses from their mothers than other children did from their own mothers. The hyperactive children asked more questions, were less likely to play by themselves, and were more negative and less compliant during play sessions with their mothers. Understandably, these children received more direction, less approval, and more negative responses from their mothers.[3] To the extent that hyperactivity is biologically based, this research shows how biological particulars can influence an individual's socialization experiences.

Not all of our physical features are genetically determined. Factors such as nutrition, surgery, cosmetics, and accidents can also affect our appearance. However they occur, our physical features help our personalities to develop into their own unique forms.

Other biological features affecting our personalities are not visible to other people, but seem to be largely inherited. Individual behavioral differences are evident in the first weeks of life, presumably before any substantial shaping by social experiences.[4] One study found that shortly after birth, infants displayed distinguishing traits regarding activity level, general mood, ability to adapt to changes in the environment, and attention span.[5] Such personality features can be presumed to be biologically based because of their early occurrence and their persistence over a 14–year period in the study.

Another invisible biological factor at work in personality development is hormones, which are chemicals secreted by the endocrine glands. Hormone levels affect our behavior patterns indirectly, as when they help create unusual height or weight, thus possibly affecting the person's self image. Hormones also affect our moods and our behavior patterns regarding sex and aggression.

Inherited personality features or tendencies, such as high or low activity level, adaptability, or aggressiveness, can also affect the way other people react to a person. The fussy baby will probably get a different parental response than will a quiet baby. In one study, infants labeled as "difficult" by their mothers were also more likely to be viewed as irritating and fussy by other women.[6] The fussy babies in this study did not simply cry more often; they injected greater urgency in their crying techniques, and elicited a less positive response in their mothers and in other women. The responses of parents and other significant members of the child's social world are important to the child's personality development, and these responses are influenced by some of the child's inherited behavioral tendencies. The importance of biology in socialization is not stressed by most sociologists, but it cannot be ignored as a significant factor in the process of individual development.

One researcher in behavioral genetics, Robert Plomin, cautions us against assuming that there is any such thing as a "fussy gene" or an "aggression gene." Plomin asserts that few single-gene influences exist, and that most behavioral traits result from multiple genes.[7] Furthermore, Plomin explains that new discoveries suggest that genes turn on and off during an individual's development. The influence of some genes is less constant and stable than was previously thought. This means that genes do not lock us into permanent behavior tendencies.

Some researchers argue that genes affect our personalities because of the ways that other people respond to our appearance and hormone-directed behavior. Beyond this, "It must be that the unique genotypes and experiences of individuals shape the development of personality and interest patterns."[8] It may be that genes help direct our choices regarding the people with whom we will interact. Scarr and McCartney, two researchers of human development, suggest that we select our social environments in accordance with our "motivational, personality, and intellectual aspects of our genotypes."[9] In other words, they argue that people choose their own niches, the social environments they find most compatible, and these choices are influenced by genes. This new theoretical approach is not widely accepted, but it points to the underlying importance of genetic particulars regarding personality formation.

As we see in this section, social scientists do not see the developing human as a passive, shapeless lump of clay to be molded by others, but as raw material which already has some biologically determined shape of its own. To some extent, then, we are unique individuals at birth, before society begins its shaping process.

SOCIALIZATION AND HUMAN DEVELOPMENT

As far as we know, only humans have a sense of self, a personal identity, an awareness of themselves as distinct from other objects and other people. Apparently only humans can be self-conscious; that is, conscious or aware of their identities as objects. Rather than merely reacting to their surroundings, humans can experience selfness; they can think about who they are and what they want to be.

Human Need for Socialization

The self is the very essence of our humanness, the center of our personality. The self is a product of our interaction with the people around us, our social environment. Socialization is the process through which this interaction creates the self.

At birth we seem to have no self-consciousness, no awareness of ourselves as distinct entities. In fact, the human infant does not

SOCIALIZATION: The process through which the social environment shapes the self.

SELF: A person's awareness of who he/she is.

seem to realize that he or she is a distinct, separate person until the age of about six months. We are not born with an awareness of our self-identity; this develops through our experience with others. The development of self may begin much sooner than was previously presumed. Until recently, the newborn infant was seen as a passive being with little awareness of self or of much else. However, it is now assumed that newborns are able to appreciate to some extent the attention and messages given to them. As an example, infants in one study seemed to structure their facial expressions and behaviors in appropriate response to their mothers' simulated expressions of depression.[10] The infants showed a distinct, specific change in their gaze and emotions when they believed their mothers were depressed. Such a response clearly shows awareness of others at an early age. The early sensory awareness of humans suggests that even infants and children can experience social deprivation. As soon as a human becomes aware of what messages and attention she is receiving, she can presumably feel a lacking of the same. Some researchers believe that difficulties even in the first few hours of life can cause later developmental problems for a child.[11] While ethics forbid scientists to experiment with humans regarding social deprivation, some valuable research has been done with animals.

The most famous deprivation studies have been done by psychologist Harry Harlow.[12] Harlow deprived monkeys of normal social interaction. Baby monkeys reared from birth in isolation displayed clearly abnormal behavior. Lacking social experiences, these monkeys did not know how to respond normally to other monkeys. Some were withdrawn, others hostile. Some of these deprived animals would not even mate. Some of the females who did give birth neglected or abused their offspring. Social contact is clearly essential for the normal development of monkeys. But what about humans?

While such animal studies do not prove anything about the need of humans for socialization, they offer valuable suggestions. The behavioral patterns of animals are much more biologically determined than is human behavior. From this it is reasonable to presume that animals depend much less on social experiences than do humans for developing social competence. Then, if animals display such dramatic consequences of social deprivation as seen in the Harlow studies, we can easily imagine how much more dramatically social deprivation would affect humans.

There is some descriptive research that offers valuable insights. One of the most famous case studies involved the "Wolf Boy" of Aveyron. The twelve-year-old boy had been found by a French physician, Jean Itard, wandering in the woods. It was quite apparent that the child had been deprived of much socialization. Itard worked intensively with the boy, who eventually learned some writing and arithmetic skills, but never acquired reading or speaking ability. The boy's potential seemed to have been lowered greatly because of his extreme lack of human contact. Extreme social isolation, it seems, reduces our human potential.

Our early experiences with the people around us have a strong influence on our developing sense of self.

Another famous case of social isolation involved "Anna," an illegitimate child kept in an attic room for her first six years of life. The girl could not walk or talk when she was discovered, and her mental and sensory capacities were seriously stunted. With intensive teaching, the girl developed some basic human abilities, but the damage done to her by early isolation was clearly substantial.[13]

Such cases of social isolation are uncovered all too frequently even today. Depending on how young the children are when put into some degree of isolation, they show various levels of retardation. Both the mental and physical development of such children suffer. It may be that sensory deprivation, such as a lack of rocking or touching, is imprinted on the brain, impairing a child's mental and social capacities. The young child without adequate human contact can be likened to a young bush with too little water and sunlight. Both the bush and the child will survive, if at all, only in a stunted, shadowy form of what they could have become.

Humans can be stunted by early social isolation, but they may not be as easily damaged by traumatic experiences as was once thought. Many scientists, as well as nonscientists, have believed that neglect, abuse, or other trauma early in life produce permanent damage in the developing child. Some recent studies by psychologists have begun to question this belief. In a longitudinal study, children were studied beginning before their birth until they reached age 18. The researchers watched for any events which would be expected to hinder a child's social adjustment. Some children showed considerable resiliency, remaining well-adjusted despite difficulties suffered in the womb or later. Factors such as emotional support at home helped the children shrug off troublesome events.[14] While none of these cases included the deprivations of the "Wolf Boy" or "Anna," they suggest, along with other research, that children need social contact, but not an idyllic childhood, to develop into well-adjusted adults.

Socialization Theories

The socialization of a human being is a very complex process, and so there are several theories which offer differing views of the process.

Charles Horton Cooley (1864–1929) explained that the self-concept or self-image is based on how we think other people see us.[15] He used the phrase *looking glass self* to describe how we use others as a mirror to build a self-image. The reflection we see as we discover other peoples' judgments of us is the self we accept. According to Cooley, the formation of self involves three elements. First, we imagine how we appear to others. Then we imagine how others react to what they see in us. Last, we evaluate ourselves in accordance to the judgments we imagine that other people have formed of us. From this unconscious process we gain some feelings, either positive or negative, about ourselves.

Imagine first graders undergoing this looking-glass process as they meet their teacher for the first time. Each child imagines his appearance in the eyes of the teacher ("I must look sloppy in these old clothes"). Then the child imagines how the teacher judges that appearance ("The teacher doesn't seem to like the way I look"). Last, the child forms some self-feeling based on the teacher's imagined judgment ("I guess I'm a little slob").

The looking glass can offer distorted images. The first grader may misinterpret his/her teacher's reactions ("There is a shy little sweetheart"). Whether or not it is distorted, the image of ourselves we believe we see in the responses of others is the image we use to build our self-image. We may enhance our self-image unrealistically if we perceive an image in the looking glass that is distorted in a positive direction. Or, like the first grader just described, an image distorted in the other direction can lead us to undervalue our worth.

Cooley's explanation of how the self is formed takes us only so far. It does not explain why we respond strongly to one person's judgment of us and can ignore the judgments of others. Also, Cooley does not explain how children learn to respond effectively to other people's judgments. Just how does this socialization process work?

George Herbert Mead (1868–1931) went beyond Cooley and other theorists of the day by explaining how the self is developed. Rather than beginning with some preexisting mind, Mead's description begins with a basic social process: a conversation of gestures among biologically human individuals. From this social process language arises, and from language the self arises.

Language, the use of what Mead called significant symbols, transforms the merely biological individual into an organism with a mind, a self, a self-consciousness. By using a vocal symbol, the individual becomes able to call forth the same response in himself as the symbol calls forth in other individuals; the individual can then affect himself as he affects others. We might say that the individual holds a kind of conversational interchange with himself. As Mead explains, humans, through vocal symbols or gestures, are "continuously arousing in ourselves those responses which we call out in other persons, so that we are taking the attitudes of the other persons into our own conduct." [16] Language thus enables the individual to look back on himself from the perspective of others; by looking back on himself he becomes an object, and he becomes aware of his self's existence. Through such a conversation of significant symbols, humans become conscious of their objective existence, and they thus acquire a sense of self and a mind.

According to Mead, this development of the self involves two stages of role-taking. In the play stage, the child assumes a specific, other role, and addresses herself as, for example, a parent or teacher. In the game stage, the child must be able to take the roles or attitudes of all of the other individuals involved in some game or common activity. All of those roles must be related to one another. The child "becomes" all of the others involved in the common activity so that she can successfully play her own part. She assumes not the role of a specific individual but of any "other" participating in the common activity. She takes the attitude or role of what Mead called the "generalized other."

Taking the role of others is part of our development of self, according to Mead.

The attitudes of all the others in the generalized other are organized by the individual and taken into one's self, becoming what Mead called the "me." The me reflects the social structure surrounding the individual. Beyond the me is the I, the principle of action, impulse, and morality. It is through the I that the individual can exert some willful change on the social structure.

Through the I the individual creates and reconstructs society, even as the me is formed through the social process. In other words, through the social process the biological individual gets self and mind; impulsive animal becomes rational human. By internalizing the social process of communication, individuals gain reflective thought, and can see self as an object set within a social world. The individual becomes conscious of self and the self's actions and goals. Individuals regulate their behavior and contribute to the organization of human society by taking the role of generalized others. In sum, the society shapes the individual and creates a self which can in turn change society.

While Cooley and Mead saw society as working essentially in harmony with the self, and helping to construct the self, Sigmund Freud (1856–1939) contended that society's task is to control the expression of the human's unruly nature. According to Freud, the socialization process is mostly a matter of conflict. The child's inborn, unconscious drives for aggression and selfish gratification clash with society's need for order and personal restraint. Freud also contended that the way these conflicts are resolved during childhood would affect the later adult personality. While Freud's pioneering work in the area of the unconscious has made a lasting impact on our ideas about human behavior, few theorists today agree with his emphasis on the nearly irreversible effects of early socialization.

Social learning theorists maintain that observational learning, through modeling and imitation, is the basis of the socialization process. In this view, the child observes other people (who serve as models) and imitates their behavior. Along with a few other species, humans are able to examine the actions of their fellows closely enough to be able to duplicate them to some degree. This modeling process obviously saves a great deal of time for the developing animal or child. Rather than learning by trial and error, the imitator can acquire new behaviors by intelligent observation, thus copying some behaviors rather than originating all of them.[17] How do we decide which behaviors to imitate? We do not use all of the people around us as models. We are more likely to imitate significant others. Not surprisingly, we more readily imitate models whom we see being rewarded, though this condition is not necessary. Also, we tend to imitate models who are prestigious, rewarding to us, competent, and who control rewards.[18]

Social learning theorists point out that sometimes imitation does not follow from observation. We may want to imitate some model, but we may lack the physical or cognitive ability. We may lack the coordination to follow the dance step, for example. Or we may be too young to relate our own body to the model's actions. Also, modeling sometimes requires that we know when to display some mastered behavior. We may be able to imitate a behavior but may not know when it is appropriate to do so. Also we can learn a behavior without performing it at that time, saving it for proper occasions in the future.

These principles of observational learning are used by social learning theorists to explain the socialization process. These theorists argue that the process is more than a matter of simply molding the individual via rewards and punishments (as behaviorists would contend) and more than taming the individual's instinctual urges (as Freud said). More individual freedom and discretion are implied in the social learning viewpoint. In other words, it is argued that we are not merely responding blindly and directly to the actions of other people; rather, we react in more indirect ways to our social experiences as we learn how we should behave.

Cognitive development refers to the process in which we become able to use our intellectual capacities (as opposed to our emotional or physical capacities). This approach to child development, which can be applied to the socialization process, was established largely by the work of the Swiss psychologist, Jean Piaget. Piaget described four main stages of intellectual development, each one allowing the socialization process to work more fully within the individual.

The sensorimotor stage lasts for approximately the first two years. During this stage infants become aware of how their actions affect the environment. Children discover that they are distinct from other objects, and that they can manipulate other objects to some extent. Also during this stage, children learn that objects have permanence, that objects do not disappear when they can no longer be seen by the children.

Language is acquired in the child's next five years, a stage Piaget called preoperational. In this stage the child still sees the world as revolving around him/her, and thus cannot easily take the viewpoint of others. Also, only gradually does the child learn to go beyond visual impressions to understand that, for example, the number of objects remains constant even if the objects are rearranged.

In the concrete operational stage, between ages 7 and 12, the child becomes able to think logically. The child can classify objects and order them according to size. Also the child in this stage becomes able to understand how concrete objects are causally related to one another. Besides manipulating objects logically, children in this stage learn to consider the viewpoints of other people, an important stage regarding socialization.

By age 11 or 12, the typical child reaches what Piaget called the formal operational stage. At this point the child can reason not only with concrete objects but also with symbols. This means that the capacity for abstract reasoning develops, and children can thus begin to solve problems by forming hypotheses and applying theories and general principles. With abstract reasoning, children can go beyond what they see, and can conceive of other possibilities dealing with ideals. Questions of politics and religion can now be addressed by the child. The socialization process can now include a wide variety of significant experiences.

The sequence of stages described by Piaget has been verified by other researchers, though the ages at which individuals reach the stages can vary with many factors, including intelligence, cultural background, and social class. Some theorists suggest that reasoning levels exist beyond the formal operational levels described by Piaget, and that distinct, more complex forms of systematic reasoning are part of the developmental process.[19] Also, while Piaget's sequence is accepted by many theorists, some questions have been raised concerning his view of the dynamics of personality formation.[20] One researcher claims that Piaget's evidence fails to hold up under close scrutiny. For example, it seems that children have been taught to do things that Piaget would say they could not learn at their age.[21] Despite these criticisms, on the whole, Piaget's work offers insights into the progression of the socialization process.

SOCIALIZATION THROUGH THE LIFE CYCLE

The socialization process certainly does not end when the infant achieves a sense of self. Nor does the process end when the child displays behavior that is recognizably human. Throughout our lives our behaviors, goals, and sense of self change to reflect the different experiences we encounter. To adapt to such important personal changes we must continually learn, through socialization, what is expected of us and, more fundamentally, who we are. Socialization, then, is a lifelong process.

Childhood and Adolescence   The socialization agents that impinge on us during our first two decades of life are different from those of the rest of the lifespan. In these early years, parents, peers, and the school are powerful agents. For the most part these agents attempt to shape us from innocent incompetents into knowledgeable, productive members of the social order.

The goal of childhood socialization has varied through the ages. For thousands of years, since the beginning of civilization (and of formal education), children were seen as wild animals in need of taming. Unruliness had to be beaten out of the child. Because children were seen as potentially valuable workers, socialization was aimed in part at shaping them into producers, and discipline was generally seen as the key to success.

During the twentieth century, children have come to be seen in the U.S. as beings with tremendous potential, and parents have been challenged with the task of not merely taming their children but nurturing their development.

The Family as Socialization Agent.   Since the dawn of civilization, socialization goals for children have been changing, and so have socialization tactics. Through this time, however, the agents of socialization have not changed much. The agents remain the family, peers, and schools, though mass media have entered the picture, especially with the advent of television in the 1950s. Through all these years and all these changes, however, the family is still the most important socialization agent.

As everyone knows, parents face a formidable challenge in dealing with the child's developmental processes. But we might say the parents have the upper hand, at least in the beginning. The parents are the infant's world. They control many of the child's experiences and stimuli. The parents are the mirror of the infant's self, and as they perceive the infant, so the infant sees him/herself. Furthermore, parents provide infants with their first view of the world, giving the infants their first taste of life. From parents, infants receive their first hint of how the world will treat them.

This power of the parents regarding the child's development has been shown in many research studies. One shows, for example, how parents begin teaching their infants how to express emotions.[22] In the study, mothers prompted pleasant emotional expressions in their three- to six-month-old infants. The mothers did this by reinforcing pleasant infant expressions with positive facial expressions, such as those of enjoyment and interest. Such apparent attempts to moderate the infants' emotional expressions may or may not be unconscious, but could have a significant effect on the child's personality formation.

The socialization power of parents is evident also with older children, though the power is then moderated by other factors. Parents serve as important models, and as the child begins to grope for some idea of what kind of person she wants to become, other adults and peers can serve as models. Parents, however, are usually the most available, and potentially the most powerful. The child's perceptions of the parents' judgments affect the power of the parental model, as shown in a study involving girls age 7 to 11. The girls who perceived their mother as having more power than their father preferred careers that were less typical for women. (Boys were not affected by the mother's perceived power.) Girls whose fathers dominated the home tended to choose "women's jobs." The girls perceiving an even power balance between the parents tended toward neutral or masculine jobs. The study's results also found that the girls' choices were not determined by whether or not the mother worked outside the home. The vital factor was the mother's perceived power in the family, reflecting "an underlying dynamic of modeling" based on the mother's personality.[23]

The socialization power of the family has been clearly demonstrated in many studies regarding the child's intellectual ability. The parents' income and educational level have been linked to children's scores on intelligence tests.[24] Another approach has been to explore the association between parents' attitudes about the child's abilities and the child's achievement attitudes. One study along this line found that children's attitudes about their achievement abilities were influenced more by their parents' attitudes about those abilities than by their own past achievements.[25] Furthermore, the study found that parents' attitudes varied with the sex of their children, especially regarding math achievement. For example, the parents of girls believed their children would have to work harder to achieve in math than did parents of boys. Also, advanced math was considered more important for boys than for girls. These attitudes were reflected in the children's attitudes concerning their ability to achieve. Therefore, the children were learning, through socialization, about their personal abilities.

The socialization influence of the parents is like a powerful weapon. The weapon is loaded, but how should it be used? In other words, what is the most effective way to raise a child? For years, two contrasting parenting approaches have been offered. One, called the authoritarian approach, stresses the child's need for discipline and a strong authority figure. This approach assumes that the child is liable to run wild if allowed to develop outside a deeply grooved channel. The other parenting approach is permissive, giving the child a great deal of freedom and support. The child is assumed to be responsive to trust and to love. Rather than relying on orders, permissive parents are more likely to use reason, compromise, and flexibility. A third alternative has been suggested: authoritative parenting.[26] According to this view, authoritarian parents view children as having many responsibilities but few rights, and permissive parents demand few responsibilities of their children while giving them rights similar to those of adults. Authoritative parents, on the other hand, view their own rights and responsibilities as complementary, and not identical, to those of their children's. It can be said that permissiveness deprives the child of the firm guidance he/she needs, while authoritarian parents back the child into a corner, forcing rebellion or surrender.

The School as Socialization Agent.   With a loving hug and an encouraging word, the family sends the child to his/her next adult-controlled socialization agent, the school. The child must then make some drastic adjustments, because the school differs from the family's socialization efforts both in goals and in methods.

The socialization methods of the school give the child his first taste of what the broader, "outside" world is like. The school's approach, unlike the family's, is largely impersonal. The child can no longer expect to be loved and accepted without question, as may have been true at home. Most parents accept and praise their children regardless of how smart, fast, or strong they are. They love their children because of who they are, not what they can do. At school the child must earn acceptance through performance. The child is not simply accepted as a person worthy of love, but is evaluated as an achiever—or a nonachiever. Also, parents will usually respond to their children's whole package of personal qualities. The school, on the other hand, focuses mostly on math and language ability, ignoring the child's ability to climb trees, help with cooking, or dive into the pool head first. Also, children relate to their parents on an emotional level, obeying or not on the basis of love-hate feelings. At school, the teacher must be obeyed simply because she is the teacher, regardless of how the child feels toward the teacher. Rules are applied impersonally in the school, and children eventually realize that they can and will be treated in the larger society as part of the mass of humanity. In the school, the child learns to adapt to the impersonal, performance-based world beyond the accepting, personalized family environment.

As the socialization methods of the school and the family differ, so do their goals. The family usually aims to fulfill the child's potential for happiness, and deals with all facets of the child's capacities. The school has two narrower goals. First, the child is to be prepared for contributing socially. The school aims to equip the student with appropriate job skills, built on an academic base. Parents may teach personal grooming and table manners, but the school's job involves math and science, and the like. Second, the school aims to prepare the child, through socialization, for the regimentation, impersonal authority, and discipline of rules that the child will encounter in the adult world.

Recently, the schools have not been so limited to these two goals. In fact, the schools have been criticized for invading the socialization territory of the family by offering courses in subjects such as sex education and social adjustment. This reaching out by the schools is an effort to ensure that all children are exposed to the necessary socialization experiences. However, some questions remain as to how well the schools can compensate for the socialization failures of families.

The Peer Group as a Socialization Agent. As the child enters school, another socialization agent increases its own influence: the peer group. This agent is actually several groups. Any one of the child's peer groups consists of people who are similar to the child, holding similar statuses such as those regarding age and sex. The child naturally associates with others holding the same traits and interests, thus forming peer groups.

This natural association among peer group members is one reason these groups are significant socialization agents. Unlike the family and the school, the child's peer groups are not controlled by adults. The child chooses his/her peer groups, though these choices are largely accidental for young children. In peer groups, therefore, children escape somewhat the decisions and control of adults. Within this freedom, the child can learn important lessons that parents cannot teach.

The child learns valuable lessons from peers, such as how to deal on an equal basis with other people. Unlike parents, peers are unlikely to "pull rank," to use authority in their relationships. Interaction processes such as exchange and cooperation can be learned more readily with peers than with parents, who always hold a trump card. Among peers the child gets a chance to make more decisions, to establish rules and enforce conformity. Within the peer group the child has the opportunity to lead and to deal with hostility on his/her own.

The peer group also affords the child a more honest appraisal of his or her personal traits. Within the adult-centered socialization agents of the family and the school, the child is unlikely to hear entirely candid descriptions of him/herself. Peers, however, can be brutally, but perhaps helpfully, truthful in pointing out one's faults. It is in the peer group that one is most likely to discover, as one must, that one has huge ears or funny teeth or an unfashionable hairstyle.

The candidness of peers is due in part to the fact that peer group members are not necessarily friends. All the members of one's first grade class can be considered one's peer group, even though only a few of them are close friends.

Peer groups, then, can be cruel but still valuable, especially as one enters adolescence. For most people in industrialized countries, where this stage is found, adolescence is a difficult transition stage, and the teenager needs some help in dealing with its challenges. A major task in adolescence is ending one's dependence on parents. This is something we all must do, but it is difficult while we actually depend on parents for food, clothing, and shelter. The peer group offers an important source of independence because it allows one to participate in the subculture of adolescence. This subculture is sometimes a counterculture, rejecting such mainstream cultural values as proper manners, respectfulness, and orderliness. By rejecting at least some of the adult world's values, the adolescent can begin to detach herself from the influence of the family.

It is likely that the adolescent subculture, which flourishes in teenagers' peer groups, is becoming increasingly important in industrialized nations. As parents are removed from the home by greater economic and social demands, the peer group will take up the socialization slack created by the parents' absence. Many children, then, will shift their loyalties early from the parents to the peer groups, and socialization patterns will reflect the adolescent subculture more than ever.

Adulthood   Researchers of socialization have come to recognize the continuing influence of that process throughout our lives. Earlier studies focused on the socialization of the infant and child, assuming that these experiences fixed the basic personality of the individual. The research focus has shifted to the total lifespan, with increased emphasis given to the latter half of the life cycle.

Socialization during adulthood is no longer seen by researchers as a matter of rather uniform experiences interrupted by crises. Rather than crises, transitions are the framework within which adult life is now viewed by many socialization theorists. According to one such theorist, adult socialization is mostly a matter of two kinds of transitions.[27] First, the individual drops some roles and adds new ones. For example, a person may drop the role of student and gain a new occupational role in its place, which is later replaced by the role of retirement. Many lost roles are replaced by new ones, and in early adulthood we are more likely to gain more roles than we lose. Later in life, we usually lose more roles than we gain. The second kind of adulthood transition is the changing expectations or definition of roles we hold over the years. For example, we may hold the role of spouse for several decades, but we may also define the rights and responsibilities of spouse differently over time. Such changing expectations of ourselves and of others are part of the transitions of our adult socialization.

Transitions are not necessarily crises, because most are expected, and are considered a normal part of adulthood.[28] Retirement and widowhood, for examples, are expected by most people. Most people realize that in time they will face such transitions, and they prepare themselves for those changes. However, such transitions may come at an unexpected time, resulting in crises. Widowhood, for example, is less likely to catch us by surprise, and thus create a crisis, when we are 70 than when we are 30. Also, inadequate socialization can produce a crisis out of a transition. For example, young adults of parenting age may be caught unprepared emotionally and financially for the birth of a child. The common occurrence of this situation suggests that socialization for parenthood is inadequate in our culture.

The particular transitions in a woman's life are, not surprisingly, likely to differ from those of a man. In many cultures, women experience an increase in their personal powers with the onset of menopause. With no babies on the way, and many of her children grown, the middle-aged woman has time for other pursuits besides childcare. Also, with less nurturing and maternal behavior expected of her, she is free to develop the more "masculine" side of her personality. This flowering of self-assertiveness and independence is more common in traditional than in Western societies, largely because of differing cultural expectations. Thus, menopause can be a crisis for one woman, but a peak for another, depending in part on the way the socialization process is interpreted by the woman's culture.

In our culture, it is difficult to describe how middle age is interpreted by women. According to one essay, the changes in socialization patterns over the last few decades have produced different views of women's transitions.[29] Midlife transitions are experienced differently by American women, depending on earlier life events. As major social trends change the early socialization experiences of women in our society, they will face their midlife changes differently from older women. For examples, the postponement of marriage and childbearing, the higher frequency of divorce, and earlier career entry are trends that will affect the women in their twenties when they reach their fifties.

According to social scientist Lois Tamir, the middle-aged male in America is likely to be at his peak performance, but may also be anticipating his personal decline.[30] During his forties the man may experience worries and problems, such as the deaths of peers and his parents, ill health, and the loss of his earlier career hopes. These problems often lead to either desperation or a quieter turning into himself and his family. On the other hand, he may seek drastic changes in his life as a way of grasping at his last chances. He may leave his family, change jobs, or suddenly imitate the lifestyle of younger men with a new hair style and a sports car. On the other hand, the middle-aged man may turn away from his career and toward his own responsibilities concerning future generations, especially his own family.

RESOCIALIZATION: The reshaping of a human personality; the process by which new values replace old values.

The process called resocialization shows how strongly socialization can shape us even in adulthood. Resocialization is the process by which we learn new values and unlearn old ones that are no longer appropriate. The process is part of every social transition we make. For instance, when we leave school and take a job, we drop the values and behaviors of the student and take on those of the worker. For some people, the resocialization involved even in ordinary transitions, such as parenthood and retirement, is painful because of financial or emotional unreadiness. For most of us, however, resocialization is simply part of the flow of life.

A more powerful form of resocialization is not part of a normal transition, but is aimed largely at remaking the person entirely. Extreme cases of such resocialization are often called "brainwashing," which occurs in a controlled environment.

The most common form of intense resocialization is military training, in which the civilian is to be transformed into a soldier. Many civilian values and attitudes are ridiculed and rejected, to be replaced by military attitudes. The recruit lives in a controlled environment, exposed to a limited array of people and ideas. The recruit is given a new hairstyle, new clothes, a new label—a new self. Values such as obedience and aggressiveness are promoted, values that serve well in combat but may require a new resocialization process if the soldier is to adjust to civilian life again.

Resocialization methods are also used in prisons and in some religious cults. From Jim Jones's "People's Temple" to prisoner-of-war camps, the aim is the same: the creation of a new self for the individual. In all such cases, the individual is required to deny all former values and behaviors that do not conform to the new self which the person is to assume. In cases in which the individual's captives have total control over the environment, resocialization can be powerful but not absolute, so resocialization methods have not usually been successful in replacing a person's self with another. Many resocialization efforts aimed at prisoners have been woefully ineffective. Even victims of "brainwashing" often gradually reestablish their former selves. The limited influence of this type of resocialization may be seen as evidence of the strength of socialization early in life.

SUMMARY

Human growth proceeds through several stages from conception, through the prenatal environment, then infancy, childhood, and adolescence.

The typical behavior patterns of the individual can be explained by factors categorized as nature and nurture. The basic human package contains a nervous system and a lack of constraining instincts, allowing great variety of personality types. Each individual's "nature" contains some behavioral predispositions as well as a blueprint for physical appearance features which affect personality.

Socialization is the process in which social interaction shapes the human potential into a unique self. Humans deprived of social interaction show how much humans depend on socialization for the development of their potential for humanness.

Socialization can be viewed from several theoretical perspectives. Cooley used the analogy of a looking glass in which we see the reflection of ourselves in the image other people hold of us. Mead focused on how the use of language enables individuals to reflect and to see self as an object within a social world. Freud saw human nature at conflict with society's restraints. Social learning theorists contend that observational learning, through modeling and imitation, is the basis of the socialization process. Piaget described four main stages of cognitive development, each one allowing the socialization process to work more fully within the individual.

The individual is socialized by several agents throughout the life span, beginning with the most important, the family. The family controls many of the developing infant's stimuli, and this shapes the basic self of the individual. The school is more impersonal, and the child learns that his/her acceptance in the broader society is partly based on performance. The peer group allows children to control some of their own socialization experiences and allows individuals to learn more about themselves and to reduce their dependence on parents.

Socialization continues throughout our adult years, as we drop some roles and add new ones, and as we change our expectations or definitions of roles we have held. How we cope with transitions depends on our preparation and our gender. In resocialization we learn new values and unlearn old ones. Resocialization is part of each social transition, but in its extreme, it attempts to remake the person entirely.

SPECIAL TOPIC

Technology's Impact on Growth and Development

You are married and, with your spouse, have decided to have a child. What kind should it be? Should you have a boy or a girl? Should the child have blond hair, light skin, dark skin, black eyes, blue eyes—or should you not worry about all that?

Over the thousands of years that human beings have been breeding and having children, little thought has gone into the results of the activity. We all want healthy children, but until recently we have not been able to do much more than check the general health and form of our partners and hope that the genetic combination will result in a normal child.

In groups where a healthy partner was a matter of life or death, more attention was given to the physical qualities of the partner. One of the partners would have to be capable of protecting the family, hunting through winter, and living long enough to provide children. A woman might be chosen only if she would not have a difficult time bearing children or carrying a pack on the trail. Later, the ability to pull a plow was important.

In days gone by, we knew our neighbors' shortcomings and virtues. Indeed, most isolated people were related in one way or another. If a person did not measure up to the mental or physical requirements of a group, there were ways to eliminate the strain from the breeding pool. Tests at puberty probably did much to eliminate many young people before admission to the group. Imagine the odds against the asthmatic child who had to climb a mountain to get the tail feather of an eagle. The nearsighted warrior in a night raid would soon be eliminated. The clubfooted, the crippled, the hemophiliac, and those who suffered other disabilities were not common in the past—because they tended to die young.

In recent years our ability to deal with physical shortcomings has allowed us to extend life for many who would have died young. The U.S. Public Health Service once released an estimate that 40 percent of the people alive in the United States today would not have been alive if they were living under the conditions present in 1900. In other words, if you look around your class, subtract four of every ten students and assume they would have been dead of pneumonia, scarlet fever, whooping cough, abscess, infection, broken bones, flu, or any one of a hundred illnesses uncommon today. These illnesses are either uncommon because of innoculation or inconsequential because of our ability to treat them medically. As late as 1938, treatment for pneumonia was a mustard plaster on the chest and boiling water with wintergreen in the room. There was also aspirin. Today, unless there is a viral form present, pneumonia can be knocked out more easily than a common cold. There have even been changes in human form, a result of medical care. An example is our propensity for small-hipped women, which may have led to an alarming increase in Caesarean section babies.

Desirable physical characteristics have led certain people to be overrepresented in the breeding pool. Today we may accomplish our heart's desire in quite another way. Many medical procedures are aimed specifically at correcting a perceived deformity. No longer is the plastic surgeon occupied only with repairing the results of disfiguring accidents. We have become accustomed to the repair or reduction of noses; we are becoming accustomed to accepting breast reduction, shaping, or enlargement; we are able to do "tummy tucks" for the flabby; we do thigh reductions for those without muscle; and there are face lifts, ear replacement, and jaw reduction, enlargement, or realigning. In addition, we can hide the effects of the cleft palate and hairlip, we can turn the club foot, and we can replace organs.

At this point, organ replacement is done only in cases of life or death. We can look forward to the time when various organs will be replaced to maintain youth, or the feeling thereof. An older athlete may receive a heart-lung transplant or even muscular supplements.

We have been discussing the changing of what we have. What then of the young couple thinking of having a child? Will they continue to take yesterday's chances with all the possibilities available today? Let us discuss exactly what the new developments in genetic choice have been.

For some years, cattle breeders have been using the frozen sperm of prize bulls. In the dairy breeds, a prize bull's offspring will give plenty of milk. In the beef breeds, the calves will grow quickly and put on more weight with less feed. But while the sperm of a prize bull can father thousands of calves, a prize cow can still have but one calf a year.

In recent years, however, it has become possible to cause prize cattle to ovulate at an accelerated rate. In plain terms, cattle are induced chemically to release many eggs at one time. These eggs are bathed in the sperm of a prize bull and are thus fertilized. The fertilized eggs of the prize bull and prize cows are then placed in what are called scrub cattle, ordinary, everyday cattle that eat too much, gain too little, and give not enough milk. It is the difference between a minor league cow and a major league cow. In nine months our scrub cow will give birth to a major league son or daughter that has none of her distressing characteristics.

In the human world there have been avenues available to women whose husbands have not been able to provide viable sperm. The usual route is artificial insemination using the sperm of a donor. More recently we have seen various methods of fertilizing eggs outside the body. This has been done when the prospective mother has a condition that prevents the sperm from reaching the egg, or the egg from reaching the uterus. The fertilized egg is then implanted in the mother.

At this point we can find a certain amount of grumbling and preaching against the unnatural manner in which the child was conceived. The real issue has yet to be dealt with in public. One always assumes that Dad's sperm fertilized Mom's egg and that egg was implanted in Mom's uterus to be carried to term. At worst, sperm from a donor or sperm bank was used to fertilize Mom's egg, which was then placed into her uterus.

What if selected sperm from a selected donor in storage in a sperm bank was matched to a selected egg from a woman with acceptable genetic traits, and the fertilized egg was then implanted in Mom's uterus? We can carry this theme one step further. What if a genetically acceptable fertilized egg was placed in the uterus of a surrogate, or contract, mother and carried to term? And then the baby, related by blood to neither of the prospective parents or the surrogate mother, is born and given to the parents who arranged the process?

If people could choose the parents of a prospective child, we would expect that there would be careful selection of the genetic pluses and minuses. In time, the world will come to accept such occurrences as normal. What would you do if you found that your genetic contribution might result in a deformed, unhealthy, or retarded child? Would you seek help in the manner mentioned? Would you have the child and hope for the best? Would you not have children at all?

We are left with a story about George Bernard Shaw. One day he was approached by a beautiful but flighty young lady who said, "With your brains and my beauty we really should have a child together." Shaw's retort was, "What if it had your brains and my beauty?"

SELF-TEST QUESTIONS

1. The sex of a child is determined by the sex gene it gets from which parent? _____

2. True or false: Genes have no influence on personality traits.

3. True or false: The pregnant woman's diet can affect the unborn child's mental potential.

4. True or false: Because of recent medical advances, birth poses no danger to the child.

5. During infancy, the focus of the child's needs shift:
   a. from the social to the physical
   b. from the physical to the social
   c. from the vital to the causal

6. Humans do *not* have:
   a. drives
   b. instincts
   c. reflexes
   d. inherent personality tendencies

7. Social scientists see the developing human as:
   a. a shapeless lump of clay to be molded by other people
   b. having a full set of genetically programmed traits at birth
   c. raw material with some biologically determined shape of its own
   d. none of the above

8. Studies of social deprivation show:
   a. that human infants need social contact to develop their human potential
   b. how the developing child can be emotionally crippled
   c. how resilient children can be
   d. all of the above

9. According to Cooley, the:
   a. self is based on genetic programming
   b. looking-glass self can offer distorted images
   c. self is based on hormonal tendencies
   d. self is based on the use of language

10. According to Mead, the development of self involves:
    a. viewing oneself from the perspective of other people
    b. a looking-glass
    c. innate, antisocial drives
    d. all of the above

11. According to Freud, socialization:
    a. is based on contact comfort
    b. is a matter of conflict between society and unconscious drives
    c. involves a basic harmony between society and human nature
    d. is mostly a matter of responding to generalized others

12. According to Piaget, language is:
    a. an inborn ability
    b. acquired during the formal operational stage
    c. acquired during the preoperational stage
    d. acquired at any age, depending on the skill of the teacher

13. In the school the child learns:
    a. basically how the world will treat her
    b. that the world will accept her based on her innate worth
    c. whether or not the world can be trusted
    d. to adapt to an impersonal, performance-based world

14. In the peer group the child learns:
    a. how to deal on an equal basis with other people
    b. language

    c. a basic orientation to the world

    d. whether or not the world can be trusted

15. The process which is involved in every social transition and which replaces old values with new values is:
    a. life changes
    b. peer group pressure
    c. resocialization
    d. generalization

ANSWERS TO SELF-TEST QUESTIONS

1. father	9. b
2. false	10. a
3. true	11. b
4. false	12. c
5. b	13. d
6. b	14. a
7. c	15. c
8. d	

NOTES

1. Carol Zander Malatesta and Jeannette Haviland, "Learning Display Rules: The Socialization of Emotion Expression in Infancy," *Child Development* 53 (August 1982): 991–1003.
2. J. W. Crawford, "Mother-Infant Interaction in Premature and Full-Term Infants," *Child Development* 53 (August 1982): 957–62.
3. Eric J. Mash and Charlotte Johnston, "A Comparison of the Mother-Child Interaction of Younger and Older Hyperactive and Normal Children," *Child Development* 53 (October 1982): 1371–81.
4. Nancy Hubert, et al., "The Study of Early Temperament: Measurement and Conceptual Issues," *Child Development* 53 (June 1982): 571–600.
5. A. Thomas, S. Chess, and H. G. Birch, "The Origin of Personality" in Atkinson, R.C., ed. *Contemporary Personality: Readings from Scientific American* (1970): 364.
6. Mary Lounsbury and John Bates, "The Cries of Infants in Differing Levels of Perceived Temperamental Difficulties," *Child Development* 53 (June 1982): 677–86.
7. Robert Plomin, "Developmental Behavioral Genetics," *Child Development* 54 (April 1983): 253–59.
8. Sandra Scarr and Richard Weinberg, "The Minnesota Adoption Studies," *Child Development* 54 (April 1983): 260–67.
9. Sandra Scarr and Kathleen McCartney, "How People Make Their Own Environments," *Child Development* 54 (April 1983): 424–35.
10. Jeffrey Cohn and Edward Tronick, "Three-Month-Old Infants' Reaction to Simulated Maternal Depression," *Child Development* 54 (February 1983): 185–93.
11. Charles Spezzano and Jill Waterman, "The First Day of Life," *Psychology Today* (December 1977): 110–16.
12. Harry F. Harlow, "Love in Infant Monkeys," *Scientific American* 200 (1959): 68–74.
13. Kingsley Davis, "Final Note on a Case of Extreme Isolation," *American Journal of Sociology* 52 (1947): 432–37.
14. Ruth Smith and Emmy Werner, *Vulnerable But Invincible* (New York: McGraw-Hill, 1982).
15. Charles H. Cooley, *Human Nature and the Social Order* (New York: Scribner's, 1902).
16. George Herbert Mead, *Mind, Self and Society* (Chicago: University of Chicago Press, 1934): 69.

17. Albert Bandura and R. H. Walters, *Social Learning and Personality Development* (New York: Holt, Rinehart & Winston, 1963).

18. Ibid.

19. Michael Commons, Francis Richards, and Deanna Kuhn, "Systematic and Metasystematic Reasoning: A Case for Levels of Reasoning Beyond Piaget's Stage of Formal Operations," *Child Development* 53 (August 1982): 1085–69.

20. Jack Block, "Assimilation, Accommodation, and the Dynamics of Personality Development," *Child Development* 53 (April 1982): 281–95.

21. Kieran Egan, "What Does Piaget's Theory Describe?" *Teachers College Review* (Winter 1982).

22. Malatesta and Haviland, "Learning Display Rules," 1982.

23. Linda Lavine, "Parental Power as a Potential Influence on Girls' Career Choice," *Child Development* 53 (June 1982): 658–63.

24. James Mercy and Lala Steelman, "Familial Influences on the Intellectual Attainment of Children," *American Sociological Review* 47 (August 1982): 532–42.

25. Jacquelynne Parsons, Terry Adler, and Caroline Kaczala, "Socialization of Achievement Attitudes and Beliefs," *Child Development* 53 (1982): 310–21.

26. Diana Baumrind, "New Directions in Socialization Research," *American Psychologist* 35 (July 1980): 639–52.

27. Linda K. George, "Models of Transitions in Middle and Later Life," *Annals* 464 (November 1982): 22–37.

28. Ibid.

29. Angela O'Rand and John Henretta, "Women at Middle Age: Developmental Transitions," *Annals* 464 (November 1982): 57 +.

30. Lois Tamir, "Men at Middle Age: Developmental Transitions," *Annals* 464 (November 1982): 47–56.

SUGGESTED READINGS

Erikson, Erik H. *The Life Cycle Completed.* New York: Norton, 1982.

Papalia, Diane E., and Olds, Sally W. *A Child's World.* New York: McGraw-Hill, 1982.

Rainwater, Lee. *And the Poor Get Children.* New York: Franklin Watts, 1960.

Rose, Peter I. ed. *Socialization and the Life Cycle.* New York: St. Martin's Press, 1979.

Serlin, Florence R. and McGlynn, Angela P. *Living with Yourself.* Englewood Cliffs, N.J.: Prentice-Hall, 1979.

5 PERSONAL ADJUSTMENT

Born To Be Wild?

They say you are dangerous. You have never hurt anyone, but you are classified as a potential criminal, a person who will probably commit a violent crime. Society may say that you have a tendency to behave like everyone else who shares your genetic attributes and that therefore you cannot be changed.

Some years ago a book entitled *Brave New World* told the story of a society that could breed people who would share such behavioral traits. This has not been a safe topic among sociologists and biologists. Over the years, patterns of behavior and intelligence have been said to be associated with racial groups or religious groups or national groups or any other group that could be identified. When dealing with topics of this nature, one must be sure that the criteria used to judge are not based on cultural prejudices.

In recent years sociobiology has linked behavior to genetic background, but the extent of the genetic sharing of human beings has not been established. Certainly these groups or genetic pools will be far smaller than the poorly defined groups that have been called races.

Perhaps we can look to the tightly controlled breeding of various breeds of dogs or cattle. Within certain limits, one can describe the typical poodle, golden retriever, or bloodhound. The same generalization can be made regarding breeds of cattle. Some are gentle, others rough; some can be fenced easily, others cannot; some are devoted mothers, others are not. A Hereford cow who is not a good mother goes to slaughter, and her genetic combinations are thus wiped from the slate. Cattle with acceptable patterns of behavior are bred again and again, reinforcing desirable traits.

Variation from accepted norms may in some cases be attributed to one's genetic makeup. What do you think?

Why are some people around you so hostile or dangerous while others are so pleasant? Why does your own behavior range from one extreme to the other from time to time? As the chapter preview asks, how much of this is due to genetic attributions? These questions touch on the topic of this chapter.

In Chapter 4 we studied the various influences on a person's development. Here we will explore the theories that try to put all those pieces together in a meaningful way, to explain in a broad way why people behave the way they do. Another important concern here is why some people do not fit well into society. Because it is in our best interest to learn how to deal with problems of personality, the inability of individuals to meet the needs of both themselves and society will also be explored.

THEORIES OF PSYCHOLOGICAL ADJUSTMENT

Society's concern with the behavior of its members is probably as old as human society itself. Our first glimmerings of organized inquiry date back to the Greek philosophers, most notable of whom were Plato and Aristotle. Plato's view of a universe was comprised of two parts: mental and material. This differed greatly from the universe as conceived by Aristotle. Aristotle believed that elements of the environment activated the sense organs and then expressed them as thoughts and ideas. This element of interaction provides the basic difference between the two points of view.

Viewpoints on this matter differed in the past, and the differences remain today. They provide the bases for various schools of psychology that will be discussed here.

PERSONALITY: The traits, forms of behavioral adjustment, that characterize the individual in relation to others in the environment.

When dealing with the human personality, we must realize that its component parts are based in all the psychological and physiological processes. While human personality can be defined as the way in which an individual typically reacts to his environment, it is also the manner in which the elements of the environment converge on the individual and act to determine behavior. The various schools of psychology essentially disagree on the importance or effect of the elements of the environment upon the individual.

Freudian Psychology

We have mechanisms that we use to maintain stability in our adjustment processes. They were outlined by Sigmund Freud, but before we present them, we must understand Freud's conception of the structure of personality.

As conceived by Freud, the personality is composed of three basic parts: the id, the ego, and the superego. If we each examine ourselves, we may find that these concepts will not present anything unfamiliar.

ID (Freud): The source of humanity's basic, instinctual urges; seeks immediate gratification.

Freud viewed the id as the part of our personality that contains repressed impulses and desires, often sexual or aggressive in nature. If we examine our daydreams, or if we can remember our dreams after we awaken, we will probably admit, at least to ourselves, that they can be wild. Under normal circumstances we

Greek philosopher Aristotle, author of works on such topics as logic, ethics, politics, and poetics.

REPRESSION: A defense mechanism whereby anxiety-provoking material is blocked from entering consciousness, although it exists on the unconscious level.

would not discuss these thoughts even with a close friend. In our society, a man walking down the street may have fantasies about the females he sees. Most men, however, never even consider turning their thoughts into reality, because their culture and its rules have repressed the performance of these small dramas.

Although many have dealt with the fantasies of women, few people in our society have had the opportunity to hear a firsthand description of those fantasies. If the male id is repressed in our society, then the female id has been so repressed that even its existence has until recently been denied.

The id, then, is concerned with a person's unexpressed thoughts and desires. In theory, we could predict that without the repressing effect of our cultures we might act out those desires. Another opinion on the matter asks whether we might not have the thoughts at all if they were not repressed by the limitations placed upon us.

The superego occupies the other end of the scale. If the id is concerned with the forbidden, the superego is concerned with the individual's conscience, the center of guilt and concern for punishment. The superego acts to block the impulses of the id. We can imagine the typical plight of people faced with a strong moralistic sense reinforced by an overactive superego and an active id. On one hand, there are entertaining thoughts that fill them with self-loathing; on the other hand, they rather enjoy the stimulation of the thoughts that they fight unsuccessfully to control.

In the middle, between the id and the superego, lies the ego, the rational planner within each of us. Where the id seeks immediate gratification of desires and the superego attempts to block it, the ego attempts to allow gratification within an acceptable cultural framework. The ego attempts to confine gratification to the proper place, time, and situation.

Defense Mechanisms

In everyday life we may find that it is easier to resort to the use of a defense mechanism than it would be to face the resultant anxiety many situations would bring. Blame it on Charlie, don't recognize the problem exists, fall back to a comfortable pattern of behavior familiar from earlier days, all are examples of an endless list of formats associated with defense mechanisms. People who use various defense mechanisms are not aware of their use, or at least do not face up to the reality of their use because it would defeat the anxiety reducing aspect of the defense mechanism.

SUPEREGO (Freud): The part of the personality that imposes on the individual the restraints and moral precepts of the external world.

EGO (Freud): The rational self that satisfies the needs of the id.

Freud felt that the ego developed defense mechanisms whenever the id impulses threatened to get out of control. The ego actually fears the punishments that would result from realization of the unapproved id desires. These mechanisms, all the product of the unconscious self, are aimed at warding off feelings of anxiety. They also tend to distort reality. Freud felt that since the defense mechanisms were products of the unconscious, they were attempts to deceive other people but in reality were also self-deceptive.

DEFENSE MECHANISMS: Reactions to anxiety or frustration that enables people to adjust to themselves and to society.

BEHAVIORISM: A school of psychology advocating the objective study of behavior.

Other, more recent psychological theories of the "behaviorist" school suggest that the defense mechanisms used by the individual are learned. The behaviorists conclude that since defense mechanisms are part of our learned behavior, they are also a product of our conscious means of responding to a situation. In a psychoanalytic framework, while most of us utilize one defense mechanism or more during the course of our lives, we are unaware of what they are.

Some of the more common defense mechanisms are repression, regression, and projection. Repression, probably the most basic of all these mechanisms, is the unconscious inhibition of a need. The individual unconsciously refuses to be aware of or to remember a need, desire, fantasy, or feeling. People may repress certain needs and desires because they feel threatened by what those needs and desires represent.

In dealing with repressed desires, we might examine the cultural influences that require a clergyman to deny his sexual feelings when he is confronted with attractive women. Our literature abounds with stories of clergymen who did not repress those desires. Also, for many years after the Victorian period, women in our society tended to repress their sexual activity and thought.

Among certain groups, the need to control overt emotion is also an example of repression. The stereotypes of the inscrutable Oriental or the expressionless, unfeeling Indian of history are examples of repressed emotion. Their cultures do not accept overt displays of emotion; therefore such feelings must be repressed. How many men have felt that they wanted to cry but couldn't because it was not "manly"? How many women feel free to discuss their sexual fantasies? Would they admit even to having sexual fantasies?

Many of us are actually frightened by the contents of dreams and daydreams. People commonly imagine themselves in what they would consciously view as despicable situations. For example, some people have found themselves with incestuous thoughts that disturb them deeply; they usually suppress action in these forbidden areas.

REGRESSION: The escape from frustrating or anxiety-provoking situations by retreating to earlier forms of behavior.

Regression. Regression is the defense mechanism employed when people who are emotionally threatened revert to patterns of behavior practiced in a more secure period of their lives. A typical example of this pattern is the behavior of a five-year-old child who suddenly finds that he has a baby sister. His secure world of being the only child is shattered, and he reverts to the infantile pattern of thumb-sucking. The child is regressing to a period of emotional security where his position was relatively unthreatened.

PROJECTION DEFENSE MECHANISM: A means whereby people remain oblivious to their own undesirable qualities by attributing them to others, thus reducing their own feelings of anxiety.

Projection. Projection is another common defense mechanism that many individuals practice. When using this mechanism, people project their unconscious feelings to another person. People feeling depressed might ask a friend why he or she is depressed. In a sense, they are seeing a mirror image of their feelings in another person.

DISPLACEMENT: Application of a thwarted frustration on a substitute person or thing by someone who cannot show anger toward the true cause of the frustration.

Displacement. Another variation of the defense mechanism theme is displacement. Frequently we are placed in positions where it is impossible to vent our anger. An instructor or employer might have made excessive demands or acted unfairly. Under the circumstances, we would have to grin and bear it. When we left school or work to return home, we would seize upon a victim for our pent-up anger. We might pick a fight with a waiter, blow the horn at a pedestrian, or wave a fist at another motorist.

As we have said, Sigmund Freud was the first person to attempt a comprehensive explanation of personality development. Freud believed that an individual did not behave in a specific way without a reason. He felt that a person acted the way he did because of a stimulating factor and not from mere chance or accident. Freud's structuring of his views around the basic tenet that action was determined by situation or occurrence categorizes him as a "determinist."

DETERMINIST: Describing the belief that given complete knowledge of conditions, one would know precisely how a person will, indeed must, act.

Most of us have heard of the phrase "Freudian slip" used to describe an instance when someone accidentally says what he unconsciously meant to say. In our pattern of culture, we rarely vocalize our actual thoughts. The person who blurts out, "I'm sorry you could make it to dinner," instead of "I'm glad you could make it to dinner," is unconsciously revealing his true feelings. The Freudian slip illustrates the action of unconscious processes. Freud is credited with popularizing the concept of the unconscious. When we say that a person is motivated by unconscious processes, we are saying that the individual is acting in a specific manner without knowing the reasons for the behavior. Freud felt that the greater part of human behavior was motivated by the unconscious. As a result, people's unconscious forces them to behave the way they do.

Freud developed a form of therapy known as psychoanalysis, which is designed to delve into a person's unconscious to discover the underlying causes for behavior. Freud believed that by the age of five an individual's personality was fixed and relatively inflexible. He further stated that only after years of psychoanalytic therapy could the personality begin to change.

Some psychoanalysts still advocate Freud's teachings, and they are called classical psychoanalysts. Others have remained faithful to Freud's basic tenets but have made significant changes in his theory. These are referred to as neo-Freudians.

Behaviorism

Freud's approach to personality is only one of many involved in the study of personality. Some other approaches to the study of personality are behaviorism. Gestalt psychology, phenomenology, and existentialism.

In order to understand the first of these, behaviorism, we must consider two earlier schools of psychology: structuralism and functionalism. In the late 1800s these schools were concerned with the study of conscious behavior. With the advent of Freud's theories, there was a shift to the study of the unconscious as a determining factor in behavior. During the developing years of

Freudian psychoanalysis in the United States early in the twentieth century, John B. Watson developed the basic theories of behaviorism, which was in a real sense a reaction against psychoanalysis and other forms of psychology. In its claim that the conscious or unconscious processes were entirely too subjective, behaviorism made a radical departure from the accepted forms of psychology. It held that to be more scientific psychology had to focus entirely on behavior since behavior is observable, repeatable, concrete, and measurable. If the basic requirements of the scientific method were satisfied, behavior was considered to be worthy of study.

The focal points for the behaviorists were concrete aspects of personality: what they could see, touch, and measure. Another major contention of the behaviorists was that a person's behavior was learned entirely through conditioning and shaping. An important tenet of behaviorism is that "for every stimulus there is a response, and for every response there has been a stimulus." Behaviorists who wished to study the cause of a person's behavior felt that they had only to search for the stimuli that led to that particular response. The two major goals of the behavioral approach are prediction and control.

In trying to make a simple comparison of psychoanalysis and behaviorism, we must first note that they are based on different philosophies and strive for different goals. The techniques used for the treatment of individuals also differ considerably.

The Freudian psychoanalyst will try to find the unconscious motivation for a person's behavior, while the behaviorist will attempt to understand how the person has "learned" the troublesome form of behavior. The Freudian feels that helping patients gain insight into the unconscious base of their problems will be a first step toward the solution of those problems.

The behaviorist's therapy is known as behavior modification. As the name implies, the therapist believes that former conditioning can be nullified and that the person can be reconditioned along healthier lines. Behavior modification emphasizes controlling, changing, and manipulating the behavior of the patient and not dealing with the individual's internal conflicts.

B.F. Skinner, a leading contemporary behaviorist, proposes in *Beyond Freedom and Dignity* that freedom itself is a myth.[1] He suggests that since our conditioning processes determine behavior, those processes and our environmental forces have determined the way we behave. We are then nothing more than products of our past history. Because Skinner believes that we are not really free, he suggests that we should surrender to a behaviorally engineered society. In such a society, we would all be conditioned to behave in ways that are good for society. His proposal seems to have considerable merit until we begin to wonder who would choose the manner of conditioning.

Gestalt Psychology During the years of controversy between the members of the psychoanalytic and behaviorist schools in the United States, an entire-

GESTALT PSYCHOLOGY: A school of psychology that emphasizes the whole as more than the sum of its parts.

ly different school of psychology developed in Germany. Three men, M. Wertheimer, Ian Kohler, and Kurt Koffka, founded Gestalt psychology. "Gestalt" literally means "whole." The difference between the Gestalt and behavioral schools is easy to see. The behaviorists feel that one must separate behavior into its smallest parts, study each part separately, and then recombine the parts to see the behavior as it originated. The behaviorists believe that all behavior can be reduced, at least in theory, to biochemical components.

The Gestaltists objected to this reductionist view and claimed that by the reduction we might lose something. They believed that the "whole is greater than the sum of its parts" and that behavior is not reducible to a biochemical base. We must not only consider the "whole" behavior, we must also give considerable attention to the situational context of behavior. The Gestaltists are also noted for their research in the area of perception.

Social Perception

Perception is the manner in which we interpret our sensory data. A class may look at the same tree, but each member of that class may perceive it in a different way. In a political or religious discussion, we are aware of the fact that several people using the same data or facts treat this information in entirely different ways. They will come up with opposing values drawn from the same material. Each person sees or perceives the material in a different light.

The influences upon our perceptual abilities are many and interactive. In other words, they are not isolated from one another but are built upon the complex whole that constitutes an individual's personality makeup. Perception, then, is a product of our intellectual ability, previous learning patterns, conditioning experience, attitudes, culture, and sex.

While this list of influences upon perception is by no means complete, we may use it as a base to enlarge upon.

When discussing the various factors affecting perception, we are able to use only the broadest terms, such as intelligence, sex, and cultural influences. A person's intelligence may be based upon heredity or social conditioning through the environment. Certainly in our society our tests for intelligence are based to a degree upon previous learning, conditioning, and experience. The very attitude necessary to take a test and score well or poorly may depend upon social conditioning and experience.

An individual's sex calls for different values and rules in our society, which in turn affect perception. A male child is taught to perceive colors, pictures, paintings, music, and women in a manner far different from his sister. His very walk and gesturing pattern is different. In some segments of our society, he may not allow himself the luxury of crying as the result of specified stimuli. While the female's perception of an event may require her to be tearful and sad, a boy is called upon to be harsh and brutal. Training in sex roles calls for a different view or perception of the same stimuli:

A story about an anthropologist illustrates the cultural influences upon perception. He was working in the North African desert, in the marketplace of a small oasis town. While purchasing supplies, he noticed a group of men watching a baby camel strangle on a plastic bag. They were laughing and thoroughly enjoying the spectacle. The anthropologist, having been raised in a culture that stressed kindness to animals, perceived the event as blatantly cruel and abhorrent. He was shocked and saddened at the spectacle. Two cultures viewed the same event in different ways based upon the values, roles, attitudes, and their cultural conditioning in general. How we perceive the world is largely a function of our personality makeup.

A generally hostile, selfish person may project those feelings to other people and to society at large. The bases of personality assessment lie largely in the subjects' ability to verbalize or to speak about their views of themselves. In addition to self-perception, it is also important to find out how these people perceive other people and the world around them.

People's self-concepts, or how they see themselves, are tools we may use to measure adjustment. Perception exists at different levels. Carl Rogers suggested the notions of real self and ideal self. The real self refers to people's images of themselves and how they believe others see them. The ideal self refers to the personality combination that the individual desires. Each of us daydreams about what we would like to be. If we are well adjusted, we usually know the difference between our real self and our ideal self.

When the distance between the real and the ideal is small, we may assume that a person is relatively well adjusted. If the ideal self inhabits a dream world that has no relation to the realities of a person's life, that person will probably feel dissatisfied with himself or herself. Some of us may have experienced such dissatisfaction. Our concept of our physical self may well affect our actions and manners. If we want desperately to be famous models or ballet dancers but realize that we resemble mud fences and that we cannot walk across the room without tripping, we may have a problem. If we cannot bring ourselves to speak two consecutive sentences to a young lady, let alone hold her hand, yet dream of ourselves as the prime seducers of the twentieth century, we may have an adjustment problem.

Humanist Psychology

PHENOMENOLOGY: The view that behavior is determined by the phenomena or direct experience, rather than by external, objective, physically described reality.

Phenomenology is the study of immediate experience. This approach suggests that the scientific analysis of experience may result in a loss of the essentials and the richness of human behavior. Existentialists believe that the emphasis should be placed on existence or "being." Some major themes in existentialism are freedom, choice, and death. The phenomenologists and existentialists believe that human beings differ from other animals because of their reason, imagination, uniqueness, complexity, and self-consciousness. We are free, they feel, to choose our own destiny, and while we may be products of our own history, we are still capable of understanding our condition to the extent of making changes both in our life and in our behavior.

The phenomenologists maintain that personal perception of the world determines forthcoming reactions. Perception, in particular what individuals perceive themselves to be, is of primary importance to those individuals in determining what they will be. In this sense, people's *concepts* of their ability and/or lack of it is far more important than their actual ability. Phenomenologists emphasize an individual's perceived world rather than the objective measurable aspects of that world. The humanists have recognized the value of direct observation and empirical research, but they feel that the very precision of this form of research has reduced psychology's ability to be creative. Psychologists have concentrated on insignificant issues for which there is adequate research. In other words, humanists feel that they rely on methods rather than attempting to deal with more important issues with less precision.[2]

EXISTENTIALIST PSYCHOLO-GY: A view that the task of psychology is linked to the observation and description of the existent data or contents of experience.

The humanists have extended therapy into daily life, an example of which is "group experience." The aim of the group experience is to increase sensitivity and to allow for the transfer of learning. Traditional sensitivity-group experience can be painful as one inspects interpersonal relationships. The value of such groups depends upon the training of the leaders and the goals of the individual participants. The aims and goals of the humanists are acceptable to psychologists of other persuasions, but areas of method have met with considerable resistance. Critics contend that the bases of humanism are poorly specified. They also maintain that while the humanists reject much, they affirm little.[3]

DEFINING THE BOUNDARY LINE: NORMAL AND NOT NORMAL

When all the theories have been discussed and all the developmental history has been presented, we are left with several important issues. Among them are:

1. What is normal behavior?
2. What is abnormal behavior?
3. How do we define normal and abnormal behavior?
4. Why do we define them in the manner we have chosen?
5. What do we do about abnormal behavior once it is defined?

Normal Behavior

Someone once said, "All the world is crazy, except for you and me, and sometimes I wonder about you." If we use a subjective model, we may claim, "I am normal." Convinced of our own normalcy we may further reason that all people who act as we do are therefore "normal." The person professing normalcy may well be a patient in a mental hospital. According to his or her definition of normality, all mental patients would be normal while nonmental patients would be abnormal.

The statistical model may also be used to determine normal behavior. This model claims that what happens most frequently

Depression is a growing problem
among adolescents.

Skill Reinforcer 5-1*
Which measure of central tendency applies here?

can be considered normal. Although the limits used by the statistical model are wider than those used by the subjective model, the
results once more depend upon the population sample used. The
subjective model uses the individual as its population sample; the
statistical model uses a population grouping that may have any
sort of criteria. The statistical model assumes that the middle-of-
the-road, most frequently occurring activity is normal. Anything
that deviates from the middle-of-the-road is considered abnormal.

Because of its emphasis on most frequently occurring forms of
behavior, the statistical model presents mediocrity as the ideal.
Variations from the norm are judged not by quality but by the degree of deviation. If we consider the need to reflect the total personality by means of a model, we find the statistical model lacking.
Because it cannot isolate the quality personality variables, it cannot deal with the subtle complexities present in all individuals and
with personality disturbances.

The sociological model claims that behavior which conforms
to the group's norm is indeed normal. To accept this model, we
must first recognize that the group itself defines normalcy; therefore, the value system of that group is normal insofar as the group
is concerned. Accepting this model also means accepting the view
that normality differs in different groups.

The range of normal behavior is wide and flexible. What is
considered normal in one society may well be considered abnormal in another. When we analyze behavior, we must always
consider the context in which that behavior takes place.

If we observe two people jumping from a bridge without considering the context or situation of their action, we may be tempt-
ed to put both jumpers into the same category.[4] If we consider the
situation, however, we may find that one jumper was indeed attempting suicide, which is abnormal behavior in our society. The
other bridge jumper may have been attempting a rescue, which is
ideal behavior in our society. When we question the normality or
abnormality of suicide itself, we are left with even more unan-
swerable questions.

The Japanese student who fails final examinations may take a
one-way hike up a steep mountain. Traditionally, the Japanese
who has lost face has had no option but to commit suicide. Suicide
was so institutionalized that the steps and methods for the action
were ritualized. People would dress and position themselves in a
specific manner and then proceed to disembowel themselves.
Since disembowelment is not a painless or quick death, once it
had been accomplished, the aid of a second person was usually
enlisted to decapitate the person with a sword. By the standards of
our society, such behavior is clearly abnormal. The abnormality of
the action has resulted in almost no American incidents of Hari-
kari to date. The Japanese, as we have stated, accepted the action
as normal behavior under specific circumstances.

Americans were treated to another form of what we consider
abnormal suicide in the 1960s. Vietnamese monks signified their

political displeasure by dousing themselves in gasoline and lighting up. While this was thoroughly abnormal by our standards, the pattern caught on in the United States, and several instances of self-immolation occurred here. While the actions in Vietnam were not happy events, they were accepted there as a form of normal protest. Few Americans would agree that the self-immolators in this country were participating in a normal form of suicide or protest. Suicide is not considered thoroughly normal behavior in our society, yet there are common procedures of accomplishing the act. Carbon monoxide, natural gas, sleeping pills, barbiturates, poison, and small caliber bullets are more acceptable than other means of suicide.

The recent sharp rise of teenage suicide in the United States has been a source of consternation. A large number of studies, papers, and seminars have been directed toward finding the reasons behind this phenomenon. In brief, many psychologists associate the higher levels of substance abuse common today with the increased rates of adolescent suicide. In addition, there is some feeling that the relatively high rates of depression also common among adolescents has a sociological base. It is difficult to quantify the effect of a high divorce rate, lowered possibilities of upward social mobility, shifting economic fortunes, and demographic imbalances upon the world view of a generation. Perhaps in the last analysis the rate of social change has accelerated beyond the point of easy assimilation. We are left with a question: Is suicide on the verge of being considered a normal alternative for specific age groups in the United States? The use of the term normal should in no way be considered acceptance as a desired alternative, but the practice may, by virtue of increasing frequency, be seen by various groups as being within culturally accepted normative patterns. Eating disorders such as anorexia nervosa and bulimia have their base in our culture's perception of beauty. The Duchess of Windsor was quoted as saying that, "One can never be too rich or too thin." Our society's view of the ideal woman, at least in the eyes of young women, is thin is best. The result is a psychological and physical disorder in which eating eventually stops altogether. It is not unusual to hear of young women dying of these socially-inspired disorders. An objective observer could equate the bound feet common to Chinese women of days past, normal for its time, to many of our accepted but destructive practices, normal for our time and culture.

As we can see, normality depends upon both the context of the situation and the cultural value of a particular society. We may also see differences in the concept of normal behavior when we survey social classes. It is acceptable and preferable for upper-class people to defend their idea of honor, but lower-class people are expected to react more physically to situations than upper-class people. What is normal? We are left with a question but no clear-cut answer.

Abnormal Behavior

DIAGNOSIS: The act or process of deciding the nature of a diseased condition by examination.

While we have ended our discussion of normality with a question, we may realize that as individuals we have been able to point clearly to abnormal behavior in others. There seems to be a nearly universal quality concerning the labeling of abnormality.

Abnormal behavior in a person is primarily diagnosed as mental illness. Various cultures refer to abnormal behavior in other ways, but it seems to boil down to the idea that certain people are "not all there" mentally, or "not playing with a full deck."

Each language has had a word for abnormality. Examples of words common in our own language are "lunatic," "mad," and "crazy." The common thread in all cultures appears to be an understanding on the part of society involved that the individual in question exhibits behavioral patterns that are unpredictable and sometimes uncontrollable.

Frequently the reasons given for this lack of control have been unsophisticated. It was once popularly assumed that an individual acting in an abnormal fashion was possessed by a spirit or the devil. Many persons still believe in spirit-possession. Fortunately, in our society the label no longer carries the weight it once did.

Through a long and painful period in the history of Western society, an effective cure for abnormal behavior was to burn the person accused at the stake. The results were certainly conclusive; any devils lodged in a person so treated were expelled. The history of Europe and America is replete with stories of the termination of senile old men and women and younger people, which made mental treatment unnecessary.

A typical method of dealing with a person who appears to be talking to the wind is to assume he or she has a direct connection with the forces of nature. Many cultures have recognized the epileptic, the cataleptic, or the person possessed with abnormal traits as holy. While in a trance or otherwise unable to communicate with other people, he or she was assumed to be talking to the gods. In some societies subjects who were unable to convince the gods to act in a particular manner were killed.

CATALEPTICS: People who suffer from catalepsy, a condition in which consciousness and feeling are suddenly and temporarily lost.

Running amok has been one pattern of behavior that most societies have been unable to handle. This pattern occurs when stress becomes unbearable for an individual and usually results in violent action directed toward anyone around. The person who runs amok is restrained, if possible, or killed if restraint is impossible. We normally do the same thing through police action.

The history of the development of mental treatment reads like a horror story. For the most part, abnormal behavior has prompted mistreatment rather than treatment. The first mental institutions appeared in fifteenth-century Europe and resembled nothing more than the worst prisons. Care consisted of chaining, whipping, locking away, and denying the amenities of life.

Beginning in the late eighteenth century and into the nineteenth century, there were some major developments in the care of mental patients. Chains were removed, and an attempt was made to alter the image of mental patients. They were presented

Bedlam, London's madhouse, epitome of uproar and confusion.

as "sick" rather than "possessed,"[5] a change which tended to make others act in a more humane manner. By the middle of the nineteenth century, care reached its peak, but it slowly declined as the small hospitals became overcrowded. The demonic concept once more gave rise to restraints and a "keeping" policy, since cures seemed impossible.

Recent innovations have produced more direct results. Once more people are no longer chained, but they are frequently illegally imprisoned. Imprisonment is the only term that can be applied to a situation in which egress is limited and no treatment is given. Patients are not often rehabilitated, even by modern methods. Long-term institutionalization seems to produce deterioration. The longer people stay in an institution, the less their chances of getting out and leading a more normal life.

The causes of these problems are easy to find. Patients far outnumber their doctors, who can rarely do more than check patients as they enter. Two or three observations per year per patient is typical in many institutions. Attendants are often underpaid, poorly educated, and insensitive to the needs of the patients. Physical force and brutality are common, since many attendants feel that the patients are dangerous and do not understand how to cope with them. In addition, being with other disturbed people seems to reinforce the patients' disturbed behavior.

Institutions have evolved for a number of reasons. The realization that institutionalization should be a last resort and the emergence of outpatient and semi-controlled halfway houses seem to have reduced funding for the development and maintenance of institutions. Treatment itself is confused. Another complicating factor is the economics of the times. The costs of doctors, food, building upkeep, attendants, and associated equipment have risen greatly. Another factor, our population growth, the fastest in the Western world, has supplied patients to our institutions at an ever-increasing rate. It is difficult to foresee the answers to these huge problems.

Modern techniques for the treatment and/or cure of mental illness have had their wilder moments. The director of a major state mental hospital found that a patient had a remarkable recovery from schizophrenia after her teeth had been extracted. As a result, all patients afflicted with schizophrenia in that hospital had all their teeth removed. Unfortunately, there were no further cures.

Brain operations (psychosurgery) turned many possibly violent people into living vegetables, but they were no longer violent. The operations were performed on a large number of people who were not violent and only questionably ill. Needless to say, they never again became violent—or anything else.

Theft from and sexual and physical abuse of mental patients has long been one of the fringe benefits accepted by some low-paid hospital attendants. After all, who would believe a crazy person? Even today the daily life of some mental patients defies description. Because of the low proportion of doctors to patients,

SCHIZOPHRENIA: A psychotic reaction in which the basic symptoms are withdrawal from reality, distorted or disturbed contact with reality, regressive behavior, erratic thought, inconsistent emotional relationships, hallucinations, and delusions.

it has become standard procedure to treat only those cases for which a cure is expected. The remainder of the less hopeful cases are merely kept. "Keeping" may mean solitary confinement without clothes or such basic amenities as toilets, sinks, glasses, books, razors, knives, forks, spoons, or any other objects with which the person might injure himself. Recalcitrant patients in some institutions are supposedly helped back toward the right path with electric-shock treatments.

RECALCITRANT: Refusing to obey authority, custom, or regulation.

Shock treatments are given in an attempt to reorient the individual. No one can say with any assurance exactly what shock treatments do to a person. We know that they are very painful, that they can cause muscular spasms of such intensity that bones break, and that they occasionally bring a person closer to what we call normal. The scientific community does not know what shock treatments actually do, and there is much about the use of shock reminiscent of the practice of driving out evil spirits. Now, instead of roasting people slowly on a spit or at the stake, we shock the devil out of them. For further information on the dedication of modern people to the concept of spirit possession, read *The Exorcist* by W.P. Blatty.

We must at this point make a further distinction between the forms of abnormal behavior. On the one hand, we have those features of pathological behavior that are constant in human populations. These features appear in all societies, and they may be recognized as universal human afflictions, although the particular symptoms may vary. On the other hand, those incidental abnormalities that are culture-dependent vary from society to society.

PATHOLOGICAL: Due to or involving disease.

The universal psychological disturbances found in all societies include traits that interfere with the individual's attaining an effective, satisfying personal and social adjustment. The traits subject to disturbance are in the areas of communication volition, thought, emotion, and general conduct. Any person with clear defects in these highly critical psychological areas would be considered abnormal in almost any society.

COMMUNICATION VOLITION: Willingness to communicate.

The culturally dependent aspects of abnormality frequently show themselves in the outward forms or surface symptoms of such disturbances. In addition, the interpretation of such disturbances by an individual's society varies from culture to culture.

In other words, people whose society considers them disturbed act in the manner that their culture provides for mentally disturbed people. Each culture provides models or patterns of expected actions for certain situations. The teacher in our society plays a part when facing a class. Students act in a manner suitable to their position. When in uniform, the police officer reacts to specific situations in an accepted manner.

The social environment of mentally ill people forces specific patterns of behavior upon them to fit their roles. In our society a depressed woman is likely to seek only certain modes of suicide. As a rule, she will not usually disfigure herself; pills, gas, and drowning are acceptable. Men in our society are likely to shoot themselves, but women rarely do. Our culture regulates even our abnormal behavior.

In a primitive society, an accepted mode of behavior for depressed people may be to develop "moth sickness." They have heard of and seen moth sickness, so they know that when people feel as they do, they should fear moth sickness. If the pattern is completed, they will jump into a campfire, drawn to it as though they were moths, and die.

There are many examples of the power of a culture's influence over a person's mind. At this reading, someone somewhere is dying because a witch put a curse on him. It may sound foolish, but if we had been raised in a society that believes in witchcraft, if we knew what it could do, and if we then found that we were the subject of a curse, we would die. We might spend a few days telling ourselves that the curse would have no effect on us, but in a matter of time we would stop eating and waste away.

Such deadly influence is the result of a culture's acceptance of patterns of action and reaction. The common criteria used in determining disturbed behavior should be emphasized: behavior is uncontrolled, and functions are impaired. In our society, the next step is to evaluate the behavioral pattern to determine whether it is harmful either to the individual or to society.

Under normal circumstances, if the person is judged harmless, he or she remains in society and is considered a harmless kook. On the other hand, if judged to be harmful, the individual may be locked away in an attempt to prevent injury to himself or herself or to others. The decision-making processes in use today leave much to be desired. We apparently have many dangerous people walking the streets. Our societal pattern calls on us to succeed in our attempts to cure individuals. We do not like to accept the concept of hopelessness, yet our ability to deal successfully with most forms of mental illness is extremely limited.

In our approach to the study of abnormal behavior, we have touched upon some aspects of supernatural possession. There have been numerous other approaches to the same problem. In the nineteenth century, people revived an ancient Greek idea that attributed abnormal behavior to an underlying brain or biochemical defect. "Diseases of the mind" became a useful term to fit psychological problems into the medical framework. Once this adjustment was accomplished, mental diseases were categorized according to symptoms. By using this system, it was felt that science could then find specific organic causes for the disturbances.

Once more, an evenhanded approach was lacking. Little or no attention was given to other possible causes of abnormal behavior. Nonphysical traumas, such as personal frustrations, conflicts, and other debilitating factors of a purely psychological nature, were almost ignored.

Recent psychological opinion has tended to find fault with the medical model of mental deviance. The basic assumption of that

Skill Reinforcer 5-2
What is the major problem in finding the cause of mental imbalance?

Will their personalities and intellects be molded by their environment or genetic makeup?

Brain anomalies

Some are diseases & Psyc do advance Medical Tx as well as

model was the physical cause of mental disease. Many medical people believe that the presence or lack of specific trace elements in the body influences or causes forms of mental imbalance.

There is considerable evidence that direct links exist between physical or biological conditions and some psychotic reactions. To illustrate this point, we must consider that identical twins share the same genes, whereas fraternal twins do not. Gottesman and Shield (1966) found that when one of a set of identical twins is schizophrenic the chances of the other being schizophrenic are five times greater than those of fraternal twins.[6] Evidence also supports the transmission of schizophrenia from parent to child.[7]

Glandular defects, chemical imbalance, and metabolic disturbances have also been observed in schizophrenics.[8] When serum extracted from schizophrenics has been injected into otherwise normal human beings, they have exhibited schizophrenic symptoms.[9]

In reality, a shift from the medical model to a more psychologically based model is taking place. We can only hope that a blending of the models can be attained.

A major flaw in the medical model, as seen by psychologists, is that the labeling caused by the words "disease" and "sickness" has affected the patient's self-concept. In addition, these labels have directed society's reaction toward the affected person. While we must admit that the labels "disease" or "sickness" are more enlightened than "witch," "devil-possessed," or "sinner," the stigma attached is almost as damaging.

Various psychologists have suggested that we replace the concepts of mental disease or illness with the concept of problems in living.[10] Under this broad heading would fall such categories as norm deviance, which would serve to describe abnormal behavior.[11] Others have proposed that we view the mentally disturbed as people who have been unable to establish acceptable social identities and roles.

Any future answer must be a combination of the medical and psychological models. At present we are left with an assortment of approaches to a touchy set of problems. Today the most acceptable view is that the factors which have been described are as complex, varied, and interactive as those factors that lead the rest of society toward what we consider normal behavior. To explain thoroughly why a person is mentally disturbed, we must know that person in entirety. This includes that person's history, genetic background, physical and social environments, and the totality of personal experience.

A Continuum?   There are two other major approaches to the disturbed versus the normal behavioral patterns: the discontinuity approach and the continuity approach. With the discontinuity approach, we must divide all people into two groups: the "healthies" and the "sickies." Such a method is simplistic in its design, and it divides society with a blunt knife. Perhaps better would be the continuity approach, which claims that all people and behavior can be ranked on a continuum, ranging from normal to severely disturbed. By using this method, we see all people in society as though they were on a long staircase but in different positions. Those at the bottom may be categorized as severely disturbed and those at the top as normal. As one ascends the stairs, people exhibit fewer and fewer abnormal personality traits, until they reach the point of normality.

In essence, the continuity approach seems reasonable in that it views all of society as possessed of the same traits, with those at one extreme more disorganized and less controlled than those at the other extreme.

TYPES OF MENTAL DISORDERS

It may be enough to label someone as abnormal and let it go at that, but when in the position of having to deal with such a person, we want to be more specific in our labeling.

An attempt to divide mental disorders into categories is subject to the basic limitations and flaws of any labeling system.[12] The categories that follow should in no way be considered the last word on the matter. While examples of the types of mental illness are not all-inclusive, they will give some idea of what is to be found in the area of mental disorder. Two major categories of mental disorders are brain disorders and mental retardation. Brain disorders include organic brain disorders, acute brain disorders, and chronic brain disorders. The causes of mental retardation are numerous. Retardation sometimes results from the mother's having contracted rubella (German measles) during pregnancy. Other common causes may be poor prenatal care or birth difficulties. Down's syndrome (mongolism) is a result of genetic mishap. The mongoloid receives forty-seven chromosomes instead of the usual forty-six. No matter what the cause, the retardation may be described as mild, moderate, severe, or profound.

Brain disorders and mental retardation are not considered emotional or mental disorders in the general sense. The basis for these disorders is physical, but emotional disturbances may develop either from the actual symptoms, which result from a disturbed thinking process, or from the manner in which other people react to the subject's individual symptoms.

Besides these first two types of mental disorders, there are others that we will study in greater depth here.

Psychosomatic Disorders

Psychosomatic disorders involve physical symptoms unrelated to a physical cause. The psychosomatic patient suffers, in a very real sense, from a physical ailment that has developed as a result of emotional tension, usually anxiety. Examples of ailments caused in this manner are colitis, ulcers, frigidity, impotence, skin disorders of various kinds, gastritis, asthma, migraine headache, hyperten-

Not True

They are Visceral Responders to Stress etc result in Physical illness

sion, and anorexia nervosa (excessive aversion to food; excessive weight loss). It must be reemphasized that many of the examples given may have a physical basis, in which case they would not be considered as psychosomatic disorders.

People maintain a different degree of concern for the victim of psychosomatic ailments that is different from their degree of concern for victims of other diseases. In reality, the psychosomatic patient suffers every bit as much as the patient with a physically based disease. We would have to watch a child near suffocation from an asthma attack to appreciate the actual physical symptoms of a psychologically based ailment. In asthma, the bronchial tubes are affected, the muscles connected with chest expansion may atrophy, and the heart may suffer from the strain of repeated attacks.

Neuroses

Neuroses are classed as mild disturbances that do not prevent functions in society. We all have neurotic tendencies. The fine line between the neurotic person and the normal person is barely visible and quite arbitrary. People may be labeled neurotic if they are unhappy with themselves or if the people around them are dissatisfied with their behavior. Some neurotic reactions are anxiety reaction, phobia, hypochondria, depressive reaction, obsessive-compulsive reaction, and dissociative reaction, such as amnesia and multiple personality. We are familiar with many of these neuroses in ourselves and people we know.

If neurotics seek treatment at all, they usually do so on an outpatient basis. Generally there is no need to hospitalize the typical neurotic. Because of the high cost of psychiatric and psychological treatment, the typical people undergoing therapy are at least middle class and relatively well educated. Probably they seek treatment more often than their lower-class counterpart, who may have a subcultural disposition to accept neuroses as part of life. People undergoing therapy are probably more in touch with their feelings and problems than neurotics not seeking therapy.

One of the more familiar neuroses is the phobia, an unreasonable fear of particular phenomena, such as heights, bridges, tunnels, darkness, or insects. Not all irrational fears are phobias. People may have learned fears as a result of conditioning. Such people are the hypochondriacs who are always ailing or checking themselves for the symptoms of any popular disease. The hypochondriac has perhaps contributed to the great affluence of the American medical profession.

Another familiar neurosis is obsessive-compulsive behavior. Who among us has not had the opportunity of watching someone overclean a house? A prime example of obsessive-compulsive behavior is in the play, movie, and television series *The Odd Couple.* The plot centers around two male roommates, each the product of divorce. One of the roommates is a slob, the other is a diligent housekeeper who wants everything spotless and in its proper place. The conflict and comedy of the story arise from the clash

---

PSYCHOSOMATIC DISORD-ERS: Physical disorders that originate in or are aggravated by emotional difficulties.

NEUROSIS: A functional behavior disorder which, though troublesome, is seldom sufficiently severe to require institutionalization; chronic, inefficient, partially disruptive ways of dealing with personal problems.

AMNESIA: Loss of memory.

PHOBIA: Fear; intense feelings of anxiety associated with objects or situations.

OBSESSIVE–COMPULSIVE REAC-TION: Psychoneurotic behavior in which anxiety is associated with unwanted ideas (obsession) and with persistent impulses to repeat certain acts over and over.

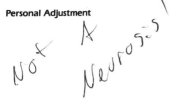

between the slob's casualness and the housekeeper's obsessive-compulsive cleanliness. The librarian who labors against the compulsion to have all the books on the proper shelves all the time may be exhibiting obsessive-compulsive behavior.

Some neuroses are classified as dissociative reactions. Amnesia, a type of dissociative reaction, is an attempt to wipe out memory. Another type of dissociative reaction is multiple personality, an extremely rare neurosis in which a person develops several different personalities.

DISSOCIATIVE REACTION: Repression of a thought or experience that an individual is unable to cope with.

Personality Disorders

MALADAPTIVE BEHAVIOR: Behavior whereby people do not adjust to themselves or to environment.

Personality disturbances are mental disturbances that lie somewhere between and frequently overlap neuroses and psychoses, the more serious category. The person suffering from personality disturbances has an ingrained maladaptive personality. The sociopath, the sexual deviant, and the addictive personality are varieties of personality disturbances, and admittedly, extreme examples. (Many personality disorders are less debilitating than neuroses.)

The sociopath participates in antisocial behavior without the controlling factors of anxiety or remorse. People who brutally torture or kill other people as calmly as if they were swatting a fly may well be classified as sociopaths.

Sexual deviants are far less dangerous to the public than sociopaths, except where they involve another, possibly unwilling partner. The majority of their acts involve either animals (beastiality) or dead people (necrophilia) or transvestism. The transvestite usually cross-dresses, frequently in private, and attains sexual gratification through masturbation.

Psychoses

PSYCHOSIS: A serious mental disorder in which the individual loses contact with reality and thus becomes unable to manage the problems encountered in daily life.

People suffering from psychoses are those who are "most severely disturbed." They are frequently hospitalized, because they suffer from severe disorganization and have major emotional and thinking difficulties. The major psychoses are schizophrenia, manic-depression, and paranoia.

Schizophrenia is a catchall term for a mental disturbance for which no other label exists. Some schizophrenics, severely withdrawn and unable to relate to people, exhibit disorganized thinking. Still others are able to function in society with marked inefficiencies in limited areas. Simple schizophrenics are people who never quite operate near their native capability. Others giggle like children; still others stand like statues, unable to move, needing someone else to reposition their arms and legs. One variety of schizophrenia is childhood schizophrenia, which tends to become more apparent in late adolescence.

Any possibility of curing the schizophrenic lessens with prolonged institutionalization. Treatment of schizophrenia depends on the interpretation of the cause of the onset. Since schizophrenia appears to run in families, there has been research suggesting

a genetic predisposition for the malady. It is not that schizophrenia is definitely inherited but that the subject's environment may well be the factor governing whether or not the individual will develop schizophrenia. Some people inherit a higher risk factor which, when exposed to a maladaptive environment, will tend to increase their chances of developing schizophrenia.

Treatment of schizophrenia depends to a large degree upon the theoretical interpretation of the cause of the affliction. In recent years, attempts to control the symptoms have been effective. "Effective" does not mean that a cure is produced, only that the symptoms are controlled.

MANIC-DEPRESSIVE REAC-TION: A psychotic reaction characterized by swings in emotion from one extreme to the other, either very depressed or very excited.

Severe changes in mood and outlook characterize manic-depressives. One moment they may be extremely happy, the next moment they seem to bear the weight of the world on their shoulders. They are beset by anxiety and severe depression.

PARANOID: Having delusions of gradeur and/or persecution.

Paranoid people typically feel that the world is filled with people who have no purpose other than to spy on or find fault with them. Paranoids may spend most of the time looking over their shoulders. While the psychotic syndrome paranoia is quite rare, the paranoid personality is common.

There is a famous story about a European peace conference of the last century that illustrates paranoid personality. After all the ambassadors of the major European powers had gathered one night, the Russian ambassador suddenly died. The first comment made by the ambassador of another nation was, "I wonder what he meant by that?" This brief question gives the reader an insight into a personality that sees threatening significance in every occurrence.

PERCEPTION: The process of becoming aware of and interpreting objects or events that stimulate the sense organs.

Many psychotics hallucinate. Hallucinating can be hearing voices that are not there (a misperception of reality) or having delusions that are a misinterpretation of reality. As the result of hallucinations, people may find themselves in an imagined situation that appears to be reality. Remembering our last daydream, we can try to conceive of believing that what occurred in that dream was real. The inability to separate the dream from reality is an example of a psychotic hallucination. The typically normal person is aware of the difference between imagination and reality. When the distinction blurs and the real and unreal merge into a single sequence, the dreamer is in trouble.

HALLUCINATION: Imaginary or unreal perception, often experienced by psychotic individuals.

TREATMENT OF MENTAL DISORDERS

The treatment of mental disorders has increased greatly in recent years, as shown in Figure 5–1. The surge of such treatment is probably not the result of any great increase in the occurrence of mental health problems. Instead, it may be the result of greater availability of treatment or a heightened awareness of the nature of mental disorders.

The treatments of psychoses and other mental disturbances vary greatly. The detailed description of forms of treatment for

FIGURE 5-1.
Occurrence of
Treatment in
Mental Health
Facilities,
1975–81.

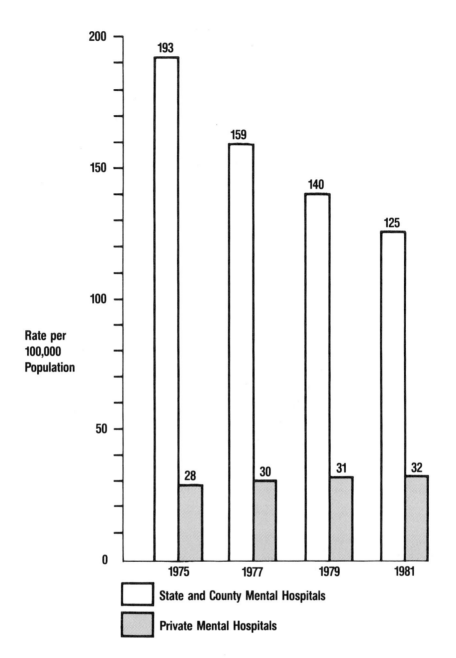

SOURCE: U.S. Bureau of the Census, *Statistical Abstract of the United States: 1986* (Washington, D.C.: Government Printing Office, 1986), p. 113, no. 106

Rate for each year includes total number of people treated in inpatient and outpatient facilities. Excludes private psychiatric office practice, all types of psychiatric service in hospitals or outpatient clinics of federal agencies other than Veterans Administration. Also excludes outpatient cases of VA hospitals and all partial treatment cases.

mental disorders is far too complex for discussion at this time. A brief illustration of some major forms of treatment follows, but by necessity the listing is sketchy and the descriptions are generalized.

SKILL BOX

Reading Graphs

Social (and natural) science often deals with large bodies of quantitative data (pieces of information that can be measured or counted). Very often, the scientists want to compare various parts of such data. A valuable way of doing this is the graph.

In reading a graph, read the title first, then any notes given just under the title. It is often important to check the source of the data, because that may alert you to how reliable the source is. (None of the examples here has an authentic source.) Make sure you understand what is being counted, and in what units.

Bar graphs are useful for comparing sizes of different things, or of one thing at different times. The bars can be either horizontal or vertical. In the following horizontal bar graph, what is the number of hats produced by Nairhair Hats in 1960?

FIGURE A

Hat production by
Nairhair Hats
(1950–1980).

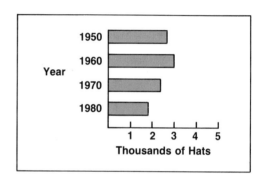

(Answer: 3,000 hats)

Line graphs show changes in amounts over time. The line in such a graph is determined by plots on the horizontal and vertical scales. Each point on the line is thus read in terms of both scales. In the following line graph, what is the average number of hours spent watching television on Sundays?

FIGURE B

Average number of
hours spent daily
watching television for
5,000 residents of
Happy Falls, Montana
(1980).

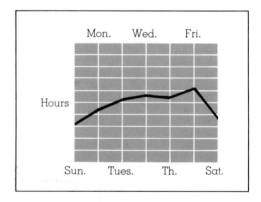

(Answer: 3)

The circle graph shows how something has been divided into several parts, and the proportion of each part. In other words, such a graph shows the percentages of the whole that the parts make up. In the following circle graph, the relative sizes of production of Bigtime's various products are clearly shown.

FIGURE C
Products of Bigtime
Corporation (1980).

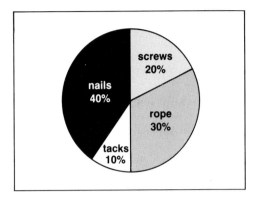

Sometimes picture graphs are used because they are easy to read. However, such graphs cannot present data precisely; amounts can be shown only in rough terms. As seen in the graph below, it is difficult to show the amounts except in whole units.

FIGURE D
Apples used by Mother
Humble's Pies
(1960–80).

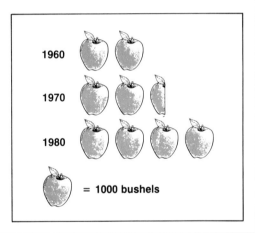

PSYCHOTHERAPY: Systematic attempts to have people understand their problems and adjust their behavior accordingly.

1. *Psychotherapy.* Psychotherapy includes a number of different techniques. These are psychoanalysis, group therapy, family therapy, transactional analysis, and rational emotive therapy. This list shares one feature: The treatment is not physical in nature, but consists primarily of verbal exchanges.
2. *Behavior therapy.* Behavior therapy aims to modify actual behavior patterns. This form of therapy employs the principle of learning, like reinforcement of some behavior aspects and efforts to eradicate other aspects.
3. *Child psychiatry.* The field of child psychiatry is explained by its title. It consists of applying the basic psychiatric methods to younger, more formative patients.

CHEMOTHERAPY: The treatment
of mental disorders by use of drugs
and chemicals.

4. *Chemotherapy.* This therapeutic method uses various drugs and chemicals in order to treat the symptoms of mental disturbance.

5. *Electroconvulsive shock therapy.* This form of treatment, discussed earlier in this chapter, consists of applying severe electric shock. It is a questionable technique used less often today than in prior years and sometimes administered to depressed patients. No one knows why this technique works at some times and not at others. We do know that shock treatment has some side effects, such as some loss of memory and learning ability. In less ethical institutions, this form of treatment, because of the severe pain involved, has been used to discipline recalcitrant inmates. Some 83 percent of New York psychiatric hospitals and units employ shock therapy.[13]

6. *Hypnotherapy.* Hypnotherapy makes use of hypnosis to treat some mental disorders. Subconscious suggestions and regression are major points of concern with this technique.

7. *Psychosurgery.* Psychosurgery, when first explored, was thought to be the answer to many problems of severe mental disorder. During the 1930s and 1940s an operation called the prefrontal lobotomy was performed on many unfortunate patients. The purpose of the operation was to separate the frontal lobe from the remainder of the brain. Sometimes the depressive symptoms were reduced, but patients often lost a considerable portion of their memory and basic personality. While the operation was performed to reduce either depression or aggression, the result was frequently a higher degree of aggressive behavior. Such surgery has occasionally produced a person with a "blah" personality. "Blah" is, of course, neither a medical nor a psychological term, but it is certainly descriptive. Because control and alteration of personality are frightening prospects, the technique is also morally suspect.

SUMMARY

Theories of psychological adjustment disagree on many issues, including the relative importance of genes versus environment. Freudian psychology views the personality as having three basic parts. The id is the source of our basic, instinctual urges. The super-ego is the conscience. The ego is the rational part of the personality which helps to fulfill the id's desires within an acceptable cultural framework. Sometimes the ego develops defense mechanisms when the id's impulses threaten to get out of control. These mechanisms include regression, projection, and displacement.

In behaviorism, the focus is not on unconscious forces but on observable behavior. This approach is based on the belief that every behavior is a response to some stimulus. Therapy involves manipulating stimuli causing the problem behavior. This contrasts with the Gestalt approach, which focuses on the broader personality picture and the social context within which one behavior takes place.

The social perception approach deals mostly with how our social world affects the way we see things and thus the way we believe.

Humanist psychology focuses on the way the person feels and how he or she experiences the world.

The boundary line between what is normal and abnormal is not clearly identified. Indeed, there is no consensus about how to define normal behavior. It depends on the culture's values and the social context of the behavior. Likewise, abnormal behavior is defined in several ways. Throughout history, many people unlucky enough to be classed as abnormal have often suffered cruel treatment. Today treatment is less cruel, but cures are still all too elusive.

There is a wide range of mental disorder types. They include mental retardation and the several types of brain disorders. Also included are psychosomatic disorders, which are physical ailments with mental causes. Mild mental disorders are sometimes called neuroses. They can include phobias, obsessive-compulsive reaction, and dissociative reactions. More serious are personality disorders. The most serious disorders are psychoses, including schizophrenia, manic-depressive reaction, and paranoia.

The treatment of the wide range of disorders is also broad. Treatments range from drugs and surgery to verbal exchanges.

SPECIAL TOPIC

Something Is Wrong

Something is wrong, things are not falling into place. When I was younger, the sisters at school thought that I was the nicest, smartest, and most motivated student they had seen in years. They would always tell my mother what a grand child I was. In high school I always made the honor roll, and like as not I would get straight A's.

Something started to go wrong in high school. I was a successful student, but I had little social life. My family and friends stopped saying how cute or good-looking I was. In college and then graduate school, I did well and I did have a girlfriend for several years, but she went home to New York with her master's degree.

I have a graduate degree but no job. I have held several jobs, one in the library and others for only a few weeks. The people could not see that they were doing things incorrectly, and eventually I was fired for attempting to put things right.

The character described above is a somewhat abbreviated version of Ignatius J. Rielly, the hero of John K. Toole's *Confederacy of Dunces.*[14] While a good bit of Ignatius's character is exaggerated, enough was there to let me recognize the person on whom the caricature was based. The difference between my old friend and Ignatius was that my friend could cope with life. He made adjustments to allow himself to compromise with his problems and, as such, they were simple neuroses.

He could or would not cross high bridges, so he would either require the driver to stay on the inside lane while he shut his eyes or planned trips taking ferries. Ferries are harder to find these days, so he probably does not travel as much. He would not fly in airplanes, but there were always buses and trains.

Ignatius J. Rielly had a worse set of problems; he almost could not cope. He was on the edge of psychosis. Each week saw him spending longer and longer periods of time buried in his room. The room itself became messier and messier because he would not allow his mother to clean. He became more protective of his life's work, his journal, which was strewn about the floor in the small lined notebook of the type used by grade-school children.

As the years passed, Ignatius became less charitable in his opinions of the outside world. He saw most people as barbaric, uncivilized, and generally without taste. He had less and less patience with the shortcomings of others. His worst trait may have been his total indifference to the things that were of importance to others. If an event, duty, or norm had no importance for Ignatius, it could be ignored or violated with impunity. A prime example of this pattern of behavior occurred when Ignatius was finally forced by his mother to find a job. He was hired as a bookkeeper in a failing pants factory. The factory manager did not really expect Ignatius to do anything constructive, but he did not expect him to be destructive either.

Ignatius found that the job was too demanding, in addition to the inconvenience it caused him. He could not stand the idea of piles of unfilled orders and correspondence. In his detached way, Ignatius solved the problem of overwork and piles of material to be filed. He simply put it all in wastebaskets. With the offending correspondence out of the way, he felt much better and less imposed upon. He had eased his own problem, but he gave no thought to the calamity he had created for the pants company.

In time, letters began arriving demanding to know the status of orders. The office manager could not find any reference to these orders. Ignatius was outraged that his peace and quiet should be disturbed by department stores in places like Little Rock, Arkansas. He took pen in hand and composed nasty responses to these inquiries. If this was not bad enough, he signed the letters with the name of the factory owner. When the inevitable lawsuit was brought against the factory for slander, libel, and other assorted legalities, Ignatius did not admit his guilt but rather accused an ancient secretary. It did not occur to Ignatius that he was hurting someone, the factory owner, who had never done him harm. It did not occur to Ignatius that the secretary could be hurt by his actions. Even if it did occur to him that these people could be hurt, he did not care. The important thing for Ignatius was that *he* was not inconvenienced or hurt.

Several other examples of this nature can be found in this discussion of the personality structure of Ignatius J. Rielly. The most striking and telling of these occurred when Ignatius was being arrested. His physical characteristics would make him a prime candidate for suspicion of any number of activities. During the disturbance, an old man came to his aid and questioned the arresting officer. Their discussions grew heated, and the police officer arrested the old man. Ignatius quietly moved off center stage, saw his mother, and walked away with her. She asked him about the disturbance, and he said it was nothing but an old man. Never once did he admit that the old man had gotten in trouble to save Ignatius. That was not important. In his mind Ignatius was the only one who should be saved.

The story ends on an upbeat note, but with a sinister prediction of the future.

His old girlfriend is somehow convinced to drive from New York to New Orleans to save Ignatius. She arrives just in time to help load Ignatius and his manuscript and dirty clothing into her car. They start north to New York City and pass the ambulance coming to take Ignatius to the mental hospital. After all this time, Ignatius's mother has been persuaded by her friends to have her son put away. Our story ends with Ignatius sitting in the back seat of his girlfriend's car, heading north to new adventures.

This could be the end of the story, but you are probably asking, "Why is he in the back seat?" The reason is that the front seat is dangerous and Ignatius will not take the chance of being hurt in an accident. His girlfriend must sit in the front seat and face that danger. Ignatius is still free and will be able to walk the thin line between the real world and the unreal world. As long as there are people to help pull his major chestnuts out of the fire, he will remain in society. If he somehow violates a major norm or becomes too noticeable, he may be classed as disturbed and committed to an institution.

There are quite a few Ignatius J. Riellys on our streets, some worse off than others. In fact, there is, as you know, a school of thought that has each of us closer or further from what could be called normal. Have you given any thought to your position relative to *normal?*

SELF-TEST QUESTIONS

1. True or false: Psychologists agree that genes are more important than environment in determining a person's ability to adjust.

Match numbers 2–4 to the descriptions on the right:

2. id   a. conscience
3. ego   b. referee for the other two; rational
4. superego   c. combination
               d. pleasure-seeker; irrational

5. When the id's impulses threaten to get out of control, the ego may develop _____.

6. Escaping from a threatening situation by retreating to earlier forms of behavior is called:
   a. projection
   b. displacement
   c. regression
   d. phobia

7. Behaviorism focuses on:
   1. self-concept
   b. unconscious forces
   c. observable behavior
   d. assumed behavior

8. Which focuses on the "whole" of the personality?
   a. Freudianism
   b. behaviorism
   c. phenomenology
   d. Gestalt psychology

9. Humanist psychology focuses on:
   a. self-concept
   b. behavior
   c. ego
   d. social perceptions

10. True or false: Science has drawn a clear boundary line between normal and abnormal personality.

11. The most severe form of mental imbalance is:
    a. psychosis
    b. personality disorder
    c. neurosis
    d. phobia

12. True or false: The treatment of mental problems is limited to chemicals.

ANSWERS TO SELF-TEST QUESTIONS

1. false; there is no agreement	7. c
2. d	8. d
3. b	9. a
4. a	10. false
5. defense mechanisms	11. a
6. c	12. false

ANSWERS TO SKILL REINFORCERS

5–1. The most frequently occurring number in a set is the mode. Therefore, the behavior that occurs most frequently could be called the mode, or the normal.

5–2. Remember that to estimate a cause-effect relationship, control of all variables is required. This means that in an experiment to test whether a certain factor causes mental imbalance, we would need to control the lives of two similar groups of people. Both groups would be limited to the same set of experiences, diet, and so on (except for the one factor being tested, to which only one group would be exposed). Such control over peoples' lives is bad enough, but there are also the ethical questions of exposing humans to a factor that might cause them to lose their normal behavior patterns. These two concerns make it difficult to prove that a certain factor causes mental imbalance.

NOTES

1. B.F. Skinner, *Beyond Freedom and Dignity* (New York: Alfred Knopf, 1971).
2. A.H. Maslow, "A Philosophy of Psychology: The Need for a Mature Science of Human Nature," *Main Currents in Modern Thought* 13 (1957): 27–32.
3. J.F.T. Begental, *Challenges of Humanistic Psychology* (New York: McGraw-Hill, 1967).
4. J.D. Page, *Psychopathology* (Chicago: Aldine-Atherton, 1971).
5. T.S. Szasz, *The Myth of Mental Illness* (New York: Harper & Row, 1961).
6. Irving I. Gottesman and James Shield, "Schizophrenia in Twins: Sixteen Years' Consecutive Admissions to a Psychiatric Clinic," *British Journal of Psychiatry* 112 (1966): 809–19.
7. P.H. Wender, "The Role of Genetics in the Etiology of the Schizophrenics," *American Journal of Orthopsychiatry* 39 (1967): 3.
8. R.G. Hoskins, *The Biology of Schizophrenia* (New York: W.W. Norton, 1946).
9. R.G. Heath, et al., "Behavioral Changes in Nonpsychotic Volunteers Following the Admissions of Tarafein, the Substance Obtained from the Serum of Schizophrenic Patients," *American Journal of Psychiatry* 114 (1958): 917.
10. Szasz, *Myth of Mental Illness.*
11. T.R. Sarbin, "The Scientific Status of the Mental Illness Metaphor," in *Changing Perspectives in Mental Illness,* ed. S.C. Plog and R.B. Edgarton (New York: Holt, Rinehart & Winston, 1969).
12. American Psychiatric Association, *The Diagnostic and Statistical Manual of Mental Disorders* (Washington, D.C., 1968).
13. G.M. Asnis, M. Fink, and J. Saferstein, "ECT in Metropolitan New York Hospitals: A Survey of Practice, 1975–1976," *American Journal of Psychiatry* 135 (1978): 479–82.
14. John Kennedy Toole, *A Confederacy of Dunces* (New York: Grove Press, 1981).

SUGGESTED READINGS

Cousins, Norman. *Anatomy of an Illness as Perceived by the Patient.* New York: W.W. Norton, 1979.

Emde, R.N., and Brown, C. "Adaptation to the Birth of a Down's Syndrome Infant." *American Academy of Child Psychiatry* 17 (1978): 299–323.

Skinner, B.F. *Beyond Freedom and Dignity.* New York: Alfred Knopf, 1971.

Toole, John Kennedy, *A Confederacy of Dunces.* New York: Grove Press, 1981.

6 SOCIAL INTERACTION: IN GROUPS AND IN COLLECTIVE BEHAVIOR

No Pain, No Gain

Escaping pain, failure, unpleasant smells, and even the pain and fear of death—these are signs and goals of human progress! Not so, says H. Wayne Hogan in a recent essay.[1] In fact, he says, our efforts to escape the negative aspects of human existence are denying us our humanness and thus threatening our social system. We must take the good with the bad. Or, as a football coach might put it—no pain, no gain.

Hogan's thesis is much deeper than the coach's statement. Hogan sees in many aspects of modern life an escape from a personal burden that holds the social system together: social responsibility. Though we all have a responsibility to help deal with social problems and to face our own personal problems, we try our best to do neither, he says. This threatens our social world.

On the personal level, says Hogan, we are detaching ourselves from the pains and duties that are part of the human condition. We try to duck responsibility; an example of this is "no-fault" divorce. Also, we avoid facing the naturally negative aspects of death. In fact, Hogan describes several parts of the trend toward passive (he says, less rewarding) acceptance of death. Rather than experience dying to the fullest, we try to make it easy and less human. Even our use of drugs, mouthwashes, and hairsprays shows how we are trying to delete from our lives parts of its humanness. We are unwilling to face life at its fullest, even with regard to unpleasant moods, smells, and sights.

On a social level, Hogan points to several policies that have the effect of leading us further away from our humanness. By offering solutions to social problems, some policies make it too easy for us to wipe our own hands of responsibility for our fellows. Instead of fulfilling our human duty to help deal with the poor, with criminals, and with helpless people, we let the experts take care of such unpleasant matters. If the experts cannot solve the problems, they often focus instead on protecting themselves. After all, no one wants to feel guilty or inadequate. In turn, we see their failure and shrug and say, "It's *their* [the experts'] responsibility."

Hogan says that by refusing to take the bad in life with the good, we lose touch with our humanness and thus lose touch with our basic values and duties to other people. And by avoiding responsibility while seeking only comfort, we become less able to live together in a healthy, functioning social system. The system depends on the humanness of its members. As those members avoid their humanness, the system is threatened.

While reading this chapter on how we interact with other humans, think about Hogan's point. Do we have a natural sense of social responsibility that makes human social systems work? Are we losing that part of our nature?

When we deal with other people, we are engaged in social interaction. Such interaction is full of hidden forces and patterns which social scientists try to reveal to us. For example, sociologists reveal to us that conversation contains power plays, unseen attempts to dominate the other person: "control over everyday procedures in talk becomes a mechanism of interactional domination. . . ."[2] One such procedure, or power play, is to demand literal accounts of facts, without adding any context to the answer. For example, the parent asks the child, "Did you finish that chore yet or not?" The child is not allowed to add any reasons or explanations—no context, simply yes or no. In this interaction we see the parent's domination. Conversations usually involve individuals with different abilities to use such power plays, and the interaction thus is revealed by social science as a micro-power struggle. Our interaction with other people is full of such unseen processes, some of which are revealed in this chapter.

Before we get to the micro- or small-scale picture of everyday interaction, we need a bit of orientation. The broader context in which a street corner conversation takes place is the society. A society is a large, enduring grouping of people. These people share a territory as well as a culture. Such a grouping is not considered a society until it lasts more than about three generations.

SOCIETY: A large, enduring grouping of individuals who share a territory and a culture.

Note that the term "society" is often confused with "culture." While the culture is a way of life, the society is the people who share the culture. The society is the people themselves; the culture is the way they live.

What happens as the members of a society deal with one another? Their interaction often follows basic patterns or processes, which will be explored here. Much of this interaction occurs within various kinds of groups, which this chapter will describe. Sometimes the interaction breaks through the confines of the usual rules and patterns, and people engage in collective behavior, another topic covered in this chapter. Finally, an increasingly important setting for social behaviors, the bureaucracy, will be explored in this chapter's Special Topic.

PROCESSES OF SOCIAL INTERACTION

As we react to the presence of the other members of society, we are influenced by them. In turn, the actions of those others are influenced by their awareness and perceptions of us. This mutual influence is called social interaction. While most of us interact with others many times each day, there are some basic patterns to this interaction. Here we will look at four of these patterns, called social processes.

Exchange

"You scratch my back and I'll scratch yours." "I'll never speak to her again, after she ignored me like that." Exchange, is repayment for some action, be it pleasant or vicious. This "give and get" is part of most human interaction. We exchange ideas, goods, favors, and injuries. Exchange is the most basic social process. Indeed, as the chapter preview mentioned, the exchange of responsibilities holds a social system together. When too many people begin to avoid their social duties, to get from but not give to the system, the system is threatened.

EXCHANGE: The social process in which the actions of people or groups are based on the expectation that those actions will be repaid appropriately.

Exchange occurs at the group level and at the personal level, when both parties derive value from the interaction. One group helps another obtain political power in the hope that its own ends will be furthered. Or two groups may exchange attacks or insults. Personal relationships are based on an exchange of affection, loyalty, and other rewards. When we send a gift to someone, we expect to be repaid either with a gift or with gratitude. In fact, the gift itself may be payment for some previous favor received from the other person.

Exchange is basic not only to our social system but also to all others. All cultures depend on this process to give some order to human interaction. It is found in all times, in all places, and at all levels of human interaction.

The result of this exchange process is better social functioning. Exchange of goods and favors helps cement alliances and boost economies. It also works in more subtle ways. Because we know we are likely to "get," we will "give." Thus, most people are willing to fulfill their social duties. They feel safe in giving their goods and energies because they know they will be repaid. We work for our boss, our community, and our family because we expect benefits from our giving. So long as we are paid for our efforts, we will do our part and thus keep the system working.

Cooperation

Showing up for softball practice or bringing a covered dish for the big dinner—in both cases we do our part along with other people

Cooperation is people working together to achieve some common goal.

so that we all share some reward. This is cooperation, another basic process in human interaction. Cooperation is defined as people or groups working together to achieve some common goal.

Cooperation is often essential, because we depend on one another in so many ways. Because we have become so specialized, we often lack all the talents needed for a certain task. We must then combine our efforts with those of others whose talents we need.

Cooperation is encouraged in varying degrees in different cultures. In some cultures, children learn that this process is the preferred approach in achieving goals. This is true in some primitive groups as well as in the Soviet Union and China. Children in such cultures who compete with others for approval or other rewards will be criticized for not being "team players." They may be urged to work hard, but it is for the benefit of the group, not just themselves.

COOPERATION: Individuals or groups combining their efforts to achieve a common goal.

Competition

COMPETITION: A struggle in which individuals or groups try to obtain the same goal, which is limited in quantity.

You put in extra hours so that you will be the one to win that big promotion up for grabs. You study hard so that you will earn one of the few A's to be given out in your class. You are involved in both cases in competition, which contrasts with cooperation.

People or groups compete when they strive separately for the same rewards, rather than working together for them. Competition occurs when the rewards are limited, so that only some of the people competing can win. This serves to discourage the people from pooling their efforts, because not all will win the rewards. There may be only one office, one person's favor, or one contract to win. It then makes little sense to cooperate with someone when he or she, rather than yourself, may end up with the prize.

Competition is often impersonal. Two teams can compete with each other, but the members can direct their efforts at the other team instead of its players. The focus is on the struggle, not the other players.

In addition, competition is carried out within a framework of rules. The teams' efforts are limited by an accepted system of guidelines. Because of this, it is possible to compete in a safe and friendly manner.

Conflict

CONFLICT: Individuals or groups trying to defeat one another while pursuing the same goals; this interaction is carried out without a framework of rules.

Another social process, conflict, also involves struggle. Conflict may or may not be limited by a system of rules. It differs from competition by its intent. Conflict aims to destroy or deprive the opponents. The focus is defeating the other "players," not just winning a struggle.

Robin Williams describes three sources of conflict.[3] First, people may lay claims to the same scarce resource. These claims may cause only competition, but they may grow into conflict. Second, people may hold beliefs or values that clash violently with those of others. Such clashes can result from commitments to very different people or ideals. When one group can no longer tolerate others' loyalties, conflict can arise. Third, conflict may be based on anger felt toward something we believe has caused us problems, such as a part of a social system (the schools) or some group (police). These three sources account for much of the world's conflict.

Conflict can have its positive side. When two groups are in conflict, the members of each group feel more unity, because people draw together against a threat from outside. Conflict can also direct attention to problems that have been ignored. It can force us to face injustice and to resolve issues.

On the other hand, conflict wastes and destroys. It can leave resentment and death in its wake. It can involve cruelty, suffering, and wasted resources. Because of potential conflict, we spend billions of dollars to support our military forces. If the conflict never came, these dollars would have been wasted. Though this spending may prevent conflict, it represents wealth diverted from other needs. If the conflict did come, it would cause even more wealth to be destroyed.

These four social processes may work together. For instance, an exchange of aid is one way to cooperate: "You help me with math, I'll help you with science, and we'll both earn grades so as to stay on the football team." Or people may cooperate in order to compete better or fight with others: "Let us work together so we can win the war." These processes may be interwoven, but their threads are still distinct. They comprise the fabric of much human interaction.

GROUPS: SCENES FOR STRUCTURED INTERACTION

When we exchange favors or threats, when we cooperate or compete, and when we engage in conflict, we most often do so within some kind of social structure. Often this structure is a group. For scientists, the term "group" has a special meaning, which other people commonly ignore. Indeed, the term is often used by lay people, or nonscientists, to refer to any gathering of people. Scientists must be more precise. Here we will explore what scientists generally mean by "group." Also, various kinds of groups will be described, as will the inner workings of the group.

Defining Groups

GROUP: Two or more people who ordinarily interact more than once, share something significant, identify with one another, and whose interaction is structured.

A group might be defined as a gathering of two or more people, but this description includes many social units that are not groups. To be considered a group, those gathered people must meet several criteria: (1) They ordinarily must interact more than just once. Under special circumstances, such as an airplane hijacking, group formation can occur in one intense "meeting." Typically, however, a group exists beyond one meeting, though the meetings may or may not be numerous or scheduled. (2) A group also has some structure, which can include rules, patterns, or expectations of behaviors. (3) The members of a group have a "we-feeling": they are aware of their membership and they know who belongs and who does not. The group members feel bound together as insiders. (4) Group members share something in common.

They may hold the same goals, beliefs, territory—anything that in their eyes sets them apart from others.

An example of a nongroup can help us grasp what social scientists mean by "group." Ten people, gathered on a sidewalk to watch a building being torn down, do not constitute a group. They will never meet again as a unit. The gathering has little structure and few rules or patterns beyond basic, unwritten norms about how we are to behave among strangers. Nothing special is expected or required of the people. There are no leaders, no special rules. Nor is there a shared identity. The people are not conscious of any social boundary around them; they do not feel set apart from others. They are not a "we," but merely a collection of "Is." They do share something—an interest in the building's destruction—but this is probably not enough to give them a feeling of shared identity with one another.

A typical classroom is an example of a group. These people meet more than once; in fact, they meet on schedule, at least through the school term. The classroom is a very structured setting. The students know the pattern of events, the rules they must follow and the duties they are to fulfill. The students often form a we-feeling with the others in a classroom of normal size. They know who belongs and who does not. If a nonmember comes in and takes a seat—a seat that probably "belongs" to a member—the members may well see him or her as an intruder. Finally, the members of the class share interests and goals—the subject matter and academic credit—that set them apart from other social gatherings.

If we wish to use the term "group" in such a proper manner, what do we call those gatherings and groupings that are not groups? Sociologists give us only a little clear direction here. People who are merely in the same place together can be called a collectivity, a cluster, or an aggregate. Such gatherings are crowds if, like our example of ten people, their members share one focus of their attention. We are given another label for those people who share some trait or traits but who never interact: social categories. Men, women, students, football fans, blondes, infants, and short people are examples of categories.

Such nongroups may begin to act like groups if some special event draws them together. For instance, if the people in a stalled elevator share fear or anger, they can begin to identify with one another and organize themselves. Left handed or very tall people may sense common needs and form a club. From the one shared trait, such people can build a group.

All this defining may not seem worth the effort. The reader may see little importance in clearly defining groups and nongroups, but we must thoroughly describe something we want to study. And we want to study groups because they are not only pleasant for us but essential.

Groups are important, even vital, parts of our lives. From the moment of birth—and even before—we depend on groups to protect, nurture, and satisfy us. The family group is the most important; this and other groups shape us into humans. They shape our views of ourselves and determine the extent to which we will blossom. They are the structures within which most significant human interactions occur. Their nature can even affect that interaction. Because of the importance of groups, social scientists have spent much time not only defining them but studying their structures and dynamics.

Types of Groups

When we are with our study group, the things we do, say, and expect will not be the same as when we are with our family group. The ability to recognize the various types of groups will help us adjust our actions to different group situations. From their research, social scientists have described several types of groups. They commonly use three broad categories to classify group structures: primary-secondary groups, out-in groups, and reference groups.

From Intimate to Impersonal.

Primary groups. A classic view of groups is that of Charles H. Cooley, who coined the term "primary group."[4] Under his scheme, groups are ranked by the degree of intimacy involved. While all groups have some degree of intimacy, primary groups have a high degree of intimacy. Primary groups are comprised of primary relationships. These relationships are based on three factors: special responses, special communication, and built-in satisfaction.

PRIMARY GROUP: A small, cooperative, intimate group based on primary relationships.

First, our response to the other person in a primary relationship is a unique one. It is based on a thorough knowledge of his or her personhood. When we respond to the person, we consider the many aspects of his or her self. We tailor our response to this detailed, unique profile of the person. This means that the response cannot be transferred to other people, because no one else has the same self.

PRIMARY RELATIONSHIPS: Unique interactions based on deep, extensive communication and giving personal satisfaction.

The group involves shared goals and recurrent interaction within a structured setting.

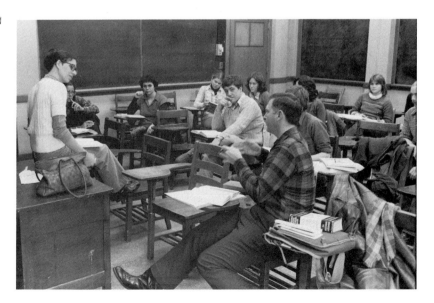

Disciplined Observation

One of the main techniques used to study groups is disciplined observation of the group in its natural setting. As we shall see here, this requires that we discipline our looking so that we see effectively. This is helpful not only to scientists but also to us.

We must take care in accepting the results of casual observation. What we "see" may not be what is in fact there. Our eyes may play tricks on us, as in optical illusions or magicians' tricks. Or our mind may alter input from our eyes, so that we believe we see what does not exist. Our mind may fill in the gaps of what our eyes see, so as to complete our mental picture of what we view.

Further, when more than one person sees the same event, they are likely to report seeing different things. This is because what is observed depends on each person's state of mind at the time, that person's interests and knowledge, and other factors. An attentive, calm sailor observes something in the night sky and labels it a comet. A frightened, tired tourist can observe the same thing and "see" something quite different.

Also, if we observe too casually, we may miss a common, constant part of our surroundings. We may notice a noise only when it stops, and we might not observe the salt in our diet until it is removed.

For these reasons, it is valuable for all of us to try to sharpen our observing skills. This can help us in our daily lives. For instance, let us say you want to discover why your child always gets in fights at the playground. The child says she doesn't know why. Disciplined observation can help us gather data to help solve the problem.

In trying to observe in a disciplined way, the first thing to remember is that the presence of an observer can affect what happens in the scene. If you, the parent, go to the playground to observe, the children may not act the same as they would in your absence. This can be overcome by letting them get used to your presence over a few weeks or, better in this case, by observing them without them seeing you. These are the same things the scientist would do in the field.

There is another problem in trying to observe in a disciplined way. As a parent, you would not be able to observe objectively. Your attachment to your child would bias your mind, distort what you observe. It may not be clear to you that your child is a bully. An objective observer, not affected by such emotions, would be more likely to see that. Scientists try to be objective.

Of course, the cause of the problem may become clear with one visit to the playground if you observe all relevant factors. For example, the age or size of the other children may explain the friction between them and your child. But if this is not the case, you must observe more closely, as would the scientist.

To do this, you must decide what it is you want to observe. You need a focus. You cannot observe everything, so you use a theory or, more likely in this case, a guess to direct you. You may guess that perhaps the cause of the fighting is social-class differences. Your observation will thus be focused on such clues.

> You must beware of following your guess or focus too intently. Disciplined observing means considering other answers. In casual observing, we may well see only what we expect or want to see. We may thus miss other facts or connections among facts. Disciplined observing requires that we focus on one line of thought while being alert for other promising lines. This skill does not come without practice and, indeed, discipline.

This response is also accepting. We know much about the other person, and we accept what we know. This acceptance permits a free and spontaneous interaction. There is little need to cover up or be on guard. We can relax and freely let our selves show.

Second, a primary relationship requires special communication. There are few limits put on topics or methods. We can use touch, signals, and informal language. We reveal some of the deep layers of our selves. Such communication is thus both broad and deep, as in a "heart-to-heart talk."

This communication is often face-to-face. It is difficult to maintain such a relationship over the phone or through the mail. But face-to-face communication does not in itself make a relationship primary. We have many contacts every day that are impersonal, even though they are face-to-face. An example is the talk we have with the police officer who has stopped our speeding car.

The third special quality of primary relationships is that we maintain them because they in themselves give us satisfaction. We need no ulterior or hidden motives. We accept people because of what they are, not for what they can do for us.

To the extent that a group's relationships are primary, it can be classed as a primary group. Such groups take on certain traits. They are usually small; it is easy to see how hard it would be to maintain such intimate relationships with a large number of people. Also, primary groups have a strong influence on their members, shaping their goals and their selves. They help us learn who we are and what we should become. The groups create basic rules for the members to follow. Furthermore, the tone of such groups is one of cooperation. The members, to the extent that the group is primary, pull together and share a very strong we-feeling.

Some social scientists see primary groups as a useful tool for fighting social problems. Since these groups have such a strong influence on their members' values, it is thought that the values of delinquents and other "problem" people can be changed by such groups. Primary groups can be used as therapy when used to transmit acceptable social norms to their members. And in the end primary groups may be our last hope in preventing the social breakdown feared in the essay described in the chapter preview. That is, the members of these groups feel responsible for each other; therein lies the core of our social system.

Intimate communication and acceptance are features of the primary relationship.

SECONDARY GROUP: One based
on utility and impersonal relations.

Secondary groups. On the other end of the spectrum built from Cooley's writings is the secondary group. Secondary groups are based on impersonal relationships and task performance. The members are interested in the usefulness of each member more than the self of each member. Communication is limited in breadth of topics and methods used. These kinds of responses can be transferred.

This is not to say that secondary groups are bad or to be avoided. There are times and places in which they are more useful than primary groups. When the performance of a task is of utmost importance, primary relations may impede the group. The members' intimate needs and feelings must not be allowed to disrupt the required discipline. Police officers could not enforce the law if they built primary relations with their suspects. The teacher would find it hard to give an "F" to a student who had become a close friend.

On the other hand, we cannot ignore the value of primary groups. In such groups, we can relax and enjoy being accepted for ourselves. We can confide in the other members. The intimacy of the primary group seems to fulfill a basic human need. Such rewards are among those things, for example, that make a marriage a good one.

Perhaps it is because we derive so much pleasure from primary groups that they often grow within secondary groups. In impersonal settings such as the work place and the classroom, primary groups can often arise. Once they have formed, they can influence their members to undermine or support the aims of the secondary group.

A Matter of Belonging. Another way to classify groups uses in-groups and out-groups. These two types are classified on the basis of a person's feelings: Do I feel a part of or apart from the group? This feeling is what defines a group as "in" or "out."

IN-GROUP: A group defined by a
person as a "we," to which the
person feels he or she belongs.

In-groups. If we consider ourselves members of a group, it is an in-group for us. This feeling of belonging is based on a sharing of traits with the other members. The members share such things as interests, backgrounds, and outlooks. With these people, we feel at ease and accepted. In some cases, we know just by glancing at a person if he or she is "one of us." The age, dress, race, or grooming of the person might suggest whether we share much in common with that person.

In-group loyalty varies with each group and with each situation; that is, the feeling of we-ness is a matter of degree. This loyalty is much stronger for our family group than it is for our in-group of fellow Americans. This feeling also varies with time and place. Two students in the class of a horrible teacher may feel this we-ness, though this lasts only as long as they share that teacher. But these in-group feelings can shift. At a football game, those same two students may cheer along with that teacher against the rival school's team.

Out-groups. Those groups we reject or feel rejected by we can call out-groups. We feel we do not belong with those people; we ignore them or are ignored by them. These feelings are based largely on a lack of shared beliefs and background. Furthermore, such differences serve to prevent any such sharing from occurring. Thus if we don't know "them," they may remain an out-group, perhaps to our loss, unless something throws us together. Even worse, the force causing us to feel a bond with our in-group members also causes us to feel alien or even hostile to those in our out-groups. This hostility is the greatest problem with out-groups. Indeed, it may be that today we too easily classify other people as being in out-groups, and thus deny any responsibility for them, as the chapter preview says.

Reference Groups: Yardsticks for Ourselves. "I'm a success. After all, I've been invited to join the Blue Nose Club." We use reference groups to evaluate our degree of social success and self-worth. These groups serve as standards to which we refer ourselves, much like we use a yardstick to measure the length of something. We base our self-judgments on the degree to which we share the values and traits of these groups. We try to reduce the gap between what we are and what we think the members of the reference group are like. In this way, reference groups can affect our actions, our goals, and our views of ourselves. For example, medical students may model their manners, dress, and hobbies after doctors they know.

Most of our primary groups serve as reference groups for us, but this is not always the case. One such exception, for example, would be the rising business executive who loves his or her family but rejects their world as inferior. In fact, secondary groups often serve as reference groups. The executives at our work place may serve as models for us even though we are not on intimate terms with them.

We may not be a member of some of our reference groups. Indeed, some reference groups are not groups at all. We may use "the jet set" as a reference group, though it may be only an image or a category to which we refer when judging our life-style. In any case, we need not belong to a reference group, even if it really exists. It can be a group to which we aspire or which we hope to join. We can still use it as a model, a standard.

"If one of *them* does that, I *never* will." Reference groups can also tell us what we want to avoid. Using them as negative models, they still give us direction and self-judgment. A negative reference group is one whose actions and traits we try to avoid.

Some reference groups are forced upon us. The classic case is the second-oldest child whose older brother or sister is an excellent student. This child may be forced by parents and teachers to judge herself against excellent students rather than merely good students. She may always be unhappy about her own school performance, even if it is good—just not excellent. Or she may re

---

Skill Reinforcer 6-1*

What conclusion could be logically deduced from these two premises?

1. Reference groups are groups used by people to evaluate themselves.

2. Joe uses the male models in the *Keen* magazine advertisements to evaluate himself.

3. So . . .

---

*Answers to the Skill Reinforcers appear at the end of the chapter.

ject that reference group completely, take the pressure off herself, and let her grades slide.

Whether or not we freely choose our reference groups, we use them to help determine how fulfilled we are. Because of this, we might stop to identify our reference groups. We may decide to reject some of them or add others, and be happier for it.

Group Dynamics

"It is not wise for two roommates to add another person to their group." "We are more likely to join a group with people we live close to." From experiments and observations, scientists have learned not only about the types of groups but also about the inner workings of groups—group dynamics. They have discovered processes and principles that affect what goes on inside a group, and we will explore some of them here.

Size Affects Dynamics.   As a group changes size, its inner workings change. Simmel noted that the most important difference in size is that between the two-person group (dyad) and the three-person group (triad).[5] Adding one member to a dyad has a profound influence on the interaction. While the dyad can be an intimate setting, "three's a crowd." In a triad, it is likely that two members will form an alliance, leaving the third party feeling alone within the group. Because of this, having two roommates is much different from having only one. Among four roommates, two pairs are likely to form.

The addition of new members to any group increases the number of relationships greatly. The number of pair relationships increases from one in a dyad to three in a triad. In a group of five members there are ten possible pairs. In one of seven people there are twenty-one. The interaction within a group can thus grow much more complex when just a few members are added.

The quality of interaction is affected by the group's size. The members of a dyad can feel very close to each other. Research shows that members are likely to feel the we-ness more strongly in small groups than in large ones. In a smaller group, more interaction with each member is possible. Also, in a small group the members depend on one another more. This is seen most clearly in the dyad, where one person can destroy the group by leaving it. The larger the group, the less important each member is. Thus, while there is strength in numbers, there is reduced intimacy, too. Perhaps this is why we tend to limit our casual work and play groups to two or three members.[6]

How Groups Form.   One reason people form a group is that they share something in common. A common purpose is one strong basis for group formation. People will link themselves with others in pursuit of the same goal, be it passing an exam, making a profit, or sharing affection. Sharing the same background also helps form ties among people. For example, people are more likely to form a group if they are all of the same race or social class. Com-

Skill Reinforcer 6-2
How could a cause-effect relationship be established between the addition of one member to a dyad and the interaction within the resulting triad?

mon needs and problems can also help join people together. When people become parents, they are likely to establish social ties with other parents.

Besides being alike, people who are physically close to each other are also more likely to form a group. Research has shown that we are more likely to form friendships or groups with people whose front doors are even a few feet closer to us than the doors of other people.[7] Likewise, we are more likely to enter into a group with people whose apartment building is only one building, rather than two, away from us. While we all could have guessed that closeness, or proximity, can be a factor in group formation, such research has shown us just how important it is.

It is not hard to understand how proximity works to encourage group formation. Living or working near someone makes contact with that person more probable and frequent. This makes it more likely that we will discover common interests. Nearness presents opportunities for forming social bonds.

Sticking Together: Cohesion.　　Once a group is formed, it can develop a high degree of cohesion. Members of a very cohesive group will often speak of "we" rather than "I." They will interact often and enjoy it. They will defend the group and work for it. They will choose many of their friends from among the group's members.

You may someday want to produce a high degree of cohesion in a group. There are several tactics you could use. You could try to require that members make a strong commitment to the group. Toward this end, some religious sects and cults require their members to give up all their worldly goods. You could also enhance the group's cohesion by accepting new members only in small numbers, because the more stable the group's membership, the more cohesive it is. Also, you might prevent the group from getting too large. This helps promote interaction, and thus cohesion, within the group. If possible, you might even want to confine the group members to a somewhat limited space. By enforcing a degree of proximity, cohesion could be enhanced.

A consequence of cohesion is that it affects the degree of conformity found within a group. The more cohesive a group, the more likely its members are to conform to the group's norms. One reason is that the frequent contact within such groups makes their members' opinions more alike, and this produces more conformity. Also, members of a cohesive group value their membership highly. They derive important rewards from the group and thus are willing to conform so as to preserve their place in the group.

All Members Are Not Equal.　　A great deal of research has focused on the important question of how power within a group is acquired and used. This research has discovered what leaders are like and what functions they serve. Some of this research is presented here (with the cautionary note that such laboratory re-

One way in which leaders are different is the higher prestige they enjoy.

search may not always give us an accurate picture of real-life leadership dynamics).[8]

Leaders are different. They tend to have higher status than the other members. We are likely to choose as our leader the person who has some mark of prestige—a title, a degree, or another symbol of competence. We seem to assume that a person successful in some sphere will be better qualified to guide our group, no matter what the group's task. Furthermore, leaders tend to be larger and better looking than the other group members. They tend to be smarter too.

Leaders are different from their followers, but effective leadership is not simply based on the force of the leader's personality. Effective leadership is based on several principles, such as candor, trust, respect, conflict resolution, consensus, and mutual support.[9] Many effective leaders share such features which suggests that leadership abilities can be acquired.

Another skill or ability of an effective leader is to control the members' interpretations of a situation. Such a leader can get the members to accept the leader's interpretation of reality, and to use that interpretation as the basis for their actions.[10]

Leaders serve two needs of the group: direction and harmony. First, the group must be helped to achieve its goals; it needs a boss. But the group also needs a peacemaker. A group without harmony and affection among its members will offer fewer rewards to those members. It is difficult for one person to serve both these needs of a group. Few people can wield power and still be popular.

The sexes are not equal in human social interaction. This is proven in many research studies. For example, many studies have shown that men typically dominate women in conversations, and that women generally assume a supportive role when speaking with men. Further, men typically talk more than the women to whom they are speaking, and men interrupt women more than women do men.[11] These status and power differences between men and women are often expressed through nonverbal cues, such as touching, as well as interrupting.[12] And when working with men in task groups, women generally have less prestige and influence than they objectively deserve.[13] When women and men perform similar jobs, they are usually assigned different job titles, and the jobs are typically performed in different parts of the organizational setting.[14] Furthermore, men have more numerous contacts and more contacts with both sexes within voluntary organizations than do women.[15] Even though such gender inequalities can be reduced, according to one study, "it is still 'better' to be a man than a woman," in mixed-sex groups.[16]

COLLECTIVE BEHAVIOR: INTERACTION BEYOND GROUPS

All our social interaction does not occur within groups. Our social behavior extends beyond the talk at the dinner table to include conversations with strangers on the bus and screaming with other fans at the football game. Much of this social interaction outside the structure of a group can be labeled "collective behavior." In

COLLECTIVE BEHAVIOR: Spontaneous, unpredictable, transitory, relatively unstructured actions of a set of people.

contrast to a group's actions, collective behavior can be placed on the other end of the spectrum of social interaction. By contrasting collective behavior with the behavior of groups, we can explore the several traits of this special kind of behavior.

Traits of Collective Behavior

We have seen that a group's actions are influenced by principles and patterns, or structure. This lends an air of order and control to the group's behavior. There is no such structure to restrain collective behavior. Such behavior usually follows no routines or rules. Unlike group behavior, it is given no direction; it has few limits.

This lack of restraint can produce extremes of behavior. Because they feel released from the controls of group ties and the official controls of the law, people engaged in collective behavior base their actions on feelings of the moment. They make up most of their rules as they go along. This may result in either heroic acts or horrible acts. These acts can range from risking one's life helping others to destroying property or life. The people may commit acts they would not commit normally. Herein lies the great danger of collective behavior: it can result not only in great deeds but also terrible ones.

This lack of structure also helps make collective behavior unpredictable. Therefore, it can begin and end before the authorities can gain control of it, or before scientists can study it. It is often a spontaneous occurrence. Rather than being planned, it bursts into existence on its own. And once it begins, it is hard to predict what direction collective behavior will take or how long it will last. This is in sharp contrast to the routine nature of most groups, where meetings are often scheduled and the course of events is often the same each time.

Collective behavior is also transient. It does not last very long, but rather comes in a burst. It is often a brief flash of action, which also makes it hard to control or study. In contrast, a group can be somewhat enduring, lasting for years, as in a family.

All this can be put together to contrast collective behavior with group actions. We have already seen that the students in a classroom are a group. The group has structure; its members share a purpose and get together more than once. Those same people can leave the classroom and gather on the campus to listen to a protest speech. They now form a crowd, which can erupt into collective behavior. This behavior will not last throughout a school term, as will that of the classroom group. And unlike a group, it will have little or no structure, so its course will not be easily predicted.

Types of Collective Behavior

Riots, mobs, and panics are all forms of collective behavior. Even the following of fads and fashions can be seen as collective behavior. (Fads and fashions are treated in Chapter 9 as guidelines to behavior.) The audience at a concert is a collective behavior, as is the women's movement. The changes in public opinion are also studied under this title, as are revolutions. Some forms of collective behavior deal with trivial subjects, such as hair styles; some can result in a change in the power structure of a nation. This diversity of collective behavior makes it hard to study, yet fascinating too.

Some collective behavior involves an assembled set of people—a crowd. We will start with this type. Other forms of collective behavior need no such gathering. The rumor is one example of this form; it will be examined later in this chapter.

Collective Behavior Within Crowds.   Much of collective behavior is crowd behavior. A crowd is defined as a large number of people gathered and sharing a common focus. A crowd, like all collective behavior, is temporary.

CROWD: A large, temporary gathering of people who share a common focus for their attention.

There are many types of crowds, but it is useful to distinguish between active crowds and passive crowds.[17] An audience is a passive crowd. The people gather for a specific event. They all respond to the same stimulus, but they need not respond to one another. The audience is usually orderly, but it can turn into an unruly, active crowd. When a crowd is aroused and violent, it can be called a mob or a riot. These clearly are active crowds, in which frightening and destructive forces can be unleashed.

MOB: An emotionally aroused, perhaps violent crowd, the hostility of which is directed at a particular target.

Mob.   A mob is an active crowd that focuses its violence on a specific target. Mobs have their origins in some perceived social wrong. Such a crowd often aims to correct the problem by using violence. The results may range from something like the Boston Tea Party to a lynching.

Some mobs are not violent. In these types, the peoples' emotions are aroused, but the people merely want to release tension or express intense feelings. Pep rallies or victory celebrations are examples of this type, called expressive mobs.[18]

RIOT: A violent crowd with no specific target; its hostility is randomly directed.

Riot.   The riot is an active crowd too. It differs from the mob in that its violence lacks a specific target. It grows from social unrest and explodes into a hostile rampage. Its intention may be the same as a mob, but a riot is not focused on a single group or person. It may be triggered by one event, but its real cause can be traced to some general social problem. A riot can be born of a mob that loses its narrow focus and attacks a broader target, such as the members of a particular race.

PANIC: On a collective level, this involves a hysterical flight from some perceived threat; the behavior of a mob bent on escape.

Panic.   In a panic, the people involved are trying to flee from some real or imagined threat. Panic occurs when a collection of people perceive a threat and become frenzied in their efforts to flee. The problem is worsened when the people feel they must compete for the means of escaping. On the other hand, if there is no hope for escape, panic is unlikely. Also, if there are plenty of ways to escape, a panic is less likely. The danger lies in the struggle that can develop over scarce means of reaching safety. This is seen in the case of too few lifeboats on a sinking ship or too few exits in a burning building. In such cases, some people show a total selfishness and will disregard all ethical standards. This may involve trampling over someone in an effort to reach the crowded exit or snatching a life jacket from someone else.

Collective behavior is unpredictable and can involve extreme actions.

RUMOR: An unconfirmed story, circulated usually by word of mouth and usually in an atmosphere of anxiety or stress.

Collective Behavior Without Crowds: Rumor. Mobs, riots, panic, and the audience are all one kind of collective behavior. They are all based on the existence of a crowd. Besides crowd behavior, collective behavior also includes what may be called mass behavior. Here we will look at one such type: rumor.

A rumor is simply an unconfirmed story, most often passed along by word of mouth. It may or may not be true, and the source is often unknown. A rumor's transmission is often rapid and uncontrolled. All this makes rumor dangerous, especially because it can also cause other types of collective behavior to occur.

Rumors are based on fear. They often arise during times of stress or anxiety. During such times, people often require information about some unsettling topic. They need a tool with which they can try to control or combat an unclear situation. The rumor meets this need, though often with distorted or groundless information. The rumor may be examined or discussed at great length in a search for comfort or hope. If they feel fear and stress, people are more likely to listen to and pass along anything they hear.

Besides fear, other conditions can cause rumors to form. Turner lists two such factors.[19] First, rumor formation is more likely when something occurs that people are not familiar with. The stranger the event, the more help people need to understand it. They may turn to rumor if they lack other bases for understanding the strange happening.

Second, rumor can be born of a wish for entertainment. It lends a bit of excitement to the normal routine of living. A rumor may be used as an excuse to break from the routine. On the other hand, we could expect that people who are engaged in important tasks would be more likely to be "too busy to listen to rumors."

Once a rumor is formed, several factors affect how likely it is that people will accept it.[20] Educated people are less likely to pass a rumor on without first checking its accuracy. Also, we are more likely to accept a rumor if it supports what we already believe or expect. Further, the more useful we see a rumor to be in coping with the situation, the more likely we are to accept it.

Dynamics of Collective Behavior

We have seen that collective behavior, because of its unpredictable and unstructured nature, is hard to study. Still, there are several reasons why its dynamics *should* be studied. In some of its forms, collective behavior can look like a mysterious, fearsome beast. It can be wild and destructive. It is thus within our interests to wonder why and how the beast moves. Beyond this, we are all likely to be involved in some of the milder forms of collective behavior. The crowd, rumor, and the audience are parts of our experience. Social science offers some insight into the forces working on us in such situations. Such knowledge of these dynamics makes it likely that collective behavior in some of its destructive forms can be controlled.

A French scholar writing near the turn of this century, Gustave LeBon seems to have been accurate in his suggestion that the twentieth century would be the century of collective behavior. His predictions aside, however, LeBon deserves attention here because of his explanations of collective behavior. He focused on the psychological impact of crowds upon individual behavior. He noted that crowds create their own "mental unity" that dramatically changes an individual's behavior. Indeed, being a member of the crowd transforms the individual into part of a "collective mind" where normal restraints are temporarily forgotten or ignored. Under this influence people can act like crazed animals, displaying their worst impulses.

While this view of individuals being transformed into a collective monster is not widely accepted today, LeBon did give us some important concepts about crowd behavior that sociologists still find useful in doing their research. These concepts are anonymity, suggestibility, and emotional contagion.

With anonymity the individual feels that he is a part of a mass in which he loses a sense of individual identity. As members of the crowd, people feel free to act out their true feelings, because their inhibitions have been reduced. Participating in the Mardi Gras or attending a wild rock concert, the individual becomes anonymous and is thus freed to engage in extraordinary behavior.

Suggestibility means that people under certain circumstances are more apt to be receptive to information, especially rumors. Suggestibility is heightened in crowds. When this happens, filtering out the truth from the fiction in a rumor, for example, is not so important. Guidelines to acceptable behavior are more easily ignored when we are no longer sure just what we should believe, and realizing the consequences of one's behavior becomes less important, freeing us to follow suggestions we would not normally even consider.

Feelings easily become shared in an emotional contagion situation. These shared emotions take the place of the social structure during collective behavior. Values, goals, norms, and roles are all forgotten as the emotional aspects become paramount. The crowd becomes a psychological unit, rather than merely a socially structured grouping of individuals. During emotional contagion, norms are likely to emerge under the direction of some authoritative leader. These norms may include looting and shooting, which can be perceived as acceptable behavior in such an emotionally charged atmosphere.

These concepts borrowed from LeBon can easily lead to comparisons of humans with a stampeding herd of cattle or a mindless mass of lemmings. Though these concepts are unflattering, they are still useful and interesting to theorists studying collective behavior. From LeBon's concepts, other theories have developed.

Convergence theory explains that crowd behavior is the result of people with similar predispositions gathering and acting together. Unlike the helpless crowd members described by LeBon, convergence theory suggests that only people with certain feelings will respond to the crowd. Only those people already leaning in the same direction will use the chance to act out their impulses in the crowd situation.

Emergent-norm theory holds that individuals in a collective behavior situation may not at first hold the same feelings or ideas about what action should be taken. Instead, the rules of proper conduct, the norms of the collective behavior situation, emerge among those people gathered together. Members of the crowd communicate to one another their feelings about what is happening and what should be done. From this discussion, common norms emerge to guide the whole group.

The urban riots of the 1960s spawned more ideas about the causes of collective behavior. One of the most influential theories arising from this was Neil Smelser's value-added theory.[21] Smelser identified the basic cause of such riots as a conflict between the established structure of society and emerging, challenging contradictions. As old norms come in conflict with new ones, mobs, riots, and terrorism are likely to develop.

Because we are probably faced with more urban riots in our future, Smelser's theory holds a special attraction. His theory offers help in managing or controlling such crowd behavior. Smelser describes the patterns of a riot or mob as it develops, identifying six stages or determinants, all of which must be present before hostilities actually break out:

1. *Structured conduciveness.* This means that some preexisting situation prepares individuals for conflict. Unemployment, injustice, or inadequate housing are all examples that create conflicting interests. For example, the people in a ghetto neighborhood may feel, "We have nothing."
2. *Structural strain.* In this stage, a lack of adequate communication or trust among parts of the community creates a strain. The ghetto residents in this stage have concluded that, "We should have more than we do."
3. *Generalized belief.* The reality of some perceived injustice becomes a source for social action. A general agreement forms as to the specific cause of the problem and the solution. "It's *their* fault, and we need to . . . ."
4. *Precipitating event.* All riots begin with an event that triggers an expression of collective behavior. "That's the last straw! "
5. *Mobilization for action.* Mobilizing a group for action is often encouraged by community leaders for legitimate purposes. Sometimes these are converted from peaceful demonstration to violence. "Let's go! "
6. *Social control.* At any stage, the response of the police or other authorities can determine how fast and how far the collective behavior will develop.

Theories such as Smelser's spring from the sociologists' need to understand why the social structure failed to function more smoothly. Functionalists are especially likely to search for factors related to social functioning. On the other hand, conflict theorists assume that social events can be explained by looking at exploitation and oppression rather than smooth functioning. But even though sociologists approach a phenomenon from different perspectives, they all attempt to offer theories explaining the phenomenon.

SUMMARY

With the processes of exchange, cooperation, conflict, and competition, people construct a social web. These processes are the basic tactics, the raw materials, of social interaction.

Much of our social interaction occurs within structures called groups. Social scientists have identified several types of groups. These range from closely knit, intimate (primary) groups to loose, impersonal (secondary) ones. We can also classify groups according to how strongly we feel that we belong to them (in-groups or out-groups). Those groups to which we belong or want to belong are used as bases for self-judgments; these are reference groups.

When people interact outside the confines of group structure, their behavior is hard to predict. It is called collective behavior, which is unstructured and transient. Most collective behavior involves a gathering of people. If the gathering simply shares a common focus, it is called a crowd. A mob has violent intentions directed at a specific target. The violence of a riot lacks such a target. A panic results when people feel a desperate need to escape some threat. Rumors, or unconfirmed stories, often cause other forms of collective behavior.

Collective behavior shows us how much humans need the stability of group membership. Without such group controls, people become more likely to be caught in collective behavior, wide-eyed and adrift. Whether this is beneficial cannot always be predicted. The unpredictability of collective behavior makes it often dangerous but exciting to study.

SPECIAL TOPIC
Bureaucracies In Our Lives

In a chapter that introduces groups, it is proper to introduce another type of social structure: the formal organization. This structure differs from most groups in that it does not arise by itself. Instead, it is created purposefully, for the achievement of one or more clearly stated goals. While other groups may accomplish things, the formal organization is built with specified ends in mind. These kinds of structures range all the way from prisons to the Boy Scouts. Here we will focus on only one type of formal organization with which we must all deal, the bureaucracy. As we will see, a bureaucracy is a formal organization based on hierarchy, specialized tasks, and explicit rules.

THE NATURE OF THE BEAST
Bureaucracies can be troublesome to deal with, and many of us must deal with them almost every day. It thus makes sense to explore their nature so we can have more understanding, and maybe even success, when dealing with them. We will do this by looking at the traits of bureaucracies.

Weber's Model
Much of today's thinking about bureaucracies is based on the model constructed by Max Weber.[22] Weber used a model to show the traits that all bureaucracies share to some degree. It is a picture of an ideal, a smoothly

functioning machine. No real bureaucracy will display all the traits of the model. This model, like others, serves to tell us what to look for in the real world. It tells us what to expect in a real bureaucracy. By studying this model, therefore, we can better anticipate what we will encounter in our dealings with these social machines. Here we will examine several traits of Weber's model.

Division of Labor. First, there is division of labor. Each worker has a clearly defined part to play in the bureaucracy's total workings. To do his or her job, each person must have specified skills and is given certain rights and powers. In this way each member is expected to perform a specific role for the bureaucracy.

Hierarchy. The bureaucracy is also based on hierarchy, which is a chain of command in which each member has authority over other people at lower levels. In a hierarchy the members are aware of who their boss is and whom they are to boss. This means that everyone knows his or her place in the bureaucratic power structure.

Rules. The bureaucracy is based on rules rather than on feelings or friendships. Rules lend discipline to the structure. They offer clear statements of what kind of treatment one can expect. The rules (as well as every other action of the bureaucracy) are recorded in writing. Though this recording can be cumbersome and annoying, the rules help make the tasks and the members' actions more standardized. This helps prevent biased treatment of some members. All members are to be treated fairly, in accordance with these objective rules.

Public. A bureau or office of a bureaucracy is public not private. The office and its property belong not to the holder of the office but to the bureaucracy, which can distribute those resources as it sees fit—according to the rules, of course. Furthermore, while members are expected to be loyal to the bureaucracy, they must keep private lives separate from bureaucratic life.

Merit. Hiring and promotion practices are based on merit, at least in the model of the ideal bureaucracy. The special skills demanded for each position are specified and required through test scores, degrees, and other means. This helps guarantee that each member is qualified. Further, the requirements for promotion are specified. If people show the specified skills, they can expect to move up the hierarchy.

These essential traits of bureaucracies give those structures their flavor—unpleasant for many. But even these basics do not always completely set the tone of the bureaucracy. Remember, we described the ideal. Within the real bureaucracy, people are not as objective, rational, and controlled as the ideal implies.

Beyond Weber's Model

No formal bureaucratic plan can cover every detail in the day-to-day setting. The members find they must at times make their own informal decisions because the formal rules offer no guidance. Also, when some new or unexpected need arises, people must go beyond the formal plan. Further, the formal plan may not be so rational in all situations. In these cases the members may disregard the rules and use common sense instead.

A good example of the variance of the real bureaucracy from the ideal is the informal network of primary groups that develops among its members. We have seen that the interactions of the members are supposed to be restricted by the rules and the chain of command. Rules also aim to control the flow of information among the people. But an informal network arises outside the formal plan. This is based on personal relations, not rules. Such ties may disregard the goals of the bureaucracy, or they may be used to get around the cumbersome chain of command, the formal network. They can either undermine the bureaucracy's goals or support them. Though they are often unplanned, such networks are hard to prevent.

Working Within the Bureaucracy: What Its Traits Mean for Its Members

In some ways, the description of the bureaucracy's nature can be comforting to a person who belongs to one. After all, the bureaucracy is intended to be a reasonable organization, so it should be easier to work with and work for. Besides this, there are other attractive things about working in a bureaucracy that help offset its negative traits (which will be explored in a later section). While we can expect no special favors from the bureaucracy, we should get fair treatment. While it is cold and impersonal, it is not supposed to intrude into the private lives of its members. While our job in a bureaucracy may be specialized to the point of being boring, we at least know exactly what is expected of us, and the task should be within our range of training. Also, while each person has a boss, that boss's powers are limited by the rules. This means that we are not at the mercy of a bureaucrat's moods or biases. And the rules, not the boss, determine whether we get that promotion. At least, that is how it is supposed to work.

Of course, the bureaucracy can be so rigid that it does not serve our personal needs. Sometimes, unless we tap into an informal network, we may get no satisfaction from working within the bureaucracy. And its "rational" rules may drive us crazy when they defy common sense, as they sometimes do.

The point here is that, despite this, working within the bureaucracy is not always as unpleasant as popular notions suggest. The bureaucracy is probably easier to deal with if one is a member than if one is not, maybe because the machine wants its cogs to fit comfortably so they will work well.

ADVANTAGES OF BUREAUCRACIES

Bureaucracy is almost a dirty word to many people. The word brings forth a picture of waste, inefficiency, and frustrating red tape. Bureaucrats are seen as paper shufflers, not producers. A bureaucracy is seen as a machine that disregards people, a monster, the enemy.

The fact remains that we could not get along without the bureaucracy in our modern world. Imagine the chaos that would result if the Pentagon allowed all its workers to "make up the rules as you go along" or to "play it by ear." There would be little agreement on rules, and mass confusion would reign. If the chain of command was erased, control and coordination would collapse. People might work only on tasks they enjoyed and neglect vital projects. If bosses somehow still retained power, and hired and fired people on the basis of their personal feelings, the competence and morale of the workers might drop.

While we may curse bureaucracies, we do not destroy them. In fact, we value bureaucracies—even need them. Let us look more closely at why we not only tolerate but depend on the bureaucracy.

First, bureaucracies work; they get things done. They can work for us, even on a very large scale, in an orderly, rational way. They can coordinate large numbers of people so as to accomplish very big tasks. Despite their neg-

ative image, bureaucracies work. And if we consider the alternative, the chaos of personal decisions, bureaucracies look very productive.

The other advantage of the bureaucracy is that it is stable. Not only does it serve us, but it can be depended on to continue. Indeed, the bureaucracy could almost be described as immortal. Some part or other may "die," but the whole lives on. The bureaucracy can survive the death of many of its members because its parts are replaceable. The very nature of the structure assumes that the tasks are so standardized and clearly defined that most workers can be easily replaced.

Many bureaucratic tasks require such a narrow range of competence that many people can acquire, or already have, the required skills. This may be the reason the term "bureaucrat" is not often used as a compliment. The more easily replaced people are, the less respect they get. Such is the plight of the lower-level bureaucrat.

The bureaucracy is stable also because it does not allow much change in the way each task is performed. This helps protect the stable performance of the total machine. After all, such changes might threaten the health of the bureaucracy, just as nonprescribed medicine might threaten a person's health. Thus the bureaucracy will remain stable as long as the rules describe exactly how its members are to perform their appointed tasks.

One weakness in this regard is found at the very top of the bureaucracy. The leader, who may be appointed from outside the bureaucracy, has the power to change the goals of the bureaucracy. This may threaten its stability if the changes are drastic. Also, the death of this leader may shake the structure. The leader's personal image can have a strong, motivating effect on the bureaucracy's members; his or her death can bring a time of stress for the structure.

FLAWS OF THE BUREAUCRACY

Though the bureaucracy seems to be immortal, it is far from perfect. You need not be told that it has flaws. Here we will explore why the bureaucracy sometimes fails to serve our needs as well as it should.

Going to Extremes with the Model
The main reason for the horror stories we hear about dealing with bureaucracies is that these

machines sometimes follow their strategy to extremes.

Rigidity. One such mistake bureaucrats often make is following rules blindly and rigidly. While the bureaucracy requires conformity to the rules, there exists in them the danger that the structure will become inflexible and inefficient. When followed too closely, rules can limit the number of ways to do the job. We have all heard of cases in which the bureaucrat is too accustomed to the routine, or too afraid, to consider an alternative method of achieving a goal.

Means Become Ends. At its worst, blind conformity to rules leads to a confusion of means and ends. The routine, which is a means toward the ends, sometimes becomes an end itself. Workers may become so wrapped up in the paper-shuffling ritual that they lose sight of the goal of the ritual. They may continue to shuffle the papers even when it no longer helps—even hinders—accomplish the ends.

Poor Management. It is also no secret that bureaucracies do not always manage their human resources as well as they could. They fail in two ways. First, they do not easily rid themselves of nonproductive workers. Second, they do not always place workers where they can function best.

Keeping Incompetents. The nonproductive worker can hide in the large-scale bureaucracy. The screening devices that are used to ensure that only qualified people are hired do not work perfectly. When an incompetent person is hired, he can often find a quiet corner in the bureaucracy and dig in. If he breaks no rules, and if his fellow workers will cover for him, his incompetence may never be noticed by his bosses.

The Peter Principle. Even competent workers are sometimes misused by the bureaucracy. These workers are usually the ones given promotions. Some workers function as well or better at the higher level as they did at the lower one. They will probably get another promotion. But sooner or later the workers will be promoted over their heads, beyond their competence. There they will stay. It seems that all workers tend to rise within the bureaucracy until each one reaches his or her level of incompetence. This is called "The Peter Principle."[23] It is also a poor use of human talent.

Because of their flaws, bureaucracies sometimes annoy, frustrate, and even abuse us. But these machines have gained a foothold. They have been woven into our social fabric. And we depend on them. So for all their failings, we can only hope that they will improve. They will not disappear.

SELF-TEST QUESTIONS

Match numbers 1–4 to the descriptions on the right:

1. exchange
2. cooperation
3. competition
4. conflict

a. working together toward a common goal
b. aims to defeat others
c. working separately toward some goal not all can share
d. give and get; payment in kind

5. True or false: The patrons in a restaurant typically are a group.

6. Which are true of a group?
   a. transiency
   b. interaction occurs more than just once
   c. "they" feeling
   d. "we" feeling
   e. members share something in common
   f. unstructured
   g. structured

7. Which are true of primary relationships:
   a. they are unique
   b. they are based on exploitation
   c. communication is deep
   d. the other person is accepted.

Match numbers 8–9 to the descriptions on the right:

8. in-groups   a. we judge ourselves by

9. reference groups   b. we are leaders of

                   c. we feel we belong to

10. Collective behavior is:
    a. structured
    b. well-planned
    c. enduring
    d. unpredictable

Match numbers 11–13 to the descriptions on the right:

11. crowd   a. violence focused on a specific target

12. mob   b. violence, but no specific target

13. riot   c. people gathered together and sharing a common focus; no violence

14. A rumor is:
    a. unconfirmed
    b. false
    c. usually passed along by word of mouth
    d. often the cause of other forms of collective behavior

ANSWERS TO SELF-TEST QUESTIONS

1. d	8. c
2. a	9. a
3. c	10. d
4. b	11. c
5. False, though the "regulars" at a restaurant could form a group.	12. a
	13. b
6. b, d, g, e	14. a, c, d
7. a, c, d	

ANSWERS TO SKILL REINFORCERS

6–1. Conclusion: Joe's reference group is the male models in the *Keen* magazine advertisements. The first premise is a general statement, a definition of reference groups in general. The second premise describes a particular case. From the general definition of all reference groups, we move to a particular case, which we relate to the general definition.

6–2. It is easy enough to suspect that one thing causes another, but in social science such relationships are hard to prove. The following description of an ideal experiment shows the difficulties.

The ideal way to establish a cause-effect relationship between these two factors would be an experiment beginning with two large sets of groups. One set of groups would have been randomly assigned to be the experimental set. The other groups would be the control-group set. In this ideal experiment, all the groups would have to agree to have their membership controlled. The control groups would not be allowed to add a member; the other groups would be forced to add a member. These added members could not differ among themselves too much, ideally. After a specified time, during which all the groups would be limited to similar outside stimuli, the interaction of the groups within the two sets would be measured by some acceptable device. The interactional quality of the two sets would then be compared. This would determine if any difference in interaction had been produced by the addition of a member.

The extensive control of the people's lives required in this ideal experiment makes this kind of research very difficult to carry out. Because of this, social scientists must usually rely on research that renders less than conclusive proof of a cause-effect relationship.

NOTES

1. H. Wayne Hogan, "Killing Society with Social Irresponsibility," *Etc.: A Review of General Semantics* 38 (Spring 1981): 12–19.
2. Harvey Molotch and Deirdre Boden, "Talking Social Structure," *American Sociological Review* 50 (June 1985): 273–88.
3. Robin M. Williams, Jr., "Social Order and Social Conflict," *Proceedings of the American Philosophical Society* 114 (June 1970): 217–25.
4. Charles H. Cooley, *Social Organization* (New York: Charles Scribner, 1909).
5. Georg Simmel, *The Sociology of Georg Simmel*, trans. Kurt H. Wolff (New York: The Free Press, 1950).
6. A. Paul Hare, "Group Size," *American Behavioral Scientist* 24 (May/June 1981): 695–708.
7. Leon Festinger, Stanley Schachter, and Kurt Back, *Social Pressures in Informal Groups* (New York: Harper & Row, 1950).
8. Fred Fiedler, "Leadership Effectiveness," *American Behavioral Scientist* 24 (May/June 1981): 619–32.
9. Robert Blake and Jane S. Mouton, "Theory and Research for Developing a Science of Leadership," *The Journal of Applied Behavioral Science* 18 (1982): 275–91.
10. Linda Smircich and Gareth Morgan, "Leadership: The Management of Meaning," *The Journal of Applied Behavioral Science* 18 (1982): 257–73.
11. Peter Kollock, Philip Blumstein, and Pepper Schwartz, "Sex and Power in Interaction," *American Sociological Review* 50 (February 1985): 34–46.
12. Cecelia Ridgeway, Joseph Berger, LeRoy Smith, "Nonverbal Cues and Status," *American Journal of Sociology* 90 (March 1985): 955–78.
13. M.D. Pugh and R. Wahrman, "Neutralizing Sexism in Mixed-Sex Groups," *American Journal of Sociology* 88 (January 1983): 746–62.
14. William Bielby and James Baron, "Men and Women at Work," *American Journal of Sociology* 91 (January 1986): 759–99.
15. J.M. McPherson and Lynn Smith-Lovin, "Sex Segregation in Voluntary Associations," *American Sociological Review* 51 (February 1986): 61–79.
16. D.G. Wagner, R.S. Ford, and T.W. Ford, "Can Gender Inequalities Be Reduced?" *American Sociological Review* 51 (February 1986): 47–61.
17. Roger Brown, *Social Psychology* (New York: The Free Press, 1965).
18. Ibid.
19. R.H. Turner, "Collective Behavior," *Handbook of Modern Sociology*, ed. R.E.L. Faris (Chicago: Rand McNally, 1964): 382–425.
20. Ibid.
21. Neil Smelser, *Theory of Collective Behavior* (New York: The Free Press of Glencoe, 1963).
22. Max Weber, *The Theory of Social and Economic Organization* (Glencoe, Ill.: The Free Press, 1947).
23. Laurence F. Peter and Raymond Hull, *The Peter Principle* (New York: William Morrow & Co., 1969).

SUGGESTED READINGS

Cooley, Charles H. *Social Organization*. New York: Charles Scribner, 1909.

Goffman, Erving. *The Presentation of Self in Everyday Life*. Garden City, N.Y.: Doubleday & Co., 1959.

Hall, Richard H. *Organizations*. 3rd ed. Englewood Cliffs, N.J.: Prentice-Hall, 1982.

Kanter, Rosabeth Moss. *Men and Women of the Corporation*. New York: Basic Books, 1977.

Ridgeway, Cecilia L. *The Dynamics of Small Groups*. New York: St. Martin's Press, 1982.

Smelser, Neil J. *Theory of Collective Behavior*. New York: The Free Press, 1963.

Toffler, Alvin. *The Adaptive Corporation*. New York: McGraw-Hill, 1985.

Whyte, William H. *The Organization Man*. New York: Simon & Schuster, 1956.

7 SOCIAL STRATIFICATION

PREVIEW

Poor Man and Rich Man

We are ranked unequally in our social world, and these rankings have a great effect on how we live. They are based largely—though not solely—on how much money we have. Of course, how we spend the money we have is important too. Still, a person with little wealth probably will have more limited opportunities, less respect, and less influence than the rich person. The contrasts in the following two cases show just how much difference social rankings make.

First, we have a man who does not make much money. He happens to be a garbage collector. This man spends his evenings the same way many other people with similar social rankings do. After work, he goes home, grabs a beer, and sinks into his easy chair to read the paper or watch television. After a modest dinner, it is time for chores. He is proud to be a home owner, but there are always repairs to be done. His days are spent working—messy, grueling work. His leisure time is a blur of television and beer. All he hopes for out of life is "maybe a little vacation every few years, decent food and clothes for the family, and a bit of peace and quiet every so often."

In contrast, the rich man moves in a different world. His worries are few because his resources are so great. His evenings are spent in activities that stimulate his refined tastes. Rather than decent food and clothes, this man expects the finest in all material comforts for himself and his family. What work he chooses to do is satisfying. The reason he faces no chores can be seen from a description of some of the homes of the late nineteenth century: "The mansions of the rich were staffed first of all by an all-important butler or butlers, a valet for the master, and ladies' maids for the mistress and her daughters. Then came ten or twelve footmen, who worked under the butler, a housekeeper, chef, assistant chef, and a profusion of parlor, upstairs, and scullery maids."[1] Though the homes of the rich today may have fewer servants, the masters of those homes are not bothered with chores.

This chapter explores the system within which people are ranked so differently and which affects all our lives so very much.

You probably place yourself somewhere between the rankings of the garbage man and the rich man in the chapter preview. Later in the chapter you will get a better idea of just where you are ranked, but the point here is that you are ranked socially.

Indeed, in every human society that has been studied, people are ranked socially. Even in the hunting and gathering bands, the members are ranked according to age and sex, with older males at the top. In these most equal of all societies, personal traits such as strength and intelligence count too. In more complex cultures, a person's rank is based more on how he or she fits into the economic system; those who are specialists in highly valued jobs are ranked high. This pervasive theme of inequality is seen, for example, in archaelogical evidence of the Mayans. There, an elite had superior burials and residences, and enjoyed greater longevity than the masses.[2] The Mayans are only one of many cases of social rankings in human societies.

This chapter will describe the forms and the results of this social ranking in the United States. From the basic ranking systems, we will move on to the factors that determine rankings in the United States. We will then look at the social classes in America, how they are studied, what they look like, and our chances of moving up—or down—the social-class ladder. The Special Topic will deal with the dream of social equality.

SYSTEMS OF STRATIFICATION

SOCIAL STRATIFICATION: The unequal ranking of members of a society.

Doctors are in a higher social layer than accountants, who are higher than barbers. This ranking shows social stratification, a pattern in which the members of a society are arranged in a hierarchy of unequal layers. The ranking of these layers is based on the distribution of social resources. By its very nature, such a society is an unequal one: every layer is ranked above or below another. This inequality is the basis of human social structure, more so in some societies than in others.

People are given rankings for two reasons. One is people's innate differences in talent and abilities. Potentials for such traits as beauty, strength, and intelligence are to some degree inborn, and social interpretations of our characteristics serve as bases for our rankings of one another. We neither ignore nor fail to judge such innate variations among individuals. The other reason we rank one another unequally is the socially devised system of ranks. Rules and standards are constructed (for reasons explained in the Special Topic for this chapter), and some age groups, religions, races, education levels, and other categories are given higher rankings than others. Each of us starts out, then, with some inborn features which affect our ranking. These features help determine how we will fit into the socially constructed hierarchy.

Each society ranks its individuals unequally, and each generally uses one of two systems of ranking. These two systems of stratification are caste and class.

Closed Systems: Caste

Our culture urges us to work hard and get ahead, to move to a higher social layer. In another culture we would stay in the same layer that our family had always been in. Stratified social systems vary as to how much a person is allowed to move from one social layer to the next. In open systems, described in the next section, a person is somewhat free to rise or fall socially. The degree of this movement depends on how open the system is. In more closed systems, the walls of each social layer, or caste, shut off such movement. Each caste is closed to members of the other castes.

CASTE: A closed system of stratification, based on inherited social positions.

The Nature of Caste.   A caste is an inherited social ranking or category. The caste a person is born into is the same in which his or her great-grandchildren will die. No one is allowed to move from one caste to another. Each person is socially enclosed by his or her caste's walls.

In a caste system there is rigid social inequality. A caste society is divided into strictly defined levels within an elaborate hierarchy. That is, each group is ranked above or below the other. There is little shifting among the levels; their rankings are somewhat permanent, as is membership in that caste.

Members of a caste system must follow certain rules so that the system will be maintained. An essential rule is that members may not marry outside their caste. The Cinderella story—escaping one's lowly station in life through marriage—is not possible. Another rule is that people must live out their lives in their caste regardless of how hard they work or how good they are. No one is allowed to climb up the social ladder in his or her lifetime. Another rule, more difficult than the others to enforce, is that the members of a caste system are to accept their social rankings. When this rule is followed the system can run smoothly.

An Example: The Caste System of India.   Although it has been weakened by social change over the last few decades, the caste system of India is a good example of a closed society. Both British colonial rule and the coming of industrialized culture have served to undermine the caste system. Still, the system survives and, more so in rural villages than cities, governs the lives of millions of people.

In the system, the people are divided into five layers, or castes, though the lowest layer is usually considered as being entirely outside the caste system. Along with these castes, there are hundreds of subcastes. The caste division helps bring some order to the diverse regions of India. Throughout the country, the castes are understood. Within each region or village, people are fitted into a system of subcastes. The ranking of these subcastes varies somewhat from one village or group of villages to another. The overall caste system lends order to this complex, localized subcaste system.

It is one's subcaste, more than one's caste, that shapes a person's life-style. Each subcaste is a separate social world. The

Skill Reinforcer 7-1*

Complete this syllogism:

1. A caste system is a stratification system with no social mobility allowed.

2. This stratification system allows no social mobility.

*Answers to the Skill Reinforcers appear at the end of the chapter.

members of a subcaste often live in the same part of the town, sharing values, diet, dress, and religious rites. In other words, they share a common culture. They also share an occupation, although this is less true today than in the past. Subcaste boundaries also determine whom a person may have sex with, dine with, and even touch. In some provinces, members of different subcastes must maintain minimum physical distances. The movement of food from person to person is also regulated by subcaste rules. One's subcaste determines whom one may marry. Marriage outside one's subcaste is not allowed, though this rule is changing regarding closely or equally ranked subcastes.

This system of separate, unequal social levels has been supported for centuries by Hindu religious beliefs. These beliefs include *karma,* which holds that people are born into certain subcaste levels because they deserve it. According to *karma,* people's stations in this world are based on their spiritual progress in their many past lives. Those who have lived according to *dharma,* the moral code, are rewarded with high social rankings in their next worldly life. Under this belief system, low-caste people have no reason to resent their social ranking, because it is a result of their own actions.

Aside from one's personal spiritual progress, movement from one social level to another is and has been possible in two ways. First, people can try to learn the life-style of a higher caste, go to a new town, and present themselves as higher-caste members. Second, a subcaste can adopt parts of the high-caste life-style. In this way, a subcaste can over a few generations gain a higher ranking.

The Nature of Class: An Open System

"Class" is a vague concept. You may not be sure whether you have *some* class, and social scientists do not agree if you have *a* class. In fact, not all theorists believe social class exists; some say the concept is just something created by sociologists. But many people in our culture use the idea of class, and scientists spend much time studying the concept. So, assuming it does exist, let us explore its meaning.

SOCIAL CLASS: A social layer whose members share similar amounts of power, prestige, and wealth.

Defining Social Class. A social class is a social level within an open system of stratification. The reasons people belong to a certain class are based more on their own actions than on their parents' social level. This is because movement among levels is allowed, to some degree, in social-class systems.

One way to understand class is to contrast it with caste. A class system is open, allowing some degree of movement from one level to the next. The barriers among classes are not nearly as strong or as clear as they are in a caste system. A class system is relatively open, while a caste system is closed, with no—or very little—movement allowed. Furthermore, one's class position is in theory based on one's own actions, but caste is inherited.

Another way to understand class is to explore the ideas of two important class theorists, Karl Marx and Max Weber.

Karl Marx on Class. Karl Marx (1818–1883) offered a view on social classes that still has great influence. He reasoned that society must create a system of production by which it can supply needed goods and services. This economic system determines the rest of the social structure, he said. A class is formed by people who share the same position in this system.

He saw that in most societies, there are two major classes. One class owns and controls the means of production. Because economics determines everything else in society, these people control all other major social institutions. The other major class has only its labor to offer. These people have no control over the means of production and so have no power.

Marx saw these two classes as the two basic opposing forces in societies. The one is called lords, masters, and capitalists. The term "bourgeoisie" is often used now in referring to this class. The other class, called peasants, slaves, or just plain workers, were called the proletariat by Marx. He saw the owners and the workers as always in conflict. One class exploited the other.

Marx believed that this exploitation would create such a huge gap between the two classes that eventually the workers would develop a "class consciousness," that is, the workers would see they all had common interests. They would come to realize that the only way to get a fair share of the power and the wealth they helped produce would be to overthrow the capitalists. In this revolution, the workers would seize control of the means of production and a classless society would be established. Because everyone would share in the means of production, class barriers would vanish.

Many of these ideas are not fully accepted by social scientists today, but Marx's view of conflict between unequally rewarded classes has had great influence in social science and in world events. His views point to the abuses that can occur in an open class system.

BOURGEOISIE: In Marxist theory, the owners of the means of production in capitalist societies.

PROLETARIAT: The Marxist term most commonly applied to the working class in an industrial, capitalist society.

Max Weber on Stratification. Max Weber (1864–1920) offered us a valuable perspective for understanding the factors that determine our place in an open class system. Weber said our class position is based on how much we have of three things: property, prestige, and power. Power can be defined as the ability to get others to do what we want, regardless of their wishes. Prestige is honor and respect given to us by others, based on social positions we hold. Property is income and wealth of any kind. These social desirables by which we rank one another can be called the "three Ps." We will now look at each of these factors.

Property. Weber saw Marx's class as just one factor of stratification. Class in Weber's view is measured by wealth and income—what we will call property. It is a basic factor in a person's life opportunities, determining the goods and services the person can afford. But wealth by itself does not determine social ranking.

Prestige. Weber saw prestige, or honor, as another factor in determining a person's social level. Prestige determines what Weber called one's status group, which may or may not be linked with one's class. Status is a measurement of one's position in a stratified system, distinct from class. While class is concerned with getting money, status is concerned with how one spends it—life-style more than just life chances. Members of the status group own, do, and say the same kinds of things. They like to be around those with similar life-styles. Indeed, the members of a status group feel some unity with one another. Weber did not believe classes are likely to feel such cohesion. He believed that similar incomes would not draw people together but that similar life-styles would.

Power. Weber also saw people ranked according to something besides money and prestige: social power, or influence. He wrote that power was expressed in political parties, blocs, or pressure groups. This kind of power enables a person to direct and control events and people. It is clear that people have unequal power, just as they have unequal wealth and prestige. The question now is, Who in our society has these three Ps, and how did they get them?

STRATIFICATION IN AMERICA

Suppose the daughter of two high school teachers in the United States wants to achieve a social class standing higher than that of her parents. Because our system is a relatively open one, she may indeed achieve a higher—or lower—social position than her parents. According to Weber, where this daughter ends up will be largely determined by how much of the three Ps she obtains. We will start with Weber and explore how these three factors work in America to help determine a person's social class position.

In some cases it is quite clear who has a large share of the three Ps.

How the Three Ps Are Obtained

If you win a million dollars, you can use this to gain prestige and power. Along this line, Weber recognized that the three dimensions of inequality are intertwined with one another. People who share similar amounts of wealth often are ranked similarly as to prestige and power. That is, the rich person usually has honor and influence as well as money.

This insight suggests how the three Ps are obtained in our own system. In America, one's job is the key to the three Ps for most people. And increasingly, education is the key to a job. One's job largely determines both the wealth and the prestige one receives in life. Some jobs, such as that of a judge, also entail power. Also, as Weber pointed out, these three factors are interrelated. The amount of property one owns affects the prestige and power one can command—depending on how the property is used. Power can bring prestige and even wealth. Prestige can be parlayed into power and even wealth. All three Ps can also be obtained to some extent by such personal traits as beauty, intelligence, strength, and ambition.

Property in America

So far we have seen that the daughter who wants to rise above her parents' level should probably focus on her career, because occupation is the key to the three Ps. But if she is intent on climbing

SKILL BOX

Reading Tables

Some bodies of information are expressed in numbers, such as in tables. Tables help to organize large amounts of complex information. They help us find patterns and important variations in the patterns. But tables can also be bewildering, unless we know how to use them. Here is some help.

Read the title of a table carefully. It tells us exactly what to expect in the table. Often included with the title is a headnote, which helps us explain the data. Footnotes do the same. Footnotes and headnotes can help us judge how accurate and useful the information is. So make it a habit to read the title, headnote, and footnotes before you start studying the numbers.

Next, be sure to determine what units of measurement are being used in the table. For example, are millions or thousands of dollars being discussed?

Now check the categories being used. For example, what are the labels on the rows and columns? Now you are ready to begin your search for patterns or variations.

To better interpret the meaning of each number, it helps to get an idea of the scale of the table's numbers. Do this by searching out the highest number and the lowest number. The average may also be given. These numbers give a basis of comparison for the others.

In drawing conclusions from the table, it is wise to judge its worth as a whole. Does it seem to be based on scanty data or a doubtful source? Are the data up-to-date?

the social class ladder, she must remember that her job will be only the means to the end of obtaining more of the three Ps which will translate into a higher class standing. She needs to keep her focus on those three Ps, not just on her career, to ensure her social climb. She will need to explore where the three Ps are to be found in our society. Here we will look at the distribution of those three factors, starting with property.

Distribution by States.   Where is the wealth found in America? Looking at personal incomes by states, we see a wide range.

Table 7–1 shows us the amount of income each person would receive if personal incomes in each state were distributed equally. Remember, this does not mean that each person actually gets this equal share. The table tells us nothing about how equally the income in any state really is distributed. But, all other things being equal, a person has a better chance of a high income in Nevada than in Maine. Although we must remember that all other things are not likely to be equal, the table does give us some idea of how income is distributed in the United States.

Table 7–2 gives us another view of where the property is—or is not—in the United States. With only a few exceptions, we see that Tables 7–1 and 7–2 agree about where the high and low incomes are to be found in this nation.

TABLE 7-1. Average Personal Income, Top Ten and Bottom Ten States, 1984

Ranking	State	Personal Income
1	Alaska	$17,155
2	Connecticut	$16,369
3	New Jersey	$15,282
4	Massachusetts	$14,574
5	California	$14,344
6	New York	$14,121
7	Maryland	$14,111
8	Colorado	$13,742
9	Illinois	$13,728
10	Delaware	$13,545
41	Kentucky	$10,374
42	New Mexico	$10,330
43	Montana	$10,216
44	Idaho	$10,174
45	South Carolina	$10,075
46	Alabama	$ 9,981
47	West Virginia	$ 9,846
48	Arkansas	$ 9,724
49	Utah	$ 9,719
50	Mississippi	$ 8,857

SOURCE: U.S. Bureau of the Census, *Statistical Abstract of the United States: 1986* (Washington, D.C.: Government Printing Office, 1985), p. 440, no. 735.

Wealth is not evenly distributed in the world; the rural South in the U.S. has more than its share of poverty, as do blacks.

Skill Reinforcer 7-2

Concerning high income levels and living in the suburbs, which is more likely to be cause and which effect?

Other data show that not only among the states but also within the states there are patterns of where the wealth is. For example, high-income families often live in the suburbs. Urban families living outside central cities are more likely to be in the higher-income levels. In fact, 7.3% of these suburbanites have incomes below $5,000, compared with 12% of the residents of central cities.[3]

Some People Have It, and Others . . .   The fact that you are attending college probably shows that you have some interest in making more money than you make now. What factors determine the chances of acquiring more wealth? The contributing factors depend on which theory is used, functionalist or conflict. We will use both here.

According to functionalist theory, a person's level of wealth depends on how well one's personal abilities and accomplishments fit society's needs. In this view, one's skills and work habits, plus the structure of the labor market and other economic conditions, largely determine the wealth a person is likely to accumulate. Because our society depends on skilled labor, those who possess the skills are rewarded.

Conflict theorists, however, point out that there are other factors which strongly affect a person's income level, factors which have little to do with how well a person contributes to society's functioning. Why should a person's sex, age, and race automatically affect his or her income level? In the conflict perspective, the dominant, white-male elite arranges obstacles against other kinds of people so as to protect its own economic positions. In this view, income inequalities are not the natural result of fair, open competition. On the contrary, inequality results from a rigged competition in which some people compete under usually insurmountable disadvantages.

The sex factor is a case in point. At every education level, women earn less than men. This inequality based on sex is built

TABLE 7-2.
People Below Poverty Level, by Region, 1984

Poverty criteria computed on a national basis only and not adjusted for regional variations in cost of living. Data from current population survey.

Region	Percent of People Below Poverty Level
Northeast	13.2
Midwest	14.1
South	16.2
West	13.1
Total U.S.	14.4

SOURCE: U.S. Bureau of the Census, *Statistical Abstract of the United States: 1986* (Washington, D.C.: Government Printing Office, 1985), p. 459, no. 768.

into our system, though it has been lessening in the last decade. Functionalists would explain the inequality by pointing out that women, more often than men, drop out of the labor force when they have children. This dropping out makes a high-income career difficult to maintain. Another reason is that women may be more likely than men to be working at less than their full ability. For example, a woman with a college degree is much more likely than a man to take a low-paying job such as typist. This may be because, in the past, fewer women than men felt the pressures that come with being the main breadwinner for the family. This reason is becoming less important as more single women and single mothers have taken on the role of breadwinner.

Conflict theorists counter these arguments by claiming that women are simply the victims of a male-dominated, sexist society. Women are and always have been exploited by men. The economic disadvantages of women are simply the result of their inferior social power.

Race is another factor affecting the individual's income and wealth. Blacks and other minorities are more likely than whites to find that education does not pay off as much as it could. Functionalists would point to the inferior training of blacks, lower educational levels, and perhaps poorer work habits. Conflict theorists would point to unfair hiring practices, unequal educational opportunities, and the general oppression of minorities. From the conflict perspective, then, we see a picture of exploitation of minorities. From the functionalist perspective we see inequality resulting from a meeting of historical patterns with current social structures.

Statistics help tell the story. Persons under the age of sixteen make up about one-fifth of the people below the poverty level, largely because poor families are generally larger. And poor fam-

FIGURE 7.1
Percent Of Persons Below Poverty Level: 1984.

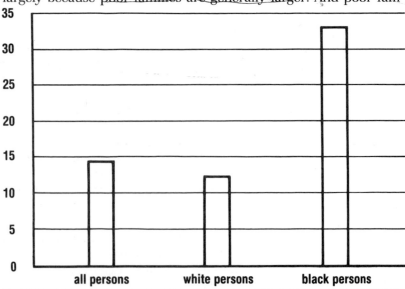

While most poor people in America are white, blacks show a much higher percentage of poverty.

Source: U.S. Bureau of the Census, *Statistical Abstract of the United States: 1986* (Washington, D.C.) 1985.

ilies are often headed by women; indeed, about one-half of all poor persons live in female-headed households.[4] The elderly as a group have climbed out of the poverty picture. More than a third of the elderly were living in poverty in 1959; now their poverty rate is close to that of the general population. Race/ethnicity is another factor regarding poverty. While most poor people in America are white, there is a much higher percentage of minorities in low-income levels. About 11% of whites are poor, compared to about 33% of blacks, and 28% of persons of Spanish origin. And, though urban poverty is more visible, more rural people than urban people are poor.[5]

Christopher Jencks tried to identify the reasons some people are wealthier than others in America.[6] He found that family factors have a significant effect on one's chances of earning a high income. These factors include the years of schooling one's parents had, the job and income level of one's father, one's race, the size of one's family, and one's ethnic background. He also found that high-income people had good test scores and positive personality traits in high school. The number of years spent in school was another influence. But Jencks and his colleagues limited themselves to studying only factors they could measure. That is why Jencks decided that all the above factors account for no more than half the influence on a person's economic success. The rest of the factors include such unmeasurable things as career changes, genes, and luck.

Functionalists might stop at this point, satisfied perhaps that economic inequality was fairly explained. But conflict theorists would point to the exploitation by the elite which prevents the oppressed members of society from sharing meaningfully in the wealth of the society. Perhaps a specific example of such exploitation is the stressful conditions of some blue-collar jobs. A recent study claims that the "noisome work conditions (hazards, noise, heat, humidity, fumes, and cold) that characterize many blue-collar but few white-collar occupations" render blue-collar workers more susceptible to schizophrenia, and thus a worsening of their quality of life.[7] Conflict theorists could point to such dangerous work-related stress as an example of class exploitation.

Prestige in America

Many people talk about wanting more wealth, but what many of us are really after is prestige. Prestige is the ultimate social goal for many people. They see wealth as a means to gain the honor, respect, and admiration given to a person who does, owns, or is something socially valued.

How We Are Ranked on Prestige. Occupation is a major factor in the prestige we can expect in our society. A person's job is an excellent indicator regarding his or her wealth, power, and, as we see here, prestige.

In ranking the occupations in Table 7–3, Americans did not base their opinions only on money. Several of the top-ranked jobs,

TABLE 7-3. Prestige Rankings of Occupations in the United States

Occupation	Prestige Score	Occupation	Prestige Score
Physician	82	Sales manager	50
College professor	78	Electrician	49
Lawyer	76	Aircraft mechanic	48
Dentist	74	Machinist	48
Physicist/astronomer	74	Police officer	48
Bank officer	72	Bookkeeper	48
Architect	71	Insurance agent	47
Aeronautical engineer	71	Musician/composer	46
Psychologist	71	Secretary	46
Airplane pilot	70	Fireman	44
Clergy	69	Adult education teacher	43
Chemist	69	Air traffic controller	43
Electrical engineer	69	Mail carrier	42
Geologist	67	Apprentice electrician	41
Sociologist	66	Buyer/shipper: farm products	41
Secondary school teacher	63	Farmer	41
Mechanical engineer	62	Photographer	41
Registered nurse	62	Tailor	41
Dental hygienist	61	Carpenter	40
Pharmacist	61	Telephone operator	40
Radiologic technician	61	Welder	40
Chiropractor	60	Restaurant manager	38
Elementary school teacher	60	Building superintendent	37
Veterinarian	60	Flight attendant	36
Postmaster	58	Brick/stone mason	36
Union official	58	TV repairperson	35
Accountant	57	Baker	34
Economist	57	Hairdresser	33
Draftsman	56	Bulldozer operator	33
Painter/sculptor	56	Bus driver	32
Actor	55	Truck driver	32
Librarian	55	File clerk	30
Statistician	55	Retail salesperson	23
Industrial engineer	54	Security guard	22
Forester and conservationist	54	Taxi driver	22
Surveyor	53	Bartender	20
Dietician	52	Waiter/waitress	20
Funeral director	52	Clothing presser	18
Social worker	52	Farm laborer	18
Athlete	51	Household servant	18
Computer specialist	51	Garbage collector	17
Editor/reporter	51	Janitor	16
Locomotive engineer	51	Bellhop	14
Radio/TV announcer	51	Shoe shiner	09
Bank teller	50		

SOURCE: Adapted from *General Social Surveys, 1972–1983: Cumulative Codebook* (Chicago: National Opinion Research Center, 1983), pp. 338–349.

such as college teachers, do not command top salaries. The income one earns is only one factor in determining a job's prestige ranking. Another factor is the job's social importance. People in the highly ranked jobs serve important functions. A related factor is the skill or talent believed to be required for the job. That is one reason the garbage collector's job is ranked so low. The job has social importance, but the individual worker can be easily replaced because the skills needed are common. This leads to another factor in determining the prestige of a job: its desirability. Note that most of the low-ranked jobs involve serving the personal needs of other people. But occupation is only one way in which we rank one another on prestige.

There seem to be several other hierarchies by which Americans rank one another.[8] Skin color, religion, gender, age, degree of schooling, marital status, and ancestry are bases for ranking one another. When one considers all the hierarchies we use, it may seem surprising that people are usually ranked at the same level in all the hierarchies. This status consistency is to be expected, however, because the three Ps are so interrelated. Thus people with much money are likely to be ranked high on power and prestige. They are also likely to be white, Anglo-Saxon, married, and male with a college degree.

Inconsistencies in Prestige Rankings. But some people are ranked high in one hierarchy and low in others. For example, the college professor has a high job ranking but is ranked lower according to income. And the professor may be a divorced, black female. This person is caught in status inconsistency. She may claim a high overall ranking based on her occupation, but many people she meets may base their treatment of her on her race, sex, and marital-status rankings. They may not give her the respect she feels she deserves. This complex matter can cause ill feelings. Beyond this, status inconsistency can prompt demands for social change—change in the weightings of the various hierarchies. To complicate the matter even more, there is still one more major hierarchy to examine.

STATUS INCONSISTENCY: The situation in which a person is ranked higher in one hierarchy than in another.

Power in America

Power, another dimension of stratification, is difficult to measure. There are two kinds of power: personal power and social power.

Personal power allows us to pursue our own goals and live the way we choose. For most of us, personal power requires money. Therefore, poor people, the very old, and the very young have little such control over their lives.

Social power involves the capacity to influence the lives of others. Conflict theorists would argue that social power is based on control of the means of production. The people who control resources, factories, banks, and other such capital control everything else. Social power flows from such economic power.

Social power cannot be measured precisely, and there is little agreement on how to measure it. Some social positions, such as that of president, confer social power, so social position can be used in measuring power. But even a president may not exercise much power. He or she may serve as a figurehead while others make the decisions. Even though it is difficult to measure, power should not be ignored when considering how we are ranked.

SOCIAL CLASS IN AMERICA

The chapter preview showed us one man who collects garbage for a living and another who collects money. Their vastly different life-styles and social rankings are based on how much of the three Ps they have. So far we have seen what the three Ps are and how they are distributed in our system. This knowledge is much more valuable when we can apply it in our everyday world. Suppose we meet a person for the first time and need for some reason to size him or her up, to determine his or her social class. How do we go about it?

Indicators of Social Class

The most valuable indicator of a person's social class is occupation. As we saw earlier, a person's job is usually the best clue to his or her three Ps. If we had to guess a stranger's social class and could ask only one question, it would be best to ask, "What do you do for a living?" The answer would give us a good idea about the other social class indicators too.

According to the conflict perspective, the best indicator of social class is the extent to which a person controls capital, or means of production. If one controls no capital, but can only offer her labor, she controls nothing. Indeed, she does not control her own life choices. So from this viewpoint we need not know a person's specific occupation, only her occupational category: worker or owner.

Income is another factor used to determine social-class ranking. Both the size and the source of income are of interest to the social scientist. But income size can mean different things in different parts of the country. An income adequate in a small town may indicate a lower-class status in a large city. Also, the ranking of income sizes changes from year to year. Because of this, source of income, rather than size, is often used to indicate class level. If most of a person's income is from inheritance or dividends, we get a good indication of that person's class level. Income from salary usually ranks higher than income from wages. Income from welfare payments ranks even lower.

Another question that might be asked on an objective questionnaire is, "In what kind of house do you live?" Is it brick or frame? How many rooms? How large is it? Answers to these questions will also help us rank a person as to social class.

The neighborhood in which one lives can indicate social class, because members of the same class often flock together. However, a person living in a high-status area may be a servant, so it would be dangerous to depend on this factor alone. The use of this factor requires thorough knowledge of the neighborhoods in a town.

A useful question in ranking a person concerns education level. Years of schooling can give us an indication of a person's social-class level. To use this factor most fully, however, we would have to evaluate the schools a person attended. A degree from Harvard, for example, should be weighted more heavily than one from a less prestigious school.

While other factors may indicate social-class ranking, those described here are most useful. Used together, they can provide a clear picture of social class level. Used alone, any one of them may give a distorted view of who belongs in which class.

Methods of Identifying Social Classes

How have sociologists managed to identify the social classes so they could be studied? The task was to find out who belonged in which class, and then to study those people to discover the traits of each class. How does one find out who is in which class?

Social scientists have developed three basic ways to discover where the boundary lines between the classes are drawn. The method used for any one study depends in part on the kind of data the researchers need. Also, each method has its strong points and weak points.

Reputational Method.   In the reputational approach, people in a community are asked to rank one another. People who know many of their neighbors well are chosen by the researcher as judges. These judges rank the prestige or reputation of the citizens they know. The researcher asks what bases the judges used in their rankings. By putting together the perspectives of all the judges, a picture of the class system for that community is obtained. A drawback of this method is that it works well only in a town small enough for people to know one another fairly well. Another drawback is the expense of interviewing the judges. In larger cities, other methods would be used.

Subjective Method.   The subjective approach is easy to use in a large city. A questionnaire is given to a large number of people. In it, individuals are asked to rank themselves as to social-class level. As the name of the method implies, the aim is to determine how the people feel about their class status. These feelings may be more important than what other people think about the individual. A problem with this approach is that the responses of a person are limited by the categories of the questionnaire. For instance, if the only choices are upper, middle, and lower class, a great percentage of Americans will label themselves middle class. If working class and various other categories are offered too, respondents are more likely to find one that really reflects their feelings. Also, there is always the danger with this method that people's true feelings are not revealed in the study.

Objective Method.   The third approach relies not on feelings but on observable data. In the objective method, researchers choose

certain factors believed to indicate social-class level. These measurable factors are applied to a sample of the people in a community. The measurements, not the feelings of the people, are used to
depict the class structure.

If all three of these methods were applied to one town, the
resulting pictures of the class boundary lines might differ from
one another. Because of this, social science can offer only a general
picture of the overall class system, with differing views on where
the class lines are drawn within the system.

The Shape of America's Class System

Although some Americans deny that a class system exists in the
United States, many have clear views about who fits in where
socially. The rich man and the garbage collector described in the
chapter preview were clearly in different social rankings. There is
some question, however, of how many rankings or classes there
are and how big each one is. Let us look now at the shape of
America's social-class structure.

Remember that, according to Marx, the class system is simple
to describe: two classes, one exploiting the other. A recent systematic investigation gives us a Marxist picture of the U.S. class system.[9] The classes were defined according to how much control is
exercised over investments, decision-making, other people's work,
and one's own work. The working class was by far the largest class
in this picture. But in between the large-scale employer and the ordinary workers were many workers who are exploited but who
also dominate other workers, and thus could be called exploiters,
too. Included in these in-between occupations is the "new class,"
consisting of salaried professionals and technical managers. There
is disagreement as to whether this new class is competing for
power with the business elite or is simply a part of the dominated
nonowner mass.[10] These many in-between workers make it difficult to see the U.S. system as simply composed of two classes.

Along a "purer" Marxist line, however, we would denote only
two classes, the upper class and the nonupper class.[11] The upper
class consists of 200–300 families who control the corporate economy through stock ownership, the tax code, monopolizing political
offices, and directing many corporations.

There are many ways of drawing the U.S. social class system.
Many sociologists would simply include three: upper, middle, and
lower. Many would draw six classes, after Warner, who used these
categories:[12]

1. The upper-upper class, comprising 2% of the population
2. The lower-upper class—2%
3. The upper-middle—10%
4. The lower-middle—28%
5. The upper-lower—33%
6. The lower-lower—25%

Warner's six-class system was based on a 1941 study but is still
often used by observers of today's class system.

Joseph Kahl takes a different view. His categories are: the upper class (1% of the population), the upper-middle (9%), the lower-middle (40%), the working class (40%), and the lower class (10%).[13] Many sociologists use Kahl's scheme. Notice that the population estimates of both Warner and Kahl produce a diagram with a bulge nearer the middle than the bottom.

Other sociologists draw nine or more classes in their pictures of the class structure. Among other things, the number depends on the community being studied. A diagram of Manhattan, for example, would be complex, with many classes; a small town might well have only three classes. The Manhattan survey would probably be top-heavy, with many highly ranked professional people. The small town might be a pyramid. For our purposes, we will assume a national structure shaped like a bottom-heavy diamond.

The boundaries among these classes should not be drawn too sharply. Not everyone in the same class will share the same amounts of the three Ps. Many people will be at the border between two classes; on a national scale, this will involve millions of people.

We might better draw the class structure as clusters of people. Many people would be near the center of each cluster because they have similar amounts of the three Ps. The density of a cluster decreases as we look outward from the center, until we near the point at which we run into people belonging to the next higher or lower cluster. It is in this in-between space that the boundaries lie.

In fact, some theorists see people ranked on a continuous spectrum rather than in discrete classes. The differences among the classes in this view are seen not as clear or dramatic but as more matters of degree than kind. The life-styles at various levels of the spectrum are seen to share many aspects. Drawing the boundaries in such a system would be quite difficult.

It is easy to understand why social scientists do not agree on the boundary lines within the U.S. class system. Not only must they work with indirect methods, but the U.S. social system is a varied and complex one. Still, the studies that are well founded can be used to learn about the varying life-styles of people in our society.

Social Class Traits in the United States

It is important to have a clear picture of what is meant by such terms as "middle class." These terms are used frequently by the media and the people around us. The attempt here will be to make generalizations on the life-styles of America's social classes. Remember, as these descriptions apply to millions of people, there are many exceptions. In addition, though these described traits are based on studies of real cities, every city's class structure is different in its own way. Still, we can offer here a sensitizing, if not definitive, description of each social class. We will start at the highest class and work our way down the hierarchy, using Warner's widely accepted six-class system.

The Upper-Uppers and Lower-Uppers. Here is a more complete picture of the life-style of the chapter opener's rich man.

For the upperclasses, education is a matter of polish rather than job training.

The upper classes hold positions, not jobs. Many have reached the point where they can enjoy their life-style without working for it. Their interests are typically in business and finance.

Though they need not worry about jobs, the upper classes still view education as important. Schooling for these people is usually a matter of polish, not job training. A degree from the "right" college is necessary to fit in socially. People from upper-class families are more likely to major in the fine arts than in accounting. And they will attend elite, private schools where they will meet the "right" kind of people.

The upper-class family is more stable than families in any of the other classes. These people marry later, have fewer children, and have a lower divorce rate. In fact, divorce rates are tied directly to class: rates are lowest in the highest classes.

Upper-class people are most likely to attend a Presbyterian, Episcopal, Unitarian, or Congregational church. The religious service is not likely to be emotional in tone. It is more likely to involve a lecture on social ethics than a sermon on the devil and the flames of hell.

Upper-class people are likely to hold conservative economic views but liberal social views. That is, they may resist political change, especially when it involves a redistribution of wealth. They are, however, likely to accept social change, such as in civil rights.

We can easily combine the lower-uppers with the upper-uppers in this section because there is only one major difference between the two. The difference is important enough, however, to make the two classes socially separate. The difference is based on money—not how much one has, but how long one's family has had it. One needs enough wealth to be able to afford the schools, neighborhoods, and resorts of the upper-class life-style. To qualify for the upper-upper class, however, the money must be old. If a family has been rich for only one or two generations, this will probably put them in the lower-upper class. This is true even if the family is more wealthy than some in the upper-upper class. In the United States, many a wealthy family traces its money back to a rough, ruthless businessman, not royalty. Time is needed to soften the image of a family's source of wealth. In time, one's ancestors may even be glorified. Indeed, lineage is something money cannot buy. To be able to boast of a noteworthy ancestor sets one apart from a person who is merely wealthy.

The Upper-Middle Class. The upper-middle class is comprised of people who are successful but still must work for a living, mostly in business and the professions. The nature of upper-middle-class occupations often demands that these people be rational decisionmakers. They are leaders, movers. If society is seen as a ship at sea, these people are at the wheel, giving orders to the crew—the classes below them. (The ship's owners, sipping brandy at home, are the upper classes.) The career of the upper-middle class is typically the central aspect of their life-style. It is vital to their standard of living.

Because they depend on their careers to maintain their life-style, the upper-middle class regards a good education as vital. It is made clear to the children in such families that college comes after high school, and graduate training may well follow that. Such parents usually know the best colleges and courses of study, and they can afford these paths for their children. Thus the typical upper-middle-class child is given every chance to succeed.

Some members of this class have conflicting urges regarding money. On the one hand, there is the desire to display the symbols of success. Having the latest fashions in clothes, fine cars, and homes is a way to demonstrate success to the world. On the other hand, there is the need to save for the future, lest some disaster strike. College for the children and retirement require restraint in spending. This class can afford luxury, but only so much. Thus, more than the higher class, the upper-middle class is often torn between spending and saving. The upper class, of course, can usually do both. Those below the upper-middle class find that there is so little surplus income that such decisions are easier to make.

The Lower-Middle Class.   The desire to save for the future is a main link between the upper-middle class and the lower-middle class. The lower-middle person does not have the upper-middle's option to display success symbols. Any surplus income is likely to be saved. The future is a typically middle-class concern, and for the middle-class family their children are the future.

The families of both the middle classes are child-centered. Many things they do are "for the children." This concern might mean buying a home in a neighborhood that is "good for the children." It might mean saving toward college "for the children."

The middle-class family is influenced by another trait held in common by the upper-middle and lower-middle classes: a concern for respectability. This is reflected throughout their life-styles. Indeed, the middle classes are sometimes criticized as being too concerned about their reputations. But this concern helps the middle class succeed.

It is hard to generalize about the jobs held by lower-middle-class people. The class includes millions of people, but it is fairly accurate to classify them as mostly white collar. "White collar" refers to work that involves the head more than the hands. This class includes not doctors and lawyers but teachers and technicians. Some researchers also include in this class highly skilled blue-collar workers; they may work with their hands, but the hands are well trained.

All these lower-middle-class jobs require a decent education. Usually some schooling beyond high school is needed, either trade school or some college. Parents of this class are likely to be disappointed if a child decides to drop out of school before this level is reached, because that might mean the child will drop into the lower class. The concern with education reflects the middle-class concern both for the future and for respectability.

The Upper-Lower Class.   Like other classes, many upper-lower-class people resent those socially above themselves. At the same time, they may be quite critical of classes with lower rankings. Members of one class may criticize those in a lower class in order to assert their higher status. The television character Archie Bunker is typical of this. Like many other working-class people, he wants to make a clear distinction between himself and "those welfare bums."

The jobs of the upper-lower class—often called the working class—require little training. Typical of these is factory work. Only a few days or weeks of training are needed for such workers, often called "semi-skilled." Some unskilled and some skilled workers are also found in this class.

The family life of the upper-lower class is less stable than that in the higher classes. They marry at an earlier age, thus lowering chances for more schooling. They have more children and fewer resources, and thus more strains in the home. Friction and divorce are likely to result.

The Lower-Lower Class.   The lower-lower-class family is much less stable than the upper-lower-class family. Divorce and illegitimacy are most common in this class. The parent typically has little warmth to give to the children. Though this is an adult-centered class, husband and wife are not often close to each other. Still, family and kin are the focus of lower-lower-class life. The outside world is viewed as hostile and brutal.

One refuge from this world is religion. It is easy to see how a person who views life as oppressive would seek escape through spiritual means; if this life has turned out poorly, perhaps the afterlife will be better. The church may be the only place such a person finds happiness. Church services are likely to be emotionally relieving. Religion can serve as an escape from the present and a guarantee for the future. But this is not the most common lower-class view of religion. Few members of this class attend church often.

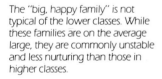

The "big, happy family" is not typical of the lower classes. While these families are on the average large, they are commonly unstable and less nurturing than those in higher classes.

The typical lower-lower-class person also has few job skills and often no job. Such people are likely to be the last hired and the first fired, which results in chronic financial distress. Debt is a constant feature in such a life-style. No wonder such people are apathetic. They seldom show much motivation. The future is not viewed with much hope, perhaps rightly so.

Time orientations can be contrasted usefully among the three main classes. The lowest class lives mostly for the present. Life has taught them that the future offers little hope for a better life. The middle-class person sees the future as full of promise and is likely to work toward that promise. Upper-class people value the past. Lineage—their family's past—is vital to them. This ancestry, along with their money, gives them their special status.

We must remember that all these comparisons and descriptions of the social classes are only generalizations. Each has many exceptions. Still, this picture of the classes can help us understand our own life-styles and those of the people around us.

Mobility Within America's Class System

SOCIAL MOBILITY: Movement from one social position to another.

At this point, we have seen that we live in a stratified system that is relatively open, that the system allows some movement from one class to another. This movement is called social mobility. Some class systems are more open—that is, allow more mobility—than others. Western industrial nations share similar mobility patterns, and all of them generally allow more mobility than agrarian nations.[14] Here we will explore mobility forms and factors in the U.S., as well as the consequences of that mobility. All this can help us evaluate our ambitions and plot our social strategies.

Types of Mobility.   To plot a strategy for mobility, one should know what forms this movement can take.

Horizontal.   One kind of social mobility is horizontal. This is movement from one position to another, but without a change in rank. For example, a college student might change from botany as a major to chemistry. Or, a man might transfer from one company to another while retaining the same job title. In both cases, there is a change in position but not in rank.

HORIZONTAL MOBILITY: Movement from one social position to another without a change in rank.

Vertical.   The more commonly studied type of mobility is vertical social mobility, which refers to movement up or down the social hierarchy. This is the type most researchers refer to when they use the term "social mobility."

VERTICAL MOBILITY: Movement up or down in a social hierarchy.

There are two types of vertical social mobility. One is the movement above or below the status of one's parents. It is called intergenerational mobility. This type is difficult to measure because the criteria for success change over time. For example, we may earn a college degree, which our parents lack, but we may end up at the same level as our parents because so many others of our generation also have college degrees. We may have to run just to stay where we are, relative to others. And a woman must run even faster.

INTERGENERATIONAL MOBILITY: Vertical social movement relative to the previous generation.

Research shows that a female in the United States is probably more likely to stay at her parents' social-class level than her brother.[15] That is, men seem to have greater chances for vertical mobility than women.

There is another kind of vertical social mobility, the movement of a person relative to his or her past rank. This intragenerational mobility is easier to determine. The amounts of the three Ps gained or lost by a person can be measured. People are also mobile as they change in education level, age, or marital status.

Even so, it is not always easy to know when one is moving up or down socially.

While recent research suggests that mobility in the U.S., both up and down, occurs in greater degrees than has been assumed so far,[16] measuring the individual's mobility can be difficult. One may move into the space in-between two social classes, where the boundary is unclear. It is not easy today to place oneself by comparing oneself to others. At one time in the past, upper-class men wore top hats and rode in carriages, while the workers wore cloth caps and walked. Today, the people around us are not easy to place. No longer is it easy to use dress or make of car to place people socially. The millionaire may wear jeans and ride a bicycle.

Factors Affecting Mobility. In the United States, as in other class systems, a person's chances for mobility are affected by many factors, some of which are beyond his or her control. So, too, our own chances for mobility are affected by our attitudes and personal traits, as well as by external factors.

Attitudes. In some ways, mobility is determined by attitude. Mobile people must often be willing to drop old contacts and make new ones as they move up in the world. Likewise, the willingness to move can be a vital attitude for mobile people.[17] How a teenager views his or her ability affects mobility chances.[18] Delaying present pleasures in order to gain some later goal is another important factor—for example, sacrificing by going to school to ensure a comfortable life-style later.

Personal traits. Personal traits can also influence chances for mobility. Intelligence, beauty, charm, and talent can make the climb easier. For instance, people born with great athletic potential have an edge on their neighbors. Good looks and charm can help in business or in finding a higher-class mate—if one knows what looks are considered good in the higher class.

While level of education is another personal factor that affects chances for mobility, one study has shown that it pays off differently for men than for women.[19] The study found that college education helps the male in the United States get a good first job much more than it helps the female.

There is some disagreement as to whether race is still the most important factor affecting a black's chances for mobility. An important study by Wilson in 1978 contended that indeed the importance of race has declined since the 1960s, when formal

INTRAGENERATIONAL MOBILITY: Vertical social movement within one's own lifetime.

discriminatory barriers diminished, allowing blacks from advantaged backgrounds to climb the social ladder, in much the same way as whites.[20] Recently, Wilson's argument has gained some empirical support,[21] but the controversy remains.

Beyond such personal features, some social conditions also affect chances for mobility. These factors are largely beyond one's control.

Family. The family has a big influence on the mobility of its children, as is seen in many studies. The wealth of one's parents influences a person's level of education and earnings.[22] Similarly, the father's occupation influences the kinds of psychological attributes and occupational values of the son, and this influence is greatest when the father-son relationship is close and empathetic.[23] Some families use private schools as a means to protect their children's social status. Private schools do help prevent downward mobility, but by themselves produce little upward mobility.[24]

The size of one's family is important, too. Many studies have shown that the fewer siblings one has, the greater are one's chances for upward mobility, even when factors such as social class are controlled. Along these lines, the firstborn son, the youngest son in a small family, and only children have better chances than other children for upward mobility. The mobility system has indeed been more open for men with few siblings; the good news is that family size is declining, and thus mobility may increase.[25]

More recent research points out, however, that our ideas about status attainment are based on samples of large families, that is, families in the past. And large families affect educational mobility more than do small families, according to one researcher.[26] If this is true, sociologists must look more deeply into family structure and its impact on mobility.

There seems to be little question that the family equips the child with speech patterns that will help or hinder mobility chances. Although most Americans speak the same language, different classes speak it differently. Because speech patterns are so difficult to change, a lower-class person is at a disadvantage in job interviews. Also, these patterns are hard to hide when one is trying to gain acceptance into a higher-status group. Beyond the family's influence are broader social factors affecting mobility.

Labor market. Changes in the U.S. labor market have affected mobility rates in the twentieth century. As technology has grown in importance, so have the number of jobs requiring highly skilled workers. Such jobs have offered higher status to those people who, earlier in the century, would have been farmers. According to one observer, however, many of the jobs now being created by new technology are routine and poorly paid.[27] The openings for white-collar professionals are few compared to those for service workers and secretaries. Relatively few good jobs will open up in the computer field. Along with this is the fact that two of the biggest agents for upward mobility, labor unions and government jobs, are declining. This view suggests that the middle class will be shrinking because of such changes in the structure of the labor market.

The nature of the work place seems to allow certain kinds of people less access to jobs with power and high pay. One study found that the attitudes and policies of employers are an important reason that women have less chance to reach positions of authority in the work place.[28]

Since 1980, some mobility researchers have focused on the organization of the labor market, which seems to be segmented or broken into different sectors.[29] For example, workers who enter the market by way of large-scale organizations with little competition will enjoy more pay and benefits.[30] Once a worker settles into either a favorable or an unfavorable sector, he or she will probably remain there.[31] Thus a person's mobility chances are strongly affected by an employment choice made early in her or his work career.

Birthrate.   Differences in birthrates among the social classes are another social factor affecting mobility chances. Though these differences have recently narrowed, higher-class families in general do not have as many children as the lower classes. While the demand for high-status workers increases, such couples may produce only one or two children. This leaves room at the top, drawing up people from below.

Results of Social Mobility.   The benefits of upward social mobility in the United States or any other class system are obvious. People rising up the social ladder are gaining more of the three Ps. Gains in property, prestige, and power give people more freedom to control and enhance their lives. Though the three Ps do not guarantee happiness, they open more doors and offer more opportunities and choices. Indeed, the higher socioeconomic status reached, the better medical care and physical and mental health will be enjoyed by the individual and by his or her children.[32] That people in higher social classes enjoy better emotional health is clear. What is not clear is whether emotionally distressed people drift into the lower classes, or lower-class living conditions lead to greater distress and emotional problems.[33]

It is easy to forget that mobility is not always upward. A person demoted or fired from a job, losing a business, divorcing, or growing old is falling in social rank. The loss of the three Ps can be devastating, because people are judged socially by these factors. Social failure may be interpreted as personal failure.

Upward mobility can bring problems too. As one moves into a different social class world, self-doubts can grow. Mobility often requires that a person drop old values and grope for new ones. The broken ties with family and friends that often result can make stresses harder to bear. Rapid mobility may even sometimes cause mental illness, although the evidence on this is unclear.

None of this means one should refuse sudden wealth. Big winners in state lotteries were found to adjust quite nicely to their new fortunes.[34] They showed little evidence of stress or breakdown due to the sudden change. To the extent that sudden and drastic upward or downward mobility—or the lack of any mobility—does put a strain on people, however, the society can suffer.

Strains on individuals can mean broader social problems. As its members suffer, so does the society. Frustration and resentment can result when disadvantaged people see people all around them moving up. On the other hand, openness can be an asset for a society. The prospect of mobility motivates workers. Because achievement is seen to pay off, workers are encouraged to achieve. Such a system will be more productive than one in which hard work matters less than family name.

SUMMARY

Social stratification, the unequal ranking of people in a social hierarchy, is a fact of human social life. Whether they are ranked by age, sex, strength, or in classes or castes, people are socially unequal.

Modern societies are divided into classes or castes. A class system is relatively open, allowing movement from one level to another. Caste barriers are more rigid and impassable.

In the United States, stratification is based on how much property, prestige, and power we have. Property is wealth, prestige is honor or respect, and power is the ability to get others to do what we want. The more of these "three Ps" we have, the higher our social ranking.

America is a class system. Job, size and source of income, location and type of residence, and level of education indicate a person's social class. Our knowledge of America's class structure has been developed through the use of three methods; one based on reports of reputation, one on people's feelings about their class standing, and the other based on objective data. From this, a picture of a class system shaped like a bottom-heavy diamond has emerged, though there is a lack of agreement among scientists as to where the class boundaries lie within it.

Warner's six-class scheme was used to illustrate the varied lifestyles of the classes in the United States. The upper classes differ from each other on the newness or oldness of their wealth. The upper-middle class differs greatly from the lower-middle class as to occupation, but the two classes share a concern for the future and for respectability. The upper-lower-class person, compared to those of the lower-lower class, is much more likely to have hope as well as a job.

Horizontal social mobility, mobility from one position to another of similar ranking, is not much studied, so vertical mobility was our focus. Vertical movement, up or down the hierarchy, occurs in two forms. Intergenerational mobility is measured by comparing the rankings of two generations. Intragenerational mobility takes place within one person's lifetime. People's attitudes and traits affect their chances for vertical mobility, as do broader forces over which they have little control, such as family background, the labor market, and the differences in birthrates among the classes. Mobility can bring increased opportunities if it is upward, or devastation if it is downward. Even upward mobility has its costs.

This chapter has offered a view of where we fit in America's open-class society. By understanding our ranking system, the boundary lines, and the game's rules, we can learn to deal with the system better. This is true whether we are moving up, moving down, or just hanging on to our rung in life.

SPECIAL TOPIC

Is Social Equality Possible?

Since the 1960s, many Americans have been demanding social equality. Billions of dollars have been spent on efforts toward this goal. Of course, equality requires that we redistribute the social goods, and this causes resentment in certain segments of society. Such an expensive and explosive issue should be thoroughly explored.

There are basically two sides to the issue. On the one hand, some people believe social equality is a goal not to be questioned, a nearly sacred ideal. They believe that social policies should be aimed toward achieving this goal. They want much more of our nation's wealth and energies directed toward equality.

Other people, however, resent this use of social resources; they see social equality as a bottomless pit into which our nation is wasting resources. They advocate equal opportunity, which would result in a just but still unequal system.

In exploring this social and political issue, we will first examine the nature of equality and inequality. Then we will look at the historical views. Next, current theories will be explored. Finally we will address the question of whether social equality is really possible or desirable.

WHAT ARE EQUALITY AND INEQUALITY?

"Equality" is often used very loosely to mean a state in which all people share the social goods to the same extent. It is also used in references to equal rights, or chances to share in those goods. Here we will focus on equal shares of power, prestige, and especially wealth.

In studying equality it is valuable to study its opposite. Inequality is the absence or lack of equality. Just as there are different kinds of equality among people, there are also several types of inequality.

First, people are unequal with regard to such traits as height or the number of hobbies they have; such differences are not often ranked, one above another. Differences that are ranked are often differences that involve such traits as intelligence, strength, and talent, which m y be to some degree inborn. If such differences are indeed inborn, inequality involving such traits cannot be altered by human efforts. The inequalities that most concern theorists are those that are used to rank people and are social in origin, not natural or inborn. An example of this type is unequal wealth. This socially devised kind of inequality is the object of most reformers. Here we will ask how much this kind of inequality can be reduced.

HISTORICAL VIEWS ON EQUALITY

Let us use history to begin our study of the issue of inequality. One theorist traces the issue back to the ancient Greeks.[35] Aristotle assumed that humans were by nature unequal. He believed that natural law caused people to be born unequal in rank. This meant that some people were born more deserving and others were placed by nature into lowly positions. Nature decided who would be the prince and who would be the peasant. This view was held for hundreds of years. Few people were willing to argue with nature's plan. Besides, nature's plan was seen as fair, because the peasants were clearly inferior to the princes. They were crude and ignorant, while the princes were polished and literate. That seemed to prove that nature was only fair in assigning unequal stations to people of such unequal traits. This traditional view of inequality was accepted until the 1750s, when Rousseau seriously questioned it. He attacked the basic premise on which inequality had been accepted for centuries: natural inequality. Inequality, Rousseau said, was neither natural nor right; social ranks were assigned not by nature or God, but by society. He contended that people were inherently equal. This was a radical idea in eighteenth-century Europe, but it gained a foothold. The traditional view would no longer go unchallenged.

Rousseau blamed private property as the cause of inequality. Karl Marx, writing in the nineteenth century agreed. Marx and Rousseau reasoned that when people began to own property, some people would get more than others. Both saw this as the beginning of an unjust social order that would need to be reformed or overthrown. Indeed, the ideas of Rousseau and Marx are linked with revolutions in France, North America, and Russia.

Not all other thinkers of those times agreed with all the views of Rousseau and Marx, but their basic premise became established. Inequality was no longer as easily accepted as natural.

The two basic views on inequality were therefore established before the twentieth century. The traditional view saw inequality as natural, as part of nature's plan, and claimed that the social order was and should be based on this plan. Opponents of that view saw inequality as an evil that need not exist. They saw the fight for equality as a moral struggle to right a wrong. The aim of the struggle was a social structure based on equality.

TODAY'S THEORIES ON EQUALITY

The battle lines today are drawn in the same fashion, but the labels attached to the theories are "functionalist" and "conflict."

Functionalist Theory

Today's functionalist viewpoint was established in the 1940s. A paper by Davis and Moore involved American theorists in the issue.[36] This view resembles the traditional one in that social inequality is not seen as an evil. On the contrary, it is viewed as an integrating factor. Unequal rewards are seen as necessary for smooth social functioning.

Davis and Moore believed that inequality provided incentive, the key to smooth functioning. This line of reasoning asserts that complex systems need highly skilled workers. People must develop their full potentials so they can function as doctors, technicians, and so on. To motivate people to develop and use their talents, rewards must be offered. If people were rewarded equally, no matter how much or how little they worked, too few people would work hard and society would suffer. Therefore, rewards must be unequal and based on how well a person fulfills his or her social role.

Davis and Moore believed that people should be ranked according to their social role. Social roles are ranked according to their social importance and the training and talent they require. If a role is important, high rewards are offered to ensure that the role is filled by a capable person. Likewise, some roles require talents that few people have. To make sure that the most talented people fill such roles, high rewards must be offered. The higher the reward offered, the greater the chance that the most highly qualified people will apply for the role. Similarly, for some roles the required training is long and hard. Who would endure the training required of a doctor, for instance, if there were no assurance of getting higher rewards than loafers would get? Ranked social roles thus are believed to help the system function well.

Conflict Theory

The conflict theorists argue that inequality does not produce smooth social functioning. On the contrary, they argue, only conflict and harm result.

These theorists contend that inequality does not ensure that important roles will be filled by the most able people. They argue that some of the highly rewarded roles will go to those who were simply lucky enough to be born with certain advantages. In addition, they say that all too often fraud or force, not ability, determines one's rewards. The competition is not fair, say conflict theorists. Those who are born socially high, stay high. Those born low have little chance to rise. In this view, the unequal rewards produce not incentive but resentment for the disadvantaged. Therefore, besides wasting human talent, such a system creates tension and conflict.

Further, conflict theorists charge that high rewards are in some cases given to people who actually harm social functioning. For example, heads of companies that produce harmful products, such as liquor and cigarettes, are well paid. This is not the same picture the functionalists paint.

While the conflict theorists have leveled sound criticisms of the functionalists, they have yet to convince their own critics that they can offer a better system as an alternative. So the debate continues.

IS SOCIAL EQUALITY POSSIBLE?

Now these two theories will be used to explore the original question.

No: Unequal Rewards
Are Necessary for Society's Survival

The functionalists say that social equality is not possible. People, they say, are not born with equal potential. Further, even if born equal, people do not contribute equally to the system. The social fabric would be destroyed if it were based on the injustice of equality. A system treating people as though they made equal contributions would be unfair to those who did the most work. Equal treatment cheats the better workers by pretending they do less than they do. These more productive workers will grow frustrated and resentful as a result of this injustice. In time, they will refuse to produce any more than they want to. In fact, all workers will respond similarly to such a system. If the rewards one receives are not based on one's work, where is the incentive to work? Without productive work, no society can survive long. Thus, according to the functionalist view, social equality is not feasible.

Yes: People Can Be Equally Rewarded
and Still Be Motivated to Perform

On the other hand, those critical of the functionalists contend that inequality is not the only way to motivate people. They claim there

are ways to motivate people that do not result in social harm and conflict.

Job Satisfaction. Job satisfaction may be such a way. If all occupations were equally rewarded, they might be filled by people who were interested in the work itself, not just the size of the paycheck. Such people would enjoy their jobs and therefore be more productive. The problem with this idea is that many roles might go unfilled because they offer no intrinsic rewards. Some jobs are so dangerous or unpleasant that no one would volunteer for them.

"Team" Spirit. Marxists believe that people can be motivated by broader social incentives. In communist countries, workers, in theory, get fairly equal slices of the social pie. They work to make the pie—and their own slice—bigger and because they are encouraged by their fellows to do their share of the work. However, those countries with economic systems based on this idea often suffer from inefficient production, except where unequal rewards are offered. Besides, there are still inequalities of income and power in such systems. Still, according to this line of thought, political incentives can replace unequal rewards.

Brainwashing. There are other plans offered to motivate people by intensive socialization. The utopia described in *Walden Two* used a kind of brainwashing to produce citizens who wanted to be productive.[37] Their personalities were shaped early in life in government nurseries, so that they were self-motivated. In this fictional system, unequal social rewards were not needed; psychological incentives replaced economic ones.

The question of freedom arises here. Such a system is based on what could be called mind control, or brainwashing. On the other hand, such intensive childhood training could be viewed as a highly effective way to produce productive and happy citizens. In *Walden Two* there was no bad parenting, no abuse or neglect of children. All children were raised by experts in parenting. Such a system could ensure that every child had a secure, warm, and effective upbringing, say its proponents. The children would be taught to value harmony and work.

The use of such a system has been promoted as offering freedom with dignity.[38] That is, people who had a highly controlled childhood upbringing would not be restrained by an insecure personality. They would be free to fulfill their potential—and society's. Inequality would not be needed to make this system work, it is claimed.

Critics of this way of providing noneconomic incentives fear abuse of such a mind-control system. They ask, Who would be in charge, who would choose the values taught the children? There is also the doubt that such a system would function smoothly. The prospect of such a system's going wrong is frightening. Many people would rather take their chances in the haphazard system we now have rather than submit their children to such an experiment.

Equal Power and Prestige Too?
So far, we have discussed the problems of erasing differences in wealth, but we have neglected the two other factors used in ranking people: prestige and power. Differences in these factors must be erased if complete equality is to be achieved. Let us examine briefly the costs of "total equality."

To equalize prestige among members of a system would require much coercion. Prestige comes from the functions that we fulfill. Will we ever respect the cab driver as much as we do the doctor? Some sort of mind control would be needed to equalize such differences in prestige. Further, the esteem we receive from others can also be based on personal traits, such as beauty. Surely we don't wish to equalize these differences. But "total equality" would include that kind of equalization.

Power would also have to be equalized under a system of total equality. The problem here is that, in order to erase differences among people, a good deal of social control is required. Great power would be needed to restrain more able people from gaining advantages of wealth, prestige—or power. Such control would mean unequal power and would perhaps be a great price to pay.

None of those who demand "total equality" want to equalize power and prestige as well as wealth, but that is what "total equality" implies. Perhaps any goal of equality should be limited to wealth.

WHAT IF WE ARE BORN WITH EQUAL POTENTIAL?
Are people born with unequal potentials? The functionalists believe that we are born unequal. If, however, we are born *equal*, would not equal social rewards naturally follow? Not necessarily.

Equal potential does not mean equal achievement. We have seen the problems in rewarding unequal achievements equally. In order to equalize the achievement of people with equal potential, the same social stimulations are needed for all. Each person's potential must be subjected to the same shaping forces. The conditions in each home must be equally nurturing. Much government control would be needed to equalize the social environment for each person. This may be seen as neither acceptable nor feasible. So even if we are born equal, we will not perform equally. When there is unequal performance, equal rewards present great difficulties.

Equal Opportunity Instead of Equal Ranking?
This brings us to the last issue: equal opportunity. If true equality is not feasible, or even desirable, perhaps our goal should be equal opportunities for everyone to gain social rewards. Our discussion of equalization of environments shows us that this issue is a matter of degree. How far do we wish to go in equalizing opportunities? Offering equal schooling, for example, is not enough. Children from poor home situations will not have an equal chance in school, so home environments would have to be equalized. But this could not occur without a tremendous amount of government interference.

There is no clear answer. While the functionalist theory is imperfect, the conflict theorists have yet to offer a clearly better system. Is social equality possible? No, but surely less inequality is possible. That leaves us with another question, however: How far should we go to equalize opportunity? This question will be answered not by the theorists, but in the political arena.

SELF-TEST QUESTIONS
1. In what ways is class different from caste?
2. _____ was the basis of Marx's views on the history of societies.

3. A layer of society in which the people share similar numbers of the social rewards is a:
   a. status
   b. hierarchy
   c. social class

4. What are the bases of stratification in the United States?

5. The U.S. social class system could be depicted as a:
   a. rectangle
   b. triangle
   c. circle
   d. bottom-heavy diamond
   e. square

6. What three methods are used to identify the social-class boundaries of a community?

7. What factors affect a person's chances for social mobility?

8. What factors indicate a person's social class?

9. True or false: Social mobility always has positive results for the person involved.

ANSWERS TO SELF-TEST QUESTIONS

1. Caste is based on ascribed status, strong barriers to mobility, and often an acceptance of the system by its members.
2. social-class conflict
3. c
4. property, prestige, and power
5. d
6. reputational, subjective, objective
7. attitudes, personal traits, family background, labor-market conditions, differences in birthrates of social classes, among others
8. job, income (size and source), type and location of residence, educational level
9. false

ANSWERS TO SKILL REINFORCERS

7–1. Conclusion: This stratification system is a caste system.

7–2. It is unlikely that an address in the suburbs is the cause of a high income. Instead, the income is probably the requirement (and cause) of the suburban home, which is likely to be more expensive than a home in the inner city or the country. It would be better to look at some other variable, such as job, as the cause of the high income, which is seen as one cause of the suburban address.

NOTES

1. Allen Churchhill, *The Splendor Seekers* (New York: Grosset & Dunlap, 1974): 159.
2. William Rathje and Randall McGuire, "Rich Men . . . Poor Men," *American Behavioral Scientist* 25 (July/August 1982): 705–715.
3. U.S. Bureau of the Census, *Statistical Abstract of the United States, 1986* (Washington, D.C. 1985): 451.
4. Ibid., p. 458.
5. Ibid., p. 768.
6. Christopher Jencks et al., *Who Gets Ahead? The Determinants of Economic Success in America* (New York: Basic Books, 1979).
7. Bruce Link, Bruce Dohrenwend, and Andrew Skodol, "Socio-Economic Status and Schizophrenia," *American Sociological Review* 51 (April 1986): 242–58.

8. David Popenoe, *Sociology,* 2nd ed. (New York: Appleton-Century-Crofts, 1974): 263, 265.

9. Erik Wright, David Hachen, Cynthia Costello, and Joey Sprague, "The American Class Structure," *American Sociological Review* 47 (December 1982): 709–26.

10. Steven Brint, " 'New Class' and Cumulative Trend Explanations of the Liberal Political Attitudes of Professionals," *American Journal of Sociology* 90 (July 1984): 30–71.

11. John Dalphin, *The Persistence of Social Inequality in America* (Cambridge, Mass.: Schenckman, 1982).

12. Lloyd Warner and Paul S. Lunt, *The Social Life of a Modern Community* (New Haven: Yale University Press, 1941).

13. Joseph A. Kahl, *The American Class Structure* (New York: Holt, Rinehart & Winston, 1957).

14. Lucienne Portocarero, "Social Mobility in Industrial Nations," *The Sociological Review* 31 (February 1983): 56–82.

15. Norval D. Glenn and Sandra L. Albrecht, "Is the Status Structure in the U.S. Really More Fluid for Women Than for Men?" *American Sociological Review* 45 (April 1980): 340–44.

16. Greg Duncan, "Years of Poverty, Years of Plenty" (Ann Arbor, Michigan: Institute for Social Research, Publishing Division, 1984).

17. William Markham, Patrick Macken, Charles Bonjean, and Judy Corder, "A Note on Sex, Geographical Mobility, and Career Advancement," *Social Forces* 61 (June 1983): 1138–46.

18. Diane Looker and Peter Pineo, "Social Psychological Variables and their Relevance to the Status Attainment of Teenagers," *American Journal of Sociology* 88 (May 1983): 1195–1219.

19. William H. Sewell, Robert M. Hauser, and Wendy C. Wolf, "Sex, Schooling, and Occupational Status," *American Journal of Sociology* 86 (November 1980): 551–83.

20. William J. Wilson, *The Declining Significance of Race* (Chicago: University of Chicago Press, 1978).

21. Michael Hout, "Occupational Mobility of Black Men," *American Sociological Review* 49 (June 1984): 308–22.

22. Russell Rumberger, "The Influence of Family Background on Education, Earnings, and Wealth," *Social Forces* 61 (March 1983): 755–73.

23. Jeylan Mortimer and Donald Kumka, "A Further Examination of the Occupational Linkage Hypothesis," *The Sociological Quarterly* 23 (Winter 1982): 3–16.

24. Lionel Lewis and Richard Wanner, "Private Schooling and the Status Attainment Process," *Sociology of Education* 52 (April 1979): 99–112.

25. Judith Blake, "Number of Siblings and Educational Mobility," *American Sociological Review* 50 (February 1985): 84–94.

26. Judith Blake, "Sibsize and Educational Stratification," *American Sociological Review* 51 (June 1986): 413–17.

27. Bob Kuttner, "The Declining Middle," *Atlantic Monthly* 252 (July 1983): 60–72.

28. Wendy C. Wolf and Neil D. Fligstein, "Sex and Authority in the Workplace: The Causes of Sexual Inequality," *American Sociological Review* 44 (April 1979): 235–52.

29. Charles Tolbert, "Industrial Segmentation and Men's Intergenerational Mobility," *Social Forces* 61 (June 1983): 1119–37.

30. David Jacobs, "Unequal Organizations or Unequal Attainments?" *American Sociological Review* 50 (April 1985): 166–80.

31. Charles Tolbert, "Industrial Segmentation and Mens' Career Mobility," *American Sociological Review* 47 (August 1982): 457–77.

32. Catherine Ross and Raymond Duff, "Medical Care, Living Conditions, and Children's Well-Being," *Social Forces* 61 (December 1982): 456–74.

33. Ronald Kessler, "A Disaggregation of the Relationship between Socioeconomic Status and Psychological Distress," *American Sociological Review* 47 (December 1982): 752–64.

34. Mark Abrahamson, "Sudden Wealth, Gratification, and Attainment: Durkheim's Anomie of Affluence Reconsidered," *American Sociological Review* 45 (February 1980): 49–57.

35. R. Dahrendorf, "On the Origin of Inequality Among Men," in *Social Inequality,* ed. André Beteille (Harmondsworth, Eng.: Penguin Books, 1969): 16–44.

36. Kingsley Davis and Wilbert E. Moore, "Some Principles of Stratification," *American Sociological Review* 10 (1945): 242–49.

37. B.F. Skinner, *Walden Two* (New York: Macmillan Co., 1948).

38. B.F. Skinner, *Beyond Freedom and Dignity* (New York: Bantam/Vintage, 1971).

SUGGESTED READINGS

Domhoff, William. *Who Rules America Now?* Englewood Cliffs, N.J.: Prentice-Hall, 1983.

Gilbert, Dennis, and Joseph A. Kahl. *The American Class Structure.* Homewood, Ill.: Dorsey Press, 1982.

Harrington, Michael. *The Other America.* New York: Macmillan Co., 1962.

Hollingshead, A.B. *Elmstown's Youth.* New York: John Wiley & Sons, 1949.

Jencks, Christopher, et al. *Who Gets Ahead?* New York: Basic Books, 1979.

Lenski, Gerhard. *Power and Privilege: A Theory of Social Stratification.* New York: McGraw-Hill, 1966.

Rubin, Lillian. *Worlds of Pain.* New York: Basic Books, 1978.

Ryan, William. *Equality.* New York: Vintage Books, 1982.

8 MINORITY, ETHNIC, AND RACIAL GROUPS

PREVIEW

They All Look Alike

"They all look alike to me." This familiar statement can be an irritant in minority-group relations. Most of us like to think of ourselves or of our groups as easily distinguishable from others. After all, each of us is unique and special, so we may resent being lumped together.

Why do people sometimes find it difficult to distinguish one face from another within other races? It may be because they have not had much contact with people from other races. Sometimes it is easier to distinguish among unfamiliar things if we spend more time with them. The study we are about to describe by Terrence Luce tested the idea that contact with members of other races improves people's ability to distinguish among them.[1]

The study used groups of white, black, and Asian-American people. The whites had many previous contacts with blacks. The blacks had the same with whites. Neither had much previous contact with Asian-Americans. The Asian-Americans in the study had previous contact with both blacks and whites.

In the study, each person was shown a page of twenty faces, all of one race. After one minute the subject was shown another page of faces, all of the same race. Some of the faces had been on the first sheet, others were new. The subject tried to recognize the faces from the first page. Each person was tested in this way on black, white, and Asian faces.

The black subjects could most easily distinguish among black faces. But even though they had a good deal of previous contact with whites, they found it difficult to distinguish among the white faces, as well as the Asian faces. It seems that for blacks, all non-blacks look alike.

The results were similar for the whites. Even with previous contact with blacks, the black faces were hard to distinguish from each other. But these whites who had had no previous contact with Asians had little difficulty distinguishing among the Asian faces.

The Asian-American subjects could easily distinguish among those of Chinese and Japanese origins. They had some difficulty with the black faces, and much difficulty with the white faces in the study.

The results suggest that we are either unable or unwilling to notice the facial features of people of other races. Perhaps it is because we have negative feelings toward those we view as outsiders. Or perhaps we see color first and need to know other people better before we can notice their other features. Perhaps when racially distinct groups are no longer seen as "others," the uniqueness of their members will be recognized.

In the meantime, "They all look alike to me" will continue to be seen as a snub, even though it may be a statement of fact. As long as we are unable—or refuse—to recognize the features of other groups, we will need progress in intergroup relations. In the meantime, we can try to understand the nature of such intergroup problems.

For a person living in the United States, as in other countries, it is more than just "too bad" that people of different racial or ethnic backgrounds so often clash. This conflict can affect politics from the local to the international level. Beyond that, it is likely that you have been affected personally by such conflict. Because of this conflict, it is worthwhile to learn something about minority-group relations.

This chapter will focus on the recent large-scale mixing of peoples and the effects of that mixing. After defining the nature of minority groups, races, and ethnic groups, we will explore patterns of interaction involving minorities. Then we will focus on those parts of the American past that led to the minority-group relations in our nation today. The Special Topic will deal with affirmative-action policies in the United States.

MINORITIES AND OTHER GROUPS

Since the 1960s, the words "minority-group relations" have become more and more familiar in this nation. Minority-group relations have become an important issue, and you will probably study the topic in other courses. This chapter offers an introduction to this important topic. We begin by introducing the concepts of minority, racial, and ethnic groups.

Minority Groups Described

What They Are.   A white American, especially a white male, will need to use his imagination in reading this section. Imagine you are marked, physically or culturally, as someone who is to be denied equal treatment. You must marry within your own group, and your group is dominated by a more powerful one that writes all the rules by which your group is to be treated. You are a member of a minority group.

MINORITY GROUP: A race or ethnic group that is dominated by others.

The main thing that makes a social grouping a minority group is the way its members are treated. A minority group is dominated by other parts of society. Its members are denied equal access to important social resources. They have little control over economic, political, or social matters.

As the label implies, a minority group is usually smaller than the dominant population, but it is possible for the minority group to be the largest subgroup in the society. The best example of this is the Union of South Africa. In that nation, the dominant whites constitute only about 20 percent of the population. The nonwhites make up 80 percent, but they are clearly a minority group because of the poor treatment they receive. Another example of a large minority group is the women in the United States. Though they outnumber men, women are considered by many to be a minority.

How They Arose.   A look at how minority groups came to be formed can tell us something about their nature. At the hunting and gathering level there are no minority groups. If a person is treated poorly, it is because of his or her personal traits, not because of membership in a certain group.

Oppression based on group membership did not exist until nation-states were formed, about five thousand years ago. When some groups in these states gathered power, others were left without it and became minority groups. Other groups were subjugated by conquering states.

Minorities developed only in societies that were arranged in hierarchies and controlled by central powers. Those in power erected barriers to protect their positions. An official language and culture were adopted. With a culture different from this, the minority group was distinct and made a clear target for poor treatment. Minorities can also be deliberately created by dominant elites for economic reasons, most clearly where economic specialization calls for an exploitable group of unskilled workers.[2]

How They Are Maintained.   There are two ways the majority group maintains the oppressive system. One is by focusing on descent. The other is by clearly labeling minority-group members.

The use of descent ensures that minority members will have no chance of moving out of their status, because they cannot change their ancestry. The members inherit their station in society. An extreme example of this concern with descent is what we now call "hypo-descent." In America's Old South, people were considered black if any black ancestry was somehow discovered in their line of descent. Such ancestry would override the actual physical features of the person.

To maintain the use of descent as a feature of minority-group status, intermarriage is discouraged. This social wall helps prevent members of the minority from moving out of their position. The rules against intermarriage are aimed at preserving the boundary lines among the various social segments.

Another method is the use of racial or cultural features to label minority group members. Language and religion are common cultural features used to distinguish members of minority groups. For example, Jews have been singled out for minority-group status because of their religion. This labeling marks the members as targets, victims, and helps make the system of oppression work.

The minority group system is also maintained by early social experiences. One study showed that black and white children preferred same-color friends when they entered kindergarten. This preference increased by the end of the school year. The researchers concluded that this same-color preference is partly the result of different black and white behavior patterns. Those differences, "combined with the lack of cross-color contacts during the preschool years, contribute to the development of children's preferences for same-color peers."[3]

Racial Groups   Here we must be careful. As was mentioned in an earlier chapter, race is a very sensitive topic, and the term "race" itself is perhaps not technically accurate when referring to humans. If there were human populations with distinct gene frequencies, we could speak of human races. But genetically distinct populations are not easily found among humans.

Drawing the Boundary Lines.   Whether people see it as tragic or proper, boundary lines are drawn among races all over the world, but the lines are rarely drawn clearly. The imprecise nature of the boundary lines is more apparent in some parts of the world, such as South America, than others. A person might consider himself or herself as belonging to one race, yet be considered as belonging to another race by other people. In South America, it is possible that the photograph of a person could be shown to villagers in a nearby village and the person could be identified as a member of any one of several races.

While ordinary people find it difficult to identify racial boundary lines, scientists have a hard time defining the concept of race clearly. Even those scientists who specialize in the study of race disagree over the number of races as well as boundary lines among races.

Many of us who are not scientists classify races without studying races. Many of us sense a need to classify things, and in doing so we proceed with the knowledge we have. If we have been taught by culture that certain boundary lines define certain races, this teaching will be used if no other knowledge is available. The popular usage of race is based not on the physical evidence offered by science but on such traditions of culture that have survived time. Because of this, the biological concept of race is imprecisely defined in common usage.

One result of this imprecise definition of race is that the racial boundary lines ignore the overlapping of racial traits. The use of skin color is a good example. Among both blacks and whites there is a wide range of skin colors. In fact, a person considered "white" may have darker skin than some "black" people. This overlapping is also true of other racial traits, such as eye and hair color, lip formation, and hair type. These and other traits show an overlap among races.

While there is much overlapping of racial traits between any two racial groupings, most North Americans are perfectly clear about their race membership. Furthermore, we do not often have trouble classifying others. Regardless of how imprecise the racial boundary lines are, Americans largely agree on where they are drawn. This agreement on racial lines is illustrated by the results of a change in the U.S. census. For the first time, the 1960 census asked people what racial group they belonged to. Before this, the census workers had classified people. This change in procedure did not seem to affect the results. That is, the workers and the respondents seem to agree on the respondents' race memberships. Such agreement on race membership in such a racially diverse so-

RACE (SOCIAL DEFINITION): An ethnic group in which members share inherited, physical traits.

ciety as ours points to the importance of the social definition of such a vaguely defined concept as race.

Race and Intelligence.   The biggest controversy concerning race involves racial differences in intelligence. While some racial groups have long held others to be innately less intelligent, the issue has become more heated during this century for several reasons, one reason being that intelligence has become more important than ever in our culture. Brawn counts less than brain. Along with this, more tests of intelligence have been developed and refined, and the scores of these tests are often used as a basis for educational decisions involving millions of tax dollars. The question of intelligence differences is of such basic importance in race relations that it deserves attention here. We will focus on the center of the storm: Are whites by nature more intelligent than blacks?

On the surface, the question of black-white differences in intelligence seems to have been answered clearly. The average intelligence scores of blacks are lower than those of whites. But—and this is a big but—there are important factors that cloud the picture.

First, intelligence tests do not measure innate intelligence. Instead, they seem to measure the intelligence as it has been developed at that point in a person's life. Few test experts contend that any test can measure innate brain quality, that is, the potential with which any one person is born. Discrimination, poverty, and neglect must be considered in interpreting the scores. The fact that such social factors affect the test scores is in itself enough to undermine any claims about the superior innate intelligence of whites. Some part—perhaps all—of the black-white gap in test scores is the result of different social environments. The tests do not tell us how big this part is.

Besides the questioned validity of the tests, we must note that the blacks and whites whose intelligence scores are compared are really mixed groupings. Several centuries of gene flow, or interbreeding, between the two groups has occurred, so we should be cautious when comparing the intelligence of these two socially defined categories.

This issue is, and may remain, unresolved. We simply do not know if there is a difference in the innate intelligence of various races. If there is a real difference, we cannot be sure what the rankings of the various races would be, because we cannot equalize environments in order to find out. Even more important, we should note that the comparisons of intelligence are of average scores. There is much overlapping here, as with other racial traits; that is, there will be members of any race found at nearly every level of mental ability. Any difference in the proportions of people from various races at any one level is usually slight. Again, these differences may be completely due to differences in environment.

Skill Reinforcer 8-1*

Evaluate the truth and the logic of this syllogism:

1. Intelligence-test scores measure inborn intelligence.

2. The average intelligence test scores of whites are higher than those of blacks.

3. Whites have higher inborn intelligence than blacks.

---

*Answers to the Skill Reinforcers appear at the end of the chapter.

Ethnic Groups

ETHNIC GROUP: A collectivity of people who share a (usually) inherited membership in a common cultural identification.

The Nature of Ethnicity.   Much more has been heard recently about ethnic groups than thirty years ago. Today, from our local Irish social club to "Proud to be Polish" bumper stickers, we can see evidence of ethnic awareness. But even more than "race," the term "ethnic group" is a vague one. It is applied in so many ways that its meaning is not always clear. Still, several features of ethnic groups can be identified.

In contrast to racial groups, an ethnic group is a socially distinct "people." Its members identify with the ethnic group and are bound together by a common culture. Membership is usually inherited and can be based on race, nation, religion, language, or traditions. Ethnic groups are sometimes minorities, and sometimes races are also ethnic groups. American blacks are a race, an ethnic group, and a minority group. American Indians are also a racially and ethnically distinct minority. But some ethnic groups are not minorities. Some culturally distinct groups are not singled out for ill treatment. Examples include the ethnic groups of European origins, such as Italian-Americans. Such people are distinct when gathered in places like a "Little Italy," but do not suffer poor treatment because of it. Also, Jews in the United States are a somewhat distinct people but on the whole enjoy high social-class status. In this light, Jews could be considered an ethnic group, but perhaps not a minority group, because they are not denied access to social resources.

Some scientists have been surprised by the resurgence of ethnic solidarity in several industrialized nations such as Great Britain, France, and Canada. Most predictions had pointed to a decline in the importance of ethnicity and in the cohesion of ethnic groups as societies became more modernized. But ethnicity seems to be strong in such nations, perhaps because ethnic group members feel a need to stick together in the intense competition for jobs. Or, it may be that ethnic members stick together because they are exploited as a group. One observer even predicts that ethnicity will grow as a "convenient basis for mobilization," a means of collective action in a complex, modern society.[4]

The Problems with Ethnicity.   A social grouping that remains very distinct runs the risk of being singled out for poor treatment. The danger of ethnicity is that people often consider "different" to be the same thing as "inferior." Those not identified with the cultural majority may become a "them," subject to poor treatment by "us."

Indeed, much of the world's social conflict in recent decades has been along ethnic lines. Instead of the class conflict predicted by Marx, the conflicts of our day are based on differences of religion, race, birthplace, language, and so forth. For many people today, their most important social ties are those of ethnicity.

Because these ties are usually inherited, we continue to be separated along ethnic lines. People are not likely to give up their ethnic membership as long as it offers them a sense of belonging that cannot be obtained otherwise. Until these lines disappear, jealousy, resentment, and scorn will mark our social systems.

INTERACTION WITH MINORITY GROUPS

In the chapter preview, we saw that the members of other racial or ethnic groups often "all look alike" to many of us. Whatever causes this mental block may also be responsible for the poor treatment so often accorded racial and ethnic groups. The causes of both the mental block and the poor treatment remain something of a mystery, but if we study the interaction between dominant and subordinate groups we may gain some insight into the domination and into why "they" all look alike instead of being unique like "us."

Prejudice

Unlike discrimination, prejudice need not involve any action and thus may hurt only the prejudiced people themselves. Still, prejudice can be viewed as the fuel for the oppression of minorities. Both the nature and the causes of prejudice will be explored here.

PREJUDICE: An emotional, rigid attitude that prejudices individuals on the basis of their group membership rather than on their personal qualities.

The Nature of Prejudice.   Prejudice is a matter of what people think and feel, not what they do. That is, prejudice is an attitude that often causes the mistreatment of minorities; it is not the treatment itself.

Looking at the word "prejudice," we can see its basic meaning: pre-judge. The prejudiced person judges certain other people before knowing them personally. That judgment is based on the group membership of those other people.

Prejudice can be positive. We can judge all the members of some group to have good qualities. For example; "The British have more class than any other people; their taste is impeccable." Or, "You just have to admit that those Japanese are the most clever people on earth." Despite such examples, the term "prejudice" is most commonly used to describe the negative judgment of members of certain groups. For example, "The British are all small-minded boors." Or, "Those Japanese are all sneaky and cannot be trusted." It is this negative type of prejudice which we will consider here.

The prejudiced frame of mind is emotional and rigid. It is not open to new knowledge concerning the group it is set against. The prejudiced person can ignore some facts and focus on others. He will not be easily persuaded by reason. It is not logic that is of interest to such a person, but support and agreement. Facts that do not fit can be explained away or distorted. In matters concerning certain groups, emotion reigns over logic for this person.

The Origins of Prejudice.   What causes this curious, damaging viewpoint? Why do people who may be reasonable in other ways grit their teeth and close their minds when certain groups are mentioned? The sources of prejudice can be grouped in three classes: psychological, cultural, and intergroup conflict.

The Ku Klux Klan aims to instill prejudice. The Klan hopes that action will result from these attitudes.

The mind. Some theories use psychology to explain prejudice. Early theories of this type saw prejudice as an instinct; this view is now largely abandoned. Today the focus is on the individual's needs. While this view ignores many other factors, it still helps us understand why some people are prejudiced.

Some of these theories are straightforward. One states that prejudice is used to enhance self-esteem. In this way a person can say "I may be poor, but I'm better than any of *them.*" Another theory states that prejudice may simply be a response to the unknown. What we do not understand, we are more likely to fear or dislike. Prejudice may also be a person's way of responding to social pressures, of conforming.

Other psychological theories are less obvious. One such view on prejudice is the frustration-aggression theory.[5] It helps explain why races or minority groups are often blamed for the problems of others. The theory reasons that frustration builds up aggression in a person. Sometimes this aggression cannot be safely directed against the people causing the frustration; the people may be too powerful. Perhaps the cause is unknown. In either case, the aggression can be displaced toward people who cannot easily strike back—a minority. In this way, a people can be blamed for the problems of others, and hated for it. There are some problems with this explanation. First, frustration does not always produce aggression. Also, aggression is not always directed toward some other people. Finally, the theory fails to explain the choices of targets.

Another mental trick that can result in prejudice is called projection. With this, the members of some minority are assumed to engage in forbidden but tempting behavior. This makes it easier for the believers to resist engaging in such behavior. After all, they wouldn't want to be like "them." In this way, some minority group or race is treated with scorn and contempt because of the belief that they break the behavior code.

Much research has been done on the prejudiced personality. This approach holds that prejudice is just one of a package of traits, which has been called the "authoritarian personality."[6] People who have this package are insecure, threatened, and repressed. They want to ally themselves with powerful figures. Prejudice is part of this package of traits. In other research of this type, the mother is blamed. Mothers who are domineering and possessive are said to cause prejudice in their children.

These personality theories have been attacked on several grounds. Some of these studies were based on peoples' responses to questions, not their behavior. Such factors as age and class were ignored. Critics charge that the list of traits is not a unified package. It is suggested that perhaps other factors, perhaps social ones, produce the package or the prejudice. While this type of theory has remained popular, it is at best a partial explanation of prejudice.

There is a problem with all these theories that are based on psychology. Many of the traits of people are caused by social background. It thus seems unwise to focus on people's inner forces and neglect the social factors.

Culture. In the cultural theories, prejudice is viewed as a part of the cultural heritage. Each generation learns that certain peoples are to be hated or scorned. Just as we learn which foods and music are good, so we learn which people are not "good." This theory does not explain, however, how the prejudice begins in the culture, or why certain target groups are chosen; it does describe the nature of the prejudiced "mind set."

Group conflict. The intergroup conflict theory explains the origins of a heritage of prejudice. It also explains why certain targets were chosen. This approach views prejudice as arising from the contact among social segments.

The conflict may be due to ethnocentrism. When some ethnic group violates our moral beliefs, friction develops. In several countries, conflicts arise over which language is to be the official one. Likewise, arguments over religious holidays and dress codes can cause conflict. For example, factions in Muslim countries argue over whether women should be required to wear face veils or head shawls. From such arguments over moral issues can come the belief that the members of the other group are immoral. This is prejudice.

Intergroup conflict can also result from competition. In some eastern U.S. seaports years ago, Irish dock workers resented the competition of blacks for jobs; later the blacks who had won some of the jobs resented Hispanic job seekers. In cases where segments of the same society compete for jobs, training, or schooling, hard feelings may arise. Competition may also be based on politics. If ethnic groups have differing goals, their power struggle may become bitter. One group may feel threatened, another cheated.

It is easy to see how a competing group can be seen as the enemy. When fighting an enemy it is helpful to believe in their bad qualities. A team's morale is boosted by a belief in the other team's inferior worth. From these feelings, prejudice can result.

Racism

It would not be proper to say simply that racism is a form of prejudice. Racism is such an important problem in the United States, as in many other places, that it deserves separate treatment.

RACISM: A form of prejudice directed against races.

The Nature of Racism. Racism is the belief that a person, because of the genetic limits of his or her race, cannot function as well as people with "better" racial endowments. Note that this belief is based on the person's race, not on personal qualities. The racist sees cultural differences as the results of innate, or genetic, differences. That is, the racist views some races as innately inferior. If a race's culture is judged inferior, the racist believes this judgment is based on the race's poor genes.

Racism in the Past.   Racism is not a modern invention. It is seen in the ancient writings of India and China. Ever since, it has been a theme in history. Before last century, most Europeans believed racial differences were due largely to environment. Humans were seen as blank slates at birth on which experience would draw differing profiles. Many people thus believed that racial differences could be easily decreased. Some thought education was the key to closing the gaps between the cultures of races. Others believed that the racial features were due mostly to climate. On the whole, Europeans before the nineteenth century saw racial differences as something that could be changed. This view often was grounds for scornful treatment of the "inferior" races. The attitude was often "Those races are not yet developed." The key word was "yet."

In the 1800s, the European view of racial differences changed. It became "Those races can never develop their culture." The earlier aim of helping other races develop was replaced by pity and disgust toward races seen as inferior. In Europe and the United States, "scientific racism" held sway. Science was used to support racism. Most writers on the subject believed that their own races were innately better than others. Rather than searching for truth, science was used to support what was already believed.

The beliefs concerning the origins of races illustrates the tone of science during the nineteenth century. A popular notion on this issue was that the races had been created different from the beginning. Rather than springing from Adam and Eve, the races were thus seen to be innately different. Darwin's ideas were also applied to this reasoning. This tact saw the races as having evolved to differing degrees. In either view, racial differences were seen as permanent and of vital importance.

Science was used to support racist fads during the nineteenth century. Various means were used to measure physical—racial—differences among people. The bumps on a person's head were studied. The skull width and height were measured. All such efforts aimed at proving that some races were less intelligent than others. The theories of scientific racism were widely accepted. They were so vague and so general that they could be made to fit any situation. Moreover, these "theories" were never tested, only supported with helpful, if biased, data.

There is irony in the words "scientific racism." Indeed, the two words contradict each other. Racism is close-minded. The essence of science is the open mind, the courage to let the facts speak the truth. Racism distorts facts to fit beliefs.

Discrimination   While prejudice, including its special form racism, is a problem in itself, discrimination is even worse. While prejudice distorts a person's perceptions, discrimination goes beyond oneself to hurt others.

Defining Discrimination.   Discrimination is behavior directed at people because of their membership in some group. The people

SKILL BOX

STEREOTYPE: A belief, based on limited information, about all members of some population.

Spotting Stereotypes

Stereotyping can be an unpleasant, even dangerous, habit. It serves as a basis for prejudice. It can cause social friction and steer us wrong. This can be avoided by learning how to recognize stereotypes.

Stereotyping may be a natural outgrowth of our daily efforts to cope with limited data. We must make decisions every day without full information on the matter at hand. When we find ourselves in this situation, we often generalize, that is, we assume that the data we have represent most or all similar cases. For example, say we must deal with a graduate of a certain college. We have already met two other people who went to the same school. Both were stuffy. We might conclude from this sample of two persons that most or all graduates of that college are also stuffy. This general picture of all such people is a stereotype.

A stereotype is a means of expressing attitudes, not describing reality. We might hold stereotypes about people who hold certain jobs, drive certain cars, or belong to certain races. The traits assigned to those people may be positive or negative, but they probably exaggerate. The essence of stereotypes is that they are based on too few facts.

Stereotypes help us simplify the world around us, but the problem is that too often they give us a picture that is too simple to be accurate. When science makes conclusions on data from small samples, the data have been selected so that they represent all the cases. A stereotype, on the other hand, is based on whatever data have fallen into our hands. It gives us a picture that is simple but likely to be wrong.

Stereotypes are not difficult to spot. When some trait is applied to all members of any large group, we should be suspicious. In no large group are we likely to find any trait in all the members. Humans are just too unique for that to be likely. "They are all like that" usually means that the speaker does not know all of "them." To spot stereotypes, look for general statements applying good or bad judgments to many people with no evidence of thorough sampling. Here are some examples of stereotyping. "Football players—well, you know, none of them are very bright." "Of course, he's hardworking. He's one of those immigrants from Southeast Asia. They're all very industrious."

DISCRIMINATION: Behavior, usually negative, directed at a person, based on that person's membership in some group.

are treated differently simply because of their membership. While we may hear of negative discrimination, discrimination can also be positive, as when a restaurant always serves the local football team first and nobody else minds. Discrimination in its most usual and important form, however, is negative. This form will be our focus here. Negative discrimination can range from snubs to restrictions to attacks and results in resentment and reduced life opportunities. It is the worst outcome of viewing people as "them" as outsiders.

Discrimination is frequently linked with prejudice, because the latter often leads to the former. That is, the behavior (discrimi-

Discrimination is one result of viewing people as outsiders.

nation) springs from the attitude (prejudice). But the opposite can also occur. The members of a group may be treated badly because they are seen as competing or as disturbingly different. To justify this discrimination, prejudice may be formed. The result: "We oppress them because they deserve it; they are inferior." We can compete much more effectively with people if we believe they are not worthy of fair play.

An example of this mistreatment is the way white settlers pushed the American Indians off the land for which the two groups were competing. Surely the government officials involved eased their consciences concerning the lies they told and the massacres they ordered by telling themselves that the Indians were only vicious heathens.

Sometimes prejudice and discrimination are not linked. One may appear without the other. The attitude may not produce the behavior for several reasons. The prejudiced person may treat the target group fairly because of fear, peer pressure, or the law. On the other hand, a person may discriminate against others without being prejudiced. This may be the result of pressure to conform, of customs, or of law.

A Short History of Discrimination. Like prejudice, discrimination has gone through a few phases in the last few hundred years. In medieval Europe, discrimination was often practiced against newly discovered peoples. The basis for some of this treatment was religious belief. Christians were viewed as fully human and therefore deserving of humane treatment. But there was much discussion about how human non-Christians were. Often such people were not seen as fully human—until they were Christianized—and so were treated as nonhumans. From this viewpoint, exploiting a non-Christian could be seen as no worse than kicking a dog.

During the nineteenth century, a new basis of discrimination evolved. Europeans based their discrimination on social class and, later, on national origin. In the United States, treatment of people was based on race and national origin in the nineteenth century and the early twentieth century. None of this discrimination has disappeared in this nation or any other nation. Still, the discrimination that came with the large-scale migrations of last century has decreased in scale. Its basis in the United States has shifted mostly from religion to race today.

Discrimination is not always obvious, or even intentional. Many educational and occupational barriers in the U.S. today are part of institutional discrimination. The job requirements, the admissions qualifications, or the money needed to take advantage of seemingly open opportunities, can effectively prevent minority participation. For example, the poll tax, a fee required of people who wish to vote, was used for decades in some southern areas to discourage black voting. Because most of the blacks in those areas were desperately poor, the poll tax prevented their political participation. In other cases, however, institutional discrimination is more obscured, and perhaps unintentional. Job qualifications may involve prior job experience or educational backgrounds which most minority group members lack. As the qualifications do not mention race or ethnic background, they appear to be nondiscriminatory, but such qualifications effectively lock out many minorities.

Institutional discrimination thus works as a screen. Just as a screen door looks open from a distance, so do many opportunities in the U.S. However, just as the screen prevents entry of "undesirables," so does institutional discrimination prevent minorities from entering fully into the economic mainstream.

How Minorities Respond to Discrimination.   Minority-group relations are the product of two factors: the policies of the majority and the response of the minority to that treatment. We have been discussing the actions of the majority; we now turn our attention to the minority response. Four major types of minority responses have been described by social scientists: assimilation, pluralism, avoidance, and aggression.[7]

ASSIMILATION: The process by which a socially distinct group takes on the cultural traits of the dominant group.

Assimilation.   Assimilation has been the most common course followed by minorities in this nation. In this process, the members of ethnic groups lose their ethnic identity. This is the "melting pot" image. Group differences tend to decrease as minority groups take on the cultural traits of the majority.

An essential part of assimilation in the U.S. is the shift from the ethnic group's language to English. The shift is common between early generations, and occurs as more intimate social contacts outside of the ethnic group are established.[8]

The dominant group too is affected by the process of assimilation. Some parts of the minority group's culture become part of the dominant culture. This may involve such elements as music, food, and language.

Even if the majority group allows it, not all minority-group members desire to become assimilated. It is true that for most minorities the process has been the road to acceptance and success and the way to escape discrimination. But assimilation has its costs. It may involve changing one's name or even one's religion. It means denying part of one's self. Ties with one's past must be broken. Some minority-group members have refused to pay such costs.

CULTURAL PLURALISM: The condition in which ethnic groups remain culturally distinct and suffer no unfair treatment because of it.

Pluralism.   In the past two decades, many ethnics have resisted the "melting pot" process. They seek to maintain their cultural identity while also demanding fair treatment. The image of a salad bowl is more appealing to these people than that of a melting pot. From this attitude come such slogans as "Irish power," "Proud to be Polish," and "Black is beautiful."

While ethnic pride is fashionable in the United States today, it was not always so. Most notably, in the nineteenth century immigrants were expected to become fully American. Strong pressures were put on these newcomers to drop their foreign ways, and most did so.

When housing segregation creates large communities with many minority members, they can develop their own occupational network to some extent. For example, when members of the majority group do not want to work in the minority neighborhood, this opens positions for minorities in teaching and community service work. A sufficiently large minority population can support a number of minority professionals, business owners, and tradespeople.[9] Thus, having one's own large minority community can force or allow the group to stand on its own.

Pluralism is appealing, but it has its drawbacks also. While it adds vigor and flavor to a culture, it fosters division too. The maintenance of ethnic lines prevents social cohesion. In addition, ethnic differences serve as bases for inequality. In our country we have learned that it is difficult to be separate yet equal.

Avoidance. Other minority responses are less common. One is withdrawal from the cultural mainstream. Some ethnic groups try to isolate themselves in order to avoid discrimination. They form colonies in which they feel more at home. Ethnic enclaves such as Chinatowns are the result.

Aggression. Another minority response is aggression. The aim of this militant approach is to change the social system in order to gain better treatment for the minority. Sometimes the goal is to turn the tables and become dominant.

The first two responses listed above, assimilation and pluralism, are part of a pattern of adaptation that developed among immigrants in the United States during the nineteenth century. In the first stage of this pattern, the newly arrived immigrants often clung to the old ways, seeking out their fellow ethnics. They were not ready to be Americanized. But the children of these people usually were ready. Because of the pressures they faced in the schools and on the streets, this second generation sought to hide their ethnicity. They jumped into the melting pot to avoid the punishments of being an ethnic. By the third generation, many groups had merged with the mainstream American culture. They were secure in their social standing, so much that they could come out of the "ethnic closet" and boast of their ethnicity. Much of the ethnic pride we see today is the result of this development.

This success story does not apply equally to all groups. Some ethnics were so similar to the dominant culture that they found it easy to fit in. Others were so very distinct culturally or racially that they remain targets of discrimination.

MINORITY GROUPS IN THE UNITED STATES

So far, our discussion of minority groups has been largely academic. We have explored the meanings of the terms involved and the general patterns of minority-group relations. It is now time to turn our attention to some of the people involved in these patterns: the major minority groups in the United States. First, the general pattern of past minority-group relations in the United States must be described in order to set the scene. Then we will be ready to deal with several specific groups.

Past Minority-Group Relations in the United States

Minority group relations are prominent in the social history of the United States. Strangely enough, the natives of the land, the American Indians, were not dominant. Instead, a struggle ensued among various immigrating ethnic groups. Some of these immigrants were attracted by the promise of America, others were escaping from problems at home. America was widely described in other countries as a land of golden opportunity, where land and jobs were plentiful. This image was conveyed by word of mouth as well as public relations efforts aimed at attracting new settlers. Other people came because of war and oppression at home. And some came in chains.

The English settlers in North America established themselves early as the dominant group. They were by far the most numerous group, and they made their culture *the* culture. They built the foundation of American culture with their political heritage, language, religions, and customs. Even today, the White Anglo-Saxon Protestant (WASP) holds a dominant position in this country.

Besides these English settlers, most other early immigrants were also white and Protestant. They came from northern Europe. These people brought with them values that fit smoothly with

FIGURE 8–1
Immigration: 1920–1984

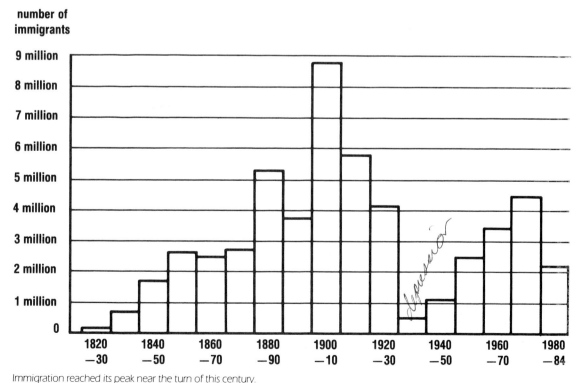

number of immigrants

Immigration reached its peak near the turn of this century.

Source: U.S. Bureau of the Census, *Statistical Abstract of the United States: 1986* (Washington, D.C.) 1985.

those of the numerous British colonists. Distinctions among the various groups were not sharp enough to create serious ethnic tensions.

During the nineteenth century, new kinds of immigrants began to make ethnicity a source of problems. During the first half of that century, the first big waves of Catholics arrived from Ireland, followed by Germans and Scandinavians. During the last quarter, people from eastern and southern Europe arrived by the millions. Not only were most people in this last wave non-Protestant, but most did not even speak English. What was worse, in the eyes of the dominant group, they did not quickly lose their ethnic distinctiveness.

All these waves of "new" immigrants were met with prejudice and discrimination. America became quite conscious of ethnicity. The dominant group feared that its status would be subverted by these foreign peoples. Though these immigrants offered their skills to our expanding economy, they were often scorned and ridiculed for their "foreign" ways. They were considered inferior and dangerous. Indeed, it seems that as a minority group increases in population size and is seen as a political and economic threat, discrimination against it increases.[10] America was willing to use immigrants as laborers but would not offer them respect if they came from the "wrong" country. From the 1890s, efforts were made to restrict the flow of this new immigration from southern Europe and Asia, though quotas allowed much immigration from northern Europe and South America. Ethnicity had joined race as a basis for discrimination in the United States.

The Immigration Act of 1965 established new, nonracist quotas. Under this law, a person's chances of being admitted to this country did not depend on race. Instead, preference was given to the relatives of those already admitted and to those with special skills. A result of this 1965 act was the admittance of more people from Asia and southern Europe.

TABLE 8-1.   Immigrants, by Country of Birth

In recent decades the primary source of immigrants has shifted from Europe and neighbors of the U.S. to Asia and our neighbors. Much of this shift is due to the Immigration Act of 1965.

	1961–1970	1984
Europe	1,238,600	64,100
Asia	445,300	256,300
South America	228,300	37,500
Africa	39,300	15,500
Australia	9,900	1,300
New Zealand	3,700	600
North America	1,351,100	166,700
Canada	286,700	10,800
Mexico	443,300	57,600
Caribbean	519,500	74,300

SOURCE: U.S. Immigration and Naturalization Service, *Statistical Yearbook* 1984.

The next major immigration legislation was the Immigration Reform Act of 1986, intended to check the increasing flow of illegal immigrants, especially from South and Central America. Under this law, employers can be fined up to $10,000 for each illegal alien they hire, and the employers are responsible for making sure that prospective workers have valid citizenship or passport papers. The law also grants amnesty to illegal aliens who can show that they entered the United States before January 1, 1982, and have lived here continuously since. Whether or not this law will prove to be effective in limiting illegal immigration remains to be seen.

Today most of the immigrants have blended into the melting pot or salad bowl, but to varying degrees many have retained some of their distinctiveness. In fact, a survey of ethnic group assimilation in recent years showed that third generation ethnic groups are still distinguishable from the core English group regarding educational, occupational, and income levels.[11]

Some ethnic pride has only recently been reborn, for others, ethnicity was never lost. Recent arrivals face essentially the same choices as those in the past. They can cling to their ethnic identity or try to join the majority culture. While more ethnics choose pluralism as their goal today, recent arrivals may find this a costly luxury. Most groups have found acceptance and success most easily through assimilation. Only after they achieved social success have most groups found it safe to enjoy their ethnicity.

Blacks in America   The plight of blacks early in the history of our nation went from bad to worse. The first blacks arrived in 1619, bound by contract for a certain number of years. Soon, however, laws were passed making blacks slaves for life.

The Slavery Era.   In the status of slave, blacks were defined as property, with few rights. They could not vote, own property, or testify against whites. Limits were placed on their public gatherings, schooling, and relations with whites. Attempts were made to destroy their families and African heritage. Even the freed blacks lived in a disdained world separate from whites.

Most blacks worked on Southern plantations. Many had had prior experience in Africa in large-scale farming or in crafts. They quickly replaced Indian slaves and whites as laborers on plantations. At first, slaves were used in tobacco-farming and later in cotton-farming. By the late 1700s, both crops were waning. Then the invention of the cotton gin made cotton more profitable and gave a boost to slavery.

White attitudes toward blacks from North to South differed only in degree. Southerners had reason to fear blacks where blacks clearly outnumbered whites. In South Carolina, for instance, blacks made up 70 percent of the population. The few blacks living in the North were seen as competitors for jobs. Though many Northerners were against slavery, few wanted blacks to be freed. Of course, there were social rankings among blacks. Before the

Since the 1960s, blacks have achieved more access to the political process. Jesse Jackson, for example, has achieved national political prominence.

Civil War, free blacks were distinguished from slaves. Among the slaves, household servants (usually of lighter skin color) ranked higher than the field-workers. But to most whites, all blacks were lumped together and scorned.

After Slavery. After the Civil War the status of blacks in the South improved for a while, but after protective federal troops were withdrawn, blacks again faced oppression. Slavery was replaced by a strict system of segregation, called Jim Crow. This system was maintained by terrorism, laws, and custom in the South. The few blacks in the North also were denied equal life opportunities.

Since World War I, blacks have been moving out of the rural South and into cities. In 1900 some 90 percent of blacks lived in the southern and border states. In 1960 the figure was about sixty percent. Most of this movement was to the factory cities, largely in the North. Today, only about half of all blacks still live in the South. Four out of five blacks live in cities, many in the largest ones. Increasingly, blacks are moving to the newer cities of the South. Still, all this movement did little to change the social status of blacks; they often moved from rural poverty to urban slums.

Since World War II, welfare spending had been increasing, largely due to the nation's increasing wealth and federal incentives.[12] This spending may have eased somewhat the plight of blacks, but not until the 1960s did the civil rights movement crack the segregation system. In 1964 the Civil Rights Act was passed and the door to equality was opened wider. Since the 1960s, each step forward for blacks has highlighted the steps still to be taken. For example, while more blacks moved to suburbs during the 1960s, probably because of federal legislation and black activism, the trend did not continue into the 1970s.[13] Another area of some advancement is athletics. Many successful athletes are blacks; few, however, are coaches, and few are found in golf, swimming, or tennis.

The social status of blacks has not changed uniformly in the U.S. Research has revealed regional variations in the amount of occupational inequality between blacks and whites.[14] Such inequality increased in the nation as a whole in the 1940s and decreased in the 1960s and 1970s. During the 1980s, however, the inequality sharply increased in the South and decreased elsewhere.

More important than any regional differences in black progress, however, are the class differences. The black middle class has enjoyed improved opportunities in jobs, housing, and education. Those blacks were the ones who were prepared with the middle-class values and attitudes when many discriminatory barriers fell in the 1960s and 1970s. This middle class has pulled ahead, while the black poor have slipped further and further behind. The plight of the black "underclass" is worsening as more poor blacks, especially young males, drop out of the labor force and add to statistics that speak of social failure. The black under-

Governor Bob Martinez of Florida illustrates the growing political power of Hispanic Americans.

class is riddled with rising rates of crime, illegitimacy, drug addiction, and welfare dependency.[15]

The general expectation has been that the rise of the black middle class and the fall of the black underclass would create a division within the black population that would shatter the solidarity of the Civil Rights era. A report for the National Urban League asserts that the gap has not been so divisive.[16] The report claims that the black elite has not been making their progress at the expense of the poorer blacks, and that blacks in both groups share similar attitudes regarding the struggle for equality. As the gap continues to grow, however, we may see increased tensions between the successful blacks and blacks without hope.

Hispanic Americans

The second-largest minority in the United States is a diverse one. It includes people with Spanish, Mexican, Puerto Rican, and Cuban heritages. These groupings are often put under one label—Hispanic—though they differ in important ways.

The Mexican-Americans are the largest part of the Hispanic population in the United States. These people are concentrated in the cities of Texas and California. They often are clustered in *barrios, or ghettos.* An unknown but probably large number of these people entered the United States illegally. The group suffers serious discrimination, in some places as bad as that shown any minority in the United States.

Hispanos include the Hispanics who became citizens when much of the southwestern part of the United States was annexed after the Mexican-American War in 1848. The category of Hispanos also includes those who have claimed "pure" (non-Indian), Spanish ancestry. Some of these have managed to retain a somewhat higher social standing than more recent arrivals from Mexico.

A growing group of Hispanics in the United States are people of Puerto Rican birth or ancestry. Their immigration to the States rose sharply after World War II. Most of these people live in New York City. Like Mexican-Americans, they suffer because of their low levels of skills and schooling and the language barrier. Another problem is that, while some Puerto Ricans are blue-eyed blondes, others have dark skin. Thus, for some, racism is an added challenge.

Since Castro took over Cuba in 1959, thousands of Cubans have come to the United States. Most have stayed in Miami. Many who immigrated earliest were from middle-class backgrounds and so were better equipped than most other Hispanics to survive in American society. The Cuban-Americans have established some strong Spanish-speaking communities with growing political clout. The largest Cuban enclave in the United States, in Miami, has developed its own local economy with many immigrant-owned firms.[17]

American Indians

The history of discrimination faced by native North Americans is one based on group conflict. When whites wanted what the Indians had, the whites would get it. The object of the struggle was land. From this conflict came the devastation of the native cultures.

From the start in the United States, relations between the farmers and the Indians were hostile. A few missionaries tried to protect the Indian, but soon massacres by both groups occurred. The "noble savage" soon came to be seen simply as a savage. Exploitative policies were used to move the Indians out of the colonists' way. As early as 1650, because of settlers' demands for land, the "reservation" policy was used to push Indians westward. By promising them ownership of the lands not then wanted by whites, the Indians were pushed farther west over the years. By 1846, with few exceptions, all Indian groups had been moved to the western half of the United States.

This removal of Indian tribes from the eastern to the western part of the nation was supported by the government. The Removal Act of 1830 supplied money to move the tribes to what is now Oklahoma. Usually the tribes were given western land for their eastern land. They were not, however, given the choice to decline the offer. The removal of the Cherokees from Georgia showed the government at its worst in this regard. The discovery of gold on the tribal land made whites eager to force the Indians off. The state pressured the Cherokees to leave. The Supreme Court ruled that the state's actions were illegal, but President Andrew Jackson ignored the ruling and the Cherokees were forced off their land. Thus began the infamous "Trail of Tears." The tribe was forced to march through a bitter winter to Oklahoma. Thousands died along the way.

Of course the West was not a harbor of safety for the Indians any more than the East was. To help transfer desirable Indian land to whites, and also to "civilize" the Indians, the Bureau of Indian Affairs was established. This bureau began as a branch of the War Department, which shows the means used to "civilize" the tribes. The Army was authorized to corral Indians into small areas in order to "tame" them. On the reservation, the Indians were to become harmless wards of the government. The Army was used against tribes who rejected this option. The "Battle of Wounded Knee" is just one case which resulted in massacre.

The government demanded that Indians turn to farming and the white man's ways. Tribal customs were discouraged on the reservations. Schools for the Indians were a prime weapon to destroy the ethnic heritage of the tribes. Later, most of the reservations were broken up into small plots of private property. This was another tactic aimed at destroying the tribal nature and spirit of the American Indian.

Native Americans today have yet to recover from being stripped of their ways and their lands. They are among the poorest of ethnic groups in this country. Many are unemployed or receive public welfare, and the level of education among Indians is generally low. The Indian's plight is better in the cities, and federal poli-

cy encourages urban migration of the Indian. Better jobs, schooling, and housing are available in the cities.

Economic success has a cultural cost for the Indian. The price is often assimilation. It is hard to compete in the game of material success and still maintain Indian values of collective cooperation. The question for the Indians, as for other ethnic groups, is whether they can afford pluralism.

Ethnics, but Not Minorities

On the whole, blacks, American Indians, and Hispanics clearly fit our definition of minorities. There are some other ethnic groups that have been minorities in the past but can be said to have climbed out of the social cellar of the United States. Two clear examples are the Jews and the Asians. Largely because of their focus on education, these groups have overcome past persecutions in this country and now enjoy much better opportunities. In fact, Jews now have a higher rate of reaching national prominence than people of English origin.[18]

But Jews, as well as Japanese Americans, still face problems. One study cites continuing subordination of even highly educated Japanese Americans, their separateness shown in their distinct value systems, family relations, and community participation.[19] While Japanese Americans still face some problems because of their ethnic membership, they have "climbed the class structure more rapidly than many white immigrant groups."[20]

Also included in the ethnic success stories are the so-called "white ethnics." This term is used to include mostly the more recent immigrants from southern and eastern Europe. These Poles, Slavs, Greeks, and Italians, many of whom were Catholic and non-English-speaking, faced poor treatment. After two or three generations they have, on the whole, risen up the social ladder, as had many Irish and Germans earlier. Their ethnicity no longer marks them for serious discrimination.

In these last groups of ethnics can be seen the promise of minority-group relations in the United States. While some of the oldest minority groups in our nation have only recently begun to draw near to social equality, most groups who were minorities in the past are no longer minorities. While the system of minority-group relations has been cruel, it has not prevented most groups from overcoming its obstacles and achieving some measure of success in our nation.

Skill Reinforcer 8-2

Evaluate this reasoning:

1. The experience of Irish and German immigrants in this nation has been typical of all other immigrant groups to this nation.

2. Irish and German immigrants in time worked their way up the social ladder in America.

3. All other immigrant groups in the United States have over time worked their way up the social ladder.

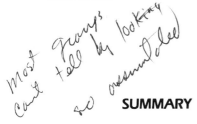

SUMMARY

Minority groups are groups of people dominated by other segments of society. Since the rise of the early nation-states, minorities have been singled out based on their ancestry and racial or cultural distinctions.

Race, in common usage, is imprecisely defined. Many of a race's traits overlap with those of other races. Because of this and the shortcomings of available tests, any intelligence differences that may exist among races are also not well understood.

Members of ethnic groups share a distinct cultural identity. Ethnic groups can be minorities and races, but they may also be neither.

Prejudice is a favorable or negative judgment of a person based on that person's group membership. Explanations of the origin of prejudice focus on the individual's mind, on cultural traditions, and on group conflict.

Racism is a form of prejudice based on the victim's racial membership. It is an ancient problem that even enjoyed the support of science during the nineteenth century.

Discrimination is the treatment accorded a person because of his or her group membership. It may cause or be caused by prejudice. The victims' responses can include assimilation (losing ethnic distinctiveness) and pluralism (retaining ethnic identity while being treated with respect). Avoidance and aggression may be responses too.

Until the 1800s, immigrants to the United States were largely English-speaking and Protestant. As these traits changed, Americans began to view immigration with less favor.

The plights of blacks, Hispanics, and Native Americans were described. These groups can still be classed as minorities, though not all ethnic groups can be.

Problems remain in our minority-group relations. Two solutions present themselves. We can try to prevent the immigration of any more "different" peoples, while we either maintain our intergroup differences or try to erase them. Or we can use education and other tools to foster tolerance for groups and just judgments of individuals, to the extent that human nature will allow. This last path seems the most promising.

SPECIAL TOPIC

Affirmative Action: A Good Tool to Help Minorities?

Before we deal with the debate over affirmative action, an introduction may be helpful. Affirmative action is a strategy born of the civil rights movement of the 1960s. It is not a law, but a policy of the federal government. The efforts of various agencies in this regard aim at improving the life chances of minority groups. Most of these efforts focus on job-hiring and admission to colleges. Schools and businesses are sometimes faced with loss of federal funds if their enrollment or hiring of minorities do not reflect population proportions. For example, if blacks comprise one-eighth of the population, it may be required that this proportion be enrolled or hired when federal funds are used. Rulings by the Supreme Court have basically upheld such goals (sometimes called quotas).

Affirmative action is one of those issues about which reasonable people can honestly disagree. There are valid arguments on both sides. Here we will explore the main questions concerning affirmative action. Both sides will be presented.

CAN AFFIRMATIVE ACTION PROGRAMS BE FAIR?

No

Affirmative action is reverse discrimination. It is clear that members of several minority groups are given preference because of these programs. The result is a decrease in opportunities for people who do not belong to these selected groups. In a democratic system, all groups are entitled to an equal chance. Thus any program that results in unequal chances is contrary to our basic social values.

People who have in no way caused the disadvantages of any minority can suffer from affirmative-action programs. Their chances for being hired are lowered simply because they belong to a group that is out of favor. In this view, affirmative action causes the blameless to suffer at the expense of individuals who are presumed to have suffered because of past wrongs done to their group. This applies not only to the person applying for a job but also to the employer. The owner of a business has the right to protect his or her interests by hiring the most qualified applicants. Affirmative action infringes on this right.

The quotas of affirmative-action programs ignore individual needs. A person who belongs to a dominant group may have suffered deprivation. Yet this person, because of his or her group membership, might lose a job to someone who enjoyed many advantages. The individual's needs are ignored in the presumptions based on group membership. Not all minority-group members need or deserve special help.

Another problem with the aim of affirmative action is the selection of targets. Blacks, women, Hispanics, and American Indians are usually the only people who are helped by affirmative action. A case could be made for other groupings, such as rural southerners, Appalachian whites, or migrant laborers. Furthermore, homosexuals, short people, and fat people suffer social handicaps. All could be described as underprivileged. All suffer disadvantages. None are offered the special protections of affirmative action. The targets selected are simply those groups that have been the most effective in promoting their interests.

If the goal of affirmative action is limited to a few minority groups, it may be feasible, though not fair. If the goal is to equalize life chances for all Americans, the target must be vastly enlarged. This would be fairer, but it is not feasible.

Another injustice of these programs lies in the nature of the enforcers. Affirmative action is largely in the hands of unelected bureaucrats, who have power of judge and jury in these cases. Enforcement efforts have ranged from lax to heavy-handed. There is no guarantee of fairness, "nor can there be."

Yes, The Programs Can Be Fair

While there are several arguments against the fairness of affirmative-action's programs, none of them can hide one simple fact: The present system, without affirmative action, would be unjust. There is a wrong—unequal opportunity—and some positive action must be taken to right that wrong.

The arguments about the unfairness of affirmative action ignore the past treatment of some minority groups that has left them disadvantaged today. That argument rarely mentions that discrimination has reduced the past opportunities of minority groups. In a discussion about equal opportunities, we cannot ignore the current impact of these past wrongs. When we hear the complaint that some people are given an unfair advantage because of their group membership, we hear little mention of the group's disadvantages. To speak of justice, we must look at the history of the problem. We cannot ignore the past.

Also, if we do indeed want to be fair, we cannot just invite everyone to take a slice of the pie. "Symbolically viewed, if we cannot tell the poor to go homestead on free land, we may have to share some unfree land with them. If we cannot siphon them off onto unclaimed territory, we may have to adjust our own claims to what territory there is." [21]

There Is No Easy Answer

The basic problem with affirmative action is that it creates conflict among the rights of the institution, of each person, and of minorities.[22] First, the institution is expected to serve society effectively. This entails hiring or selecting the most qualified candidates. But its role also entails serving the larger social goal of equalizing as much as possible the life chances of all people. At the same time, each person is entitled to just treatment. But just treatment is not always equal treatment. People may deserve a boost if they, with their group, have been cheated. This brings us to the conflicts among various groups. A minority group might be seen as deserving a boost, but it will be at the expense of others.

There seem to be no clear-cut answers to these conflicts. None of the rights discussed here are absolute, yet all must be taken into account. This is the task of the makers of affirmative-action policy. No one's rights should be ignored. Instead, it must be determined which rights are to be given more weight and how long the policy should last. To accomplish this will not be easy, but it is possible.

CAN AFFIRMATIVE ACTION PROGRAMS ACCOMPLISH THEIR GOALS?

No

For all the injustice and resentment affirmative action causes, it does not achieve its goal, which is gender and ethnic equality. For several reasons, hiring or admissions quotas will not accomplish these ends.

One reason is that too many Americans view affirmative action with disfavor. Polls show that white Americans favor helping blacks get jobs and education, but oppose the use of quotas.[23] After all, quotas threaten the prospects of white male workers. Like most other government policies in our nation, public cooperation is vital for the success of affirmative action. This is notably clear in the private sector. Corporations and private schools have the means to evade the aims of such policies. And whether this evasion is based on a lack of cooperation or on the sheer difficulty in changing a well-established occupational system, affirmative action programs face what one writer calls "structural inertia," which will insure that progress is slow.[24]

A related matter is that these programs are for many people a matter of race or gender. So long as affirmative action is seen as aid for blacks or women, many other Americans will refuse to cooperate. This will limit the success of the programs in creating true equality.

Further, affirmative action produces resentment. Data from a national survey show that whites tend to perceive widespread reverse discrimination, in favor of minorities and against whites.[25] Those who lose jobs or promotions to people advantaged by minority-group membership cannot be expected to be understanding of broad social goals. A backlash of racial jealousy and hatred may result. This is not the kind of atmosphere that will produce acceptance or equality. The unfair-

ness of affirmative action thus thwarts its own aims.

Even when affirmative action works, its benefits are spread unequally. Black women have enjoyed much more progress in the civilian labor market than black men, perhaps discouraging the formation of stronger, married-couple households. More black women have gained private sector jobs, and at a faster rate, than black men. One reason may be that employers prefer to "kill two birds with one stone" by hiring an individual who represents two favored groups, blacks and women.[26]

Affirmative action goals are stated in terms of population proportions. As Allan Ornstein, a theorist in this area, points out, these are not proper measurements of equal job opportunities.[27] He says it is unrealistic, for example, to require that 12 percent of all college teachers be black simply because blacks are 12 percent of the population. College teachers are selected not from the general population but from the highly educated segment of the nation. Only about 1 percent of all qualified people are black. The demand that colleges ensure that blacks comprise 12 percent of their staffs ignores the proportion of blacks in the pool of qualified persons.

There are two responses to this quota squeeze: greatly increase the supply of qualified blacks or lower hiring requirements. Of course, the first response is preferable, but it takes time. The institution being squeezed by quotas can often do little but resort to the second response. Thus affirmative action can accomplish its goals, if at all, by lowering standards. This dilemma will be discussed further, later in this essay.

Yes, The Programs Can Accomplish Their Goal

Affirmative action is working today. It is helping minority-group members to get education and jobs that might have been out of their reach. This will break the vicious cycle of discrimination, lack of opportunity, and poverty.

It is true that affirmative action must be accepted by most Americans if it is to work. In this regard, it must be remembered that affirmative action is not intended to be permanent. It is merely a tool to be used as long as it is needed.

CAN AFFIRMATIVE ACTION BE USED WITHOUT WEAKENING OUR SOCIETY?

No

Minorities in this nation produce a small proportion of people qualified to take advantage of job or school opportunities. The only way affirmative action can be used today is by lowering selective standards for those opportunities. That is, members of minority groups must be given preference even if they are less qualified than other people. This means that more merely average professionals will be produced by our schools. The quality of our institutions may drop. In this way, we will lose some of our productive ability. This will clearly lower the efficiency of our economy.

In some fields, pressures to hire minority-group members are so strong that some institutions cannot hire the most qualified of all applicants. Instead, the search is for the most qualified of minority-group applicants. Standards must be lowered in order to hire "qualifiable" minority applicants. Until the supply of qualified minority-group persons increases, this lowering of standards will continue to do its damage. The question is, how much loss are we willing to accept while waiting for enough minority workers to become fully qualified?

Many affirmative-action programs involve jobs where high skill levels are vital. For example, these programs can help determine who will become doctors, whose decisions on the job directly affect the lives of others. We cannot expect citizens to settle for any but the most qualified professionals. This is where merit, though it is elusive and hard to measure, is of vital importance.

Also, our institutions have the duty of maximizing our human resources. That means matching jobs and training with the most qualified people. Our government agencies should be staffed with the most able workers. Our colleges and graduate schools should fill their seats with the most promising students. If our institutions settle for less than the best, the health of our system will be damaged.

Besides hurting our production, affirmative action damages our morale. People who worked hard to qualify for rewards feel cheated when those rewards are given to someone less qualified. The resulting resentment, apa-

thy, and frustration are not healthy for any social system.

Yes, The Programs Can Be Used Without Weakening Our Society

The critics of affirmative action fear that it threatens our merit system of selection, in which rewards are supposed to go to the most able. But our system is not based solely on merit. It is neither objective nor as fair as claimed. Affirmative action aims at changing not a perfect and just system but one with built-in biases.

Admission to college, for example, is not based solely on merit. Factors other than test scores (which themselves are not perfect measurements of merit) are used to select students. Those who are from certain regions, who are athletes, whose parents are alumni are often given preference. This is not a pure merit system. Surely race, sex, or ethnicity can be considered along with these factors without causing great injustice.

The same is true of many hiring decisions. Few are based solely on such objective criteria as test scores. Often cultural criteria are used. People with excellent test scores may not have the "right" manners or values. Their life-style may not fit in with those of the people who already dominate the field. This means that people reared in a minority subculture will be handicapped, even if they are technically qualified. A "good old boy" system may thus lock out qualified women or ethnics in a so-called merit system. Even if a minority-group member is hired, the climb up the ladder may be doubly difficult for such an outsider. Even though he or she is skilled, he—and especially she—may be excluded from the fishing trips and after-hours drinks so important in many jobs. The only access the woman or ethnic member has may be through affirmative action.

Many selection systems should and do use subjective ratings of workers, not just merit. Personal traits, such as leadership and "pep," are included in some systems. The importance of "personal chemistry" should not be and usually is not ignored in evaluating applicants for a school or job. Thus, to claim that merit systems are based on objective assessments of workers is deluding. And the claim that affirmative action threatens the blind justice of "merit" systems is false.

The claim that productivity will decrease because of affirmative action is also doubtful. A system is most efficient that uses its human resources most fully. Affirmative action, while it may produce some short-term loss in efficiency, helps bring all citizens into the pool of human resources. It will help establish a foothold for minority groups in the system of success. In the long run, affirmative action will increase our production by enlarging our labor pool.

Some critics of affirmative action claim that it is unjust and dangerous because it aims to equalize rewards regardless of merit. But most proponents of affirmative action realize that merit must not be ignored in distributing social rewards. The intent of these programs is simply to delete some of the biases in the present systems of selection. While it is often not feasible to do away with all biases, affirmative action can rid systems of those biases based on race, gender, and ethnicity. The aim is not equal rewards but an equal chance to earn a share of the unequal rewards. And affirmative action is needed to help equalize those chances.

intent vs what really happens

SELF-TEST QUESTIONS

1. True or false: A minority group is always less than 50 percent of the population.

2. True or false: Minorities have existed in all times and places.

3. True or false: Races are biologically distinct, with no overlap of traits.

4. True or false: Whites are innately smarter than blacks.

5. An ethnic group can be:
   a. a race
   b. a minority
   c. both of the above
   d. none of the above

6. Prejudice is:
   a. rigid
   b. emotional
   c. an attitude
   d. behavior

7. Racism:
   a. is a form of prejudice
   b. is 150 years old
   c. has never been supported by science

8. Discrimination is:
   a. treatment of a person based on his or her personal qualities
   b. treatment of a person based on his or her group membership
   c. only one hundred years old

Match numbers 9–10 to the descriptions on the right:

9. assimilation   a. losing one's ethnic identity and taking on cultural traits of the dominant culture

10. pluralism   b. distinct ethnic groups existing peacefully side by side

11. The immigrants before and after 1800 differed as to _____ and _____.

12. True or false: The life chances for blacks in the United States have improved since right after the Civil War.

13. True or false: The term "Hispanic" includes several groupings.

14. True or false: American Indians suffered because of official government policy.

ANSWERS TO SELF-TEST QUESTIONS

1. False. A minority group can be any proportion of a population. Its oppressed condition, not its size, defines it.
2. False. Minority groups arose only with nation-states. They are not found in earlier cultural stages.
3. False. The biological boundary lines among races are blurred because of the overlap of traits.
4. Any differences in intelligence that may exist among races cannot be proved, so the answer is False.

5. c
6. a, b, c, and not d
7. a
8. b
9. a
10. b
11. language and religion
12. false
13. true
14. true

ANSWERS TO SKILL REINFORCERS

8–1. The *logic* of the syllogism is acceptable; that is, the conclusion is logically deduced from the premises. The *truth* of the syllogism, however, depends on the accuracy of its premises. The first statement, or major premise, is not recognized by most experts as being supported by the evidence. Thus, the conclusion is based on solid (deductive) logic but on an incorrect premise and should therefore be rejected as false.

8–2. The inductive reasoning works logically enough from particular cases to a general statement, but it is based on an untrue statement: the first one. Because the experiences of Irish and Germans are *not* typical of all others, we cannot generalize from these two cases to all others.

NOTES

1. Terrence S. Luce, "Blacks, Whites, and Yellows—They All Look Alike to Me," *Psychology Today* 8 (November 1974): 105–8.
2. Graham Kinloch, *The Sociology of Minority Group Relations* (Englewood Cliffs, N.J.: Prentice-Hall, 1978).
3. Neal Finkelstein and Ron Haskins, "Kindergarten Children Prefer Same-Color Peers," *Child Development* 54 (April 1983): 508.
4. Francois Nielsen, "Toward a Theory of Ethnic Solidarity in Modern Societies," *American Sociological Review* 50 (April 1985): 133–49.
5. John Dollard, L. Doob, N.E. Miller, O.H. Mowrer, and R.R. Sears, *Frustration and Aggression* (New Haven: Yale University Press, 1939).
6. T.W. Adorno, E. Frenkel-Brunswik, D.J. Devison, and R.N. Stanford, *The Authoritarian Personality* (New York: Harper & Row, 1950).
7. James W. Vander Zanden, *American Minority Relations* (New York: Ronald Press, 1972): chap. 11–13.
8. Gillian Stevens, "Nativity, Intermarriage, and Mother-Tongue Shift," *American Sociological Review* 50 (February 1985): 74–83.
9. Michael Hout, "Opportunity and the Minority Middle Class," *American Sociological Review* 51 (April 1986): 214–23.
10. Jay Corzine, James Creech, and Lin Corzine, "Black Concentration and Lynchings in the South," *Social Forces* 61 (March 1983): 774–96.
11. Lisa Neidert and Reynolds Farley, "Assimilation in the U.S.: An Analysis of Ethnic and Generational Differences in Status and Achievement," *American Sociological Review* 50 (December 1985): 840–50.
12. Edward Jennings, Jr., "Racial Insurgency, the State, and Welfare Expansion," *American Journal of Sociology* 88 (May 1983): 1220–36.

13. John Stahura, "Suburban Development, Black Suburbanization and the Civil Rights Movement since World War II," *American Sociological Review* 51 (February 1986): 131–44.
14. Mark Fossett, Omer Galle, and William Kelly, "Racial Occupational Inequality, 1940–1980: National and Regional Trends," *American Sociological Review* 51 (June 1986): 421–29.
15. William J. Wilson, "The Black Underclass," *The Wilson Quarterly*, 8 (Spring 1984): 88–99.
16. James D. McGhee, "Black Solidarity: The Tie That Binds," a report for the National Urban League, Washington, D.C., as reviewed in *Wilson Quarterly* 8 (Winter 1983): 47.
17. Kenneth L. Wilson and Alejandro Portes, "Immigrant Enclaves: An Analysis of the Labor Market Experiences of Cubans in Miami," *American Journal of Sociology* 86 (September 1980): 295–319.
18. Stanley Lieberson and Donna K. Carter, "Making It in America: Differences Between Eminent Blacks and White Ethnic Groups," *American Sociological Review* 44 (June 1979): 347–66.
19. Eric Woodrum, "An Assessment of Japanese American Assimilation, Pluralism, and Subordination," *American Journal of Sociology* 87 (July 1981): 157–69.
20. Ibid., p. 157.
21. Daniel C. Maguire, *A New American Justice: Ending the White Male Monopolies* (Garden City, N.Y.: Doubleday & Co., 1980): 27.
22. Robert J. Havighurst, "Individual and Group Rights in a Democracy," *Social Science and Modern Society* 13 (January-February 1976): 13, 25–28.
23. James Kluegel and Eliot R. Smith, "Affirmative Action Attitudes," *Social Forces* 61 (March 1983): 797–824.
24. William E. Feinberg, "At a Snail's Pace: Time to Equality in Simple Models of Affirmative Action Programs," *American Journal of Sociology* 90 (July 1984): 168–81.
25. James Kluegel and Eliot R. Smith, "Whites' Beliefs About Blacks' Opportunity," *American Sociological Review* 47 (August 1982): 518–32.
26. Gary Puckrein, "Moving Up," *Wilson Quarterly* 8 (Spring 1984): 74–87.
27. Allan C. Ornstein, "Quality, Not Quotas," *Social Science and Modern Society* 13 (January-February 1976): 10, 14–17.

SUGGESTED READINGS

Brown, Dee, *Bury My Heart at Wounded Knee.* New York: Holt, Rinehart & Winston, 1972.

Farley, Reynolds. *Blacks and Whites.* Cambridge, Mass.: Harvard University Press, 1984.

Glazer, Nathan, and Moynihan, Daniel. *Beyond the Melting Pot.* Cambridge: M.I.T. Press, 1963.

Gossett, Thomas F. *Race: The History of an Idea in America.* New York: Schocken Books, 1965.

Myrdal, Gunnar. *An American Dilemma.* New York: McGraw-Hill, 1964.

Parrillo, Vincent. *Strangers to the Shores: Race and Ethnic Relations in the United States.* Boston: Houghton Mifflin Co., 1980.

Rose, Peter I. *They and We.* 3d ed. New York: Random House, 1981.

Sowell, Thomas. *Ethnic America: A History.* New York: Basic Books, 1981.

9 THE SOCIAL ORDER: CONFORMITY AND DEVIANCE

A Look at a Deviant

The social order is the web of expectations that helps our dealings with other people run more smoothly. This web is made up of customs and laws that tell us what we should and should not do when dealing with the people around us.

In the book *Manny: A Criminal-Addict's Story* we get an insider's view of a deviant, a person who refuses to conform to the rules of the social order.[1] Manny's deviant behavior has its roots in the subculture of his early years. Illegal means of making money are offered him and, in his teens, so is heroin. Heroin use makes Manny desperate for money. He violates the rules of friendship and kinship as he exploits friends and family to support his habit.

Pretty soon the family is burned out and won't lend me any more dough, I hassle them, but before long they won't be hassled. So, I start stealing from them. I go over to my sister's house when they're all downtown and I walk off with anything that I can hock. This happens a couple of times with relatives and pretty soon they put out the word, "Manny's hooked like a dog. Turn him out like a mad dog."

So, they turn me out. Nothing else they can do. You can't have a dope fiend around the house, mainly because he'll steal everything in sight. A lush's behavior may be undependable and raunchy, but a doper is five times worse than a lush. Once you are wired behind scag, it is life, nothing else lives. A lush flops, passes out, quits. But a dope fiend hustles, scores, and fixes so he can get down. And he has no regrets. He doesn't care at all. If somebody gets wasted in the process of hustling, scoring, and getting down—so . . . what? The doper is a true isolationist. He doesn't give a dam for others. Only insofar as they are a means to score.

Manny's addiction to heroin leads him to an addiction to crime.

One time I remember we'd made two good "withdrawals" in one day, both chain grocery stores. When we'd divvied up the take we each came away with over three thousand. That buys a lot of dope. Besides, I had over an ounce on me at the time. Not actually on me, but stashed. So I didn't need to do any robberies for a while to score bread for dope. But that very same evening I went out with Izzy and we hit two candy stores. Now, what the hell you going to get outa candy stores? Money? Not much. There's the same thrill though when you back those people off and stand there like god and demand that they move like you got them on the end of a string. . .

I was hooked on dope, and hooked bad, during this whole period, but I was also hooked behind robbery.

Prison does not change Manny. He quickly turns to a life of reckless disregard for the social order.

We pulled jobs every day sometimes. Small jobs draw a certain amount of heat because they are the ones that you have to do more often. But they also take a lot less planning. We'd just jump in the car and ride around until we saw a place that might have money. And we'd hit it. Sometimes we only got twenty or thirty dollars, and we'd taken the same risk of having to injure or kill the clerks as if we'd got a million. We thought nothing of it, though.

That last sentence captures Manny's attitude. His story, up until his eventual reform, shows how important it is for the social order to hold a person in check.

Perhaps it is true that love makes the world go 'round, but something more than love is needed if we are to enjoy social interaction fully. What is needed is social order.

SOCIAL ORDER: The web of expectations, in the form of customs and rules, that describes the form our social interaction is to take.

The rules and customs that make up the social order give us some degree of security so that we can live and work with other people. Think for a moment about what it would be like to live among other people without those rules and customs. Would you feel safe walking down the street? What would prevent people from robbing or attacking you? What would it be like to drive a car if there were no rules for drivers to follow? Every outing in your car would be dangerous. Without social order we would all feel threatened, insecure.

CONFORMITY: Compliance; here we are dealing with how much a person complies with, or follows, the rules and customs of the social order.

The social order is based on conformity. The people in society must follow the customs and rules of the social order. To the extent that people do that, we can relax in the knowledge that they will do what is expected of them. To the extent that people fail to conform, we cannot enjoy the security that the social order can bring. Behavior that does not conform to the social order is called deviance.

DEVIANCE: Failure to conform to the social order.

In this chapter we will explore how the social order is maintained and defined. First we will study two means for ensuring that most people conform to the social order. Then we will deal with the failure to conform to the social order: deviance.

TWO TOOLS FOR CONFORMITY

Norms

NORMS: Guidelines to appropriate behaviors.

What Norms Do: Giving Guidance and Comfort. Don't talk with your mouth full. Say "thank you." Do not covet your neighbor's wife. These are all norms, or rules to which members of a system are expected to conform. Norms define for us what behavior is expected and proper for a situation; they act as guidelines for our behavior. Norms tell us what the ideal patterns are. Norms tell us which behavior follows these guidelines and which does not.

Norms provide more than just social order; they give us the comfort of knowing that a certain act will be considered proper by others. If we are in a strange place with people we do not know, we want to find out what rules those people are using. When we have learned the norms, we need not spend so much time guessing what each person's reactions to our behavior will be. We can feel more at ease, because norms mark for us the accepted path. We need not leave this safe path unless we want to.

Why We Follow Norms: Going Along to Get Along.   Why do we not talk with our mouths full, and why do we say "thank you"? Most people conform to most norms most of the time. Few of us see the need for, or any payoff in, challenging established norms. Most of us want to fit in with—rather than fight it out with—society. Those who follow the norms of a group are accepted as members. Those who defy the norms are rejected, as Manny in the chapter opener was rejected by his family. Most of us would rather belong.

Bierstadt lists other reasons why most of us accept most norms [2]. First, we are socialized to accept the established norms of our group. Once a code of conduct has been agreed upon, it gains great force and weight for later generations. It is difficult to resist such a powerful part of our culture. From the moment of birth, we learn which behaviors bring reward and which bring punishment. In this way, we are encouraged to follow the norms of the culture.

Another reason most people conform to most norms involves habit. Once we have learned to conform to certain norms, we tend to continue. Habits are comfortable. Challenging patterns are likely to be seen as a more difficult path. We stick with those patterns that make us feel secure. Thus we conform to established norms.

We also conform to norms because it is practical to do so. We submit to their discipline because it allows us to get things done. On the job, on the highway, or waiting in line, most of us realize that norms are useful. By limiting to some degree the freedom of each person, we can enjoy the rewards of cooperation.

Kinds of Norms: From Manners to Murder.   Rules that tell us to say "thank you" are in a different class from those that tell us not to say "Your money or your life." Norms range from matters of manners to those of murder. They can be grouped into three major types. William Sumner described two basic kinds: folkways and mores.[3] Supporting these two types are laws, which are formalized norms. These three categories introduce norms for us.

FOLKWAYS: Norms of no great consequence or weight which deal with everyday, routine matters; they define what is proper and polite.

Folkways.   Some norms deal with everyday actions. They guide us through daily routines. They define what is correct behavior when we greet people, enter a church, eat in a public place, and so forth. They tell us what to wear, how to sit, and what to say. This kind of norm defines what is tasteful or disgusting. It defines what is proper for men, for women, and for children. These norms are called folkways.

Though they deal with routine matters, folkways would surely be missed if they disappeared. Without rules of politeness, we would experience friction many times each day. We would constantly be faced with behavior we found unpleasant. Each person would act on his or her own feelings, so every meeting with a stranger would be something of an adventure. That person might use nearly any greeting, from hugging, to pinching the cheek, to arm wrestling. Such encounters, if not controlled by folkways, could be quite wearisome. Folkways help grease the machinery of social interaction.

Besides reducing social friction, folkways help us to conserve our energies. Because of these guidelines, we need not spend our energies making decisions about routine matters; the decisions have been made for us. This saves us energy as well as embarrassment.

Because folkways do not deal with particularly grave matters, they are supported by only mild sanctions. Rewards for conforming to folkways include smiles and words of praise. These signs of approval and the feelings of acceptance they give are effective rewards for most people. For those who violate folkways, scorn and ridicule are used. Frowns, smirks, and gossip can be effective punishments. The violator of folkways can expect to face discomfort, but not serious attack.

Though folkways are established customs, they can change. Styles of dance and dress seen as indecent in the past are now largely accepted. Courtship is no longer confined to the parlor, and asking a woman's father for her hand is regarded by many as quaint. Indeed, some folkways are very changeable.

FASHION: A short-lived folkway, conformity to which brings esteem.

Fashions and fads are part of these changeable guidelines. Both can be viewed as very temporary folkways. "This year ladies will be wearing short skirts, high shoes, and long hair." "Everybody who is anybody is drinking apple juice and whisky this summer." Fashions such as these can be seen as folkways because they help direct our behavior. They offer guidance concerning not only clothing but also art forms, philosophy, and many other parts of life. Fashions tell us what is—for a while—respectable and proper. Having been chosen by those people whose tastes are respected, fashions serve as beacons to guide us through a confusing array of options.

Unlike most folkways, fashions are not well grounded in custom, so they change quickly. While fashions help us cope with a fast-changing world, they are difficult to follow because they change so rapidly themselves. But this may be the very reason that following fashion brings esteem. While everyone is expected to know and follow the usual folkways, only people "in the know" can follow fashion and thus gain the esteem.

FAD: A very short-lived, intense fashion followed by a limited segment of the population.

"Wearing loincloths and animal skins to class was the rage among students in Boston colleges last month." Folkways like this one that guide only a few people, and only very briefly, are called fads. They have an even shorter life and a narrower following than fashions. While fashions are generally accepted, fads are intensely followed by only small parts of the population. In fact, most people see fads as foolish or silly. Fads often involve songs, slang, or clothing and rarely reappear once they have been dropped.

Fads are followed by only small parts of the population.

MORES (rhymes with "forays"): Serious norms, considered vital to the welfare of the group.

Skill Reinforcer 9-1*

What is the missing statement in this syllogism?

1. Violations of mores are punished severely.
2. . . .
3. Murderers are punished severely.

LAW: A formalized norm, officially decreed and enforced by specified sanctions.

* Answers to the Skill Reinforcers appear at the end of the chapter.

Mores. "You must not kill, rape, or rob." Another kind of norm defines not just what we *should* do, but what we *must* do. This type of norm is not merely a matter of what is nice or proper and what is not. These norms define what is right and wrong, what will and will not be allowed. They are called mores.

Mores are believed to be vital to the welfare of the group. Whether this belief is accurate or not, one who violates one of these norms arouses the wrath of the group. For instance, the person with more than one spouse will be regarded as more than just impolite. Likewise, the person in our culture who abandons a baby, who attacks others at will, or eats human flesh will be seen as a threat to the social fabric, to the welfare of the group.

Because of the perceived importance of mores, they involve strong emotions. Their violation can cause horror or disgust. In fact, a person can feel so strongly about some such norm that he may be unable to violate it himself, even if pressured to do so.

Punishments regarding mores are severe, and can be imposed both by oneself and by others. First, the wrongdoer is likely to feel great guilt as a result of the intensive socialization he or she received from the culture. Such guilt is self-inflicted punishment. Second, besides this internal punishment, the wrongdoer may face anything from beatings and torture to exile and death—all imposed by others.

While mores define what is essential to the order of any group, they vary widely as to time and place. A change of place can bring special circumstances. Westerners who usually would view cannibalism with disgust have in some cases resorted to the act themselves when faced with starvation. Likewise, the cannibal and the baby-killer are not viewed as threats in all cultures because some cultures' mores support such acts. The horrid deviant in one culture may be seen as a solid citizen in others. The definition of mores can change over time too. What was wrong in the past is not always wrong in the present.

Laws. Isn't it good we don't just say, "It is not polite to kill and rob," and leave it at that? Isn't it comforting to know that such norms are backed up by something a lot stronger, so as to control people like Manny, in the chapter preview? Supporting some folkways and most mores is the third kind of norm: laws. Laws are formalized norms. This means they are written (if the culture has writing) and publicly decreed by officials. A special authority is established to enforce these codes of conduct. Specific punishments are carried out by specified people. Enforcement is not left to public opinion.

Laws are not found in all cultures. They are not needed in simple societies, where there is general agreement on social norms. In complex social systems there are more viewpoints on what is right and wrong. There, informal means of social control, such as folkways and mores, are less likely to work. In such cases, more formal norms are needed—laws.

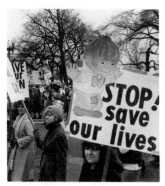

The drive for an anti-abortion amendment illustrates an attempt to legislate morality.

Laws work at various levels of importance. Some laws enforce mores and thus involve strong feelings. For example, the laws against murder and rape are taken quite seriously by most people. Other laws, such as those on illegal parking, arouse little emotion. These kinds are merely ways to minimize disorder. They can be viewed as formalized folkways.

When laws conflict with folkways or mores, they are not likely to be effective. There are many examples of laws that try, without success, to counter such well-established norms. Perhaps the most famous was the Eighteenth Amendment, which banned the making and selling of liquor in the United States. This law was unable to change custom and was abolished. Likewise, many Americans ignore the laws against smoking marijuana.

Still, it is sometimes possible to legislate morality. That is, laws can sometimes change informal norms. Fair employment acts and other laws springing from the civil rights movement of two decades ago have provided the context for changed norms regarding race relations in the United States. This has been possible only because a substantial part of the U.S. population no longer sees equal rights for blacks as a threat to the social welfare.

So far we have explored one means of keeping members of a social system in line. Humans need norms to ensure some degree of social order. Only with such guidelines can we maintain order without inborn controls.

Role and Status

At some point in our childhood we learned that kings are rich, slaves are not free, and that the police officer is either our friend or our enemy. We also learned what little boys and girls are supposed to do and not do. In such cases, we were learning about role, which is another tool that helps ensure that we conform to the social order. Role is what is expected of a person holding a certain social position. Like norms, roles give guidance and direction to our behavior. In this way they help maintain social order. Unlike norms, roles are always linked to specific statuses, or social positions.

We cannot fully explore the concept of role without also dealing with status, so in this section both will be covered. After defining role, we will explore status, from which roles spring.

ROLE: Behaviors and traits expected of a person holding a certain status.

Role: What You Are to Do.   Kings do not beg, slaves do not boss, and police officers do not steal. These are things most of us have learned to expect in the social order. These expectations are the things of which roles are made.

A role is a set of expectations. It defines some of the behaviors and traits that society allows and demands of a person who holds a certain social position. It includes rights as well as duties. It is a script to follow whenever the role comes into play. The roles we are to follow are determined by our status.

STATUS: Socially recognized position.

Status: What You Are. A status is a social position, such as queen, son, or nurse. Such positions or titles are socially recognized; that is, they have meaning to other people. For example, when we hear that some person is a king, we understand what that status implies: wealth and power, a crown and a castle. Each status has a role attached to it, so that certain behaviors are expected of each status.

Many of the most important statuses, such as wife and husband, are paired. Parent-child, boss-employee, student-teacher are other examples. Often the power within such pairs is unbalanced, though this varies from one culture or one time to the next. For example, the husband-wife power balance may be greatly tilted toward the husband in one culture, toward the wife in others, or it may be more balanced in still others. The student-teacher pair shows the change over time. Years ago, the teacher had great power over the student. Recently, the balance in some places has tilted to the student, as the increasing number of assaults on teachers testifies.

Status confused with prestige. There is some confusion about the word "status." Sometimes it is used to mean prestige, or honor. Discussions may consider, for instance, how high or low the "status" of some job is. Some statuses, such as king, do indeed have high prestige. Also, sometimes "status" is used to mean social class. This adds to the confusion. "Upper status" may mean "upper class." Because these usages of the term are so confusing, we will avoid them. "Status" here will mean "social position," whether it is ranked high or low or not ranked at all.

Status confused with role. Status is also confused with role. These two concepts differ from each other but are sometimes used as though they were the same thing. Remember, status is the position, and its role is the behavior expected of that status. In other words, a status helps define what you are; a role is what you are to do.

To show this distinction, we can look at status and role throughout the world. Some statuses, such as mother and father, are found in all cultures. They are universal social positions. But the *role* of mother or father varies from one culture to another. What is proper for mothers in one culture might be considered abuse or neglect in others. Any one status may thus have different roles in different cultures.

Two Types of Status: Work and Luck. Some of our statuses we earn, like champion or hero. Others, such as princess or prince, we are given no matter what we do. Statuses—and with them their roles—can be classified into two types: ascribed and achieved.

ACHIEVED STATUS: Status gained through a person's efforts.

Achieved. Achieved statuses are those we gain through our own efforts. They are the results of things we do and choices we make. They can range from spouse or student to bum or burglar.

Likewise, it is because of some choice or action on our part that we take on the statuses of parent, college graduate, or, like Manny in the chapter opener, drug addict.

ASCRIBED STATUS: Status assigned to a person, regardless of his or her efforts.

Ascribed. Ascribed statuses are those which are assigned to us. Most of these are given to us at birth. Instead of being based on our achievements, ascribed statuses determine the chances we will be given to achieve rewards. These statuses are based on membership in some group or category. Those memberships are not chosen by us but forced upon us. We might have thrust upon us that status of sister, teenager, or Eskimo.

Some statuses are ascribed to us at birth but may be changed later through some choice or effort on our part. We are assigned to a certain social class position by our family membership. Later, we may achieve a different class level. Likewise, we may be assigned by our family to membership in a religion. Later, we can choose to drop it and perhaps take on some other religious beliefs.

Ascribed vs. achieved. Cultures vary as to whether certain statuses are assigned or achieved. A status that is achieved in one culture may be ascribed in others. In the United States, job is an achieved status, but people elsewhere might have no choice but to accept their parents' job status. One's religion or even political status are assigned by some social systems to their members.

In our culture today, more attention is paid to achieved status than in the past. The past two decades have brought more truth to the belief held by many in the United States that what you do is more important than who you are. In the U.S. today, one's chances of being hired are more likely to depend on training and grades than on such ascribed traits as race, age, or sex.

ROLE CONFLICT: Simultaneous incompatible demands on a person resulting from the expectations of two or more statuses.

Role Conflict: Trying to Be Two Things at Once. Anyone can have many achieved statuses and several ascribed ones. It is easy to see how some of the roles accompanying these statuses might

Ascribed statuses such as royalty are often assigned at birth.

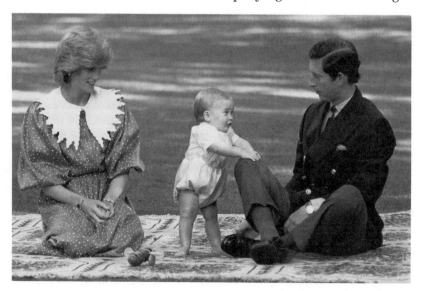

conflict with one another at some point in time. That is, a person may be expected to be or do two or more things at the same time. This is called role conflict.

GENDER: Social aspects of sex; attitudes and expectations related to being male or female.

Gender: A Special Role.   Gender refers to the social aspects of being male or female. The expectations, feelings, and roles of the male or female have a huge impact on the individual. In North America, a male learns that he cannot always hug when he feels like it. Besides this and other restraints, he has also learned, for example, that he does not have to leave his job when his child is born—he is free of such expectations. A female has learned a different set of rules, a different role. Like the male, her role has a great influence on her life; it affects her throughout each day and throughout her life. Because they have such a powerful influence on our lives, roles deserve special attention. Here we explore how gender roles—often called sex roles—are assigned, how they vary among cultures, and where they come from.

Achieved or Ascribed?   Both gender status and gender role are assigned, but each by a different agency. Gender status is clearly ascribed. It is determined by the sex genes that come from one's father. While some persons have their gender status changed through surgery and hormone treatment, it is for most of us a status assigned to us at conception. While gender status is assigned by biology, gender roles are assigned by culture. The culture determines what male and female behaviors are proper.

The Many Forms of Masculine and Feminine Roles.   The variation of gender roles is shown quite clearly in a classic study by Margaret Mead.[4] Mead studied three cultures living within a one-hundred-mile area of New Guinea. There she found extreme contrasts in gender roles. While two of the cultures assumed little difference in the temperaments of the sexes, the other one defined the male and female roles very differently. In one culture, males and females both were expected to be gentle, mild, and maternal. Such a person would be considered feminine in the United States. That culture contrasted sharply with a second one, where both sexes were expected to be fierce, competitive, and aggressive. A "feminine" American woman would be little admired there. Nor would she be given much respect in the third culture Mead studied. There, the U.S. roles were reversed. In this rare case, women were the bosses. They clearly dominated their culture and their men. These females were responsible, no-nonsense breadwinners. They acted in ways that we might expect a "real man" to act in the United States. The men of that culture were dependent on the women. They wore curls and much decoration and spent most of their time on gossip and art. They tried to please and earn praise from the women.

Mead's study shows how very much the temperaments of the sexes can vary. Because of this, cultures can mold a woman or man into any emotional form it wants. Thus one must stop and think before saying that it is not "normal" for a man (or woman) to act in a certain way. What is defined as normal or masculine/feminine varies widely among cultures.

Origins of gender roles. Why is it that little boys are not supposed to cry or wear dresses? Where did such rules come from? Researchers have asked this question, but it is not clear what the gender roles in any one culture are based on. There are several theories offered to explain the origins of gender roles. Maccoby and Jacklin describe three such theories and conclude that biology cannot be ignored.[5]

One of these theories says that small children are molded to gender roles by rewards and punishments from adults. When a child turns to some behavior the parents think is not proper for the child's gender, he or she is discouraged, perhaps by a frown or a slap. The child is likewise praised for behavior seen as correct. The problem with this theory is that few parents seem to do this enough to explain the very early gender identity that children show.

The second role-learning theory contends that gender roles are the result of imitation. That is, boys do what their fathers do and girls do what their mothers do. There are some problems with this theory too. First, girls, for example, choose girlish things even if mother does not. Second, children seem to choose their sex-role behaviors before they choose their same-sex models.

Both these theories contend that the feelings and actions of boys differ from those of girls because the two sexes are treated in different ways. In these viewpoints sex differences are based on childhood learning.

A third theory described by Maccoby and Jacklin says the behavior differences between boys and girls have a physical basis. In this view, the sexes find different tasks and roles easy because each sex is equipped with tendencies that make certain roles more appropriate than others. (It does not matter whether these innate tendencies really exist; what counts is what society believes.) Roles are built upon these perceived tendencies. Children are expected to fit these images of male and female. This theory is supported by recent research.[6]

U.S. Gender Roles: Vague, Unequal, . . . and Changing. Whatever their origins, our gender roles are clearly a force to reckon with. Dealing with these roles is made more difficult by the fact that a person may not be so very sure just what is expected of either sex. In the United States, the roles are growing less distinct but remain clearly unequal.

How distinct are masculine and feminine? If you had been born in Mexico, your gender role would have been different from the one you would have been assigned as an Eskimo. In either place, however, you would have known quite clearly what was expected of you as female or male. While gender roles vary from one

The status of female is ascribed by biology, but the role of the woman is assigned by culture, and can be changed or rejected.

SEXISM: The belief that, compared to men, women and their roles are inferior and less valuable.

culture to the next, in most places the roles of male and female are clearly distinct from each other. Different jobs are assigned and certain personality traits are expected, according to gender. The prescribed pathways are distinct from one another.

In the United States today, gender roles are not distinct. Over the past decade the line between the female and male roles has become less clear. American women spend less time and energy on their families and more on study and employment.[7] At all social levels women are gaining access to jobs that were once "for men only." It is not as rare as it once was to find a woman working (for pay) outdoors. More women now have jobs that include executive powers. Likewise, men in this culture have been moving into jobs reserved in the past for women. This is most evident in the home. In many homes one can no longer guess with confidence if the dishes are washed by him or her. The process of adjusting to the changes in gender roles continues in the United States.

Still unequal. Women in the United States remain socially unequal to men, even though the two gender roles are less distinct than they once were. Not only are women less likely to finish college, but those who do tend to make only a little more than half as much money as males with the same level of schooling. Most of the well-paying jobs are dominated by men. Also, few women hold power in politics or business. In the home, many women with full-time jobs outside the home still shoulder most of the housekeeping chores. In all these areas, things are improving for women, but the basic inequalities remain.

The inequality regarding income has received the most research attention. Why do women in general earn only about two-thirds that of men? Several explanations have been explored. Some studies point to sexual discrimination as the cause of the male-female salary discrepancy.[8] Also, women still tend to find themselves in college majors having lower income potential, perhaps because of discrimination within the allocation process at the college level.[9] Other studies point to an earlier discrimination, a form of sexism in which teachers assume that girls are less talented than boys in mathematics.[10] While there is some reason to suspect that boys are better than girls in mathematics because of a genetic difference in that regard, the cultural stereotype of females' math weakness may explain most of the discrepancy.[11] In other words, if female students were encouraged more to succeed in math, they would succeed, and many of the higher paying careers, such as engineering, would be opened to them, and the male-female income gap would diminish.

However, the male-female math gap seems to begin early in life. One study found that parents of daughters had different perceptions of their children's math ability than did parents of sons.[12] Even when boys and girls performed equally well in math, parents believed that girls had to work harder than boys. Furthermore, the girls' attitudes about their own math ability were more strongly influenced by their parents' attitudes than by the girls' actual performance. The cultural stereotype of the "math-dumb" girl seems to be deeply rooted in our culture.

When women enter the career world, they face further disadvantages. In industrialized societies, women are less likely to move up the career ladder.[13, 14] Men are generally more willing to move than their more family-oriented female competitors, and this gives men an advantage in getting career promotions.[15] Also, occupations have become defined as masculine or feminine, which helps lock women into less lucrative career channels.[16] Still another piece to this income-gap puzzle is the fact that women have less prestige and influence in mixed-sex task groups, which may make it more difficult for women to perform up to their potential.[17] On top of all these disadvantages, women in general are assumed by many people to possess personality traits that are not typical of normal, healthy adults. Women are not considered normal if they act like a man, but are considered unhealthy if they show the personality traits of the stereotypical female role.[18] The differing cultural expectations and social opportunities women face pose formidable barriers to gender equality.

The role of the American male is surely not one with all rewards and no costs. Though men in our culture enjoy more legal and social power than women, they also face the stress that power and privilege bring. Men have higher rates of suicides and stress-related diseases than women. They are compelled to compete—and pressured to win. The cost of greater social opportunity is possible failure.

"Liberation"?   In the past two decades, women in the United States have gained more social opportunities. Jobs in education for women have increased, and as women participate in the labor force, gender role attitudes have changed. Mothers who hold less traditional gender role attitudes transmit those attitudes to their daughters.[19] Women today face fewer obstacles to income equality, though obstacles do remain.

Recently a few voices have been raised for "men's liberation." The male role is being studied in a new light, and more notice is being taken of its pressures and restrictions. Just as some women want more freedom to perform, some men want fewer expectations of their performance. Rather than restraining emotions and pretending to be tough and aggressive, some men want more freedom to be warm and gentle. While the women's movement has focused on social changes for women, some men seek more emotional freedom too.

It is not clear how far changes in, or liberation from, our sex roles will take us. History may label these times the "human liberation" movement, but it is unlikely that differences between sex roles will disappear. Perhaps our descendants will have much more choice in their social and personality traits. Perhaps people will be more free to choose the traits they feel most comfortable with, instead of accepting those required by society's sex roles. Some people envision an androgynous society in the future. In

ANDROGYNOUS SOCIETY: A society in which members have the psychological and social traits of both sexes.

that setting, each person would, to a greater extent than is true today, have some of the personality traits of both males and females today. That is, there would be no emotional or social distinctions between the sexes.

The question facing you is, How much of this "liberation" do we want? Many would agree that we should take some of the pressures and restraints off of males and open more social doorways for women. But many people feel threatened by more basic changes in sex roles. They enjoy what they see as the romance and mystery of sex-role distinctions. While it might be healthy to presume nothing about people based on their sex, we might soon begin to yearn for such guidelines to use in forming relationships with people. Roles limit, but we have seen that they also give our social interactions valuable structure.

Age Status.   Another important ascribed status is that of age. People of various ages are expected to play quite different roles. As with sex, the age status is a fact of life, assigned in this case by the passing of time rather than genes.

The age role is also similar to the sex role in that it can be shaped into many forms, depending on time and place. As to place, there are several ways in which the age role varies among cultures. In one culture, an old person is expected to give valuable advice; in others the aged are expected to try to imitate the young. One culture may see a child as a tender seed to be nurtured into a lovely blossom. Other cultures see a child as a wild animal to be tamed. We can see how age roles change over time by looking at U.S. culture. In the times past, children were expected to be less independent and more obedient. Teenagers had fewer rights. The role of the aged included more power. (The role of the aged will be explored in detail in this chapter's Special Topic.)

To this point, we have looked at how norms and roles help make sure that social order is maintained. Norms direct our actions. Roles also direct us, but are linked to certain statuses. While all these guidelines restrict us, they also free us from the fears and discomforts of social disorder.

DEVIANCE: FAILURE TO CONFORM

When people fail or refuse to follow roles and norms, social life can become threatening, as it did for the people around Manny, the deviant described in the chapter preview. At other times, this nonconformity can just make life more interesting for the actor as well as the onlookers, such as when a person colors his hair green. Here we will look at the nature and causes of this lack of conformity, called deviance.

What is Deviance?

Deviance can be defined easily enough, but it is difficult to describe just what fits this description. Deviance can be defined as behavior that fails to meet social expectations. The problem here is that there is not always agreement on what the expectations are.

Is climbing a wall deviant behavior—even criminal behavior? It is in Berlin. The definition of deviance varies greatly from one time and place to another.

Thus we may or may not define the atheist, the working mother, or the homosexual as deviants. It depends on our culture and our personal point of view.

The deviance of an act depends on several factors. Time is one such factor, because cultures can change over time. Behavior that fifty years ago would have been labeled deviant is accepted as normal today. And while public drunkenness is considered deviant at most times during the year, it may not be so on New Year's Eve. Special circumstances affect how an act is defined. Killing a human is not deviant in certain wartime settings or police actions. Abortion is considered murder by some people, a matter of a woman's rights by others. Cultural values lead to different views on the same act. Most people consider car theft a deviant act, but some delinquent subcultures do not. And one's role helps define what is and is not deviant. For example, kissing strangers may be allowed for a female who is four years old, but not for one who is forty. The deviance of behavior depends on the time, status, subculture, and other circumstances.

According to conflict theory, deviance is defined according to the value system of the dominant elite. The group with sufficient power to impose its values on the rest of the population rigs the normative system in its favor. Because the corporate elite controls our society, corporate crimes are not treated as severely as are crimes more likely to be committed by the lower classes. The justice and law enforcement sectors concentrate on protecting the property interests of the elite from encroachment by the masses. In this view, the nature of deviance in any particular society reflects the nature of the dominant elite.

Deviance: Criminal or Just Out of Line?

Are people who eat eggs with their hands deviants? Yes, but are they criminals? How about the person who comes to church in a bathing suit? Again, the behavior is deviant, but not criminal. Is the Communist or the heavy drinker a deviant? How about the murderer? These cases suggest that there are many kinds of deviance, ranging from the illegal to the merely improper. Here we will look at both criminal and noncriminal forms of deviance.

Social Problems as Deviance: Not Conforming, But Not Criminal. Some deviance causes social problems, even though it is not threatening enough to be made illegal. While a person may choose to play the deviant by shaving his or her head, that behavior does not cause trouble for the social order. It may be interesting, but it is not worth our study here. But some of a person's behaviors may be considered part of a social problem. It is worthwhile to take a look at two such behaviors.

Drug use. Even when people use a legal drug, they may be seen as a deviant. The deviant label here depends on how much they need the drug to function normally. If they cannot get along emotionally without the drug, they deviate from a social norm of personal freedom from such chemicals. They are likely to be seen as addicts, deviants, though not criminals.

There are exceptions; not *all* addicts are deviants. In our culture, the person addicted to—or dependent on—nicotine or caffeine is not seen as abnormal or even deviant. This is because the use of these drugs is widespread and the addicts are unlikely to have their supplies cut off. So even if a person *needs* tobacco, coffee, tea, or cola, he or she is not a deviant.

Dependence on alcohol is seen as a social problem and thus as deviance. Alcohol abuse is one of the most destructive and widespread drug-linked forms of deviance we have in the United States. Certainly alcohol is the most widely used drug in our culture. But it is not known how much of this use is in the form of abuse, or dependence. Being so widespread, the consequences of this form of deviance are serious. Alcohol abuse kills thousands of people yearly through liver ailments and traffic accidents. The poor appetite of heavy drinkers can result in malnutrition and serious disease. And the lost production caused by the abuse of alcohol is huge. Because of these results, alcoholism is a social problem and a form of deviance.

Sexual (mis)behavior. Sexual behaviors may also be seen as deviant and as part of a broad social problem. Sexual actions may not conform to widely held standards or norms, and because some sexual deviance is seen as a threat to either society's moral health (as in pornography) or its pocketbook (as in some of the premarital sex resulting in pregnancy), it is a social problem.

As in most areas of deviance, we are faced here with varying definitions of what is allowed. This makes sexual behaviors difficult to classify as deviant or normal. Still it is clear that homosexuality, pornography, and premarital sex are regarded by some people as forms of deviance, and social problems. Depending on local laws, some of these behaviors are considered criminal, others merely immoral. Furthermore, while adultery, various sex acts, and cohabitation (unmarried living together) are in most places illegal, people engaging in these behaviors are rarely considered criminals—sometimes not even deviants. Because of all this, sexual deviance is very difficult to define.

Deviance as Crime. Now we turn our focus to criminal forms of deviance. As we have just seen, it is not always clear what is deviant, nor is it always clear what is criminal. Some deviance, such as murder, is clearly criminal. In other cases, the question of whether a deviant act is a crime is debated without end. For example, is sex between two unmarried people really a crime, even though it may be against the law? Despite such questions, there are many acts defined by most people in our culture as criminal. It is this domain—criminal deviance—that will be explored here.

Table 9–1 gives some idea of the many kinds of criminal deviance dealt with by our society.

There are several categories within the domain of criminal behavior. Many people probably think first of murder, robbery, assault, rape, and the like when they think of crime. Indeed, these

TABLE 9-1 Total Estimated Arrests, United States, 1985

Totals based on all reporting agencies and estimates for unreported areas.

Type of Criminal Deviance	Persons Arrested
Murder and nonnegligent manslaughter	18,330
Forcible rape	36,970
Robbery	136,870
Aggravated assault	305,390
Burglary	443,300
Larceny, theft	1,348,400
Motor vehicle theft	133,900
Other assaults	637,600
Forgery and counterfeiting	87,600
Fraud	342,600
Embezzlement	11,400
Stolen property; buying, receiving, possessing	127,100
Vandalism	259,600
Weapons; carrying, possessing, etc.	180,900
Prostitution and commercialized vice	113,800
Sex offenses (except rape and prostitution)	100,600
Drug abuse violations	811,400
Gambling	32,100
Offenses against family and children	58,800
Driving under the influence	1,788,400
Liquor laws	548,600
Disorderly conduct	671,700
Drunkenness	964,800
Vagrancy	33,800
All other offenses (except traffic)	2,489,200
Suspicion (not included in totals)	12,900
Curfew and loitering law violations	81,500
Runaways	161,200

SOURCE: U.S. Federal Bureau of Investigation, *Crime in the United States* (Washington, D.C.: U.S. Government Printing Office, 1985).

are among the most frequently reported, serious types of crimes. But such a listing hides the fact that crimes are likely to be committed in very different circumstances and for very different reasons. To best deal with such a variety of crimes, it is helpful to use other crime categories. A few of these categories are offered here to provide a fuller view of the many forms criminal deviance can take.

Organized crime.   Organized crime differs from most other types. First, unlike other types of crime, it is based on a bureaucratic organization, which protects the big crime bosses and makes their prosecution difficult. This type of crime is also different in that it began only recently, during the Prohibition era, when criminal organizations were established to sell illegal alcoholic beverages. Another difference is that organized crime prospers by supplying what the public demands. This includes drugs and gambling, as well as some products and legal services.

Professional crime. Professional crime is based on special skill rather than organization. That is, professional criminals most often work alone or in small groups. Because of their levels of skills, they often claim higher prestige than other types of criminals. Depending on knowledge rather than force, these people often hold themselves above other kinds of "common" criminals.

Among the various types of professional criminals are the confidence man or woman, the pickpocket, the sneak thief, the shoplifter, the jewelry substituter, the hotel thief, the forger, the counterfeiter, and so on. The professional participant in a crime such as shoplifting should not be confused with the typical amateur teenager or housewife who picks up an item here and there. The professional makes a living from this activity.

Ordinary career crime. Like the professionals, ordinary career criminals limit their crimes to providing money for themselves. There are, however, some basic differences among the kinds of people to be found in the two groups. The professional criminal is at the top of the social hierarchy, and the ordinary criminal is at the bottom. An ordinary criminal does not normally develop into a professional criminal, as one would rise through the ranks of the armed forces.

Ordinary career criminals normally have lower-class origins and a long history of contact with the law. They usually have worked their way from minor crimes to major profit-making ventures. In all areas, the professional has a much higher degree of skill, finesse, and technical aptitude than the ordinary criminal. While the ordinary criminal will resort to force and weapons, the professional criminal studiously avoids them. The ordinary criminal will either become part of a large organized group, operate individually, or work with several compatriots. Organized crime then forms a third subcategory.

Ordinary career criminals do not exhibit various traits commonly associated with criminal types. They think of themselves as business people. On the personal level, they are pleasant, generally even-tempered, and levelheaded. They try to limit their associates to people whose actions are controlled, since unbalanced types may get everyone in trouble. Their criminal activity does not raise any moral issues on the personal level. Ordinary career criminals are not compulsive in their actions; instead, they are likely to be deliberate in the execution of their various activities.

Skill Reinforcer 9–2

How does the skill of recognizing stereotypes relate to the prosecution of white-collar criminals?

White-collar crime. White-collar crime is a very different type of crime, involving a very different kind of person. White-collar criminals usually depend on their jobs to create the opportunity to break the law. Many hold high-status jobs that give them access to large amounts of money. Accountants, bank officers, and business executives have the chance to engage in crimes that can range from embezzlement to computer theft. Those who violate antitrust laws, federal trade regulations, and tax laws are also white-collar criminals.

While white-collar crimes are often largest in scope, involving many victims in many places, and much money, "persons located in the employer class do not receive sanctions commensurate with these crimes."[20] Such offenders are more likely to be accused of violating a governmental regulation rather than a crime.

Juries and judges sometimes find it hard to define or to treat white-collar criminals as "real" criminals. A white-collar crime is often seen as a special case. Because of this, such criminals are not treated the same way as others who may do the same amount of damage. They are less likely to be arrested, face trial, or be convicted. This may be because of the nonviolent nature of their crime, as well as their high social status and other "respectable" traits.

Our criminal justice system recognizes the need for different treatments for different kinds of criminals. The white-collar criminal is not treated in the same way as the violent criminal. People who are unable to control their actions require different treatment, as do habitual criminals.

Making sure that different treatment is fair treatment is not easy. The car thief may be treated much more harshly than the person who embezzles one hundred thousand dollars. Until the system decides which crimes are the most serious, and whether the nature of the crime or of the criminal is to be the basis of society's reactions, our justice system will be less than just.

Moralistic crime.   Another type of crime involves much controversy because the line between deviance and crime is very hazy. This type of deviance, called moralistic or victimless crime, is defined by many people as immoral but not criminal. It offends the morals of the community but does not hurt anyone, at least directly. Examples are gambling, pornography, prostitution, and the use of illegal drugs.

It is debatable whether some of these crimes are really without victims. The gambler's family may suffer financially. Prostitution involves exploitation and sometimes violence. It is argued that the moral tone of the community is damaged by pornography. The users of addictive drugs are victims, as are the people robbed or killed by addicts desperate for money to support their habits.

On the other hand, there are several reasons why many people urge the repeal of laws regarding such moralistic crimes. One line of reasoning is that the victims of gambling are only very indirect victims, in the same way that the person killed by a car is the victim of the corporation that sold the car. People can be hurt playing football, too, but we do not ban the game. Another point made is that instead of wasting efforts policing victimless crimes, our tax dollars could be better spent fighting crimes that directly threaten us. In this view, police should be freed to spend more time tracking down thieves instead of rounding up prostitutes. Further, it is argued that enforcement of such laws pertaining to such crimes breeds disrespect for other laws and invites police corruption. In fact, otherwise respectable people form links with the criminal world in order to get what they want but are forbidden by these laws to have.

There is another way to label some crimes as moralistic. Some crimes, rather than offending the community's morals, are attempts at enforcing those morals. Indeed, such actions may not be crimes at all, but morally motivated actions. In traditional societies, assassination, beating, confiscation or destruction of property, and humiliation are simply socially condoned methods of conflict management or social control. Where there is no formal justice system or police, the people must administer justice on a private basis.

In modern society, much crime is conflict management in the form of punishment or restitution. Some assaults, murders, and robberies may be responses to adultery, domestic disputes, affronts to honor, or debts. Such crimes can be seen as a form of self help, a form of social control, and a way of enforcing ideas of right and wrong.[21]

We have seen the great variety of ways by which people deviate from the norms. Some involve laws, others the sense of decency or normality of at least some part of society. Because of the varying definitions of deviance within our culture, nearly all of us could be considered a deviant of some kind. Most of us have failed to meet some expectation, as defined by some police officer, church group, or subculture.

Causes of Deviance

Because there are people who do not conform to the social order, we must be on our guard with strangers, lock our doors, and avoid certain places. If deviance, especially the criminal type, could be prevented, we could relax and enjoy life more fully. Social science has tried to help by developing many theories about why some people do not conform to society's rules. For the most part, these theories are quite different from one another. This is partly because of the many different kinds of deviance. Any one form of deviance may be better explained by one approach than another. Among all these theories, there are three basic approaches.

Physical. Are deviant people born with a tendency to be deviant? Some theories center on the physical causes of deviance. An early exponent of this view was Lombroso, who contended that criminals were in a less-advanced state of evolution.[22] He looked for the physical traits that he thought would identify a criminal type. However, other people noticed that entirely respectable citizens possessed the traits Lombroso identified as "criminal." Later, Sheldon suggested that a muscular body type is linked to criminal tendencies.[23] These theories have been criticized because of the methods used to gather proof. Still more recently, research has suggested that body chemicals are linked to criminal behavior. A correlation has been found between trace-metal elements in hair and violent personalities.[24] While a recent study has perhaps finally disproven the supposed link between epilepsy and crime,[25] another study suggests that society may react differently to people with different genetic heritages.[26] Research continues, searching for a link between biology and crime, but so far none has been es-

Now Disproved

tablished. Evidence has been gathered to suggest a link between a rare chromosome pattern and crime.[27] It was discovered that a large percentage of men with an XXY chromosome pattern (males normally have an XY pattern) were found among people convicted of violent crimes. But we must note that not all violent people have this pattern, and there is no proof that the pattern causes violence. While males commit more crimes than females, the gap between the sexes is narrowing in this regard.[28] This suggests that the higher crime rates for men cannot be explained only in terms of the physical differences between the sexes. Sex may be another blind alley in the search for physical causes of crime. All this shows that, though there may be a link between criminal tendencies and biology, none has yet been clearly proven.

Psychological.   Another approach for explaining the causes of deviance is based on psychology. The focus here is on personality types. It is thought that some types are more likely to deviate than others.

Skill Reinforcer 9-3

Could a cause-effect relationship be proven between the XXY chromosome pattern and criminal tendencies?

Anti-social Personality - Not a cause but a Dx - was Psychopath or Socio path

The Freudian viewpoint is one of several such approaches used to explain deviance. Its focus is on a person's ability to control the deviant impulses found to some degree in all people. According to this view, we must learn to resolve the conflicts between selfish drives and conscience. Some people have poorly developed consciences. This leaves them unable to empathize, and they feel little guilt for the harm they inflict on others. Deviance can easily result from this, as it can when inner impulses overwhelm a conscience. Or there are people whose conscience may be *too* strong and who feel so much guilt that they commit deviant acts in order to receive the punishment they feel they deserve.

The frustration-aggression theory is also based on psychology.[29] According to this theory, frustration can cause people to strike out at others. The targets of this aggression may have nothing to do with causing the frustration, but unless such people can control their impulses, the target is attacked.

Another psychological explanation of criminal deviance involves incompetent parenting. Behavioral psychology can perhaps be used to improve the behavior of even serious delinquents, especially those who have not yet reached adolescence. And it is hoped that raising children in more controlled environments will help "prevent the frenzied or apathetic incompetence of so many families from producing monsters."[30]

Social.   The third approach to deviance looks at its social causes. Such theories focus not on how the deviant is different from other people but on the person's social surroundings as causes of the deviances. The forces causing the deviance are presumed to be more social than personal.

The oldest sociological theory on crime causation traces its roots back to Durkheim's concept of anomie. Anomie refers to a condition of weak or absent social norms. Robert Merton used anomie to explain deviance. According to Merton, individuals in modern societies are more likely to experience a lack of clear, consistent, relevant guidelines, and such people are more likely to disrupt the social order.[31]

Merton described deviance as the result of strain between social goals and the approved means for achieving these goals. In other words, some individuals are caught in a bind between the goals that the culture tells them they want, and the means offered by the culture for attaining these goals. Deviance results when such people lack access to the legal means of achieving their goals.

Another feature of the social environment that may help explain crime is social class. Some researchers argue that there is no proven link between class and crime rates. While lower-class people seem to have higher crime rates, this may be because "lower-class crimes" are over-represented in police records. Self-report surveys show no significant link between class and crime, except perhaps that people at different social class levels tend to commit different kinds of crimes. Conflicting data continue to be gathered, some showing higher crime rates among lower classes.[32, 33] The link between class and crime has not been fully established.

Cultural transmission theory focuses on the opportunities that the social environment may offer for learning deviance. In some parts of society, children are taught to value education, to mind their manners, and to work for respectability. The "teachers" (mainly the parents) in such homes are themselves usually winners in the competition for social success. Other children are taught by drug pushers, thieves, and pimps. Deviance can be seen as a lesson learned through interaction with the role models in one's cultural environment. The array of opportunities presented by the environment affects whether the individual learns to hustle stolen cars or to succeed in an academic setting.

Like other cultural transmission theories, Edwin Sutherland's theory of differential association is based on the idea of social learning.[34] In this view, most criminal behavior, like other behaviors, is learned in intimate social settings. The direction of the learning (toward or away from deviance) is determined by the relative strength of delinquent as opposed to nondelinquent attitudes to which the individual is exposed. Although we are all exposed to both socially acceptable and socially disapproved attitudes, it is the balance of the legitimate and the illegitimate that determines our behavior. The learning mechanisms are the same in any social setting; the difference in the delinquent group is the direction of the learning, or what is being learned.

Along a similar vein, Shaw and McKay observed that delinquency seems to be transmitted culturally through the play groups and gangs in a neighborhood. Shaw and McKay noted that as one ethnic group moved out of a neighborhood to be replaced by another, the delinquency rate did not change. As the new ethnic group gradually moved into the area, they learned delinquent behavior by interacting with the remaining members of the delin-

SKILL BOX

Using the Hypothesis

The attempt by science to explain the causes of crime is based on the tool of the hypothesis. The use of this tool is an important skill not only for scientists but also for people trying to find out the whys and hows of their world.

The hypothesis is an informed guess about the solution of a problem. It is informed insofar as it is based on some knowledge of the problem area. Some form of research is then used to test the accuracy of this guess.

For example, to find out how you can improve your study habits, you could form a hypothesis on the basis of your knowledge about proper study habits. That knowledge might suggest that your habit of beginning to study at midnight should be changed. Your hypothesis might be: Beginning my studies at 9 p.m. instead of midnight will improve my grades. You would now be ready to put this guess to a test.

One way of testing this hypothesis would be to try the new study schedule for a school term and compare the grades thus earned with those earned with the old midnight schedule and a similar study load. Another test would be to study at midnight for one course, at nine for another course for which you would expect to make the same grade as the other course. The results might suggest a modified hypothesis. That is, you may try studying at some other time, in a different place, or for a longer time each night.

The use of the hypothesis tool can be much more complex than this. For the scientists or any serious problem solvers, the hypothesis directs their research, their probing into the unknown. It also helps them anticipate and understand what they will find in the realm of the unknown. These two functions of the hypothesis are described more fully below.

The hypothesis is our probe. With it we reach from the known into the unknown. From the clearly drawn limits of the known, we can use the hypothesis to enclose a part of the unknown within a dotted line. By applying the process of science, the area within the dotted line may become part of our region of the known—if our guess was correct. A hypothesis found to be incorrect may cause us to erase all or part of the dotted line, or to move it to some other part of the unknown. Then, with a modified or new hypothesis, we can continue to probe the unknown. The hypothesis thus suggests our research directions by focusing our search on the area inside the dotted line. The terrain within this line will suggest various experiments and observations. Based on the facts that emerge from our exploration, new hypotheses will lead us further or elsewhere.

The hypothesis also helps explain the significance of objects or events we may find within the dotted line. It tells us what to expect, as well as how discoveries relate to the realm of the known. The hypothesis gives structure and meaning to the emerging facts.

In dealing with the causes of crime, for example, the hypothesis maps out the scientists' research. It probes into the facts and figures and identifies the areas most likely to yield other useful data. It frames new evidence with expectations, giving the discovery meaning.

As an example, imagine a scientist has reason to form the hypothesis that a certain level of a certain hormone helps to cause violent crime. The hypothesis helps the scientist to map out the research. The scientist will compare the levels of the hormone in violent criminals with those in people who have not committed violent crimes. As the data from this comparison come in, the scientist knows to expect a certain level of the hormone in one group but not in the other. The hypothesis tells this, and it tells the scientist how big a difference in hormone levels would be significant. These expectations, based on the hypothesis, give structure and meaning to the incoming data.

The case of crime causation is just one example. In all realms of exploration, the probe of the hypothesis tells the scientist where to look and what to expect. It is the vanguard of science's progress.

quent group that had not yet left the area. Shaw and McKay also observed that the delinquency rate decreased as one moved away from the center of the city. The poorer neighborhoods near the urban core are usually less stable socially than others, and this may help explain the effect noted by Shaw and McKay. Even though this ecological picture no longer seems accurate, the link between crime and community stabilization and adaptation still seems to hold true.[35]

Labeling theory has attracted a great deal of attention in recent years. This viewpoint maintains that the reactions of society play a very important part in labeling some people as deviants. Deviance is thus socially defined, not by some universal code but by the time, place, and persons involved in the situation. The critical factor is not the act but the reaction to that act.

Once an individual's act is defined by others as deviant, the individual defines him- or herself as a deviant as well. The label of deviant serves to deny the individual access to nondeviant, or "straight," roles. The doors to respectability are to some degree closed to the deviant, and thus the "deviant" label helps create future deviance. Society's reaction is the key factor at work.

Several other social approaches explain deviance. Research has suggested, for example, that effective socialization in the home is important in preventing delinquency. Effective parenting, according to one study, consists of three parental tasks: monitoring the child's behavior, recognizing deviance when it occurs, and punishing it.[36] In other research, unemployment has been linked to crime.[37] And mass media portrayals of violence have been linked to violent behaviors in the general population (however, these studies have been criticized).[38, 39] All such approaches focus on the impact of the social environment on people's behaviors.

We can learn from this sociological view of deviance how deeply deviance is embedded in the social structure. Individuals are shaped by social forces, as we have seen in preceding chapters, and their actions are then interpreted by the social environment. Deviance can thus be seen as a social product and a socially defined phenomenon. Even though this connection may be more clearly apparent in the case of deviant behavior, our other behaviors are socially defined phenomena as well. Individual behavior is a social product.

SUMMARY

To many of us, the word "control" has an unpleasant ring. It implies a lack of freedom. Yet you may have reflected that the nature of human beings makes some form of control necessary if we are to have social order.

Norms are social devices for maintaining this order by helping to control our behavior. Norms range from matters of politeness (folkways) to matters of social survival (mores). Folkways include fashions, which are short-lived guidelines that define what is tasteful, what will bring us esteem. Fads are of even shorter duration and are followed by only a small part of the society. Like many other folkways, fads and fashions are not—as most mores are—enforced by formal sanctions, or laws.

Along with all these types of norms, roles also help regulate our social interaction. Roles are expectations attached to certain social positions, or statuses. Some of these statuses, such as those of age or sex, are ascribed, or assigned to us regardless of what we do. Achieved statuses, such as hero or dropout, are based on our efforts. Gender roles seem to be based somewhat on physical differences between male and female but are still changeable. Indeed, many people in the United States have been pressing for changes in the role of the female so as to decrease the social inequality of the sexes. Some people have urged the "liberation" of both the sexes from limitations.

These two tools of conformity, norms and roles, cannot give perfect control of our behavior. Behavior that fails to conform to these guidelines is called deviance and can range from merely improper behavior to criminal behavior. There is a wide range of types of crime. Organized crime is based on bureaucratic structure. Professional criminals depend on skills, while white-collar criminals depend on their jobs to give them access to their crimes. In contrast to these types, the ordinary career criminal is more likely to be of lower-class origin and to use violence. The moralistic criminal offends the morals of the community and may not produce any victims. Explanations of the causes of crimes range from physical to psychological to social approaches.

Deviance is usually a problem, but not always. Challenges to the social order are most likely to be damaging to the well-being of other people, but without it, little social reform would occur. Total conformity means stagnation, something we do not want until a perfect social order is reached.

SPECIAL TOPIC

The Role of the Aged: Problems and Promise

Old age can be a problem. One of the reasons lies in the way society defines the role of the aged. Other reasons involve physical, financial, and emotional factors. Many of the problems with old age can be solved, but solutions must be based on an understanding of the role of the aged. This Special Topic offers a beginning toward that understanding, in order to show the possibilities of old age as well as the problems.

WHAT IS OLD AGE?

Americans do not share a common picture of old age. Many of us are unsure what to expect of old people, or even what to call them. Because the role of the aged is defined so vaguely, adjusting to it is hard.

The way old age is defined depends greatly on the kind of culture in which one grows old. While the role of the aged is viewed with honor in some cultures, in others it is not. In traditional, agrarian cultures, old people are often respected. This is especially true in non-literate cultures. There the old person is the source of wisdom and knowledge about the past. In such cultures, where knowledge changes slowly, the status of the aged is one of honor and prestige. In cultures such as ours, based on factories and cities, the honor given to the aged is not so great. Where change and new ideas are valued, the old person is often seen as behind the times. The skills a person develops over decades can be replaced quickly by new technology. The aged are seen by many people as outdated and of little social value. The status of old age is thus given little honor.

Besides this low valuation of aging, there is little agreement in the United States as to when old age begins. Retirement may mark the entrance to old age, and many government and retirement programs define old age as sixty-five and over. Because of this arbitrary number, many people feel they become old at that age.

But age clearly cannot be counted by years alone. Some people at sixty-five are physically old, while others are in fine shape. And age is defined not just by the body but also by mental outlook. This is seen in the way social classes differ in their perceptions of aging. In contrast

Sex does not necessarily end when we reach old age.

to the upper classes, people with manual jobs and from lower-class backgrounds are likely to see themselves as old long before they reach sixty-five.[40] It is difficult to say how much of this gap is due to physical factors and how much to mental factors. It is clear, though, that the boundary line of old age is not clearly defined in our culture.

More of us will occupy this status for a great number of years. Because of this, it is valuable to find out what lies in store for us. Here we will examine the problems and the possibilities of aging.

THE PHYSICAL PROCESS OF AGING

We define aging partly by bodily changes, which involve a gradual loss of functioning. The loss of the senses normally starts with eyesight. Next hearing and tasting abilities decrease. The sense of touch weakens, resulting in a weaker grip and less balance. Along with this, strength and endurance lessen. Wrinkling of the skin, baldness, and weight gains are other common conditions of aging for some people.

A part of aging that is still widely misunderstood is the change in sex drive. Most women after the age of fifty can no longer become pregnant. At a later age, men begin to be less able to father offspring. But these developments in themselves have no effect on the sex drive. Despite this fact, many men and women past fifty or sixty feel they are over the hill sexually. While arousal may be less frequent and take longer than before, a person of seventy or more can still derive full satisfaction from sex. While the body may be able, the mind may not be willing, perhaps because of cultural beliefs. What is considered virile for a male of twenty may be viewed as disgusting for one of seventy. As the facts of age and sex become more widely known, perhaps more people will be able to enjoy sex in their later years.

Another physical fact of aging is that old people are threatened by disease more than younger people. A national study found chronic illness increases with age, especially after seventy-five.[41] Cancer, heart disease, diabetes, and arthritis are major threats to the aged.

Women survive the aging process longer than men. On the average, a woman lives about eight years longer than a man in the United States. Even before birth, males have a higher death rate than females. Part of this gap may be the result of the greater stresses and dangers faced by men. But it may also be that women's bodies are built so that they can withstand the rigors of life better.

Physical aging affects mental processes, but advanced age need not bring an end to mental sharpness. The mind loses some of its quickness and short-term memory, but it need not lose the ability to deal with concepts and data.[42] These and other findings show that learning and thinking do not decrease with age as much as many people think.

AGING AND MONEY

Money problems afflict too many old people. The proportion of elderly people living below the poverty line is higher than that of the general population. The reasons for this involve retirement and the special costs of old age.

Only a small percentage of the elderly work. Many are forced to retire. Others are no longer able to keep up the pace required by their jobs. Some are displaced by new machines and new skills. Once an older person loses his or her job, it is difficult to get another one. Few training programs want to take the time for someone who will only work a few more years. Some employers assume that an older worker will be too slow, weak, and often absent—none of which is necessarily true.

While some retired people have their own financial assets to depend on, most have only social security, which is hardly enough. While most old people are among the many who take advantage of this program, the benefits are small. It seems that many people regard the program as a retirement income in itself. Instead, it is intended only as a supplement to a family income. Still, the social security program eases the money strain for many elderly people, largely because of its cost-of-living increases, which help the elderly cope with inflation.

As people age, they may need even more money because of new expenses. Not only do medical bills increase, but paid aides may be needed to perform the chores the elderly are no longer able to do. Cooking, house maintenance, and transportation may be beyond the ability of the aging person.

The handicaps and costs of aging can be clearly seen in the transportation problem. Not only the price of a car, but also repairs, maintenance, and insurance all put driving out of reach for many old people. And the problem is not only one of money. Driving skills are diminished with age. Public transportation is not often accessible for the old person for whom a walk to the bus or subway is an ordeal. Taxis are ideal, but the cost is too high for many old people. This dilemma shows how aging can be complicated by money problems.

This leads us to another problem that is aggravated by the limited incomes of most old people: housing. As mobility is decreased, home becomes more important for a person. Though many elderly people own their own homes, much of this housing is old and found in high-crime areas. Old people are less able to maintain and repair their homes by themselves. Repair costs thus rise, as may insurance rates. The aged are more likely to feel discomfort from cold and thus need more heat too.

Most of the elderly seem to prefer these housing problems to living in a nursing home. Only a few people over sixty-five live in such "homes." Most nursing homes are run for profit, and many complaints have been made about them. Common among these are poor food and medical care. Residents may face overcharges, neglect, and even abuse. There are some excellent nursing homes, but again the problem is money.

We must not forget that many old people have no money problems. For them, retirement can release them to enjoy the fruits of their previous decades of work.

AGING AND SELF

Major challenges of aging are the social and emotional adjustments tied to this status. Our sense of self may change when we are treated as different people because of our new age status, but many people enter this new status with a sigh of relief. Still, the transition to the status of the aged can be a difficult one.

Retirement clearly shows this challenge. For people with other sources of satisfaction, retirement is a blessing, but some people feel useless when they no longer work. Our culture values work so highly that some of us cannot enjoy retirement. The loss of one's job may mean some loss of self-respect. Adjustments must be made to cope with these feelings.

In one way, old age brings freedom, but with freedom a person can feel either free or lost. The role of the aged, as we have noted, is unclear, for fewer guidelines are given. This may be perceived by a person in that role as freedom from many restrictions. On the other hand, such freedom may be perceived as a loss of direction, a sense of aimlessness. Time can thus be either a boon or a burden.

The role of the aged may also include isolation. The loss of job contacts and mobility, and the death of friends and spouse, become more likely as one ages. These factors can lead to loneliness, though most of the aged have enough contact with relatives, especially their offspring, that they escape loneliness.

It is most likely the husband who will die first, leaving the widow with perhaps another decade of life. It can mean for her a loss in not only income but also in love and sex. In this light, it is fortunate that it is the wife who most often maintains contacts with friends and family over the years. She is less likely than her husband to be isolated when the spouse dies.

TOWARD A NEW ROLE FOR THE AGED

We have thus far focused largely on the problems of aging, noting that while not all people face those problems many do. Adjustments to the role of the aged is a challenge, but one which can be met successfully. The chances of success depend on each person's resources, but society can help too.

Retirement policies have been made more flexible. Fewer people today are forced into retirement. Others want to retire, but not as early as sixty-five. As the birthrate drops and there are fewer young workers to replace older ones, a later retirement cutoff could be used. This would help protect the income level and self-respect of the older person.

Construction of more old-age communities can help too. People living in such places are less likely to feel lonely. They can relax and be less concerned about what younger people expect of them.

More community work by the elderly benefits both the old and those whom they help. Working in child-care centers and other service projects, older people can earn extra needed money and a sense of satisfaction. The community can benefit from the experience and wisdom of the aged. More of us will learn that most of the elderly have much to offer.

SELF-TEST QUESTIONS

Match numbers 1–5 to the descriptions on the right:

1. norm   a. norm followed by only a very limited segment of society
2. folkways   b. serious norms
3. mores   c. any kind of behavior guidelines
4. fad   d. norms involving matters of politeness
5. law   e. officially decreed, formalized norm
6. Fads and fashions are:
   a. laws
   b. mores
   c. folkways
   d. roles

7. Norms prohibiting cannibalism and child abuse are:
   a. fads
   b. folkways
   c. mores
   d. roles

Match numbers 8–9 to the descriptions on the right:

8. role   a. what you are; social position
9. status   b. what you are to do: expectations of a social position

Match numbers 10–11 to the descriptions on the right:

10. achieved status   a. based on one's efforts
11. ascribed status   b. assigned to a person regardless of his or her efforts
12. Age status is:
    a. achieved
    b. ascribed
13. True or false: A particular act can clearly be defined as deviant or not, regardless of the time, place, or kind of person involved.
14. True or false: All deviant acts are criminal acts.
15. True or false: No link between biology and criminal tendencies has been clearly proven.
16. Differential association theory is based on:
    a. body chemicals
    b. Sutherland's idea of social learning
    c. the concept of anomie
    d. body types (Sheldon)
17. Which theory focuses on society's reaction to the person who has been designated as a deviant?
    a. cultural transmission
    b. anomie
    c. conflict
    d. labeling

ANSWERS TO SELF-TEST QUESTIONS

1. c
2. d
3. b
4. a
5. e
6. c
7. c
8. b
9. a
10. a
11. b
12. b
13. false
14. false
15. true
16. b
17. d

ANSWERS TO SKILL REINFORCERS

9–1. Second premise: Murder is one of the mores. This bit of deductive reasoning may not be accurate (some murderers go unpunished), but it is logically valid.
9–2. Stereotypes assume that all members of some category or group share some particular traits. In this case, a jury member who believes that all criminals are lower-class would be unlikely to declare the bank officer guilty of, for example, embezzlement.

9–3. Remember that to prove cause-effect the important thing is to control all other possible causes of criminal tendencies. Here, since we cannot assign the XXY pattern randomly to people, we can only compare those people *with* the pattern with people *without* the pattern. To prove cause-effect, both groups could differ only in having the pattern or lacking it, and would somehow have to be alike in other ways that might cause crime, including their psychological outlook and social background. The chances of matching two groups in these ways is obviously small. Because of this, it is unlikely that the XXY pattern can be proven to cause criminal tendencies. Scientists can only try to measure the degree to which these two factors are linked, and thus suggest to that extent the possibility that one causes the other.

NOTES

1. Richard P. Rettig, Manual J. Torres, and Gerald R. Garett, *Manny: A Criminal-Addict's Story* (Boston: Houghton Mifflin Co., 1977). Excerpts from this book, pp. 38–39, 59, and 155, are reprinted with permission of Houghton Mifflin Co. © Copyright 1977 Houghton Mifflin Co.
2. Robert Bierstedt, *The Social Order,* 4th ed. (New York: McGraw-Hill, 1974): 235–37.
3. William G. Sumner, *Folkways* (New York: New American Library, 1960).
4. Margaret Mead, *Sex and Temperament in Three Primitive Societies* (New York: Dell Publishing Co., 1935).
5. Eleanor E. Maccoby and Carol Nagy Jacklin, *The Psychology of Sex Differences* (Palo Alto, Calif.: Stanford University Press, 1974).
6. Alice Rossi, "A Biosocial Theory of Parenting," *Daedalus* 206 (Spring 1977): 1–31.
7. Daphne Spain and Suzanne Bianchi, "How Women Have Changed," *American Demographics* (May 1983).
8. William Remus and Lane Kelley, "Evidence of Sex Discrimination," *American Journal of Economics and Sociology* 42 (April 1983): 149–52.
9. Kenneth L. Wilson and Eui Hang Shin, "Reassessing the Discrimination Against Women in Higher Education," *American Educational Research Journal* 20 (Winter 1983): 529–51.
10. Penelope Peterson and Elizabeth Fennema, "Effective Teaching, Student Engagement in Classroom Activities, and Sex-Related Differences in Learning Mathematics," *American Educational Research Journal* 22 (Fall 1985): 309–35.
11. Aaron Pallas and Karl Alexander, "Sex Differences in Quantitative SAT Performance," *American Educational Research Journal* 20 (Summer 1983): 165–82.
12. Jacquelynne Parsons, Terry Adler, and Caroline Kaczala, "Socialization of Achievement Attitudes and Beliefs: Parental Influences," *Child Development* 53 (1982): 310–21.
13. Therese Baker, "Class, Family, Education, and the Process of Status Attainment," *The Sociological Quarterly* 23 (Winter 1982): 17–31.
14. Lucienne Portocarero, "Social Mobility in Industrial Nations: Women in France and Sweden," *The Sociological Review* 31 (February 1983): 56–82.
15. William Markham, Patrick Macken, Charles Bonjean, and Judy Corder, "A Note on Sex, Geographic Mobility, and Career Advancement," *Social Forces* 61 (June 1983): 1138–46.
16. L. Murgatroyd, "Gender and Occupational Stratification," *The Sociological Review* 30 (November 1982): 574–602.
17. M.D. Pugh and Ralph Wahrman, "Neutralizing Sexism in Mixed-Sex Groups," *American Journal of Sociology* 88 (January 1983): 746–62.
18. Wray Herbert, "Curing Femininity," *Science News* 124 (September 10, 1983): 170–71.

19. Arland Thornton, Duane Alwin, and Donald Camburn, "Causes and Consequences of Sex-Role Attitudes and Attitude Change," *American Sociological Review* 48 (April 1983): 211–27.

20. John Hagan and Patricia Parker, "White-Collar Crime and Punishment," *American Sociological Review* 50 (June 1985): 302–16.

21. Donald Black, "Crime as Social Control," *American Sociological Review* 48 (February 1983): 34–45.

22. Cesare Lombroso, *Crime: Its Causes and Remedies* (Boston: Little Brown & Co., 1911).

23. William H. Sheldon, *Varieties of Delinquent Youth* (New York: Harper & Bros., 1949).

24. Janet Raloff, "Biochemical Aggression: Locks—A Key to Violence?" *Science News* (August 20, 1983).

25. M.J. Oliver, "Epilepsy, Crime and Delinquency," *Sociology* 14 (August 1980): 417–40.

26. David Rowe and D.W. Osgood, "Heredity and Sociological Theories of Delinquency," *American Sociological Review* 49 (August 1984): 526–40.

27. Menachem Amir and Yitzchak Berman, "Chromosomal Deviation and Crime," *Federal Probation* 34 (June 1970): 55–62.

28. Douglas A. Smith and Christy A. Visher, "Sex and Involvement in Deviance/Crime: A Quantitative Review of the Empirical Literature," *American Sociological Review* 45 (August 1980): 691–701.

29. John Dollard et al., *Frustration and Aggression* (New Haven: Yale University Press, 1939).

30. James Q. Wilson, "Raising Kids," *The Atlantic* 252 (October 1983): 56.

31. Robert K. Merton, "Social Structure and Anomie," *American Sociological Review* 3 (October 1938): 672–682.

32. Terence Thornberry and Margaret Farnworth, "Social Correlates of Criminal Involvement," *American Sociological Review* 47 (August 1982): 505–18.

33. John Braithwaite, "The Myth of Social Class and Criminality Reconsidered," *American Sociological Review* (February 1981): 36–57.

34. Edwin H. Sutherland and Donald Cressey, *Principles of Criminology,* 7th ed. (Philadelphia: J.B. Lippincott Co., 1966).

35. Bursik and Webb, "Community Change and Patterns of Delinquency," *American Journal of Sociology* 88 (July 1982): 25–42.

36. Travis Hirschi, "Families and Crime," *Wilson Quarterly* 7 (Spring 1983): 132–9.

37. David Cantor and Kenneth C. Land, "Unemployment and Crime Rates in the Post-WWII United States," *American Sociological Review* 50 (June 1985): 317–32.

38. David Phillips and Kenneth Bollen, "Same Time, Last Year: Selective Data Dredging for Negative Findings," *American Sociological Review* 50 (June 1985): 364–71.

39. James Baron and Peter Reiss, "Same Time, Next Year: Aggregate Analysis of the Mass Media and Violent Behavior," *American Sociological Review* 50 (June 1985): 347–63.

40. Bernice L. Neugarten, "Adult Personality: Toward a Psychology of the Life Cycle," in *Readings in General Psychology,* ed. Edgar Vinacle (New York: Dryden Press, 1968).

41. U.S. Public Health Service, *Working with Older People: A Guide to Practice,* pub. no. 1459 (Washington, D.C., Government Printing Office): vol. 2.

42. J.L. Horn and R.B. Cattell, "Age Differences in Fluid and Crystallized Intelligence," *Acta Psychologica* 26 (1967): 107–29.

SUGGESTED READINGS

Becker, Howard S. *Outsiders.* New York: Free Press, 1963.

Clinard, Marshall and Robert Meier. *Sociology of Deviant Behavior.* 6th ed. New York: Holt, Rinehart & Winston, 1985.

Giele, Janet Zollinger. *Women in the Future.* New York: The Free Press, 1978.

Goldberg, Herb. *The New Male.* New York: William Morrow & Co., 1979.

Hess, Beth B., and Markson, Elizabeth W. *Aging and Old Age: An Introduction to Social Gerontology.* New York: Macmillan Co., 1980.

Rothman, David. *The Discovery of the Asylum.* Boston: Little, Brown & Co., 1971.

Rubin, Lillian. *Women of Certain Age: The Midlife Search for Self.* New York: Harper & Row, 1979.

Silberman, Charles E. *Criminal Violence, Criminal Justice.* New York: Vintage, 1980.

Traub, Stuart and Craig Little, eds. *Theories of Deviance.* 3d ed. Itasca, Ill.: Peacock, 1985.

10 THE FAMILY

Family and Marriage in the Future

No one can be certain what will happen in the future, but some guesses can be made based on current trends. Some of the predictions offered here may tempt you, others may terrify you. The point is that some may actually affect you one day, either as an issue to confront, a decision to make, or even a law to obey.

Mate selection in the future may be less casual and more scientific. People may find it wise to base such a vital decision less on feelings and more on facts. Couples may take tests to see how compatible they are then and would be later. Society, hoping for more stability, may even require such tests before marriage licenses can be obtained.

More weddings in the future may occur in places other than a church or courthouse. And whether a wedding takes place under water, thousands of feet above ground, or simply in a private home, it may center upon the signing of a document written by bride and groom: the marriage contract. Such a written agreement would specify the rights and duties of each spouse and is used by some couples today.

The marriages of the future will probably be based on even more freedom of choice than today. More marriages will be tailored for, and by, each couple. Sex roles will be based less on tradition than on choice, as will the type and frequency of sex relations. Perhaps the number of sex partners and even the number of spouses will be less limited either by law or by custom.

Childbearing will also be more controlled. It will ''just happen'' less often, as people become more aware of even more effective methods of contraception. Having children by choice and not by accident will become more common also, because children will seem more of a burden to people with too little money or time for child-rearing. In fact, child-rearing may become a luxury, enjoyed mostly by people with leisure and wealth. Meanwhile, the poor who do not choose to be sterilized may find parenting even more expensive and worrisome than it is today. Besides this, society may decide that certain kinds of people should not be allowed to have children. Couples might even be required to pass tests of their intelligence or their emotional health before being certified as legal potential parents. Child-bearing may well become more a conscious decision, for the person or society, rather than a matter of fate.

People in the future may decide not just if or when to have children, but what kind of children they will have. It may not be long before parents will be able to choose the genes their children will be born with. From hair color to hormones, parents will be able to construct their ideal child, with no worry about birth defects.

Do you find this picture terrific or terrible? Whichever your reaction is, the future world of the family will offer more conscious choice and control by humans. To deal with this, you need a fuller understanding of the forms and functions of the family, and an awareness of the trends involved today. This chapter offers some help in this regard.

FAMILY: A group of people related to one another by blood or marriage.

The families of your parents (your family of orientation) and of your children (your family of procreation) are probably the most important groups of your life. They are the sources of some of your most intimate and satisfying personal ties. But because you are so close to your family life, you may never have studied it and therefore may not fully understand it. You may not have thought about the ways in which your family is different from or like all others in the world. Furthermore, while you may at times see your family as something of a bother, it performs for you several important functions of which you may have been unaware.

This chapter will help you think about the family in these ways. In addition, the chapter will look at some of the major changes taking place today in the American family. The Special Topic will explore the rewards and the costs of the working woman. Overall, the chapter will offer perspective: a broader, more fully informed view of the family.

DESCRIBING MARRIAGE AND FAMILY

A useful perspective of the family is based on a grasp of the essence both of the family and of its core—marriage. In defining the words "family" and "marriage," we learn something about the essence of both concepts.

Marriage: Its Essential Features and Its Varied Forms

Chances are high that most of us will marry someday, if we have not done so already, so it can be valuable to know what marriage is and what it can be. This section explores the essence of marriage as well as the various forms it can take. It begins by defining marriage.

A Definition for All Marriages. How many husbands make a marriage? How many wives? Is the spouse chosen from within the family or outside? These questions give an idea of the wide range of marriage forms throughout the world. Because the arrangements that are called "marriage" vary so much from one culture to the next, the term is difficult to define. Our search for a definition of marriage must take into account this wide range of variations.

The Nayar of India are the most famous example of an unusual marriage form.[1] Young women of the Nayars once went through a wedding ceremony that linked them to official "husbands." After the ceremony, a woman's link with her husband dissolved, and she was allowed any visitor she wished, one per night. Any children she had would have to be recognized by one of her lovers, whether he was the real father or not. This "father" would not live with her. In fact, like other Nayar men, he would live with his sister. His "wife" would live with her children in the household of her brother. From this example we can see the problems theorists face in trying to define marriage in such a way that both the Nayars and our parents' marriage are covered.

Also, we might reasonably assume that marriage involves a man and a woman. A worldwide definition of marriage could not

Skill Reinforcer 10-1*

What are the premises that might lead deductively to this conclusion: Those African "marriages" are not really marriages at all. Evaluate the syllogism.

* Answers to the Skill Reinforcers appear at the end of the chapter.

even specify that a man was involved. In some African cultures, a woman already married to a man can be said to marry some other woman. The "female husband" allows her "female bride" to have children by selected males. These children come under the control of the "female father."[2] Because this is considered a marriage, it must be covered by our definition.

In searching for the essence of marriage, science has found one trait of marriage that seems to exist in all cultures. This trait is that marriage gives children a legal place in society; it makes them legitimate. The children are recognized as those of the husband. This is the basis of any definition of marriage.

Because all the many types of marriage forms must be considered when marriage is defined, the result is a description of marriage that does not sound familiar. Marriage is here defined as the relationship between at least two people—of any sex—which makes the child legitimate.

Universals of Marriage. Beyond this bare definition of marriage, science has found several worldwide elements in marriage. Even though the number and gender of the people involved, and their living and sexual arrangement, may vary, marriage in all cultures has the same core of traits. Saxton points out that marriage everywhere involves a contract, a ceremony, and division of labor.[3]

Contract. Marriage is made legitimate either by a civil contract or by a sacred contract, which spells out the duties of the partners both as spouses and as parents. It legally or morally binds the couple to their duties.

In Western society, the contract has gone from a religious focus to a civil focus to a personal focus over the past one hundred years.[4] Until the late nineteenth century, marriage was viewed as a holy contract sanctioned by God. Then more governments began to see marriage as a civil agreement. Today many people hold that the personal commitment of marriage is more important than the civil or sacred frameworks.

This trend toward a personal contract is based on two developments of the twentieth century.[5] First, as people began to choose their own mates, through dating, mate selection came to be based more on the person than on the person's family. Along with this, romantic love came to be a large part of the picture. This view of love is based on a view of mating as something exclusive and intimate—something very personal.

The chapter preview suggests that custom-made personal contracts may be a common part of future marriages. Such contracts are sometimes drawn up by lawyers and signed by the bride and groom. Though this arrangement has long been used by wealthy people to safeguard the family estate, some moderate-income marriages are now based on contracts too. These contracts often specify many parts of the marriage bond. The personal relationship is made legal (though such a personal contract cannot over-

MARRIAGE: The relationship between two or more people which gives any child born of it a recognized place in society and full legal birthrights.

In the wedding ceremony, the marriage contract is recorded in public.

Not all cultures restrict marriage to monogamy.

ride a state law). Contract clauses might specify how money is to be shared and spent, who does what chores, and how many children—if any—there are to be. In this way, the partners can agree on the ground rules before they make the final commitment.

Such personal contracts are much more detailed than the state marriage laws. The civil contract described by state laws specifies broader requirements concerning age, incest, number of partners (only one per person is allowed in the United States), witnesses, and other such matters. A civil contract is required in the United States, but it sets only general requirements.

Ceremony. In the wedding ceremony, the marriage contract is recorded in public. The partners make public commitments to the contract and to each other. In front of witnesses, the spouses are tied to a new set of duties and rights. The partners step into new social statuses during the ritual.

The chapter preview mentioned that wedding ceremonies are taking place in many nontraditional places. A related trend is for the couples to write their own script for the ceremony. In this way, the bride and groom can specify their agreed-upon commitments and add a personal touch to the ceremony with their favorite music or poetry. Like the marriage contract, both these trends show that the wedding ceremony is becoming more personal.

Division of labor. The third worldwide element of marriage is the division of labor, which is often assumed to be part of the marriage contract. The jobs and roles of the partnership are usually determined by the culture, but even when spouses work out their own division of labor, as often happens in our culture, some agreement between the partners is needed. Without this, resentments would build up and chores would not get done.

Variations. Contracts, ceremony, and division of labor can be found in marriages all over the world. Despite this, marriages take on varied forms among the world's cultures.

Number of spouses. The basic marriage framework just described can vary as to the number of spouses it contains. Marriages can be classed as monogamous or polygamous. Monogamous marriage involves one spouse per person; polygamous marriage means several spouses per person. Our culture takes the unusual position of outlawing plural marriage, or polygamy. Most cultures allow a person to have more than one spouse.

There are two main classes of plural marriage. In polyandry, one wife has several husbands. In polygyny, it is the husband who has more than one spouse; this is the most common form of polygamy.

There are several reasons why polygyny is so popular throughout the world. One is that more children can be produced. Where children help produce wealth, or care for the parents in old age, they are clearly an asset. Polygyny also makes sense from the viewpoint of sociobiology, which suggests that our genes urge us

MONOGAMY: Marriage involving two people.

POLYGAMY: Plural marriage, consisting of more than two spouses.

POLYGYNY: Marriage of a man to two or more women.

to maximize their chances of being passed along. In this view, polygyny helps ensure that the genes of the superior man—one who can afford many wives—will be reproduced in greater numbers. Polygyny can also help solve an imbalance in the sex ratio. If there are many more women than men, this type of marriage can help prevent too many unmarried women. In some cultures, frequent violence creates a high death rate among men. There polygyny offers the widow and her children a haven. Furthermore, polygyny benefits the man who can afford it. His several wives offer him a varied sex life and prestige. Despite this, while polygyny is allowed in many places it is practiced by few men because it is so expensive.

A potential problem in polygynous marriages is jealousy among the wives. This is not often a problem, however, for two reasons. One is that wives are often given definite ranks and chores and therefore do not compete with one another directly, even helping to lighten the work load for one another. Another tactic is for a man to marry women who are sisters to each other. The sisters have already worked out their power balance and share loyalty to the same clan. Still, this is not to say that jealousy does not occur in polygyny, though it does not seem to be a major problem.

Polyandry is rare. Where it does occur, it is often fraternal. That is, the husbands are brothers.

There are several reasons for polyandry.[6] When too few women exist, this marriage form gives more men the chance to have a marriage household. Also, in some places, land is passed on through the males. If the brothers of a family marry the same woman, the land is not split up into less valuable pieces. Polyandry also means that fewer heirs will be produced to claim the land.

In only about one out of four human societies is monogamy the only marriage form allowed.[7] Polygamy is in most places preferred. In actual practice, however, one wife per husband is the most common marriage form. This is because the number of males and females is usually balanced. Leaving too many men or women without mates can be disruptive, so monogamy often prevails. Also, as already mentioned, sharing spouses presents problems of expense and jealousy. Because of this, even in a polygamous society most of the marriages will be monogamous.

Mate selection. Marriages can also vary as to the rules for choosing a spouse. Religious, ethnic, and other kinds of groups have rules concerning marriage with outsiders. The rule of endogamy requires people to marry within their own kind, for instance, within their own religion, class, tribe, ethnic group, or race. This helps maintain the unity of the group and ensure that the group's values and traits will be passed to the next generation. To help avoid incest—mating between close relatives—and the total isolation of the group, exogamy is used. This rule requires a person to choose a spouse from an outside group. Such a practice ensures

POLYANDRY: The marriage of several men to one woman.

ENDOGAMY: The requirement that people marry their own kind.

EXOGAMY: The requirement that people marry outside their kin group.

links with other groups, which can be helpful for a group's trade and defense.

The Various Forms of the Family

So far we have seen that marriage is basically a relationship based on a contract, a ceremony, and a division of labor. This relationship is used to place children socially. Around this forms a family, which must care for those children placed in its care.

Just as the marriage of a person's parents was the basis of that person's childhood family, so that person's own marriage is the core of his or her own adult-level family. That is, marriage is the core of the family. Now that we have studied the core, we are ready to study the various forms the family can take.

NUCLEAR FAMILY: The unit consisting of a husband, his wife, and their unmarried offspring.

Types of Family Organization. The basic family organization is the nuclear family: husband, wife, and their unmarried children. In about half the world's cultures, the nuclear family serves as the unit on which extended families are based. Extended families include the nuclear unit as well as other relatives, such as grandparents, aunts and uncles, and in-laws.

EXTENDED FAMILY: A family organization involving a nuclear family and additional relatives.

In our culture, the nuclear family is much more important than the extended family. While this gives the married couple the advantage of independence and privacy, there are disadvantages too. To the extent that the couple is independent of the extended family, the spouses are dependent on each other. Each spouse must meet all the other's emotional needs. The couple must divide the household chores between two people instead of perhaps as many as twelve. Also, extended family members are not so available for child care or for help in a crisis. And there are simply fewer people to love or to be loved by in the smaller, nuclear family setting. Despite these drawbacks, the nuclear family is the most important type of family organization in our culture.

BILATERAL DESCENT: Ancestry traced through both male and female ancestry.

MATRILINEAL: Tracing the family line through the female lineage.

PATRILINEAL: Tracing the family line through the male lineage.

Descent Rules. Families can also be classed according to their rules regarding descent. In the United States we are equally related to kin on our father's side and our mother's side. This is a bilateral (two-sided) system. In most cultures, however, descent is reckoned on only one bloodline. In a matrilineal system, a person belongs to the mother's line. In such a system, a man who marries remains part of his mother's descent line, but his children will belong to his wife's line. A patrilineal system is just the opposite; all people are placed according to the father's line.

PATRILOCALITY: A married couple moving in with the family of the husband.

MATRILOCALITY: A married couple moving in with the family of the wife.

NEOLOCALITY: A married couple establishing a household separate from that of their parents.

Residence Rules. Families can also be described on the basis of residence rules. In a patrilocal system, the newly married couple moves in with the husband's parents. Matrilocal residence would be with the bride's parents. Neolocal residence means that the couple would establish their own household, apart from the parents.

FUNCTIONS OF THE FAMILY

It may be true that if the family breaks down and ceases to do what it now does for us, our society will also cease to function as well as it does. The social functions of the family are truly vital. The family can be called culture's most important institution, the foundation of the social system. As the family performs its functions, it touches its members' lives intimately, from sex to parenting to money. Here these functions of the family are explored.

Sex and Reproduction

Having sex and having children are naturally linked activities, but over the past century they have become more and more separated from each other. Because of this change, they will be treated here as being somewhat distinct.

The Sexual Revolution. In our culture, love and marriage are supposed to go together, as are sex and the family. One of the family's functions is to control the human sex drive, to limit sexual behavior to the confines of the family.

The family has had a difficult time. It has been faced with what has been called the sexual revolution. Since the 1960s, dramatic changes in Americans' sexual behavior and views on sex have taken place, and this has affected our ideas about the family's functions regarding sex.

Views on sex. The most dramatic changes in this sexual revolution have been those in our views on sex. Throughout the 1970s, premarital sex has come to be viewed more favorably. This attitude change has occurred among both sexes, all social classes, and both blacks and whites.[8] Also, sex is now discussed openly and studied thoroughly. Teachers, researchers, counselors, and nearly everyone else find the topic no longer one to be neglected. Perhaps this will result in fewer sexual problems, because so many of such problems are caused by ignorance. In any case, the openness toward the topic has clearly affected sexual behavior, the other part of the sexual revolution.

Sexual behavior. The changes in sexual activity during the sexual revolution have been biggest among young females. The level of sexual activity among young females had increased by 1970 and remained fairly stable through that decade.[9] It seems that, in this regard, the sexual revolution came and stayed.

For many young people, sex has become a part of courtship. As a result, the number of unwed pregnancies has soared since World War II. Illegitimate births tripled between 1940 and 1960 and have continued to increase, though at a slower rate, since then.[10]

The sexual revolution has also affected sexual behavior in marriage. Open discussion and increased knowledge about sex can influence sexual expression between spouses. The revolution has made available more counseling, stimulating books and films, and varied value systems. Of course, such changes can bring both confusion and freedom and can either help or damage marital sex.

Class Differences in Sex.   Based on the chapter on social stratification, we should expect that sex attitudes and behaviors vary according to social class. Research has confirmed that, indeed, working-class and middle-class people of both sexes differ in their typical sex-life histories.[11] For the most part, the lower their social class, the more inflexible and traditional people's sexual attitudes are likely to be.

Reproduction: How Many Children?   Besides shaping and controlling our sex attitudes and behavior, the family also has the job of reproducing each generation. As mentioned in the chapter preview, science will soon be able to offer parents more control over the number—and perhaps the kinds—of children they will have. In the meantime, social science offers some insight into which families are likely to have many children or few children. Social class and residence (whether urban or rural) both affect family size.

If we had to guess the size of some unknown family, our best hope would be to find out the social-class level of that family. Since the late nineteenth century in this nation, middle-class women have, in general, had fewer children than lower-class women. This has been partly the result of different attitudes toward birth control, which may be viewed by a lower-class person as being neither moral nor desirable. The class differences in birthrates have also been based both on knowledge and on the lack of knowledge. Until two decades ago, poor women had little access to family-planning information or facilities. On the other hand, middle-class women could afford a private physician.

Besides social class, we might also use the size of a family's town or city in an effort to guess the number of children in that family. Rural or small-town families are in general larger than families living in large cities. Children on a farm are extra hands to help with production; the big-city family may see a child as another mouth to feed.

These urban-versus-rural and social-class differences in reproduction have held even while the overall rates for the United States have risen and fallen. In this century, the nation's birthrates were dropping until the mid-1930s. New contraceptive methods and the Depression helped cause the downward trend. After World War II, the rate went up, as it usually does after a war, and stayed high through the next decade.

The Shrinking American Family: Factors Affecting the Birthrate.   For the last two decades, the birthrate has been low, and the average size of the American family has continued to decrease. In the mid-1970s the average size of American households slipped below three persons, and the size has continued to decrease. While 9.7% of families had four or more children in 1960, only about 3% do now.[12] This shrinking tendency was due in part to the development of the Pill and the improvement of other means of birth control. Also, more lower-class women have gained access to contraceptive methods. The concern over population growth led some people to restrict their childbearing. Young people are waiting longer to get married, others are influenced by the high cost of raising a child. Another big factor is the feminist movement; more women are avoiding marriage and childbearing in favor of careers.

Indeed, more American couples are completely ignoring the childbearing function of the family. Half of all families have no children under the age of eighteen.[13] The percentage of families with children dropped about 4 points during the past decade.[14] The trend toward childless marriage seems to result from the same factors responsible for the low birthrate.

Parenting is difficult. Another reason for today's lower birthrate is that the task of parenthood is viewed as more difficult now than it was a generation ago. No longer are parents assured that the approach they are using is the ''right'' one. A lack of agreement on what is the best way to rear children is cause for anxiety among parents.

Parenting is hard on a marriage. Marriages of couples with young children tend to last longer, at least in the short run.[15] When children are present, a marriage is more likely to endure, regardless of how old the parents are or whether they have been divorced before. Parents are more likely to stay together, perhaps because they cannot afford the cost of a divorce or because they want to do what they think is best for the kids.[16] However, marital satisfaction tends to drop as more children are added to a family. One reason for the drop is the financial and emotional strains imposed by the demanding job of child-rearing. It is clear to anyone that children cut down the time parents spend being companions to each other, thereby affecting the degree of satisfaction in a marriage. Indeed, many parents today feel unprepared for their new role. After all, a two-person household must adapt to a very demanding third party. Fatigue and a lack of leisure time are common. The parent may resent the infant, then feel guilty about such feelings. If this is the case for a couple, their first child may be their last.

Socialization   Having produced children, a family is given the vital task of shaping them into members of the social system. As we have seen in an earlier chapter, the child must be humanized through socialization. This is a major function of the family. In performing this task, parents face several duties. Benson lists several jobs of child-rearing.[17]

Tasks Involved in Child-rearing.
Meeting physical needs. First, the parents, and in most cases the mother, must meet the survival needs of the child. It is doubtful that any other agent will ever take the place of parents in this task. Infants need so much attention that a system of caring for them would require too many adults.

Teaching.   Parents must also teach the child basic living skills and habits. The child must be taught what is right and wrong. The parents serve as models and teachers.

Guiding.   Another, related task is discipline. Parents are responsible for enforcing basic standards of behavior, for which there are many different techniques. Though it is not a pleasant duty, the parent cannot shirk it without neglecting the child's needs for guidance.

Loving.   Benson says that another duty of parents is to love their children. Children are no longer to be merely tolerated or used as farmhands. Love of the child is expected to mature into respect. This can be a joyful part of the overall duty of socializing the child.

Releasing.   Another duty not often recognized is that of releasing the child. Children must some day establish their own households. The parent must help in this process by releasing the child at the proper time. This time is being delayed in many families today. Growing numbers of mature children return to live at home after college.[18] When jobs are difficult to find and the costs of living on one's own are too high, some parents are finding it hard to release their children.

Benson's list of the jobs of child-rearing gives the total picture of the socializing task of the family. It shows that this job of shaping human infants into functioning members of the social system is a complex one.

Social Class Differences in Child-rearing.   The way a child is socialized varies according to the family's social class level. In fact, even during pregnancy and the birth experience, social class differences are apparent.[19] Compared with middle-class women, working-class women are more likely to have negative feelings toward their pregnancy, partly because they have fewer resources for finding rest and relaxation. These women also are more apprehensive about labor and delivery, and are less interested in "natural birth." The level of mother-child interaction varies with social class, beginning during the child's first two years.[20] The parents' level of income and education affects the kind of attention they give their children. The parents' social class will influence the child's views toward church and school, toward sex and marriage. The child's view of the future and the government, and his or her politics, will be affected by the family's social class. Besides this, higher-class parents can provide better food, housing, and schooling for their children. This world of comfort and security contrasts starkly with the world of a lower-class child.

Child-rearing Approaches: In Search of the Best Way.   Families have different ways of rearing their children. The important question is: Is there a *best* way to raise children? We want to do what is best for our children, but social science does not tell us what is best. Child-rearing seems to be more an art than a science;

Laissez faire
authoritarian
authoritarian

that is, it is based more on values than on facts. Still, social science can offer descriptions of the various approaches to child-rearing. Such descriptions can help people choose the approach that best fits their own values.

Democratic vs. traditional. Most child-rearing approaches in the United States today can be classed as either democratic or traditional. The democratic approach, sometimes labeled permissive, is more typical of middle-class families. The democratic and traditional approaches differ most on the issues of power and control.

The traditional approach to child-rearing views the parent as boss; the children are expected to adapt to the boss's rules. Above all, the parent is to be obeyed. Physical punishment, such as spanking, is seen as the most effective means of control.

The issue of physical punishment is at the heart of the difference between these two child-rearing approaches. Few experts view physical punishment, even spanking, as the best means of child control. It is said to teach violence and cause resentment, and it can even be viewed as a form of child abuse. Further, physical punishment is not regarded by the experts as being very effective. They say that in the long run punishment is not as effective as praise, perhaps because punishment is aimed more at the child than at the behavior. In fact, experts urge parents to criticize the child's improper behavior, not the child.

The democratic approach to child-rearing tries to aim more at the child's actions, while at the same time accepting the child himself. The parent is seen as an adviser or counselor, rather than as a boss.

However, the democratic approach has its drawbacks. It can easily become permissiveness. The parent may be so concerned about the children's need to grow that the children are allowed to direct their own upbringing to a large extent. The parents might in this way neglect their task of socializing the children. Also, the democratic approach can be very demanding of both parents and children. The methods of control used can produce guilt and anxiety in the children. And the parent must do more adapting to the children's needs, which is very demanding.

Parenting models. E.E. LeMasters offers another way to classify the various approaches to child-rearing.[21] He says that parents adopt one of several parent models in socializing their children. A review of these models can provide some insight into the ways this function of the family is performed, and perhaps which way is best for any particular parent.

Many parents, says LeMasters, adopt the martyr model. Nothing is denied the child by such a parent. This approach produces guilt on the part of the parent and resentment in the child. The martyr model may be the most harmful model for children, even worse than neglect.

In the buddy or pal model, the parent believes in being a pal, a peer for the child. LeMasters says, "Only the superior parent can play the buddy game with his or her children without losing their respect and their obedience."[22]

The police officer model is very strict. It is used in an attempt to keep the child out of trouble. It meets much resistance in the child and unduly limits his or her behavior, says LeMasters.

A model popular with middle-class parents is the teacher-counselor model. In this approach, the parents are held to be almost completely responsible for the growth of the child. The child is seen as having tremendous potential, and if the child does not reach this potential, it is the fault of the parents. Such parents are often plagued by guilt and anxiety; the children often suffer from an inflated sense of importance.

LeMasters advocates for many parents the athletic-coach model. This role demands of the child fitness, skill, and discipline. The parents encourage and instruct. In many ways, LeMasters says, this model is appropriate for socializing children in our culture.

Parenting guidelines. There is no parenting model or approach that is perfect or best for all parents. The experts can help us only so much. The recipes they offer vary with the scientists' own basic premises. Because we will not subject children to the required experiments, there is little proof to support any specific technique.

Still, some general advice can be gleaned from the experts. Balance seems to be a key to successful child-rearing. Whatever techniques are used, the parent must avoid the extremes of overindulgence and rejection. Rules must be clear and consistently enforced. Yet while giving guidance and direction, the parent must also allow the child freedom to grow into an independent adult. The parent who is firm but loving will be most successful in the vital child-rearing role.

Economic Functions

A person's standard of living is determined by the total income of the nuclear family. Along with this personal economic function, the family is also the basic unit of a society's economic system. In meeting its members' material needs, the family consumes the production of the nation. It is at the family level that the economy is sustained.

While the family in our culture still has a vital role as a consumption unit, its role as a productive unit has been largely lost. During the nineteenth century, families owned most businesses and most men were self-employed. For its standard of living, the family depended on its own production. With the advent of corporate industry, however, this situation changed. Increasingly, people worked apart from the family. The family functioned less as a productive unit and more as a consuming unit.

In carrying out its role as consumption unit, the family has been adapting in two main ways. One is the divergence of the economic roles of husband and wife. The other change is the employed wife. The wife today often works, but not with her husband.

Spouses' Economic Roles Grew Apart.   The economic roles of husband and wife grew apart as the family's functions shifted from production to consumption. As the home lost its productive role, the wife lost her role as a producer in the home. Where she had in the past been a co-producer, a kind of vice-president in the family business, her role now does not center on production. While today many American women work, the wife's family duties still focus on homemaking and shopping for the family, not bringing in a paycheck. This role does not demand that she work outside the home, though increasingly it does allow her to do so.

The husband's role also changed as the family's economic function shifted away from home-centered production. No longer is he the owner and boss of the family business. Seldom does he have an intimate involvement in the family's production, or even in its daily activities. His economic role has been pared down to that of provider.

More Employed Wives.   Even though the economic roles of husband and wife grew apart during the nineteenth century, the trend of the working wife has been growing stronger recently. Since World War II, an increasing number of married women have joined the labor force. While the roles of some wives had settled into focusing on consumption and homemaking, other women were becoming paid producers.

This is now so common that production may once again become part of the wife's duties. We may even see changes in laws that require a husband to support his wife. Most of these laws do not require a wife to support her husband, unless—in some states—he is unable to work. Insofar as the laws reflect our views on the roles of spouses, they may change to add production to the wife's duties.

Emotional Security

Where Else but the Family?   Most of the love we find in our life we find within our family. Indeed, the function of providing intimacy and emotional support has emerged as one of the family's most important tasks. As our society has become more impersonal, the family has become the main source of intimacy.

This is in contrast to the other functions that have been in part taken over by other agencies. The family has lost much of its socializing function to the schools. Sex today is less confined to marriage; even reproduction may become more and more the province of scientists. We have seen how the family lost its production function over the past century. Not all families today provide religion, recreation, protection, or medical care for their members.

The broad social changes that have caused the family to lose many of its functions have at the same time enhanced the importance of emotional support. The rise of an urban, industrial society has broken down the primary relationships that give people a feeling of belonging. The people around us today are likely to be

Warmth and intimacy: where else today but the family?

strangers. Because emotional ties are difficult to establish in such an impersonal world, the family becomes even more important to people. Even as we depend on the family less for our other needs, we depend on our family and marriage for most of our intimacy. As the outside world becomes more impersonal, even hostile, we see our family as a haven.

The Family Is Not Always a Haven. Not all families were or are havens. Recent research has focused attention on the violence found within some families. Only very recently has violence in families been thoroughly studied. Violence can be directed against any member of the family. Spouse abuse is mostly wife abuse, though battered husbands have also been reported. Aged parents or grandparents have been attacked by younger family members. Siblings do violence to one another. The most important type of family violence is child abuse, because it tends to produce people who will become abusers themselves. It is difficult to say how common family violence is, for surely not all cases are reported.

In this section we have seen that the functions of the family have been changing over the past one hundred years, and even more so since World War II. Some people see these changes as threatening the family's survival. Others see them as necessary adaptations to a modern world. However, if the family changes to the extent that it does not perform some of its vital functions, some other agency must step in. It is doubtful that any such agency would be able to meet in an acceptable way our needs for sex, reproduction, child-rearing, and intimacy. Because of this, we must carefully judge the changes we see in the family.

CHANGES IN THE AMERICAN FAMILY

The essential question asked about today's American family is: Is the family dying? The chapter preview envisions greater freedom and variety for family members. It suggests that today's trends are in fact progress toward a more fulfilling family life. We're all aware of soaring divorce rates and the increase in single-parent homes; it seems that the family is disappearing in the United States. Increasingly, in divorce cases neither parent wants custody of the children. Violence among family members is now well publicized. Wives are deserting their families the way only husbands seemed to do in the past. Illegitimacy rates have leapfrogged during the last two decades. The disintegration of the American family seems to be only a matter of time. However, most people will marry, and most first marriages will last until death. And most people who leave one marriage will enter another one. Is the American family collapsing or adapting? Either way, it is certainly changing.

Changing Family Structure

The kinds of families we see around us are quite different from those our parents were accustomed to. This is due to the big changes that the structure of the American family has undergone in recent years. These changes are seen in several statistics.[23] While

2.3% of Americans were in the divorced category in 1960, in 1984 the figure had climbed to 7.3%. In 1970, 708,000 divorces occurred; the figure was over 1,170,000 in the early 1980s. In 1970, 72.5% of all white households were based on a married couple; in 1984 only 61.2% were. The family with a working father, a nonworking mother, and one or more children is no longer the typical family structure in the United States.

Many people in our culture who agree with the critics of our marriage structure cast their votes by simply avoiding marriage in any form. The number of people living alone rose dramatically over the last decade, mostly because young adults are remaining single longer, and because more divorced and widowed people are living on their own. In fact, singlehood is viewed by more people as a desirable life-style, not a lonely stage before marriage. Clearly, many people no longer see marriage as the only acceptable route. Research suggests that the recent decline in marriage rates is not due to increased barriers to marriage but to the fact that women have more options open to them besides marriage.[24]

While more people today choose to live alone, another trend is that more people are living together without being married. Such couples make up only about 2% of all households in the United States, but this arrangement seems to be gaining acceptance. People living in this kind of union cite various reasons for avoiding marriage, including feminist mistrust of marriage and memories of parents' bitter marriages.

Another change in the American family's structure is the increase in young, middle-class families living in their parents' homes. Economic pressures have forced more of this sharing of households, and this sharing is expected to increase. Interfamily tensions will accompany this trend, as disagreements and misunderstandings arise regarding such matters as shared expenses and chores.[25]

Other options to our traditional marriage structure range from a flexible monogamy to group marriage. First, some people aim for personal and, in some cases, sexual freedom within a monogamous framework. This may include swinging, or sexual spouse-sharing. It is impossible to say how many people attempt swinging and how many such attempts actually succeed in enhancing personal freedom. Group marriage and communal families are also part of this picture of our changing family structure, but they seem to draw more attention than followers.

Changes in American marriages inevitably affect the childhood experience. Compared to children born in the early 1950s, children born in the early 1980s will experience a dramatically different childhood.[26] By age 17, about 70% of today's children will live at some time with one parent. For blacks the figure is 94%. And white children will spend about 69% of their childhood with both parents, compared to 92% for the earlier generation. Black children will typically spend only 41% of their childhood with both parents. Clearly, the changing American family structure translates into a different kind of childhood experience.

Changing Family Dynamics

Over the last two decades, our culture has focused more than ever on individual freedom. While we have long valued political freedom, many Americans have recently been demanding personal freedom from social restraints. Some people view freedom to grow personally as a right. Along with this, certain groups in our nation have aimed at removing social restraints on their members.

Such concern with freedom has been reflected in the family's inner workings. One distressing result has been that with its adults going their separate ways, "the conjugal family . . . has begun to divest itself of its responsibility for the young." [27] This divestiture is mostly a matter of absent fathers. The search for personal freedom has also created far-reaching changes regarding divorce and freedom for wives. These two changes will be explored here, because the life of each one of us is affected by them, often in important and very personal ways.

Freedom for Wives. A prime example of Americans' demands for freedom has been the women's movement. This movement has altered the attitudes of many women and men concerning sex roles and as a result has had a profound effect on the dynamics of many marriages.

Many women have begun to demand more freedom in their marriages to explore their life options. They are refusing to accept the limits of the traditional housewife role, which, insofar as it hinders personal growth, is seen as something to change. There are several areas in marriage in which some wives have demanded this freedom.

Sex. Sexual fulfillment has been one such area. Some women have claimed the right to cast off many of the sexual restraints put on women in the past. They refuse to accept the double standard, which allows men more sexual freedom than women. More women now feel free to explore various sources of sexual pleasure. Fewer middle-class women than ever before view sex as an unpleasant wifely duty (this has spread to the working class, though to a lesser extent). They view sex as something that should give pleasure to both partners. Because of childhood training, this change in attitude is not easy to accomplish, but many have succeeded. In fact, some husbands complain that their wives are too sexually aggressive. Thus, while some husbands with such a partner are quite happy about it, others feel threatened by their wives' demands. As is often the case, one person's gain in freedom can cause problems for another.

Chores. The increased freedom for wives has also led to changes in the division of labor in some marriages. More women are refusing to accept the division of chores and powers they saw in their parents' marriages. Rather than limiting themselves to the past, such wives examine the role images they carried with them into their marriages. If they find these images are not really what they want, they seek a new arrangement. Of course, this attempt works well only when both partners' views coincide. If only one spouse accepts changes in the division of labor, a great strain is put on the partnership. And when the husband does take an active parenting role, he typically feels more strain than do traditional fathers. Being an involved father is satisfying, it seems, but difficult.[28]

Paycheck. A central part of the women's movement has been the demand for freedom to work outside the home. While some women feel they must work because of financial pressures, many also see their jobs as giving them freedom for greater personal growth.

The soaring number of working wives has required important changes in the marriage's balance of power, which is based on each partner's relative strengths. During the first half of this century, the "normal" allocation of household money was based on the dependent wife receiving a "housekeeping allowance." Now there seems to be a demand for a deconcentration of money within households.[29] When the wife brings home a paycheck, she can gain a great deal of power. With more financial independence, she can more readily risk the anger of her spouse by asserting her own wishes. Her spouse may not only get angry at her self-assertion, he may suffer lower self-esteem.[30] Clearly, adjustments are required in a marriage's inner workings when the wife brings home a paycheck.

Increasing Divorce. America's divorce rate has generally risen since the 1860s (a drop during the 1950s being an aberration). Ninety percent of children today will marry, 50% will marry and divorce, and 33% will marry, divorce, and remarry.[31] The demand for personal freedom may be partly responsible for the rise in marriage instability. As women have gained financial and emotional independence, they have less need to remain in lifeless marriages. Also, as more married men and women demand freedom to explore their options, more couples will grow apart.

Skill Reinforcer 10-2

Is there a clear cause-effect relationship between increased freedom for wives and increased divorce?

FIGURE 10-1
Divorce Rate (divorces per 1,000 married women, 15 years old and over), 1960–1982.

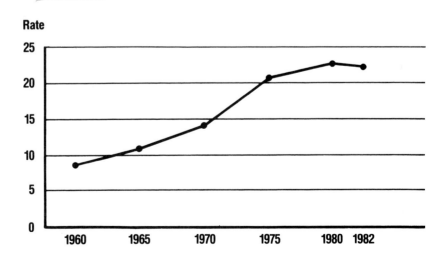

SOURCE: Based on U.S. Bureau of the Census, *Statistical Abstract of the United States: 1986*, 106th edition (Washington, D.C., 1985), p. 79, no. 124

SKILL BOX

Understanding Divorce: Statistics Can Mislead

Divorce data are useful in showing how statistics can give us an unclear or distorted view of a social trend. Divorce statistics can be especially confusing and can be used to give quite different pictures of divorce trends. There are several reasons why, including the way data are collected and the differences in the ways divorce is measured.

First, many divorce statistics are incomplete. Not all states give complete reports to the federal government. Thus some data are based on what might be a biased sample. For example, if most of the states not reporting data have low divorce rates, the national picture would reflect a higher divorce rate than is true.

The main problem in grasping divorce trends is that there are several different ways divorce can be measured. For example, if we compare the number of divorces against the number of marriages in a year, we can get a distorted picture. In a recent year there were about 2,444,000 marriages formed and 1,179,000 divorces.[32] Proportionally, this gives a divorce rate of about 49%. This, however, is a distortion, because the number of divorces should be measured against all marriages, not just the ones formed that one year. Also, people who divorced that year for the fourth time are counted along with those going through their first divorce. This method of measuring divorce tells us nothing about the chances a new marriage has of remaining intact. It also tells us nothing about how one generation's rate compares with another's. The divorced group for any one year might contain a high percentage of old people or young people. Thus we cannot tell if it is only the new crop of marriages that is failing or if divorce has spread throughout other age-groups. So, though it is a simple one to use, this method of measuring divorce is of limited value.

Simply counting the total number of divorces per year is another way of measuring divorce. We might thus compare the number of divorces over the years. If the yearly totals get larger over time, we could conclude that divorce was becoming more common. The problem here, of course, is that the growing number of divorces may merely reflect a growing population. The rate of divorce could actually be growing smaller.

If we count the number of divorces per one thousand people, we can then compare these rates over time. Still, this does not give us a true feel of the incidence of divorce. The one thousand people in our count will include many who could not get divorced anyway. Thus two divorces out of one thousand people looks good, until we consider that a large portion were children or eighty-year-old widows. The picture is in this way distorted.

A better method is to count the number of divorces per one thousand married women, perhaps adding an age range. This gives us a more accurate picture of divorce trends.

Statistics are also reported giving the likelihood of divorce for persons in certain age-groups. For example, of the marriages of women born between 1945 and 1949, some 17 percent had ended in divorce by 1975, and 38 percent were expected to end in divorce.[33] For the men, 34 percent may end their marriage with divorce. These figures give us the best feel of the impact divorce has on today's marriage.

These variations in divorce measurements suggest that statistics must be viewed with caution. We must ask questions about how complete the sample is and what measurement techniques were used. Only then can we begin to trust the divorce statistics.

The rise in the divorce rate is not caused only by the women's movement. Instead, it is valuable to view that movement as just part of the demand for personal freedom which has spread throughout our culture. As husbands, wives, and even some children demand more freedom, they are less likely to sacrifice for the sake of family bonds. While personal freedom allows us the chance to further develop our potentials, it also allows us to ignore the needs of other people.

Several other social trends are correlated with divorce since World War II.[34] Most clearly, as more women participated in the labor force the divorce rate has gone up. And surprisingly, as the unemployment rate went up so did the divorce rate. Economic prosperity apparently makes divorce more affordable, even though it seems to reduce the pressures and strains which can cause divorce. Divorce rates are also related to several other social factors. Higher divorce rates are more likely to be found among people with lower educational, occupational, and income levels, and people who marry at an early age.[35]

It is helpful here to contrast humans with a flock of birds, which, when released from a cage, will soar, free, together. On the other hand, when humans are released from the "cage" of social controls, each may take his or her own path. Some soar, and some stay where they are. Many will find themselves alone in their freedom.

Though the divorce rate is not always clear, statistics do show that divorce has become part of many people's family lives. Many people see that fact as a social disaster. Others, including support groups for the divorced, see divorce as an escape from damaging personal relationships. No matter which view is more common, the increasing divorce rate clearly affects the family's ability to meet the needs of its members. Our survey of the family's functions showed that society depends on the family in several ways. In this light, it is clear that the upward trend in the breakup of families affects not only the spouses who divorce and their children, but also the rest of society.

SUMMARY

The essential features of marriage can be found in its definition. The search for a universal definition of marriage turns up some unusual marriage forms. All these forms can be included in our definition of marriage as a relationship between two or more people which makes a woman's offspring legitimate. Other essential features of marriage are a contract, a ceremony, and division of labor, which are found in various forms in all cultures. Beyond these universal essentials are variations in the number of spouses and the rules for mate selection. Marriages can range from monogamy (one spouse per person) to polygamy, which includes both polygyny (several wives per husband) and polyandry (several husbands per wife). It may be required that mates be drawn from within one's own group (endogamy) or from outside one's immediate family (exogamy).

The group of related people centered around the marriage is called the family. The spouses and their children are the nuclear family; any wider family network is called the extended family. Within the extended-family network, descent can be traced through the mothers' line (matrilineal system), the fathers' line (patrilineal system), or through both lines (bilateral system). The nuclear family resides with the husband's family in a patrilocal system, with the wife's family in a matrilocal system, or with neither in a neolocal system.

The dramatic changes in the 1960s and 1970s in the sexual behaviors and attitudes of Americans have shown that the family has not been fully able to control the sexual drives of its members. The related function of the family, reproduction, is fulfilled to varying degrees, depending on the family's social class and the size of the town in which it lives. Birthrates have recently been falling, the main reasons being the view that children are expensive and the view that parenting is hard on parents and on the marriage bond.

Once the family produces children, it is expected to socialize them. This child-rearing function includes several tasks: meeting physical needs, teaching, guiding, loving, and, finally, releasing the child. Child-rearing methods, goals, and values vary with the family's social-class status. The democratic child-rearing approach focuses on the child's feelings and inner controls. The traditional approach focuses more on obedience. Besides these two basic approaches, there are several parenting models that can help describe how various parents raise their children. These models can include the martyr, the pal, the police officer, the teacher, and the coach.

The family also has the job of meeting its members' material needs. In performing this function, it consumes the goods and services produced by the economy. In the past, the American family also produced many of those goods and services, both spouses producing within the home. Today the husband's role is that of producer, while the wife's role is more that of the consumer, except in those families in which the wife works outside the home.

As the family has been losing many of its traditional functions, the function of giving love and security to its members has become more important. The family has become for many of us the only source of emotional security, even though too many families are rocked by violence among their members.

It is unclear whether the family is being destroyed by change or merely adapting to a changing world. In either case, it is changing. This change is seen in the family's structure in that the typical family membership and marriage form are no longer what they were a few decades ago. The family's dynamics are also changing, as wives gain more freedom and the marriage bond is subjected to more pressures, resulting in higher rates of divorce.

Even though the family and marriage in America are showing some dramatic changes, these institutions are in all cultures basic to the healthy functioning of the social system. Because of this, we can expect that while the marriage and family in our culture may change, they will not—they must not—lose too much of their ability to fulfill their vital social functions for the society and its members.

SPECIAL TOPIC

Working Women, Wives, and Mothers

Will you, as a wife, work outside the home? Or will you, as a husband, want your wife to do so? Whatever your personal decisions have been or will be, the employed wife is becoming more common in American families. Chances are high that this trend will touch or has touched your life, so you want to learn something about it. Toward this end, this Special Topic will look at the broad issue of employed women. Then the rewards and costs of the working wife and the working mother will be examined. All this can help us make informed personal decisions on this issue.

A HISTORY OF THE WORKING WOMAN

Women have always worked. Like men, they have always had their chores and duties, though these vary among cultures. In our culture, however, it is only recently that women have been working outside the home, for pay. Furthermore, this is not seen as a temporary condition. That is, many women today are not just working until they get married or until the economy improves. They are planning careers, not just hanging onto jobs for a while. In this way, these women play a work role that differs from that of earlier times.

The woman in hunting and gathering cultures was a worker, of course. Her role was centered on the domestic scene. Because she was the childbearer and the nurse, she was assigned the domestic chores. This was based not so much on her physical strength as on the restrictions of pregnancy and nursing. Her chores might involve heavy labor, such as carrying water or clearing farmland, but they could be done with her child close at hand. Thus, the earlier work role of woman was domestic, based on her special maternal role.

The woman in farming cultures retained this domestic role. Along with her husband, she helped run the family production efforts. Still, her role confined her to the farm; rarely did her duties take her away from the household.

As we saw in this chapter, the work role of women began to change as America industrialized in the nineteenth century. At first, young unmarried women were employed in factories. These early jobs were seen as a proper enough means of easing a family's finances and keeping her out of trouble until she married. But soon, married women were hired in the factories, though this was not accepted as the proper woman's role. It was mostly poor, immigrant women who were forced to help their husbands provide for their families. The woman who worked outside the home was viewed in the same way as the unmarried woman. Neither was considered to be fulfilling her proper role—her unpaid, domestic-work role.

World War I brought little change. The women who worked in the defense plants during the war were replaced by men right after the war. And most of the women who held the few "women's jobs" after the war were single; few respectable married women worked outside the home. During the Depression of the 1930s, in fact, married women were in some places barred from the better jobs. They were seen as taking good jobs away from married men whose families depended on them. The proper place for a woman was the home. The married woman who worked outside the home was viewed as neglecting her home duties and her children.

This view changed with World War II. Women were again needed in the war plants to support the men fighting overseas. The female defense worker was seen as doing her patriotic duty. After the war, many of these working women stayed in their jobs. And since the war, the working woman has been seen less and less as an oddity, as out of her place. In fact, women now make up over 40 percent of the work force, and about half of all adult women hold jobs. The working woman is now largely accepted, especially if she has no husband or children.

WOMEN IN TODAY'S WORLD OF WORK

This is not to say that women, because they are free to work outside the home, have easy access to financial independence. A woman is still likely to need a spouse's paycheck in order to have a decent standard of living. (This is becoming increasingly true of men too.) The average income of women in the United States is about two-thirds the income of men at the same level of education, and the gap has broadened over the last twenty-five years.[36] Further, the unemployment rate is higher for women than for men, and women are more likely than men to hold low-paying jobs. So, while more women are holding jobs, many of them still seek marriage for the financial security they cannot gain by themselves.

There are several reasons that women are in many cases less likely than men to be hired or promoted. One is the belief that the female worker does not really need the money. Some employers reason, not without some basis, that a married woman's paycheck will be used for luxuries, while a man's income goes for family needs. That is, if a woman is refused the job it may mean only that her family will not be able to travel abroad that year, but if the man is denied the job, he may have to sell his house. That many women are heads of families is too often ignored in this reasoning. Even when a woman is head of a household, an employer may assume that she will miss more days than a man because of illness or child care (there seems to be no basis for this fear). There is also the pregnancy issue. Will she disrupt production with maternity leave? Will she work only until she gets pregnant? For these and other reasons, women face special problems in the world of paying jobs.

THE WORKING WIFE: IMPACT ON MARRIAGE

Many of our cultural values working against employed women are directed at the married woman. It has long been accepted that a woman on her own should be allowed to support herself—even though being on her own was not quite proper. It is when the woman's job is thought to conflict with her family duties that many people object. We shall now look at the female worker who is married.

The last generation has seen great changes in this regard. Since 1940 the percentage of women employed has doubled, and the percentage of married women employed went from 16.7% in 1940 to over 54% today.[37] From the typical woman as homemaker we have come to the typical woman as homemaker *and* employee outside the home.

The working wife has recently had a big impact on American marriage. First, the woman with a job enters marriage for different reasons and in a stronger bargaining position than before. With her own paycheck, a woman today feels less pressure to marry. She is more able to delay marriage if she wishes. She need not commit herself to marriage simply because she needs someone to take care of her.

Impact on the Wife

For the working woman who chooses to marry, her job can in some ways enhance, in other ways hurt, her marriage. The benefits of a job for the wife are obvious: satisfaction and excitement. She is less likely to feel lonely or bored. And she and her husband can enjoy a higher standard of living.

However, the rewards of working outside the home depend greatly on the kind of job held. The working wife may hold a job that is boring and low-paying. The costs of working—transportation, clothing, taxes, and so on—may leave her with only a tiny financial payoff.

Furthermore, the employed wife may get little help from the husband with the housework. Her job may be viewed as a minor part of her work role; the housekeeping is often still all hers to do. This division of labor is especially hard on the wife who holds a full-time job outside the home. In such cases, the working

wife is faced with strain and fatigue and the marriage will be affected by that strain.

The working wife may also face emotional strain. For instance, it is difficult for the woman who may feel guilty about neglecting her wifely duties to enjoy the fruits of her job.

Impact on the Husband

The husband of an employed wife can face problems too. He must either help with the housework or face a resentful and exhausted wife. If he does some of the housework, he may feel some role strain himself. That is, he may feel uneasy about his earning power: "If I were a good provider, my wife could stay home where she belongs." Also, his wife may expect more power in the marriage because of her job earnings. If his self-esteem is threatened in these ways, the marriage bond may suffer.

On the other hand, the husband of an employed wife may enjoy some benefits. He may welcome the added income insofar as it spares him financial pressure. He may be released from the pressure to accept overtime work. In addition, his working wife might be a more stimulating companion.

These changes, good and bad, are all likely to have an impact on a marriage when the wife takes a job. This picture is more complex than the one for a single woman, with more possible problems. When children are added to the picture, there are even more difficult issues to be resolved.

THE WORKING MOTHER: IMPACT ON THE CHILDREN

The working mother is no longer unusual. In fact, over half of U.S. mothers hold paying jobs. This is astonishing when one thinks that just a few decades ago a working mother was seen as neglecting her child-rearing duty.

In 1970, 30.3% of married women with preschool children were in the labor force. By the mid '80s, 53% of such mothers were working, and 68% of mothers with school-age children work.[38]

It is often difficult to make a decision about whether the mother in one's family should hold a job. The costs and benefits of a mother working outside the home are measured in terms of effects on the children. If the mother's job interferes with parenting duties, then the rewards enjoyed by the parents may come at

The parent-child bond is a major factor to be considered when a mother decides to take a job.

too great a cost. Here the impact of the mother's job on the children will be explored.

To some extent, as parents feel less financial pressure and more satisfaction because of the mother's income, the children benefit. Satisfied, happy people are better able to be loving parents. The time parent and child spend together may be of higher quality when mother does not feel tied to the children all day. The mother's job may free the father to spend more time with the children.

On the other hand, the children of a working mother may have parents strained with guilt and fatigue. When the working parents come home at the end of a day, they may be too tired or too busy with housework to give love and attention to the children.

This is the core of the issue concerning the employed mother: Will the children receive enough loving, socializing attention when both parents work? This in turn involves the question of child-care centers. Can they meet the emotional needs of children? The question of child-care centers cannot be easily answered, for we cannot put children through experiments to see how much care and attention is enough.

This research restraint has not prevented experts from giving their opinions. In the 1940s and 1950s, mothers were told that an infant needed full-time mothering. More recent research has provided no clear proof of this. When experts say an infant is not harmed by the mother's working, they usually presume that the child is left with a loving caretaker. Also, it seems that the child needs to have one continuous caretaker (other than parents), not several; this lends a needed stability to the young child's world. The need for stable, loving nurture is presumably greater for infants than for older children. Many child-care centers do not meet this need for children, but neither do some mothers. Some homes are so lacking in nurture that the children fare better in child-care centers than at home.

Though the evidence is not yet clear, it seems safe to say that infants need more attention than many child-care centers offer. This makes the trend of mothers of young children taking jobs even more dismaying. Still, if par-

ents can find high-quality care for their infant, there is as yet no evidence that the baby will suffer because it is given loving attention by someone other than a parent.

As is true in other such issues, social science cannot decide for us whether a wife or mother should work. Because people and their personal worlds vary so much, little advice can fit all people. Each person can only use the data offered by science to make his or her own choices.

SELF-TEST QUESTIONS

1. The most basic function of marriage in all cultures is to:
   a. make sure the spouses have sexual relations with each other
   b. provide companionship for the spouses
   c. legitimate the children

Match numbers 2–5 to the descriptions on the right:

2. monogamy   a. more than one spouse per person
3. polygamy   b. more than one husband per wife
4. polygyny   c. one spouse per person
5. polyandry   d. more than one wife per husband

Match numbers 6–7 to the descriptions on the right:

6. endogamy   a. the rule that mates must be selected from within one's cultural group
7. exogamy   b. the rule that parents choose one's mate
              c. the rule that mates be selected from outside one's immediate family

Match numbers 8–10 to the descriptions on the right:

8. matrilocality   a. the newlyweds move in with the husband's parents
9. patrilocality   b. the newlyweds move in with wife's parents
10. neolocality   c. the newlyweds alternate residence with the wife's and the husband's parents
                   d. the newlyweds establish their own residence

Match numbers 11–13 to the descriptions on the right:

11. bilateral   a. descent reckoned through the mothers
12. matrilineal b. descent reckoned through mothers and fathers
13. patrilineal c. descent reckoned through fathers
14. True or false: The American family has been growing in size since World War II.
15. True or false: Children generally have a negative impact on marital satisfaction.
16. True or false: The tasks of child-rearing include releasing the child at the proper time.
17. True or false: Child-rearing is affected by the parents' social-class level.

18. Which kind of parents are most likely to use the democratic child-rearing approach?
    a. working-class
    b. superior
    c. middle-class
    d. inferior
    e. neglectful

19. What has happened to the American family since the nineteenth century?
    a. The family became more a consumption unit than a production unit.
    b. The husband's economic role became typically that of a producer outside of the home.
    c. The wife's economic role became centered on consumption more than on production.
    d. Recently more women have been joining men in the work place.
    e. All of the above.

20. Which family function has grown in importance this century?
    _____ .

21. True or false: Monogamy is still the only marriage form considered by Americans today.

22. According to the author, the dynamics of the American family have been most affected by Americans' demands for _____ .

ANSWERS TO SELF-TEST QUESTIONS

1. c	12. a
2. c	13. c
3. a	14. false
4. d	15. true
5. b	16. true
6. a	17. true
7. c	18. c
8. b	19. e
9. a	20. providing emotional security
10. d	21. false
11. b	22. personal freedom

ANSWERS TO SKILL REINFORCERS

10–1. The following two premises would lead deductively to the conclusion that those African "marriages" of two females are not really marriages:
   1. A marriage is a bond between a man and a woman who have sexual relations with each other.
   2. Some of the "marriages" in this African culture are between two women.

The syllogism formed by these two premises and the conclusion is logical; that is, the premises lead inescapably to the conclusion. However, we may not wish to accept the conclusion if we do not accept the truth of the major premise. That is, the premise may be too narrow or based on ignorance of the world's many marriage forms.

10–2. The difficulty in establishing cause-effect relationships is always that of controlling all the factors that might influence or cause the effect. Many factors besides increased freedom for wives might affect divorce rates. It would be very difficult to design and carry out an experiment that could prove cause-effect. Instead, broad trends must be searched for in an effort to discover some link between the two factors being studied. But without tight control of other relevant factors, a clear cause-effect relationship cannot be proved.

NOTES

1. E. Kathleen Gough, "The Nayars and the Definition of Marriage," *Journal of the Royal Anthropological Institute* 89 (1954): 23–24.
2. R.S. Oboler, "Is the Female Husband a Man? Woman/Woman Marriage Among the Nandi of Kenya," *Ethnology* 19 (January 1980): 69–88.
3. Lloyd Saxton, *The Individual, Marriage, and the Family,* 2d ed. (Belmont, Calif.: Wadsworth Publishing Co., 1972): 184–91.
4. Ibid., p. 185.
5. Ibid.
6. Peter B. Hammond, *An Introduction to Cultural Anthropology* (New York: Macmillan Co., 1971): 161.
7. E. Adamson Hoebel, *Anthropology: The Study of Man,* 3d ed. (New York: McGraw-Hill, 1966).
8. B.K. Singh, "Trends in Attitudes Toward Premarital Sexual Relations," *Journal of Marriage and Family* 42 (May 1980): 387–93.
9. Evelyn M. Kitagawa, "New Life-styles: Marriage Patterns, Living Arrangements, and Fertility Outside of Marriage," *Annals* 453 (January 1981): 1–27.
10. Ibid.
11. Martin S. Weinberg and Colin J. Williams, "Sexual Embourgeoisment? Social Class and Sexual Activity: 1938–1970," *American Sociological Review* 45 (February 1980): 33–48.
12. U.S. Bureau of the Census, *Statistical Abstract of the United States,* 106th ed. (Washington, D.C., 1985): 44.
13. Ibid.
14. Ibid.
15. Linda J. Waite, Gus Haggstrom, and David Kanouse, "The Consequences of Parenthood for the Marital Stability of Young Adults," *American Sociological Review* 50 (December 1985): 850–57.
16. Robert Ranking and Jerry Maneker, "The Duration of Marriage in a Divorcing Population: The Impact of Children," *Journal of Marriage and Family* 47 (February 1985): 43–52.
17. Leonard Benson, *The Family Bond: Marriage, Love, and Sex in America* (New York: Random House, 1971): 11–13.
18. "The American Family: Bent—but Not Broken," *U.S. News & World Report,* (June 16, 1980): 48–50.
19. Margaret Nelson, "Working-Class Women, Middle-Class Women, and Models of Childbirth," *Social Problems* 30 (February 1983): 284–97.
20. Dale C. Farran and Craig Ramey, "Social Class Differences in Dyadic Involvement During Infancy," *Child Development* 51 (March 1980): 254–57.
21. E.E. LeMaster, *Parents in Modern America,* rev. ed. (Homewood, Ill.: Dorsey Press, 1974): chapter 12.
22. Ibid., p. 195.
23. *Statistical Abstract of the United States: 1986,* p. 81.
24. Frances Goldscheider and Linda Waite, "Sex Differences in the Entry into Marriage," *American Journal of Sociology* 92 (July 1986): 91–109.
25. Michael Winerip, "Married Couples, Squeezed by Recession, Squeezing into Parents' Homes," *New York Times* CXXXII (February 25, 1983): 14.
26. Sandra Hofferth, "Updating Children's Life Course," *Journal of Marriage and Family* 47 (February 1985): 93–115.
27. Sammuel Preston, "Children and the Elderly in the U.S.," *Scientific American* 251 (December 1984): 44–49.
28. Wray Herbert and Joel Greenberg, "Fatherhood in Transition," *Science News* 124 (September 17, 1983): 172.
29. Jan Pahl, "The Allocation of Money and the Structuring of Inequality Within Marriage," *The Sociological Review* 31 (May 1983): 236–62.
30. Zick Rubin, "Are Working Wives Hazardous to Their Husbands' Mental Health?" *Psychology Today* 17 (May 1983): 70–72.
31. Andrew Cherlin and Frank Furstenberg, Jr., "The American Family in the Year 2000," *The Futurist* (June 1983).

32. *Statistical Abstract of the United States: 1986,* pp. 80, 81.
33. Paul Glick and Arthur Norton, "Marrying, Divorcing, and Living Together in the U.S. Today," *Population Bulletin* 32, n. 5 (October 1977): 19.
34. Scott South, "Economic Conditions and the Divorce Rate: A Time-Series Analysis of the Postwar U.S.," *Journal of Marriage and Family* 47 (February 1985): 31–41.
35. Kristin Moore and Linda Waite, "Marital Dissolution, Early Motherhood, and Early Marriage," *Social Forces* 60 (September 1981): 20–40.
36. W.G. Steglich and Margaret Knoz Snooks, *American Social Problems: An Institutional View* (Santa Monica, Calif.: Goodyear Publishing Co., 1980): 151–2.
37. *Statistical Abstract of the United States: 1986,* p. 398.
38. Ibid., p. 399.

SUGGESTED READINGS

Blumstein, Philip, and Pepper Schwartz. *American Couples.* New York: Morrow, 1983.

Cherlin, Andrew. *Marriage, Divorce, Remarriage.* Cambridge, Mass.: Harvard University Press, 1981.

Skolnick, Arlene and Jerome Skolnick. *Family in Transition.* 4th ed. Boston: Little Brown, 1983.

Stein, Peter J., ed. *Single Life.* New York: St. Martin's Press, 1981.

11 EDUCATION

The Home as the First School

To see how differences in home life can affect a child's success in school, we will look at the early years of two children, Bobby and Nancy.

Bobby was born into the best kind of home. His parents are well educated and looked forward to his birth. During pregnancy, his mother followed her doctor's advice. She drank very little alcohol. She even stopped smoking. And she was careful to eat well, having heard how important a good diet is for her child's growing brain.

Because Bobby was an only child, and his mother could afford to stay home for a few years after he was born, he got plenty of attention. He talked and played with people who used proper grammar and had good vocabularies. Exploring his home, Bobby found stimulating toys and books—plenty of books. He saw his parents reading often. When he asked, his parents were glad to read to him. Soon he was going with them to the library. The games Bobby's parents played with him often involved letters, shapes, and numbers. From an early age he felt at ease with these concepts.

When he asked what school was all about, Bobby heard that it was pleasant. He learned from older children that school was a place where he could enjoy success. Adults told him that the teachers would be his friends. Every day Bobby saw all around him proof that education works, that it pays off with a comfortable life-style. Neither he nor his parents ever doubted that Bobby would some day enter college.

With this ideal background, Bobby has a good chance to make the most of his mental equipment. He will probably succeed in school. But another child, in another neighborhood, faces a different future.

Nancy's parents had little schooling and many children. Her mother rarely saw a doctor and did not know the importance of a good diet. With too little protein during her vital early months, Nancy's brain could not develop to its potential.

There was plenty of stimulation in Nancy's home, but it was mostly noisy and distracting. There was too much television and too little reading. The games Nancy played rarely involved numbers or letters. The verbal and reasoning skills in her home were not very advanced.

Nancy did learn about school. She heard that school is a demanding, restricting place where children are often punished. The teachers, she was told, do not understand children and do not like them much either. For Nancy, school became an object of both fear and hostility.

It is unlikely that these two children will succeed in school to the same degree. Bobby has a much better chance of being seen by teachers as a bright, well-mannered student. Nancy, with few skills in her head and fear in her eyes, will find that life's inequality has already weighed her down before she even reached school. We will deal more with such inequality later in the chapter.

Our social and our personal worlds are shaped and made possible by education. Earlier chapters in this book have described how one's personality and one's culture depend largely on what certain people taught others. This teaching process is called education. There are two types of education: formal and informal.

Informal education can also be called socialization. Socialization is the process by which a society teaches its young the proper things to do, to want, and to think. The child learns from society what is right and wrong, good and bad. The child learns how to perform men's or women's work and how to get along with other people. There are only a few special or secret skills to learn. The necessary job skills are learned by watching the adults. This is the kind of education found in simpler societies. There is little need for formal education.

INFORMAL EDUCATION: Socialization.

Other societies need both formal and informal education. They must socialize their members, but they also depend on skills and knowledge not possessed by all their adult members. Such things may be too technical, too sacred, or too complex to be learned by just observing adults. Schools and teachers are used to pass on such knowledge to the next generation. Such education is no longer informal, but formal.

FORMAL EDUCATION: Systematic instruction, in schools and other full-time training institutions, by teaching specialists.

Formal schooling involves special people called teachers and special places called schools. A planned program of teaching is carried out to give children the knowledge and skills they would not get just from being around most other adults. This process will be the focus of this chapter.

First we will look at the functions of education in all cultures. Then we will shift our focus to the United States and look at two things expected from our schools: social mobility and equality. Next the framework of control of the American school system will be explored. The Special Topic will examine the debate about mental testing in our schools.

FUNCTIONS OF EDUCATION

Formal education is needed for the transmission of complex knowledge.

There is only one thing more important for a culture than education: producing children to carry the culture into the future. But once those children are born, they must be educated. In fact, the main function of education is to transmit a culture's knowledge to the next generation. This function is linked to another one, that of integrating the people by uniting them with the same set of values and cultural identity. These two functions are vital to the survival of a way of life, but another function deals with something beyond survival.

Some ways of life are more complex than others and depend on education to do more than ensure social cohesion and the culture's transmission. In such cultures, new knowledge is highly valued and schools are expected to produce it. In most modern societies, the schools are also expected to meet many other needs of the student, from nutrition to equality, but in this section we will focus only on the three major functions of education: transmission of knowledge, cultural integration, and creating new knowledge.

Transmission of Cultural Knowledge

The most obvious task for the schools is to teach knowledge to students. And despite recent criticisms of American education, there is evidence that schools do their job in this regard. As the researchers put it, "Our results indicate that schooling . . . plays an important role in fostering cognitive growth."[1] If an education system did not teach students thinking skills and knowledge, the culture would not be effectively transmitted. If a culture is not transmitted from one generation to the next it will die. Some form of education is needed to pass along the knowledge that will maintain the culture. The culture's knowledge must be passed on because humans must be taught everything. We do not possess a way of life at birth; one must be taught to us if we are to maintain it.

Transmitting Simple and Complex Cultures.   Transmission of cultural knowledge sounds simple—the culture is passed from the old members of society to the young. The young are tamed, saved, humanized—shaped into responsible, productive adults. In simple cultures, such shaping *is* simple. As long as the culture changes very slowly, as simple cultures do, the educational function is simply a part of other cultural activities, such as farming and hunting. This is possible because so little knowledge is added to the culture that all adults know everything the children need to learn. Informal education can transmit the culture as long as the storehouse of knowledge is small and changes slowly.

As some cultures became more complex over time, formal education became necessary. No longer could the process of transmitting knowledge be blended with the rest of the culture. Knowledge became too complex and was added too quickly for all the adults to be adequate teachers. In those early, changing cultures, specialists took over much of this education function.

Since the Middle Ages, the Western cultural storehouse has expanded greatly. More scholars produced much new knowledge, and more scholars were needed to transmit the knowledge to new scholars. Education kept pace with the demand of cultures for new knowledge: an army of scholars was put to work producing and transmitting knowledge.

Today, this education function remains as vital to complex cultures as it is to simple ones. Modern cultures are dependent on the transmission of their huge, complex funds of knowledge, just as simpler cultures depend on transmitting their cultures informally.

What Knowledge, and for Whom?   The need for formal transmission of cultural knowledge is clear, but fulfilling this need is not a simple task. Two important issues are involved, and neither is easily resolved: What knowledge is to be transmitted, and to whom?

What knowledge? First, a decision must be made about which knowledge to transmit. In modern cultures, so much knowledge has been produced that there is no way to transmit all of it to everyone. Someone must decide which knowledge to give to whom.

Whoever makes this decision clearly helps shape the direction of the culture. For example, the tone of the culture will differ if the schools transmit mostly art or religion or science. Along with this, other questions arise. Should schools produce specialists or generalists, scientists or priests, followers or free-thinkers? The answers may simply be based on the values of the culture, but in complex cultures various groups often disagree on these basic issues. This leads to arguments over which knowledge is most valuable. For example, some people want more religion in the schools, others want less. Some want traditional knowledge and values taught, other people see the old knowledge as irrelevant.

In a modern, fast-changing culture, the question of relevance is a vital one. The debate often becomes one of old knowledge versus new knowledge. On the one hand, traditional subject matter is attacked as no longer meeting the needs of the students or the culture. The argument is that, rather than preserving the old knowledge, schools should help students cope with the flood of new knowledge. In this view, adjusting to the future requires that this cultural transmission function of the schools focus less on the past and more on tomorrow. On the other hand, there is the argument that the storehouse of knowledge built in the past is much more valuable than anything that can be built on the shifting currents of today's values. People who have this view claim that the traditional approach gives students the strongest tool for dealing with any demands that they may face in the future. After all, they say, no one knows what will be needed in the future, so we had best keep what we have and use it to help us adjust to whatever comes our way.

This debate can be described in terms of the rock in a lake versus the raft. The traditional fund of knowledge is the rock: sturdy, solid, and formed long ago. The problem is that the water level of the lake, representing cultural demands, has been rising so that one can scarcely keep head above water when standing on the rock. Should we continue to offer students the rock, or should we offer them a raft? The raft looks promising, but it is new, untried, and might sink. Another concern is that the raft may float away from the rock, from the culture's heritage, and leave the students with no way to orient themselves. We must face the certainty that fast change will be a basic part of the future, as it is of today's world. Students must be equipped with knowledge that helps them deal with a constantly changing culture. Perhaps the solution is to give students a raft so that they may cope with rising water and shifting currents, but to tie the raft securely to the rock, for security and stability.

The issue of what parts of the culture to transmit also involves a debate over the academic versus the vocational. Should the schools focus on knowledge for the rewards it can bring in itself, or should they focus only on knowledge that will help the student do a certain job? Our culture requires that people be trained (equipped with job skills), but should they also be educated more broadly? For example, should plumbers be exposed to art and science, to broaden their knowledge and make them more aware, sensitive, and open-minded? Some people see this part of cultural transmission as a nuisance and a waste of time and money, for example, engineering students who might complain that they must take an art course. But others feel that a narrow focus on job training, to the neglect of broader education, would produce a society of shortsighted people content to live in a limited, desolate world.

The question of what parts of the culture to transmit is not a simple one. It will continue to be a vital issue for all cultures with systems of formal education. And it is not the only question raised concerning this function of education.

Who gets what knowledge? Second, it must be decided to whom the knowledge is to be transmitted. In a complex culture, it is not practical to give the same knowledge to everyone. Not everyone can be given the skills of the lawyer or the engineer. Specialists are needed. People must be screened and sorted, then matched with appropriate skills.

In most modern cultures, except for the United States, the decision about who gets what knowledge is often based on scores of tests given to students in their early teens. Only the highest-scoring students are offered a college education. The other students are offered different areas of knowledge and thus less opportunity for social success.

In the United States, everyone is encouraged to reach for the highest knowledge pathway possible. College is not just for the elite. In America, the college system is like a swimming pool into which many people are encouraged to jump and see if they can stay afloat. Those who cannot keep their heads above water come to realize it themselves—rather than being denied entry to the pool by a test. Some students flail around in the water for a while before returning to the side and deciding to get out of the pool. For those students, the sorting process is less abrupt than it would be in most other countries, where those students would not have been allowed in the pool at all.

Questions of control and equality arise concerning this decision of who gets what. For example, who decides which students learn what job skills? It could be left to each student to decide, or some agency could direct the students in accordance with a certain policy. If not the student, then what agency and what policy? Furthermore, who makes the policy?

We have now come to the issue of control of the schools and the shaping of the direction of the culture. The section on control of America's schools (later in this chapter) will describe how much any one of us can influence such decisions. Related to the control issue is the issue of equality, which concerns the fairness of the decisions of those in charge of the school system. Equality will also be explored more fully later in this chapter.

Cultural Integration

The first function of education, transmission of knowledge, helps ensure that the second function, cultural integration, will be performed. To the extent that students are exposed to the same cultural knowledge, through cultural transmission, they will take on the same values, goals, and identity. They will come to share the same manners, myths, and language. They will be fitted into their culture.

In homogeneous societies, the process of cultural integration is simple and natural. There is only one cultural identity, one way of life to be transmitted. No special process is needed to make sure children are integrated into their culture. But in societies with subgroups of diverse cultural backgrounds, schools are often seen as tools of cultural integration.

A Prime Example: Americanizing the Immigrants. America is a good example of a society built from diverse subgroups. The cultural integration function of education took on great importance during the nearly three hundred years when immigrants were pouring into the nation. The diverse ethnic groups had to be taught a common culture. It was seen as proper that they give up their old customs for those of the country to which they had moved.

In the past, immigrant children were given little choice about becoming integrated into the American culture. In fact, the schools have been accused of being brutal in their approach. Students were sometimes ridiculed or punished for using language other than English in the classroom. Native American children, often treated like foreigners, were sometimes put in state-run boarding schools to separate them from their parents' "un-American" ways. When the flow of immigrants slackened by the 1930s, the schools turned from immigrant children to others who needed to be fitted into the cultural mainstream: children of the lower class.

Cultural integration of various ethnic groups was a more important goal of our schools in the past than today.

Integrating the Lower Classes. Another function of the schools in many modern cultures is to bring students from lower-class backgrounds into the cultural mainstream, the middle-class world. Such students may thus be forced to choose between the values of home and school. Schools demand self-discipline, persistence, and cooperation. In contrast, the home may foster aggressive, assertive behavior. Such behavior, rewarded at home, may be punished at school. The price of school success for such students may be detaching themselves from home and parents. In this way the school's attempt to integrate lower-class children into the middle-class world can create a dilemma for the children. But to the extent that the school does integrate these children, their chances for social success are increased.

**Creation of
New Knowledge**

The third major function of education is the creation of new knowledge. Some cultures took advantage of the great expansion of knowledge that occurred over the last three hundred years. Those cultures advanced to positions of dominance. They grew wealthy and strong. Their citizens became more secure and comfortable. All these benefits came from the new knowledge that poured forth from the growing number of scholars and scientists. Without formal education, the new knowledge on which these advances depended would not have been produced.

This function of education is as important today as it was in the past. Modern cultures depend on the creation of new knowledge to meet ever-growing social and economic needs. Economic growth is based largely on new technology. New ideas are needed to solve the new problems that develop in fast-changing cultures. The transmission of old knowledge is not adequate; knowledge must be created, not just conserved.

Education functions in two ways to create new knowledge. One is the direct production of new technology and ideas. Many scientists and scholars work in college settings, reaching beyond existing knowledge to expand the storehouse of knowledge.

Education also works indirectly to perform this function. It produces the scholars and scientists who will create the new knowledge. The lowest levels of a school system must equip students with basic academic skills. Colleges can then broaden and deepen the minds of the students, some of whom will become researchers who will expand the storehouse of knowledge. The goal of the educational system is to form people able to put together pieces of the old knowledge to bring about new knowledge. Such people help keep the wheels of a culture turning by offering new tools, new ideas, and new solutions.

**SOCIAL MOBILITY:
A FUNCTION OF
AMERICAN SCHOOLS?**

This chapter takes the reader through the steps people follow in a system of education. The first section, like the elementary grades, offered a broad, general introduction. That stage provided background information needed for more specialized areas. Just as in our early schooling we went from the basics to more specific subjects, this chapter moves from a general study of education to specific study of the American school system.

In the United States, one function of the school system is to increase people's chances for social mobility. In fact, that may be part of the reason many people attend college. Some people are studying so that they can get a job that may raise their social-class status. Likewise, parents may expect their children to be lifted socially by education, to be "better off than I am."

Though we may expect the school system to perform this function, there is some debate about whether the system does allow social mobility. Both sides of the debate will be explored here.

One View: The System Is Rigged Against the Lower Class

Some people see schools as a tool the powerful in our society use to preserve the social-class structure. One such writer contends that the "schools reflect the dominant ideology and power in any society, whatever its organization, and in the United States this means the furtherance of monopoly capitalism."[2] In this view, education can be seen as a game that the middle and upper classes can play well and therefore use as a requirement for success. It is as if the best jumpers (the higher classes) chose the high jump as the contest that decides who gets the prizes in society. The lower classes are handicapped, perhaps because they have had little practice and poor coaching.

Conflict theorists such as Bowles and Gintis have pictured America's schools as a means of the dominant elite for reproducing the capitalist system.[3] The schools are rigged against the lower classes in two ways. First, the schools help higher-class families transmit their social status to their children, because a student's success is determined by his/her family's wealth more than by the student's own abilities. Second, the schools train students to fit into specialized, alienating work roles, meeting the needs of the capitalist system for docile, exploitable, productive workers.

The schools are also often seen as demanding irrelevant skills. Critics argue that the skills required for school success, such as memorizing and test-taking, are not the skills that most jobs actually require. But to get the good jobs, people must show they have these irrelevant skills. It is like proving one is a good high-jumper before one can get a job driving a truck. From this point of view, the school system is an unjust barrier to social mobility.

The key to getting over this barrier may be social class, not ability. A person's chances of making good grades and of going to college are much greater if his or her parents were middle or upper class. Some see this as proof that the schools are biased against poor children. Perhaps the system is rigged.

The school is often viewed as a biased gatekeeper. The teachers decide which students will attain success: those who are like the teachers. Middle- and upper-class students are more likely to be seen by the teacher as winners, it is said. These students know the rules well and are comfortable with them: being polite, quiet, and obedient. Lower-class children have learned that different traits are required in their social world. Children from lower classes do not select and organize meanings in ways which the schools demand. Such children have more difficulty adapting to the schools than do middle-class children.[4] To get the approval of the school, lower-class students must take on middle-class values and behaviors. Middle-class students are not required to make such a huge change. Thus the lower-class students are seen by the schools' critics as having less chance for using the school for up-ward social mobility.

Some critics have argued that the schools, not these lower-class children, should be required to change. By accepting differ-ent rules and using different strategies, the schools could be places where more lower-class students could succeed. The schools are urged to not base their treatment of all students on a middle-class perspective. In this view, the students' backgrounds and needs should be considered in setting school programs.

The Other View: The Schools Offer the Chance for Mobility

The second point of view sees the schools as making social mobil-ity possible—though still not easy—for children from the lower classes. According to this view, the lower-class students should adapt to the schools' middle-class values. The reasoning here is that since our society plays by middle-class rules, it is improper to allow the lower-class student to depend on the wrong set of rules. To succeed, the student must learn to play the middle-class game by which our society is run.

Skill Reinforcer 11-1 [*]
Build a syllogism from this major premise: A school system that gives all students the chance to equip themselves with socially valuable skills is a tool for up-ward social mobility.

In this light, school is seen as the place where children can get those things lacking in their homes. The school equips the stu-dents with the skills and values required for success. Lower-class students will not be so limited by their family environments. In the classroom, the deprived child can be exposed to reading, mental stimulation, and proper speech patterns—advantages most middle-class children get at home. This means that those children born into poor families are given a chance in the classroom. Their chances are not as good as those of higher-class children, but some of these students will rise to the challenge.

Back to our question: Do the schools just preserve the social class structure or are they a ladder by which all students can climb to their limits? The answer is not clear. Although today fewer children are denied a chance to climb the ladder, the class struc-ture seems to be changed little by the increased chances for education. So maybe the schools can only do so much. Indeed, perhaps it is the family, not the school, that most determines a child's future success. The family gives the child his or her direc-tion in life. The school cannot easily change that direction. We will explore this more later.

WHY AMERICAN SCHOOLS ARE NOT THE GREAT EQUALIZER

As we have just seen, there is serious doubt that America's schools offer all students a chance for social mobility. Our schools have been burdened with another task under which they have strug-gled with only partial success. That task is to offer all students an equal education.

At first one might think that the schools should make sure all students achieve equally well in school so that all have an equal chance to achieve after their education is finished. But equal achievement for all students is not a feasible goal for our school system. There are both innate differences in potential and differences in motivation among people. To equalize achievement, we would have to lower the performance level of all to that of the lowest student, which would be unjust.

But we can work to create a fair system. In such a system, if a student did poorly, it would not be because he or she lacked an opportunity equal to any other student. The proper goal is to equalize the opportunity to use the schools. A person's opportunity to achieve in school is affected by the home, the school, and the racial factor in this country. We will examine each of these factors here.

Home Environment

The chapter preview showed how important the home environment is for a child's later school success. It is clear that Bobby's chances are much better than Nancy's, even before they get near a school. Here we will go beyond the story of Bobby and Nancy and examine how differences in home environment work against the goal of social equality.

The Importance of Social Class.   The parents' social-class status is the single most powerful predictor of a child's performance in school. The higher the social class of the home, the higher the student's test scores, grades, aspirations, and attainment. It does not seem to be a matter of just money. Other factors are thought to play a part in this connection. What is it about the life-style of higher-class families that gives their children a better chance to do well in school?

One guess is that the genes of these higher-class parents are superior. These genes helped these people succeed. The genes passed on to their children are therefore likely to be of high quality. Thus the children succeed in school tasks.

Another reason for the link between social class and school success may be the quality of the home environment of higher-class students. It boils down to the constant question of social science: Is the cause mostly genes or social surroundings? In this case, as in most others, it is hard to prove either way. But the fact remains that the higher the social class of the parents, the better chance the child has to succeed in school.

What Can Parents Do for the Home Environment?   What does all this tell the parents of school-age or younger children? What can they do to enhance their home environments for their children? Parents cannot control the genes they give to their children, and they have only a little control over their social-class status. But there are things parents can do to improve the home environment.

Parents have some control over the number of children they have, and family size is one home condition that seems to affect a child's intelligence. The larger the family, the lower the intelligence of the children.[5] This may be caused by the dilution of the mental climate by too many children. But it may also be a result of the fact that higher-class families are often small families. Is it the social-class life-style or the number of children that affects the child's intelligence? The evidence is not yet clear, but we do know that school success is clearly not just a matter of social class.

This means that there are ways low-income parents can help their children to succeed in school. One key seems to be the parents' aspirations for the children. Although school success requires more than just support from parents, this factor can override social-class background. Another such factor is parent-child interaction. Boocock found that the ideal seems to be a mixture of love and pressure to do well. The children should be told what their parents expect of them.[6]

Boocock also found that how well parents fulfill their roles as homemakers and providers affects the child's school success. Evidence is limited, but it seems that students do poorly when their father is absent or out of work. But two parents are not needed. It seems that it is the quality of the parenting, not the number of parents in the home, that is the key.

There are still other home factors linked to school success. Good students are likely to come from homes where the parents read well and enjoy reading. Many books are found in such homes. School-related games are played by preschoolers who later succeed in school. The parents of such children show interest in their children's school progress. These young children are offered books and reading opportunities. All these factors depend on the parents.

Beyond the Parents' Control. The parents of Nancy (in the chapter preview) could do only so much to help prepare her for school. They could offer support and skill practice. But while there are several ways parents can improve the home environment, there are some factors beyond the control of parents. For example, moving from one home to another seems to hurt the achievement of lower-class students more than middle-class students. Likewise, the number of years between children in a family may affect school achievement; more spacing may help. Birth order seems to be a factor too. Firstborn children succeed in school more often than others. So far, the research can only suggest, not prove, the above connections.

School Environment

Even children with the same home conditions and the same innate potential can reach unequal heights of school success. If the homes and the genes of two students are roughly equal, and their grades and test scores still differ a great deal, the differences must be due to the school environment.

School Factors That Make a Difference. Many school factors affect a student's chances for making the most of the school's offerings. The teaching methods and books that work well for some students may not work for others. The school's rules and demands may be acceptable to some students but not to others.

SKILL BOX

Correlation

It does not follow from the studies on home environment that school success is caused directly by home conditions; many studies show only correlations. This means that academic scores are found to be *related* to home factors. For example, a factor like many books in the home might be linked to school success. That is, children from homes in which there are many books would be to some degree more likely to succeed in school than others. The more often this link was found, the higher the correlation.

The problem is that the factor of books in the home may not in itself explain school success. The two factors are only found together, and only for some children. The cause of the success may be some third factor, such as social-class values, which causes both the books to be put in the home and the home climate that helps the child succeed. Or perhaps the child's success in school causes the parents or the child to keep books in the home. A correlation study cannot untangle the causes and the effects.

So correlations offer only a little help in solving problems, because they can only suggest the real causes. But such studies do help us predict. For instance, in a classroom in which many students have books at home, we might expect high test scores. But to find the real cause of such success, we would need to run an experimental study.

Correlation studies can point the way to possible causes but cannot by themselves prove cause.

CORRELATION: The measured strength of a relationship between two factors.

Nevertheless, some schools have been proven to be effective, and such schools share some general principles of leadership, classroom management, and school climate.[7] And recent research suggests that if students are allowed to use their own initiative, thought, and judgment in schoolwork, they will learn to think and to direct their own lives.[8] Beyond this, sociologists have been arguing over whether private schools provide better education than do public schools.[9, 10] Besides these considerations, there are more factors in the schools that help account for unequal chances for student achievement. Three of those factors will be explored here.

Skill Reinforcer 11-2
What might have been the hypothesis used in the research study described here?

Teacher expectations. The power of the factor of teacher expectations was shown in a clever research study.[11] All the children in one elementary school were given standard I.Q. tests at the start of the school year. The teachers were told that the scores showed some children—whose names were actually chosen at random—were expected to show an intellectual spurt that year, but in reality, there was no reason to expect those children to do any better than the others. When these "special" children were later retested several times, however, they showed a greater gain in I.Q. scores than those children not selected. The gains were more dramatic among the younger children, which suggests that they are more easily influenced by teachers' attitudes. Among the older children for whom the trick worked, the gains were smaller but longer-lasting. (A question of research ethics is raised here, a

A basic part of unequal educational opportunity is the unequal funding of schools among various districts.

common one in social science: What about the students who were not lucky enough to be chosen as "special"? Was it right to have denied those children the chance for big academic gains?)

Explaining these dramatic results, the researchers said, "By what she said, by how and when she said it, [by] her facial expressions, postures, and perhaps by her touch, the teacher may have communicated to the children . . . that she expected improved intellectual performance." [12] An excellent teacher performs this magic with many students. Indeed, all children deserve this kind of powerful treatment, but this depends on which teacher—or school—a child is assigned.

Some popular notions portray teachers as applying biased expectations to students, the biases being based on such factors as sex, race, and ethnicity. If teachers systematically expect less of students in such categories, these biases could have powerful and negative effects on students' school experiences. However, researchers find that teachers base their behavior toward students not so much on a student's sex or race as much as on the student's behaviors.[13] As one researcher put it, "the analysis failed to uncover any evidence of conscious or unconscious racial bias." [14]

School funding.   Schools are no more equal in quality than teachers are. One reason for the variation in quality among schools is the amount of money spent on them, though the impact of money on quality may not be as large as was once thought. Still, school funding varies among states (see Table 11–1) and among districts. Those districts with little property to tax spend less money per student than do other, more wealthy districts. Court decisions have forced some states to devise new ways of funding schools so as to give all students more equal schooling quality.

Tracking.   Even in the same school, not all students get the same quality of education. There are, for example, various "tracks"

TABLE 11-1. Funding of Public Schools

Average expenditure per pupil.
Top ten and bottom ten states, 1985.

Top Ten		Bottom Ten	
Alaska	$6867	Georgia	$2692
New York	$5226	South Carolina	$2650
New Jersey	$5220	Indiana	$2638
Wyoming	$4809	North Carolina	$2588
Connecticut	$4477	Tennessee	$2349
Delaware	$4155	Arkansas	$2344
Maryland	$4101	Idaho	$2290
Rhode Island	$4097	Alabama	$2241
Pennsylvania	$4002	Mississippi	$2205
Montana	$3968	Utah	$2181

SOURCE: U.S. Bureau of the Census, *Statistical Abstract of the United States: 1986*, 106th ed. (Wash., D.C., 1985).

in high school: vocational and precollege. This "tracking" in high schools clearly offers some students better schooling than others. Is this tracking fair; that is, is it based on a student's merit or on the wealth of the student's family? Conflict theorists believe that tracking reflects not individual ability but the inequalities of the social class structure of the United States.[15] Other research concludes, in contrast, that individual merit, not family class status, is the key to a student's progress.[16] The debate continues.

Race   So far we have explored the influence of the home and school environments on students' chances for succeeding in school. One cannot help but notice that a student's social-class background is an important part of the picture. Now we move from the factor of social class to race as a factor that affects a student's chances in school.

A History of School Desegregation. The racial factor has changed over recent decades as students of different races have been mixed in the schools. This mixing began with the famous 1954 case of *Brown* vs. *Board of Education,* in which the U.S. Supreme Court held that separate schools are inherently unequal schools. From this came hundreds of court-ordered desegregation plans.

Social science had a hand in these plans. The conclusions of James Coleman's report on school equality helped support the idea of mixing children of different races in the schools. Coleman and his associates claimed, among other things, that such mixing would help the school achievement of minority-group students and have no effect on that of white students.[17] It is not that simple, of course. Coleman dealt with other factors required for success, such as acceptance by teachers and by other students, teacher expectations, and teacher and student morale. Still, hopes were

Despite various degrees of resistance, school desegregation has shown some benefits, such as an increase in the achievement of black students.

raised by Coleman's findings that racial differences in test scores would decrease if the students were mixed. Busing has been the main tool used to achieve racial mixing in the schools.

Today busing presents a confusing picture, but one pattern has emerged. The South has largely desegregated its schools. The least mixing is to be found in large northern and western cities. There, the inner-city schools consist mostly of black and other nonwhite students. Because of what has been called "white flight," most of the white students in the big northern and western cities are found either in private schools or in the suburban public schools on the fringes of those urban cores. Due to desegregation, at least for a few years, "substantial numbers of whites seek to avoid attending schools with blacks." [18] Desegregation, then, has proved to be most difficult. There are too few white students to achieve racial balance. The schools in many areas remain mostly black in the city, mostly white in the suburbs. Busing has not been very effective in such places. Why not? There have been several reasons.

One reason that busing has failed in some places is that since a 1974 decision the Supreme Court has usually refused to allow busing from such city cores across district lines to the suburbs. Only when these district lines are proven to have been drawn so as to segregate the schools can busing be ordered. This frustrates attempts to prevent separate and unequal schools for different racial groups.

The Supreme Court has also set other limits on busing to achieve racial balance. For instance, court busing orders may be used only in cases of intentional segregation. And once a busing plan is carried out, no further action is required. That means that if the schools are later resegregated (as a result of changed housing patterns), they can stay that way. Still, unlike other branches of government, the courts have aimed to desegregate schools.

Meanwhile, Congress has been fighting such efforts. Several strategies have been used, including attempts at an antibusing amendment to the U.S. Constitution. Also, some southern states passed laws allowing public schools to be closed when desegrega-

TABLE 11-2. College Freshmen, in Percentages

Since the Civil Rights era of the 1960s, blacks are now attending college at a rate (about 10%) nearly equal to their percentage of the general population (about 12%).

	1966	1984
BLACK	5	10
WHITE	91	86

SOURCE: U.S. Bureau of the Census, *Statistical Abstract of the U.S.: 1986*, 106th ed. (Wash., D.C., 1985).

tion was ordered by courts. State funds were offered to private schools. Federal financial pressure largely foiled these tactics, however.

Further resistance to busing is found among American citizens. Many accept the principle of desegregation but oppose busing. Some whites fear a decline in school quality as a result of such programs. And some blacks want separate but equal schools to preserve ethnic pride.

Results of School Desegregation.   In light of all this resistance, what has desegregation accomplished? The earlier hopes for equal school environments have been fulfilled in only a few areas. Still, some gains have been recorded. There has been some increase in the achievement of black students in all learning areas.[19] In early elementary grades, desegregation has enhanced black achievement by about one grade year.[20] Interracial contact in high school produces only small improvements in blacks' scores, those improvements due mostly to the higher academic standards demanded in predominantly white schools.[21] Many formerly black schools have been improved. More minority students are attending college. And students from different racial and ethnic groups have become acquainted.

Disappointments remain. Achievement scores are still not equal among racial groups. Minority students still do not attend college in the same proportions as others. Most black college graduates still get their degrees from predominantly black colleges.[22] The hopes raised by Coleman's report have not been realized on a large scale. This may be because the "cure" of racially mixed schools has not been given a full trial. Also, even though many schools are racially mixed, many are not truly integrated. That is, students who sit in the same classroom still sit at different lunch tables.

With the goal of racial harmony so far out of reach, there seems to have been a shift to a new goal, that of educational quality for our schools, instead of racial mixing. Either way, much remains to be done.

Do We Want Equal Education?

As stated earlier, the proper goal of the schools is to provide an equal chance to fulfill one's potential. As we have seen, people's chances in the system are tied to some factors beyond their control. This is not fair, but at the same time, equal education may not be the answer.

If we did provide excellent schooling for everyone, regardless of social class, the gap between the lower- and the higher-class students might widen. Students from some homes would be better prepared to take advantage of such offerings. They would soar while other students were taking their first steps. This would bring us no closer to equalizing everyone's chances to grow to their own limits.

It seems clear that the preschool environments must be made less unequal. The schools' agents would have to reach children from poor home environments at an early age, so that those children could be brought up to the starting line, where the middle-class children already await the starting gun.

Any government plan to equalize preschool environments raises several important questions concerning the right of parents to control the social environment of their children. Not all parents want "help" from government preschool programs. Do parents have the right to prevent their children from attending such programs? Do the children have a right to a good preschool environment? In Massachusetts Bay colony in the seventeenth century, parents who neglected their children's schooling could have their children taken from them. Is equality so vital today that it overrides the parents' rights? All these questions spring from one basic question: How far should the government go to equalize all students' chances for growth and success?

Another point may be raised: Who is to pay for these preschool programs, and who benefits? The middle-class parents might protest that, though they pay more taxes than the lower-class parents, less money is spent on their children. Middle-class tax dollars would be spent on lower-class children to make up for the neglect shown by some parents. There seems no way around the fact that unequal treatment will be needed to give all children an equal chance in school.

CONTROL OF AMERICA'S SCHOOLS

Who controls the American school systems? Despite the recent growth of nonpublic schools, education in the United States is still mostly public. And control of the public school systems rests largely in the hands of government agencies. This means that taxpayers still have some control over the nation's system of schools. However, the taxpayer's influence is decreasing because control has been shifting away from local agencies, where the taxpayer's control is greatest.

Since the 1830s, there has been a trend toward more central control over the schools, even though the U.S. Constitution puts the job of schooling in the hands of the states, not the national government. This trend runs counter to the fondness with which many Americans view local controls. Still, over the last century, more control has shifted from the local to the state to the federal level.

Federal Government

Supporting this trend toward centralized power has been the idea that federal control is needed to ensure that all students get schooling of more equal quality. States vary greatly in the amount of money they spend on their students; some spend twice as much per student as others. Federal control is intended to help decrease these differences. Also, educational standards among the states could be made more uniform through federal control, making transfers easier for the increasing number of students who move from one school system to another.

Of course, there has been resistance to the idea of more federal control. Many see federal aid as interference, even though it accounts for only about one-tenth of the government money spent on education. Still, many school systems depend on those funds to build and equip the schools and to help students with special programs.

Colleges have been complaining about federal interference. In an effort to ensure equal opportunity, colleges are required to fill out many forms and keep many records. The schools complain not only about the cost of such paperwork but also about the attempt to gain some control, even in private schools. Because schools have been unable to get federal money without federal control, federal aid to education will continue to be a source of controversy.

State Government

State education agencies are also seen as gaining too much control. One study traces the increasing power of the state government in the schools to the early part of the twentieth century.[23] At that time, efforts were under way to improve the quality of the schools through state enforcement of certain standards—the same argument now used also for federal control. "In organization, instruction, personnel, and many other matters the states have imposed a broad and detailed mandate on local schooling."[24] The extent to which this has occurred varies widely from state to state, but control clearly seems to have been shifting from local boards to the state capitals.

This trend is seen in a recent movement in several states toward more state, and less local, funding of education. An increase in the proportion of state funding would result in lower local property taxes. This would decrease the variation in funding among the school districts throughout each state. The undercurrent theme is: central control decreases inequality.

All this has given state departments of education the power to not merely suggest but also compel local districts in matters of equal opportunity and minimum standards. Still, this increasing state control has not been criticized as much as federal influence has. Despite their gains, the state agencies have left much freedom to local districts. While the job of the state departments of education are to enforce standards and provide leadership and service, the local school boards are left with more everyday concerns.

Local School Board

The school board sets local policies regarding such things as teacher salaries and student promotion. The board also usually appoints the superintendent and approves his or her recommendations concerning the actual management of the schools. It is through the local board that the taxpayers are given some school control. Or are they?

The local school board members—who are in most places elected—should represent the voters. Critics argue, however, that the poor are often not well represented on the boards.

Nongovernment   Where do the average taxpaying citizens fit into this power picture? They may be involved in local school board matters, or they can join some of the citizen groups which exert some control—though often not much—over the schools. The government has mandated Local School Advisory Councils, but they seem to have little real power. Parent-teacher associations (P.T.A.s) still have millions of members and over 40,000 local units but their influence seems to be waning. The P.T.A.s are accused of being run by the principals and teachers and thus resisting change. Some businessmen's clubs and other booster groups have influence on the school boards. But what little power the average citizen has seems to be found today in grassroots efforts. When not begun by school officials, such community groups have sometimes been effective. Activist groups of parents are sometimes viewed by school officials as troublemakers, but such spontaneous expressions of citizen interest are becoming more common.

There are other groups fighting for power. For example, in the past two decades teacher groups have grown in size and power. However, the National Education Association and the American Federation of Teachers have so far had more impact on state policies than on federal policies. And success on the local level has varied greatly from place to place. Still, through collective bargaining, teachers can be expected to increase their influence in school decisions and to protect their own working conditions.

Despite all these groups fighting for more control of the schools, the trend is clear. More power is shifting to state and federal governments.

SUMMARY   There are two types of education. The informal kind (socialization) is sufficient for simple cultures. For most complex cultures, a formal system of education, with teachers and schools and specified programs of learning, is needed.

Education serves several functions. One important function is that of transmitting cultural knowledge. All cultures need this, but in complex cultures a decision must be made about what parts of the huge storehouse of knowledge are to be transmitted. A major issue here is which knowledge is most relevant and valuable. Another decision involved in this function is who will get what knowledge. Another function of education is cultural integration. This need was seen clearly in the story of American immigrants, whose children were often forced to join the mainstream culture. In modern cultures, education systems are also expected to create new knowledge.

In America, education is expected to create chances for social mobility and to produce greater social equality. Some people maintain that the school system serves to maintain the social-class structure. Others believe that the schools offer lower-class children a real chance to rise above their social-class backgrounds.

While education in America is still largely public, the taxpayer's influence over the schools is decreasing. This is because control has been shifting from local agencies to more central agencies in an effort to achieve more efficiency and equal opportunity.

Americans expect the schools to provide equal opportunities for all students. This goal is not easy to achieve, largely because the home environment affects so much how well a student does in school. While there are some things parents can do at home to improve their child's school success, some factors are beyond the parents' control. Though the school environment is important for a student's chances for later social success, that environment offers unequal opportunities to different students. This is seen in the differences in teacher expectations and school funding, as well as in the tracking system. Race is another factor that affects a student's chances for equal educational opportunity. School desegregation is the main tool used to make sure fewer students loose their chance for a good education because of their race. The results of this tactic have varied from place to place; overall, many disappointments remain.

SPECIAL TOPIC
Arguments About Testing

Most students have taken many tests during their school careers, but some of the most important tests were also the most criticized. Have the students been treated unfairly because of some of the tests they took? This Special Topic will explore this question.

In recent years, the debates concerning mental testing have become more heated. To the issue of testing intelligence has been added testing of basic school skills—competency tests. The tests have been attacked by minority groups, teachers' groups, and some experts. Such tests have been taken to court and have been banned in several school districts, yet they are still widely used and are defended by many experts. Here the debates surrounding both kinds of tests will be explored.

INTELLIGENCE TESTS

The most heated debate surrounds intelligence tests. It involves four basic questions.

What Do the Tests Measure?

First, can a test tell us how good a brain a person was born with? The issue here is how well the tests measure innate mental ability. There is little agreement among experts. Arthur Jensen has been at the center of this controversy since his 1969 article claimed that the I.Q.—intelligence quotient—tests do in fact measure innate mental ability.[25, 26] One of his many critics says that Jensen's reasoning shows "a classic case of the substitution of social prejudice for social science."[27] Furthermore, many experts charge that the tests measure mostly the quality of the person's background rather than that of the person's brain. As one researcher puts it, "we must remember that the fact that a test score is (or appears to be) precise does not mean that it is valid."[28] The I.Q. tests are sometimes labeled tests of achievement rather than tests of intelligence. Which is right? Social scientists do not agree, but the answer might be that most believe the test scores reflect the background of the person more than some vague notion of inborn intelligence.

What Is Intelligence?

On this second question, most experts agree that intelligence is some mixture of various mental abilities.[29] Herrnstein says the basic ability measured by the tests is that of finding relationships among pieces of information and applying these to new data.[30] Intelligence itself is a vague notion, but a person scoring high on one test will probably do well on others. There does seem to be some basic, underlying ability measured. But how much of this ability is inborn?

There is great variation among estimates of the amount of intelligence that is controlled by genes. One researcher found a range of from 40 percent to 80 percent.[31] Others do not give percentages, but say that, "in spite of the significant and increasing influence of genetic factors during (the child's early years), the importance of environmental factors cannot be overlooked."[32] Intelligence tests can measure how well a person is able to function mentally. The unanswered question is how much this functioning is based on innate mental ability—brain quality.

Are Intelligence Tests Biased?

This third question is a little easier to answer. The evidence shows little bias in the widely used tests of intelligence.

This is disputed by people concerned about those groups that have a lower average score than the population in general. Because the average black I.Q. score is about fifteen points lower than that of the average white (100 is average), the tests are called biased by some people. But a meter stick is not biased just because it shows one group to be taller than another. Furthermore, Japanese and Jewish children have higher average scores than the majority group. These scores suggest that there is no cultural or racial bias in favor of the majority group. It seems that the tests simply point out group differences that exist for some reason other than test bias.

Other evidence shows the lack of bias in these tests toward blacks. The ranking of test questions in order of difficulty for blacks is the same as the ranking for whites. In a culturally or racially biased test, the rankings would be different. Also, researchers state there is "overwhelming published evidence . . . showing that I.Q. tests are not unfairly biased against the even more severely disadvantaged black population in the U.S."[33]

Should These Tests Be Used?

This is the most important of these four questions for a student, a parent, or a concerned taxpayer. There is no agreement among experts as to how much these tests measure brain quality, but it is clear that the tests do predict academic performance very well. The score for a six-year-old child gives the school a very good picture of his future achievement test scores. And though such tests are not very relevant for most jobs, the mental abilities required in high-status jobs are measured in intelligence tests. So applicants for some kinds of training slots could be screened with the tests. For scarce rewards that should be awarded on the basis of mental ability, the intelligence tests are a valuable tool.

If intelligence tests are used, the danger is that the tests may serve to label some children as unable to learn. Remember, there is a great deal of doubt whether the test scores can accurately measure potential ability. A low-scoring student is sometimes written off by the school or teacher as unable, not just undeveloped. So the tests must be used carefully.

COMPETENCY TESTS

Another testing issue concerns competency tests. Many states now require that students pass basic skills—competency—tests to graduate, to be promoted, or both.

Those who promote the competency test claim that it will motivate students and give some meaning and value to a high school diploma. In many places now, a diploma means only that the student stayed in school long enough to get the diploma. It is no guarantee that the student learned very much. It is hoped that competency tests will restore the diploma to its status of proof of achievement. Also, the tests are intended to help motivate students to learn. If students know they will be required to show competence in certain mental skills, they may make more effort to learn. The tests may or may not accomplish these goals, but they are fast becoming a part of most state school systems.

Competency tests are not accepted by everyone. There are several questions about the effectiveness and fairness of the tests.

Some people fear that ethnic groups that fail these tests at high rates will be faced with poorer job chances and that more students may drop out of school. It is argued that a worthless diploma may be better than none at all for a person who has not learned the skills expected of a high school graduate. It is claimed that minority-group students should not be forced into the same system of demands with students from separate and superior school systems.

There are other fears. One is that the minimum skills may become the average or standards of student performance. By teaching to the test skills, the teacher may slow the advance of those students able to go beyond the minimum. There is also concern that the passing scores are arbitrary and may be too high or low.

Competency tests are further criticized as being merely punitive. Those students who— for whatever reason—have not mastered those skills chosen for the tests are punished, not helped, unless the school offers extra aid for those students. In some states, the tests are not given until the students near graduation. By this time, some students are several years behind. A special class or summer program may be too little too late for such students. Perhaps the tests should be given every year or so.

Critics of these tests ask other questions. Just what are these skills, anyway? What skills are needed in society? Who decides? What should we expect of a high school graduate? Do the tests accurately measure this? Will we demand only those skills that are easily tested? Will other goals be ignored in the classroom? Will the tests focus the teacher's attention too narrowly, to the neglect of subjects not tested, such as art? Will the entire domain of values be ignored?

Some of these criticisms of competency tests are justified, but if the tests can avoid the pitfalls pointed to by the critics, the schools can take a big step toward raising standards and quality. When used to diagnose rather than punish, the tests may be able to help the schools to meet the needs of all students. Learning and teaching may be enhanced. It depends on the use for which they are intended.

Mental testing is an area in which social scientists can help. Firmer ground is being reached by science concerning such tests. Progress is slow, but it is being made. Science is reaching answers that can and should be used in making social decisions in such areas. But in the end, it is the citizen who must use the facts to make decisions. And the schools must prepare the citizen for that job.

SELF-TEST QUESTIONS

1. True or false: All societies use a great deal of both informal and formal education.

2. All societies demand that their schools:
   a. transmit the culture
   b. integrate the cultural parts
   c. create new knowledge
   d. provide social-mobility opportunities
   e. provide social equality

3. The American school system can be seen as:
   a. clearly promoting social mobility
   b. clearly hindering social mobility
   c. both the above

4. According to this textbook, the proper goal of our schools is equal opportunity rather than equal _____.

5. The best predictor of a child's academic success is _____.

6. True or false: There is nothing parents can do to override the effect of their social class on their child's school success.

7. List two school factors that affect the quality of education available to students.

8. The Coleman report helped promote _____ .
9. True or false: The hoped-for results of school desegregation have generally not been fulfilled.
10. Over the last century, control of America's public schools has shifted, in the name of ensuring greater quality and equality, more to:
    a. the federal level
    b. the state level
    c. the local level
11. Which nongovernment group has recently been increasing its influence concerning the public schools?
    a. P.T.A.
    b. local school advisory councils
    c. teachers' organizations

ANSWERS TO SELF-TEST QUESTIONS

1. false: some societies use very little formal education
2. a, b, c.
3. c
4. achievement
5. Parents' social class
6. false
7. teacher attitudes or expectations, funding, tracking
8. school desegregation
9. true
10. a
11. c

ANSWERS TO SKILL REINFORCERS

11–1. This is practice in deductive reasoning. It shows how such logic proceeds from a general statement to one concerning a specific case to a conclusion concerning that case. You may supply a minor premise based on either of the two points of view described in the section on the schools' function of producing social mobility. The conclusion would follow inescapably from the major and minor premises, as shown here:
   1. A school system that gives all students the chance to equip themselves with socially valuable skills is a tool for upward social mobility.
   2. The American school system does (or does not) give students from all social classes the chance to equip themselves with socially valuable skills.
   3. The American school system is (or is not) a tool for upward social mobility.

11–2. Even from the brief description of the research study's results, it is possible to guess what its guiding hypothesis was. The study's intent seems to have been to measure the extent to which teachers' expectations affected students' I.Q. scores. Remember that the hypothesis is the researcher's informed, well-founded guess as to what the experiment may show. Taking all this into account, we can guess that this study's hypothesis was something like this: Heightened teachers' expectations of students will result in (specified) improvements in the students' intellectual performance over (a specified) period of time.

NOTES

1. Karl Alexander, Gary Natriello, and Aaron Pallas, ''For Whom the Bell Tolls: The Impact of Dropping Out on Cognitive Performance,'' *American Sociological Review* 30 (June 1985): 409–420.
2. Edward Berman, ''The Improbability of Meaningful Educational Reform,'' *Issues in Education* 3 (Fall 1985): 99–112.

3. Herbert Gintis and Samuel Bowles, "Contradiction and Reproduction in Educational Theory," in Barton, Len, et al., *Schooling and Ideology and the Curriculum* (Lewes, Falmer Press, 1980).

4. Janet Holland, "Social Class and Changes in Orientation to Meaning," *Sociology* 15 (February 1981): 1–18.

5. Lala Carr Steelman, "A Tale of Two Variables: A Review of the Intellectual Consequences of Sibship and Birth Order," *Review of Educational Research* 55 (Fall 1985): 353–386.

6. Sarane Spencer Boocock, *An Introduction to the Sociology of Learning* (Boston: Houghton Mifflin Co., 1972).

7. Donald Mackenzie, "Research for School Improvement: An Appraisal of Some Recent Trends," *Educational Researcher* 12 (April 1983): 5–17.

8. Karen Miller, Melvin Kohn, and Carmi Schooler, "Educational Self-Direction and Personality," *American Sociological Review* 51 (June 1986): 372–90.

9. James Coleman, Thomas Hoffer, and Sally Kilgore, *Public and Private Schools: A Report to the National Center for Education Statistics* by the National Opinion Research Center. University of Chicago, March 1981.

10. J. Douglas Willms, "Catholic-School Effects on Academic Achievement: New Evidence From the High School and Beyond Follow-Up Study," *Sociology of Education* 58 (April 1985): 98–114.

11. Robert Rosenthal and Lenore Jacobsen, *Pygmalion in the Classroom* (New York: Holt, Rinehart & Winston, 1968).

12. Ibid., p. 180.

13. Gary Natriello and Sanford Dornbusch, "Bringing Behavior Back In: The Effects of Student Characteristics and Behavior on the Classroom Behavior of Teachers," *American Educational Research Journal* 20 (Spring 1983): 29–43.

14. Emil Haller, "Pupil Race and Elementary School Ability Grouping: Are Teachers Biased Against Black Children?" *American Educational Research Journal* 22 (Winter 1985): 465–83.

15. Jeannie Oakes, *Keeping Track: How Schools Structure Inequality* (New Haven: Yale University Press, 1985).

16. Richard Rehberg and Evelyn Rosenthal, *Class and Merit in the American High School: An Assessment of the Revisionist and Meritocratic Arguments* (New York: Longman, Inc., 1978).

17. James Coleman, et al., *Equality of Educational Opportunity* (Washington, D.C.: Department of Health, Education, and Welfare, 1966).

18. Franklin D. Wilson, "The Impact of School Desegregation Programs on White Public-School Enrollment, 1968–1976," *Sociology of Education* 58 (July 1985): 137–53.

19. Nancy Burton and Lyle Jones, "Recent Trends in Achievement Levels of Black and White Youth," *Educational Researcher* 11 (April 1982): 10–14, 17.

20. Robert Crain and Rita Mahard, "The Effect of Research Methodology on Desegregation-Achievement Studies: A Meta Analysis," *American Journal of Sociology* 88 (March 1983): 839–54.

21. Martin Patchen, Gerhard Hofmann, and William Brown, "Academic Performance of Black High School Students Under Different Conditions of Contact with White Peers," *Sociology of Education* 53 (January 1980): 33–51.

22. Whitfield Ayres, "Desegregating or Debilitating Higher Education?" *The Public Interest* 69 (Fall 1982): 100–16.

23. Frederick M. Wirt, "What State Laws Say About Local Control," *Phi Delta Kappan* 59 (April 1978): 517–20.

24. Ibid., p. 520.

25. Arthur Jensen, "How Much Can We Boost IQ and Scholastic Achievement?" *Harvard Educational Review* 39 (Winter 1969): 1–123.

26. Arthur Jensen, *Bias in Mental Testing* (The Free Press, 1980).

27. Philip Green, *The Pursuit of Inequality* (New York: Pantheon Books, 1981): 26.
28. Robert Sternberg, "What Should Intelligence Tests Test?" *Educational Researcher* 13 (January 1984): 5–15.
29. Joseph Horn, "The Texas Adoption Project," *Child Development* 54 (April 1983): 268–75.
30. R.J. Herrnstein, "In Defense of Intelligence Tests," *Commentary* (February 1980): 40.
31. Bruce K. Eckland, "Genetic Variance in the SES–IQ Correlation," *Sociology of Education* 52 (July 1979): 191–196.
32. Laura Baker, J.C. Defries and David Fulker, "Longitudinal Stability of Cognitive Ability in the Colorado Adoption Project," *Child Development* 54 (April 1983): 290–97.
33. Robert A. Gordon and Eileen E. Rudert, "Bad News Concerning IQ Tests," *Sociology of Education* 52 (July 1979): 174–90.

SUGGESTED READINGS

Ballantine, Jeanne H. *The Sociology of Education.* Englewood Cliffs, N.J.: Prentice-Hall, 1983.

Bowles, Samuel, and Herbert Gintis. *Schooling in Capitalist America, Educational Reform and the Contradictions of Economic Life.* New York: Basic Books, 1976.

Collins, Randall. *The Credentialist Society: A Historical Sociology of Education and Stratification.* New York: Academic Press, 1979.

London, Howard B. *The Culture of a Community College.* New York: Praeger Publishers, 1978.

Parelius, Ann Parker, and Robert J. Parelius. *The Sociology of Education.* Engleglewood Cliffs, N.J.: Prentice-Hall, 1978.

Silberman, Charles E. *Crisis in the Classroom.* New York: Random House, 1970.

Spindler, George D., ed. *Education and Culture: Anthropological Approaches.* New York: Holt, Rinehart & Winston, 1963.

Zwerling, L. Stephan. *Second Best: The Crisis of Community College.* New York: McGraw-Hill, 1976.

12 RELIGION

How Old Is Religion?

How old is religion? No one can say, but the urge to deal with the world beyond this world is older than any church. Indeed, the earliest, though perhaps not the first, traces of this otherworldly concern are found deep in the past, hundreds of thousands of years ago.

Some of the skulls of Peking Man (*Homo erectus*) suggest some gory ritual that may or may not have been religious in nature. In one of Peking man's caves, the human skulls were so broken as to suggest the brains had been removed, probably to be eaten. Brains may be eaten for reasons of diet or for ritual. While we can only guess, it may be that those hunters and gatherers ate the brains of either friends or foe to gain some power, perhaps from the spirit of those others.

A much earlier case for the earliest religion is found among the Neanderthal. These early humans buried their fellows with some ritual effect. In one case, a ring of goat horns surrounds a child's grave. In another, flowers were included in the grave. Tools, weapons, and perhaps food were left with other bodies. Another site appears to have been a family burial ground, with the bodies arranged with care. Indeed, in many of these early human burial sites the bodies were clearly not just thrown into a pit. A few years ago, evidence of an ancient shrine was uncovered in northern Spain.[1] In a small room inside a cave were found two mounds made of animal parts and colored clay. On one mound was a large stone slab that seems to have been an altar. Topping the other mound was a stone head. Half the head's face was humanlike, the other was more like that of a beast. It is not difficult to guess that the slab and the head may have been used as part of some ritual. At an age of 14,000 years, this cave room seems to be the oldest shrine yet found.

All this evidence suggests strongly that early humans were thinking about an afterlife. The funeral rituals show us the respect given to a dead person, perhaps because of some belief that the person's spirit lived on. The articles left in the grave suggest that these people thought about the needs of people after life.

All we can do is guess what these early humans believed. But the evidence makes it seem likely that the beginnings of religion are far back in the human past. In fact, if we could ever know for sure what those beings of long ago believed, we might discover that religion appeared with the first humans. In the absence of any more proof, it is easy to see that the desire to relate oneself to a world beyond this, which many of us feel today, is at least as old as humans themselves.

Whether we go to church every week or not at all, an interest in the world beyond this one is a part of our way of life. At the least, this interest is a part of the culture in which we live and affects our social world in many ways. At the most, this interest is part of our deepest, most personal feelings. Because of the social and personal influences of this ancient interest in the other world, it deserves a place in a book on the social sciences.

The job of social science here is not to judge whether or not beliefs in the other world are true. The other world lies beyond the world of our senses and of facts. Therefore, it lies beyond the reach of science. The attitude of science is agnostic. The role of social science is to help us better understand the role these beliefs play in our culture.

AGNOSTIC: A person or attitude claiming that with regard to God or ultimate reality nothing can be known. This is distinguished from an atheist viewpoint, which denies the existence of God.

In this chapter we will examine the nature and development of this human concern with the other world. Then we will focus on the functions, both social and personal, of this interest. Next, the form this interest has taken in the United States will be explored.

RELIGION: WHAT IT IS AND IS NOT

Demons and drugs and visions and ghosts—these are among the many things used by humans all over the world as they try to deal with the world beyond the natural world. If social science is to help us understand this human concern with otherworldly matters, science must first label it, then define it. This task is more difficult than expected, which we will see as we follow the efforts of an imaginary social scientist as she explores what she will label religion.

The Essence of Religion

Forming a Definition. Our scientist knows that before she can study something she must know just what the object of her study is. She must define the essential traits of what she has labeled religion. If she were to study several cultures herself in order to discover these essential traits, she would run into some problems.

The first problem our scientist would encounter is that religion is deeply embedded in cultures. It lies near the center of cultures and its influence spreads throughout the cultures. Religion is often combined so intimately with other parts of the culture that it cannot easily be set apart and defined. Because of this, it is hard to mark the boundary of religion, to say where religion ends and where the everyday begins.

Skill Reinforcer 12-1*
What are some ways disciplined observation might be used by a scientist studying religion?

Another problem for our scientist is that religion is found in all cultures. This means that any definition of religion must cover a variety of forms. It is hard to capture the essence of religion when faced with such a variety. For example, religions have different numbers of gods. Indeed, some have no gods, but center on spirits of various kinds.

RELIGION: A system of beliefs and practices organized around ideas of the sacred.

Despite these problems, if our scientist studied all religions, she would find that there are some features that are seen in all of

* Answers to the Skill Reinforcers appear at the end of the chapter.

Religion involves sacred practices, or rituals.

SACRED: A person or thing set apart from the profane, everyday, and understandable world.

PROFANE: Ordinary, rooted in the everyday, natural world.

them. There is everywhere, in all human cultures, a belief in supernatural forces, forces beyond those in nature. Along with these beliefs there are ideas about the proper behavior concerning those beliefs. These beliefs and behaviors are the essence of religion.

This leads our scientist to a definition of the concept. Religion could be defined as a culture's system of beliefs and practices concerning supernatural forces or beings. With a definition, she can further explore the essence of religion.

Durkheim's Three Elements of Religion. In her continued search for the essence of religion, our scientist would read what other scientists had found. She would surely run across the writings of Emile Durkheim, a pathfinder for social scientists in many areas. Durkheim explored three basic elements of religion: the sacred, beliefs and practices, and believers.

The sacred. Durkheim pointed out that all religions deal with the sacred, which he saw as one of the three elements of religion.[2] To make clear the sacred domain, he distinguished it from the profane. The profane is that which is natural and ordinary; it is part of everyday life. We can be more familiar and at ease with the profane than with the sacred. The sacred is set apart from daily life. The sacred demands more than a casual attitude; it can arouse great attraction or dread. A feeling of awe and a sense of mystery arise from the sacred. The sacred demands reverence and special commitments. The sacred has power which lies beyond logic and natural experience. It cannot be observed or dealt with in usual ways. Humans deal with the sacred through religion.

The sense of sacredness can be attached to an object, place, time, person, and other things. Plants, animals, even nonliving things have been assigned sacredness. Sacredness can be attached to a cross, for example. The symbol of the cross thus takes on special meaning for Christians. Similarly, the star of David has special meaning for Jews. These symbols have no meaning in themselves, but sacredness is assigned to them by religion. Likewise, people can be assigned sacredness. Examples are Christ, Mohammed, and, for Shintoists, one's ancestors.

Beliefs and practices. Durkheim wrote that beliefs and practices are the second element of religion. Both are related to the first element, the sacred.

The beliefs of religions are built around the sacred. In fact, most religions are based on a belief in God, a sacred being. Such beliefs in God are for some religions so ancient that their origins are lost in time. Other beliefs are more recent in origin and can be traced to individuals, such as Christ, Gautama Buddha, and Joseph Smith. Not all religions involve a belief concerning the existence of God; Buddhism is an example of such a religion. Still, all religions do share some system of beliefs that are based on the sacred.

Also based on the sacred are religious practices, or rituals. These behaviors are the expressions given to the religious beliefs. They can take many forms, such as praying, bowing, singing,

RITUAL (religious): Rite; a practice or behavior associated with the sacred.

dancing, and offering sacrifices. The rituals are saved for special occasions. Such special behaviors are a way of keeping the sacred apart from the ordinary.

There are other functions of ritual. Ritual serves to bring the believers together. It organizes them in relation to one another and to their God. Ritual directs the believers in the proper, safe manner to behave toward the sacred. The sacred is awesome and dangerous, and ritual serves to decrease our dread by defining the safe behaviors to use regarding the sacred. Further, relief can come from the knowledge that one has done one's duty toward the sacred.

The funeral rite for a Trobriand Island man shows how duty toward the sacred, and toward family members, can be expressed in ritual.[3] The widow must spend six months to two years in quiet isolation to mourn her husband. Her head is shaved, and she may not leave a small, dark hut during the entire period. Meanwhile, the corpse is caressed and made to move as if still alive; then it is buried. The mother of the deceased lies on the grave, wailing throughout the night. The second morning after burial, the body is dug up and the dead man's sons remove the bones from the rotting corpse and clean them (in the past, the sons had to suck from the bones any decaying matter). The bones, hair, teeth, and nails all become mementos of the dead man. While these rituals may seem grisly or cruel, they enable the family to show great reverence for the dead person. After such ritual, the family members should feel no guilt about showing too little respect for the dead man.

Rituals can become sacred in themselves. Prayers, for example, can be regarded as sacred. Likewise, objects used in rituals, such as a book or a cup, can be assigned sacredness.

Community of believers. After the sacred, and the related beliefs and practices, Durkheim saw the third element of religion as a community of believers. These people are held together by their beliefs and practices. They share a religious loyalty and identity. To ensure that the religion will continue, tasks must be performed, such as building churches, training clergy, and conducting rituals. The believers are organized so these things will be done.

With the help of Durkheim, our scientist has by now captured the essential traits of religion as a part of culture. These traits all fit together in our definition of religion as the beliefs and practices shared by a community of believers as they relate themselves to the sacred or supernatural.

Religion Versus Magic   How is the Star of David different from the voodoo doll? Both deal with the supernatural. The same question applies to the local preacher and the witch doctor. What is the essential difference in both these cases? This question shows that the social scientist's job is not yet finished. She has shown us something about what religion *is;* now we need her to contrast that with what religion is

MAGIC: A set of practices aimed at manipulating supernatural forces that are believed to be subject to human control.

not. That should give us an even better understanding of the nature of religion.

Our scientist will review her survey of the world's cultures and, with a little insight, distinguish for us religion from magic. Of course, here we are not dealing with the stage magician's tricks. Rather, here magic refers to the belief that otherworldly forces can be controlled. Magic is more typical of primitive cultures, as seen in the chapter preview, but traces of it can be found in the religions of advanced cultures too.

A Matter of Attitudes. After surveying the various ways people deal with the world beyond nature, the scientist notes that there are two basic attitudes toward otherworldly forces. In what has been called religion, the believers see these forces as being all-powerful. The people are thus humble, submissive, and reverent toward those forces. Humans are seen as completely dependent on the will of the forces, on gods. The only hope for the people is that the forces will find favor in them. Prayer is the tool used to maintain a link with the otherworldly forces. Through prayer, the believers can communicate with, though not control, those forces. By contrast, in the context of magic, people view the supernatural forces as something to be controlled. The magician feels he or she has power over these forces. Bribes and even threats may be used to control them.

Nature of the Forces. Our scientist notices another basic difference between magic and religion. Both are based on a belief in supernatural forces, but religions usually see these forces as humanlike. The forces have human form or traits. The forces are more like beings than just forces. People can thus relate personally to them. Sometimes the wind or the sun are seen as such beings, with personalities to which the people can relate. In magic, the ultimate forces surrounding people are seen by the magician as impersonal. The sun may be seen as a force more than a being. It is something to be controlled or exploited, not prayed to—as we might use a fire for its warmth but not relate to it as a being.

Goals. The scientist finds another way of contrasting religion and magic: by their goals. In magic, the goal of one's efforts is likely to be worldly, personal, and immediate. There is little concern for ultimate values. The goal may be a cure for disease, victory in battle, or rain. The goals are narrow, concrete, and specific. In religion, the goals of a person may sometimes be personal and even worldly, but they are likely to be seen as part of the ultimate goals of life. That is, a religious person may pray concerning a disease, but is likely to ask for strength or understanding in the crisis, rather than merely for a cure. The focus of religious goals is likely to be salvation or inner peace. Such goals deal with one's relationship to God and with the meaning of life. Magic deals with more worldly comforts and concerns.

Secret or Shared? Another difference between religion and magic is found in their rituals. The magician is often approached by a client and hired to do a job. The ritual sought may be secret because the magician does not care to share power with others. In religion, the believer approaches rituals with awe and reverence, sometimes through a priest. The rituals are shared and usually performed in public. Indeed, the believers in a religion are sometimes required to learn the beliefs, prayers, and songs and to take part in the rituals.

Effectiveness of Magic. What are the results of religion and magic? The results of religion, such as closeness to God, are difficult to measure. This means that the effectiveness of religion is often unclear. Magic, however, sometimes clearly seems to be effective. Headaches are sometimes cured and battles are sometimes won after magic is used. There are several reasons why magic seems to work.[4]

Coincidence. First, results may follow magical ritual by coincidence. If enough time is allowed, surely the headache will go away or some battle will be won. Though a scientist would not be fooled by this into believing that the ritual causes the effect, many people would be fooled. (This is a matter of being able to identify cause-effect relationships, as described in the Skill Box in Chapter 1.)

Suggestion. Magic also works by means of the power of suggestion. If magic is directed against a person who believes in its power, he or she may fall prey to the magic. Sickness and even death can result from such belief. Magic can also work in a more positive way. For example, a believer can be given a boost in confidence by magic. This can make one work harder and thus be more likely to succeed. If one's belief is strong enough, the results may be only imagined. Warriors who use magic to achieve bravery may act no differently than before, but they may believe themselves to be braver and thus testify that the magic worked.

Fraud. Another reason magic sometimes seems to work is fraud. The magician may use tricks to deceive the client. For example, the magician may perform a ritual and at its climax pretend to pull out of a sick client an object that is claimed to be the cause of the problem. Again, if the client's belief is strong enough, the problem may be solved.

Our scientist has noted that some people mix a bit of magic into their religion. They may ask for a new job, a new car, or relief from disease. They may give promises or money to God to get what they ask for. The scientist, of course, does not label this mixing as bad. She merely notes that religion and magic are not as distinct in life as they are on paper.

Although religions often use a certain amount of magic in their rituals, churches are hostile to magic. This is because their basic attitudes conflict with each other; in magic people are in command, but they are in submission in religion. The gap between magic and religion will never be fully bridged.

**PAST AND PRESENT
FORMS OF RELIGION**

From the good luck token to ghosts and fairies to temples and priests—so religion has developed. After thousands of years of such development, religion today assumes a rich array of forms, from widespread and powerful churches to small, intense sects and fanatic cults. This section of the chapter will follow the line of religion's development through the ages until the current scene is reached. Then our picture of religion will broaden to include the many religious structures and forms of today's world.

**The Development
of Religion**

The churches and temples we see around us today are merely the latest, and maybe not the last, stage of religious development. Today's structures did not arise at the beginning of religion. Other forms came before them, and these older forms still exist in many parts of the world. To see the whole range of religion, we must follow its development from its beginnings.

The origins of religion are found only in the world of human beings. As far as we know, the world of the supernatural is of no concern to animals. To reach out to the supernatural, a brain is needed that can reach beyond the world of the senses. The brain must be able to reflect on one's surroundings. The brain must be able to ask questions about one's origins, one's nature, and the meaning of life. At the point when a brain that could do these things developed, religion must have developed too.

In the Beginning: Religion's Foundation. The chapter preview showed us something about early efforts to reach out to the world beyond this world: special treatment of the dead, especially the skulls. But keeping a skull around the house is hardly a common practice in our culture today. It is part of an earlier stage, which is where our story of the development of religion begins.

We can examine the earliest religious forms by describing the two bases of supernatural ideas: mana and animism. While these ideas are important in cultures with older forms of religion, they are much less important in the religions of our own culture.

MANA: The force believed to reside in certain living and nonliving things.

Mana. Mana is supernatural force. It is the power to do exceptional things. This force exists within certain beings and objects. A person can possess mana, as can a "lucky" horseshoe—or a skull. The concept of mana is used to explain unusual qualities of both living and nonliving things. A warrior or artisan with unusual ability may be said to possess mana. The unusual rock and the exceptional tool or weapon can also be described this way. Thus a net that catches many fish or a spear that kills many deer has large amounts of mana. Mana transcends the usual, the natural. It is part of religion's foundation. As mana is today part of many cultures, it was probably part of the first human attempts to explain the supernatural.

ANIMISM: The belief in beings with souls or spirits.

Animism. To the mana of the rabbit's foot we add now the idea of ghosts and angels, which is animism, the second basic religious form. Animism is the belief in beings with souls or spirits. They may be called ghosts, fairies, devils, gods, and so on.

Their basic trait is that they are nonmaterial—having no substance. Yet these spirits are believed to exist and to have power.

An early theorist, E.B. Tylor, suggested that animism developed as part of the human effort to explain mysteries, such as death.[5] He reasoned that early humans saw two parts to a person: body and soul. The soul is the vital force of a person. When this soul leaves the body, the body dies. The soul, or spirit, however, may still move about in the world.

Animism is found in all cultures today. Spirits and souls are basic parts of all religions. Surely such a belief was part of the origins of religion, as was mana.

Since the Beginning: Religion's Evolution. In an attempt to reconstruct the earliest religions, we face the problem that religion began before written records were made. As we saw in the chapter preview, ritual treatment of the dead occurred among early human cultures. From this type of evidence we can only speculate on the religious beliefs of early humans.

Fossil and other remains show clearly how the burial practices became more elaborate over time. While they were still hunters and gatherers, later humans showed great concern over burials. At one site, for example, skulls were colored and placed in shallow pits. Ornaments and tools were included. Further, all the skulls faced west, a practice found today in many cultures.[6] Surely such rituals had religious meaning. At this point in cultural development, religion was probably centered in the home or village. Perhaps each family devised its own rituals and worshiped its own sacred objects. There were no full-time priests. Religion was not controlled by any one part of the group.

Once humans began to farm and thus settle down, religion changed. It became a special, separate part of the culture. In time, powerful full-time priests controlled it. Religion became a tool of the ruling elite. The religions of the earliest states took on new functions, compared to those of earlier stages. Elaborate systems were devised, aimed at controlling not only nature but the people too. In many of the early states, religion clearly dominated the rest of the society.

From this brief sketch of the evolution of religion, we see the various stages of religious development. Religions can range from a family-centered endeavor to one which controls the people through a powerful, formal system.

Religious Forms Today From the times dominated by lucky charms and hovering spirits, our story has come to the current world of religions. Now we are ready to explore the various religious structures that have developed from this heritage of mana and animism. We will begin with the world scene, then narrow our focus to the religious forms in America.

Religious Forms in the World. Many people have only a vague idea that there are some religions in the world that are very different from their own religion. This chapter gives a broader and deeper view of religion. In this section we offer a broad view by surveying the major religions in the world.

To make some sense out of the many world religions, they must be classified. One way to classify them is by the central object of worship, be it a god, a group of gods, or something else. Under each type, the larger religions will be briefly described.

MONOTHEISM: Belief in one god.

Monotheism. The type of religion most familiar to Americans is monotheism: the focusing on a single god. Examples of monotheism are Judaism, Christianity, and Islam. Judaism's God is Yahweh of the Old Testament, as revealed to Moses and the prophets. From this heritage sprang Christianity, based on the teachings of Jesus. From the teachings of the prophet Mohammed came Islam. Followers of Islam are called Muslims, Moslems, or Mohammedans; they worship Allah and regard the Koran as sacred scripture.

POLYTHEISM: Belief in several gods.

Polytheism. Another category of the world's religions is polytheism. The largest polytheistic religion is Hinduism, practiced mostly in India and Pakistan. Hindus believe in many gods, who are ranked from local to regional and from lesser to more important ones. A Hindu believer can worship any of these gods, depending on the god's special interest, such as childbirth, and the god's location, such as the local well. Hinduism may be the world's oldest religion.

Religions of the way. Besides these god-focused religions, there are other types less familiar to most Americans. Some religions lack the notion of a personal god. In Buddhism, Confucianism, and Taoism, sacred principles, not gods, are the center of worship. These could be called "religions of the way." Religions of the way stress ethics and proper behavior. Their principles define the way to moral excellence, which is the goal of these religions.

Buddhism arose in India during the sixth century B.C. The various sects of Buddhism all center on the "enlightened one," Buddha.

Confucianism is based on the teachings of Confucius, who lived about five hundred years before Christ. Because this system includes no priesthood or required doctrine, it is not considered a religion by some people. Social and personal perfection is the goal of its followers.

Taoism is another religion of the way. It grew from a mixture of early Chinese cults into a popular religion. Divided into dozens of sects, Taoism uses mystical practices, and sometimes magic, to search for the divine way of the universe.

Ancestors. Another religion that centers on worship of something other than a god is Shintoism. This is the traditional faith of Japan. Its focus is the worship or honor of one's ancestors. Rituals and rules of conduct are built around this focus.

Memberships of the World's Religions. From this brief survey of the world's major religions, we get some idea of the various forms religion has taken. Such a survey should include a comparison of the sizes of these religions. Table 12–1 gives a rough estimate of the sizes of religious memberships. From the table we see that the two largest religions are monotheistic. The major polytheist religion is the third largest faith in the world. These numbers must not, however, be viewed as totally accurate.

Skill Reinforcer 12-2

Apply the process of thoroughly reading a table to Table 12–1.

World religion membership figures are inexact for several reasons. While some churches keep exact membership figures, others are rather casual about it. Even so, even some of those religions with exact counts will not release the numbers. Another problem is that some churches with strong ethnic connections sometimes assume that all members of the ethnic group are members of the church. Also, some nations have not taken a census. In others, persecution makes it impossible to achieve an accurate count. Also, in Southeast Asia, a person may belong to several religions at the same time. All this lends confusion to the task of counting world membership of religions.

Religious Forms in America.   What do the River Brethren, Moravians, The Schwenkfelder Church, and the Vendanta Society

TABLE 12-1.   Global Adherents of Religions, Mid–1985

Rounded to nearest million. Figures are projections based on a variety of sources, mostly surveys conducted from the mid-1960s through the 1970s using church organizations as well as field surveys.

	Adherents	% of World Population
Christians	1,549,000,000	32.4
Roman Catholics	884,000,000	18.5
Protestants	293,000,000	6.1
Nonreligious	806,000,000	16.9
Muslim	817,000,000	17.1
Hindus	648,000,000	13.5
Buddhists	296,000,000	6.2
Atheists	211,000,000	4.4
Chinese Folk Religionists	188,000,000	3.9
New Religionists	106,000,000	2.2
Tribal Religionists	91,000,000	1.9
Jews	18,000,000	0.4
Sikhs	16,000,000	0.3
Shamanists	12,000,000	0.4
Confucians	5,000,000	0.1
Baha'is	4,000,000	0.1
Afro-American Spiritualists	4,000,000	0.1
Jains	3,000,000	0.1
Shintoists	3,000,000	0.1
Spiritists	3,000,000	0.1
Parsis	171,000	0.0
Mandaeans	35,000	0.0
Other religionists	1,000,000	0.0

SOURCE: David B. Barrett, ed. *World Christian Encyclopedia*. Nairobi: Oxford University Press, 1982, Global Table 4, p. 6.

have in common? They are all religions found in the United States.[7] Even when we narrow our study of religions to this nation, we find a wide range of forms: denomination, sect, and cult. One form missing in the United States is the ecclesia, which is a religious organization that dominates a society. Supported by the state, an ecclesia largely controls the culture. In the past, the Church of England was close to this type, as was the Catholic Church in France. The ecclesia in this view is the "only game in town" and tends to be conservative, thus protecting its power.

Denomination. A denomination is not state-supported. It may be part of a larger religious category, such as Protestantism. When Americans today say "church," they are often referring to a denomination.

A denomination is a large, wealthy, and respected religious structure. Its members are often born into it, and membership is based less on the spiritual traits of a person than on the social traits. Members are largely middle-class, though this is not true of all denominations. The daily lives of the members are not heavily controlled by doctrine. Such structures are usually led by full-time, trained clergy. Religious services tend to be unemotional and rather intellectual. These structures are well-established within the broader social system, endorsing and supporting it.

Sect. Fragments of denominations sometimes split off to form sects. A sect is a structure formed in protest against the larger structure from which it split. In fact, sects are generally at odds with society too. The world is seen as evil; members focus on the next world. Sect members see their way as the only way and are typically intolerant of other religions. They accuse denominations of having compromised too much on matters of belief.

These sects are usually small and of limited wealth. Members are more often from the lower classes than middle or upper classes. A person is not just born into a sect. To join, one goes through an emotional conversion. The sect services are also emotional, with members often participating. The members' lives are subject to much control by the sect's rules and beliefs. For example, diet and dress are more likely to be controlled in a sect than in a denomination. Scriptures are accepted as literal truth. Sect leaders are typically self-trained and are often part-time.

The life of a sect is intense, but often short. That is, a sect often either disappears or grows into a denomination. If it does survive to become a well-established structure, it tends to lose its sectlike intensity. In time, sects may split from this structure and the cycle begins again. The disciples of Jesus can be seen as an example of a sect that grew into a church, from which sects have split. Another example is the Quaker sect, breaking from the Church of England in the 1600s. The Quakers, or Society of Friends, may now be seen as a denomination.

Cult. Cults are another type of religious structure. They can be compared with sects in several ways. Cults are even further removed from the established social order than sects. They are also

ECCLESIA: A highly institutionalized religious organization to which virtually all members of the society belong.

DENOMINATION: A well-established religious structure larger than a sect and often part of a larger religious grouping, as Methodism is part of Protestantism.

SECT: A relatively small religious organization, usually not wealthy and usually not identifying closely with dominant social values.

Some churches with wealthy members spend lavishly on impressive architecture.

CULT: A small, unconventional, somewhat religiously based group under the leadership of a strong leader.

less stable. While a sect leader is important to the structure's success, a cult leader is central to the cult's existence.

Many cult leaders possess charisma, the gift of inspiring great loyalty. This personal gift can produce tremendous feelings in others. Followers may believe these leaders are divinely inspired or superhuman. Such leaders have great power over their followers. Thus, leaders with charisma can move people in dramatic ways, inspiring them to follow even extremist paths. Such paths may be destructive. For example, the followers of Jim Jones' Peoples' Temple were led to their deaths. On the other hand, leaders with charisma may lead their followers to better lives, though this is less typical. This leadership is so vital for cults that many such structures die when their leaders die. The nearly hypnotic power of the leader is the only force that holds such groups together.

Cults are not only more loosely organized than other religious groups; many cults are not very religious in tone either. Some have no religious framework to give meaning to the members' actions. Instead, the members seem bound together more by emotional forces than religious forces. Their goals may be more secular than spiritual.

Who joins a cult? A study of several cults described the members as having dependent personalities.[8] Typical members were upper-middle-class students. Their parents were college-educated and determined to give their children everything. The members were sheltered and dominated at home, given little chance to be independent. Such people develop a need for external controls, and when they leave home they look for someone to take over the parents' role. The cults fill this need. Another study described people who joined cults as being in transitional states, such as between family and school, or school and job.[9] Many were going through a personal crisis when they joined. Often they had come from another minority religious group. They were attracted to the cult's simple answers to life's complex questions. Some young people join cults in a search for deep meaning and service within an alternative life-style.[10]

WHAT RELIGION DOES FOR US AND TO US

So far we have seen what religion is and how it differs from magic. We have seen how religion began, built upon beliefs in supernatural forces and spirits. From these bases, religion developed into the several forms seen in the major types found in the world today. Religion has thus been presented as an ancient and, today, widespread part of human life. Knowing all this, social scientists wondered *why* religion has existed for so long and in so many places. This question has led scientists to the study of the functions of religion. They concluded that religion is so much a part of human cultures because it does so many things for us.

In this section we will explore the things religion does for us and to us, both on a personal level and on a social level. We shall see that the effects are not always positive; that is, in some ways religion can be socially harmful. It will become clear, however, that the benefits outweigh such effects.

Religion and the Individual

Serving Our Needs. An assumption of a great many people is that "religion is good for the human psyche." [11] But religion can be restrictive, even fanatical. It can be the basis for war and bigotry. Despite its negative aspects, great multitudes of humans have been drawn to religion. Why?

Explanations. A major reason humans have turned to religion for thousands of years is that it gives our existence meaning and purpose. We seem to need an answer to our questions: Why are we here? Why do we suffer? Why do we die? We also need to understand the physical world. Religion has always explained the awesome, frightening conditions surrounding us. Earthquakes, storms, and dreams can be less terrifying when explained in terms of otherworldly powers. Anything can be less frightening when it is explained.

Comfort. In this light, another of religion's functions—comfort—is evident. Explanation can bring comfort. Religious views of earthly trials can give us strength and support. We need consolation as we face the uncertainties of life and the mystery of death. Indeed, religion's comfort is most clearly seen in regard to death. Most religions offer some kind of hope and comfort concerning death. It can thus be much easier to face our own death or that of a loved one.

Identity. Another kind of comfort offered by religion is identity. Religion helps us to understand who we are. We are given a place in the universe by the framework of our faith. Our link to divine powers is defined. Likewise, our place on earth is made clear by religion. As a member of a religion, we gain a feeling of belonging somewhere, of being connected to a body of fellow human beings. This bond with the other members of a religion is especially strong because it is based on strongly felt beliefs and values.

Affecting Attitudes and Status. Besides serving some of a person's emotional needs, religion also has effects that are not spiritual. For example, involvement in religious activities seems to cause less deviant behavior in certain social situations. [12]

Religion can also enhance the individual's marriage stability. Religion can be a source of unity between spouses, and religious laws may force the couple to work out their problems rather than split up. Besides keeping spouses together, religion can also improve the quality of their marriage. One study showed that the more religious the spouses were the more likely they were to have established a strong marital adjustment. [13] Religion promotes personal sacrifice, it provides a clear set of norms, and it may make life more satisfying in itself, all of which would enhance the quality and the durability of a relationship.

Religion also seems to affect an individual's politics, education, income, and career. A Gallup Report shows that Jews and Catholics are mostly Democrats, while Protestants are split between the two major parties.[14] Religious preference also predicts income: most Catholics and Jews earn over $15,000 a year, while Protestants overall earn less. Within the Protestant category, however, there are important distinctions. Baptists are more likely to earn below $15,000, but Presbyterians and Episcopalians are often in higher income brackets. Similarly, Jews and then Catholics have the highest education levels, but within the Protestant category, Presbyterians and Episcopalians generally have high education levels and Baptists do not.

These social-religious rankings have changed little over the 40 years that the Gallup Organization has conducted these surveys. During that time, the highest income and education levels have been found among Presbyterians, Jews, Episcopalians, and Congregationalists, followed increasingly closely by Catholics, then Methodists and Lutherans. Baptists, with a high proportion of blacks and southerners, usually are ranked lower. Religious affiliation, then, is clearly associated with several social class indicators.

What Religion Does for Society

Religion has built the pyramids in Egypt and the huge cathedrals of Europe. It has been the cause of wars as well as peace marches. It has reached out to feed hungry children and to oppress nonbelievers. Religion serves several important functions for society, usually but not always for the social good.

Cohesion. In Durkheim's view, religion serves the need of every society to regularly reaffirm its shared sentiments and ideas. By this he meant that every society needs to worship itself, and religion is the means for this self-affirmation.

Religion helps unite people into a community, giving them a sense of oneness. As they share their rituals and beliefs, social cohesion results, and the social web is thus strengthened, even though the preference for friends of the same faith seems to have declined in the United States.[15] Still, religion provides a way of reaching out socially to other members of the community. Indeed, religious commitment has been linked to a person's greater involvement not only with family but also with neighbors and community.[16] That is, religion serves to link us to other people.

Sometimes this unity is based on ethnocentrism. That is, the members may feel their religion is the only true religion. This may result in a hostility to "non-believers." Thus, while producing unity within groups, religion can produce conflict among groups. Many wars throughout history have been fought in the name of religion. During the Middle Ages, for example, Christians fought Muslims in the name of God.

Also, because it sometimes creates and maintains ethnic differences, religion plays a part in causing conflict among groups within a society. Catholics still fight Protestants today in Northern Ireland. There are also ethnic divisions within the Catholic

Church. Religion sometimes serves as support for such divisive ethnic differences. Along this line, Marxist theory sees religion as another means by which people are enslaved and alienated. Through religion, the true and positive self-consciousness of humans is suppressed, making people easier to exploit, according to Marx.

Control.   As religion unites its members, so it controls them. Teaching through the church and through the parents, a religion defines right behavior and wrong behavior. Religion justifies and upholds the laws and the government of the dominant elite, according to conflict theory. Since the religious concepts of good and evil are believed to come from divine sources, they hold great weight for the members. Such a moral order can have a substantial influence on society too.

Even when there are many competing religions, as in America, the codes of the various faiths may converge. The result is a common moral order that enhances the control of each religion. Because of this, the members of any major faith in our culture may be seen as subject to the same basic moral controls.

Harmony.   Most major faiths involve a love not only for God but also of all human beings. In this way nearly all religions promote social harmony. The members of most religions are taught the basics of good citizenship. A person actually following such a moral code is not likely to be a criminal—so long as the code and the laws do not conflict.

Religion can also create harmony among other social institutions. This harmony is more evident in some cultures than others; in the United States, for example, the government is separate from religion. But often the values of religion are also the basis for the family, the economy, education, and government.

Effect on Change.   A side-effect of the control religion has and the harmony it creates is a hindrance of social change. The existing social system is sometimes supported by the church, even though the system may deserve change. According to Marxist perspective, religion is a diversion through which oppressed workers are told to be patient and to wait for reward not in this life but the next. In the meantime, workers are encouraged to work and to support the social order, thus serving the needs of the exploitative economic elite. Religion, with its false promises, said Marx, lulls the masses into submission. Marx called religion, "the opium of the people."

While religion sometimes hinders change, it can also encourage it. More so now than in the past, religions in the Western world have worked to better the worldly conditions of humans. Their goals have involved abolition, civil rights, prison reform, urban reform, and charities. Religious organizations maintain homes for the aged, schools, hospitals, and provide assistance during disasters. They also provide for the poor. Missionaries, while spreading their faith, spread literacy and improved health practices.

While not all changes caused by such efforts meet the peoples' needs, religion can bring about reform as well as hinder it.

RELIGION IN AMERICA TODAY

In this chapter, we have gone back in time to the origins and essential traits of religion. Then from the past we have moved through the development of religion up to the present. We have seen the forms of today's religions throughout the world and in America. This study has led us to probe into the nature of religion and its many forms. We are now ready to explore the current scene near at hand: religion in America today.

Challenge and Change

Since the trauma of World War II, religion in America has gone through two stages. One writer sees the first stage as one of revival for major religions, followed by a second stage, one of upheavals and crises.[17]

The revival occurred in the late 1940s and the 1950s. Church membership peaked during the 1950s. Belief in God, in prayer, and in an afterlife was high. Sunday school enrollment, church construction, the sale of religious books, and attendance at revival meetings were all increasing during the decade. Never before had a religious surge been so widespread, touching all denominations.

Challenges. By the end of the 1950s, however, the revival had begun to fade. Church membership was dropping. Other signs were also beginning to foretell the next stage; crisis and challenge.

Rejection of the mainstream. One sign of this second stage of challenge was the rejection of Western religion, especially among young people. The major religions were losing their appeal. Some people turned to Eastern religions in a search for spiritual satisfaction. Mystical approaches had great attraction. Buddhism, Yoga, and other movements appealed to many young people. Drugs and the occult replaced traditional faiths for many others. The major religions in America found themselves in a crisis. They were accused of being out of touch with social reality.

Many religious groups answered the challenge by getting involved in various social causes. Some church leaders joined movements involving civil rights, antiwar protests, and other causes. By effecting social change, these members of the clergy felt they were fulfilling the ideals of their faiths.

Besides the rise of non-Western tendencies and the social activism of some churches, there was another sign that religion in America was entering a phase of upheaval. This was the "Jesus movement." These people tried to imitate Christ's life and sought to be filled with the Holy Spirit. Their efforts often involved them in social causes. The "Jesus people" often did not fit into the established denominations. Instead, they challenged those structures.

Recent religious movements have, in many cases, challenged the more traditional churches.

Another challenge faced by the major religions in our society is what has been called the "privatization of faith."[18] Some individuals trying to cope in our modern society build their own systems of values and sacred meanings. As more people turn inward for their religious direction, their loyalty to mainstream religion may weaken or disappear.

Changes in the Numbers.   The challenges faced by American churches over the past few decades are also reflected in surveys of attendance and membership. Church and synagogue membership has declined overall since 1936, when a Gallup poll began measuring this factor [19] (the United States Bureau of the Census staying away from religious subjects). Church attendance, too, has declined from its 1950s peak of 49% to around 40% in the 1980s. Most of the loss of membership has been seen in the mainstream churches, while some sects and cults have flourished.

Changes.   How have the major faiths in America been affected by this period of challenge and crisis? They have been forced to change. Perhaps the biggest changes have been seen in the Catholic and Jewish faiths.

Catholics.   By the 1960s, the Roman Catholic Church had become large and powerful. It was no longer the struggling church of poor immigrants. In this respect, it was ready for the changes brought by the Second Vatican Council called during that decade by the Pope in Rome. The council called for an end to the hostilities against Protestants and Jews. This spirit of cooperation affected all the major faiths in America.

Other results of the council were a number of changes intended to make the Catholic Church more relevant. Changes in the worship services and in rules of conduct were involved. Some Catholics saw these changes as a fresh breeze of relevance. Many saw it as not enough—or as too much—change. Indeed, attendance figures suggest that the changes caused many Catholics to turn away from their church. Catholic attendance fell 22% between 1958 and 1978, bottoming out at 52% in the early 1980s.[20]

Other issues were creating turmoil in the Catholic Church in the United States. Perhaps the biggest issue was birth control. An increasing number of church members refused to accept the church's ban of any artificial means of contraception. Catholic efforts to get federal aid for their schools was another source of controversy for the church. According to one writer, the diversity of opinions and beliefs within the church today has increased "to the point of confusion and doubt."[21]

Jews.   Meanwhile, Jews in the United States have also felt the challenges of the 1960s and 1970s. Widespread among Jews today is concern about the survival of Judaism. Many Jews, especially the young, are seen as drifting away from their Jewish identity. Their social mobility—based on a strong belief in education—is often accompanied by a weakening of their ethnic and religious ties. Jewish groups battle this trend by promoting Jewish identity and discouraging intermarriage with non-Jews.

Protestants. Protestants were not immune from the challenges of recent decades. The large, liberal Protestant church groups have been losing members. At the same time, conservative groups such as Southern Baptists and Seventh-Day Adventists have been gaining members.[22] Smaller sects are growing too. Within the main-line churches, splits have occurred between the evangelical faction and the liberal faction. On the one hand, evangelicals believe in born-again salvation and the Bible as absolute, word-for-word truth. More liberal members interpret the Bible in light of science and social changes.

All three of the major faiths in this country have faced challenges. They have been shaken just as the larger social system has. Like other parts of the system, religion has had to adjust to the times.

Church and State

An ongoing adjustment for churches in this nation has been the one between religion and government. The First Amendment to the U.S. Constitution states: "Congress shall make no law respecting an establishment of religion . . ." In practice, however, this separation of church and state has not been easy to maintain. Many disputes arise because of this. Some of these disputes concern churches and the state's schools. One dispute revolves around this question: Should prayer be allowed—or prevented—in public schools? The other involves public funding of church-run schools.

Prayer in the Public Schools. The issue of religious practices in public schools has a long history. During the nineteenth century, Bible reading and morning prayers were common in public school classrooms. In 1900, however, only one state required these practices. By 1946, thirteen states did so. At that time there was a growing demand to include religious teaching in the public schools. This trend gained force until 1963, when such religious practices in public schools were declared to be in violation of the First Amendment.

Today several states still permit or even require a "moment of silence" for prayer or meditation. Students can choose not to pray during that time. Several other states require teachers to invite voluntary prayers in the classroom. The idea has been attacked as a violation of the doctrine of separation of church and state. Other critics argue that such rules give parents an easy way out of giving their children religious guidance at home. The issue is not likely to be resolved in the near future.

Public Funding for Church Schools? A related debate concerns state funding of church-run schools. Supporters have argued that church schools help serve the public interest as well as public schools. The government gets a bargain by merely helping such schools rather than teaching all those students itself. Why should Catholic parents, for example, not only support their church

The Supreme Court of the United States ruled in the 1963 case of School District of Abington v. Schempp that laws requiring prayer and Bible reading in public schools are unconstitutional.

schools and also be taxed to support public ones? Care need be taken only that one church's schools not be given more or less support than any other. Some people favor only indirect support of these church schools, such as free lunches, books, and transportation. Such aid benefits the children, not the schools directly. Others see any aid to any church school as unwise and probably in violation of the First Amendment.

Both these disputes continue. While the relationship between church and state in the United States has deep roots in both law and tradition, it continues to be a source of tension in our society.

In these and other socio-political issues, religious leaders, especially those of conservative political bent, have been exerting significant influence. Television evangelists such as Rev. Jerry Falwell and Rev. Pat Robertson have been involved in politics, and have displayed some political power. It has long been common for American politicians to invoke the name of God and to use religious themes in political issues, but recently religious leaders have shown political power more openly than has been true for many years. This is another way in which the mixing of religion and politics creates tensions in America.

SUMMARY

Religion is the beliefs and practices shared by a community of believers as they relate themselves to the sacred. In contrast to magic, religion is based on a humble attitude toward what are seen as all-powerful supernatural forces. Magic involves an attempt to control those forces; religion aims to build a relationship between God and the believer. Unlike religion, magic is often secret. Whether the goals of religion are reached cannot be clearly seen, but magic sometimes works, or appears to work because of coincidence, suggestion, or fraud.

Religion began on the bases of mana (a supernatural force found within objects or beings) and animism (the belief in spirits). From what were probably small-scale, family-centered efforts, religion grew into large and powerful institutions.

Today's major religious forms range from those believing in one god (monotheism) to those believing in two or more gods (polytheism) to those that focus on moral pathways or the honoring of ancestors. In the United States, religions are classed as denominations (large, widely respected structures), sects (smaller, protest-based structures), and cults (radical, leader-based forms). In the United States, when we speak of a church we mean not a single, dominant structure but rather a denomination.

Religion can affect us on a personal level and a social level. It can provide explanations, comfort, and personal identity. Religion also is linked to a person's social attitudes and social standing. On a social level, religion provides cohesion, control, and harmony and both promotes and hinders social change.

In recent years, religion in America has faced challenges. Mainstream churches have been rejected by many people. In general,

SKILL BOX

Sampling

Do surveys such as the Gallup poll really reflect the thinking of over two hundred million people? The answer depends largely on the sample used, because only a small number of people are surveyed. The Gallup poll interviews a few thousand adults in a national survey. The pollsters claim that 95 percent of the time this sample is in error no less than three percentage points. That is, the results of the sample rarely differ from what would be shown by the entire population. Here we will see how sampling works.

In designing a social science study, selecting a population is important, because the population is the people to which the research results will apply. For example, the aim of the scientist may be to make some kind of general statements about all left-handed persons in Texas. Such people would be the study's target population.

If the scientist finds it impractical to study all members of that population, he or she must study a sample: a certain number of left-handed Texans who represent, or are typical of, all such people. The sample must be carefully chosen. If only urban members of the target population are included in the sample, it would be dangerous to apply the results of the study to the rural left-handed Texans too. Also, if the target population was 55 percent male and 45 percent female, the sample should be close to this proportion, if sex is relevant to the study. The sample should accurately reflect the other relevant traits of the entire population, such as age, race, and social class.

In order to ensure that the sample is representative of the population, one of several sampling methods may be used. The ideal method is simple random sampling, in which every member of the population has an equal chance of being chosen for the sample. Choosing names from a hat is an example. The selection of one member must not affect the chances of others for being selected. Since such sampling is seldom practical for a large population, other methods may be used.

In area, or cluster, sampling, the person is not the unit of sampling. Rather, the units used in a study of a city population, for example, might be census tracts or city blocks. A simple random sample of all city blocks could be drawn. All residents of each selected block would be then studied.

The multi-stage sampling method would go one step further. For the above example, a simple random sample would be drawn from the residents of each selected city block. Only these selected persons of each selected block would be included in the study. This decreases the costs, but also the accuracy, of the sampling.

When the study requires comparisons among several subgroups of a population, stratified sampling is used. For example, we might wish to compare the sexual values of students at various grade levels in three colleges. We would divide the students in those colleges into freshmen, sophomores, juniors, and seniors. We would probably also wish to group them as to sex. Our groups would then be male freshmen, female freshmen, male sophomores, and so on. From each of these eight groups, we would draw a random sample. This would prevent a random sample of, for example, 60 percent male freshmen being drawn otherwise.

These and other such sampling methods all attempt to give an estimate of how some factor, such as voters' opinions, is distributed in the total population. The estimate is considered accurate if statistical tests assure us that repeated sampling of the population would produce the same results as this single sample. This tells us that our sample gives us results similar to those that would be obtained by studying the entire population. Thus, by properly using an established sampling method, social scientists are assured that their samples reflect the total population.

Another point to consider in evaluating the sample of a study is the sample's size. The larger the size, the smaller the sampling error. This error is the difference, measured by statistical means, between the traits of the sample and those of the population.

To the extent that a scientist gives proof of proper sampling method and reasonably large sample size, we can be sure that the study's results can be applied to the entire population.

Americans do not belong to or attend churches or synagogues to the extent they did twenty-five years ago. In the face of these challenges, the major faiths in this nation have had to make adjustments. Part of the picture of religion in America today is its relation to the government. The debates over prayers in public schools and public funding of church-run schools go on.

Religion will continue in the future of all cultures. The basic human needs served by religion will not be met completely by science or other worldly means. There are questions that will always lie beyond the power of science to answer. Because of this, the religious urge will always be part of human culture.

SPECIAL TOPIC
America's Religions

How many times have you passed by a church or synagogue and wondered what it was all about? How many times have you met a person and wondered what his or her religious label meant? What does the fact that a person is a Jew, a Mormon, or a Lutheran tell us about that person's beliefs? This Special Topic is concerned with such questions.

In the United States, religious freedom has resulted in a great variety of religious options. They create a rich religious fabric. Surrounded as we are by these many groups, it is valuable to have some understanding of their history and basic doctrines. We shall look at ten of the largest religious bodies.

Determining the sizes of the groups is not easy. While some bodies keep very accurate accounts, others offer only rough estimates. Also, requirements of membership and commitment vary greatly. Some count all persons baptized, including infants. Membership for others is based on ethnic background; for example, all Jews living in Jewish communities are counted as members. Therefore, the data in Table 12–2 should be seen as only an estimate.

The descriptions offered in the Special Topic are based on an authority [23] and on selected spokespeople.[24] Their views may be different from those of some members of these religions. Since the views of all individuals cannot be giv-

TABLE 12-2. Membership of Religious Groups in the United States

(Based on the *World Almanac* questionnaire and the 1980 *Yearbook of American and Canadian Churches*)

1.	Roman Catholic	49,602,035
2.	Baptist	24,726,564
3.	Methodist	12,942,525
4.	Lutheran	8,532,472
5.	Eastern Orthodox	4,179,500
6.	Jewish	3,985,000
7.	Presbyterian	3,648,011
8.	Latter-Day Saints	3,369,236
9.	Episcopal	2,825,254
10.	Pentecostal	2,577,813

SOURCE: *The World Almanac & Book of Facts*, 1981 edition, copyright © Newspaper Enterprise Assn., 1980, New York, N.Y., 10166.

en here, these descriptions are offered as only basic introductions to these religions.

ROMAN CATHOLICS

The Roman Catholic Church dates its origins from Christ's choosing of the apostle Peter as earthly guardian of the faith. The influence of the church was later spread throughout the Roman Empire. In the year 1054, the church split in two, forming the Roman Catholic and Eastern Orthodox churches. The Roman Catholic Church was clearly dominant in the Western world until the 1500s. At that time, largely in response to corruption within the church, the Protestant Reformation occurred. Then, various splinter groups broke away from the church, some growing into the established denominations of today.

Roman Catholic influences in North America began with the earliest Spanish and French explorers. Missionary priests were among the first Europeans to come to this land. The church grew slowly at first in the English colonies. Roman Catholics founded Maryland in 1634, but neighboring Protestants dominated the colonies until the Revolution. It was not until the mid-1800s, in fact, that Catholics were found in any great numbers in this country. Starting with the 1820s, a flood of immigrants from Catholic countries—notably Ireland and later Italy—continued until the 1930s. These people were fleeing hunger, religious oppression, and economic crises. This flood of immigrants made the Catholic Church the largest in the United States today.

It is valuable here to compare Roman Catholics with Protestants and Jews concerning beliefs, or doctrines. Catholics and Protestants, but not Jews, accept the New Testament, and believe that Jesus was both God and man, the promised Messiah. Two major differences between Catholics and most Protestants concern the Bible and the priesthood. Protestants hold that each believer should interpret the Bible, but Catholics see the church as appointed by God to interpret the Scriptures. Most Protestants view all believers as part of the priesthood, while Catholics view the clergy as being the only people specially ordained for that function.

BAPTISTS

In the 1500s, Anabaptists were found in small numbers all over Europe. They were attacked because their practices, based on a literal reading of the Bible, included rebaptizing adults and communal living. The first Baptist church was organized in England in the early 1600s.

Roger Williams came to America in 1631 and established a Baptist church in Rhode Island. A "great division over slavery came in 1845, when the Southerners 'seceded' to form their own Southern Baptist Convention."[25] This split over the issue of slavery occurred in other religious groups as well. Such splits still exist today.

Today the largest Protestant group consists of over two dozen Baptist denominations. Each of these is independent, but they share the same basic principles. In fact, this local independence reflects a major basis of the Baptist faith: religious liberty. Another distinctive belief is baptism—by immersion—only of people old enough to understand its meaning.

METHODISTS

Methodism began with a small group of students at Oxford University (England) in 1729. Part of the group were John and Charles Wesley. The Wesleys and others spread their beliefs throughout England, gaining so many converts that an organization apart from the national Church of England was formed. By 1766 Methodism had spread to America. There, it swept through the colonies by way of circuit preachers and camp meeting revivals. Membership soared, and Methodism became one of this nation's major religions.

This Protestant faith has emphasized such beliefs as justification by faith and the need for conversion. Methodism's name derives from the methods or rules followed by its followers.

LUTHERANS

Martin Luther, the founder of this faith, was the first Protestant. His break with the Catholic Church in 1517 set off the Reformation. His major argument was that the Bible, not the church, was the final authority in religious matters. People had to justify themselves through faith, he said, not through church rituals. He saw religion as a matter of people relating directly to God—a church or priest not being necessary.

From Germany, the Lutheran faith spread throughout northern and eastern Europe. Immigrants from Germany and Scandinavia brought the faith to America in the early 1600s. Various synods or councils were later formed to serve the needs of more Lutheran immigrants.

Articles of faith are the basis of Lutheranism. In fact, one writer describing the Lutheran church says, "Lutherans, more than most of the other Protestants, emphasize doctrine." [26] For Lutherans, faith is the focus, more so than rules of conduct.

EASTERN ORTHODOX CHURCHES

In 1054, the Christian church was split into two branches. The Roman church with its Latin background, and the Eastern, Greek-oriented church separated. The reasons for the split were many, including politics and differing beliefs. The question of the Roman Pope's authority was a major factor.

The Eastern Orthodox Church has always been divided into several national groups, headed by a patriarch. From the countries of eastern Europe and Russia, the Orthodox faith was brought to America. Now there are over twenty Orthodox groups in this nation.

PRESBYTERIANS

There were two original Protestant branches. One followed the lead of Martin Luther, and the other was the Reformed Church, based on the ideas of John Calvin. From the latter grew the Presbyterian religion and others.

Calvin's ideas are important because they affected so many religions. He believed that humans have no power, that salvation is a gift from God. He maintained that some people are predestined, or fated, to be offered this salvation. A person must totally surrender to God to be saved. Beyond this, good works show that a person is gaining in grace, so followers of Calvin tended to be hardworking and successful. Calvin's ideas were the basis for the Dutch Reformed Church and Presbyterian groups in England, Ireland, and Scotland. This religion was brought to America in the early 1700s, mostly by Scotch-Irish (Scots who had been transplanted to Ireland). These people spread their faith throughout the colonies, making it the first one to be found in every colony.

PROTESTANT EPISCOPAL CHURCH

The Protestant Episcopal church sprang from the Church of England. The Church of England was founded after a long period of bitterness concerning the authority of the Pope. King Henry VIII asked the Pope for a marriage annulment. The Pope refused, and Henry's break with the Pope established the long-awaited freedom of the Church of England from the Roman Catholic Church. The Church of England retains many ancient Catholic beliefs and practices. The major differences between the two churches concern the Pope's power. This is also true of its American counterpart.

Chaplains from the Church of England accompanied some of the earliest explorers to North America. With the early English influence came the church's influence. As it was closely linked with the British Crown, however, the church in this nation was nearly destroyed during the Revolution by anti-British feelings. In 1789, the Protestant Episcopal Church was founded. Though still closely linked with the mother Church of England, the American church is independent and self-governing.

CHURCH OF JESUS CHRIST OF LATTER-DAY SAINTS (MORMONS)

Joseph Smith was the founder of this church. He testified that at the age of fifteen in western New York he had a divine vision. The vision told him that the gospel of Jesus Christ had to be restored through a church to be founded by Smith. The church was organized in 1830. As membership grew, so did opposition to the Latter-Day Saints, largely because of their practice of polygamy. The group moved westward, and Smith was murdered by a mob in Illinois. Brigham Young took over the leadership and brought the group to the land around the Great Salt Lake in 1847, where the church is now centered.

Christian but not Protestant, the Mormon faith is based on the Bible and on the writings of Smith. Smith's writings, based on direct, divine revelations, include the Book of Mormon, which is believed to have been translated by Smith from ancient golden tablets discovered by him with the help of an angel.

The Church of Jesus Christ of Latter-Day Saints has established a strong, loyal membership and in recent years has become one of the country's fastest growing religions.

JUDAISM

The religion of Judaism is based on the Torah and the Talmud. The Torah is the Five Books of Moses in the Old Testament. The Talmud consists of sixty-three books containing the ancient laws and traditions of the faith. The principles of Judaism include the worship of God, good deeds, and a love of learning. Judaism looks forward to the coming of a Messiah and a divine kingdom on earth. Jews share with Christians the heritage of the Old Testament. The two groups differ mostly in that Jews accept neither the divinity of Christ nor the concept of original sin.

Jews first came to the United States by way of Brazil in 1654. Later groups came from southwest Europe. They mostly settled in the coastal cities. Great numbers immigrated from Europe and Russia in the nineteenth and twentieth centuries.

In America there are three types of Judaism. The Orthodox Jew strictly follows the rules and traditions of the Torah. Reform Jews are much more liberal in defining the proper rules of conduct; they see a need for adapting some traditions to the modern world. Conservative Jews are between the other two, resisting extreme changes, but accepting others.

PENTECOSTAL CHURCHES

Pentecostal churches are a diverse lot and cannot be grouped together as one church. But as a category of religious beliefs and practices, Pentecostalism can be distinguished by its focus on the Holy Spirit and the literal meaning of the Bible's words. Worship services in such churches are often very emotional, often including speaking in tongues and sometimes divine healing. The various Pentecostal churches were founded in the United States, most during the twentieth century.

SELF-TEST QUESTIONS

1. Which is *not* part of Durkheim's three elements of religion?
   a. the sacred
   b. community of believers
   c. the profane
   d. beliefs
   e. rituals

2. Which are traits of religion?
   a. humble attitude toward God
   b. attempt to control supernatural forces
   c. worldly, concrete goals
   d. shared beliefs and practices

Match numbers 3–5 to the definitions on the right:

3. mana   a. shared system of beliefs and practices
4. animism   b. supernatural force
5. monotheism   c. belief in spirits
                   d. belief in several gods
                   e. belief in one god

Match numbers 6–9 to the definitions on the right:

6. denomination   a. religious organization that dominates the society
7. ecclesia   b. small, leader-based, very unconventional
8. sect   c. small, poor, at odds with dominant social values
9. cult   d. large, widely respected

10. True or false: Religion has some effect on a person's social standing and attitudes.

11. True or false: Religion's impact on society is always for the social good.

12. True or false: Since 1960, the major religions in the United States have gained in membership.

13. True or false: The issues of public funding of church schools and prayer in public schools were both finally decided by court decisions in the 1970s.

ANSWERS TO SELF-TEST QUESTIONS

1. c	8. c
2. a, d	9. b
3. b	10. true
4. c	11. false
5. e	12. false
6. d	13. false
7. a	

ANSWERS TO SKILL REINFORCERS

12–1. If the scientist is observing a people's religion firsthand, she must remember that her presence may affect the way the people present their religion. That is, certain points of the religion may either be hidden or made to seem more important than they really are. To avoid this effect of her presence, the scientist would observe secretly or only after her presence had become common and accepted.

The scientist would also need to take care that her own religious beliefs and her emotions did not bias what she saw, either in person or in print.

Finally, she should not observe any one religion until she has acquired some background on the subject through thorough study. This background should include enough theory to give her observation some guidance, to tell her what she might expect and how to interpret what she does see.

12–2. The Skill Box in Chapter 7 described the several steps for reading a table. First, read the title carefully. Note that Table 12–1 is a listing only of estimates and only of the membership of principal religions. Next, check the headnote (none here) and footnotes. Those footnotes for the row and column titles and "populations" are of value; the object of your search determines the value of the other footnotes. The next step is to check the units of measurements used, in this case individual people. The next step, checking the meanings of the columns and rows, requires use of the table's footnotes.

NOTES

1. "Stone Age Religion," *Discover* 3 (February 1982): 10–11.

2. Emile Durkheim, *The Elementary Forms of Religious Life,* trans. Joseph Ward Swain (Glencoe, Ill.: The Free Press, 1954).

3. Charles Lindholm and Cherry Lindholm, "Sex and Death in the Trobriand Islands," *Science Digest* 90 (February 1982): 82–85, 105, 112.

4. E. Adamson Hoebel, *Anthropology: The Study of Man,* 3d ed. (New York: McGraw-Hill, 1966): 469–70.

5. Edward B. Tylor, *Primitive Culture: Researches into the Development of Mythology, Philosophy, Religion, Language, Art, and Custom* (London: J. Murray, 1871).

6. Annemarie De Waal Malefijt, *Religion and Culture* (New York: Macmillan Co., 1968): 129–31.

7. *The World Almanac and Book of Facts 1981* (New York: Newspaper Enterprise Assoc., 1980): 334–35.
8. Lita Linzer Schwartz, "Cults: The Vulnerability of Sheep," *USA Today* 108 (July 1979): 22–24.
9. Patricia Thomas, "Targets of the Cults," *Human Behavior* 8 (March 1979): 58–59.
10. David Martin, "Revived Dogma and New Cult," *Daedalus* 111 (Winter 1982): 53–71.
11. Mary Douglas, "The Effects of Modernization on Religious Change," *Daedalus* 111 (Winter 1982): 1–19.
12. Charles Title and Michael Welch, "Religiosity and Deviance," *Social Forces* 61 (March 1983): 653–82.
13. Erik Filsinger and Margaret Wilson, "Religiosity, Socioeconomic Rewards, and Family Development," *Journal of Marriage and Family* 46 (August 1984): 663–670.
14. Gallup Organization, "Religion in America: The Gallup Report," report # 222 (March 1984).
15. James McRae, Jr., "Changes in Religious Communalism Desired by Protestants and Catholics," *Social Forces* 61 (March 1983): 709–30.
16. William McIntosh and Jon Alston, "Lenski Revisited: The Linkage Role of Religion in Primary and Secondary Groups," *American Journal of Sociology* 87 (January 1982): 852–82.
17. Leonard Pitt, *We Americans* (Glenview, Ill.: Scott, Foresman & Co., 1976): 767.
18. Wade Clark Roof, "America's Voluntary Establishment: Mainline Religion in Transition," *Daedalus* 111 (Winter 1982): 165–84.
19. Gallup Organization, report # 222.
20. Ibid.
21. Richard McBrien, "Roman Catholicism," *Daedalus* 111 (Winter 1982): 73–83.
22. " 'Old-Time' Religion on the Offensive," *U.S. News & World Report,* April 7, 1980: 40–42.
23. Frank S. Mead, *Handbook of Denominations in the United States,* 4th ed. (Nashville: Abingdon Press, 1965).
24. Leo Rosten, ed., *Religions in America* (New York: Simon & Schuster, 1963).
25. Mead, *Handbook,* p. 34.
26. G. Elson Ruff, "What Is a Lutheran?" in Rosten, *Religions in America,* p. 114.

SUGGESTED READINGS

Bergerv, Peter L. *The Sacred Canopy: Elements of a Sociological Theory of Religion.* Garden City, N.Y.: Doubleday & Co., 1969.

Fowler, James W. *Stages of Faith.* New York: Harper & Row, 1981.

Glock, Charles Y., and Bellah, Robert N., eds. *The New Religious Consciousness.* Berkeley: University of California Press, 1976.

Hadden, Jeffrey K., and Swann, Charles E. *Prime Time Preachers: The Rising Power of Tele-Evangelism.* Reading, Mass.: Addison-Wesley, 1981.

Robbins, Thomas, and Anthony, Dick, eds. *In God We Trust: New Patterns of Religious Pluralism in America.* New Brunswick, N.J.: Transaction Books, 1981.

Stark, Rodney, and Bainbridge, William Sims. *The Future of Religion.* Berkeley, Calif.: University of California Press, 1985.

13 SOCIAL CHANGE

PREVIEW

Future Shock: Too Much Change in Too Little Time

You may be in a state of shock and not realize it. The shock referred to here is what Alvin Toffler calls "future shock" in his book by that name. It is kind of an illness caused by a dizzying rate of change.

Future shock will not be found in Index Medicus *or in any listing of psychological abnormalities. Yet, unless intelligent steps are taken to combat it, millions of human beings will find themselves increasingly disoriented, progressively incompetent to deal rationally with their environments. The malaise, mass neurosis, irrationality, and free-floating violence already apparent in contemporary life are merely a foretaste of what may lie ahead unless we come to understand and treat this disease.*

Future shock is a time phenomenon, a product of the greatly accelerated rate of change in society. It arises from the superimposition of a new culture on an old one. It is culture shock in one's own society. But its impact is far worse. For most Peace Corps men, in fact most travelers, have the comforting knowledge that the culture they left behind will be there to return to. The victim of future shock does not.

Take an individual out of his own culture and set him down suddenly in an environment sharply different from his own, with a different set of cues to react to—different conceptions of time, space, work, love, religion, sex, and everything else—then cut him off from any hope of retreat to a more familiar social landscape, and the dislocation he suffers is doubly severe.

Now imagine not merely an individual but an entire society, an entire generation—including its weakest, least intelligent, and most irrational members—suddenly transported into this new world. The result is mass disorientation, future shock on a grand scale.

This is the prospect that man now faces. Change is avalanching upon our heads and most people are grotesquely unprepared to cope with it.[1]

Toffler sees this avalanche of change roaring down at us. While the future holds much promise, he believes that the speed with which we approach it threatens our mental and social well-being unless we learn to cope with it. This chapter won't save you from "future shock," but it will make you more aware of the nature of social change and perhaps help you deal with it more effectively.

The United States has changed. From a few thousand English set-tlers, we have grown into 226 million people from dozens of eth-nic origins. The yeoman farmer has become the pencil pusher or the technician. Our arrest records now feature vicious assaults rather than such offenses as missing church on the Sabbath. While we once depended on the long rifle, we now rely on—and fear—the "Saturday-night special" as well as the nuclear missile. While we once believed that we should work hard, save, and thus get ahead, many of us now aim to avoid work, spend money as soon as we get it, and then borrow so we can spend some more.

The only way people can prevent change in their social world would be to withdraw into a very limited world, for example, join the monks in a monastery or become hermits. Instead of prevent-ing social change, we can hope for an understanding of social change, and perhaps, from this, some greater degree of control.

This chapter describes what social science has to offer toward controlling the changes swirling around us as a society. First we will explore the nature of social change, and then its sources. This will lead us to descriptions of the theories that try to explain change. The results of social change will then be examined. Final-ly, the Special Topic will ask whether we humans have—or will ever have—any control over this change.

WHAT IS SOCIAL CHANGE?

If we are to control social change, or even cope with it, we must understand it. In an effort to understand change, a good place to begin is to define it. First, change will be defined, then social change and cultural change, then the several dimensions of social change.

According to Nisbet, "Change is a succession of differences in time in a persisting identity." [2] This description contains three ba-sic elements: differences, time, and a persisting entity. In this view, change involves not only differences of conditions in the same thing but also differences that occur over time. Thus, differ-ences must exist in different times before they can be considered change. Furthermore, these differences over time must relate to the same object that persists through that time, not to several objects.

SOCIAL CHANGE: Differences occurring over time in a particular social structure; often used to in-clude cultural change.

When we apply this description of change to social change, so-cial change is defined as differences over time occurring in some persisting social system. Social change would thus include changes in the size and composition of a population. Also involved would be any changes in the way the system's members or groups relate among themselves. Any change in the way the people are structured or organized would also be defined as social change.

CULTURAL CHANGE: Differences occurring over time in a particular way of life of a society.

Social change very often involves cultural change too. Cultural change is a difference over time in the life-style of a people. This could include changes in technology, values, and customs. Rarely does a change in the social structure not also involve a change in way of life. Because of this, the term "social change" usually includes cultural change. Sometimes the term socio-cultural change is used. In this chapter, it will be assumed that social change includes cultural change.

Some examples will clarify what is and what is not meant by social change. The difference between the average family size in 1900 and that in 1980 shows social change. It shows a difference over time in a part of the social structure. On the other hand, the changes seen in a child as he or she matures is not social change but individual change. Likewise, the difference between the parenting goals of lower-class and middle-class families is not social change because there is no time dimension involved and because we are describing two different social entities. The difference between middle-class parenting goals in 1950 and those of today would show social (or cultural) change: differences over time in the same part of the social (or cultural) structure.

Along the same lines, Nisbet points out that interaction, motion, and variety are not in themselves social change.[3] Interaction among people and the motions they go through during their daily lives are continuous and found in all social settings. They do not, however, imply any differences over time in the social structure. Also, the scenes that confront people will vary at least to a small extent throughout even one day. There is variety in the stimuli a person faces in the morning and the afternoon. But just because a person sees various daily scenes does not imply change over time in any parts of the social structure. Such variety is not change.

Sociologists Donald Light and Suzanne Keller offer several dimensions that help distinguish among different kinds of social change.[4] They point out that social change can vary as to scale, duration, continuity, and direction.

One social change could differ from another as to scale. For example, if the teacher in one classroom uses a new teaching method, this change is on a much smaller scale than if all teachers in the state switched to the new method. Also, the scale or size of change is related to the scale of the social structure. Ten families trying a new child-rearing approach in Brooklyn would be small-scale change. Such a change in ten families in a hunting band of twenty families would be large-scale for that system. The scale of social change also depends on how many parts of the structure it affects. For example, the women's movement of the last few decades touched on courtship, employment, child-rearing, and sex in our social system. This is large-scale change.

Some changes take place within a short period of time, while others may require many years. For example, in the United States a huge change in the number of mothers working outside the home occurred in just two decades, while the Industrial Revolution—a shift from a farm- to a factory-focused society—required over one hundred years.

Some social changes bring an abrupt break in basic social patterns; others are gradual changes within those basic patterns. For example, the closing of churches in this nation would be an abrupt social change, a clear break with the past. The change from liberal to fundamentalist viewpoints within some churches would be more within our basic religious patterns.

Finally, social change can take various directions. It may represent a move forward or backward, or it may be part of a cycle. It may move along a circular path or in a straight line. The Industrial Revolution is an example of social change moving in a straight line away from the past. On the other hand, marriage rates go up and down over the years.

By using these dimensions, we can understand any specific social change better. Using them all, we can say that, in general, large-scale change is more important than changes of smaller scale, especially if it is a drastic break with basic patterns and happens quickly.

SOURCES OF CHANGE

The chapter preview describes a common view of our society's rate of change: We are dizzy from change. Despite this idea of future shock, there is a great deal of inertia—an unwillingness to move or change—in social structures. In fact, a noted student of social change, William Ogburn, said, "The persistence of culture at times appears so strong that it seems as though culture actually resists change." [5] Indeed, once a part of our social structure is seen as useful, we often balk at changing it. This inertia makes our social system somewhat stable.

In the face of such resistance, what can cause social change? We will look at three ways that change is caused. First we will examine the extent to which change is affected by the nonhuman factors of the physical environment. Then we will see how change occurs within a social system. Last, we will explore how change results from contact between societies.

The Physical Environment

What does a forest or an ocean have to do with social change? One does not need to think very hard to see how such factors affect the way people live. A long-term drought can force huge changes in social structures. A shocking example of the impact of drought (along with social factors) is the story of the Ik, briefly described in Chapter 3. When forced to turn to farming on a dry and barren land, the Ik began to starve. This caused enormous changes in all parts of their social structure. Cooperation, family ties, and love became unimportant to the Ik; selfishness reigned supreme. In fact, the Ik can be said to have suffered from future shock; they faced too much basic change too quickly.

How Much Influence Does the Environment Have?   To some extent, physical environment determines the culture its human inhabitants produce. One theorist argued that human culture advances most easily in temperate climates. [6] This line of reasoning proceeds from the fact that Egypt and Greece, early centers of cultural advancement, enjoyed such climates. It is easy enough to

The physical environment can influence such social factors as population patterns and the economy. Here, fertile soil originally attracted a substantial population and continues to have an impact on the area's economy.

Skill Reinforcer 13-1 *

Is the conclusion that "temperate climate causes cultural advancement" an example of the use of inductive reasoning or deductive reasoning? On what would you base your evaluation of this conclusion?

see, however, that these nations are no longer in the vanguard of the world's cultural advance. Further, some other climates enjoyed a temperate climate but never held a place of world leadership. Because of these arguments, a view that depends too heavily on the environment is not widely accepted among social scientists today.

We would be safer in following theories that focus on how the environment sets limits on and shapes the direction of change. For example, in a region where food is scarce, such as a desert, it is unlikely—but not impossible—that an urban center will develop. Such a land would not support a large concentration of people. Likewise, nations without great natural resources are unlikely to rise to positions of power and wealth. The environment can clearly set limits on social change.

The environment can offer opportunities as well as limits. Witness the changes open to oil-rich countries today. Also, people whose environments include access to sea routes have a distinct advantage over landlocked groups. Or a land—and its people—might be blessed with rich soil, precious minerals, or great forests. Physical environment can play a large part in a people's social development.

It follows that if the environment can help shape a social system, it can also account for some similarities among systems. Among human societies, there are "similarities . . . of life which are the result of the exploitation of similar possibilities." [7] In other words, similar environments may result in similar cultures. Still, we must remember that the environment is only one of many factors that affect the form a culture or social system takes.

The Early North American Colonies as an Example.   The influence of the physical environment is evident in the case of the early settlement of the United States. The ocean, mountains, and other factors had some influence in the social structure that was produced here.

Ocean.   The ocean gave to early America two ingredients for independence: isolation and protection. The wide expanse of ocean did not allow the early colonists to depend too much on England. The early settlers knew that the next supply ship might be months in coming. The need to be self-sufficient was an early lesson taught the colonists by their isolation. Later, this ocean vastness would serve to protect the colonists in their attempts to change their relationship with Britain. It acted as a buffer against the might of England, as well as that of other powers.

Once the ocean currents deposited them along the coast, the settlers had to deal with other aspects of the environment.

Soil.   Glaciers and the soil they carried helped determine where many early immigrants settled.[8] Four or five times glaciers had moved down from Canada to the northern and central America. The glaciers scoured parts of Canada and pushed soil and minerals into what is now the United States. From the southern

---

shores of the Great Lakes to the Gulf of Mexico, America offered early settlers fine, rich soil, much of it "imported." Many of the farming centers that affected America's growth were themselves the results of glacier movements.

Mountains.   The mountains of eastern North American also helped shape early social development.[9] The early settlers were hemmed in between the coast and mountains. The Appalachian mountain system is about 300 miles wide and 1,300 miles long. Before gaps were discovered in this huge wall, settlers had to go around the southern tip of the mountains or through the Hudson and Mohawk valleys. Contained by this wall, the early colonists developed a unity that was of great help during their revolution. Without the mountain wall, the settlers would have spread earlier over the continent, which may have averted the showdown with England that produced the Revolution.

Forests.   Likewise, the great forests of eastern North America affected the culture that would develop there.[10] The early settlers faced a land nearly covered with trees from the East Coast to the Mississippi River. A new way of life was needed to deal with this factor. Changes included house construction and the design of rifles, axes, and other tools. Most important, the forest slowed the spread of the culture. In doing so, it may have forced the culture to mature and integrate its parts.

These and other physical factors clearly had an influence on the social and cultural development of early America. These factors set limits and offered possibilities. They influenced, but did not determine, the changes that took place.

We should pause here and note the all-too-obvious fact that social change affects the physical environment just as the environment affects social change. As urban areas spread, the landscape is subdued. As populations expand in many undeveloped nations, forests are stripped and irrigation ensues. As industrialization proceeds, the earth is befouled with pollutants. As social change occurs in technologically powerful societies, the physical environment is changed dramatically.

Innovations

Just as a culture can be changed by a drought, so it can be changed if someone comes up with a new thought or machine. Consider the impact, for example, of the idea of Karl Marx that violent revolution is needed to establish a just society. Any additions produced within a culture are called innovations and are a source of social change. Cyrus McCormick's reaper was an American innovation that helped transform the United States into a farming giant. Since a society produces innovations by itself, this source of social change can be controlled. With control possible, and in order to prevent future shock, the nature and impact of innovations deserves our study.

INNOVATION: Addition of new elements to a culture from within the culture.

How Much Change Will an Innovation Bring?   The change an innovation brings depends on factors within the culture. For ex-

Although the idea of steam-powered machines was employed in this second century gadget, the innovation had no impact on the culture of the times because there was plenty of slave power available to do the work; there was little need for steam power.

ample, the culture must see a need for the new element. Also, the addition must be compatible with the culture's values and power structure.

Needed? If a social system sees no need for a new element, the innovation will cause no social change. An innovation with great potential social impact may be ignored. For example, the ancient Greeks knew about steam power. They even used the principle in small steam engine models. This new power source caused no social change, however, because that culture saw no need to replace slave and animal power with steam power. Another example is the slide fastener, or zipper, which was invented in 1851 but was virtually ignored for decades. Only when the U.S. Navy used zippers on galoshes in World War I did the invention gain widespread acceptance.[11]

Compatible? A new element may cause no social change if it does not fit in smoothly with the existing culture. It may be that existing values view innovation as dangerous. There is a "traditional hostility . . . towards the new among some peoples, particularly those with the simpler cultures."[12] Modern cultures are usually eager to consider the benefits of new elements, but even then a newly available element may meet the resistance of vested interests. Powerful groups or social classes can often minimize the impact of a new element if it threatens their position of advantage.

An example of vested interests opposing an innovation is the 250 mph train. Japan and West Germany are working on this machine, called the maglev, which zips along on a thin magnetic cushion. But in the United States, we may not be able to use these swift trains. "Under pressure from the railroad companies, the Department of Transportation cut out almost all financial support for maglev in 1975."[13]

INVENTION: Creation of a new cultural element.

Invention Versus Discovery. There are two kinds of innovation occurring within a culture. One is invention: the creation of a new element, something that never existed before in the culture. The other is discovery: the act of becoming aware of something that had already existed. Both are often accidental, but with the right cultural conditions they can cause social change.

DISCOVERY: Establishing awareness of an element that had already existed.

The difference between these two sources of innovation can be important. An invention can be patented, a discovery cannot be. For example, the creation of a new kind of food freezer would be an invention for which a patent could be obtained. On the other hand, the idea of preserving food through freezing would not earn a patent, because that relationship between food and temperature has always existed.

How Do These Things Happen? Invention and discovery often happen in different ways, because of their different natures. While a discovery often "just happens," an invention usually requires the right kind of people with enough relevant knowledge.

Invention often depends on a person's having high mental ability. A good mind is required to manipulate available knowledge in order to produce a new element. Inventions in our culture today are often made by research groups of such people in large laboratories. These research scientists must have a grasp of available knowledge and the creativity to go beyond it.

An invention is based on the existing cultural knowledge. The inventor alters the resources or combines them in a new way, producing a new form. The existing resources are the raw materials of further inventions. Because of this, a complex culture will produce more inventions than a simpler culture.

Discoveries are often accidental. They require less mental ability than intentional discovery or invention but can still result in great social change. The use of penicillin and the vulcanization of rubber are good examples. Both were accidental discoveries. One had a tremendous impact on the world's fight against disease. The other affected the world's need for natural rubber.

Innovations: Social or Technological.   Innovations can involve changes either in technology or in moral and social ideas. If you produce something that challenges existing ideas and values, it is likely to meet greater resistance than an innovation involving technology. People's minds are harder to change than their tools. As the inventor of a more efficient machine, you may be called a genius. As the creator of the new moral viewpoint, you may be called a radical, a heretic, or a fool. The point is that these two classes of innovations are distinct.

Technology.   New technology can cause important social change. Witness the impact of the wheel and sail on transportation, the plow on farming, and the printing press on world history. In the southern United States, the appearance of the cotton gin encouraged and increased the use of slaves and trade with Europe, two factors that helped cause the Civil War. Another example of technology breeding social change is the case of the British railroad system. When this technology was being adapted, a need arose for a system of standardized time zones rather than local

TABLE 13-1.
Patents Issued for Invention, United States.

Each invention makes future inventions more likely, creating an accelerating pace of innovation.

Year	Number of Patents Issued for Inventions
1884	19,118
1904	30,258
1956	46,817
1984	67,200

SOURCE: U.S. Bureau of the Census, *Statistical Abstract of the United States: 1986* and *Historical Statistics of the United States, Colonial Times to 1957,* Washington, D.C., 1960.

time zones.[14] Similarly, the invention of metal eyelets allowed the development of corsets that could be laced very tightly. Tight lacing became so extreme that middle-class British women, the victims of this fashion, experienced a sharp decline in fertility, a result of displaced internal organs.[15]

The invention of the automobile is perhaps the most dramatic example of the social change that can be caused by new technology. The economic impact has been enormous. The rubber, oil, and steel industries boomed, while railroads declined. The automobile helped the suburbs to expand and city cores to decay. Leisure pursuits, including dating customs, were affected by the automobile. The car came to be seen as a necessary part of our lifestyle and a prestige symbol. It offered the freedom of mobility while it also created the confinement of traffic jams. Government's role was expanded to include the regulation of driving and the building of more highways. Sales of gasoline and automobiles brought in more taxes. Engines fouled the air and burned enormous amounts of oil. Millions of people have been killed and injured because of this invention, yet medical care, for example, is more accessible because of the automobile. The impact of this invention is found everywhere in our culture.

Today we must also note the pervasive influence of the computer on social change. The innovation of the silicon chip has led to revolutionary changes in the way information is stored and retrieved. Computers, with their logic-based systems and massive data banks, are changing the way businesses operate, the way students learn, and perhaps even the way people reason. The work force is becoming more efficient, police can track criminals more effectively, and scholars can base their conclusions on broader knowledge, all because of computers. On the other hand, computers have led to displacement of many workers, computer crime, and the prospect of accidental, "computer-error" nuclear war. The social changes reverberating from the introduction of the computer have only begun.

Social. Of course, like technological innovations, social innovations can also cause important social change. New religions, for example, have affected economies, family structures, governments, and other parts of social systems.

Once new social innovations have been released into a social system, they can produce social conflict even more than technological innovations. Social conflict can occur when two groups actively oppose each other regarding a new social or moral idea. This might involve political, religious, or other interest groups. Karl Marx saw conflict between social classes as the basic cause of social change. Change can result from such social conflict when one group wins the struggle for dominance and imposes its viewpoint on other members of society. Such conflict is much more likely to occur when the innovation is a new religion rather than, say, a new machine.

Cultural lag occurs when some parts of a culture change faster than others.

CULTURAL LAG: The differences in the rate at which various parts of a culture change.

Cultural Lag. Problems can result when the various parts of a culture do not change at the same rate. This difference in the rate of change within a culture was labeled by William F. Ogburn as cultural lag.[16] This lag produces confusion and friction. Ogburn pointed out that the material parts of a modern culture often change at a faster rate than other parts of the culture. In this way our technology may make some social values obsolete. For example, easy and cheap methods of contraception cause many people to rethink traditional values concerning sex and childbearing. This rethinking causes clashes over such values.

Another example of cultural lag is seen in Japan's modernization during this century. Becoming modern in general meant becoming Europeanized, but this Europeanization did not proceed in all aspects of Japanese life. For example, Japan's traditional music did not combine easily with modern European music; indeed, only since mid-century has Japanese music become "modern." [17] Thus while the nation's technology raced ahead into the modern world, its music lagged for decades.

Contact Between Cultures

So far we have seen that social change can be influenced by the environment or by additions from within the culture. Cultures have little control over the first factor, and the second factor is not a common occurrence. The third factor in social change is by far the source of most social change and can be more easily controlled by humans. This third source of social change is contact between cultures. Such contact results in diffusion, or the spreading of elements from one culture to another. As we have seen, the introduction of new elements into a social system can cause social change. This is as true when the elements come from outside the system as when they come from within.

DIFFUSION: The spread or transmission of elements from one culture to another.

Social Contact and Diffusion Go Together. If we lived in a small society far from the world's main pathways, imagine how little social change we would face. No danger of future shock there. The environment might influence our culture, but other change would have to come from among our own group. Unless we were a very creative group, there would be few additions to our way of life. What little social change there was would come from changes in the environment. But once an outsider found our little group, change could come pouring in.

The more contact one culture has with other cultures, the greater the rate of social change in that culture. Social contact means social interaction, and social interaction brings social change. Such changes are sometimes seen as progress. Throughout history, urban centers, with their many contacts, have been in the forefront of cultural advance. Cities and countries along major trade routes have experienced a great deal of social change. Jerusalem was located on the major caravan routes, and New York grew from a harbor town into a world trade center.

Contact between cultures can be caused by many factors. War, migration, and trade are obvious examples. New people and goods bring new possibilities into a culture. Intermarriage among royalty can cause an exchange of cultural traits. Some special-interest groups send missionaries to spread social and moral viewpoints. From such contact can come diffusion.

The Mechanics of Diffusion. Diffusion often is neither smooth nor regular. A diffused trait may be resisted if it does not fit the receiving culture's basic values and social patterns. Such resistance has hindered the spread of casino gambling into more parts of the United States. Enough people view casinos as a threat to established social values that its diffusion has been slight. Any spreading trait must fit or be made to fit the new culture. Rarely, if ever, is a new trait accepted without being altered to some degree. It will be reworked to fit easily into the receiving culture. Since professional soccer was imported to North America, there have been efforts to adapt the rules to allow more scoring and thus satisfy the fans' demand for more explosions of excitement. Also, traits coming from the same culture may not spread at the same rate or to the same distance. American men may accept the idea of wearing French cologne, but not the French designers' idea of carrying purses. A culture may accept some traits and reject others from the same culture. For example, a culture may accept another's weapons but not its religion.

Problems can result when only one part of a package of traits is diffused into a culture. The idea of bottle-feeding by itself could bring disease and death if it were introduced alone, without ways to sterilize bottles and refrigerate milk. Likewise, the spread of health practices, without contraception, results in soaring population growth rates.

Diffusion can cause disruptive social change in other ways. One culture may come face-to-face with another culture that has a clearly superior technology. This can cause severe moral problems and may lead to desperate attempts to close the gap through diffusion. There might follow a political or religious revolution that changes the old culture beyond recognition.

Most Social Change Comes from Diffusion. Diffusion plays a huge role in social change. Kroeber points out, "All cultures are largely hybrid composites of material that once entered them from outside."[18] He says that just as humans learn most of what they know from each other, so cultures depend on other cultures for most of their traits.

In fact, more of the world's social changes are the result of diffusion than internal innovation. Diffusion does not require genius; it requires only contact with a culture trait that is useful and that fits the overall receiving culture.

The importance of diffusion is not always acknowledged. As we saw in Chapter 3, the ethnocentric view is found in all cultures. This sometimes causes people to ignore the role of diffusion, that is, they choose to focus on their own culture's contributions. Such a focus can give a distorted picture of one's cultural heritage. The importance of diffusion is greater and more easily seen in young cultures, such as that of the United States. This culture did not start from a cultural zero. Instead, it began forming on a large cultural base that already had a long history. A good example of such a large borrowed cultural base is seen in the language and political and religious institutions of the United States. These institutions can in large part be traced back to England. Indeed, if we were to take away the British heritage from the North American culture, our culture would be difficult to recognize.

Of course, England and its colonies were an ocean away, but usually the closer two groups are to each other, the more diffusion is likely to take place. There are many cases, however, of neighboring groups borrowing little from each other. One example of little sharing between neighbors is the United States and Mexico. The one nation formed its culture largely from England, the other from Spain. Furthermore, the similar cultures of neighbors may be the result not of diffusion but of similar responses to the same environment. For these reasons, among scientists today diffusion is not as popular an explanation of how cultures change in the same direction as it was in the first half of the twentieth century.

ACCULTURATION: The cultural changes resulting from contact between groups having different cultures.

Acculturation Results from Diffusion. Acculturation is the change that results from diffusion. Whenever two cultures come into contact with each other and diffusion occurs, acculturation may result. Acculturation is a form of cultural change produced in a culture through the influence of another culture. Acculturation and diffusion are closely linked: the latter causes the former. Anthropologist A.L. Kroeber helped explain the relationship between these two terms: "Diffusion is a matter of what happens to elements or parts of culture; acculturation, of what happens to cultures."[19] In other words, acculturation and diffusion are the same process viewed from different angles.

VIEWS ON CHANGE

To understand social change, or maybe even to produce some social change, we must go beyond a knowledge of what it is and what its sources are. We need a broad view that explains *how* social change occurs. That is, we need a theory, and there are several from which to choose.

The basic premises on which social theories are built have changed over the years. Before last century, people in Europe tended to view change in religious terms. Social systems were seen as stable and controlled by God. Major change was often seen as the result of divine intervention. An invasion by an enemy would be viewed as proof that the gods were angry, that the gods were testing the people of the homeland. The dramatic changes coming from the Industrial Revolution made it difficult to maintain this religious view. Stability was replaced by change as the basic feature of society. It was seen as a problem if a culture was *not* changing and was thus losing out on opportunities. Change has been sought so much that today we hear talk about future shock, caused by too much change happening too fast. Most social systems are no longer seen a stable; in fact, they are seen by some people as spinning out of control.

Today it is clear to even the most casual observer that change is a basic part of social life. Social scientists believe that it is important to go beyond this knowledge, to find out how and why the change occurs. If the causes and patterns of social change could be discovered, we could more effectively deal with the present and plan for the future. With a better idea of where our social system is heading, we might waste less of our energies trying to cope with social change and its "shock" effects. And a knowledge of social-change patterns might help us better control the process. Such an important topic has attracted much attention from social scientists who have developed several types of theories to explain social change.

Evolution Theories

Does the world move like a game of golf, from one station to the next toward some end? If we assume the world is headed down some path toward a certain state, we may find the evolutionary social-change theories the most helpful. These theories try to fit social change into an orderly set of developmental stages. Such theorists see change as moving cultures from simple forms to more complex forms. Many theorists in the nineteenth century held this view, but it fell from favor in the early 1900s. In the last two decades, this view of social change has made a comeback. Indeed, it seems that this kind of social-change theory has itself evolved over time.

Evolution: Popular in the Nineteenth Century. Evolutionary theory became popular in the nineteenth century as European explorers came into contact with primitive societies in various parts of the world. Some idea was needed to explain the huge gap between these simple social systems and the complex systems of Europe. Most theorists came to agree that the gap was the result of some cultures lagging behind others along the path of evolution.

Comte. One of the earliest evolutionists was Auguste Comte (1798–1857). He believed that social systems evolve through stages based on how people think about the world. In the first stage, supernatural forces were seen as the moving forces of the world; the gods were seen as being in direct control of the world. People in second-stage societies use abstraction, or speculative reasoning, to interpret the world. Comte believed that all social systems tend to move toward the third stage, positivism. The positivist is not interested in speculation about ultimate reality, or in anything else beyond the reach of our senses; he wants to deal only with what can be proven to be true. The outlook of this third stage is scientific, explaining the world through natural causes.

Comte's view shows the unilineal, one-line, nature of early evolutionist theories. He and other theorists assumed that societies move along a single path. All social systems were seen as moving through the same stages, though at different rates.

Morgan.   L.H. Morgan (1818–1881) was another unilineal evolutionist of the nineteenth century. He argued that all cultures evolve through the stages of savagery, barbarism, and civilization. Morgan stated that all cultures would be limited to these stages because people are so similar mentally. Like most other early theorists, he viewed the final stage as the best stage. That is, change was generally viewed as progress.

Marx and Engels.   Karl Marx (1818–1883) and Friedrich Engels (1820–1895) used Morgan's view to formulate their theory of social change. Though their theory pictured social systems evolving through various stages, it also assumed that this process would need a boost from revolution at some point. Marx and Engels assumed that the class struggle between the exploiters and the workers was the basis of social change. From this struggle, workers would form a dictatorship that would lead to a classless system—communism. Like most other theorists of the nineteenth century, Marx and Engels saw only one pathway for change, and change was progress.

Social Darwinism.   Another theorist, Herbert Spencer (1820–1903), believed that society would evolve naturally toward perfection. He agreed with Charles Darwin's view that change is a process of natural selection. As "Darwinism" stated, organisms that do not adapt well enough to the demands of the environment will become extinct. Spencer believed that the development of societies was much like the development of the plants and animals of which Darwin spoke. Spencer saw social change as a process of natural selection, so his viewpoint is often called Social Darwinism.

Spencer argued that this orderly, natural process should not be disturbed. At any one time, what *was* was what *should* be, he said. Thus Spencer believed that governments should not interfere with the natural competition among people. He described change as a struggle for the "survival of the fittest." As the socially "fit" won out, progress would result. Interference in this struggle by, for example, welfare or free schooling for the "unfit" poor would only serve to impede progress, according to Spencer.

Some of us have heard someone make a comment that sounds much like Social Darwinism: "The poor deserve what they get because they are inferior." The flaw in this reasoning is that those born at the bottom of the social structure were not necessarily less "fit" than those on the top. What *is* is not always what we might think *should* be, because it is in many cases not the result of a fair

Skill Reinforcer 13-2
What is the conclusion of this syllogism:

1. What *is* is what should be.
2. Children of poor families do have a high death rate, so. . .
3. Then . . .

process. The competition is rarely free and open. Some people are held down by artificial barriers. Some people are kept up at the top by artificial supports. Because of this, a person's social position does not clearly indicate his or her innate "fitness."

Durkheim. Emile Durkheim (1858–1917) was one of the few early theorists who did not assume that change was progress. He saw that change could bring more problems, not perfection. In his view, people in simple social systems held many values in common. This gave these systems unity and little conflict. As the population grows, Durkhcim said, the system must become more specialized to better exploit the dwindling resources. As more people specialize, they begin to have differing outlooks on life. Their unity weakens, and conflict more easily arises. More formal control is needed. This picture is not one of progress toward perfection, but Durkheim was less intent than other early theorists to see how social change *should* happen. He was more interested in describing how change *did* in fact occur.

The empirical approach, which demanded factual basis before theory could be built, has rejected the nineteenth-century evolutionary theories. Many of the early theorists built theories without bothering to gather facts. Few of them ever studied social systems. Rather, they often relied on the accounts of tourists and other travelers. As social scientists rushed out into the field early in the twentieth century to study the quickly disappearing primitive cultures throughout the world, facts came pouring in. Much of this new knowledge exposed flaws in the old evolutionary theories. By the middle of the 1920s, these theories (except for Marxism) were dead—or so it seemed.

New and Improved Evolutionary Theories. Over the last twenty years, evolutionary theory has been revived. It has always been obvious that there exists some sequence of social development. Some social changes do happen in an orderly way. A political empire cannot be built before people learn how to produce a surplus of wealth. Algebra cannot be developed before the concept of zero is grasped. The basic approach of social evolution is still plausible, and recently new theories have been offered that try to avoid the flaws of earlier efforts based on this approach.

Part of the new face of these theories is the search for more than one path of change. Rather than fitting all examples of social change into one line, multi-lineal (more than one line) theory looks for parallel paths. In the multi-lineal view, a social system may not go through the same stages others went through. The economies of the world's developing nations may skip some stages of development. For example, some developing nations might even go from a simple farming base to a system based on computer data processing, skipping the heavy industry stage altogether.

Also, most evolutionists today restrict themselves to specific cases of social change. This is in contrast to the theories of the nineteenth century, which offered grand explanations of broad cultural forms. Still, some theorists today attempt to describe broad-scale trends—based, of course, on facts.

A major feature of today's evolutionary theories is that change is not always viewed as progress. Theorists today recognize that we cannot be sure change has a goal. There may be no ideal, perfect system toward which change takes us. While some specific changes are clearly improvements, a culture's overall direction and ultimate goal are not always clear. Indeed, it might be argued that our system is moving away from perfection, however we might define it, rather than progressing. Perhaps we cannot be so sure that our culture is better today than it was in the past.

On the whole, evolutionary theory today still provides insight into social change. Most theorists using this approach are more cautious, empirical, and modest than those of the past. This makes their work more valuable.

Cyclical Theories

If we believe that our culture's pattern of change is more like a yo-yo or merry-go-round than a golf game, if we see the social world around us changing, but not toward anything new, the cyclical view of social change might suit us best.

Since World War I, several theorists have suggested that social change can be explained best in terms of cycles. These theorists searched for long-term, regular patterns of change that recur over time. Unlike the evolutionists, these theorists believe that some trends repeat themselves rather than move things along in one direction. While evolutionists view change as a hand pushing cultures along a path, cyclical theorists see change as a force that repeatedly knocks a culture from one phase to the next, fashioning a new culture in the process. That is, rather than viewing change as progress along some path, the cyclical theorists view it as fluctuating within some pattern. Some of these theorists view change patterns in terms of a rise and a fall. Others see a pendulum motion in social-change patterns.

Rising and Falling.

Spengler's growth and death. An early cyclical theorist was Oswald Spengler (1880–1936), who saw social change as resembling the process of birth, growth, maturity, decay, and death.[20] In this view, Spengler believed that a culture passes through the same phases as a person. He saw decay and death as something no culture could escape. This is an unpleasant theory to accept; it is a pessimistic view, especially in light of the fact that Spengler claimed that Western societies are in their declining phase. A follower of Spengler might point to socialist or developing nations as being on the rise.

Toynbee's challenges. Arnold Toynbee (1889–1975) also saw social-change cycles in terms of growth, decay, and death.[21] His theory is more firmly based on research than Spengler's and is more comforting. Toynbee believed cultural decline can be avoided, though it involves a struggle. The struggle is based on challenge from the environment, to which the culture responds. It is during times of challenge, Toynbee said, that cultures have the chance either to grow or to edge closer to death. As a culture successfully meets challenges, it grows toward perfection. Thus Toynbee saw social change being played out in a cycle of challenges and responses. Some cultures rise upward while others fall by the wayside.

Compared to Spengler, Toynbee's theory is more pleasant to accept and perhaps more valuable. While Spengler offers no hope for a culture, Toynbee's theory urges us to gird ourselves for challenges, assuring us we can survive and prosper if our response is a strong and proper one. Of course, we cannot know for sure which theory is accurate, if either is.

Swinging Back and Forth. If neither of these two theories seems acceptable, there is another to consider in the cyclical camp.

Pitirim Sorokin (1889–1968) described a pendulum theme of social change.[22] Rather than a rising and falling pattern, he envisioned a swing between two types of stages of cultures: ideational and sensate. Although a culture contains both types to some degree, Sorokin believed that a culture would tend to develop toward one of the types until it was countered by a swing toward the other. Thus a culture might be moving toward what he called the sensate stage, when a backlash might swing the culture back toward the ideational stage. The sensate stage stresses objective, empirical sources of truth. Its search is for what can be perceived through the senses. An ideational culture, on the other hand, looks for truth beyond the human senses, beyond human reason. The cycle Sorokin saw was a pendulum motion, a swinging between these two extreme states of mind.

Like Toynbee's theory, Sorokin's viewpoint does not assume that any culture is faced with certain death. But Spengler's follower might again speak up and ask if we have reason to believe that our culture is so special that it will never die. Because all life cycles in nature include death, it is difficult to talk of eternal human social systems. While it is good for a group's morale to believe that it will never die, this belief may be misleading.

Functionalism   Functionalism will be appealing if one believes that social change is simply what social systems use to keep on an even keel, to keep things functioning.

Functionalists are different from the other theorists mentioned so far. Rather than searching for master patterns of change, they look at how the inner workings of a system tend toward a state of stability. These theorists believe that a social system will not move toward any goal or in any direction unless some outside force acts on it. Functionalists thus have a more limited, smaller-scale view of social change than the other theorists.

Talcott Parsons is a major functionalist. His study focuses on social stability rather than change. He sees a society as a system of parts, each actively working for healthy functioning of the system. Economic, political, and cultural subsystems are seen as the major parts of society. Each subsystem performs its own function. As one subsystem changes, this tends to produce changes in the others, all of which are aimed at adjusting to the initial change. Left to itself, with no outside forces interfering, the system will remain stable. Thus, internal social change is seen as tending toward stability, not movement.

A study of peasant rebellions supports this functionalist viewpoint. Large-scale rebellions by Russian peasants in 1905–7 seem to have been caused not by class struggle but by increasing economic insecurity.[23] In other words, internal change, in the form of rebellions, occurred when the stability of the existing system broke down, not because peasants wanted something new. In the functionalist view, internal change aims at maintenance of the system as it is.

An analogy illustrates this functionalist theory. Compare a social system to a human body. The subsystems of society are like the body's major organs, each one working in its own way for the overall health of the system. In the morning, the body is basically the same as it was the morning before. Only a few minor changes have occurred—a few hairs were lost, some new skin was added. The organs have all been active in maintaining this state of health, this equilibrium. Despite the body's inner adjustments, little overall change has occurred. This state of health may be disrupted, however, by agents from the outside. Germs or other objects, such as bullets, can cause major changes in the body, just as diffusion can change a culture. This analogy can be carried only so far. A cyclical theorist might ask if this state of health lasts forever, if the body does not die. Someone else might ask if a culture never produces innovations itself, which change the culture from within.

The functionalist viewpoint offers a different approach to change by focusing our attention on stability. It is another rather optimistic view on change. Unlike the other, grand-scale theories, functionalism places us up close to a changing social system and bids us look at its inner workings rather than its overall direction.

Conflict Theories

Some might see the functionalist viewpoint as just too cozy and pleasant to be realistic. And they might think human social systems are more likely to show selfishness than cooperation, conflict rather than smooth functioning. For those who think along these lines, the conflict theories will fit their beliefs and enhance their outlook.

In sharp contrast to functionalism, the conflict theories assume the groups comprising a social system are working against one another, in this way constantly producing change. Rather than working together for the system's health, each group clashes with others in a constant struggle for power. Even on a world-wide scale, societies can be seen as competing and exploiting. Social scientists describe the world as a system in which each nation has its niche or status. Some nations are dominant, others are "dependent" and "peripheral." [24, 25]

A leading conflict theorist today is Ralf Dahrendorf. He focuses on the struggle for power and the change this struggle produces. Because power is not distributed equally, he says, there is always some social group that is dissatisfied and wants change.[26] As long as some group is unhappy, social change will occur. Those without power want more, while those with power strive to keep what they have. Dahrendorf paints a picture of constant strife and struggle. He states that every social system rests on the constraint of some of its members by others. This produces conflict, and the conflict causes change. Change is constant and found in all groups in all social systems, in Dahrendorf's view.

This constant struggle need not be viewed as wholly unpleasant. Indeed, the changes it produces can better reflect the interests of the people. The change may well be reform, but the struggle will continue because other groups will have new reforms to suggest.

Karl Marx based his evolutionist scheme on a conflict model. In his view, conflict between the owners and the nonowners is constant and cannot be avoided. This struggle between economic classes would lead to an ideal, classless society. Marx saw change as leading to a better future, though the path would be bloodied with revolution. He saw conflict as a necessary part of the overall process, the fuel for progress, the basis for change.

Some conflict theorists assume, unlike Marx, that change has no overall goal, that social conflict fuels an engine that is headed in no particular direction. The scheme of Marx adds to that picture a destination, however unreal it may be.

The social theories described in this section are of more than academic concern. Accepting one of these viewpoints helps us find order in the world's social changes. It makes us aware of large-scale patterns, some of which we may want to avoid, others we may want to work for. Which viewpoint we accept will greatly influence our perception of the changes swirling about us.

MODERNIZATION

Whichever theory is used to view it, social change has produced several modern social systems. Because the term "modern" is often used too loosely, here we will explore what modernization means as well as how it happens. Then the effects of modernization will be examined.

The Nature of Modernization

The social-change theories just described explain *why* some societies have become modern and why others have not. Now we will explore *what* the label "modern" implies.

Some of the oldest cultures in the world are just beginning to modernize. Here a somewhat updated version of the donkey cart makes its way through ancient ruins in Egypt.

"Modern" Often Means "Better" and "Western."

Progress.   If Americans tried to define modernization, they might use an evolutionist viewpoint. Modernity is easily viewed as a stage along a path of change from simple to complex. Furthermore, this stage is usually described as industrialized. Modernization, then, is the social change that takes a social system from a simple, agrarian stage toward a complex, industrial stage. This modernizing trend is usually considered—by "modern" people—to be progress, advancement. It does involve an improvement in the use of resources, so that more goods per person are produced. Greater knowledge and more skills allow production to be more efficient. More energy is used, and used more efficiently.

Western.   Modernization is often used to mean Westernization. That is, the process brings societies closer to the culture of the Western nations, the ones that industrialized first. As these nations searched for the resources needed by their economies, they spread the germ of modernity. They showed other peoples the riches, comforts, and power that it could bring. Their contact with undeveloped countries created desires in the latter to modernize themselves, to become "Western."

Modernization in the World Today.

Where.   Today this form of social change is occurring in many places, though some countries in Africa, Latin America, and Asia are not engaged in the process of becoming modern. Newly rich oil-producing nations are rushing with breakneck speed to bring into their cultures many of the comforts and skills of modernity. Even advanced nations are still modernizing. For instance, in the United States, the modern world is still spreading to a few groups and regions that have remained somewhat isolated to this day.

Rate.   The rate of modernization varies greatly from one case to another. Today's advanced, Western nations modernized over a period of several hundred years. Japan started a little later and took only about one century. Many of the nations only recently starting to modernize are trying to complete the process in a matter of decades. As is usual, the pioneers took longer to blaze a trail than those who followed. Those traveling the path later can learn from earlier experiences and avoid many wrong turns.

How Modernization Happens

Having defined the process of modernization, we will explore how it happens. Though there is no widely accepted theory explaining the "how" of the process, several things do seem to be needed before the process can begin. Enough skill and resources are needed to produce a productive surplus. Along with this capacity, a social system needs certain attitudes.

Are People Ready to Modernize if Just Given the Chance?

One survey of several social-change theorists asks whether modernization begins with new attitudes or if it can be started by arranging incentives and then just letting it happen.[27] The latter view argues from the assumption that people will work for the social changes leading to modernity if given the chance to do so. It assumes that, in most societies, there are enough people moved by economic self-interest to use any chance given them to move the society toward economic development. Likewise, some of these theorists believe that people would value democracy if they were given the chance, or if they were so motivated by their government. The underlying belief is that a government can provide incentive and motivation so as to manipulate people to work toward modernity.

You may have noticed that this view would fall right in line with an evolutionary theory of change. That is, modernity can be viewed as the next stage, just waiting to happen. The government needs only to give the people a shove, and they will move along the path to modernity.

Inkeles and Smith suggest that the proper attitudes for modernization are linked to education, job experience, and exposure to mass media.[28] They found that the numbers of years of schooling people had was closely associated with how modern their attitudes are. Likewise, experience with factory work and the mass media seem to teach modern attitudes. A government might reason from this that these attitudes can be produced by building factories, schools, and television stations, then allowing the attitudes to grow naturally. This follows the assumption that the urge to modernize exists in many people, that they only need a chance and a little shove.

Or, Must People First Acquire the Proper Attitudes? Other theorists believe that the urge to modernize is not found naturally in people, that most people lack the necessary attitudes. According to this view, modernization will not happen until these attitudes develop. So government modernization programs will accomplish little until these attitudes somehow develop. Various studies have tried to identify these necessary attitudes.

Protestant work ethic. Sociologist Max Weber suggested that the Protestant work ethic is the basis for the social change leading to modernity.[29] Based on the ideas of John Calvin (1509–1564), the work ethic urges a person to work hard to achieve success. Worldly success is taken as a sign of God's favor. Success thus becomes doubly attractive, for material reasons and spiritual reasons. Many of the early colonists in America, such as the Puritans, were influenced by Calvinism. "Work hard and get ahead" became part of the rules of the game in this nation. The work ethic, according to Weber, was largely responsible for the rapid economic development of early America.

Need for achievement. Another theory arguing that the process of modernization begins with the proper attitudes is that of David McClelland.[30] He argues that the "mental virus" that leads to economic growth is the need for achievement. This mental trait causes a person to act in an energetic way, to be concerned about doing things well. If this "virus" spreads enough, the society will begin to produce more and will be able to modernize.

From these differing viewpoints we can see that the theorists do not agree on a strategy that a government might use to begin the march to modernity. It seems clear that once the people's attitudes are modern, the social changes will follow. It is not clear whether a government can easily cause these attitudes to develop.

The Effects of the Modernization Process

Now that we have seen what modernization is and some ideas on how it happens, we can look around and see some of its effects. Here these effects will be classified into four types, then they will be weighed, the good against the bad.

Four Kinds of Effects.

Economic. With modernization comes less inequality, both within and among nations. As a poor country becomes more modern, the gap between its rich and poor people is likely to become smaller, because a modern state offers more opportunities to more of its people. In addition, a modern state is more productive, so there is more wealth to be spread around. Modernization also narrows the gap of wealth between rich nations and poor nations. These results are easy to judge good. More wealth means more comfort and better life opportunities. More equality means that more people will enjoy the wealth.

Political. The political aspects of modernity are not as clearly positive. In a modern state, power becomes centralized. The government controls more parts of the social system. Further, if a system is in a hurry to become modern, it is likely to reject the slow pace offered by democracy. A dictator can move a nation along much faster than a democratic government can. Thus it is often the case that economic growth is accompanied by the growth of the government's power, but not the people's power.

Social. There are several social aspects of modernization. The school system becomes more accessible. Religion loses some of its social power. The family becomes smaller, with more women working outside the home. It also becomes more of a consuming unit than a producing unit. Both cities and bureaucracies grow in size and influence. The communications media grow in importance. Also, health care is usually improved as a state becomes modern. As a group, these changes are difficult to evaluate. Some are clearly improvements, while others are part of the reason we sometimes lament the passing of the "good old days."

Psychological. Modernization also involves changes in the mental outlook of people. These changes may be the most important, because they affect us most intimately.

Alex Inkeles and David Smith described several psychological aspects of modern people.[31] Such people are likely to be well-

TABLE 13-2. Some Social Effects of Modernization.

Modernized nations differ from others regarding such things as the quality of health care and the amount of mass communication. These differences are clearly seen by contrasting a developed nation with a developing one in these two regards.

	U.S.	Kenya
Infant mortality rate: number of deaths of children under 1 year of age per 1,000 live births in a year	11	83
Life expectancy at birth (years)	75	54
Telephones per 100 population	76	1.3
Daily newspaper circulation, copies per 1,000 population	269	12
Television receivers per 1,000 population	790	4

SOURCE: U.S. Bureau of the Census *Statistical Abstract of the United States: 1986,* 106th ed. (Wash., D.C., 1985).

informed not only about local affairs but also about broader affairs. They also believe in their power to control their own lives, rather than putting their faith and trust in fate. Modern people refuse to be confined by traditional sources of authority, such as parents and priests. Also, modern people are apt to be open-minded toward new experiences. Contrary to what some people might expect, modern people were not found to suffer from more mental stress than traditional people. Nor do they seem to be less kin-oriented than traditional people, or more blindly wrapped up in material success.

Skill Reinforcer 13-3

If your research problem is to find out more about the psychological results of modernization, what might your hypothesis be and what use would it serve?

Evaluating Modernization. Present-day college students can be assumed to be already part of the modern world, but there are many people throughout the world who are not. In fact, even in our own home town there may be some people who in their own lifetime will move out of the pre-modern world. Is it best for those people to take that giant step into modernity?

To evaluate modernization, all four of its effects must be considered. The psychological changes do not seem to be threatening to the well-being of a people. The economic changes involved are mostly beneficial. Some of the social aspects of a modern state are irritating and some are dangerous, while others are positive. But the political changes that come with modernization open the door for frightful abuses of power, frightful in the amount of power made available to modern governments.

Only when the process of social change is brought under greater control, perhaps with the aid of social science, will people have more choice about whether to modernize. Until then many people will have to take what comes their way and hope the benefits outweigh the costs.

SKILL BOX

Ethnographic Research

The word "ethnography" means literally "study of people"; it is in fact the study of the way people live. To social scientists, especially anthropologists, it is a useful tool for studying not only a culture but also the changes a culture undergoes. It gives insight into a way of life before, during, and after social change.

In the past, ethnographers focused on non-Western cultures, many of which were European colonies. The first descriptions of these cultures had often come from missionaries or government agencies. Later, social scientists entered the field, hoping to describe these cultures before they disappeared under the tide of cultural change flowing from the modern world.

Recently, ethnography has been also looking at modern cultures. The process and effects of modernization can be studied close-up through this method. The researcher who uses ethnography to get to know very well the people undergoing modernization can better understand the effects of that process.

Ethnographic research is not simply taking notes on the natives. The description of a culture must be based on some theory, which gives a direction to the scientist's work. The worker must also learn as much as possible about the culture he or she is to study before arriving among its people. This requires a review of relevant research.

The scientist also needs training in the proper research method. The chief method of ethnographers is participant observation. This research method requires that the ethnographers, armed with research goals and some knowledge of the culture, become part of that culture. They must gain acceptance among the people so that they can actively observe the way of life. The ethnographers must take care that what they observe is a typical sample of the peoples' lives. People of all ages, sexes, and ranks should be included in the records. Usually the study lasts a full year, to sample all seasons in the culture.

There are several problems faced by ethnographers. The biggest problem is trying not to distort, by their own feelings and values, what they are studying. They must strive to be objective while being sympathetic enough to understand the people they observe. The scientists must also take care not to let their presence influence the people's actions. They must melt into the group they study, becoming a part of them while remaining detached enough to study them.

The descriptions written by ethnographers become the building blocks of anthropology and social science. They are used to build theories that try to explain better the concept of culture as well as socio-cultural change.

SUMMARY

Differences occurring in a society or a culture over time are called social change. Social change can be large or small in scale, abrupt or gradual, quick or slow, and repetitive or not.

Change can be influenced, even caused somewhat, by the physical environment, which sets limits to change and offers opportunities for change to a culture. This was evident in the settlement of the American colonies, which was affected by the ocean, soil, mountains, and forests.

Change can also be caused by innovation, that is, new elements being added to a culture from within. This can include inventions (the creation of new elements) or discoveries (the new awareness of an already existing element). Technological innovations are more readily accepted than social ones. Cultural lag results when parts of a culture change at different rates.

Social change is most often the result of diffusion, or the spread of elements from one culture to another. Such change, resulting from intercultural contact, is called acculturation.

Several kinds of theories have been developed to explain social change. Evolutionist theories assume that change moves social systems through stages along one or more paths. Cyclical theorists believe that societies change through either a rising and falling cycle or a cycle swinging from one extreme to the other. Functionalists focus on the stability of a system, while conflict theorists focus on the frictions that produce social change.

Modernization is the social-change process that brings at least some societies into an advanced (that is, complex and industrial), Westernized stage. Theorists do not agree on whether the process will happen if people are simply given the chance—and perhaps a little shove—to become modern. When modernization does occur, however it is caused, it results in more economic equality and more centralized political power. Also resulting are many changes in the social sector, as well as changes in the mental outlook of the people. While some of the results of modernization are frightening, the process also offers excitement and opportunity.

The knowledge concerning social change given in this chapter can be of value for leaders and policymakers. It can help them understand and thus control somewhat the changes a social system will go through. Likewise, we can use the knowledge to help us understand the direction our system is taking. While the knowledge will not help us control that direction, it will help us adjust to it.

SPECIAL TOPIC

Is Social Change Out of Our Hands?
Leslie White's Cultural Determinism

In this chapter we have examined social change from several angles. We explored various theories and the sources of social change. While reading about how and why cultures change, it is easy to assume that humans are somehow in control of it all. This assumption is comforting, but according to one line of

reasoning it is not justified. Here we will examine this reasoning, as stated by Leslie White. His view is called cultural determinism. White offers the discomforting view that humankind cannot and does not control culture.[32] He says that culture makes and directs culture, that social (and cultural) change is out of our hands.

WHAT DOES NOT DETERMINE CHANGE

In arguing that cultural change is determined by culture itself, White attacks other explanations of change. This leads him to discussions of biological and psychological, as well as cultural, explanations.

Race Does Not Determine Culture or its Changes

White is not the only scientist to reject the idea that cultural differences are due to race. He agrees with most other scientists that racial differences are mostly superficial. These physical differences have nothing to do with cultural behaviors. There is no physical reason for a member of one race to speak a certain language or to like certain foods or music. There are only cultural reasons. In this view, social change is not affected in any serious way by race.

White points out that biology has some effect on culture in general. Each species has a range of expected behaviors. For humans, however, this range is broad enough to include many variations. Biology has nothing to do with the fact that some races developed cultures that are different from cultures of other races. That is, while culture in general is an expression of human physical traits, specific cultures and the changes they go through cannot be explained in terms of biology. Biology only sets broad limits on the development and the changing of culture.

And Culture Is Not Explained By Psychology

"Human nature" or "the human mind" are sometimes used to explain why cultures include certain behaviors. White says that the human mind is no more useful than biology in explaining culture. He says that while psychology is used to explain individual behavior, it cannot explain cultural differences or changes. He contends that it is not human (mental) nature that causes slavery, private property, or war. Rather, it is culture that explains these elements. In fact, a study of social change using White's viewpoint would proceed by ignoring human behavior as well as psychological factors.

CULTURE DETERMINES CULTURE

White argues that our way of life—our culture—is best explained in terms of culture.

That culture makes, and changes, itself may seem like an empty statement. To better understand that statement, we must explore the concept of culture as White sees it.

Culture: A Product of Past Additions

Culture is the way of life devised by symbol-using humans. Its elements are transmitted from one generation to the next. In White's view, culture flows continuously. It is like a stream flowing through time. New elements enter into the stream, swelling it. Over time, the stream of culture becomes larger and more complex. At any one moment, it is a product of the elements that have entered it in the past.

Humans of course started culture. Culture exists only as long as humans do. But humans do not control culture. Once it has begun, culture has a life of its own, according to White.

From White's view, we could say that if culture is like a stream, people are like the fish that depend on it for their existence. Their bodies surely influence the ways they live, but it is the stream that determines the ways they must live to survive. The stream supports and nurtures the fish, but the fish must adapt to the stream's demands. We are like the fish in that we humans have no control over the medium in which we live: culture.

This is not to say that humans live within a monster that is now out of control. Whatever opinion one may hold of culture, it is not, according to White, out of control. Once under way, culture has not only a life of its own but also its own laws. Like a stream in its channel, culture even has direction. It progresses toward greater control over nature, and thus greater physical security for humans.

Culture Controlled By Culture

Another analogy is useful to explain White's view of how culture is controlled. People are as necessary for culture as actors and actresses are necessary for a play. The actors and actresses are needed to speak their lines, to carry out the script; without them there would be no play. But they do not write the script, nor do they control it. The play has its own existence once it is written. It is the expression of the script, using actors and actresses for this expression.

To understand what controls culture, we would thus look not at the human mind but at culture. Culture—within biological bounds—

determines the human behavior that carries out the cultural process. Culture thus directs the cultural process. Culture directs itself.

Through this reasoning, White contends that humans do not control the social-change process. In fact, he argues that change should not be explained in terms of human behavior, even though change results from it. That is, though human behavior produces social change, that behavior is produced by culture. Humans are merely the medium through which the culture controls and changes itself.

But what about the Great Man, the genius, the leader, whose invention or ideas cause important events to occur? Do not special people influence social change? White would answer that indeed such persons are involved in changing cultures. However, he would add, these people's behaviors are products of their cultures. Even the genius is thus seen as a function of culture.

White says that genius occurs readily at peaks of a culture's development, that is, the culture produces many geniuses at such times. He says that the genius may not have great ability, but merely the talent required by the culture at that one place and time. History and culture can be seen as conspiring to bring about change. The person called genius is one who is caught up in the resulting trends. Like any other person, the "genius" can at best respond to cultural trends, but cannot cause or control them. White describes the Great Man or Great Woman more in terms of circumstances than ability.

White would say that even the person whose ideas seem to cause great reforms in, say, a school system is merely acting out the cultural forces that have shaped his or her ideas. That person, like all humans, is at the mercy of external (cultural) forces, plus his or her biological traits.

Like the individual, human groups and institutions only reflect their culture. They cannot control cultural change. For example, the school system cannot be used to modernize a culture. Instead, the schools merely give expression to the cultural process and its trends. If the culture is moving toward modernity, the schools will show symptoms of it as they change in accordance with that trend.

One might ask, if we cannot control culture, why study it? White answers that a study of culture can give us a greater knowledge of the cultural process. This knowledge will not help us control the process, but it will help us adjust to it. Control, he says, is only one way of adjusting to the world. While we must adjust, we need not control. With knowledge, we can learn to predict the changes as they develop from the process.

White believes that the key to understanding culture and cultural change is energy. Because we use technology to transform energy for our use, technology is a way to study the rest of culture. All other parts of the social system are related to it. Thus, White says, to understand social change we should focus our study on technology and the changes flowing from it as technology changes.

THE PREMISE OF CULTURAL DETERMINISM: NO FREE WILL

Because of the basic premise of his theory, Leslie White's views of social change are not comforting. White's arguments flow from his belief that we do not have free will. We do not freely decide what we will do, he says. Culture decides; we respond. This is for many people an unpleasant, perhaps frightening, prospect.

The denial of free will also conflicts with most religious systems. The Christian belief system, for example, rests on a belief in free will. In that system, people are threatened with eternal punishment if their behavior is of the wrong kind. But if people are not free to choose between right and wrong, it does not seem fair to judge them on their behavior, and unfairness makes a religious system hard to accept. One might argue, from Leslie White's viewpoint, that people's wrongful actions are the fault of their culture, not their mind or will. In this light, White's theory does not mix with the Christian belief system.

White's contention that we lack free will is not a fact, but a belief. There can be no experiment to prove or disprove the existence of free will. Arguments on either side can be offered. Some may be more appealing than others. On the empirical side, one can argue that there is no hard evidence for the existence of free will. Others contend that many things exist beyond the reach of science. In fact, it might be argued that in the realm beyond our senses lie the most important things. So to reach a decision on the existence of free will, we must first decide whether we will limit our beliefs to those things that are within the realm of science, or whether we will choose to believe in some things such as free will.

The choice is between faith and a demand for empirical evidence. As is true of our acceptance of any theory, we should decide what sort of evidence we will accept. Have you decided to accept White's theory of social change? Your very decision, White might say, will be determined by your cultural experiences, not "free will."

SELF-TEST QUESTIONS

1. True or false: The difference between the size of the average high school in 1900 and the average college today shows social change.
2. True or false: The physical environment determines the direction and form of social change.
3. True or false: An innovation may cause no social change.

Match numbers 4–7 to the definitions on the right:

4. invention
5. discovery
6. acculturation
7. cultural lag

a. new awareness of something that had already existed
b. social change resulting from diffusion
c. creation of a new cultural element
d. differing rates of change among various parts of a culture

8. Most social change comes from:
   a. physical environment
   b. diffusion
   c. discovery
   d. invention
9. True or false: A technological innovation is more easily accepted than a social one.

Match numbers 10–13 to the descriptions on the right:

10. evolutionary theory
11. cyclical theory
12. functionalist theory
13. conflict theory

a. culture works to maintain stability
b. social change is based on struggles
c. sees pendulum or rise-and-fall movement of cultures
d. change moves cultures through stages down one or several paths

14. True or false: Modernization is usually seen as movement toward Western culture.
15. Modernization brings:
    a. more economic inequality
    b. more centralized political power
    c. more social power for religion
    d. more mental problems

ANSWERS TO SELF-TEST QUESTIONS

1. False: The example shows differences in time, but not in the same entity.
2. False: Physical environment sets limits and offers possibilities: it influences but does not determine social change.
3. True: An innovation must be perceived as needed by and compatible with the existing culture.
4. c

5. a
6. b
7. d
8. b
9. True
10. d
11. c
12. a
13. b
14. True
15. b

ANSWERS TO SKILL REINFORCERS

13–1. The conclusion that there is a relationship between cultural advancement and climate is a result of shaky inductive reasoning. It proceeds from several specific cases in which the relationship did hold true and generalizes to all other similar situations. It goes from the specific cases to the general statement.

In evaluating the accuracy of this relationship, we should ask how representative the supporting, specific cases are of the other, similar cases covered by the generalization.

13–2. Conclusion: The high death rate of poor children is what *should* be. A logical conclusion, *if* one accepts the major premise (a big *if*).

13–3. There are many possible hypotheses for this problem. One might be: Modern people are more trusting (of relatives and merchants, for example) than traditional people. This hypothesis would be useful in that it would focus research on a specific area of the general area being studied. Rather than simply being on the lookout for any psychological differences between modern and traditional people, attention would be directed and focused, so one would be more likely to notice relevant data. (By the way, Inkeles and Smith discovered that the hypothesis was not supported by their data.)

NOTES

1. Alvin Toffler, *Future Shock* (New York: Bantam Books, 1970): 11–12. Copyright © 1970 by Alvin Toffler. Reprinted by permission of Random House, Inc.
2. Robert Nisbet, "Introduction: The Problem of Social Change," in *Social Change,* ed. Robert Nisbet (New York: Harper & Row, 1972): 1.
3. Ibid., pp. 4–5.
4. Donald Light, Jr., and Suzanne Keller, *Sociology* (New York: Alfred A. Knopf, 1975): 536.
5. William F. Ogburn, *Social Change* (1950; reprint, Gloucester, Mass.: Peter Smith, 1964): 145.
6. Ellsworth Huntington, *Mainsprings of Civilization* (New York: John Wiley & Sons, 1945).
7. Henri Berr, "Forward," *A Geographical Introduction to History* by Lucien Febvre (New York: Barnes & Noble, 1966): xi.
8. John B. Brebner, *North Atlantic Triangle: The Interplay of Canada, The U.S., and Great Britain* (New Haven: Yale University Press, 1945).
9. Ellen C. Semple, *American History and Its Geographic Conditions* (Boston: Houghton Mifflin Co., 1903).
10. Richard G. Lillard, *The Great Forest* (New York: Alfred A. Knopf, 1947).
11. Lewis Weiner, "The Slide Fastener," *Scientific American* (June 1983).
12. Ogburn, *Social Change*, p. 170.
13. Dennis Overbye, "Trains That Fly," *Discover* 3 (February 1982): 33.
14. Eviatar Zerubavel, "The Standardization of Time: A Sociohistorical Perspective," *American Journal of Sociology* 88 (July 1982): 1–23.
15. Mel Davies, "Corsets and Conception: Fashion and Demographic Trends in the 19th Century," *Comparative Studies in Society and History* (October 1982): 611–641.
16. Ogburn, *Social Change*, pp. 200–13.
17. Mamoru Watanabe, "Why Do the Japanese Like European Music? " *International Social Science Journal* 34 (1982): 657–65.
18. A.L. Kroeber, *Anthropology*, rev.ed. (New York: Harcourt, Brace & World, 1948).
19. Ibid., p. 425.
20. Oswald Spengler, *The Decline of the West* (New York: Alfred A. Knopf, 1926).
21. Arnold Toynbee, *A Study of History* (New York: Oxford University Press, 1946).

22. Pitirim Sorokin, *Social and Cultural Dynamics* (New York: American Book, 1941).
23. J. Craig Jenkins, "Why Do Peasants Rebel? " *American Journal of Sociology* 88 (November 1982): 487–514.
24. Patrick Nolan, "Status in the World System, Income Inequality, and Economic Growth," *American Journal of Sociology* 89 (September 1983): 410–19.
25. Heather-Jo Hammer, "Comment on Dependency Theory and Taiwan;" *American Journal of Sociology* 89 (January 1984): 932–37.
26. Ralf Dahrendorf, "Toward a Theory of Social Conflict," in *Social Change,* ed. E. Etzioni-Halevy and A. Etzioni (New York: Basic Books, 1973).
27. Myron Weiner, ed., *Modernization: The Dynamics of Growth* (New York: Basic Books, 1966): 5–12.
28. Alex Inkeles and David H. Smith, *Becoming Modern* (Cambridge, Mass · Harvard University Press, 1974).
29. Max Weber, *The Protestant Ethic and the Spirit of Capitalism,* trans. Talcott Parsons (New York: Scribners, 1930).
30. David C. McClelland, *The Achieving Society* (Princeton: Van Nostrand Co., 1961).
31. Inkeles and Smith, *Becoming Modern.*
32. Leslie A. White, *The Science of Culture* (New York: Grove Press, 1949).

SUGGESTED READINGS

Bell, Daniel. *The Coming of Post-Industrial Society.* New York: Basic Books, 1973.

Chirot, Daniel. *Social Change in the Twentieth Century.* New York: Harcourt Brace Jovonovich, 1977.

Hagen, Everett. *On the Theory of Social Change: How Economic Growth Begins.* Homewood, Ill.: Dorsey Press, 1962.

Lauer, Robert H. *Perspectives on Social Change.* 3d ed. Boston: Allyn and Bacon, 1982.

Lipset, Seymour Martin, ed. *The Third Century: America as a Post-Industrial Society.* Chicago: University of Chicago Press, 1979.

Naisbitt, John. *Megatrends: Ten New Directions Transforming Our Lives.* New York: Warner Books, 1982.

Toffler, Alvin. *Future Shock.* New York: Bantam Books, 1971.

Toffler, Alvin. *The Third Wave.* New York: William Morrow, 1980.

Wallechinsky, David; Wallace, Amy; and Wallace, Irving. *The Book of Predictions.* New York: William Morrow, 1980.

14 POPULATION, RESOURCES, AND ENVIRONMENT

PREVIEW

Volcanoes and Food

Mount Saint Helens blasted a mountain of dust into the air. Other volcanoes, in the South Pacific, South and Central America, Asia, and the Middle East have become active after long periods of dormancy or have increased activity. The volcanic ash in the sky is visible as a light haze. It tends to block the sun's rays and allows the earth to cool.

The farmers are complaining about changes in the seasons. The growing season appears to be shortening. The winters are longer and colder; something is happening.

You have never seen food prices so high. Foreign countries have been paying big dollars for our food surplus. In fact, there seems to be no surplus at all.

The population continues to grow, but our ability to feed the increase diminishes. The gains of the green revolution have receded. Such countries as Indonesia have tended to go back to native crop strains rather than maintain the high cost and high fertilizer demands of new strains.

The fabric of our world may be about to tear. The population question may be settled by nature rather than human planning. Will you move south, dig a shelter, or start putting away large amounts of canned food?

Over the past several decades we have become increasingly concerned about the interaction of human populations and their
natural environment. As some populations have increased at
alarming rates, we have seen with shocking clarity the strain those
peoples' needs put on the world's resources. This strain raises
political and moral questions that require a thorough knowledge
of the issues involved before we can come up with some answers.
To ensure at least a fundamental knowledge of such issues, this
chapter delves into population, natural resources, and the interaction of humans with their physical environment.

POPULATION

The demands made upon the world's resources have become one
of humankind's major problems. Unrestricted population growth
has combined with accelerated use of resources to place human
beings in a position they have never before occupied: Our population may well be approaching the limit that earth can support, at
our present level of technology.

If we do not control population and resource consumption,
we may place ourselves in the position of having insufficient food,
water, breathable air, and other natural resources necessary to
continue life. Never before have humans approached the limits of
their environment; they have always had a place to go and untouched resources to develop.

The social implications of our new situation are many and
complex. Shortages of basic requirements in food and energy have
brought about worldwide economic shifts that lowered the standard of living. This standard is uneven, and its downward course
will force new political and governmental alignments as efforts to
maintain life increase. If population density continues to increase,
it will also continue to affect social norms. The form of the family,
residence patterns, social control, social stratification, and all our
other basic institutions will continue to adjust to the changing
patterns of life.

In the past, nations have warred to control food-producing
areas and resources, and we can expect this pattern to accelerate.
We are seeing a replay of informal population movements with
both official and unofficial immigration from underdeveloped areas, to the highly developed nations. Examples of this movement
are the waves of boat people who take to the sea in desperation
and the thousands who cross our borders from the south. Less noticed are immigrants, also unofficial, from developed nations who
find it very easy to meld into our population without question.

Population Viewed Historically

The population problem is old, only its times and circumstances
change with each situation and generation. If a community of only
one hundred people produces inadequate food and other necessities to keep its residents living and eating well, it has a population
problem. Nature provides a ready-made solution for societies that
cannot produce enough food for their members: the people die.

CRUDE BIRTH RATE: Number of births per 1,000 of population.

CRUDE DEATH RATE: Number of deaths per 1,000 of population.

Historically, birth rates in marginal societies have always been high, but then so have high death rates. Among such groups, disease, malnutrition, and exposure to severe climatic conditions have always taken their toll.

An analysis of the age distribution differences in developed and underdeveloped nations will show that the high death rate in a developing nation will present a young population with relatively few older people. A developed nation will have a more equal distribution of persons in all age brackets.

Thomas Malthus (1766–1834) published in 1798, "An Essay on the Principle of Population." He pointed out that while population tended to increase in a geometric progression (2–4–8–16–32), our ability to produce foodstuffs seemed to increase arithmetically. The choices seen by Malthus were to have an ever lowering standard of living, marry late in life, have fewer children, and be subjected to the kindly corrections of starvation, pestilence, and war.

In the early days of industrialization, population was not considered a problem, because the conditions that prevailed in early urban centers killed people at a phenomenal rate, and labor was a needed resource.

A description of London at the time of the Black Plague reads like a horror story to the average American overconcerned with smells and detergents. In the homes of the poor, one might find a dozen or more people sleeping on the floor in the same room. Livestock, up to and including cows and ponies, shared the common residence. The combination of tainted water and lack of proper methods for the disposal of human waste created an atmosphere that could be cut with a knife.

When Americans go abroad today and find themselves in underdeveloped countries, they must be prepared with various immunizations and what has often been described as a portable environment. Our military bases are frequently merely extensions of the United States, and their inhabitants rarely leave the perimeters. Those living on the bases frequently consume food and water imported from developed areas. If people are brave enough to eat and drink locally produced items, they usually develop such diseases as amoebic dysentery, which may be endemic in the local population.

It is estimated that around 8000 B.C.[1] some 5 million people inhabited the entire world. With the beginnings of agriculture and the resultant production of a surplus of food, the world's population began its rapid rise.

BLACK PLAGUE: An epidemic spread by fleas on rats which swept Europe several times in the late Middle Ages. It wiped out a significant portion of the population.

One should not imagine the rise in population as one of a steady, uninterrupted nature, but rather as one of growth and corrections, which came disguised as war, famine, and pestilence. History is replete with examples of these corrections—possibly the most noteworthy being the bubonic plague—epidemics that worked wonders in the area of population control.[2] The two great plagues of fourteenth-century Europe reduced the continent's population by an estimated 25 percent. An interpretation of the records of those plagues in England shows a population loss of 50 percent.[3] Corrections of this sort have a distinctly upsetting effect on a society's social and economic structure.

It should be apparent that under such situations a society has a high death rate. People die younger, and death pays more frequent visits to average households there than to those in modern, developed nations. Not only is disease caused to a great extent by an accumulation of filth prevalent in such a situation, but the individual, by virtue of poor diet and weakened condition, is also far more susceptible to it.

Controlling Population   In a situation where the replacement of people is a problem, considerations of birth control and family planning are not important.

Land, once valuable because of total ownership, becomes vacant and worthless. Labor supply, once cheap and abundant, becomes short and expensive. The society that maintains power through the ownership of land must readjust to a situation where the land is of little value. Relationships of power and authority change with the removal of the basis of that authority. Food becomes priceless in times of short supply or famine, and gold loses its value when there is no surplus. Accumulated wealth, then, disappears, and a new social structure forms. Improved modes of transportation in recent years have eliminated famine in the developed countries of the world and somewhat reduced its toll in underdeveloped countries. The instances of famine today are due primarily to the primitive methods used in the transport of foodstuffs. A crop failure in central India could become a major disaster because of India's inability to unload and move foodstuffs from port facilities to the blighted area. The difficulties in the distribution of food encountered in the sub-Saharan region emphasizes this point. An added problem for many undeveloped societies is their inability to pay for continued supplies of imported food and/or manufactured items. Debt service and an increased cost base of these items have placed them out of reach for large areas of the world.

Consider the differences between a country such as the United States and an underdeveloped nation. The United States has a sophisticated network of interlocking air, rail, and highway facilities. These in turn link with large, well-equipped ports with storage and loading facilities geared to the quick movement of immense quantities of bulk items. The problem involved in gathering and shipping grain or other foodstuffs to a famine-stricken area on short notice is negligible.

Problems arise when a ship the size of a Great Lakes grain carrier arrives at a port with its cargo. The underdeveloped nation may have no facilities to unload this ship other than long lines of men and women carrying baskets.

Once the cargo is unloaded, there is no provision for its short-term storage in an adequate facility. At this point rats consume as much as human beings, and spoilage ruins another large percentage. Instead of thousands of specially designed railway cars and trucks available to transport the food, one may find ox carts or a converted passenger train. By the time one ship is unloaded, a dozen more may lie at anchor in the harbor, waiting their turns to disgorge their cargoes. Under such conditions, ships may linger several months before unloading, while, within two hundred miles, thousands of people starve to death.

Through the ages, wars have also contributed to the unconscious efforts of human beings to control population by means other than birth control. In addition to deaths caused by combatants in actual battle, war nurtures the situations that provide for disease and starvation. The Taiping Rebellion in China in the middle of the nineteenth century is said to have caused up to 10 million deaths. It is not necessary to travel abroad or into antiquity to note our own contributions to the death rate. The casualty lists of the American Civil War provide good reading for death-rate enthusiasts. In the twentieth century, the two world wars have, in the face of improved medical techniques, exceeded most death tolls of the past. Of the 74 million men mobilized for war in World War I, an estimated 13 million died. This figure excludes the large number of civilian deaths.

Without going into detail over the world wars, we can estimate that more than 50 million people died either in or as a direct result of both conflicts. Obviously, we have done our best to control population through the traditional means of famine, pestilence, and war, but if recent growth rates are considered, we must look elsewhere to solve this problem.

The Study of Population

The study of population (demography) includes a number of current avenues to be explored. These include at least nine:

1. Death rate
2. Birth rate
3. Distribution of the death rate
4. Population density and its change
5. Population growth and its rate of increase
6. Arable land and percentage tilled
7. Increase or decrease of food supply
8. Relationship of this increase or decrease in food supply to the population growth rate
9. Social effects of population growth

While we refer frequently to the current rise or fall of the birth rate, the death rate and its distribution is a more important item to consider. The rate of death (usually stated per 1,000) is a major factor often overlooked by the uninitiated because, of course, everyone dies. The point is, however, when people die.

Do they die before they are able to have children? Do they live to a ripe old age, or do they die as infants? If children die early, they do not contribute to the growth statistics because of their in-

Will tomorrow be worse?

ability to reproduce. If, as we have seen, disease and nutritional problems are corrected to a degree, children tend to grow up and procreate. While this is not to be construed as a bias against children, it has led to a jump in the rate of population growth.

Witness the example of Chile, where infant mortality dropped from 150 per 1,000 in 1945 to 100 per 1,000 in 1950.[4] In response to better health care and available drugs, the rate has continued to fall. Comparative statistics are available for most of the world's underdeveloped nations. While we see, then, that the death rate has been tampered with, only recently have we given thought to reducing the birth rate to compensate for this change.

Consider that the rate of infant mortality in the United States is 10.8 per 1,000 and that life expectancy in the developed nations of the world is about seventy years.[5] In Southeast Asia, the life-expectancy rate averages about forty-five years of age, and some African countries have a life expectancy of only twenty-seven years.[6] Even this result derives from our recent ability to wipe out the malaria-bearing mosquito in the tropical areas of the world, subsequently lowering the death rate and lengthening life expectancy. At best, the underdeveloped world is seventy-five years behind the developed areas. At worst, a life expectancy of twenty-seven years corresponds to that of fourteenth-century Europe.

By 1650, the world's population is estimated to have been only 545 million persons. As medical technology improved, the population continued to climb. In one hundred years the estimated population had risen to 728 million (1750), and by 1800, only fifty years later, the figures jumped to 906 million. The rate of increase had accelerated, allowing an increase of about the same number of people in only half the time. In other words, it took one hundred years for the world's population to gain 185 million people (1650 to 1750), but only fifty years to gain 178 million people (1750 to 1800). By 1900 the world population was 1,608 million,[7] in 1964 it was 3.22 billion,[8] in 1975 about 4 billion,[9] and in 1985, 4.762 billion.[10]

The answer to a rising population in the past has been merely to place more land under cultivation. Unfortunately, not only is

TABLE 14-1. Population of the World and Eight Major Areas, at 25 + Year Intervals, 1950–2075 (in Millions)

	1950	1975	2000	2050	2075
World Total	2,505	3,988	6,406	11,163	12,210
Northern America	166	237	296	339	340
Europe	392	474	540	592	592
U.S.S.R.	180	255	321	393	400
Latin America	164	326	625	1,202	1,297
Africa	219	402	834	2,112	2,522
East Asia	673	1,005	1,373	1,760	1,775
South Asia	698	1,268	2,384	4,715	5,232
Oceania	13	21	33	50	52

SOURCE: United Nations publication, No. F.74XIII.4.

arable land limited, but it actually decreases with use. Many areas of Mexico that had been cropland have suffered from erosion and exhaustion. These lands no longer produce crops, and in many regions they have become little more than desert. In some areas of the world, large-scale projects have been undertaken to provide more acreage for agricultural products. The projected figures for population growth illustrate that these cases are not extreme when considering the world's future.

Even if the figures presented are high estimates, they tend to bear out what has been discussed. Note that in 1975, the population for all Latin America exceeded the population of North America by 89 million. In 1950, the population of North America was larger than that of Latin America, illustrating the larger percentage rise in population of that underdeveloped area. In all areas considered, by the year 2000 the underdeveloped nations will total more than two times the world's population in the year 1950. If this seems a long time away, consider that a person twenty years old in 1990 will be only thirty years old in the year 2000 and eighty years of age in the year 2050.

If these projected population figures seem too high and the problem exists only as a figment in the minds of alarmist scientists, we must point to past mistakes. For the most part, these errors have been on the low side. In 1948 the United Nations Food and Agriculture Organization predicted a world population of 2.25 billion in 1960. Everyone considered the figure too high, yet in 1960 the actual world population totaled 3 billion. Predictions in the late 1940s and early 1950s placed the world population of the year 2000 at about 3 billion, a figure exceeded by 1960. In most cases, figures of these denominations mean nothing to the reader. They may be shocking, but we rarely consider what a million or a billion people mean. It is impossible to visualize the needs and consequent effects of population when it reaches stages such as those predicted. A more meaningful line of approach might point out the doubling time these statistics indicate.

The area of highest rate of growth, Latin America, may expect as a result of its growth rate (2.9 per year) to double its population

TABLE 14-2. Population Growth Rate with Doubling Times

Growth Rate (Percent per Year)	Doubling Time (in Years)
0.1	700
0.5	140
1.0	70
2.0	35
4.0	18
5.0	14
7.0	10
10.0	6

every twenty-four years. In retrospect, the population of this area was 91 million in 1920 and 326 million in 1975, and it will approach or surpass 700 million by the year 2000. In plain terms, in the year 2000 this region will contain eight times as many people as it did in 1920. This increase represents only eighty years lapsed time during the life span of a resident. Africa has a doubling time near that of Latin America. Its current growth rate, which is 2.8 per year, will double every twenty-eight years. Asia's rate is only 2.0 per year, and its doubling time is set for every thirty-five years. The numbers in this region exceed those elsewhere, and this continent numbers its population not in millions but billions.

Europe and most of the other developed countries of the world have the relatively small growth rate of 0.08 per year, a doubling time of every eighty-eight years. The North American area's rate is somewhat higher, 1.4 per year, or a doubling rate of every sixty-six years.[11] The doubling time is equal to seventy years (essentially a life-span) divided by the growth rate.

A yearly increase of items needed to maintain the population of Asia on a par with the living standard now enjoyed in Japan calls for the following annual supplements: [12]

5,000 billion gallons of water	14.3 million tons of meat
90.4 million tons of rice (world crop now 172 tons)	300 million living quarters
	10 million hospital beds
11 million tons of wheat	120,000 elementary schools (100 pupils each)
198.4 million tons of vegetables	
66 million tons of food fish (world catch now 35.3 million tons)	1 trillion kilowatt hours
	disposal facilities for 500,444 tons of waste per day additional

Future Population Trends

An indication of the pattern of things to come lies in recent sales of grain and other foodstuffs to Russia and China. In effect, while these sales provide needed monies to balance the trade deficits, they result in lowering the standard of living in the United States. The scarcity of feed grains and the rise of meat costs directly affect the average American's diet. What will happen when we either refuse to sell more or reach the limits of our own production can only be imagined.

The world has a limited number of acres available for agriculture. Many of our conceptions about the location of vast, untapped agricultural lands have no basis in fact. Three great fertile areas of the world exist. The Great Plains of the United States, the Pampas of Uruguay and Argentina, and the Ukraine. The recent atomic reactor disaster at Chernobyl (1986), north of Kiev, may have far reaching effects upon the future of the Ukraine. Compared to these regions, all other parts of the world have minimal fertility. The world averaged 1.25 acres of tilled land per person in 1950. Of this, only the United States, Russia, Argentina, Australia, and Cana-

A man carries a starving infant in a camp in Northern Ethiopia where thousands of refugees gather hoping to escape starvation following the severe drought which for consequent years has affected the area.

da had over 2.5 acres tilled per resident. Countries with minimal tilled acreage per person were Japan, 0.14; Egypt, 0.26; Peru, 0.42; and the United Kingdom, 0.34.[13]

As the world's population increases, residences and urban areas will cover more and more agricultural land, and pollution, erosion, and exhaustion will further deplete available land. Such great tropical basins as the Amazon Valley are composed of leached-out soils and climates not conducive to human habitation.[14] There are examples available of nature's retaliation when faced with human invasion of areas thought unsuitable for agricultural development. This does not mean that nature has a mind or will stand between people and their desires, but it does mean that when new land is placed in cultivation it frequently displaces former residents who tend to fight back. In the case of India, large amounts of former forest land have recently been put to the plow. The reasons for the expansion of the agricultural land are obvious. Well over 730 million people are resident in an area half the size of the United States. Two hundred years ago about 60 million people lived in India; today's population living in the same area looks forward to doubling every twenty-eight years. As farmland was increased, predators were wiped out to provide safe living areas. In response to this, the monkey population became serious competitors for the crops. Rats, elephants, crows, and cattle ate large holes in the produce before it was harvested. The more animals killed, the better breeding ground remained for the survivors. Army units had to be called out to fight the animals for the crops, and essentially, they lost. The estimated loss in grain to crows alone equaled approximately 10 percent of that produced in the United States. Although in twenty-eight years the country's population will double, India can maintain only 300 million people on an adequate diet. Translated into a diet equal to that of the United States, only 90 million could be served by the country's agriculture. Two-thirds of Indian women today show signs of malnutrition and suffer from anemia. Of the total population, some estimates rate only 10 million persons as having an adequate caloric intake.

Table 14–3 indicates that if the present growth rate continues, by 2400 A.D. the population density over the surface of the earth will reach a level of 30,000 persons per square mile in excess of that enjoyed on Manhattan Island in 1960 (77,194 per square mile).

When density, population growth, and tillable land figures are analyzed, it becomes apparent that a crisis will occur if population growth neither slows nor abates. Even now the underdeveloped countries of the world are experiencing the serious effects of overpopulation. As a result of malnutrition, the infant mortality rate has risen with the rate of natural deaths. An estimated adjustment of the male-female ratio in India is taking place. One estimate places males as outnumbering females by more than 20 million in that nation. One school of thought blames the disparity of rampant anemia and diseases related to malnutrition. Another

TABLE 14-3. Projection of World Population
Assuming an Annual Increase of 17 per 1,000

Year	Population (in Billions)	People Per Square Mile
1964	3.22	61.4
1975	3.88	74.0
2000	5.94	113.3
2025	9.08	178.3
2050	13.89	265.0
2075	21.25	405.3
2100	31.51	620.1
2200	177.93	3,394.0
2300	973.99	18,578.8
2400	5,330.39	101,677.2

SOURCE: David M. Heer, *Society and Population: The World Population Picture* (Englewood Cliffs, N.J.: Prentice-Hall, 1968), p. 14.

school predicts large-scale famine and death as a result of the increased susceptibility to disease of people weakened by inadequate diet. Even with the creation of new forms of food production and the improvement of old forms, there is no hope that production will in any way meet the demands of the rising population. Conceivably, worldwide wars might be waged on the pretext of conquering areas of higher crop yield.[15]

Migration from Overpopulation

For many years, people have been migrating from areas of heavy population and short food supply. Indicative of these movements and their effects are the numbers of Indians who have moved into Burma and Africa; the Japanese who have moved to Manchuria, Korea, Taiwan, and Brazil; the Latin Americans who are moving north to the United States; and the Chinese who have moved in all directions. Half the Malaysian population is Chinese, and large numbers now live in Tibet, Mongolia, and Sinkiang (15 million). In addition, Chinese residents number over one-half million in Java and like numbers in other parts of Oceania.

The one large productive land mass that has been denied the Asian population is Australia, which has historically restricted Asiatic migration while encouraging European immigrants. The influx of European immigrants since World War II has had a noticeable effect on the country's diet. As a result of the postwar immigration of only 2 million persons, the protein intake of the Australian population has dropped 10 percent. Even while Australia might appear to be the salvation of Asia in terms of food production and living space, some staggering statistics disprove this theory. The small islands of New Zealand have a larger surplus of meat production than Australia. In the past several hundred years the overdrilling of wells has been responsible for a vast drop in the ground water level on that subcontinent.

Although thought to be the center of the future food production in the Pacific area if its full potential is reached, Australia will be able to feed only one-third of the area's yearly population increase. To clarify this statement, we must point out that this increase is one-third of the growth of a single year. The explanation of this sorry statement can be illustrated graphically. When one considers Australia's major effort to create almost 2 million new acres of rice-producing land in the northern portion of the continent, the development's projected thirty-year production goal is 3 million metric tons annually. Each year, the rice-eating population grows by 30 million people. The annual growth, translated into rice needs, equals the entire result of the thirty years of development; thus, after thirty years of development, the aim of feeding the increased population is short by twenty-nine years. To add to the troubles of development, wild geese annually strip the new fields of almost half their grain crop.

OTHER OPTIONS, A DIFFERENT FUTURE

As a result of these dire predictions, some societies have attempted to alter the course of unbridled population growth while others have continued pronatalist policies. The Peoples Republic of China, for instance, has attempted to bite the bullet. With a 1983 population of over one billion people—a number equal to half the world's population in 1940 and the entire world's population in 1850, they felt forced to institute strict controls over reproduction. A couple could have only one child. If a woman became pregnant with a second child, she came under severe pressure to have an abortion. Because the Chinese value sons over daughters, it has not been unusual for female children to die at birth. Additionally, if a second child is born to a couple, it is said that one of the children is killed. The Chinese explain that they do not wish to kill children, but that they are in a serious position insofar as sheer numbers of people are concerned. They can not continue to see their standard of living and quality of life suffer without attempting a remedy. In response to the Chinese attempt to meet their population crisis, the American government has withheld population control funds until the Chinese back away from their hard line. (There has been some relaxing of the population control regulations and the 1987 unofficial birth rate for China has risen dramatically.)

From the viewpoint of the casual observer, one must look to the future and try to construct a society with a heavy population skew in favor of males. If only one in ten females is allowed to live, the future birth rate would be severely restricted. If only one in ten female children reach maturity, they (the females) would enjoy a position of desirability and favor rarely known. After a period referred to as the birth dearth (1964 to 1980), the United States has once more seen a dramatic rise in birth numbers. Most of the rest of the developed world appears to have birth numbers under control. Undeveloped nations, without forms of social security, still have birth rates running wild. If we can see China as an example of future control, there may yet be a chance. The technology for determining a child's sex before birth is available and could save the male-desiring Chinese the problem of disposing of unwanted female children. If a sufficiently large proportion of male children were produced, the population problem in China could solve itself. Many demographers feel that the population problem is overstated and that the future will balance itself in a relatively painless manner. Perhaps people will become accustomed to lower caloric intake and high density living. Perhaps we will continue to ignore areas of dessication and famine until the people go away, and we can say in truth that there are no people or very few people living in a particular area. Perhaps we can ignore the periodic rehabitation of sea-level islands off the coast of Bangaladesh that are just as regularly swept clean of people by typhoons. This pattern continues because there is available land, if for only a few comfortable years of life.

NATURAL RESOURCE EXHAUSTION

The natural resources of the United States are being exhausted. They had reached the turning point by the 1950s, making us a have-not nation. That decade saw for the first time the necessity of importing more than we produce if we were to satisfy our own needs. In recent years, we have felt the first pangs of energy shortage. Other peoples have been inured to these matters for generations. Around the world it has been an accepted fact of life that one could not drink water from the tap or that all of the lights went off at 10 P.M. Only in the last decades have we felt it necessary to restrict building in certain parts of our nation because of a water shortage or an inability to deal with human waste. When the prediction of oil, gas, and electrical shortages reach only months and years into our future, we should be able to read the handwriting on the wall.

Will we become accustomed to heating our homes only during the coldest of times? Will we soon be turning on our water heaters only when we need them? Will the use of bricks in toilet tanks to reduce the amount of water used with each flush become passè in favor of flushing once a day? Will the private automobile be phased out due to the high cost of gasoline and the resultant pollution levels in the air? The vast forests and other inexhaustible resources of the past have visible limits. Although coal appears to be available for use for some time in the future, other fossil fuels have reached a point of crisis. Conceivably oils can be on their way out in the near future. Ores of the better grades have been fast disappearing from the face of the earth, and new methods for extracting lower-grade ores will have to be developed. We are seriously considering the possibility of mining the sea for its mineral content. The labor and energy expended make these processes more expensive than treating pure or relatively pure minerals.

Where will we find the water to allow the processing of our wants? An estimated 100,000 gallons of water goes into the production of a single automobile. If our water is in short supply, the only alternative is to produce fewer automobiles. But what of food itself? While it takes 2,500 gallons of water to produce a single pound of meat, it takes only 69 gallons of water to produce a pound of wheat. As you can see, the availability of water directly affects the table. While in the most fertile areas of the world a beef animal (bovine) requires an acre of ground, the same area may produce 140 bushels of corn. As acreages decrease and people increase, farmers will tend to produce more grains for direct consumption. In many of the grazing areas of the world, a beef steer requires from 20 to 50 acres of ground to survive. While it is difficult to predict when our nation will experience the first real shortages, we can assume that they will arrive before many of us are ready to forego steak. The United States may have to rely on agricultural products for its major export items in the future, but only if our population is maintained near present levels or reduced.

Our energy reserves in oil are diminishing so rapidly that we may have to leap into nuclear fusion for our basic energy form or risk even further environmental pollution through returning to the use of low-grade coal.

Europe, the slowest growing area in the world, is overpopulated when we consider its food supply and production. When the day arrives that population pressure has eradicated the food surplus other countries used to trade for Europe's manufactured and finished products, that continent will have to face a major reorientation of values. Even though countries like Denmark export finished beef, they depend upon the importation of feed for the finishing (graining) of the product.

Food habits will change, and all other sources of protein will be explored, ranging from more economically produced chicken and pork to the newly heralded fish flour with the taste of your choice. In a relatively short period of time, the dangers of cholesterol and high-fat milk will convince the average citizen that meat and its animal by-products are unhealthy. The soya hamburger and fish-flour cake painted with the charcoal-flavored taste will substitute nicely.

Under any circumstances, we will see more nuclear power until the development of a nonpolluting power source, possibly solar energy, wind systems, or someday nonpolluting atomic energy. Our system of built-in obsolescence will have to go in favor of items that do not waste the limited resources now available. We may well live to see the day of the 500,000 mile car.

Recycling materials and the treatment of waste products will be major processes to be developed if we have any hope at all of maintaining minimal standards of living in the next twenty-five years. Today's junk yards and garbage dumps may be the treasure troves of the future. If we do not tend to these matters, we may

SKILL BOX

Reasoning Errors Based on Ambiguity

Some reasoning is invalid because some word or phrase within it is ambiguous, or of uncertain meaning. Of course such errors can be accidental or not, subtle or not. In any case, we should be able to identify them and thus avoid them.

If unclear words are the problem, the error is called equivocation. In this error, the same word is used in different senses within an argument, making the conclusion incorrect. A double meaning in a word can lead to a strange conclusion:

The crime rate of Phoenix is the second highest in the U.S.

The size of our city's crime rate is greater than that of Phoenix.

Therefore, our city's crime rate is the greatest!

This example shows that the danger of equivocation is that it may cause us to reach or accept an incorrect or improper conclusion.

In amphiboly, it is the arrangement of the words that is unclear. Instead of double meanings of a word, the problem is awkward or vague sentence construction which gives a double meaning to the whole sentence. An example is "wrapped up in a paper bag, the woman carried a dozen roses." It is not clear whether the woman or the roses were wrapped in the bag. When a double-meaning sentence is part of an argument, it can produce an incorrect conclusion. This is the danger of amphiboly.

Another error based on ambiguity is one which is more likely to occur in writing than in speaking. It is a matter of accent. A written argument may have different meanings, depending on which words are accented when read. An argument with an unclear or shifting meaning is of little legitimate value. When an unintended meaning is drawn from an argument, or when a quotation changes the accent of an argument, the result is a reasoning error. An example of this problem is seen in the statement:

We should not kill our neighbors.

If the accent is put on the last word, we are left to wonder whom we *may* kill. If the word "kill" receives the accent, we wonder what sort of treatment we *should* give to neighbors. The wrong conclusion can be drawn from such a vague statement, especially if the statement is used as a premise:

We should not kill our neighbors. (Put accent on the last word.)

John is not our neighbor.

Therefore, it is OK to kill John.

Here a deadly error is based on an uncertainty of what accent was intended.

have to face some painful decision-making in the near future. We will, for example, be forced to forego maintenance of the elderly past the point of their productive lives. The insane and the mongoloid will be labeled liabilities whom we will be unable to maintain.

Perhaps genetic matching and counseling will be required in order to acquire a permit to have a child. Donor sperm and ovum or genetic sculpting may allow avoidance of detrimental traits.

OUR CHANGING PHYSICAL ENVIRONMENT

In recent years, the environment has become a popular topic for discussion and argument. It is as though the concept of the environment and its effects on human beings had just been created. This is hardly the case. Humans have been exposed to environmental change since they first walked the face of the earth.

Environmental changes come in two major categories: natural and man-made. Each category has spelled disaster or benefit for the world's human and animal populations. A major environmental change may have caused the demise of the dinosaur, and perhaps a similar change will lead to the disappearance of humankind.

Natural Changes

The ancestors of humans lived at the mercy of natural changes in the environment until developing cultures taught human beings how to adapt to those changes. The use of technology made these adaptions possible. As humans used those methods and tools to adapt to environment, they in turn affected the environment.[16] Indeed, the more developed the society, the greater the change in the environment.

To comprehend the extent of natural environmental changes as well as their effects on our patterns of living, we can look to both geological history and to cultural history for examples.

The history of humankind has been linked with the Pleistocene epoch, which is usually referred to as the Ice Age or Age of the Glaciers. This epoch encompassed four major and many minor advances of glaciers. In turn, the glacial action caused major climatic changes in the environment. Naturally, the presence of many hundreds of feet of solid ice in glacial form limited human and animal residence. The mere presence of such a mass of ice also greatly affected ice-free areas. Due to the immense amounts of water contained in the glaciers, the water level of the world's oceans dropped from 300 feet to 1,000 feet, exposing vast areas that had been and are still covered by water.[17]

Land bridges between continents permitted human and animal migrations. One such land bridge, now called the Bering Strait, linked Asia and North America. It has been estimated to have been as much as one thousand miles wide. This natural environmental change allowed human occupation of an entire continent. Also, the Bering land bridge enabled the ancestors of our

PLEISTOCENE: Geologic epoch associated with the earliest man and what is called the period of glaciation (Ice Age).

Changing conditions may bring us a new ice age.

ECOSYSTEM: A community of plants and animals together with the interacting unit of nonliving material.

modern horse to migrate to Asia and Europe. The beast died out in the Americas but thrived in its new home. Consider the effect of a horseless history on Asia and Europe; somehow it is difficult to imagine the thundering hordes of barbarians walking into battle. Our own history of rapid transportation and power based on the horse would have been limited severely if not prevented.

Cultures rose and fell according to changing climatic patterns caused by the glacial actions. In glacial times, regions that we associate with sandy deserts were exposed to heavy patterns of rainfall. Human and animal life there reacted accordingly when these regions began to dry out as the glaciers retreated. The desert regions of the American Southwest and the Sahara are examples. These areas were once lush and supportive of animal and human life. As the glaciers retreated, the rains decreased, dislocating both human beings and animals. In many areas this process continues. It is clear that the Sahara desert is moving south over a broad bank in Africa, converting savanna into desert. This land, long the home of herd animals, both wild and domesticated, is also used for farming. As it becomes increasingly drier, people and animals either die or move south.

In 1986, a series of unrelated articles appeared in and on television, newspapers, and magazines, dealing with the extremely high water in the Great Lakes, that year over five feet above normal, and the flooding of the Louisiana swampland and delta. Additionally, various states along the eastern seaboard noted higher than normal water levels combined with severe beach erosion. Couple this with a changing weather pattern that may well dry the southeast and there could be evidence of large scale ice-cap melting.

Human contribution has complicated the largely natural phenomenon of the disruption of this ecosystem.[18] Overgrazing, breaking the soil through farming, and lowering subsurface water levels by overuse of wells are only some of the factors that human beings have added to the environmental picture. The introduction of specific domesticated animals has added to the environmental decline of the Middle East. Goats, when overgrazing, tend to strip the countryside of vegetation. They eat young trees and shrubs and strip and kill older trees. When grass is too short, patterns of erosion develop; topsoil disappears, as does the area's ability to retain water. The next phase is a desert that can support very few people.

Two areas are notable examples of cultures dislocated by environmental change. Although the result was the same, the causes differed: one cause was natural changes, the other, the contribution of humans.

The Indus Valley culture consisted of a series of rather advanced farming-based cities on the northwest coasts and plains of the Indian subcontinent. The cities were located on the Indus River or on smaller regional rivers that flowed through a flat plain to the sea. It seems that a minor natural change erased the entire civilization. Parts of the earth's surface are constantly in the process of being raised or lowered, and these movements account for some of our major mountain ranges. A similar movement on a very reduced scale ended the Indus valley civilization. A minor lifting of a section of the earth's surface near the point where the Indus entered the sea caused that river's waters and others to back up. The waters formed lakes and swamps, which covered what had been open plains. At the same time, further inland on the subcontinent, another change occurred in the tilt of the earth's surface. This seemingly minor shift in the tilt of the surfaces of the earth had major consequences.

Water tends to seek its own level; in other words, it runs downhill. As a result of this minor shift, the huge Ganges river system found it more natural to flow to the east of the Indian subcontinent than to the west. City after city abandoned for many centuries can be seen today on the banks of dried rivers. Imagine what would happen if a similar shift in the earth's surface redirected the flow of the major East Coast rivers into the Mississippi drainage system.

A natural shift of a riverbed is causing great concern in the city of New Orleans. An old bed of the Mississippi, today called the Achafalaya River, is receiving more and more of the Mississippi's water. The Army Corps of Engineers is attempting to end the apparent shift in channels, but one huge flood may well result in the river's flowing through Morgan City, Louisiana. This would leave New Orleans with no port facilities. These examples of environmental impact upon human beings are the results of natural changes.

Changes Resulting from Human Activity

Human beings have also made an impact upon their environment. One usually links environmental problems with the recent industrial process. The rapidly multiplying world population has also placed a great strain on the environment. Yet, in surveying history, we find graphic examples of people who altered the face of the earth enough to make it unfit for human life. This happened even in preindustrial times.

The Fertile Crescent of the historic Middle East, which flourished as one of the first of the world's agricultural centers, is a case in point.[19] Many cities and large numbers of people lived in this now sparsely occupied area. The story of what occurred is simple and devastating. Each year as the rivers flooded, the people of the region captured the floodwater in holding ponds to allow its gradual use during the growing season. Over the years, water evaporation in these holding ponds left a mineral residue behind. In time, the minerals became so concentrated that further farming was impossible. The people of the region began this practice near the mouths of the rivers. As more and more land was ruined, they abandoned older cities and built new cities upstream.

Today a visitor to the region will be rewarded with the view of a white landscape covered with a glistening crust of mineral salts. This desert was once called the Fertile Crescent.

These examples of environmental impact upon people and their culture should not be dismissed as irrelevant to modern society. Natural change in the environment continues even with our feeble attempts to alter the inevitable. People have increased the rate of destructive change in the environment, but they have a poor track record for improvement. In view of our recent attempts to recreate a more desirable landscape, we can look to several major projects at home and abroad.

One of the largest projects has been the Aswan high dam on the Nile River in Egypt. In addition to the creation of electric power badly needed in the country, the dam was constructed to raise the level of the stored water to a height that would allow the irrigation of what is referred to as the low desert. The low desert was being cultivated to feed Egypt's growing population, but the population growth far exceeded the production gain.[20]

In addition to the discouraging results of the farming program, there have been environmental problems that may be of disastrous proportions. As water piles up behind a dam, evaporation reduces the actual water and leaves behind its mineral content. The example of the Fertile Crescent illustrates this action, which left to future inhabitants of that area the crusted earth. The irrigation project itself tends to increase the mineral content as it seeps through the earth and reenters the river. The increased salinity of the water affects the river's delicate balance of life. As the water sits captured behind the dam, or as it is used for irrigation, its temperature tends to rise. This makes it unsuitable for many of the forms of plant and animal life which have adapted to that environmental niche. These forms typically react by dying out.

Human beings dependent on these forms suddenly find that they must readjust their lives. The dam also prevents yearly flooding of the valley floor, which refertilizes the soil. Other unforeseen results of the dam included lowering the river level, and thus the flow of Mediterranean salt water into the Nile delta region, reducing its fertility. The reduced flow of water has, in turn, affected the ecosystem in the Mediterranean itself. Water entering the sea usually has a higher nutritional level than the sea itself. As a result, the environment can support a much larger population, which in this case is comprised of many edible varieties of fish and other sea life. With the reduction of the Nile's flow and the reduction of nutrients, the population of sea life has also decreased sharply. A disastrous reduction in the amount of human food harvested from the sea resulted.

Our own nation has seen many parallel situations. We may view a classic natural water capture, such as the Great Salt Lake, as an extreme example of what may occur in time at the sites of many of our man-made lakes. People tend to think of the environment as unchanging, while the ecologist knows that a swamp is a silted-up lake. All lakes eventually die; how soon they die is frequently up to humans. The use of dams for drinking water and crop irrigation with no provision for building a forest watershed

SALINITY: Having the quality of salt; the quality of being salty.

NICHE: Place of activity or existence.

WATERSHED: The area drained by a particular body of water.

MARGINAL: Just barely acceptable.

Skill Reinforcer 14-1 *

What is the difficulty in establishing a cause-effect relationship between population growth and extinction?

MEGALOPOLIS: A "super city" formed when several cities grow together into one urban area.

* Answers to the Skill Reinforcers appear at the end of the chapter.

with the project is quickly changing marginal lands into tomorrow's deserts, and fertile lands into marginal regions.

The American West, barely a century old, has been used in ways that would never in thousands of years have occurred naturally. Water tables have dropped disastrously and cannot be replenished at this point. Forests have been cut, further reducing the watershed. Overirrigation has reduced soil fertility with mineral-laden water and wasteful farming techniques.

The situation would not be so dangerous if it did not occur at a point of fantastic demand brought on by this century's increasing population pressure. An organism, and people are organisms, can survive only as long as the environment can support it. Over and over in the history of the world, populations of one sort or another have grown out of proportion to their niches in the environment. Experiments conducted with everything from fruit flies to bacteria show populations that tend to grow up to and exceed their natural limits. At this point, the population reduces rapidly to extinction.

For many years it has been accepted that laboratory experiments of this nature do not apply to people because they do not live in a closed system. Historically, humans were wanderers. They would eat an area clean and then move on to greener pastures. Unfortunately, this situation has changed. Greener pastures are no longer available. The vast open spaces of the New World are filling in, and while humans have a few places to hide, not many remain.

For several generations the escapists of the United States have run away to California. California today has the largest population in the country. In many areas of the state, drinking water and breathable air are major problems. The Los Angeles megalopolis is rapidly stretching through the orange groves to grasp San Diego to the south, and in time it may reach Santa Barbara in the north. A motor trip along the Pacific Coast may well open the eyes of the unconvinced. After spending a short time admiring the scenery, one becomes very conscious of another element composed of people, all wanting to escape from something. The coastal highway is filled with groups of people, all seemingly seeking the wild, unsullied country no longer present. The escapists stand facing the sea with no place to go.

It is time that we start to walk back inland to survey the devastation of our environment and plan what might be done to salvage the remains. To consider the problem properly, we must first conquer basic desires. The most basic, it seems, is the desire to look at the world and to feel that it is too big to kill.

The forests can die, and they do die, as they are dying today from acid rain. The Great Lakes can die—one is already dead. The oceans themselves can die, and they are in the process of doing so. Major fertile areas of the world can die, and some have already done so. Witness the Fertile Crescent and our near miss with the Dust Bowl of the 1930s. The midwestern drought of the mid-1970s seriously affected winter wheat production in 1976. National weather forecasters foresee the possibility of a four- to six-year continuation of this dry cycle. Also, our "vast underground reserves of water, deposited over thousands of years, have been seriously depleted in a matter of decades," largely by greatly increased irrigation.[21]

The answers to our environmental problems are difficult to find and more difficult to follow through. If our population is to continue to grow uncontrolled, we may expect more large-scale famines like those that have already begun in sub-Saharan Africa and in parts of Asia.[22] As population pressure increases the drain on the environment, established ecosystems will collapse. This will leave those surplus-producing areas of the world to make a choice that will be painful regardless of the decision. It will be necessary to ship needed food from surplus areas in a vain attempt to hold off ultimate famine, or to let vast numbers of people die immediately.

This line of reasoning is practiced on a smaller scale in hospitals around the world. If a major accident occurs involving a large number of people, normally an attempt is made to save first those having a better chance of survival. In other words, a doctor or another person in authority weighs each case and selects the person to treat first. People with minor injuries may wait, but doctors abandon marginal cases to ensure the survival of the greatest number possible.

It will come to pass within our lifetime that a choice of this nature will be made on the level of millions of people. At that point, we may expect either the quiet death of a significant portion of the world's population or a major series of food wars.

SUMMARY

We have by no means dealt with all of the major environmental threats or changes. The subject of our environment has already been responsible for a wave of research and writing that fills many library shelves and grows larger by the day.

Throughout our short history humankind has had the ability to ruin a landscape and move on. That ability no longer exists. Our natural resources are quickly being consumed by our population, which has grown to such an extent that, in the course of our lifetime, we may experience a worldwide population reduction of disastrous proportions. Some of the possibilities and causes of this impending reduction have been discussed in reference to our depletion of fertile soils, air, climatic alteration and safe drinking water.

Experiments with various animals forms have clearly indicated that there is indeed a limit to population density. Experiments with bacterial colonies have shown them to grow rapidly until they outgrow the limits of their environment and die. Tests with fruit flies provide the same evidence: a rapid population rise, a period of equilibrium, and, as the environment is polluted, a quick decline of population to zero. Observation of the natural cycles of growth and decline of animal population shows much the same configuration. When food is plentiful and the living space adequate, there is a population rise. When the food supply at the lower levels of the food chain is depleted, population falls.

We find it difficult to view the death of vast numbers of our kind realistically. Objective scientific studies have for quite some time pointed to the exhaustion of our environment, yet we forge ahead toward disaster, safe in the false knowledge that we can conquer the problems that have spelled extinction for other species. This knowledge is based on our past performance in a time of small population and ostensibly unlimited resources. It is difficult to understand or comprehend the human adaptions necessary to enable us to survive in a poisoned environment and with insufficient food at present levels. The human organism may well survive in greatly reduced numbers and at a much lower standard of living.

SPECIAL TOPIC
A Balancing Act Between Hot and Cold

We have all heard about pollution, about the ways people have damaged the environment. Geographers and other scientists have been studying the topic for years. They have pointed out to us just how close to disaster we have come. This Special Topic will explore how delicate the balance between disaster and survival has become.

As part of this chapter we have seen how humans have affected their living space, but on only a small scale. Today we see that the scale of this damage has been enlarged. For example, earlier studies have shown that even a slight shift in temperature can enlarge or shrink the earth's ice caps. Also, the action of just one volcano can have resounding effects on the world's environment.

The volcanic eruption in 1815 of Mount Tambora in Indonesia threw enough ash into the world's atmosphere to affect the climate in distant continents significantly. The northern portion of the United States found that the year 1816 brought no summer. In July the temperature in England was five full degrees below the average. Records show that the lowest average temperature in England coincided with volcanic eruptions in Japan, Indonesia, and Iceland.[23] The most interesting fact is that in each instance the climate was noticeably affected for periods of more than ten years.[24]

Volcanic eruptions can still occur; Mount Saint Helens is a good example. A general increase in eruptions adds more heat-reflecting pollutants to our atmosphere. That could cool the earth and be the straw that breaks the camel's back. The lowered agricultural yield of a world subjected to noticeably cooler temperatures could trigger famines in some parts.

While nature causes volcanic pollution, humans have complicated this picture. We make agricultural, industrial, and personal additions to the atmosphere. Taken as part of a larger picture, our air pollution has caused a much greater reflection of the sun's heat than in times past. Those who study climate only partially agree on the cause-and-effect relationships of many of the newer forms of atmospheric pollution.

They agree that the movement of the storm track and jet streams to the north or south greatly affects climate. In turn, the presence and size of the polar ice caps affect the positioning of the storm track and jet stream. If, for example, these phenomena should adopt more northerly courses, the Great Plains of the United States could quickly become the greater American desert. Also, the ice caps would enlarge and begin a new glacial advance. The enlargement of the southern polar cap could have even greater consequences.[25] If that ice cap shifted into the sea by virtue of its greater weight, the resultant tidal wave could flood major portions of the world. The sea level could rise as much as 100 feet. This would place most of the world's coastal areas under the sea.

This enlargement of the ice caps could also start our next ice age. If the sun's rays are reflected, heat loss is experienced. In other words, rays of the sun falling on snow or ice will be reflected back into the atmosphere rather than being absorbed as heat. Anywhere from 30 to 90 percent of the possible heat energy can be lost, depending on the condition of the ice and snow.

On the average, forests and farmland reflect anywhere from 10 to 30 percent of the possible light energy. The change of a forest region to desert will reduce the amount of heat the region absorbs. We must consider the greater heat loss of a desert.

In the late 1800s, less than 10 percent of the earth's surface was classed as desert. In a period of twenty years, the total desert region had increased to over 23 percent of the earth's total land surface. Today the Sahara desert is advancing southward in Africa at an average rate of two miles per year over a distance of thousands of miles.

Although the average advance of the Sahara has remained constant for a period of time, the pace seems to be increasing in several areas. In the former French West Africa, the desert is advancing at a rate of as much as thirty miles a year in response to the area's disastrous drought.[26] This region includes six countries: Chad, Mali, Mauritania, Niger, Senegal, Gambia, and Upper Volta. The affected area covers more than 5.5 million square kilometers.

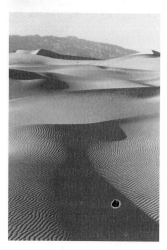

The growth of deserts serves to cool the atmosphere.

The area of the Thar Desert of western India, once a jungle, increases in every direction at a rate of one-half mile per year. This newly created desert now covers over 60,000 square miles, and in time it may rival the Sahara. As these deserts grow, the earth actually absorbs less heat and, as a result, the atmosphere begins to cool.

The world's balance between hot and cold is also affected by the heat arising from the creation of energy. All energy except incidental solar energy must eventually wind up as heat that warms the atmosphere.

We have already seen the beginnings of major effects of pollution in this area of the world. For example, a common weather broadcast reads, "thirty-two degrees in the city tonight, and somewhat cooler in outlying suburbs." It might be assumed that suburbia is simply cooler.[27] Cities, particularly U.S. cities, consume vast quantities of energy. The loss of some of this energy in the form of heat—thermal pollution—has caused what are referred to as heat islands around cities. There is also the added consequence of many large buildings blocking normal wind action. Another factor is the heat-reflective qualities of vertical building surfaces. The situation becomes even more complex when these factors are considered.

In the past, the prime concern in construction was the commercial advantage of location. Next came the need for an economical structure suitable for its functions and pleasing to the eye. In Boston a large office building with a permanently sealed glass surface was constructed. Until the windows were replaced, the areas around the building were used only at great risk, because the large plate-glass windows continually popped out of their frames and whirled to the street below. An unpredictable channeling and compression of the wind around buildings in the area had created this abnormal situation. As more and more large buildings are erected, these abnormalities will persist.

The heat-reflective qualities of buildings are another matter. Rather than striking one surface, the rays of the sun bounce from one building to the ground, to a second and sometimes a third building. Each of these structures retains some of the heat energy that under natural conditions would be lost. The construction materials of the buildings and the ground cover tend to retain more heat than natural ground cover. If we sum up these conditions, we find the following factors, among many others, that affect the climate of urban areas:

1. Less solar radiation on horizontal surfaces
2. Less ultraviolet radiation
3. Lower mean relative humidity
4. Lower annual wind speed
5. Lower speed to wind gusts
6. Higher frequency of calms
7. Higher frequency of cloudiness
8. Almost twice as much fog and smog
9. A higher annual precipitation
10. A greater number of days with minimal precipitation

A 10– to 15–degree temperature difference between the city and the surrounding area seems to exist regardless of the size of the city. Size of the urban area makes a difference in the total climate.[28] Small cities differ climatically from their suburbs less often than do large cities. Large cities appear to have weather unlike the patterns that could be expected if the city were absent.

The city's climatic situation and air pollution is an extreme in the study of the effect of humans on environment, but they indicate a future worldwide trend that we can expect as population density increases. Today we can find evidence of air pollution in isolated areas in the South Pacific, thousands of miles from major industrial or urban centers.

Concentrations of people have brought about other disturbing changes in the environment which will haunt us in the future. The items are too numerous to discuss in detail, but some of humanity's major crimes against nature may prove interesting. We have seen that people have affected climate and that through this action the climate has affected the nature of the environment. For example, people cut down trees, overgraze some land, and overfarm other land. In turn, nature reacts by creating desert areas. If there is no watershed to absorb runoff or to receive and retain solar energy, we can expect the erosion of topsoil and the disappearance of moisture. If we interfere with the atmosphere, we can expect the storm track and jet stream to shift. As these changes occur, the nature of our environment shifts, and deserts are created. Deserts may have been created anyway, but people have certainly aided and abetted their growth.

We will see if the pollution added to the atmosphere in recent decades will affect the climate enough to push us into a new ice age, but there is no use in looking over our shoulder to the north, expecting to see immediate signs of approaching glaciers. Still, if things continue to operate as they have in the past, by the time humankind acknowledges the danger it will be too late to do anything. If the ice cap melts, we have a problem; if the ice cap grows, we have a problem.

The changes in the delicate balance of hot and cold have been caused by two major sets of stimuli. On the one hand, the world's climatic environment has constantly undergone change naturally. The appearance in recent geological times of an entire series of glacial advances and retreats should have been sufficient warning that our present era is merely a period between major glaciations. There is no logical reason for the mere presence of human beings suddenly to cast nature into an unchanging, balanced state. On the other hand, humans have increasingly added the elements of their culture to the environmental whole, and these, in turn, have seriously increased the pace of change in our environment. This change has served to make the balance between hot and cold more delicate, and disaster much closer.

SELF-TEST QUESTIONS

Determine whether each of the following statements is true or false.

1. Our population growth has a base in an altered death rate rather than a change in the birth rate.
2. Demography deals with the physical features of the world's surface.
3. The Aswan Dam has proven a great success in Egypt's fight over food shortage.
4. Our developed technology will have no trouble providing for a population of 12 billion by 2050.
5. We can always increase farm acres for agriculture.
6. We may well see famine and disease control our population for us.

7. Our environment changes due to both natural and human causes.

8. Humankind is associated with the Pleistocene.

9. Human actions have changed the desert into what is called the Fertile Cresent.

10. It is possible that future famines may be ignored by food-producing nations.

ANSWERS TO SELF-TEST QUESTIONS

1. true	6. true
2. false	7. true
3. false	8. true
4. false	9. false
5. false	10. true

ANSWER TO SKILL REINFORCER

14–1. To prove cause-effect, we need an experiment in which all relevant variables are controlled. As the sentence in the paragraph notes, "laboratory experiments of this nature do not apply to people because they do not live in a closed system." That is, our ethics do not permit scientists to subject humans to the amount of control needed in an experiment aimed at proving cause-effect. In this case, to prove that overpopulation leads to extinction we would have to require a group of humans to live under the strains and dangers of overpopulation in an isolated (closed), controlled environment. We can do this with mice and keep our consciences clear. We cannot do so with humans.

NOTES

1. *Population Reference Bulletin,* vol. 18, no. 1 (Washington, D.C.: Population Reference Bureau, 1962).

2. Daniel Defoe, *A Journal of the Plague Year* (London: Dent, 1908).

3. William Langer, "The Black Death," *Scientific American* 210 (February 1964).

4. "Recent Mortality Trends in Chile," *National Center for Health Statistics,* series 3, no. 2 (Washington, D.C.: U.S. Public Health Service, 1964).

5. National Center for Health Statistics, 1984, vol. 35, number 6 (Washington, D.C.: Government Printing Office, 1984).

6. *Population Bulletin of the United States,* no. 6–1962 (New York: United Nations, 1963).

7. A.M. Carr-Saunders, *World Population: Past Growth and Present Trends* (Oxford: Clarendon Press, 1936).

8. United Nations, Department of Economic and Cultural Affairs, *Statistical Yearbook 1965* (New York: United Nations, 1966).

9. United Nations, *The World Population Situation in 1970–1975 and Its Long-range Implications,* Population Studies no. 56 (New York: United Nations, 1974).

10. National Geographic Society, 1985.

11. U.N., *Statistical Yearbook 1965.*

12. Georg Borgstrom, *The Hungry Planet* (New York: Macmillan Co., 1965).

13. U.N., *Statistical Yearbook 1965.*

14. Darryl G. Cole, "The Myth of Fertility Dooms Development Plan," *National Observer,* April 22, 1968.

15. Donella H. Meadows et al., *The Limits of Growth* (New York: Universe Books, 1972).

16. D.R. Hughes and D.R. Brothwell, *The Earliest Population of Man in Europe, West Asia, and North America* (Cambridge, Eng.: Cambridge University Press, 1966).

17. K.W. Butzer, *Physical Conditions in Eastern Europe, Western Asia, and Egypt Before the Period of Agricultural and Urban Settlement* (Cambridge, Eng.: Cambridge University Press, 1965).

18. Ibid.

19. Ibid.

20. Paul R. Ehrlich and Anne H. Ehrlich, *Population, Resources, and Environment* (San Francisco: W.H. Freeman, 1970).

21. "The Browning of America," *Newsweek,* February 23, 1981, p. 26.

22. "On the Road to Agadez, Nigeria," *The New York Times,* August 12, 1973.

23. Ehrlich and Ehrlich, *Population, Resources, and Environment.*

24. Harry Wexler, "Volcanoes and World Climate," *Scientific American* 186 (April 1952).

25. A.T. Wilson, "Origin of Ice Ages: An Ice Shelf Theory for Pleistocene Glaciation," *Nature* 201 (January 1964).

26. United Nations, "Drought in Africa: Questions and Answers," Office of Public Information, June 18, 1974.

27. William P. Lowry, "The Climate of Cities," *Scientific American* 217 (August 1967).

28. Ibid.

SUGGESTED READINGS

Bates, Marston, *The Forest and the Sea: A Look at the Economy of Nature and the Ecology of Man.* New York: Random House, 1960.

Borgstrom, Georg. *The Hungry Planet.* New York: Macmillan Co., 1967.

Brown, Harrison. *The Challenge of Man's Future.* New York: Viking Press, 1954.

Lanegran, David, and Palm, Risa. *An Invitation to Geography.* New York: McGraw-Hill, 1978.

Witthuhn, Burton, et al. *Discovery in Geography.* Dubuque: Kendall/Hunt Publishing Co., 1976.

Zimolzak, Chester, and Stansfield, Charles. *The Human Landscape: Geography and Culture.* Columbus, Ohio: Charles E. Merrill Publishing Co., 1979.

15 CITIES

My City Has Changed

You lock your door, once with the latch, once with a chain, and then with a bar. Your windows are nailed shut, and you have hung wire mesh on the outside. You are safe, to a degree, but you cannot go outside until morning. The streets swarm with groups of teenagers and young adults, many of whom would just as soon hit you over the head and rob you as they would say "Good morning."

In the morning you will call your friends and neighbors and see if any of them want to go shopping. If enough people go together it will be safer. At lunchtime a van will come to take you to the senior-citizen center to eat and spend some time. When you return, you will lock yourself into your fortress, watch television, and hope no one breaks down the door.

You grew up in this city, and it never used to be like this. How did it change? Why did a friendly, safe, enjoyable city become a prison? Why are the streets so dirty? Why are you afraid to sit on your front porch? Years ago, old folks spent their old age outside in the sun. In the evening they had lawn bowling and quoits. People would go to friends' houses for evening coffee. Now people lock themselves in their homes.

Why did your children move from the neighborhood? When you grew up, you married and found a home in the same neighborhood, but your children live a thousand miles away and come to see you once a year. They call on your birthdays and on holidays, but they are not here to help you. The only people here today are other old people and strangers. The question remains . . . What caused my city to change?

My City Has Changed— A Second Scenario

My family has lived in this house in the same neighborhood for as long as I can remember. We have gone to the same house of worship, with the same people since my Grandfather came to this country before the turn of the century. The bakeries and the food stores all smell familiar and are not at all like the supermarkets. Yet something has changed. There are new owners of some of the local taverns and restaurants. The people who go to these places are new and very well dressed. The television is not tuned to the ball game and very few people order beer and a shot. Quiche has replaced the free lunch.

New people are buying houses on the street and the prices they pay are very high. Ten years ago you could get a house for twenty thousand dollars, but the same house today sells for four hundred and fifty thousand dollars. The people that pay these prices smile and think they have found a bargain. They say that the same house across the river in New York would cost two and a half million dollars. As the new people buy and rebuild our houses, the real estate taxes go up so high that many of us do not make enough money in an entire year to pay these new taxes. There are more people selling out and moving away, the churches do not have enough members to continue and they sell. The streets are clean, the bakeries smell different, and the food stores sell gourmet items. I do not recognize anyone anymore and feel as a stranger in my own home town. I will have to move out, but where shall I go? Where has my town gone?

URBAN: Of, in, constituting, or comprising a city or town.

As you read this page, you are most likely engulfed by an urban environment. The scene outside is probably dominated by objects made by humans rather than by nature. There may be more people than trees, more cars than wildflowers. Even if you are outside an urban area, you cannot easily escape its influence. Most of your politics, your entertainment, and your goods and service come from the city.

CITY: A settlement that consistently generates its economic growth from its community.

Because of the ways the city touches your life, you are somewhat familiar with it. And if you live in the city, you know the city, right? To some extent, yes. In this chapter, however, you have the chance to look at the city in new ways, which can enable you to anticipate its challenges and enjoy what it has to offer.

First, we will define a city, and in doing so, explore its nature. Then you will learn why the city changes and look at some specific changes, such as urban decay, which affect you in ways you may not have realized.

DEFINING A CITY

How should we go about defining a city? We could talk about the number of people that live in a city, but a city is better defined in other ways. We will approach this task by exploring the factors essential for the birth of a city—its prerequisites. Further, we can contrast the city with a noncity—a village. Last, we can explore the various types of cities. This process will define the nature of the city for you.

Prerequisites for a City

Before we can deal with the problems of cities, we should understand the conditions that called for their creation. What led to the establishment of a city? What conditions must there be before we recognize that a city is needed? Why must these preconditions continue in order to ensure the lasting viability of the urban unit? Last, what happens if the preconditions that led to the establishment of a city suddenly no longer exist?

Exposure to history, legend, and the mass media has shown us idealized versions of the establishment of various cities. Romulus and Remus, for example, suddenly appear and choose a pleasant hilly section on the banks of the Tiber, where they decide to build a city. Our children are impressed by the idea that these two gentlemen, after spending an enjoyable childhood as the stepchildren of a friendly she-wolf, just happened on the idea of building a new city. The story suggests that a city comes about merely when someone desires to build one. After construction is well under way, it is decided that the city needs women, so the new Romans capture the women needed from their neighbors, the Sabines.

This is a simplistic view of the birth of Rome, an urban center that was, in time, to rule most of the known world. We may smile and feel superior to the uncomplicated natives of ancient Rome, but we have only to see a movie or a television show that depicts the settlement of a U.S. city to realize that our legends are similar. A wagon train suddenly stops; everyone gazes at the valley extending for miles. The wagon-train leader states, "Here the new city of _____ will be built." The viewer has had no indication why that particular place was chosen. The point is that we are not concerned ourselves with the basic economic and social requirements of the city.

One way to study the prerequisites for a city is to contrast the city with the village. Villages and cities are opposites, and if a residential area does not meet the requirements for a city, it is a village. Keep this in mind as we explore the prerequisites for a city.

First, an urban center or city must have a settlement much larger than a village. Population density would have to increase to the point where the residents could no longer produce enough food for their needs.

Along with this, a controlled countryside must provide food on a regular basis. To provide enough food to support the city, a system of specialized "agriculture" must produce a significant food surplus.[1] The surplus allows the development and maintenance of all the other prerequisites for an urban area.

SPECIALIZATION: Following a special or limited line of endeavor.

In a society lacking true specialization, the division of labor is based upon age and sex.[2] Children have specific duties and responsibilities. When children reach adolescence, they are assigned chores based once again on their age and sex. Adolescent males may be charged with gathering firewood and learning to hunt, or they may be trained as warriors. Young girls learn to gather roots, cook, plant and harvest crops, care for children, and develop homemaking skills. Men clear the land for their wives, protect the community, and hunt; women bear children, plant, harvest, and gather food. The aged are expected to perform similar duties according to their ages and their abilities. The unspecialized society depends little on skill, since all its members engage in most of its activities.

In addition, the development of cities requires predictive science. For example, for food production, the ability to predict the seasons accurately is vitally important. Contemporary people find it difficult to comprehend the difficulties involved in such predicting. In brief, people must be able to note and record relevant and consistent changes in the position of the sun, moon, and stars. Years of trial and error passed before a satisfactory system of measuring time evolved. One of the first attempts to deal with this problem was probably associated with the occurrences of full moons. While many people believe that there is a full moon every month, in actuality twelve full moons comprise only almost a year. Twelve lunar months equal approximately 354 days, but the solar year is 365.25 days. So we would not have to use the lunar calendar for many years before we would find so-called winter holidays falling in midsummer. The measure of a year demanded a formula more accurate than the lunar calendar. Eventually people figured out that the earth reached the same position in the sky every 365 days. Once more they had erred, but only by one-quarter of a day, or slightly more than six hours. If this situation had remained uncorrected, the correlation between the actual position of earth and the calendar would be accurate only every 1,460 years. Thus, unless the people can correct the error in the 365-day year by adding a full day every four years, the calendar is not really serviceable. Once this ability was developed, the city could more readily arise.

The ability to compile written records is also a prerequisite. Written records enable the compiler of calendric data to record pertinent materials for future use.[3] And an area with surplus goods demands a means of recording debts and credits arising from trading such goods. Written records are also necessary for planning and implementing public projects. Records are necessary to keep track of the tax and/or tribute collected. Here the predictive science too is necessary, to forecast need and supply of all monies and materials involved in projects.

Another prerequisite is the establishment of a central community authority to plan and carry out the building of monumental or public works such as pyramids or canals.

The availability of luxury items is another prerequisite for a city. As a rule, people do not assume responsibility without some extra reward for their services, which takes the form of more of the better things of life awarded to specific individuals, who have the ability to work, a sense of responsibility, or inherited position. Better and more food, clothing, servants, luxury items in general—such things separate the mass of people from those enjoying this higher level of existence. We are describing a stratified society where some people live better than others in exchange for efforts directed toward the initiation and construction of monumental works or public projects.

Long-distance trade enlarges the scope of items offered to the members of any society. In an area where nothing is desired, there will be little work expended above the level of the typical person. If the products of specialists are available for consumption both in our society and in societies more distant, there will be a desire on the part of the people to work for such goods.

The last urban prerequisite discussed here deals with the state's assumption of authority, as opposed to the authority held by the family. While this may sound complicated, it is not, and its effect on social reaction, while not always apparent, is great.

CLAN: An early form of social group, composed of several families living in residential proximity, with group ownership of land and major items. Usually unilinear in nature integrating some affinals and alienating some blood relatives.

In a society where an extended family or clan holds the authority and power, we might find restricted urbanization. Under such a system, individuals do not necessarily own goods, land, and other items. Ownership—and thus authority—is community-oriented and held by the kin group. Because the family owns all, individuals are reluctant to leave home, for they would face the loss of their rights to the family property. And because the family would assume any items acquired or commodities earned, there is also reluctance to extend oneself. The ability of an individual to own and hold property is of primary importance for the development of an urban situation.

In sum, prerequisites for an urban area include:

1. Larger settlement size and associated surplus
2. Craft specialization based on criteria other than age and sex
3. Predictive science
4. Written records
5. Monumental or public works
6. Capital gained through tax or tribute
7. Luxury items
8. Stratified society
9. Long-distance trade
10. Centralization of the state power to the detriment of familial ties

City or Big Village? It is easy to list prerequisites for what we call the urban condition. It is more difficult to understand what the presence or absence of the same criteria means in the life of an individual or a group. Many residential centers around the world which are home for thousands of people do not qualify as cities.

In India, villages with a population of 20,000 or 25,000 people are common, yet they remain villages. Uninformed visitors would classify these residential centers as villages even without knowing the prerequisites for urban development. They know somehow that they are actually visiting a village.

Village life is based upon face-to-face contact between residents. This is generally of an informal nature.

We may link agriculture, which permits a relative residential stability, with a developing technology. People engaged in agriculture are forced to remain sedentary. They are bound to the land in that a cleared field is an investment in time and labor and a planted field must be nurtured, guarded, and later harvested. With the crops harvested, the mere bulk calls for storage, for its purpose is to provide foodstuff for the months when the fields are idle. The work in the growing season results in survival in the off-season. In most instances, work on the site provides sufficient reason for the farmer to remain near the fields to prepare the next season's crop. The surplus expected from agriculture allows either the farmer or some specialist to work on methods of easing labor and improving crop yield. This is the basis of a developing technology. For example, storage facilities are only one product of the newly developing technology. Humans had to invent a whole complex of ceramic arts in order to produce the jugs, jars, and large grain vessels needed for food storage.

GESELLSCHAFT: Transitory and impersonal life style typical of urban or city life.

GEMEINSCHAFT: Intimate, face to face relationships typical of small village life.

NOMADS: Members of a group having no permanent home but moving constantly in search of food, pasture, etc.

Beyond this, the village differs from the city mainly in its attitudes toward life. These changes in attitude stem from the manner in which village life is lived with face to face contact and intimate informal relationships prevailing (see Gemeinschaft), as opposed to the impersonal, unstable, and anonymous life encountered in cities (see Gesellschaft).

A third category, the thoroughly rural, nomadic wanderer, will clarify the understanding of villagers and urban residents. (The difference we are describing is a matter of degree.)

While villagers are generally assumed to be conservative in nature, city life is shaped by and accommodates rapid, sometimes violent, change. The term "conservative" refers in this case to an attitude aimed at preserving the status quo, or the pattern in practice. The perpetuation of systems and statuses seems to characterize village life. The rigid social system associated with stable, extended-family oriented communities reinforces this essential conservatism. In such communities, simple age and sex categories may determine social position. If the community is built upon a land-based economy, the land itself will be owned and controlled, allowing little change in ownership. Commonly, people inherit their land. A strong land-based economy, where one may acquire the land only through inheritance, blocks the lines of social mobility. This leaves little opportunity for social or economic improvement based on personal achievement.

Urban life differs greatly in that inherited position, while important, is based more frequently on fluid assets more likely to be exchanged outside a family situation. While land is constant and always here, money and other fluid assets fluctuate. Skilled craftspeople cannot always pass on their talents to their children. While children, because of early and constant exposure, tend to develop knowledge and skill in a parent's craft, inheritance of a skill differs from inheritance of land.

Types of Cities

Cities fall into two major categories: administrative centers and commercial centers. Accessibility is the main requirement for an administrative center. If a city is created to house an administration of government, religion, or other large organizations, we can assume that the necessary surplus of foodstuffs will be available from the group served. The available surplus will ensure support of craft specialists and allow public works. The organization itself will provide the stratified status requirement that calls for luxury items and trade. The surplus mentioned also provides for all the other requirements. Washington, D.C., is a fine example of an administrative city. The vast number of government employees and specialists provides the economic core. Attendant services that have been created live off the surplus provided by the public payroll.

The other basic form of city is based on commerce, or industry. If we consider the world's early cities, we find many examples of urban placement in a proper commercial location. The ancient city of Troy sat in a desirable commercial location, near the juncture of the Black Sea and the Mediterranean Sea. There the commercial aspects of receiving goods from each area and selling them to other areas could not be overlooked. Most of the history taught in schools neglects the wide region to the north and east of the Holy Land. The first knowledge students receive of that region is normally with the romanticized journey of Marco Polo during the Middle Ages. The Polos followed an old trade route from the Mediterranean area to China. Goods may well have been shipped eventually through Troy during those earlier times.

If we examine a map of North America, noting the location of our early cities, we can see the reasons for these establishments.

The construction of the Erie Canal is considered this period's greatest technical feat.

Montreal and Quebec, both located on the St. Lawrence River, control access to the interior of the continent via the Great Lakes system. Boston, Salem, and Plymouth have good harbors, and they are protected by Cape Cod. In addition to maintaining the import-export trade, these ports and others served as bases for the whaling industry. New York has a fine harbor suitable for import trade, and it has access to the Hudson and Mohawk river system for trade to the interior. The creation of the New York State barge canal enhanced New York's position as a commercial center and allowed quick access and trade to the interior via Buffalo and the Great Lakes. A number of New Jersey cities were located on the fall line in a manner typical at the time when water power was in vogue. Cities such as New Brunswick and Trenton, which located then at the head of navigation on the Raritan and Delaware rivers, had the advantage of water power to serve their growing industries. In time, the Delaware and Raritan canal system linked these cities.

Often, early cities in the United States, such as Norfolk, Charleston, Baltimore, San Francisco, and, later, Seattle are known once again for their port facilities and their access to interior trade. New Orleans is located in a place that could be described only as a setting for a pest hole, but it has one attribute that makes it an important commercial center. Located near the mouth of the Mississippi/Missouri river system, New Orleans serves as the seaport for the entire middle of the United States.

Placement, position of convenience, and control of commercial trade routes give the partial list of cities discussed something in common. They share an orientation of commerce through trade and manufacturing.

Other cities created from the discovery of mineral deposits have had boom and bust periods. Cities have been known to die when their commercial bases falter. Our boom towns of the West disappeared when silver or gold deposits ran out. Unless other industry had developed during the period of the boom to supply the surplus needed to support the complex operation of an urban center, the city had no further reason to live. This is important to remember when dealing with difficulties experienced by some of our present-day cities. Removal of the economic bases means death.

WHY CITIES CHANGE

As we watch the evening news on television, we might see a report on a city slum. The buildings, streets, and services are clearly decaying. A few minutes later, a news report offers a glimpse of another city, a shining new one. There business is booming and the people prosper. We have just seen two cities changing in opposite directions. Reflecting on the contrasts, we wonder uneasily which direction the city in which we live or on which we depend will take in the next decades.

Skill Reinforcer 15-1*

What kind of reasoning would proceed from knowledge of these several cities to a general statement concerning all such cities?

* Answers to the Skill Reinforcers appear at the end of the chapter.

Several factors affect the way cities change. These include economics and the related factors of energy and transportation. You can watch these factors in your own city if you are trying to predict the changes it will go through next.

Economic Factors   Modern examples of the change in economic conditions affecting various cities are easy to find.

Any one of a large number of smaller single-industry towns died after the industry closed down and the need for the city vanished. The ghost towns of the West still serve as mute reminders of the days when they had an economic purpose. The gold or silver that stimulated their growth either disappeared or became uneconomical to mine, and the city died. It no longer needed the specialists who had gathered to service producers from the mining industry. After all, who needs a first-class laundry, restaurant, jeweler, barber, blacksmith, doctor, or anyone else if no one with money remains to purchase these services?

The same situation occurred at a later date in cities built around the railroad industry. Entire economies were based on the wage earner employed at the local railroad repair house or transfer yard. When this industry died, a victim of the vanishing age of steam, towns dried up in much the same way that mining towns evaporated.

Mines are not responsible for the Newarks, Oaklands, and Chicagos, so what really happened? The answer involves many interrelated causes and contributing factors. These cause-and-effect relationships will be treated simply, without attendant graphs, charts, and figures, but their meanings are apparent. In days past, the typical major industrial city was generally a high-density entity. In other words, large numbers of people lived, worked, and shopped in a restricted area. Those were the days of the townhouse and row tenement. The factory town is an example of this form of residence-work pattern.

There was a reason for this residential distribution pattern: transportation.[4] How far could people live from the site of their work if the only mode of transportation available was the horse? The commuter train had yet to come about, and while trains were available they were expensive; in addition to the price of train travel, schedules were inadequate for mass transit. Eventually the train and subway replaced the horse-drawn trolley, and the city limits extended further afield. Although these limits were extended, however, they were still bound by the availability of transportation. Only the arrival of the automobile age and the death of steam extended cities far along the new corridors offered by growing highway networks.

When dealing with urban change in the United States, an economic factor to consider is the pressure brought on by the Depression in 1929 and by World War II. Prior to this time, there had been a normal replacement of structures in the central urban com-

The one-time flourishing coal mining town of Madrid, NM, has been sold to an investment group for California, who say the ghost town will be restored and made into a tourist attraction.

SKILL BOX

Post Hoc Fallacy: False Cause

A bitter worker complains: "My hometown, Sordid Falls, died right after the Grinch Company moved its plant to another town. Yessir, that company killed off the town." With a few questions, we might learn from the worker that an interstate highway by-passed the town five years before the company moved. The worker's statement may have been a case of false cause.

The aim of much of your thinking, like that of science, is to determine the causes of effects. This is the way to discover the "how" of things. In our effort to link two things together as cause and effect, however, the cause may be incorrectly identified. This may involve the reasoning error called *post hoc*, which comes from *post hoc ergo propter hoc*, or "after this therefore because of this."

The *post hoc* fallacy occurs when one event happens just be-fore or at the same time as some other event and is assumed to cause the other event. This error is likely to happen when a person takes a shortcut while trying to explain a complex set of events. It may be tempting to believe that we finally passed an English test because we ate steak for breakfast on the morning of the test. Such a belief simplifies and explains things, giving us a feeling of control. The danger in this reasoning is that we may de-pend on the wrong cause to pull us through. Instead of studying, we might rely on eating steak.

Besides fooling ourselves, we may fall prey to *post hoc* if we are not careful when reading or listening to advertisements. We may be misled by others. For example, a commercial might claim, "Mr. Jones had a terrible headache, took our pill, went to bed, and woke up with no headache!" The error in this reasoning is easy to spot. Just because one event (headache disappearing) followed another (taking the pill), there is no basis to claim that the first event *caused* the second one. In the Skill Box concerning cause-effect relationships (Chapter 1) we learned the kind of evi-dence to demand of a supposed causal link between two events. Much more than being related in time is required, but many advertisements ignore this fact, and so, we might guess, do many consumers.

plexes. With the Depression, new building and replacement slowed to a halt; only after World War II did new building become once more economically feasible. With the end of the war, some-thing happened to throw the nation into a shopping-center and peripheral-housing phase.

PERIPHERAL: Located away from the center of something—relating to external boundaries.

During the Depression, no one had money to buy much of anything, and during the war, even though money was available, there were no consumer goods to be bought. As a result, when both money and consumer goods became available after the war, the nation saw an enlarged seller's market. As the shortages of a war-time economy presented themselves, wholesale houses had only limited salable items for distribution, available only to estab-lished customers. People wishing to go into business had to face the extreme difficulty of getting materials needed to build a store and to stock it. People in business prior to the beginning of the war had an established allotment of materials from suppliers. They might not get nearly as much stock as they had prior to the war, but there was almost enough to stay in business. It was common for a small department store to receive an allotment of only a dozen pairs of nylon stockings. No store had a problem selling whatever merchandise became available.

When the war ended and merchandise once more became available, Americans went out to buy everything they had done without during the Depression and the war. Building owners felt no need to improve their properties, since they were selling everything they could lay their hands on. People stood in lines for new cars, refrigerators, stoves, and every other imaginable commodity. Because business was good, the value of business properties increased. If new businesses were to establish themselves, they would have to buy expensive old buildings in the business districts located in the centers of the old cities. However, they would have no way to provide parking for new cars and less reason to remodel older structures.

It did not take too long for America's business people to divine that ten acres of ground on the outskirts of a city at a cost of $1,000 an acre was a better investment than a half acre of center-city ground at a cost of $1,000,000. Not only would the initial expense be less, but a new building could be erected and assessed at tax rates far below those in the center of the city. Salespeople could be hired at lower salaries because of job competition in a suburban center. Fewer jobs had been available in the suburban areas, and the possibility of new positions uncovered a large pool of untapped labor.

The sudden availability of the automobile and the resultant push of the highway lobby opened the countryside for development. After seventeen years of little upkeep or replacement of center-city facilities, businesses found the move to inexpensive land of the countryside easier and more profitable. Once more the economics of the situation played an important role in the development of the countryside and the abandonment of center-city areas.

In a brief aerial view of an old European city, we can see the following outline in the streets, walls, and structures: in one section of the city, the lines of an original Roman camp are visible. The defensive nature of the medieval stronghold, complete with walls, moats, and fortress, will exist either in an overlay or on a site adjacent to the original Roman settlement. The haphazard streets of the late Middle Ages wind outside the walls of the fortified town. This shows the growth of urban economic life at that time. The invention of the cannon and the breakdown of the controls of the estate system led in many cities to the presence of wide boulevards that functioned originally to provide a good field of fire for crowd control. Today many European cities have new suburban shopping plazas modeled on the American originals. These centers developed in response to the same stimulus—the automobile. With the long-term view of the life and changes in the pattern of European cities, a certain curiosity arises as to the inevitable change in our own cities' patterns.

The heart of any city tends to relocate as other areas build and replace old centers.[5] New Yorkers have raised a great cry bemoaning the fact that Times Square, the home of massage parlors and pornographic moviehouses, is run down. The activities of the area residents and business people offend official New Yorkers and the various nostalgia merchants who wail about a return to the good old days; the "good old days" means the high point of the legitimate theater and other forms of acceptable business that have either moved away or ceased to operate. Why have many firms moved from Times Square? At other times the heart of New York's life was located in other places on the island, for business and residential patterns change if the face of the city is altered.[6]

Energy and the City

Another factor affecting change in the city is closely involved with economics: energy. Energy can help explain the fate of Times Square, as well as neighborhoods near you.

In today's marketplace, old buildings do not serve as well as new ones. One reason is the need for energy. New lighting forms, air conditioning, heat controls, copy machines, batteries of telephones, high-speed elevators, and all the other appliances of which we are so fond reflect the added thirst for electrical energy. Not only is the power distribution in older buildings inadequate for air-conditioning, but the structures themselves prohibit installation of the units. Insufficient insulation and space make these necessary refinements uneconomical, if not impossible to operate. In the days of lower building costs, high ceilings and large rooms were legion, but in a world of inflating land costs these structural forms are impossible to deal with. It is preferable to move to a new building, where modern technologies can better be served at an economical rate. In a word, our technological growth has victimized older sections of the center city.

As our city centers have declined, the surrounding areas have flourished. The reasons for this change are obvious. Property values have continued to climb, even for the old buildings in the center of the city. In many instances the new development occurs beyond the political boundaries of the older, established city. This causes the citizens to claim that the city is dying, when it is only changing shape and moving.

In the past, before the accelerated growth of our cities, urban areas were compacted and clearly defined. The reasons for the high-density city have been touched on with reference to available transportation forms. In addition to transportation limitations, other factors include available energy sources.

Before we deal with the effects of energy on urban forms, we must note that political divisions were originally based on cities as they appeared to the residents. Based on knowledge at hand, which all but eliminated provisions for the future, the people included within the city limits the land area they considered sufficient to allow for all possible growth. As cities spread and grew at an ever-increasing pace, these areas filled and overflowed into the surrounding rural/political entities. In other instances, separate and distinct cities and towns grew to their mutual borders, creating a situation where people might enter and leave distinct political units merely by crossing a city street.

To a degree, newer cities have avoided this problem by extending their boundaries to include larger areas of the surrounding countryside. There is room for the growth of these units now, but it is possible that they too will fill and overflow even these ambitious boundaries.

The crux of the issue is that as cities and towns grew into one another, their forms changed. The "city" has grown to incorporate all such entities, but not its political boundaries. But that is another issue. Elements of culture lag color this situation in that the realities of modern urban development clearly show an enlarged and changed urban center, while political entities of a former century survive.[7]

The modern American city is a creation of the industrial age, limited by energy and transportation. Because energy is the basis of the form of transportation, we should first look at the effect of energy on the form and development of a city.

When water power was the most important source of energy for the newly developing industries of our nations, clusters of factories grew naturally along rivers. Since the site of an industry was tied to its power source, in this case direct water power, and since there was a lack of efficient transportation systems, workers had to find residences near the work site. As a result, a series of industrial/residential complexes spread along the banks of any river that supplied sufficient power for industrial development. The introduction of the steam engine made it profitable for industry to enlarge individual plants, because the steam-power source had to be near the machines it powered. Furthermore, in the mechanics of steam power, large power sources were more efficient than small units. This led to clustering plants with satellite residence centers. To ensure a constant labor supply, many of these units were established near existing villages and commercial towns. In time, the addition of heavy industry changed the character of the original urban or preurban settlements as drastically as dispersal and regionalization are changing modern cities.

Energy and transportation had other effects on the urban centers of that early period. The first cities founded in what would be the United States were based on commerce, not industry. Ports for the transshipment of raw materials from our continent and manufactured goods from abroad were important. Access to the expanding interior of North America accelerated the growth of some cities and limited the growth of others, depending on the size of the interior area the commercial cities could exploit. Opening the near West by various canal systems and later by the railroads set the restricted limits of satellite centers. Many towns began to spring up along established routes of the new commerce.

The early needs for servicing centers for the transport vehicles themselves formed the economic base for such settlements. Even today, canal ports maintain an existence although their original reason has disappeared. The names of such towns as Lockport, Brockport, and Coalport tell the story of their original service functions. The requirements of the transportation system mandated the location of settlements in specific areas, while a horse and wagon traveling over dirt roads favored a dispersal tendency, spreading towns over a wide area.

The inability to negotiate steep hills restricted canals and steam locomotives to specific areas. Canals had to follow the water supply and to maintain a relatively level path, or the water would flow too fast for animal-drawn barges to negotiate. If the canal encountered a rapid fall in the level of the land, it was forced to use a lock to raise or lower barges. Many canals had to maintain their level by departing from the area adjacent to the river and running along the sides of the hills bordering the river valley. Under any circumstances, the ease of digging and the lay of the land determined the routes of the canals.

Steam railroads were similarly limited in their choice of routes. The steam engine is confined to a grade of not much more than two feet per hundred. This means that one hundred feet of track must be laid to take care of a rise of two feet in altitude. Thus the availability of easy grades determines the route of any railroad.

With the emergence of the steam age arose the importance of the location of the power source: coal. Urban industrial centers were a natural outgrowth of the routes of rail communications. Areas not served by rail tended to wither and die.

The cities that grew in this age of burgeoning industry were filthy communities with extremely high death rates and infant mortality, much higher than in preceding centuries. Housing was dismal, with inadequate water, light, and sanitation facilities. As the value of land increased, industrialists made every effort to squeeze as many workers as possible into the smallest possible area. Yet as poor as conditions in the cities were, they were usually better than those in the rural areas of that time.

A journey through the old industrial cities of the eastern United States shows block after block of row houses and tenements. The gloomy comment this panorama evokes is that many of these units, substandard in the last century, continue to be used today. Beside its slum, the high-density, industrial city had the added presence of the mansions and townhouses of the wealthy. While the wealthy in any such community enjoyed a higher standard of living, they were still exposed to the environmental problems brought on by unrestricted industrial development.

We still have the slag heaps, waste piles, despoiled landscapes, and dead rivers as a legacy of this period. Acids, other chemical wastes, and live sewage are only a portion of what was and occasionally still is pumped into our rivers. The quality of the air breathed by residents of coal-burning cities was a health menace. Today we have vast wastelands devoid of vegetation because of the acid quality of air and waste runoff from industry. Even with our present relatively clean industry and environmental activity, we face the prospect of the Great Lakes dying and becoming nothing more than vast inland seas of putrid water.

The cities of the early industrial period were filthy, unhealthy, noxious places in which to live. Zoning was nonexistent, and as a result, residences, factories, power plants, and sewage-disposal installations shared the same little area. Lack of efficient transportation, and therefore access to outlying areas, limited residents from fleeing the hellish aspects of urban life. The people did not realize that their life-styles were suffering. Those who could afford to leave the cities usually refused to consider such an action; they adapted to the life-style at hand.

Modern Transportation and Its Effects

With the advent of the motor age, life became dependent on the automobile. New highway construction opened the countryside for development. The old city center was just that, the center of an enlarging area. Once more the changing pattern of urban development was based on energy. The introduction of oil and its by-products has equaled or surpassed coal and water power in changing the face of the nation's cities. Government-subsidized highway construction opened the road to the suburbs. The ability to transmit power via electrical lines opened new areas to industry. As town and residential areas had once clustered along rail lines, rivers, and canals, they now began to rise beside the new arteries of transport, the highways. The failure of the family farm, and the inevitable move toward the corporate farm with its vast landholdings and small labor force, encouraged millions more rural Americans to seek employment in the urban centers. Yesterday's slums were evacuated by yesteryear's poverty-stricken, as they moved en masse to the more spacious and comparatively luxurious possibilities of tremendous developments.

After World War II, in response to new affluence and a housing shortage, individual developments such as the various Levittowns of the East Coast built upward of 18,000 houses on single tracts of land. These homes offered the public a relatively spacious single home, compared to possibilities in the deteriorating center-city area.

Suburban development on the nation occurred with no thought for its consequences. The addition of new highways, turnpikes, and interstate systems to the growing complex of existing federal, state, and county roads accelerated development along their routes.

In urban areas, time became a substitute for distance. Travel is concerned with time necessary to commute between two points rather than with the mileage involved. In many instances, commuters can travel from their urban work areas to their suburban homes sixty miles away in less time than it takes to make a ten-mile trip in the city.

What has happened as a result of the growing abandonment of the older residential centers by middle- and upper-class people? The result of the modern gas shortage and high-priced transportation has resulted in a growing shift away from the suburbs and back to the cities. This has caused more displacement of long-term residents.

URBAN DECAY, RENEWAL, AND GROWING PAINS

As is true with nearly every other part of our modern culture, one of the few things in the city that doesn't change is the existence of change. Taking a moment to survey the urban environment nearest to you, what kind of changes do you see being caused by the factors just discussed? Do you see a city that is decaying, or one that is being reborn? Or is the outstanding feature the spread of suburbs?

The Rotting Core

The state of the center city is much worse than our casual expectations.[8] Many unseen variables are beginning to haunt the area. Its original water filtration plants are aging and, in many cases, no longer capable of living up to the demand. Distribution pipes for drinking water are beginning to deteriorate beyond the point of incidental replacement. Many older cities have found it necessary to begin replacing entire systems. Sewage lines and treatment plants are either deteriorating or unable to meet the recent higher standards that governmental pollution controls have set. Disposal of garbage and other waste materials is becoming increasingly expensive, since landfill areas are moving farther and farther from the centers as suburban residential areas build on their peripheries.

As the capital investment of these cities continues to deteriorate and call for replacement, the tax base continues to shrink. Heavy industry, in aging plants left from the old days of industrialization, has moved with greater frequency to the countryside or to the rural states that new highway complexes now connect to marketplaces. As industry abandons the old city, more and more of the tax burden falls on the remaining residents in the form of property tax needed for increased police protection, fire protection, and public schools.

The increasing need for these services becomes mandatory with the changing population of the urban centers. A larger percentage of lower-class inhabitants with larger families has moved into homes vacated by new suburbanites. Stately mansions and large single-family residences have been divided into many apartments, increasing the strain on overloaded public facilities. Rental

Waiting for gentrification—where will they go?

properties are not kept in repair, as were private residences, and their overloaded electrical circuits, designed for another age, have become fire hazards.

Streets have turned to parking lots as new multi-family houses have no off-the-street facilities to accommodate their residents. The enlarged population of the neighborhoods has made it impossible for the city to collect accumulated refuse. The many cars always at the curb have made street-cleaning impossible.

Occasional explosions occur as ancient gas mains develop leaks and demolish houses. With the demise of tight neighborhoods based on long-term associations of people, control becomes far more difficult. As the transient population spreads to surrounding neighborhoods, more middle-class residents flee to the suburbs.

The tax base for the community is reduced further as property values drop. As real property value begins to fall, it endangers the investment of the remaining property owners. The need for revenue to maintain the city remains, and property taxes continue to rise.

In time, businesses and homes become uninsurable. Urban dwellers must then face life with no protection against loss from theft or fire. From a property owner's viewpoint, increased risks of fire and theft make this position untenable. Properties already declining in value because of the previously mentioned variables face a new threat. Mortgage companies and banks withhold mortgage money for the purchase of these properties.

The choices left to the last holdouts of the middle class in center city are difficult. They can sell out to real-estate companies at extremely low prices. They can walk away from the property and let it decay. They can rent to whoever will move in and gouge them enough to reclaim a portion of the value of the property. Or, if in business, they can raise prices to the point where the investment return will in some way compensate for the risks. None of these alternatives is geared to improving the condition of the area. In fact, lack of reinvestment for upkeep of risk properties hastens the cycle of deterioration. Few people care to invest new money in an area that has hit bottom in property value.

Rehabilitation   While many believe that we should not attempt to salvage decaying cities, attempts to rehabilitate many urban areas are being made. In many cases, major attempts have been made to revive and maintain a form that no longer has economic value.

Some of the measures aimed at saving the city have been in the areas of rent control and urban redevelopment. Rent-control programs have had an effect. By virtue of bureaucratic decree, rents on old properties have been frozen or allowed to rise minimally. As a result of such programs, landlords endeavor to profit from their property as much as possible. They fail to perform all the necessary normal maintenance, and the building's deterioration accelerates. Older buildings require more costly and frequent repairs than newer buildings.

Landlords expect a return on their investment to exceed that returned by low risk bonds and securities. It does not pay landlords to remain in the rental business if they cannot exceed what they would earn by not working at all. A person might even invest in forms of tax-free bonds, which raise the actual return on invested money well above the level of interest received.

In light of rising taxes, repair costs, general upkeep, and a control on income level, landlords face a situation that may cause some of them to abandon their buildings to the city for unpaid taxes. It is a matter of record that the owner of most of the worst housing in the city of New York is the city itself.

Other efforts to reclaim many urban centers have been made through the process referred to as urban renewal.[9] An urban-renewal project can be described as a device to promote real-estate activity and building. Large tracts of selected deteriorating blocks are demolished to stimulate contractors to erect new buildings on the newly cleared site. The construction of new buildings would then stimulate investment in nearby areas and gradually upgrade a larger area. In reality, new urban-renewal sites have become parking lots and remained so for years, since building costs are on the increase and investors hesitate to risk loss on such projects.

A major side effect of such projects is that slum residents move from the original demolition sites and relocate in other areas of the city. Their relocation leads to the destruction of the neighborhood structures that had developed in the area selected for urban renewal. As these people spread to better neighborhoods, they bring with them the process of deterioration, as overcrowding and decreasing normative control take effect.

The city itself loses many tax-ratable properties for the considerable period between condemnation and rebuilding. In some cases, sites of future urban-renewal projects remain open fields of flattened rubble reminiscent of some European cities after aerial bombardment. All too frequently, loss of taxable properties to urban renewal has struck a near death-blow to many of our older cities. Someone must pay the lost taxes, and that burden falls on the city's remaining property owners. This rise causes increased urban desertion and deterioration.

BLIGHT: An impaired, damaged, or poor condition.

Public housing projects have been favorite methods of dealing with urban blight. Public housing is a wonderful concept, but it has its disadvantages, primarily the removal of large areas of vital land from the tax rolls. In addition, rents charged the inhabitants of such projects do not cover the original investment. More inequity develops with sliding rental scales. It is foolish for middle-class people to pay middle-class rates to live in a city project. They would pay essentially the same rates in a privately owned apartment house.

While many planners espouse the idea of mixing social classes in residence areas, the concept is impractical in application. Dif-

Public housing is a great concept with many disadvantages.

ferent social classes have different life-styles. What is important to one group may have no importance to another. The concern of the upper-lower class with cleanliness exists. The quest for security and respectability is equally vital to the life-style of middle-class groups. Because life-styles differ, people are more content when they live among others who have the same values. As a result, middle-class homeowners sell out and run when the building next door suddenly houses more residents than they think proper or when the yard loses its grass. They run when a wrecked automobile has been permanently parked in the street or driveway. They panic when burglaries increase and schools deteriorate. Nothing will force a middle-class family out of its home more quickly than threats to or abuse of its children. Whether the threats be real or imagined, they will soon result in a new suburban resident.[10]

The city's financial problems become increasingly difficult because of the large number of tax-free structures based in the hearts of urban regions. Nonprofit organizations do not have to pay property taxes in most parts of the nation. This means that churches, foundations, educational facilities, and the like pay no taxes on property they own, even if it is an apartment building, a store, or a commercial parking lot. If a city is unlucky enough to find itself the state capital, it will discover that the growing physical plant used to house the bureaucracy operates on a tax-free basis. The city must provide all the essential public services, such as police and fire protection, but it must write off as tax-free the property occupied by the governmental agencies.

Numerous institutions with tax-free status own considerable amounts of property in urban centers. As a result, the tax burden falls more heavily on the remaining individual owners, even though the various institutions serve a geographical area far larger than the city itself.

The presence of the United Nations in New York City is a reality. The nation's desire that the United Nations remain in New York is a reality. If it is beneficial for our nation to retain these headquarters, and those of the numerous embassies that dot the city, let the nation reimburse New York City for the tax loss it has incurred. Why should New York City residents pay for police officers to guard the entrances of those embassies? Why must one city bear the cost of protecting and providing city benefits for a world government?

The obvious answer to many if not all these problems is to eliminate the outdated political boundaries that plague most of our nation. The city is not dying; it has grown and changed.[11] If a city draws its workers from a population spread over a fifty-mile radius, and if the city center provides tax-free land on which our basic institutions have their property, it should either tax that property or spread the burden of its upkeep over the entire population.

While we must spread the burden imposed by nationwide benefits, we must also become more realistic in our attempts to deal with poverty supplements in center-city regions. If the property in a center-city region is too expensive for low-income people without subsidy, perhaps they should look elsewhere for a place to live. As matters stand, several possibilities arise. One is that center-city property values will fall to the point where large-scale demolition will enable the emergence of a low-density area resembling the surrounding areas. Or the city will replace deteriorating sections with institutional structures and large apartment houses. A third possibility remains: Values will fall, the middle class will continue to leave, and the institutional structures will also leave. In such a case, the only thing left to do would be to fence the area and examine it in about twenty years to see what happened.

The last possibility may be near reality, if we can judge the reasoning behind the architectural form of the "Gateway" in Newark, New Jersey. On leaving the train in Newark, a person can enter the "Gateway" via a protected and enclosed walkway. Access to the rest of Newark from the "Gateway" is limited and controlled. The complex is effectively separated from Newark, the city, and it is there in name only. We may well anticipate more structures of this nature: walled and protected enclaves of the middle and upper classes in the cities of the poor.

Captives of the inner city will fall into several categories. The new immigrant, if from a rural area, has probably arrived lacking the skills necessary to do much more than survive in a technological society. The second group has become accustomed to the inner city and will probably remain there. The aged, if they or their families cannot afford the luxury of nursing homes or communities for the elderly, are forced to remain in the inner city. There services are still within walking distance or available by public transportation not yet common to the suburbs.

The New Urban Residents

Considerable attention has been given to the return to various city centers of a breed referred to as the YUPPY (Young upwardly mobile professional). Not all yuppies are professional, or really very young. What they seem to be is well off and unburdened by many children. In addition, they may not be married, though they usually have a relationship with a person of either the same or opposite sex. Whatever their residential or social makeup may be, the new center city resident changes the face of his neighborhood and the city itself.

The process of gentrification has been associated with the arrival of well-to-do or upwardly mobile persons in areas of marked decline. The housing stock is undervalued and can be rehabilitated for far less than new structures can be constructed. The rising cost of suburban building sites and construction costs have allowed a new look at the Brownstones and other residences lately occupied by ever lowering class members. If a group does not have to worry about schools for nonexistent children, or other amenities associated with large family life, they can pour their resources into the redevelopment of houses for their own use. Several questions come to mind when considering the new residents of our center cities. First, what happens to the old residents who are displaced by the movement of higher income persons into their housing areas? Do they become members of an increasing number of homeless persons no longer able to afford reasonable housing? Must they move to other, less expensive regions of the country? They certainly will find it difficult paying the higher property taxes and rents associated with an upswing residential area. The suburbs surrounding most of our cities are too expensive, and the rural areas beyond the suburbs provide little employment, because of the depressed farming industry.

A second and new problem comes into view. Since 1980 there has been a major upturn in births after years of decline. Are the births the result of women who had deferred having children in favor of careers now having them to beat the biological clock? Has there been a change in the basic normative pattern that once more sees children as a necessity? For whatever reason, new schools are being built to replace those closed during the birth dearth. This will result in new taxes and possibly a replay of those conditions that caused the decline of center cities in the first place. Whatever happens, the city will continue to change.

The Suburbs and the Megalopolis

WATER TABLE: The level below the ground which is saturated with water.

SOIL PERCOLATION: Manner in which water is absorbed into soil and eventually evaporates.

Meanwhile, the suburban areas are undergoing unfamiliar problems. Overdevelopment has strained their natural resources. For example, the first home in a rural section could make do with a well and a septic system. With the coming of thousands of new homes, water tables have begun to drop, putting pressure on the well-water supply. In many areas, the soil is unsuitable for the acceptable operation of septic systems. Most towns have found it necessary to require specific performance for soil percolation prior to issuing building permits. The warning of "no percolation, no permit" is heard more often these days, but not often enough. Some homeowners have seen detergent bubbling from their taps. Live sewage overflows from inadequate systems, decorating roadside ditches in many fashionable suburban areas and posing a severe health threat. Sewage-treatment plants, when erected, cannot deal effectively with detergents and other wastes. The result is that beautiful bubbling brooks, laden with waste, bubble more effusively than ever.

For many years, urban refugees purchased or built homes on flood plains with no thought given to the consequences. A long-term drought in the 1960s allowed a number of uneventful years to pass before nature caught up to the intruder with heavy rains and flash floods.

Suburban dwellers suddenly found their tax haven in the country trembling under the burden of urban requirements. Roads had to be improved to meet the requirements of heavier traffic flow. New schools had to be built to educate the increased numbers of children. School buses had to be purchased and operated over long distances to meet the requirements of the dispersed residential area. Sewers and water lines had to replace the over-loaded wells and septic systems.

Each capital expenditure raises the tax burden on suburban property and hastens the end of tax inequality. There is the possibility that tax-free equality will allow various political units to merge into more realistic entities.

After years of catch-as-catch-can building patterns in suburban regions, the specter of regional planning and proscribed land use has reared its head. This has created an increasing number of court battles with individual citizens and planning boards, on the one hand, and developers, on the other. By means of zoning ordinances, suburban communities are attempting to control the growth and development of their areas. The developers are interested in the conversion of relatively inexpensive land into expensive apartment complexes, housing developments, and shopping centers.

There is something to be said for each position, and no clear-cut statement can be made in defense of either. The semi-rural areas wish to maintain their regional character and avoid becoming part of the urban sprawl. With increased habitation, local taxes must rise to provide full-time police and fire protection and the installation of sewers and water lines. Builders argue that three-, five- or ten-acre housing sites are discriminatory and deny the multitudes who wish to escape the cities access to these regions. As they unhappily consider the prospect of inundation by what they thought they had escaped, the suburban residents privately agree.

Governmental decisions on how to put land to use is also something new to us. We have already mentioned the effects of building on the flood plains of streams and rivers; many states have acted to prohibit future building on such areas. Low-lying beachfront areas are also falling under this prohibition. With facilities strained to the breaking point in many areas, building moratoriums are becoming more frequent. Perhaps these actions will force a wider population dispersal over the face of the nation and somewhat reverse the trend toward the megalopolis.

The megalopolis is in itself a recent creation. As our cities grew together, so did suburban regions, until entire sections of the nation have become one vast city or urban region. On the West Coast, the urban sprawl of Los Angeles reaches south into Orange County slowly creeping toward San Diego. The East Coast city stretches from Portland, Maine, through Petersburg, Virginia.[12]

Recently, many large corporations are moving their headquarters from the crowded and expensive center cities into what can now be seen as another part of the urban area. It is not a matter of moving uptown or downtown in Manhattan, but rather picking up and moving wholesale to an area such as the Route 1 corridor from New Brunswick to Trenton, New Jersey. The small municipalities can be overwhelmed by the legal pressures brought to bear by major developers and corporations. The corporations have the benefits of easy highway access, rail service, airports, and relatively inexpensive land. In the New Jersey countryside, thousands of acres of farmland have been changed into major corporate centers, large hotels, and conference centers, together with attendant housing and shopping facilities. These developments spread over many communities and seem to have a life of their own, a new city that envelops existing political and social units. One firm, for instance, moved ten thousand middle and upper level employees into their new complex. It is not unusual for a major firm to hide its headquarters away on five hundred or more acres. Housing prices have increased to reflect the new demand, and pressure on housing is being felt in the old city centers as mentioned above in our discussion of gentrification. Highways and interstate routes are experiencing similar development. It is now common for people to cross several state boundaries on their way to work.

In time, we may see the abandonment not only of the city and county but also of state borders, since actual urban regions now span state lines. There are many instances of groups of states forming agencies to face the problems arising from this population spread and recognizing the necessity of sharing natural resources. The Port Authority of New York and New Jersey, the Delaware River Basin Commission, and the various agencies in the West created to divide the freshwater reserves in an equitable manner are examples of growing regionalization.

REGIONALIZATION: Development of a political or social system based on one or more geographic areas or regions.

Energy grids and transportation networks are indicative of future phenomena in urban development. To chart the physical outline of future urban development in your region, merely fill in the areas parallel to the interstate highways for an hour and a half's travel from an employment source. At each interchange place a shopping center, especially on the circular center around smaller cities. Housing developments and industry will follow.

If the costs of fuel, tolls, and mass transportation rise high enough to make commuting uneconomical, we might see a resurgence of high-density centers.

SUMMARY

The prerequisites of a city include a large population, a surplus of goods, and capital gained through taxes. Also, a city is based on written records, public works, and predictive science. The city involves luxury items and a stratified society. Long-distance travel, job specialization (beyond age and sex), and centralized state power are also parts of an urban area.

A city differs from what is merely a large village because of its developed technology and its orientation to change. Also, an urban resident's social position is based more on skill and knowledge than on inheritance.

Some cities form around a core of administration. Others are based on commerce, and their location is more closely tied to trade routes or resources.

A city can change because of economic factors, such as the closing of its only industry. Sometimes the economic causes of a change are more complex, as seen in the postwar shifts to the suburbs in many U.S. urban areas.

Related to economics, and to each other, are the change factors of energy and transportation, both of which greatly influenced the development of American cities. This is seen basically in the shift from a dependence on water to a dependence on oil for both energy and transportation.

These and other factors have caused changes along three basic themes in American cities. First, many city cores are decaying as they attract less investment and as their tax bases erode. But efforts have been made to renew these cores. One means of renewal is rent control, which may produce more problems. Another tactic is slum clearance and replacement, which has also often been disappointing. The growth of the suburbs, for a while so full of promise, has also brought disappointment as well as environmental problems.

SPECIAL TOPIC

Gentrification

City Planner Ralph Seligman has pointed to a process that has changed the face of Hoboken, New Jersey. We have become accustomed to thinking of the old cities of the industrial North as crumbling into decay and ruin. Possibly as a result of increasing real-estate values in New York City, high interest rates, and high building costs, the old center of Hoboken began to revive. Bargain seekers bought old mansions and rebuilt them. Nineteenth-century saloons were cleaned out and redecorated. The chic set had arrived, but where were the old residents to live? The term "gentrification" has

The Yuppies are here! Where did the former residents go?

been coined to describe the raising of an area's social-class level—in other words, the reentry of the gentry.

Seligman wrote an article for *New York Affairs* entitled "Hoboken Rediscovered Yet Again,"[13] which traces the history of Hoboken from original discovery through several reincarnations up to the present. Each time, the city is reborn in another guise to serve another function. The latest turn around has come none too soon. In 1954 the city's master plan predicted that if the present rate of upgrading substandard housing were to continue, it would take three hundred years to replace or rehabilitate the cities' 6,000 substandard units. By 1967, nearly 7,500 units were classed as substandard.

With all this obvious adversity, well-planned media spots projected Hoboken as an up-and-coming haven for gracious living. Television programs and magazine articles touted Hoboken as the next good place to go.

Hoboken's history in real-estate opportunity begins with the Dutch who built America's first brewery in 1642. The Delaware Indians burned the entire town, except the brewery, in 1643. The English followed the Dutch, the

Bayard family forfeiting title by joining the Tories during the Revolution.

Colonel John Stevens bought the area in 1784 to develop the "new city of Hoboken." Stevens created a seventy-five-block subdivision and in 1811 ran the steam-powered ferry *Juliana* to and from Manhattan. The subdivision did not catch on, but by 1830 as many as 20,000 people a day would cross on the ferry to spend the day in the open, picnicking and relaxing.

By 1860, the city had become a major railroad terminal and occupied one square mile. In 1910, with a population of over 70,000, Hoboken was the nation's most densely populated city, a rail hub, and a major port.

With the boom years of World War I over, Hoboken slipped early into the Great Depression. As the rest of the nation joined it, there was some Bohemian revival in 1929. World War II provided increased waterfront activity, followed by the filming of *On the Waterfront* with Marlon Brando.

Hoboken started down once more through the 1950s. Major manufacturing and sales operations moved away from the city. As prices and real-estate values fell, lofts became bargains for artists. An article in the *Village Voice* in 1963 was entitled "Where the Depression Stopped—and Stayed." Containerization of ships killed the waterfront, and even the ferry stopped running. In 1967 a conscious effort was made by the planning board to conserve and preserve row houses in stable neighborhoods. The 1967 "model cities" application noted that the city was near Manhattan but was "technologically obsolete." The city gained the Model Cities designation as the result of this application.

Hoboken's major problem was "to change the city from a place where people live by necessity to one where they live by choice." The people sought by the city were middle-class people "like us." The early model cities staff members were from out of town with liberal arts degrees. They enjoyed high salaries and fringe benefits denied local government officials. In time, these people moved on to graduate school, leaving behind the jobs for locals to fill. The emphasis shifted from importing a middle class to retaining a middle class.

From 1972 to the 1980s, articles appeared in the *New York Times, Daily News, Christian Science Monitor,* and other newspapers citing the housing bargains available in Hoboken. Testimonials of brownstone-buyers and other solidly middle-class people told of the life-style available and to come. Gentrification had begun.

Some unexpected conflict has arisen, as many newcomers look upon their homes as investments rather than merely places to live. One of the unusual and unexpected aspects of this and other similar examples is that the people who are encouraged to settle are usually of a higher class than the local residents. The locals do not quite understand that in many cases they constitute a portion of a group classed as undesirable by the new residents. A beneficial side effect of gentrification was the ability of upward socially mobile children to remain in Hoboken rather than to move away, as had been the case before.

The other Hoboken, as seen by Seligman, includes an unemployment rate of 16 percent. More than 20 percent of households had incomes below the poverty level, and 33 percent qualified for housing assistance; in addition to this, 43 percent of the total assessed value of land and improvements were tax exempt. As late as 1977, the brick and wood sanitary sewers of Civil War times were still in use and in need of replacement.

The city discontinued its public relations attempts in the late 1970s. As Hoboken entered the 1980s, there remained an uptown and a downtown. Uptown was a middle-class haven of restored brownstones and well-kept homes. Downtown remained the place for homes of recent and earlier immigrants of identifiable ethnic affiliation.

Seligman and other planners assumed that the limits of gentrification had been reached. Housing bargains were no longer spectacular, money was hard to get, interest rates were high, and the schools were poor. It was time once more for Hoboken to go into a period of dormancy.

This did not happen. The March 23, 1982, *New York Times* contained an article that pointed to the growing entry of the well-to-do in Hoboken. In this case, it is not only the poor who are displaced but also, as Seligman points out, many people who consider themselves middle class.

In years to come, we may well see that gentrification will mean more than displacing undesirables; it may place entire sections out of reach for all but a small group of very wealthy people.[14]

SELF-TEST QUESTIONS

1. True or false: The essential difference between a city and a village is population size.
2. What is *not* a prerequisite of the city?
   a. large population
   b. long-distance trade
   c. social equality
   d. public works
   e. centralized state power
3. The two types of cities described in this chapter were (1) _____ and (2) _____ .
4. What change in urban patterns resulted from the effects of the Depression and World War II:
   a. invention of skyscrapers
   b. shift of much commerce from core to countryside
   c. development of huge specialty stores
   d. revitalization of urban core
5. True or false: The growth of a city is influenced and limited by energy and transportation.
6. True or false: The automobile has led to the abandonment of the inner city.
7. True or false: Both rent control and slum replacement are clearly effective in rehabilitating the city.
8. True or false: Tax-free structures, such as churches, add to the city's financial vitality.
9. True or false: The suburbs are clearly a story of relatively trouble-free growth.

ANSWERS TO SELF-TEST QUESTIONS

1. false
2. c
3. administrative and commercial
4. b
5. true

6. true
7. false
8. false
9. false

ANSWER TO SKILL REINFORCER

15–1. Inductive reasoning proceeds from specific cases or statements to general statements.

NOTES

1. Kingsley Davis, *Cities: Their Origin, Growth, and Human Impact* (San Francisco: W.H. Freeman, 1973), introduction.
2. Bernardin de St. Pierre, *Paul et Virginie* (Paris: Garnier Freres, 1964). This is a novel, but the depictions of the division of labor in a peasant situation apply.
3. Gideon Sjoberg, "The Origin and Evolution of Cities," *Scientific American* 213 (September 1965): 54–63.
4. Hans Blumenfeld, "The Urban Pattern," *Annals of the American Academy of Political and Social Sciences* 352 (March 1964): 74–83.
5. Lewis Mumford, *City Development: Studies in Disintegration and Renewal* (New York: Harcourt, Brace, 1945).
6. Edgar M. Hoover, et al., *Anatomy of a Metropolis: The Changing Distribution of People and Jobs Within the New York Metropolitan Region* (Cambridge: Harvard University Press, 1959).

7. Lewis Mumford, *The Urban Prospect* (New York: Harcourt, Brace, & World, 1968).

8. National Resources Committee, *Our Cities: Their Role in the National Economy* (Washington, D.C.: Government Printing Office, 1937), pp. 28–41.

9. Jewel Belliush and Murray Hausknecht, *Urban Renewal: People, Politics, and Planning* (Garden City, N.Y.: Doubleday & Co., 1967).

10. Herbert Gans, "The White Exodus to Suburbia Steps Up," *New York Times Magazine,* January 7, 1968.

11. John Walton and Donald E. Carns, eds., *Cities in Change: Studies on the Urban Condition* (Boston: Allyn & Bacon, 1973).

12. Jean Gottman, *Megalopolis: The Urbanized Northeastern Seaboard of the United States* (New York: Twentieth Century Foundation, 1967).

13. Ralph Seligman, "Hoboken Discovered Yet Again," *New York Affairs* 5 (1979): 26–38.

14. H.H. Siegal and J.A. Incardi, "The Demise of Skid Row," *Society* 19 (January/February 1982): 39, 45.

SUGGESTED READINGS

Abramson, M. "Social Dimensions of Urbanism," *Social Forces* 52 (March 1974).

Mumford, Louis. *The Urban Prospect.* New York: Harcourt, Brace, & World, 1968.

Muller, Thomas, *Growing and Declining Urban Areas.* Washington, D.C.: Urban Institute, 1975.

Salins, Peter D. *The Ecology of Housing Destruction.* New York: New York University Press, 1980.

16 ECONOMIC SYSTEMS AND PRODUCTION

PREVIEW

The Ultimate in Inelastic Demand

An item for which there is inelastic demand is an item people cannot do without. Water and air are examples of items for which demand is inelastic. There are other items for which demand is relatively elastic.

We saw over the last decade that our demand for oil is somewhat elastic. When the Arab oil embargo and price rise began, many believed that little could be done to replace oil. But in recent years, we have purchased smaller cars; adjusted our thermostats; burned wood, methane, and natural gas; and used solar and wind technologies to reduce our dependence on oil.

If you have but one functioning kidney, and that is functioning poorly, your need is inelastic. If you need a cornea transplant, your need remains inelastic. If you need any of the human organs necessary for life, your need is inelastic.

If you are in a situation where you *need* a vital organ for yourself or a loved one, you will buy it at all costs—if available; many people die before a needed organ is available. In the United States, many people carry donor cards designating their organs for use. In other nations there is a growing availability of organs on the open market. This may sound strange to Americans, but an inelastic demand frequently brings with it a price that causes the demand to be met.

Brazil is a country of widely separated social and economic classes. Members of the lower levels of the socio-economic system have little chance for upward social mobility. In recent years, runaway inflation has served to harden class lines. The rich became richer, the poor maintained their position, and what middle class there is has slipped down the social ladder. The possibility of escaping lifelong poverty grows smaller. But in the classified section of Brazil's newspapers there are such advertisements as "Wanted, a viable cornea" or "Kidney available." [1] The prices are high, frequently from $20,000 to $50,000 (American dollars). This is enough to lift a family out of poverty and give it a chance to succeed.

The people bidding for these organs frequently need them—or else. The "else" is, of course, death. A need and a desire to sell result in a price and a purchase. In this case the price is high.

The world being what it is, this market will soon be satisfied from sources other than newspaper advertisements. Today, desperate people, to meet a need, supply and buy items of inelastic demand. It is only a matter of time before less principled but certainly more highly organized groups move to supply organs from less-than-willing donors.

In the face of growing "inelastic demand," and in response to the pressure of large sums of money, healthy young people will begin to drop from sight on the streets of countries around the world. This may resemble a science fiction story, but it will come to pass soon, if it has not occurred already. People will be held and used to supply organs for other people who have the ability to pay. For the time being, the ultimate in items for which demand is inelastic will remain human organs necessary to prolong life.

The following four chapters deal with the subject of economics. This is not to say that the preceding chapters have not dealt in economic realities, and that economic considerations are not integral to the manner in which we form families and groups, and arrange ourselves in social levels and residence units. We have been using economic criteria in consideration of each of these topics.

Examples of these economic considerations can be seen in how the changing economic position of women has altered our reality, if not our perception, of family life. Looking back in history, we find examples of women as important economic units. Where this was a reality, a bride price or bride service was called for to reimburse the bride's family for their loss at the time of marriage. When women were of little economic import, the bride's family had to provide payment in the form of a dowry or other considerations to the husband or the husband's family. In recent years, because of the entry of women into the job market on a basis equal to men, there has been a lessening of the dependence of women upon men. Couples are frequently paying for their own weddings (though many couples will go through with the older pattern of showers, silver, crystal, ceramics, etc., for the ceremonial satisfaction). Prenuptial agreements, together with frequent divorce, are the rule rather than the exception. The basic reason for these changes lies in the economic equality of women. Technology has allowed this change in economic position by allowing family planning and the shift from a need for strength toward a need for intelligence.

Economics is concerned with the production and distribution of goods and services. Each society has its own method of dealing with the control of these factors. We have seen from our exposure to the daily newspaper that the differences between economic systems can lead to major confrontations between peoples within a society and between societies themselves. Our problem with the Soviet Union seems to concentrate on the difference between their perceived economic system and our perceived economic system. We say perceived because as we continue we will note that they do not have the system they are perceived as having, and we do not have the system we perceive ourselves as having. All too frequently, we tend to confuse economic systems with political systems.

This chapter will deal with two basic aspects of economics. First, we will attempt to outline the various systems different societies have chosen to control the production and distribution of goods and services. With the choices outlined, we will then spend the remainder of this chapter dealing with production. The following chapter will concern itself with who gets the product and the service. In other words, how, in a world of inherent shortages, the unequal distribution of goods and services can be justified to a society's members. Unequal distribution means someone always gets more and someone always gets less of what a society has to offer. Chapter 18 deals with the presence of government in our economy. As we will see, this is a relatively new presence in its current form. Chapter 19 deals with money in its various forms, and includes a discussion of those institutions that serve to regulate its value and flow.

Economics is usually divided into two parts. The areas concerned with the individual, firm, industry, individual markets, and producers are called "Microeconomics." "Macroeconomics" is the study of the *larger* picture, of how total production, general price level, and total employment act upon the entire economy.

TYPES OF ECONOMIC SYSTEMS

Robert Heilbroner describes three ways in which societies are organized to produce and distribute goods and services. As presented by Heilbroner, they are the traditional economy, the command economy (planned), and the market economy.[2]

Traditional Economy

When a society operates within a traditional economy, people produce and work at the trades of their parents and grandparents. Today this can apply only in an undeveloped economy. This system works best in a subsistence society, where items produced have a relatively consistent demand. Economies where specialization has remained at a low level continue to produce a broad spectrum of goods to meet basic needs. Potters may be specialists, but they will continue to produce basic food items too. In such an economy, quick changes in demand for specialty items are rare, except through outside influences or environmental changes.

The most striking feature of many traditional economies may be the lack of interdependence at a high level. In developed societies, specialization is so great that disruption of one aspect of production may affect an entire economic system. A major teamsters strike will quickly cause shortages and then close dozens of unrelated industries. A coal miners' strike will do much the same, closing steel plants and automobile component and assembly plants. This in turn will affect industries producing glass, batteries, and plastics. The resultant lack of production will affect other industries dependent upon the salaries derived from the affected industries. In time, state and federal budgets will be affected through loss of tax revenues. This will result in cutbacks in government services and employment.

The traditional economy, then, is small and largely unspecialized. Its producers are less dependent on one another than producers in command or market economies.

Command Economy. The command economy is a planned economy. People work at productive tasks as ordered. A specific number of people are allotted to road-building, agriculture, manufacturing, mining, and other jobs. The labor pool is assigned to specific tasks—to produce and distribute specified amounts of goods and services.

A traditional occupation—though not in a traditional economy.

An economy so ordered will continue to produce items after the demand has been satisfied. On the other side of the coin, demand for specific items may exist, but if no provision for their manufacture has been made, there will be no production.

Economic command is generally found with governments that have great power concentrated in one group or person. In such situations, social and economic change can be speeded up or held to a crawl, depending on the aims and desires of those in control. Regions can be opened, resources developed, and production increased by government order. At the same time, government orders can prevent other regions from developing.

Our own society and economy are not without some command aspects. Our various governments require taxes to accomplish planned activities. Heilbroner, however, distinguishes sharply between the collection of taxes and services from citizens in a democracy, and the control seen in a dictatorship. The results are essentially the same in both systems, but there is the matter of degree. In a democratic system, elements of command are largely in the hands of an elected legislative body.

Market Economy.   The market economy lies at the other end of the spectrum from the command economy. In the pure market economy, production and distribution are based on social demand. If fewer people purchase new cars, fewer cars will be produced. In time, the response to the reduced supply of an item will cause a demand greater than the supply. As competition for the available units increases, so will the price per unit. Consumer satisfaction is higher when items are scarce.

SUPPLY: Quantity of items held by seller for sale.

DEMAND: Quantity of items that buyers are willing and able to purchase.

Basic to the market economy is the concept of "Supply and Demand." The basic questions for the seller in a supply and demand situation relate to how many of whatever item he should have ready for sale. To have too many in relation to consumer demand is either to live with a warehouse full of unsold items, or to drop your price to the point where you will lose money, break even, or make a profit too small to be meaningful when considering the amount invested. It is important to note that demand must be seen in terms of how much the consumer is able to purchase at a given time. Desire for an object is not the sole governing factor in a sale, however. Each of us has seen automobiles or homes that we may well have wished to possess, yet the price may have been out of reach. In this instance, since we cannot purchase the item we are not measured as part of the demand curve. Several instances of consumer indifference and latent desire can be illustrated. Directly after World War II, a speculator purchased a sealed government warehouse. He had no idea of the contents and paid a low price. He found that he had come into ownership of five million fuel pumps for army trucks for which there was no demand. To sell any of them would require that he drop his price to the point where there would be no purpose in selling them. Four years later, the Korean War created a demand on the part of the government.

The items were in short supply on the market and the demand was high. They were needed. The speculator sold the same still-sealed warehouse back to the government for many millions of dollars profit.

In this case, consumer indifference changed to consumer desire, and the ability of the consumer—the government—allowed the desire to be translated into demand. An instance where "complementary goods" have changed the demand pattern for their complement can be seen in the relationship of cars and gasoline. When the price of gasoline increased, the price of large cars and the sales of large cars decreased. Demand increased for smaller cars using less gasoline. As the price of fuel fell, the demand for larger cars increased. As fuel became less of a price factor, the price of smaller cars also tended to rise with the production of what was perceived as "superior goods."

COMPLEMENTARY GOODS:
Goods used in conjunction with other goods. (In this case cars and fuel.)

Demand for goods of lesser quality may be high when income levels are too low to allow purchase of higher quality items. Demand for "inferior goods" falls with increased consumer income. A careful survey of the fortunes of our (American) automobile industry will provide an appropriate example of this interplay.

SUPERIOR GOODS: Those goods of a higher quality. Demand and use increase with income increase.

INFERIOR GOODS: Those goods of a recognized lower quality. Demand falls with increased income.

Demand shifts also occur with the availability of "substitute goods". When the price of fuel oil increased, many people shifted to the use of wood for heating purposes. As pressure on the wood supply increased, so did the price of the substitute. As the price of the substitute increased, the demand for oil once more increased. The rule of thumb, then, would be: An increase in the price of the substitute increases demand for the original.

SUBSTITUTE GOODS: Goods which replace other goods.

If demand is high and supply is constant, we can expect the price of an item to increase. If a substitute is available, the demand for the original will fall until the price of the substitute increases. There are instances where the supply of an item can be controlled to maintain demand at a slightly higher level than can be satisfied. It is to the interest of the suppliers of diamonds, for example, to control the number of diamonds available to the market, at a level slightly below the demand. The price is then maintained at a level which allows the supplier a satisfactory profit.

Marginal Utility

The concept of marginal utility may also be used to gauge consumer activity. Marginal utility refers to the degree of consumer satisfaction derived from the consumption of one more unit of a particular product. From the supplier's point of view, it is important that each unit of an item consumed provide the same consumer satisfaction provided by the first unit. This is a very difficult, if not impossible, goal to attain. Think of the last time you were very hot and tired after having worked or played hard on a sultry summer's day. Concentrate on the taste of that first soda, iced tea, or beer. If any soft or hard drink company could have their second bottle taste as refreshing or give as much satisfaction to the consumer as did the first taste or bottle, they would be in an

MARGINAL UTILITY: The extra amount of satisfaction buyers receive from an additional quantity of a good.

enviable position, maintaining a high degree of marginal utility. Some vendors have attempted to give the impression of such satisfaction through ad campaigns. ("The one beer to have when you're having more than one.") In other words, as each additional unit of a particular product is consumed, its marginal utility diminishes. It provides less consumer satisfaction. Marginal utility as a concept explains the law of demand. The rule here is that when the ratio of marginal utility to price is the same for all goods gained by a consumer, maximum satisfaction will be attained. If the price is raised on one item of goods, marginal utility is reduced, and the only way to increase the marginal utility of that item is to reduce consumption. (If you get less, you appreciate it to a higher degree.)

At the base of the market economy is the profit motive. People do not attempt to produce or sell items that do not bring profits. Lack of a satisfactory profit margin curtails production, while increased profits from large demand encourage production. To ensure profits, producers, sellers, and buyers must keep abreast of market demands. This adjustment allows the market economy to balance production and distribution.

The rise of competition is linked to a market economy as well as to the profit motive. Competition leads to the breakdown of social elements restricting mobility and the translation of life into monetary terms. The need to decide who gets the items produced and the services rendered requires a social order, which forms the basis of a society's economic system. Each society chooses how it will use its available resources to provide maximum satisfaction.

Capitalism, Socialism, and In Between

Today, when classifying an economic system, many people think in terms of socialist or capitalist rather than in terms of market or command economies. While all these terms refer to distinct economic forms in theory, it is almost impossible to find a pure version in practice.

Capitalism is an economic system that permits and protects legal private ownership of the means of production. For the most part, a competitive market system determines the distribution of the results of production, resources, and wealth. In pure capitalism, there is no government involvement or management in the economic world. Once the government plays any role in managing an economy, that system can no longer be described as purely capitalistic. As we have seen, our government plays a large part in the management of our economic system.

SOCIALISM: Originally seen by Karl Marx as a transitory stage between capitalism and pure communism. Pure communism would have all the means of production owned and controlled by the state, while socialism, in this transitory phase, would have the state control only those means of production necessary to promote the public ownership of the means of production and distribution. In recent years the definition of socialism has come to represent little more than a welfare state.

In many ways, socialism is the opposite of capitalism. In principle, socialism does not allow private ownership of the means of production. Instead of relying on a market system to determine the rates and means of production and distribution, socialist theory favors a planned economy.

It is one thing to describe a pure economic form in theory. It is something else to describe the many variations we see of a pure form in real life.

If we could present as an example a football field complete with yard markings, we would place pure capitalism at one goal line and pure socialism at the other. Now, where would all the nations of the world be placed on the field? We would find them scattered across the field, some close, others far away from one goal line or the other.

While the United States cannot be classified as having a pure capitalist economic system, its position on the field would be close to the capitalist goal line. We have economic controls, but they are the indirect controls of monetary and fiscal policy. Other nations, such as Sweden and Norway, would lie closer to the socialist goal line because they use overall direct economic controls and planning by a government bureau. This bureau is basically concerned with the coordination of economic activity within the nation. The fine line of how much the bureau actually influences the economic activity of the nations involved changes from time to time with shifts in the political reality. This form of planning is referred to as "Indicative Planning." A deeper entry into the economic activity of a society is called "Participatory Planning." In this scenario, the government enters the economy directly by use of a Bureau that both plans and coordinates economic activity. In France the government presence either owns or co-owns large portions of the industrial and service base. This, too, changes extensively with political swings to the left and right. A government bureau in Japan controls import and export licenses, and has the real power of protecting local industry and, to a large degree, of controlling the direction of the economy. The presence of large trading companies controlling diverse areas of production seems to set the stage for an acceptance of government control.

To the casual observer, the rush in the United States toward conglomerate mergers in recent years may well lead us into the realm of entities quite similar to Japan's trading companies. Still other nations, such as the Soviet Union and China, might lie even closer to the socialist line. China has, during the eighties, moved away from the position of relative socialist purity to encompass many aspects of an open market economy. We must remember that the movement by The People's Republic of China, while dramatic, is still subject to inertia, based on the very size of the economy and the degree of change.

The Soviet economic system operates clearly from the source of power at the top and filters down to the bottom through a series of levels within a complex hierarchy. Essentially, the Soviet system works in the following manner: The leadership of the country decides on the direction the economy will take. The political climate within the Soviet Union determines whether this' is a committee decision or rests in the hands of an individual. The portions of the economy directed toward consumer goods, industrial development, and military concerns are determined by the current leadership.

Adam Smith—He of the invisible hand.

LAISSEZ–FAIRE: Essentially this means "to leave alone;" a hands-off policy of the government toward the economy.

The actual planning and allocations necessary to meet such demands are set down in a formal manner by the state planning commission, Gosplan. These plans are then forwarded to regions and to individual plants where adjustments for reality of production are suggested. The revised estimates are sent back to Gosplan where they are set into final form. The plan is sent back to the leadership, where it is approved or modified, and when approved becomes official and is implemented. Prices play a part in the distribution of goods in the Soviet Union, but a different part than they play in an open market economy. The Soviets assign prices to goods based upon their classification as necessity or luxury. By assigning a higher price to what is considered a luxury item, the economic planners are controlling consumption. The added cost is really an excise tax, known as a turnover tax.

In the true sense of the word, we do not live in a capitalistic system. Over the years, many of our citizens have been hounded and accused of having been associated with one of the "isms." In reality, for many years our economy has been in a transitional phase, that is, our system is in some ways like several basic forms other than pure capitalism. Most Americans would hardly be content to live under a system of pure capitalism. Would we be happy with no consumer protection, no pollution control, no limits of interest, no rules and regulations, no medicare, no federally sponsored public works like the Tennessee Valley Authority, and so on?

Adam Smith saw an "invisible hand" guiding the economic system under a laissez-faire economy. In his view, profit motivation, or greed, is the basis for optimum production.[3] Laissez-faire can be translated as "leaving alone" or "keeping hands off." The economic system with a laissez-faire attitude will maintain a hands-off policy toward any control or regulation of that economy.

In a pure socialist system, we would find government management of all aspects and segments of an economy. But, as with capitalism, the pure practice does not appear to have occurred. For example, profit motives and interest on money invested have crept into the Soviet system. Even the Chinese have found no way to control a nomadic economy thoroughly. In peasant villages the garden plot with its vegetables and flowers for resale at open markets seems to evade the system. In many nations aiming at pure socialism, one can find some very unsocialistic elements.

Still, the trend may be toward more socialistic systems. The very density of the world's population forces governments to control enterprises grown too complex and possibly destructive to the life of the nation they serve. As world business increases in size and corporations become even more multi-national in character, we will see a government shift to meet the challenge. This may imply even more government control than exists today.

As we have just seen, in the United States we are not living in a capitalistic economy. Nor are we socialistic. There is nothing wrong with not being capitalistic. We live in a blend of economic systems that has evolved to answer the needs of our society. The system will change, as will the systems employed by the Soviet Union, China, Japan, Germany, and all other nations. Poland is an example of how pressures can build toward changes in an economic system. All systems change to meet the demands made upon them.

The nature of society's demands upon a system will vary with its environmental and social conditions. These pressures lead to the development of current forms of economic systems. In most if not all of the world's complex major economic systems today, one basic rule holds. It is based on the profit motive sometimes translated as "greed." [4]

We should always be conscious of the difference between economic theory and practice, on the one hand, and political form and practice, on the other. A nation with a socialistic-oriented economy can use democratic political forms. A nation with a basic capitalistic economic form may well be politically repressive. The reverse is also possible, and so is any other combination of political and economic forms. Some such combination probably is being or has been practiced somewhere at some time.

ECONOMIC PRODUCTION

The boundary lines among the various economic systems have now been laid out. Next comes the question How does each system work? This section describes some of the mechanics of economic systems, showing what each system looks like and how a system works.

How Much Will Be Produced?

Any producer must settle the ratio of production to demand. How does a person in such a position decide how many items are needed or shall be produced? A related question may be asked about pricing the items produced. Theories differ on the solutions to these problems.

Manufacturers seeking to produce and market commodities face several major considerations. First, they must decide on the amount they will be able to charge for their product. This involves the cost of production and the profit they must clear to justify their effort. They must consider how many units they should manufacture to cover expenses and eventually make a profit. What is the point of producing two hundred complex, specialized computers if they can only hope to sell five such creations?

Another consideration in production is the cost per unit versus the profit per unit, translated into the Law of Diminishing Returns. As production rises, there is the expected drop in the cost of each additional unit produced, until an element such as the basic cost factor is changed. If overtime pay is required to produce more items, the cost per unit rises. The diminished return per unit occurs when the limit of production is reached and new arrangements, such as the overtime payment mentioned above, new

LAW OF DIMINISHING RETURNS: Total output increases at an increasing rate to a certain point, after which the rate of increase will drop; eventually the extra output per additional input will decline.

SKILL BOX

Invalid Syllogisms—Part 1

1. If an economy is socialistic, there will be some government controls on the economy.
2. There are some government controls on the U.S. economy.
3. Therefore the U.S. economy is socialistic.

As this example shows, not all deductive reasoning is valid. Even if the reasoning has been put into the form of the syllogism (major premise, minor premise, conclusion), it may be misleading.

Syllogisms are often based on a major premise that contains a cause-effect relationship, an "if . . ., then . . ." statement. There are other types of premises on which syllogisms may be based, but the if/then type will be used here to describe how some seemingly logical arguments should be rejected.

The invalid if/then syllogism can take two forms. One is described in this Skill Box, along with its valid cousin. The other invalid type is described in the Skill Box in Chapter 17. In the Skill Box in Chapter 3, the syllogism was introduced. That introduction used a valid form of deductive reasoning. Using symbols and the if/then format, it can be described as:

1. If A is so, then B is so. (Major Premise)
2. A is so. (Minor Premise)
3. Therefore B is so. (Conclusion)

The logic here is airtight, valid. That is, the conclusion is forced by the logic of the reasoning. Furthermore, if the premises are indeed based on truth, then the whole argument is not only valid, but true, and worthy of our acceptance.

Related to this valid form of deduction is its invalid cousin. On its surface it may look as valid as the first form, but there is, as we will see, a fatal flaw in its logic. Its form is:

1. If A is so, then B is so.
2. B is so.
3. Therefore, A is so.

This syllogism is invalid because it ignores the possibility that B might be so even if A is not. It is like saying: When my dog is sleeping, she is quiet; my dog is quiet; so my dog must be sleeping. The premises do not force the conclusion. The dog may be in the dogcatcher's truck, peacefully chewing on a table leg, or dead—among other things.

This form of reasoning might mislead people into spending their money or votes foolishly. For example, an advertisement might say, "Joe Blow, the famous actor, drinks our beer. So should you!" Put into the form of the syllogism, this pitch reads:

1. If our product is very good, it will be used by such tasteful people as the famous actor Joe Blow.
2. Joe Blow uses our product.
3. Therefore our product is very good.

The advertisement looks silly in the form of a syllogism, but there we have it: its reasoning is silly. Joe Blow might use the product for reasons other than its quality; we simply are not compelled by the premises to believe in the product's goodness. Moreover, the premises may be false; for instance, Mr. Blow may not use the beer at all. So the advertisement's claim is not only based on invalid logic, it may also be based on false information. We probably have no way of knowing if Mr. Blow does indeed drink that beer, but because of the weak logic involved, it doesn't matter anyway.

We do not want to spend our time putting all arguments or claims into the form of the syllogism. Still, if we try it once in a while, we may acquire the habit of asking two questions: (1) Is the conclusion forced logically from the premises? (Is the argument's logic valid?) and (2) Are the premises based on accurate information? (Is it true?) The more often we ask these questions, the less often we will be misled by other people or mislead ourselves.

employees requiring supervisors, and new machines or other facilities set a new cost base. The cost per unit produced should then fall as production rises once more to the point of diminished returns.

For many years, economic philosophers have sought answers to deal with these problems. Adam Smith, considered the father of modern economics, claimed that an "invisible hand" controls production and limits it to the correct amount. Smith maintained that competition acted as a control to the proper price and amount of items produced. In a sense, each time people purchase a particular object, they are casting a vote for the object itself. This can be compared to the statement made about the large number of political refugees leaving East Germany prior to the construction of the Berlin Wall: They voted with their feet. Products can be considered in the same light. Those not purchased have received a majority of negative votes. If a product is purchased heavily, the buyers' votes have encouraged the manufacturer to produce more of that item.

Adam Smith proposed that an economy works best when completely left alone.[5] The economy left alone would find its level much as water seeks its own level. In his view, competition would control the economy.

The other extreme of economic theory contends that competition is bad. This wing of economic thought believes that a central authority must plan and carry out an economy. The advocates of a planned economy would control all aspects of economic practice. Under such an economy, the public would have no option to vote for a specific product and thus demand its continued manufacture. Poor products would not disappear even when people purchased other products. There would, of course, be no wares to compare to or to compete with the poor product.

The Soviet economic system supposedly works along the lines of a thoroughly planned economy. In the Soviet system, a central committee attempts to determine the number of acres of certain crops that will be planted. The committee also determines which and how many items will be produced in any area of manufacturing. Since in a planned economy it is assumed there will not be a need for similar products, competing products are not produced. As a result, the citizens are not allowed to vote for or against a product no matter how shoddy or useless it may be. The specific products produced are planned for the entire economy, and once more the planning is centrally controlled.

Skill Reinforcer 16–1*
How might a hypothesis be used to study this issue?

Planning how much is to be produced is not the same thing as producing. In the United States, the profit incentive motivates a farmer to work. Workers on a collective farm in the Soviet Union will receive the same return no matter how hard they work. In dollars and cents, American farmers with their profit incentive have consistently produced more than the Russian collective farm lacking the profit incentive.

The Marxist ideal that people produce according to their ability and receive from the economy according to their needs sounds good, but it rarely works out to be so. In practice, the theory that all people will work as well as they can seems not to hold true. Even in the Soviet Union the central planning committee has found it necessary to provide an incentive to ensure a higher level of production.[6] This incentive sometimes takes the form of a higher class position—which is surprising in a society that had maintained itself, in theory at least, as classless. The thesis that all producers of a specific level earn the same has also been found to be somewhat unrealistic. That is, in the real world, as Adam Smith said, people can work harder than their neighbors and thus earn more.

In the Soviet Union, workers will receive from a central committee a decree calling for the production of a specific quantity of wheat, tractors, autos, or shoes. The committee has less concern than peasants farming their own gardens for a cash sale in a local free market. The peasants know that even a bountiful harvest and a consistent demand for their products will not guarantee a decent profit. That profit also depends on how hard the peasants work. On the other hand, the same peasants, ensured a basic standard income and no chance of earning more than anyone else regardless of how hard they work, will probably not overwork for the common good.

During the years after the Russian Revolution, the basic economic plan was to increase the capital structure of the economy. In essence, the government decided to provide the basis for heavy industry at the expense of consumer goods. The fact that controlled planning of the economy interferes with the normal ratios of supply and demand becomes obvious on inspecting any Soviet government store supplying consumer items.

A visitor to the Soviet Union can see long lines of people waiting to purchase a very limited supply of consumer goods. In a free economy these lines would have been enough to encourage

Israeli kibbutz life.

hordes of different manufacturers to produce the desired items. While the people would not purchase the least desirable of these items, they would buy desirable items in great quantities. This would prompt the manufacturers to produce more. The least popular items would be phased out or improved.

The Soviet planned economy, under the restrictions imposed by a central committee, has never produced enough consumer items. It is also true that the lack of consumer items manufactured by the state has led to widespread suffering, occasional starvation, and considerable deprivation.[7] Even with these sacrifices, there is no evidence that the growth rate of the planned Soviet economy has exceeded the rate of before the revolution. In other words, without the associated shortages of consumer items, the Soviet economy would probably have grown at least as fast under a free economy as it has under a totally planned economy. In this case, the parable of the carrot and the stick seems to apply. One can encourage donkeys to work harder by promising food, not by beating them. People and donkeys appear to have much in common.

In some cases, communal work groups, with central group planning, have succeeded. This normally occurs when an outside source pressures a group or society. The Israeli kibbutz system was organized in response to religious and political pressure. While operating under those pressures, the kibbutz experiment has worked, but it remains to be seen how long the system will last when pressure from Israel's neighbors disappears. In the United States and elsewhere, various communes have succeeded for periods of time, but once more those communities have been established under pressure from society. Their members have worked for the good of the group, of their own free will. Entire societies plunged into systems lacking incentives have fared less well than in situations where members either joined by choice or because of outside pressure that threatened their very existence.

Successful ventures into communal life, with its associated sacrifices, have occurred in only a few areas. Monastic orders, where members carry on lives devoid of material pleasure for the glory of God, can make communal life work. Hardy pioneers, who choose to work the land in the face of social or political pressure, opt to do so for a purpose. Vast numbers of people around the world lack this single minded dedication to a cause. We are left with questions. Was Adam Smith right? Does an economy work properly if it is left alone?

Monopolies

It is important to understand monopolies and their effects upon the economy and the individual.[8] Briefly, a monopoly occurs when a single person, corporation, or group controls all of a particular industry's production of an item for which there is no substitute.

INELASTIC DEMAND: A small change in the quantity demanded (or quantity supplied) will result from even a large change in price.

The Role of Inelastic Demand.   The ease with which a monopoly may develop depends in part on how elastic the demand for the product is. If demand is highly inelastic—that is, if a change in price will not bring a very large change in demand—a monopoly may develop more easily, if one producer gains control of its production. Remember that in an inelastic-demand situation, a price rise causes only a small drop in consumer demand. This makes it easy for a monopoly to control prices.

On the other hand, in a perfectly elastic situation, the quantity of a product is unlimited. If a producer of such a product were to raise the price, consumer demand would be greatly reduced.

For the items we must use continually, regardless of their price, demand is inelastic. No person is likely to stop using water, for example. Because no one can live without water for very long, we can see how a monopoly could result in just about any price being asked, and paid. If a person or group gained control of our water supply, we would pay any amount. Imagine people lost on a desert with very little water but much gold. When the need for water became critical, people who had water could charge any amount for it. The demand for water can be considered highly inelastic in that, regardless of price or other factors, the demand continues to be strong.

It is easy to see how big profits can be squeezed out of consumers through inelastic demand for a product. When a product is thoroughly controlled, and demand remains constant or only slightly reduced, production and its costs can be cut. Profits increase merely by raising the price of the item. In our society we must continually worry about monopolies in certain areas.[9]

The Power of Monopoly.   We have recently seen concern over the possibility of power shortages, mostly in fossil fuels used for transportation and home heating. In the past, there have been several examples of the power of monopolies.

John D. Rockefeller, the power behind Standard Oil Company, is a good example of monopoly's power. Rockefeller controlled so much of the oil trade that he forced common carriers (railroads) to return drawback payments for any oil shipped by his competitors.[10] He also had a system of spies who ferreted out information normally held in trust by the shipping companies. This information consisted of the quantities, values, and destinations of cargo shipped. Knowledge of such things led to unfair business practices against competitors and their customers.

The by-product of the large amounts of power and money that came to such trusts was corruption. For example, the president of the Pennsylvania Railroad was found literally to have purchased the votes of a number of state legislators in Pennsylvania for his own benefit. In another case, Charles Evans Hughes established the fact that several New York State and U.S. Senators were actually on the payroll of insurance combines.[11]

Two other "robber barons" were found to have watered the stock of the Erie Railroad. Watering the stock of a corporation is an interesting and profitable pastime. It consists of selling more stock in a corporation than the corporation has in assets. One of the

ELASTIC DEMAND: A large change in the quantity demanded (or quantity supplied) will result from only a small change in price.

games in the modern oil business makes a good example of how this activity can profit even when the company that issues the stock is losing money. A lease purchased for several hundred dollars will allow an operator to drill a property for oil within a specified time. The clear-thinking operator will choose an area where the oil-bearing strata sit at a shallow level. Individuals sign an agreement known as a lease interest with the operator. This agreement gives each person a share of what the well derives, according to the amount invested. A typical agreement will call for $5,000 per $\frac{1}{16}$th interest in a lease for a total investment of $80,000. The interesting point is that operators who drill without striking oil have a total expense in the friendly neighborhood of $5,000, including all promotional aspects of the deal. This leaves the operators a profit of some $75,000. We could describe the project as being somewhat overfunded. If the operators strike oil, their total expense is still only in the area of $20,000, leaving them a sizable profit plus interest received from oil royalties. The amount of money involved in the venture has little connection with its actual value. We are dealing with watered security.

Common practice in the relatively unregulated eighties has been the purchase by speculators of undervalued stock issues by means of promise and soft money. When interest rates rise, causing stock market prices to fall, a situation arises that causes the assets of a large corporation to be worth far more than the dollar price of its stock, based on their rate of return per dollar invested. Other incidents and fluctuations cause the stock of corporations to be under-valued. Union Carbide saw its stock price fall when the Bhopal disaster rocked the world. The reality was that Union Carbide's liability in no way compared to its asset value, though the price of the stock fell far enough to interest corporate raiders who would have seized control of the corporation and sold off its parts for many times the value represented by the purchase price of the stock at market value. Another game being played on a large scale has money taken in for investment paid out at very high rates to former investors, thus encouraging new investors to buy in. They in turn are paid at a high rate of return to create even more activity. This can not go on forever and usually ends with someone leaving for Brazil, a government investigation, or a petition to the courts to protect the remaining assets of the corporation.

Watering the stock of a major corporation proceeds in much the same way on a larger scale. The actual value of the corporation may equal only $5 million, but if one sells $10 million worth of stock, we are dealing with a form of fraud.

HOLDING COMPANY: A corporation organized for holding bonds or stocks of other corporations, which it usually controls.

Holding companies to drain off "excess monies" have been used with great success. This method of business abuse uses a dummy corporation that has the sole function of owning of stock in other corporations. Picture the financial situation that can arise when 49 percent of the stock in an operating corporation is slated for sale and 51 percent of the stock held for sale is marketed to the public at the value established. The stock is then split, and even more shares than those originally issued become available for sale. Let us say that one million shares are created to sell at $10.00 each. Fifty-one percent of that stock is held by the holding company ($10 × 510,000 = $5,100,000). If 20 percent is sold publicly (200,000 × $10 = $2,000,000), 29 percent ($290,000) of the stock remains for sale, held by the corporation. The corporation can decide to give each shareholder two shares for each share held. This is called a stock split, and in a healthy, honestly run company it is a sign of high profits.

In the case of our venture into high profits and little honesty, the result is a doubling not only of the shares purchased by customers or investors but also of the shares the corporation and the holding company have held in reserve. Instead of one million shares, by virtue of the split the company has created two million shares: 400,000 are outstanding, and the company now holds 580,000 for sale. The holding company now owns 1,020,000 shares and controls the company through its 51 percent holding. In time, so many shares will be outstanding that they can have very little value. The holding company with its 51 percent of outstanding shares sits back and milks whatever cash accrues, leaving the investors with worthless paper. In extreme cases, holding companies multiply the effects of the practice.

When the citizens and smaller corporations had had enough of these practices, they forced the government to take action in the form of antitrust acts. The acts were designed to foster competition and as a result drive down prices. Specifically, the antitrust acts forbade the use of ruinous underselling and price-cutting. They also forbade the practice of forcing individuals and business into contract buying, where they had to purchase everything from their prime contractor because they were unable to purchase anything from the corporation. This could prevent the acquisition of materials necessary to stay in business. It can be likened to blackmail: buy the essential materials and the rest of our products, or buy nothing. In spite of the various antitrust laws that do protect the public to a degree, we are now faced with a variation on the same theme—the conglomerate, which will be discussed later in this chapter.

The important factor here is that unlimited control of any basic material necessary to the everyday working of a society can lead to an increase in the price of that commodity, regardless of actual production cost or supply. By manipulating supply against demand, the price of any article can be raised at the whim of a corporate group.[12]

ANTITRUST ACTS: Legislation aimed against monopolies.

Government-sponsored Monopolies. It has become necessary for certain natural monopolies to exist in specific areas. The government has tried to control these monopolies by limiting profit to a certain rate. The largest of these monopolies are the telephone company and the other public utility corporations. It is easier to see the reasons for a monopoly in the area of utilities.

Imagine the complications involved in running telephone lines for a number of competing companies in the same town. Would we be faced with having several telephones in the house, so that we could speak with friends or business contacts who subscribed to different companies? Furthermore, the expense of duplicate equipment would probably drive prices up and service down. Electricity and water suppliers are in the same position as telephone companies. Having one supplier of these services appears to be in the best interests of the community involved.

As we have said, the government has placed controls to regulate the service and profit of essential industries. The aim of the controls is to allow enough profit to motivate the industry to provide the customer with a satisfactory level of service and maintain rates at a level the customer can afford. A continuing battle develops, however, because industry attempts to avoid servicing unprofitable areas in order to reduce work and tax problems. Also, the specter of corruption hovers in the presence of so large an investment. Politicians and regulatory board members are frequently accused of allowing higher rates and poor service in exchange for future jobs, immediate payoffs, or bribes. A typical payment is land purchased at an inflated price for the building of a power plant, for example. Prior knowledge of plans for the building are leaked to the people involved so they can buy the land and resell it to the companies at the inflated price that provides the payment.

The U.S. Postal Service has been an example of a government-sponsored monopoly. In recent years, successful attempts have been made to compete directly with this government service. In some areas, notably the Midwest, independent mail companies have found that the increased rates and declining service level of the Postal Service have enabled them to provide better service at a lower price.

In time, we may come to see competition in the area of power supply trying different forms of transmission. Although we will see a good deal of infighting on the political level to bar such developments, privately owned nuclear or solar generators may come to compete successfully with electric companies. This development is far in the future, because the government prefers to keep monopolies healthy enough to provide the large-scale power possible only with a large industrial base. In many instances, the government must supply the capital needed to stimulate private investment. The capital investment is used to create the infrastructure of any economy. That is, the money is used to develop roads, power supply, and communication networks. Although not in themselves profit-producing, such things will create the framework on which profit-making industries can develop.

Industry does not operate in areas where there is only a tiny chance for profit. Because of this, a government-sponsored monopoly is good both for the government and for the people. It serves to stimulate corporate interest in areas lacking an immedi-

INFRASTRUCTURE: The capital investment on which industry can be based; examples are roads, dams, schools.

ate potential for profit. For example, prior to the Depression of the 1930s, the entire Tennessee River valley was considered a social and economic backwater. There was not enough communication and power to support a complex economy. Manufacturers were unwilling to establish factories, and the power available to serve the plants was insufficient. The network of highways and railroads needed to bring in raw materials and disperse manufacturers' products for sale was also inadequate. Because private investors had been unwilling to establish power plants, and local governments had been unable to finance modern highways, the federal government moved to make up for the lack. Unusual legislation established the Tennessee Valley Authority to control the water of that river and to provide low-cost public power. The cheap power stimulated the development of the region's economy. In later years, the Federal Interstate Highway Program further tied the region into the national economy. With the advent of cheap power and fast transportation, industry found that plants established in the region would indeed make a profit.

Inexpensive local labor and tax breaks attract new businesses to such areas, because of a combination of favorable economic factors. These include low taxes, cheap power, easy access to markets and raw materials, and a labor pool accustomed to low wages. As more industry avails itself of the situation, the competition for labor will drive the wages up to a competitive level, but the other factors will continue to act as an economic stimulant. Portions of the infrastructure of the region applied the stimulation that saved the area from many more years of slow and gradual development, or even possible decline and population loss.

The economies of scale come into play at this point. In a real sense, we can compare the ability of a large industrial installation

ECONOMIES OF SCALE: Decrease in costs as operations expand.

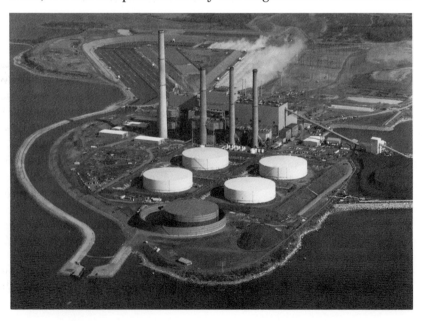

Large power plants using cheap fossil fuel are examples of the economies of scale at work.

to a water pipe. A two-inch pipe does not allow only twice as much flow of water as a one-inch pipe. Much more than twice the volume is available with twice the diameter. This may be a simple example, but the analogy does hold: In many industries a large plant has more than twice the capacity of a plant half its size. In other words, the more that is produced, the cheaper the average cost of each item produced. With the growth of large urban complexes and a possible shortage of power, the government is even more concerned about keeping these industries healthy. Toward this end, we are faced with two situations. First, while regulating their profits and service, the government encourages certain industries to be monopolistic in nature. Second, the government breaks up any monopolistic action in areas it feels will be out of keeping with the common good. At this point, a balance between industrial concentration and product efficiency must be reached. Very large firms lessen competition, but they also reduce prices. A monopoly situation that is broken up may in fact serve to raise prices. For example, the breakup of American Telephone & Telegraph (AT & T) in 1982 caused local telephone prices to rise.

Some government actions taken in recent years illustrate these positions. Upon complaint, the government found that AT & T had a policy of manufacturing its own telephone equipment, thus eliminating from the market other manufacturers of the same equipment. While there were telephone companies other than those controlled by AT & T, there were too few to support competing supply industries against the one major monopoly. The government decided that other manufacturing companies must be given a chance to compete with Western Electric (AT & T's manufacturing subsidiary) for these orders. Western Electric, the Bell Labs, and Long Lines found themselves separated from the twenty-two local telephone companies.

Variations on the Theme.   Because of the great power and profits a monopoly can bring, there have been many schemes devised toward limiting competition. Indeed, the variations on the theme of monopoly are almost endless. Here we will explore just a few.

In this area of hard-nosed business there are some funny stories. Two great robber barons of the last century were operating competing railroad lines. Each wanted to drive the other out of business, gain a monopoly, and thereby control the price of transportation in the area. They began with a price war, dropping the price of cattle shipments lower and lower. Once it became a losing proposition, the price would eventually force the weaker man out of business when he could not pay wages and taxes. In other words, the lines were trying to break each other financially. At one point, the price for shipping cattle became so low it was a joke. One of the gentlemen raised his price to the normal level. While the other wondered what was happening, the former began to buy and ship cattle on his opponent's railroad at the money-losing price.

There is no reason for complete control of an industry unless one wants to raise profits and cut expenses without competition. Some companies worry that their share of a market is too large, because too large a share might look too much like a monopoly.

One good example of a corporation in this position is the General Motors. Prior to World War II, there were many automobile manufacturing companies. Indeed, there were even more before the Great Depression of the 1930s wiped many out of business. A listing of companies that no longer exist in their own right can be compiled simply from the casualties of the past twenty years. The following automobiles can still be seen on the road, although their manufacturing companies no longer exist as independent entitics: Studebaker, Hudson, Packard, Nash, and LaSalle. Each of these companies has disappeared into other new combinations of companies or has dropped out of the automotive business. The cause of General Motors' unease has been its annual gain in the share of the automobile market. At what point did it fear that the government would step in and charge it with restraint of trade? The Japanese put an end to General Motors' worry in this regard.

Another large corporation that has faced restraint of trade legislation in the past has been International Business Machines (IBM). IBM has had a strong hold on the computer trade for a number of years.

The government has gone so far as to maintain certain corporations in losing businesses because they were the only sources of needed articles of manufacture. We can see then that monopoly need not be a winning proposition. Also, getting too close to complete control of a market in the face of government opposition may indeed be something for a corporation to avoid.

Several companies may approach a monopoly when they agree among themselves on the price for a particular item of manufacture. For example, when the major automobile manufacturers agree upon a certain level of pricing for each of their models of a corresponding market, we can say they are acting in a manner that can be defined as a form of collusion.[13] The same companies might deny access to raw materials and other controlled items in order to prevent other companies from entering into competition, and thus possibly driving down prices. They would be operating on a level similar to a monopoly. The collusion, cooperation, or even control of pricing by several companies is called an oligopoly. Properly defined, oligopoly refers to the practice of administered and/or fixed prices.

Prices can be controlled by means other than oligopoly. Sometimes corporations control the market just enough to maintain price levels. Groups of corporations have been able to set prices, thereby reducing competition. Even without formal meetings, such a group of corporations has cooperated to maintain prices. Even if price information has not actually been forwarded to alleged competitors, various interested corporations have watched one another closely and kept set prices accordingly.[14]

To the consumer this means a price level out of proportion to actual costs of manufacture. Any of the methods used has one result: It eliminates competition and keeps prices above what they would be under freer competition.

In recent years, the drug industry has been singled out for this sort of product price control. In reality, the drug industry can base its success on consumer ignorance. While the names of drugs marketed for public consumption number in the thousands, approved drug formulas number only in the hundreds. This has happened because various drug companies market a drug under many trade names, rarely under its generic name. The generic name is advertised neither to the public nor to the doctors who prescribe it. As a result, trade-name drugs, which differ not one bit from generic-name drugs, normally carry a price tag several times higher than the generic twin. Whether the higher prices of the trade-name drugs are maintained by collusion, cooperation or merely intent matters little. The result is the same: restraint of competition and increased prices for the consumer without equal increases in quality of the product.

The public is accustomed to thinking of monopoly and oligopoly in terms of large corporations, but forms of monopoly exist on a smaller scale. These forms may be no less damaging and are frequently referred to as de facto, or limited, monopolies. We see these monopolies every day, but rarely associate them with the practice. They are based on location of various retail outlets. The store located in a ghetto neighborhood, or otherwise isolated, can get higher prices for its products than it could under normal competition.

Retail stores in a position of limited competition can usually get higher prices because their customers cannot buy elsewhere. For example, coffee may cost more on a typical Harlem street in New York City than on Park Avenue. Park Avenue residents have more options than Harlem residents for shopping elsewhere. As a result, competition limits price. In instances of convenience stores, where an area lacks options for late-night or Sunday shopping, prices will rise.

In all fairness, offering services in the ghetto, in isolated locations, or at convenience times forces the vendor to meet basic expenses and other operating conditions unknown in other more competitive situations. The ghetto business must contend with more theft than businesses in typical competitive situations. In addition, lack of available financing and high interest rates make operation more difficult. Another factor is the problem of insuring for fire or theft in such neighborhoods. Business owners operating under such circumstances must make up for higher business costs.

Isolated locations and convenience stores charge the higher prices their lack of competition allows. But they must also make up for extra salespeople on Sunday, late hours, lack of business, higher transportation costs, and theft.

GENERIC: Available for common use, not protected by trademark.

DE FACTO: Concerning that which actually exists, whether or not it is recognized by law.

Large supermarket chains in some ways look something like monopolies. Various studies have shown that, though occasional prices may be lower at one market than another, their average overall price range is remarkably similar. These large markets use such practices as lower prices on a few selected items or using a "loss leader." A loss leader is an item sold below actual cost. Once the customer arrives to purchase the loss leader, the store will make up the loss on other items. One might ask why when articles of identical cost are priced differently in different markets overall shopping averages a similar price level. This similarity of price can well be interpreted as absence of pure competition.[15]

Another area of growing importance on our economic scene is the large conglomerate corporation. In simple terms, many different companies under the same corporate structure producing diverse products compose a conglomerate. In such an arrangement, one corporation can have subsidiary corporations dealing in completely unrelated services. One corporation may have a subsidiary producing printed material, another producing paint, a third manufacturing tableware, a fourth making electronic components, and still another making window frames. The same structure may also include service firms specializing in car rentals, an agency for household help or nursing, and an oil-drilling unit. One might also find a subsidiary dealing in large-scale land speculation.

Corporations diversify for several reasons. First, diversification allows the corporation to spread its investment without being dependent on one line of products. This is important because of society's swiftly changing demands and technological development. Imagine, for example, the dismay of the world's largest producer of buggy whips at the introduction of the automobile. Some manufacturers of carriages, such as Studebaker, made the transition to automobiles, but usually a single-product corporation finds itself in a do-or-die position. Today's changes come even more quickly than those in the past, and today's investments are far larger than yesterday's.

Because no major corporation can last long as a manufacturer of an out-of-date product, corporations hedging against change have tended to invest in highly unrelated products and services. In addition to this survival tactic, a corporation can shift capital funds from one area to another to bring pressure on smaller, one-product corporations—and drive many other corporations out of business, thus reducing competition. A large corporation's financial assets far exceed a typical one-product corporation operating in a limited area. As a result, the large, diversified corporation can put financial pressure in each of these areas and in turn drive prices down and force others out. When the competition is reduced, it can raise prices to regain lost monies.

In this instance, if you are a manufacturer of buggy whips—and only buggy whips—you had best make a profit on buggy whips or prepare to go bankrupt. If you are diversified and have one moneymaking industry, you can afford several other tax-loss investments.

Imagine a situation where a corporation makes $100,000 taxable profit from the manufacture of fancy hubcaps. The tax on that profit (profit is all that is left after deductions for expenses incurred in the production of the article) may be $60,000. Why pay the government $60,000 when you can invest that money and write off part of it for developing a company that will eventually make a profit? In this case the hubcap manufacturer buys a small manufacturer of poker chips. Small companies with essentially the same production costs have been producing poker chips, and the market price is about equal on all levels. With the purchase of the poker-chip company, money to be paid to the government in taxes is used instead to purchase a computerized, completely automated poker-chip machine. No one in the poker-chip industry had ever before seen the likes of such a machine. The expense of developing and purchasing such a monster could have driven every other small poker-chip company out of business, but since the hubcap manufacturer would have to pay the money in taxes, there is no expense in the purchase. The buyer writes it off as a business expense and on top of that receives a capital investment tax credit on the machine. Thus, at no cost whatsoever, the hubcap manufacturer diverts money that would have been paid in taxes to constructive investment. Furthermore, the investment is in an unrelated industry that allows much more flexibility than that enjoyed by a one-product manufacturer. The new poker-chip machine can turn out chips at a lower price than competing companies who gain no tax advantages in losing money. The monster machine obviously hauls in a larger chunk of the poker-chip market. Even though the business must pay for a large, expensive machine, it will profit through tax savings.

Buying a money-losing investment is not as necessary as one might think. Imagine a large manufacturer of automobiles on the verge of financial disaster. This company could purchase a smaller moneymaking company and write off the profits of the new company against the losses of the parent company. In other words, the deal costs the failing company nothing, and through the purchase it could retrieve tax monies to be paid by the smaller money-maker. This actually occurred with the Willys Company and Kaiser, then later with American Motors.

From these examples, we can see that modern conglomerates spread capital to work at its best advantage. It is a way to hedge a bet on a product's success. It enables the use of monies that would have gone to taxes as capital investments, giving deductions and capital expenditure credits. It will take several years before we see the effect of the 1986 tax revision on these and other activities.

Gross National Product   On newscasts and in newspaper articles we hear about the "gross national product" (GNP) when the economy of a nation is being analyzed. The GNP is an accounting tool used to measure the sum total value of all the goods and services of a nation's economy.[16] This total includes all services and products of a nation. The total of the gross national product includes all government spending, such as:

1. Defense
2. Health
3. Welfare
4. Salaries for government officials and workers
5. All government-sponsored programs, such as those of the Departments of Agriculture, Interior, Treasury, Labor and Industry, and Transportation

GROSS NATIONAL PRODUCT: The sum total of a nation's economic activity.

The GNP also includes the private sector. This covers all goods and services such as haircuts, auto sales, day workers, ditchdiggers, bootlegging, and so on. Return or interest on investments is also listed as part of the gross national product.

The GNP is merely a means, summarizing what the economy is doing at any particular time. In essence, if the gross national product is up, the economy is producing more; when it is down, the economy is producing less. If the gross national product continues to fall, the average citizen eventually notices the result.

Skill Reinforcer 16–2
You notice that the divorce rate dipped a great deal last year. Six months later, the GNP jumped upward. You conclude that the divorce-rate drop caused the GNP jump. What thinking error have you made?

Average citizens do not regularly read the financial pages to check the daily report of the gross national product, but this does not mean that they are not concerned about the economy. The condition of the economy will affect everyone in terms of the availability of money, work, products, and services. A continued downswing of the gross national product will result in less demand for most services and the products are the result of these services. A rising gross national product may mean a degree of inflation, a labor shortage, and expanding industry in general. All nations tend to follow the same rules when calculating their gross national product, but many Western economists suspect that communist bloc nations fudge a bit in their calculations of these figures.

THE UNITED STATES AND THE WORLD MARKET

How does the economy of the United States fit into the world picture? It is a modified capitalist system. That tells us something about how competition works through consumer demand and through supply arrangements to produce a specific GNP. But what is our position in the world market?

We can begin by counting our blessings. The United States is fortunate to have had enough capital on hand to invest. This investment created an infrastructure that allowed the development of our economy. Certain traits of American industry have allowed the U.S. economy to maintain its position in the world in spite of many disadvantages.

The United States has succeeded in innovating and refining manufacturing procedures. We have developed the technology of manufacture, but many items cannot or should not be manufactured in this nation. Anything demanding slow, careful, handcrafting is best imported from countries where labor is cheap.

In our relationship with other nations, we should seek importation of products that can be manufactured better and more cheaply elsewhere. By the same token, products best and most cheaply manufactured in the United States should have free access to markets. Free competition without protective tariffs would wipe out some American industry immediately, but it would also stimulate the greater number of other industries, which would benefit from a free trade situation.[17]

Another advantage we have is that the states are a group of markets with no tariffs and customs to interfere with the free movements of manufactured items. These markets are a prime factor in the development of our economy.

We must look to the rest of the world merely as another, larger marketplace for our goods. We can depend on our ability to develop and use our innovations to maintain our position in the marketplace. We must also accept the products manufactured more efficiently and cheaply by other nations. We must do this because the concept underlying all trade appears to be one of comparative advantage.

We are becoming more technologically oriented. The products that can be profitably produced in the United States result from this improved level of technology. This being so, we face a soul-searching question. We have confronted this problem internally with many painful periods of adjustment.

Many of our industries are regulated by concerns for the health and safety of workers and the public. It can be argued that this concern may not have become an issue soon enough, but white and black lung diseases, together with toxic waste dumps and a myriad of other concerns, have acted to cause us to try to save ourselves and protect our environment. These protections have caused our price per unit of manufacture to exceed the price per unit of manufacture of many other nations. They then hold a competitive edge that we are unwilling or unable to achieve. An answer to those forms of competition would be to place an environmental import tax on products whose price of manufacture was achieved under noncompetitive circumstance.

Consider old-time horse-and-plow farmers competing with the new corporate farms. The small family farmers must struggle to plant and harvest one hundred acres of corn. Perhaps they have picked up some knowledge of modern methods of soil testing, fertilization, hybrid seeds, proper conservation methods, and crop rotation. A farmer in a less developed part of the world would consider them technological experts.

Compare the same American family farmer to the corporate farm comprising thousands of acres and using efficient expensive machinery, a staff agronomist, a veterinarian, and a college-trained farm manager. There we find the same difference that existed between the American family farmer and the farmer plowing behind

One machine and two people can do the work of dozens. Pictured here. A huge, modern, turbocharged combine harvesting eight rows of soybeans.

an ox in an underdeveloped part of the world. The improved technological development of the farming has hurt the American family farmer.

As costs of labor rise, various crops are phased out, or picking procedures are shifted from hand to machine. One automated potato-picker replaces hundreds of migrant laborers in the farm industry. The same thing has happened with such crops as corn and apples. A typical highly sophisticated corn-picker and sheller can cost over $80,000. Someone farming a small parcel of land cannot afford to purchase such a machine. Without the machine, the price per bushel of harvested corn is much higher. Thus, a large corporate farm can pick and market a bushel of corn at less expense than the small-farm competition.

The technological shifts in our nation have affected or will soon affect other American industries. Doctors may find themselves replaced by computer-serviced diagnostic centers. Teachers face the prospect of being replaced by computer readers and other such innovations. Police officers on the beat and in the car use closed-circuit observation points and computer forecasting of criminal activity. What has happened in these few job areas is occurring nationwide in many other areas. Present-day economic need demands a higher degree of technical proficiency in its work force. Without this proficiency, our industry could not compete in the world market.

Historically, nations have protected certain industries from foreign competition with tariffs on imported goods.[18] An example of this protective action is the European Common Market's tariff on imported American chickens. The United States can produce chickens cut up, frozen, and ready for cooking at far less cost than farmers in Europe. In open competition, the European chicken farmer would face bankruptcy. What customer would pay a higher price for a chicken of the same quality? The Common Market placed an import tax or tariff on the American chicken. The added price of American chickens allowed French chicken farmers to maintain their prices and served to dry up the American market.

The United States follows much the same procedures with many other industries. The American dairy industry cannot compete with imported dairy products. Rather than see American dairy farmers fail, our government has placed quotas on imports which limit competition between foreign producers and the American farmer. Another innovation has acted to reduce the advantage held by American dairy breeders: The export of viable cattle embryos has allowed farmers in the rest of the world to upgrade their stock cheaply and quickly.

Anyone who has bought an automobile knows the difference that import duties make in the price of a car. For many years Americans bought European automobiles while vacationing in Europe. After driving the cars for several weeks, they could then import them as used cars at great savings. American cars face the same tariff burden when exported. In the past, many nations placed import duties on automobiles equal to or more than their actual sale price. The Japanese have developed automobiles that sell cheaper than American products, even after import duty.

The removal of all tariffs would lead to pure competition. This would encourage nations to produce only items that could succeed in the market. The transition from protected industry to free competition would be painful and dangerous. The pain would result from the many people forced to sell at a loss, as well as those forced to learn new methods of earning a living. The danger would result from nations forced to depend on other nations for vital supplies of raw and manufactured goods.

Whichever road the economics of our nation and the world follows, we face great personal adjustment in the future. The future in this case will be close at hand. The shortage of raw materials, the growing world population, and continuing urbanization will strain our resources and economy to the breaking point. These factors will also strain our personal lives. Economic trends affect our diet, health care, transportation, and everything we touch. An item such as oil has thrown our nation into turmoil. Our economy and social life has developed on the basis of cheap fuel and easy transportation.

The effect of an oil embargo placed by the Arab nations as a result of the 1973 Middle East war has given the United States a forecast of the future. Without this partial embargo, which resulted in an energy shortage, we would not really have been able to comprehend the meaning of an actual shortage of fossil fuels. Our fossil-fuel reserves, worldwide, are limited, and our consumption rises constantly.

All this has been based on our improving technology and growing population. The shock given our nation by the actual shortage and higher prices for goods has shifted attention to using other forms of energy. Since at this point politics and economics have artificially caused the shortage, we have breathing time before a real squeeze to reorient our energy consumption. We should be able to see the future and imagine the consequences of an actual series of shortages in raw material and energy supply.

SUMMARY

Each society must solve the problem of production and distribution of goods and services. Three ways in which this problem is approached are the traditional, command, and market economies. Today we divide the developed world into two major camps: those with planned economies and those based on the invisible hand of the market. While the concept of such a division is comforting, few examples exist of pure market economies or pure planned economies.

The U.S. economy depends to a large degree upon the whims of supply and demand, yet it also depends upon regulation, control, and planning. It is, like so many others, a mixed economy.

Economic production is based on a few principles. One, marginal utility, is related to the fact that production level is affected by the degree of consumer satisfaction created. Another principle is that the amount of an item that is produced and the price per unit are determined by competition, planning, or a mixture of both.

A monopoly is a concentration of control of a market. It develops more readily when the demand for a product is inelastic. That is, when the demand will not be affected much by price change, anyone who controls the supply can charge nearly any price, because people will still demand the item. There are many variations on the theme of monopoly. This tactic can be seen in the stock market and in government-sponsored corporations.

The gross national product is a measure of the total value of all goods and services produced by the nation.

The United States has a mixed economy which has prospered in the world market. This success was helped by having had enough capital and having used technology well. We, like other nations, have also used protective tariffs. These tariffs hinder economic efficiency.

SPECIAL TOPIC

Importing a Lower Standard of Living[19]

Americans fear for their economic future. Real incomes are declining. Mass firings of blue-collar and white-collar employees are common. Pension benefits are disappearing, as companies such as LTV, the huge steelmaker, fail. Parents are losing the expected security of their later years, and their children are giving up the idea of living as well as their parents.

It is said that the cause of our plight is lagging "productivity"—which also is causing our huge trade deficit (now more than $150 billion a year) and thus shifting our industries and jobs abroad. In this view, the cure is to "increase productivity," by buckling down, cutting out the fat and chopping staff and research and development programs.

But this story has it backwards. It is not that productivity weakness caused our trade problems, but that the trade problems and the undercutting of American production by imports caused the decline in "productivity," the trade deficit and the exporting of our industries and jobs. Hacking away at costs through mass firings and abandonment of research and development will not save the economy, but will worsen its decline. The trade-caused economic

sickness—including the trade-caused decline in productivity—requires a trade-policy remedy. Nothing else will work.

The concept of "productivity" is widely misunderstood. Economic "productivity" does not measure how hard, how well, how efficiently you work. It measures the sales value of what you produce. Suppose you are earning an income of $10 an hour, and producing a product with a value of $10 an hour. Then suppose you are thrown into competition with people making the same product in the same way for 50 cents an hour. The drop in the price of the product causes a drop in the value of what you produce and, thus, in your productivity. The choice is, "Work for 50 cents an hour or lose your job."

When imports from low-wage nations undersell our manufacturing production, they necessarily undercut our domestic wage level and the productivity of the American worker. Thus, eventually, the shift of our industries and jobs to other countries (to produce goods for our market) reduces American incomes and productivity just as would the migration of workers from low-wage countries to take jobs in the United States. "Free trade" has the same effects as "free immigration." Both reduce the productivity of Americans by requiring them to compete against low-wage workers.

Moreover, when the Japanese and other industrializing nations used their labor-cost advantage to take over our industries and jobs, they realistically targeted first our high-income, high-productivity industries—autos, steel and consumer electronics. It is obvious that a person's productivity depends on what he or she is doing. An excellent physician may earn a high income; the world's best dishwasher will earn a low one. As Americans are bumped down to less rewarding industries, the nation's productivity necessarily declines.

Our earlier high productivity and income were caused not by any inherent superiority of Americans over other people—as Americans used to believe, and our economics textbooks used to imply—but by a unique set of circumstances. When postwar European production revived and a new world economic situation was created by the entry of low-wage nations into efficient manufacturing production, a new situation was established. Our standard of living was set up for a great fall unless the nation adopted a trade policy that prevented American workers from being thrown into competition with workers in the low-wage nations. No such trade policy has been adopted, and our standard of living is falling.

Is the productivity weakness caused by our purported lapse into sloth and inefficiency, or does it reflect the one-way flood of imports from the new manufacturing industries of low-wage nations? Let us consider the evidence:

• United States companies that are technically more efficient, generating more output per man hour, are undersold and forced out of business by imports. With wage rates a tenth or a twentieth as high (and in some cases with cheaper credit, Government subsidies, lower environmental-protection costs and worker-protection costs), a foreign producer can easily undersell the most technically efficient American production.

• While our high-wage industries were shifted to low-wage nations, productivity and income in low-wage countries rose with extraordinary rapidity. Where did our productivity go? It was transferred abroad, along with our productive industries and jobs.

• The timing of the decline and the productivity failure of our particular industries was not associated with any visible rise of management and worker sloth. It coincided with the time when imports began to undersell our industries' production and take over its markets.

• The fall in productivity did not occur only in the United States. It afflicted all high-income nations that permitted rising and unbalanced imports from low-wage nations. Much of Europe is in worse condition than the United States, though taking its productivity decline in radically increased unemployment rather than in reduced wage rates.

• The taken-for-granted doctrine of economics textbooks that differs in wage levels between nations does not cause unbalanced or damaging international trade is shown by recent experience to be erroneous. It is obvious that if Taiwanese wages were equal to American wages, for example, we would not have a large trade deficit with Taiwan and our industries and jobs would not be moving to Taiwan. Our industries are moving to Singapore and Thailand not for the climate or for low transportation costs to the United States market, but for cheap labor.

• Low-wage imports are causing our industries to suffer losses, sales declines and constant shrinkage in the face of excess capacity world-wide. This, too, damages productivity, because the industries are unable either to justify or finance the major new investments that would produce further gains in efficiency.

Conversely, the low-wage countries are enjoying rapid increases in sales, high levels of investment and ample opportunities to purchase the latest production technologies.

Given that the United States' productivity problem is caused by its trade problem, the only cure is a corrected trade policy. What is needed to replace one-sided, one-way-benefit "trade" with real trade between nations; that is, two-sided trade that exchanges our goods for their goods and benefits both nations. Only within the framework of such a policy of balanced and mutually beneficial foreign trade can the decline in productivity, income and economic prospects be halted and reversed. The future of the United States depends on whether we can face these realities—whether we can escape from the childish dream world in which "free trade" is The Good Fairy, and "protectionism" is The Wicked Witch of the West.

SELF-TEST QUESTIONS

Match numbers 1–3 to the descriptions on the right:

1. government planning determines what your job is
2. your job is the same as your parents' job
3. supply and demand make it work

    a. traditional economy
    b. command economy
    c. monopoly
    d. market economy

4. True or false: The economies of most developed countries are mixtures of capitalism and socialism.
5. A big change in price will not affect demand much when the demand is

_____.

6. It is based on the fact that production depends on the degree of consumer satisfaction created:
   a. monopoly
   b. marginal utility
   c. imperfect competition
   d. command economy
7. Adam Smith said that _____, which he called the "invisible hand," make a capitalist system work.
8. Control of a market by one person or one group is:
   a. market economy
   b. demand
   c. supply
   d. monopoly
   e. gross national product
9. A measure of a nation's total output of goods and services is a(n):
   a. benchmark
   b. cartel
   c. index
   d. gross national product
10. The success of the United States in the world market has been affected by:
   a. abundant capital
   b. technology
   c. protective tariffs

ANSWERS TO SELF-TEST QUESTIONS

1. b
2. a
3. d
4. true
5. inelastic

6. b
7. supply and demand
8. d
9. d
10. a, b, c

ANSWERS TO SKILL REINFORCERS

16–1. A hypothesis is an informed guess that is useful for finding answers to problems. Here our problem might be: Is profit incentive necessary to ensure high production from workers? The hypothesis for this could be: Worker production will increase in (a particular country) if profit incentive is used. The experiment would be to apply that incentive in one part of that country (or in one country) but not another, similar place. Productivity could then be compared. The hypothesis is a probe into the unknown; it suggests a research plan by which the hypothesis is tested.

16–2. False cause. In your search for a cause of the rise in the GNP, you have ignored the fact that many other factors (which you have not controlled in your observation) may have been the cause. Because B followed A, you assumed that A caused B.

NOTES

1. *Washington Post,* October 18, 1981.
2. Robert L. Heilbroner, *The Making of Economic Society,* 3d ed. (Englewood Cliffs, N.J.; Prentice-Hall, 1970).
3. Adam Smith, *The Wealth of Nations,* intro. by E.R. Seligman (New York: E.P. Dutton, 1910).
4. Robert Lekachman, *Greed is Not Enough* (New York: Pantheon Books, 1982).
5. Smith, *Wealth of Nations.*
6. R.A. Bauer, Alex Inkeles, and Clyde Kluckhohn, *How the Soviet System Works* (New York: Vintage, 1956).
7. George H.N. Seton-Watson, *From Lenin to Khrushchev: The History of World Communism* (New York: Praeger Publishers, 1960).
8. Edwin Mansfield, ed., *Monopoly Power and Economic Performance* (New York: W.W. Norton, 1974).
9. John K. Galbraith, "Monopoly and the Concentration of Economic Power," in *A Survey of Contemporary Economics* (New York: Richard D. Irwin, 1952).
10. Richard Hofstader, ed., *Progressive Movement: Nineteen Hundred to Nineteen Fifteen* (Englewood Cliffs, N.J.: Prentice-Hall, 1964).
11. Robert F. Wesser, *Charles Evans Hughes: Politics and Reform in New York, 1905–1910* (Ithaca: Cornell University Press, 1967).
12. R.F. Lanzillotti, "Pricing Objectives of Large Companies," *American Economic Review,* December 1958.
13. *A Study of Administered Prices in the Steel Industry and a Study of Administered Prices in the Automobile Industry,* Senate Report 1387, 88th Cong., 2d Sess.
14. Jay Gould, *The Technical Elite* (New York: Augustus Kelley, 1966).
15. Joe S. Bain, "Price and Production Policies," in *A Survey of Contemporary Economics,* ed. Howard D. Ellis (New York: Richard D. Irwin, 1948).
16. Samuelson, *Economics.*
17. Milton Friedman, *Capitalism and Freedom* (Chicago: University of Chicago Press, 1962).
18. Bela Balassa, ed., *Changing Patterns in Foreign Trade and Payments* (New York: W.W. Norton, 1964).
19. John M. Culbertson, copyright © 1986 by The New York Times Company. Reprinted by permission.

SUGGESTED READINGS

Bauer, Raymond A.; Inkeles, Alex; and Kluckhohn, Clyde. *How the Soviet System Works.* New York: Vintage, 1956.

Belov, Fedor. *The History of a Soviet Collective Farm.* New York: Praeger, 1955.

Ebenstein, William. *Today's Isms: Communism, Fascism, Capitalism, Socialism.* Englewood Cliffs, N.J.: Prentice-Hall, 1961.

Gill, Richard T. *Economic Development Past and Present.* Englewood Cliffs, N.J.: Prentice-Hall, 1963.

Josephson, Matthew. *The Robber Barons,* New York: Harcourt, Brace & World, 1962.

Kapp, William K. *The Social Costs of Private Enterprise.* Cambridge: Harvard University Press, 1950.

Loucks, William N. *Comparative Economic Systems.* 6th ed. New York: Harper & Row, 1961.

Potter, David M. *People of Plenty: Economic Abundance and the American Character.* Chicago: University of Chicago Press, 1954.

Rostow, W.W. *The Stages of Economic Growth: A Non-Communist Manifesto.* Cambridge: Harvard University Press, 1962.

Tax, Sol. *Penny Capitalism: A Guatemalan Indian Economy.* Washington, D.C.: Smithsonian Institution of Social Anthropology, 1953.

Ward, Barbara. *Five Ideas That Changed the World.* New York: W.W. Norton, 1959.

17 DISTRIBUTION OF PRODUCT AND PROFIT

PREVIEW

The Classic Confrontation

The confrontation between capital and labor may be moving to a new battle-field. From the earliest days of the employer/employee relationship there have been disagreements about who should get the major share of the profits result-ing from joint ventures of capital and labor. We may see the beginning of the end of these disputes with the large-scale introduction of robots into the work place. At this point in time, robots are used to replace people in menial jobs.

The Yamazaki Machinery Works in Oguchi, Japan, has recently replaced almost all their blue-collar workers with six self-supervising machines. Some 230 employees would be needed to accomplish the same production levels. The president of Yamazaki estimates that these six machines will save his company $5 million.

The questions to ask are: (1) Can we be replaced by robots? (2) How much profit can be realized by replacing us? (3) If the profit is substantial, how long would it take for us to be terminated? (4) What would we do for a living after we had been roboted out of work?

This scenario is much like that played when automated looms put spin-ning-wheel operators out of business.

Who gets what? The expensive sports car or the rundown house— or perhaps the car and money to recondition the house are within reach of some but denied to most people.

Of all the social questions facing us, one of the most basic and important is the topic of this chapter: Who gets how much of what is produced?

For generations people have fought and died over the division of wealth. We have seen struggles between people and nations over which person or group deserves the lion's share of production. The phrase "lion's share" beautifully illustrates the oldest method for dividing what is available. The lion takes by force, and so did our ancestors. Many nations still use force to settle economic matters.

In the days of the cave dwellers, the strongest person came out of a hunt with the major share of the kill. History documents the names of the strong, who left tales of acquiring the property of the weak. The Persians, the Romans, and the British have all had their days of taking over the production of nations less able to defend themselves.

Today we have other examples of power groups acquiring the fruits of the production of the less powerful. We can recognize examples of pure muscle in such terms as gang, cosa nostra, or possibly politicians.

The distribution of production and profit today is the topic of this chapter. We will study those who wrestle for the largest share of the production, within our own nation and among other nations. The size of our share of the production is directly affected by this struggle.

WHO GETS WHAT

The issue is who is to get the rewards of a society's production. Remember, there are more rewards than just wealth; there are also prestige and power. Here we will look at the economic rewards of production first. We will see there are two basic views on how profits should be rewarded. Then we will look at the related issue of corporation power—with the wealth that goes with it. Finally, the distribution of rewards on the basis of merit will be explored.

Labor Versus Capital

INCENTIVE: Something that causes a person to act; a motive.

The question of "who gets what" involves the terms "capital" and "labor." Capital is existing wealth; it may take such forms as natural resources, buildings, factories, highways, monies, or ships. Another factor, which has a direct bearing upon production, is what the people contribute—labor. If we combine capital and labor and add a touch of incentive, we will probably wind up with production.

Should capital receive the major part of the product or should labor? Teams on both sides of the economic game have presented many arguments to justify one, the other, or both. But in what proportion? In *The Wealth of Nations*,[1] published in 1776, Adam Smith wrote that a nation's natural resources and work would in time find a fair distribution. The English economist David Ricardo added another factor—land. He felt that the contribution or risking of land in an economic venture entitled the owner to the larger share of the production. Land and resources are not usually considered capital. But if we equate land with capital, Ricardo's view is that the person who risks capital is entitled to the greater share of what is produced.[2]

In our society we have tended to agree with Ricardo. The landowner—by virtue of capital investment—receives a greater share of what has been produced by a sharecropper. If we equate the labor involved in growing a crop on land under such an agreement, we must see that we have valued the land or capital more than the sharecropper's labor. Later, Karl Marx reversed this capitalist theory and came up with his own conclusions. Marx felt that only labor created wealth.

If we compare these differing views, we can see the base of the argument between capitalist and socialist economic systems. Because capitalists view existing wealth used for production as the most important element, they believe that the contributor of the wealth should receive the major portion of whatever is produced. The socialist view is that labor is the more important ingredient of production [3] and that therefore the people who give their labor for the production of goods should benefit most from it.

Marx saw a process of historical determinism in the industrial world. Observing the industrial nations of the world, he developed the idea that the faulty distribution of the fruits of production found in the capitalist system would cause the workers to rise and revolt. As Marx put it, capitalism contains the seeds of its own downfall in its faulty system of distribution. Marx developed his theories based on the highly industrialized areas of Europe, but it is surprising that the revolutions he predicted have taken place mostly in the rigid social and economic systems of the more backward agrarian nations, Russia and China.

The Soviet Union would not be classed as a farming nation today, but at the time of the revolution, it was largely preindustrial. While these bloody revolutions destroyed the existing social and economic order in Russia, most of the industrial nations have evolved peacefully. They have come to the point where the benefits of production have become subject to what we now call collective bargaining.

Before we discuss modern collective bargaining and the economic order as we live it, we must first discuss capital and its ownership. One form of capital includes natural resources, and we must first determine ownership of those resources. If a large oil or gold deposit is found on government land, who has the right to the major portion of the return from that deposit? This can become tricky. On government-owned land in the western part of the United States there are huge deposits of oil-bearing shale with an estimated 600 billion, perhaps even a trillion, barrels of oil locked within them.[4] If we consider that the entire Middle East has an estimated known reserve of 390 billion barrels of oil, we begin to get some idea of the size of this resource.

The question is who should benefit more from this oil. After all, it is located on land owned by the citizens of the United States. Should these valuable natural resources belong to the person who first arrives on the scene, or should the wealth of the land belong to all the citizens?

One answer to this question would be that the person who finds and develops the resource should benefit more from that resource's production. Another answer would be that the generation of people who made the use of that resource possible is responsible for the technology and the opportunity to develop it; in accepting this argument, the answer would award the benefits of production to the entire population. Socialist theory is based on the last answer. When carried further, it requires that since the actual labor necessary to create any product is of the utmost value, the wealth itself should not be inherited.[5] The capitalist system operates on the basis that the developer, the person with the ability and energy to develop, should get the major rewards. In turn, the accumulated wealth of the developer should pass on to his or her heirs. This is a basic difference between socialist theory and capitalist theory.

A further question about the share of production and labor invested in that production is at issue. Strictly speaking, socialists see an equal sharing of all aspects of production, regardless of the unequal skills or energies offered—all people should benefit equally from the results of the labor. The socialist theorist would give a skilled tool-and-die maker the same salary—that is, rights to the production of a society—as the unskilled floor-sweeper who removed the metal filings from the floor. In brief, the theoretical basis of socialist distribution is "From each according to ability, to each according to need."

Skill Reinforcer 17-2
How does average differ from median and mode?

Once more, theory and practice vary greatly. The Soviet Union has developed a managerial class with privileges and rewards far exceeding those of the working class. It is understood that the typical member of the Soviet managerial class can live better, earn a higher average income, and thus receive a greater share of society's production than the typical farm laborer. It is unrealistic to assume that a champion chess player in the Soviet Union has no more access to the good things that make life worth living than a poor chess player. It is also unrealistic not to assume that the director of a large factory will have access to more luxury items than a worker in the same plant.

In all fairness to the Soviet system as it is today, we must point out that far fewer differences exist between what is available for the managers and workers in today's Chinese society. It boils down to what one wants out of life. Those who are content to work as hard as they can, yet who receive the same benefits as the people who work very little, might be happy under a theoretically pure socialist system. If, on the other hand, the people would like to know that they can exceed the standard rate of pay by extending themselves, they might be happier in a capitalistic system. In theory, the capitalistic system allows people who put out extra effort or have greater skill or intelligence to gain a larger part of the production of their society.

Ownership of Corporations

The question of "who gets what" is reflected in the issue of who owns—and who *should* own—the corporations. A great deal of the wealth and the power in the United States is vested in corporations. Who should own it? The question at its base involves the struggle between the unions and the managers of the corporations. The unions are assumed to represent the workers. Management represents the capitalist side of the issue. The clash of these two factions is a power struggle.

Both factions have power. Control of unions themselves provides a base for power and wealth somewhat like that of corporate management. Both industry and labor put their best words forward, constantly waging a battle for public sympathy and support.

The ownership of corporations is at issue because of the natural tendency of unions to see excess profits going to a small group of exploiters of working people. Corporation management counters with the argument that a large part of the American public owns the stock shares of most companies. The incomes of many widows and orphans depend upon the profit dividends these corporations pay. In reality, most of the American public owns no stock, and only a very small percentage of our population controls most public and private corporations.

Because so very few people own the corporations, the debate focuses on the question, Who should own them? That is, should the workers gain more—or all—of the ownership? The issue of worker ownership is growing because of other factors buying into the corporation wealth. These include unions, pension funds, and universities. Despite these new factors, the real power of most corporations is held internally, regardless of the amount of stock outstanding.

This difference between ownership and control is an important point. The people who own most, if not all, of a corporation's outstanding common stock do not always control the corporation. The management of many corporations is a closed system; it perpetuates itself. The corporate officers have access to the names and addresses of the stockholders allowing them to seek proxy votes actively. On the other hand, groups that wish to unseat the current officers find themselves at a disadvantage; they do not have those addresses. For them, the stockholders are widely spread, often apathetic, and anonymous.

The top management of a corporation may consist of a small group of two or three people who control, either through ownership or voting rights, more than 50 percent of the outstanding stock. Control of a sizable block of shares of less than 50 percent is often enough. The management can push through decisions for which most stockholders would not vote. Usually these matters are out of the stockholders' hands. The lack of communication among stockholders is their major source of weakness and lack of corporate power. Through their demands for a larger portion of production, unions form the only real threat to corporate management.

Meritocracy

There is another angle from which to explore the issue of who gets what. Besides deciding between capitalists or workers, we might want to reward people directly on the basis of how productive they are, not to which faction they belong.

At once we are faced with an important question: Is this fair? People could be classed as a natural resource needed for production, so one might also reason that we must class the less productive people, as well as the more productive, as part of that natural resource. Is it fair, then, to give the less productive person fewer rewards than the more productive person?

MERITOCRACY: A system in which advancement and reward are based upon merit.

If the answer is yes, we find that we have what is called a meritocracy, a system in which advancement and reward are based on merit. Arguments can be advanced both for and against a meritocracy.

Let us use a typical corporation as an example. The president of a large corporation may receive more than fifty times the actual benefits of a production worker. For example, the president will receive in salary, expense accounts, and stock options an amount equal to more than $500,000 per year. A production worker may receive only $10,000 a year. Is the president of a corporation worth fifty times as much as a production worker? Our system answers yes. Presidents of large corporations must make many decisions that justify the salary they receive. The difference between an adequate corporate president and an inadequate one is easy to see. A proficient person may be appointed president of a failing company and, by virtue of his or her ability, turn that company into a profit maker. The president's actions may result in profits many times over the salary received. Further, the president serves to create and save many jobs for the people who work for the corporation. In this sense the president is worth the salary.

A response to this position can be made, pointing to the many instances of corporate officials gleaning large rewards even though their balance sheet shows a substantial loss and workers are asked for give-backs. The concept of the golden parachute is hardly worthy of being identified with a meritocracy. In this situation the captain of a sinking corporate ship strikes an agreement with another corporation for a takeover. Part of the agreement provides an extremely liberal pension or job responsibilities with the new corporation, at the expense of the stockholders. Let us not neglect to mention the means by which many persons come to serve on boards of corporations and hold high paying positions with those corporations. This is, of course, by owning large blocks of voting shares and in some instances being a friend of a large stockholder. This does not fit the mold set for a meritocracy either, but it occurs regularly in our society.

INSIDE THE TWO CAMPS: CONGLOMERATES AND UNIONS

From the debate on how much of production labor and capital should get, we can now move to an inside look at the two combatants. This will show us something about how the two factions are organized.

Conglomerates

Capitalist economics encourages the development of larger and larger concentrations of capital. In progression we see the single owner of a business join another person, or several people, to form a partnership. In turn, the partnership will enlarge and seek outside capital, forcing the creation of a corporation.[6] As conditions warrant, the single corporation will find that its survival may depend upon its ability to spread risk and hold still larger amounts of capital, giving rise to what is referred to as a conglomerate. A conglomerate is an interlocking group of corporations contributing to their common good and goals. The major effect of the conglomerate structure is derived from the concentration of capital.

This progression as outlined depends upon government policies. That is, the government decides the productive structure of any nation. As citizens of the United States, we have become familiar with the general form of American business. We have seen the rise and conglomeration of numerous industrial giants. At this point it would be interesting to illustrate the differences found in capitalistic systems by discussing the Japanese business structure.

Japan. The Japanese form of capitalism developed differently from the capitalism practiced in the United States. There are but two principal conglomerates in Japan, and these are referred to as *Zaibatsu.* Instead of the concept of a strong person at the top, the Japanese have developed the working model of a group of people at the controls. While this may be considered a minor point, other more basic differences exist.

The most important difference is in the attitude of both the company's managerial staff and its labor force, which can be described as a form of group ideal. The entire staff has strong feelings of company loyalty and dedication. In years past these feelings would have been called patriotism in our own society. Just as our schoolchildren may sing the national anthem each morning at school, Japanese employees will sing a hymn of dedication to their company. While the typical schoolchild singing our national anthem is apt to be mouthing words, Japanese employees are likely to be expressing real feeling and dedication to their company. The company has taken the form of a large family that binds both workers and management together with feelings of mutual responsibility toward the company goals and purpose.

The effect of this spirit of dedication is interesting. Among the managers, decisions are made by consensus. Because the major concern is the company good rather than individual power, decision-making is an elaborate process. Japanese managers are a dedicated group in that they are consumed by the work ethic.

That vacations and leisure time are rarities is more the result of personal loyalty to the company than of any prohibitions.

American executives are known for their high consumption of luxury items. The living standard of the American managerial class is much higher than that of its workers. In contrast, Japanese managers consume luxury items at a far lower rate than their American counterparts.

There are also striking differences in the workers' relationships to their companies. When people take a job with a Japanese company, it is usually for life. Given the attitude of the typical Japanese worker, there is little or no chance that they will be fired. The company maintains the attitude that if it cannot provide constant and consistent employment for the workers, it has failed one of its primary duties, which to the Oriental is akin to losing face or honor. The company is obliged to provide its employees with the basics of life. It gives the Japanese workers many benefits as a matter of course and obligation. In our nation, gaining such benefits has required strikes and collective bargaining. These expected benefits include child care for working parents, comprehensive health programs, and, most of all, job security.

Job security is a double-edged obligation in Japan. People who leave their companies are seen as committing an act of disloyalty akin to that of a bad child's betraying his or her family. Companies are dedicated to providing jobs for their employees, and in turn the employees assume a responsibility to the company on the same level. Employment from first job to death is the standard by which most Japanese operate. Many Japanese, however, are not taking part in the corporate-worker reciprocal relationships. Life for these people is not easy and their employment is dependent upon the unpredictable movements and demands of the market. A second and frequently overlooked aspect to Japanese working conditions is that while managers are not paid inflated salaries, neither are workers. As a result, the corporation has vast surpluses to invest, and the workers, both managerial and production, receive a lesser portion of the rewards than do Americans. Consumer spending is at a lower rate in Japan than in the United States, which may have been responsible for the push to export and the lack of a consumer market for imports.

United States. If we compare this form of dedication and employment patterns to America's, we see great differences. A pink slip in the pay envelope happens often enough in the United States. Standard operating procedure in major American corporations includes a general philosophy dedicated to weeding out employees felt to be no longer producing at top efficiency.[7] The American corporation tends to operate on the up-or-out standard. People who are too often passed over for promotion are seen by the corporation as less useful than a newer employee of unproven potential. People who have dedicated twenty years of their lives to an American corporation may find a pink slip telling them they are fired as of the next day. It is easy to understand that employment involving little loyalty encourages the employee to jump at any favorable opportunity. The fear of being unemployed due to merger or takeover has done little to encourage corporate loyalty.

In American business, the rule is to change jobs when the opportunity comes, and that pattern is not confined to large corporations. All the military services use the rifting procedure of weeding out their officer corps. The teaching profession has for years had the reputation of being a haven of security in an otherwise tenuous job market. While the concept of tenure has ensured teachers long-term employment, many teachers never reach it. Academic transients are well known in college teaching circles. They pass from one college to the next on one- and two-year contracts, never reaching a level of tenured professor. Only in recent years has the teaching profession felt the need to protect its position, as tenure itself has come under fire.

The giving and taking of tenure and other benefits from the teaching profession can be tied to population variations. In a period experiencing a rising birth rate, the need for teachers is high, and they may bargain with some strength. In a population downswing, as was experienced from 1964 to 1980 (the birth dearth), teachers were no longer needed in great numbers. Indeed, the graduates of the baby boom (World War II to 1964) were underemployed and willing to work cheap. Large numbers of qualified people with doctorates work at part-time jobs because tenured places are occupied by their short-birth-year seniors. As a consequence, there have been successful efforts on the part of management to break, bend, and otherwise attack the system. Look over your shoulder and see the first ranks of the new baby boom reaching school. Even in 1986 there were emergency bond issues floated to build replacement schools for those closed during the birth dearth. The mid-1990s will see this flood hit the colleges just as the depression babies retire. The numbers will be doubly large, in that women will attend in ever larger numbers. At that time the public will forget about attacks on tenure, etc., until the next fall in demand.

In a society of little employer loyalty, it is not surprising to discover employee loyalty lacking. With which system would you prefer to live—Japanese or American?

Unions   There has always been a progression in the area of labor. People worked first for themselves. In time, people began to work for other people. Later still, people began to work for the faceless entity that is the company corporation. Workers offset the disadvantage of dealing as individuals with management by banding together to form an effective power base.

History.   The history of unionism is long and, in many nations, bloody. A glance at the beginnings of European industrialism shows the pain caused by the shift from rural agriculture and

Luddites, fearing unemployment, destroyed machinery like this spinning jenny.

individual craftspeople to the factory worker. Responses to economic shifts and consequent labor reorganization have been diverse. The realignments have run the gamut from Russian class massacres to the relatively peaceful experiences of the United States and England. Although Western experiences were less bloody than the Russian example, they involved substantial pain and privation. The early 1800s in England saw violent response to industrial change.[8] The "Luddites" protested by breaking machinery and burning plants. In all fairness to both sides of this class struggle, we must remember that the situation was new and rules of behavior had yet to be developed. The worker, newly arrived from the farm, was thought to be a lazy lout who had to be kept near poverty to ensure any return in labor. It was felt that the worker from the countryside, accustomed to the free time and life of a farm, would not easily adjust to the discipline of a factory. In part this philosophy has some basis, but treatment of workers to ensure their continued efforts was, and in many areas still is, inhuman. The economic laws developed from the theories of Thomas Malthus and David Ricardo tightened to bind labor to subsistence wages.

The first unionists in the United States were not the people we are accustomed to regarding as union members today. Skilled craftspeople were the first to organize, before the Civil War. This nation has lacked the strong class feelings found in most other areas of the world. In Europe, class lines had been tightly drawn for centuries. No doubt the long-standing class differences in other countries helped cause the excesses that became a part of the industrial revolution.

In the United States there have been two basic philosophies regarding the aims and benefits to be derived from unions, one based on broad social reform, the other only on worker benefits.

Originally, the Knights of Labor did engage in strikes and boycotts, but it was primarily reformist and humanitarian in its aims. In 1884 political pressure was used to abolish the concept of the wage system. To this end, the Knights sought many changes, some of them radical. These included government ownership of railroads and telegraph lines, compulsory education, compulsory arbitration, free textbooks, income and inheritance taxes, and a series of laws that treated employers and employees equally. Much of what the Knights sought is law today. The desire for a thoroughly cooperative industrial system has not yet been fulfilled, but widespread stock ownership and profit-sharing plans are moves in that direction.

The idealistic aspects of labor-management relations were important concepts of the Knights of Labor. This early form of unionism achieved some success. The most notable occurred in 1885, when Jay Gould and the executive board of the Knights met on an equal footing and settled their differences.

For a time, modern trade-unionism, based on the other basic philosophy, concern with worker benefits, coexisted with the

Knights of Labor. Then the modern version gradually grew to replace the Knights in importance and orientation. In 1886 an alliance between national and international trade unions formed the American Federation of Labor (AFL). The aims of these new organizations were quite different from those espoused by the Knights of Labor. The Knights had philosophical and theoretical aims regarding the reform of the economic system. Its goals were reform, cooperation, and state ownership. In contrast, the AFL worked to deal directly with improving the workers' economic situation. The Knights of Labor had fought to gain power through political change. The AFL looked for its power base in the economic area. In essence, the economic goal of the AFL was "more money, now." In other words, the workers wanted a larger share of the profits of production. Labor felt a need to equalize the balance lost with the change from individual labor patterns to group labor patterns.

Strategy. A study of U.S. labor organizations will show that workers with the greatest economic power tend to band together and hold back on their skills. Since unskilled labor cannot replace them, the industry in question suffers economic strain. If all shoemakers or skilled machine operators cease working, the affected industry will have no choice but to close down.

In recent years the situation has changed. Now large numbers of unskilled workers have banded together in unions and forced shutdowns by refusing to work. Because unskilled labor can be more easily replaced, the action in itself could not cause a shutdown. Under these circumstances, the workers use pickets, force, threats, and other forceful actions to discourage replacement.

For an example, consider the truck drivers of today. If the teamsters decide upon a work stoppage, there is no reason why they could not be replaced immediately with other workers. Nearly everyone of age has a driver's license and could adapt quickly to driving a truck. However, any attempt at strikebreaking will meet violence. The violence may be directed toward the trucks, the warehouses, the replacement drivers, or all three. Business owners do not wish to see their investments burned to the ground or blood spilled, and, as a result, the industry closed down. This respect for the job holder's position comes unwillingly from management.

We have had a history of bloody battles between striking workers and strikebreakers. While strikes have brought some groups of workers much success, other strikes seem to have made little impact. A comparison of the unions of three kinds of workers is worth making.

Garbage collectors do not have training or skill that would make them difficult to replace, but the product of their labor has become increasingly important to the urban way of life. Without constant collection and disposal of solid wastes, our cities would quickly become unpleasant health hazards. Striking garbage collectors aim to prevent all disposal of garbage. In this way the

The PATCO strike marked a major change in our government's and the public's attitude toward striking union members. Most of the striking air traffic controllers were fired from their jobs.

nuisance they cause quickly becomes unbearable, and employers must yield. In a rural area, families could burn or bury their own waste, but the city resident has no such option.

Though strikes are a restraint of trade, unions received help from the Wagner Act (1935), which exempted unions from the provisions of antitrust laws dealing with restraint of trade. Governments have acted to exempt their employees from taking advantage of these provisions by making many strikes by public employees illegal.

In 1981 the air traffic controllers staged a strike against the government and the airlines. They were crushed because they were essentially middle-class people with middle-class norms. The government knew that this group of people would not destroy radar, burn cars or planes, and shoot or beat up scab workers. The strikers had relatively high salaries, too high for America's labor to build much sympathy. Worst of all, they were white-collar workers. If the strikers had been teamsters of one kind or another, they would never have been fired. They would have burned equipment and made the airfields unsafe. The American public would have understood this. But it could not accept white-collar, salaried workers on strike.

A teachers' strike also lacks the impact of a garbage collection stoppage. Even though teachers are skilled professionals who require extensive training, a work stoppage on their part does not touch the public so directly. Even if teachers succeed in closing schools and denying access to replacement personnel, the only effect of their strike is that there are children around the house. Most Americans do not feel that several weeks' or months' extra vacation from school will affect their children seriously. Sitters and grandparents are available to care for younger children, and the older youngsters can shift for themselves. As a result, the strike is not seen as an emergency.

Strikes of the milk industry, truckers, garbage collectors, transport workers, and construction workers, among others, affect our lives directly. As such, they demand an end to the problem.

Certain groups have rarely resorted to strikes. The public had classed such groups as firefighters, doctors, nurses, police officers, and teachers as performing such services that should never be stopped, yet we now see work actions and strikes among these groups. The 1976 action doctors took in California and elsewhere is a prime example of professionals withholding vital services. Some of these same types of groups have also developed the self-concept of professionalism, but they see striking as unprofessional and somehow unworthy of their status. In many cases these groups are rapidly developing strong unions. Furthermore, the future will see changes in the laws dealing with strikes by professionals and public employees.

The latest trend in unionization is the organization of totally unskilled workers such as hospital aides, food workers, service workers, and farmers. In time, strikes will gain such groups better salaries and working conditions. As the salaries gained by un-skilled groups overtake those of skilled and professional workers, we will see more effective strikes among professionals. Doctors and lawyers may set their own fee levels. Strong, interlocking unions protect skilled and unskilled workers. This leaves the teacher, the professor, and the most middle-management adminis-trators in a vacuum. Obviously these groups will exert pressure to regain lost ground.

Antiunion sentiment in the United States appears to be at a high point in the mid-eighties. For whatever reason, the typical American seems content to associate him- or herself with those segments of the economy that derive no benefit from union activi-ty. This may be due in part to the shrinking industrial base of American labor, and the strength of unions in those areas. At one time, if the coal miners or the steel workers went on strike, everything closed down. Today, with foreign supply at hand there is less threat.

COLLECTIVE BARGAINING:
Negotiation between a company's management and some other unit for the purpose of agreeing on wages and working conditions for employees.

Collective bargaining is essentially bargaining by a group of employees with their employer.[9] It may result in an artificial job monopoly. Bargaining will begin in one of the following situations. The shop or place of employment may be "open," which means that anyone can be hired without union membership. It may be a "union shop," which requires union membership after employ-ment. Or it may be a "closed shop," which means that union membership is required prior to hiring. (Closed shop agreements have been prohibited by the Taft-Hartley Labor Act [1947]. This act also empowered the president of the United States to impose an injunction of 80 days against a strike seen to imperil the country's well being. The bill also allowed states to pass "right to work laws" which did away with requirements of union membership for continued employment.) The concept behind the union shop or closed shop is that because the union benefits all the workers, it follows that all the workers should support the union. From a con-servative point of view, all people are not required to join the Red Cross, for example, yet all may receive its benefits (even though many are required to pay for those services).

The closed or union shops bring up a major question to be answered regarding union-management relations. Do workers re-ceive more than their share of what is produced? Under the threat of closing industries by virtue of their labor monopolies, the unions may indeed reach a point in their demands where it is no longer profitable for an industry to continue in business.

We can see indications of this in the publishing business, where high labor costs in recent years have put one newspaper after another out of business. The high costs are those paid not to the editorial staff but to the printing and distribution staff, whose workers have been highly organized. The organization of these groups preserved the jobs of their members, even in the face of new printing equipment which could replace them. Not only are workers kept in positions long after their services become obso-

SKILL BOX

Invalid Syllogisms—Part 2

1. If that union demands higher wages, this newspaper will go out of business.
2. The union has promised not to demand higher wages.
3. Therefore, the newspaper will not go out of business.

It is clear here, as shown in Chapter 16's Skill Box, that tricks can be played with logic. Even when it is put into the form of the syllogism, deductive reasoning can still be invalid. Here we will explore the other valid and invalid forms of syllogisms that can be found hidden within "if . . ., then . . ." claims (which are a common basis for arguments).

From the if/then premise, one can reason validly that:

1. If A is so, then B is so. (Major Premise)
2. B is not so. (Minor Premise)
3. Therefore, A is not so. (Conclusion)

A moment's thought shows that the conclusion is forced from the two premises. That is, A cannot be so if B is not so, because A always causes B to occur.

Related to this if/then syllogism with a negative minor premise is an invalid syllogism which also has a negative minor premise. It takes this form:

1. If A is so, then B is so.
2. A is not so.
3. Therefore, B is not so.

An example of this kind of argument will help show why this logic is invalid:

1. If the animal is a poisonous snake, then it is dangerous.
2. This animal is not a poisonous snake.
3. Therefore, this animal is not dangerous.

There is danger in this line of thought: The animal under discussion could be a tiger. The conclusion is not forced by the premises; it need not be true. That is, B may be so even if A is not so.

Remembering this invalid form of deduction can help us avoid making some mistakes such as voting for the wrong politician or wasting our money on some worthless product. For example, some campaign speech might be reduced to this basic line of reasoning:

1. If too many (members of some ethnic group) come to our country, then we will have a recession. (If A, then B.)
2. A vote for me will keep those people out. (A would not be so.)
3. Therefore a vote for me will prevent a recession. (B would not be so.)

The first impulse of a clear-thinking listener might be to question the truth of the major premise. That is, do those people somehow really cause a recession? If we doubt the premise of an argument, we must also doubt its conclusion. But even if we accept the premise in our example, the logic is not valid, because a recession may well be caused by things other than the arrival of some ethnic group. Even if those people *would* cause a recession, and even if they *are* kept out, a recession could still occur through some other cause. The logic is invalid.

Whenever we must judge a claim made by a politician or advertiser—or acquaintance—it is useful to ask two questions: (1) Is the reasoning based on valid logic? (2) Is the claim true, that is, is the argument based on accurate information? True premises, logically arranged, are worthy of acceptance.

lete, but the positions themselves are also often protected. As a result, new people are hired to fill positions that serve no productive purpose but have been vacated by death or retirement.

This regularly occurs in the railroad industry. There, locomotive firemen are still being maintained and hired twenty to thirty years after the last coal-burning train has permanently jumped the tracks. The consuming public itself must decide whether it will continue to pay for the additional costs of such featherbedding.

Employers are not blameless and must share responsibility for what are seen as union excesses. In what other manner could people exposed to inhuman working conditions, starvation wages, and the ills of the company store and town respond? Tales of child labor, the seven-day week, the twelve-hour day, no pension, black lung, white lung, dangerous mines, and all the other ills of the industrial revolution have been told and retold in histories and novels. The "Grapes of Wrath", "The Molly Maguires," and Erskine Caldwell's treatment of the southern cotton mill strikes are but a few examples of the struggle. In recent years we have had farm workers exposed to poisonous insecticides, industrial workers killed by unlabeled chemicals, entire water supplies fouled by toxic waste, and, of course, there is the Love Canal. This is not meant to be a diatribe, but rather to illustrate that action begets action, and that both sides in this war over the dollar have had their day.

The future will probably see an increase in the power of various unions. This increase will be due to the size of various pension funds wisely invested. If a union pension fund invests heavily in industry, the interests of the union and the industry become the same. The militancy of the union is then tempered. In time, the hierarchy of the union becomes self-perpetuating and has more in common with corporate management than with the workers they represent. Corporate management, on the other hand, may begin to represent its own interests rather than the interests of stockholders. The management class of both union and business may operate as a third interest group, apart from labor and capital.

In reaction to real and imagined ills to be found in union organizations, the Landrum-Griffin Act (1959) was passed to allow the regulation of union affairs.

THE WORLD SCENE

Having considered some of the issues involved in the question "who gets what," we are ready to apply our conclusions to the world scene. This application involves some different issues and raises some difficult moral questions.

Suppose an American company discovers oil in an underdeveloped nation. The company installs the necessary extraction equipment and builds refineries. Should the company receive the major portion of the profits from the venture?

If we rephrase that question and state it in the following manner, will our answer be the same? Let us say that a French corporation discovers, drills, and refines oil in the United States. Should it be able to extract that oil and take the profit for such a venture out of our nation? In a number of cases, national pride will call for two different sets of answers to the same basic question.

The United States has operated from a strong position in that it had the two most important elements necessary for industrial development: natural resources and capital. In the past, nations with available capital have been able to purchase resources from poorer nations. The poorer nations would have no choice in the matter because their lack of capital precluded their own development of those resources. We have come to refer to this situation as colonialism or economic colonialism. The resource-rich but capital-poor nation always received little for its product. The manufacturing or developing nation reaped the major benefits of such arrangements.

The economic history of the United States shows how a nation may emerge from economic colonialism. In the early United States, there was little capital available for industrial development. We used European investment to build railroads and factories. With that investment came foreign ownership of large segments of our economy. During World War I, the exporting of war materials recovered the European investment. This left the United States in the strong position of owning its own resources and industry, and this position enabled Americans to consume more per capita than most of the remainder of the world's people.

The United States consumes many more times the per capita figure of oil than any other country in the free world. Other brief examples of production and consumption compared with the rest of the world follow the same pattern. Per capita steel consumption in the United States is 66 times that of Indonesia, 133 times that of Pakistan, 10 times that of Mexico, and 2 times that of France. The combined growing population, demand, and diminishing resources present such big consumers as ourselves with a moral problem.

Counting resource tonnage and barrels consumed usually makes little or no impression on readers unfamiliar with the actual meaning of large numbers. After all, few people have the opportunity to see a million tons of anything. The meaning of uneven distribution of wealth and production is more easily grasped on a personal level.

A poverty-stricken family in the United States will number among its possessions and services some if not all of the following items:

running hot and cold water	electric power
drinkable water	telephone
indoor toilet facilities	radio and television
central heating	an automobile
refrigeration	glass windows
gas or electric stove	

This list contains what Americans consider essentials; few could conceive of life without most of the items on that list. To the rest of the world, such items are luxuries enjoyed by only the well-to-do, if they are available at all. In the United States, education is free and compulsory to age sixteen. College is available to almost all who wish to attend. Jobs based on these educational achievements have also been available.

Consider the situation in most of the world. Higher education is limited to the brilliant and/or wealthy. Only small numbers of the lower classes are admitted to higher education. Even in developed Western nations, the percentage of university students is tiny by our standards. By contrast, there are approximately 5,000 two-year and four-year colleges in the United States. Each year a flood of graduates find employment in the various specialized fields for which they were trained. The least capable of these graduates may have to accept alternate jobs, but for the most part plenty of positions are available.

In the rest of the world, the opportunity to acquire a higher education may be restricted. A nation may have only one or two universities. Upon graduation, there are only a few jobs available. After all, what can a nuclear physicist do in a nation that has no job openings for teachers of nuclear physics and no nuclear industry? The answer is emigrate to the United States or to another developed nation, or remain unemployed. Thousands of trained professionals leave their homelands each year for the higher salaries, higher standards of living, and greater opportunities offered by the developed nations. In a real sense, the rich get richer and the poor get poorer.

On a personal level, we can imagine ourselves as graduates of a British medical school. Under the British system of socialized medicine, we can expect to earn under $10,000 per year for quite some time. At the same time, we become aware of the public-service medical positions in the United States that begin at $50,000 per year and include a housing allowance. Private-practice specialists regularly earn $100,000 and $200,000 after several years of practice.

The lure is strong enough to draw professionals from developed nations. It is easy to imagine the effect on the underdeveloped regions of the world. A doctor or another professional in an underdeveloped nation may face the prospect of earning the equivalent of $2,000 per year. It is therefore not surprising that many people trained in the United States do their best to remain here. The looting of professionals has become so widespread that it has become known as the "brain drain."

This world picture involves the same question of "who gets what." In this framework, the distribution of profits must be seen in terms of the developed nations versus the underdeveloped nations.[10] To equalize the two, a great change in their standards of living must take place.[11]

The differences between the rich nations and the poor nations have their roots in the past and in the very nature of development. Since the beginnings of specialization and, later, industry, raw materials have been inexpensive. Conversely, manufactured materials have tended to be expensive in relation to the cost of raw materials.[12] Groups and nations involved in the recovery or production of raw materials have consequently received less of the product of their labors and of those raw materials. This has resulted in the widespread divergence of living standards common today in industrialized nations and underdeveloped nations. Nations classed as industrialized are not interested in promoting competing industry in other nations. This is most true in such nations as England and Japan, which have much industry but few raw materials. Both have depended upon underdeveloped areas of the world for most, if not all, of their raw materials. They benefit by paying less for raw materials and charging more for the products manufactured from those materials. In addition, these nations are not overjoyed

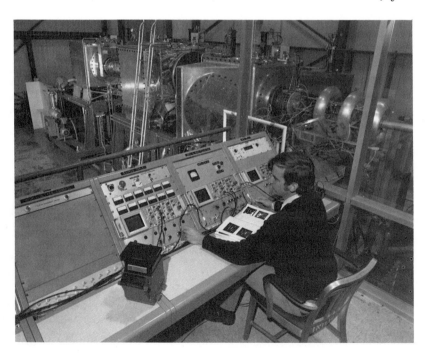

Will new sources of energy compete with oil? If this and other prototype fusion plants come on line with cheap safe energy, it could result in major social and economic changes.

at the prospect of having the supplying nations build their own processing plants.

Since capital is necessary to create industry, the industrialized nations benefit by denying capital to the resource-rich but under-developed areas of the world. This was easy to do in days when force of arms, communications, and resources were in a different stage. The British navy and the American marines, among others, often actively preserved the peace, which meant keeping friendly governments in power. Today this is complicated by the world's power confrontation and the presence of the United Nations as a forum.

The most important factor is economic, that is, the world's balance of supply and demand is changing, with demand becoming inelastic. In brief, our population is growing, and our standard of living is rising. Our demands for manufactured products and energy are rising. Our natural resources are quickly being depleted; the supply is no longer sufficient to meet immediate demand. At this point, our demand is inelastic in that we cannot support our accustomed standard of living without those raw materials. As the supply dwindles, prices will rise.

Although the consequences will be uncomfortable, this price rise must be met. This trend will make the issue of "who gets what" even more important to each of us.

SUMMARY

Throughout history, the question of "who gets what" has been a focal point of social conflict. Today the question often involves the struggle between labor and capital. On the one hand, it is said that those who contribute and risk the capital deserve the major share of the resulting production. This has been the prevailing viewpoint in our society. On the other hand, the communists, for example, point out that labor is the most important element for production. From this they reason that the workers should receive the lion's share of the profit. The question of incentive is basic to this debate. Communists want all workers equally rewarded, though this ideal yet has not been reached anywhere. Capitalist theorists say that unequal rewards offer greater incentive for production.

This issue is reflected in the struggle over corporation ownership and control. The workers' unions press for more ownership. Management argues that the corporations belong to the stockholders, not to the workers. While workers may gain more ownership, the real control of most corporations lies in the hands of a very few.

Beyond this is the viewpoint that people should be paid on the basis of merit. Those who contribute more to production in a meritocracy would be rewarded more than others.

A conglomerate offers a good picture of the workings of the capitalist faction. A conglomerate is a group of interlocking corporations that work together toward a common goal. The loyalty of the managers and workers of Japanese conglomerates contrasts sharply with the loyalty of workers in our own country.

Workers attempted to offset their disadvantage of dealing as individuals with corporations by forming unions. The union movement in this nation was less violent than in other nations, and began with skilled workers and general reform as its aim. This, in time, changed to more immediate, less idealistic goals— "more, now"—and included unskilled workers as well. The basic strategy of skilled workers withholding their labor cannot be used as easily with workers who are less skilled. Workers who are easily replaced must sometimes use violence to make their work stoppage effective.

The American union movement today has grown to include nearly all types of workers, including more and more professionals. Collective bargaining, closed shops, and union shops have also helped bring labor a larger share of production.

On the world scene, the developers and the underdeveloped countries reflect the struggle between capital and labor. The contrasts of the resource consumption and living standards of the two factions are profound. In fact, the differences serve to lure many of the few highly skilled people from the poor nations to the rich nations. With demand becoming more inelastic in the world, developed nations face basic changes in their economic strategies and positions.

SPECIAL TOPIC

Capital and Labor: Obligations

Perhaps the greatest problem facing our economy and society in the 1980s is the obligations participants in the economy owe one another.

Simply speaking, what are the expectations of capital and what are the expectations of labor? What things must capital provide for those who supply the labor? What things must labor provide for those who supply the capital? This chapter has discussed the evolution of these differences, but once more history does not appear as real to us as the strike notice, the pink slip, the closedown, or the bankruptcy. It is altogether too real if these notices appear in our mailbox or our pay envelope.

Albert Shanker, head of the New York American Federation of Teachers, presented his interpretation of the problems that face us in this decade.[13] As he sees it, our crisis depends on an interaction of a number of factors, which include our old friends the energy crisis, declining productivity, and aging cities. There are other problems, not the least of which is the

fact that as costs of conventional warfare rise, nuclear war becomes cheaper. Shanker is concerned with these problems, but his concern is centered at the point where these problems bear on education. His views may surprise many and be unpleasant reading for others.

A major point is that there is a decline in political power held by the education establishment. A glance at the 1980 census brings the sad truth. Only 20 percent of the population have children in school. Compared to the political clout held by the aged, this is rather weak.

As time passed, the educator lost stature and status. In the past, when few people were educated, the teacher held a special and respected position in the community. People in general, with less education, tended to look up to and respect those with more education. In short, as the level of education rose and more people went to college, people tended to look *at* one another, rather than up.

Over the years, teachers have come from the lower achievement levels of the college-graduate group. Competition for college graduates increases in nonteaching areas such as law, medicine, management, computer operations, and a thousand other fields that now require skilled and educated people. As educational requirements rise, the pool of teachers will tend to fall to lower levels. The private sector will continue to offer salaries commensurate with expected profits. As competition for qualified people becomes more intense, salaries can be expected to rise. If past history is any indication, teachers' salaries will rise at a much slower pace than the rest of the economy. As the need for teachers expands, the quality of those available for teaching will continue to fall. Shanker refers to this future possibility as comparable to a dropout group.

As an indication of things to come, there is considerable raiding of qualified science and mathematics teachers by industry. The reason for this is simple. People work for status, job satisfaction, and material gain. In days past, teaching offered status and job satisfaction, and the money, while not good, was above average. In recent days, we have seen that the teacher has the status level of a lower-middle-class person, at best, coupled with a salary below that of many unskilled groups. Job satisfaction has fallen to new lows for many in the profession. Physical attacks on teachers have risen astronomically. The adversary relationship that unions have established with administration have worked to lower the teachers' self-esteem. In short, by the time teacher shortages force salaries up to the point of attracting higher-level people, the jobs will have been filled and tenured.

Shanker feels that the only way the profession can be salvaged is to have the profession itself raise standards. The age-old question once more rises: Why would anyone raise standards high enough to do themselves out of a job?

Do we owe our employers proficiency? Do our employers owe us employment after their need for our services has passed?

SELF-TEST QUESTIONS

1. The argument that capitalists should receive a major share of production is based on the point that:
   a. workers are unskilled
   b. this is God's law
   c. capital is more important and essential than labor
2. Communists believe that _____ is the most important element for production.
3. Communist theory states that benefits from production should be awarded on the basis of:
   a. merit
   b. amount of production
   c. equality
4. True or false: Those who share in the ownership of a corporation share also (in the same proportion) in its control.
5. In a meritocracy, advancement and reward are based on _____.
6. An interlocking group of corporations contributing to their common good and goals is called a _____.
7. True or false: The loyalty of Japanese managers and workers to their corporations is much stronger than in the United States.
8. The early unions in the United States:
   a. demanded simply "more, now"
   b. aimed at broad social reform
   c. were comprised only of skilled workers
9. True or false: The strategy, tactics, and effectiveness of all types of workers' unions are the same.
10. The developed nations of the world:
    a. consume much more than other nations
    b. have more capital than other nations
    c. in many cases depend on cheap raw materials
    d. face no threat to their economic positions

ANSWERS TO
SELF-TEST
QUESTIONS

1. c
2. labor
3. c
4. false
5. merit

6. conglomerate
7. true
8. b, c
9. false
10. a, b, c

ANSWERS TO SKILL
REINFORCERS

17–1. This major premise is reasonable enough, isn't it? It can be used to reach a quite different conclusion, however, depending on the minor premises used. In one case, the minor premise could be:
2. Capital is the most important element of production.
3. Therefore, the capitalist deserves the major portion of the payoff.

Using another minor premise, we have:
2. Labor is the most important element of production.
3. Therefore, the worker deserves most of the payoff.
Each conclusion is based on valid logic. It boils down to which minor premise one accepts as true.

17–2. The average, or mean, is the most stable and widely used measure of central tendency. The mode is the number that occurs most often in a set of numbers. The median is the middle number in a set.

NOTES

1. Adam Smith, *The Wealth of Nations,* intro. by Edwin R. Seligman (New York: E.P. Dutton, 1910).
2. David Ricardo, *The Principles of Political Economy* (New York: E.P. Dutton, 1911).
3. Karl Marx, *The Communist Manifesto* (New York: Monthly Review Press, 1964).
4. Chris Welles, *The Elusive Bonanza: The Story of Oil Shale—America's Richest and Most Neglected Resource* (New York: E.P. Dutton, 1970).
5. Karl Marx, *Capital: A Critique of Political Economy,* 3 vols. (Chicago: C.H. Kerr, 1906–9).
6. Richard Caves, *American Industry: Structure, Conduct, Performance,* 2d ed. (Englewood Cliffs, N.J.: Prentice-Hall, 1967).
7. A. Gordon, *Business Leadership in the Large Corporation* (Berkeley: University of California Press, 1945).
8. Abraham L. Gitlow, *Labor and Industrial Society,* rev. ed. (Homewood, Ill.: Richard A. Irwin, 1963).
9. Edwin F. Beal and Edward D. Wickersham, *The Practice of Collective Bargaining,* 3d ed. (Homewood, Ill.: Richard A. Irwin, 1967).
10. Richard T. Gill, *Economic Development: Past and Present,* 2d ed. (Englewood Cliffs, N.J.: Prentice-Hall, 1967).
11. *Dirty Money, Dirty Air,* Common Cause, 1981.
12. Benjamin Higgins, *Economic Development,* rev. ed. (New York: W.W. Norton, 1962).
13. Albert Shanker to the New Jersey State Board of Education, May 8, 1982.

SUGGESTED
READINGS

Borgstrom, Georg. *The Hungry Planet.* New York: Macmillan Co., 1967.

Ehrlich, Paul R., and Ehrlich, Ann. *The End of Affluence.* New York: Ballantine, 1975.

Dirty Money, Dirty Air. Washington, D.C.: Common Cause, 1981.

Galbraith, John Kenneth. *Whence It Came, Where It Went.* Boston: Houghton Mifflin, 1975.

Marx, Karl. *The Communist Manifesto.* New York: Monthly Review Press, 1964.

Ricardo, David. *The Principles of Political Economy.* New York: E.P. Dutton, 1911.

18 GOVERNMENT AND ECONOMICS IN THE UNITED STATES

PREVIEW

Depression Today and Yesterday

The stock market has dissolved. The company for which you have worked for the last twenty-five years has decided to close its doors. In everyone's pay envelope is a notice of termination. The company is broke, its assets are gone, the pension fund went down with the stock market. You are out of a job, with no prospect of being hired by anyone.

Your wife is a schoolteacher with a tenured position. She has received notice that she may continue to work but that she will be paid in scrip. Even though she will not be out of work, she will receive no money.

Your automobile payments are due, as are the mortgage payment, the electric bill, the phone bill, your son's tuition, and a series of revolving credit account bills.

Your first move is to apply for unemployment insurance payments. That move can be made today, but it could not have been made in 1929–30. Your parents receive social security payments, but if this collapse had occurred in 1929, there would have been no social security.

Today you might consider making an application for welfare, food stamps, medicare (if of age), medicaid (if you qualify), emergency fuel assistance, a state employment service, the state rehabilitation service, various retraining services run by state and federal agencies, and so on. In 1929 you could only hope for a basket of food from a private agency or surplus apples to sell on the street.

Today the federal government could be depended upon to pour millions of dollars into the economy via Federal Reserve Banks. Congress would fund large public works projects, and defense appropriations would soar. In 1929, none of this could have happened.

As a result of the Great Depression, our government entered the economy. In 1982, the first major steps to move the government out of the economy were taken.

The health of our economy affects us in very personal ways. The job market, for example, may affect what career we choose and to what part of the country we move. If the money supply is tight, or interest rates high, we may not be able to own our own home or build our dream house. The state of the economy may even make having children too expensive.

In the past few decades, the government has been assuming more and more control over the economy. Rather than just letting supply and demand work things out, the government has tried to make sure that we are not left at the mercy of the economy. More and more, however, we find ourselves at the mercy of the government's economic policies. This chapter explores this changing role of government in the economy of the United States.

We saw in Chapter 16 that some types of economic systems use more governmental control than other systems. In pure capitalism, government is absent; in pure socialism, government controls all aspects of the economy. As we noted, however, pure forms rarely exist. In any case, average citizens can easily digest this topic of governmental controls—in theory. When they look at the effects of that control on their lifestyle, however, their healthy digestion may turn to heartburn.

The trend over the past few decades has clearly been toward more government control. The beginning of the 1970s saw the United States effectively attempt to control both the prices of items for sale and the wages of the producers of those items. The 1980s, under President Ronald Reagan, started with a new direction, called "supply-side economics" by its advocates.[1] (Detractors refer to this economic theory as "trickle-down economics.") Simply put, supply-side economics would cut taxes sharply and watch the economy expand as a result. Whether or not one approves of such government controls is irrelevant. These actions show that the "capitalistic" system of our nation is not so very capitalistic.

FISCAL POLICY: The power of the government to tax and spend in order to help bring the nation's output and employment to desired levels.

MONETARY POLICY: The regulation of the money supply to conform to policy of the Federal Reserve System.

DEPRESSION: Lower phase of business cycle in which the economy is operating with low usage of its resources and a sluggish rate of capital investment, and consumption resulting from little business and consumer optimism.

THE BEGINNINGS OF GOVERNMENTAL CONTROLS

Our government entered into economic control as a response to major economic disasters. A short history of the United States will list wars and depressions that have occurred, it seems, almost on schedule. In this chapter the wars are not an issue, but our history books neatly list depression, panics, and recessions. These events are given the same level of importance as other natural disasters. The dates of these recurrent economic depressions have been so firmly fixed in our minds that we use them as reference points. We refer to them much as an old farmer refers to the year of the big drought or the fact that he was married the year the ice house burned down.

Before the Crash

Our government reacted little, if at all, to earlier financial panics that plagued the nation. Though it is true that the government taxed whiskey, hence the whiskey rebellion, controlled customs, and the postal service, there was little other response to economic

RECESSION: Slump in economic growth.

PROTECTIVE TARIFF: A tax on goods moving across a nation's boundaries.

events. As late as the 1929 Depression, the government's most memorable reaction was to make surplus apples available for people to sell on our nation's street corners. In fact, street-corner apple mongers became the hallmark of the era. How then did we, as a nation and as individuals, become subjects of increased governmental economic control?

Tariffs.   We must link our first major experience with government control to the issues of import and export. There the government, through consumer policy decisions, acted to protect certain industries from what was considered unfair foreign competition. The fairness of the competition is not the issue. The real issue is that our nation, like many others, attempted to build its industry by protective tariff. If we could not produce a wagon as economically as other nations, we charged an entry fee or import duty on foreign wagons. The duty raised the prices of foreign wagons to equal or exceed those made in America. The buyer in the United States saw no advantage in buying a foreign product, thus ensuring sales for native industries.[2]

If we are on the right side of a protective tariff, it serves a purpose. The problem is that other nations respond by setting up the same tariffs for items that we manufacture. Also, while import duties protect some industries, they hurt others. The American poultry industry had entered the area of the European Common Market with considerable success. Until that area raised the import duties on American chickens, European growers were being forced out of business. The imposition of duties forced Americans out of the market and ruined many poultry farmers. The low duty on imported television units caused nearly all American producers of such units to cease their production.

The steel industry is about to crumble, the government has had to support automobile manufacture in at least one instance, and a number of large defense contractors are maintained as a matter of national security. In the spring of 1987, the government placed a penalty upon selected Japanese imports. This was done "to protect the American computer chip industry against unfair dumping of Japanese chips below the cost of manufacture." The American consumer will then pay more for a protected item and the American manufacturer will still not be able to export his protected wares.

One interesting concept, yet to be considered, is the imposition of import penalties on those products manufactured without meeting the same environmental standards prevailing in the United States. If we impose such standards, we should not import items manufactured without meeting the same standards. The U.S. companies that fled into Mexico and pollute the New River, which flows north into California, are exempt from standards placed on stay-at-home manufacturers a few miles away. A penalty equal to the cost of the evaded standards should be imposed on the imports.

SKILL BOX

Beware of Author Bias

"This is a typical trick of the greedy, immoral business class." If an author used this sentence, surely a reader would have taken note. It would suggest that the author had a grudge, a bias against the business class. It would be quite improper for a writer of a social science textbook to display such bias. After all, science is supposed to be objective, not biased.

The scientist's duty is to seek the truth, to uncover facts and let them speak for themselves. Some researchers, however, seek support for their own biases. Rather than being objective about their subjects, they have a strong personal wish to reach or not to reach a certain conclusion. This is more likely to be true of social scientists than natural scientists. A person studying murder, the rich, or religions, for example, is more likely to have some personal bias than someone studying rocks or stars. This means that the social scientist should take special care to avoid studying a subject in which he or she is emotionally involved. But scientists do not always do what they should. Because some scientists have tried to make their data fit or support their own biases, we must beware of author bias when reading in social science.

There are no simple rules to follow to ensure that we will spot an author's distortion of the truth to fit his or her bias. There are, however, some things to keep in mind.

First, we can watch the tone of the author's words and phrases. The scholarly writing of most scientists is quite straightforward, precise, and dry. When we spot words that tell us the author was emotional concerning the subject, we should beware. This indicates that the author was not detached, and thus not objective, but biased. For instance, scholars who call something they are studying "disgusting" or "ugly" are probably showing their personal bias. Or, if an article's title is "How Much Worse Can Men Treat Women?" we should be on guard for author bias.

The more emotionally involved authors are with a subject, the greater the chances they will be unable to keep their biases out of the research design, conclusion, or report. This means that we are less likely to be offered the straight truth. The truth may be bent by the scientist, whether the distortion is deliberate or not.

Besides watching for words that might show bias, we can look for clues about the author's interests. If, for example, authors who are part of a committee to fight poverty might unconsciously distort the data to dramatize the need to help the poor. They might write of the "sin of allowing poverty to exist." Or they might use percentages of very small samples to make their point. "Eighty percent of the poor families studied" sounds like a lot, until we find that only ten families were studied. Likewise, an author's race or religion might enter into his or her conclusions. We could expect that the author of an article entitled "Are Catholic Schools a Tool of the Pope?" has a religious bias.

Patents. The patent office is another example of early government interest in the economy. A patent guarantees a form of monopoly for a specific period of time. During the life span of the government-issued patent, the article in question is protected by governmental action, and the patent holder may license or prohibit the use of articles infringing on the patent.[3]

A hypothetical story will show how the patent process works. After years of trial-and-error testing that involved considerable expense, George Watts perfected a better mousetrap. His system was unique. It used a new concept involving a vacuum which instantly ingested the poor creature and ended its misery with an immediate explosion. The system was painless and sanitary. All this guaranteed a lasting commercial market for its use. Once the patent application was granted, the inventor owned sole rights to marketing and licensing the Jiffy Instant Painless Vacuum Mousetrap. Any company wishing to market a mousetrap using this new principle would be required by law to pay a royalty agreed upon or to pay the inventor a licensing fee.

From this story so far, we see that a patent chiefly affects the consumer by raising the price of the protected item to a level higher than it would be in a free-trade situation. The consumer is paying the inventor a bonus for the discovery. While we may feel cheated, the inventor should receive some reward for time and effort.

There are other issues concerning the monopoly held by inventors or their licensees. Perhaps the Acme Mousetrap Corporation did not want to retool or manufacture the new vacuum mousetrap. Acme, instead, would pay Mr. Watts a substantial amount to purchase exclusive rights to the new invention, but only if it could maintain control of the invention. Acme was satisfied with the sales and profit on its traditional trap and had no desire to enter into a more expensive operation. With the license safely in hand, Acme might well bury the plans in a safe place and keep this needed invention out of the market.

Possibly buried deep in the corporate records of major oil companies are formulas that would allow the conversion of water to fuel. More than likely, similar patents affecting many of our basic industries have been retired and held off the market for who knows how many years. Both holding a patent and restricting its manufacture result in higher prices for the consuming public.

Antitrust Efforts

Major moves by the government into the economy began in the latter part of the nineteenth century with the Sherman Antitrust Act. In less than thirty years the Sherman Act was strengthened by the Clayton Act. The Federal Reserve System was also formed during this period. The antitrust acts directly affected the nation's economy as well as the individual.

FEDERAL RESERVE SYSTEM:
Central banking system created by Congress in 1913.

Earlier chapters explored the effects of monopolies. We have seen that controlling an item with inelastic demand could raise its price greatly while reducing its quantity in the market. Several cases of such control in the world market show us the need for antitrust laws in the United States. For example, during the early stages of the energy crisis, control over a large part of the world's

Does "The Fed" control our economy? Pictured here is the Federal Reserve Bank of Minneapolis, one of twelve Federal Reserve Banks located in various sections of the country.

oil supply allowed a group of nations to restrict supplies of crude oil and to raise the price. As other goods and natural resources become short in supply, any nation or group of nations can raise its prices by restricting production and sale. If the United States restricted its exports of grain now and in the future, the price of grain would rise in foreign markets. Grain would become scarce abroad while the demand remained inelastic. The famous Russian wheat sales have allowed a large part of the American wheat crop to be sold to Russia. As domestic supplies fell short, the price of a bushel of grain rose from $1.62 to over $5.80 in one year. Shortfalls of 200,000 tons in the world sugar market are enough to throw that market into chaos.

These examples in the area of international trade show the dangers of domestic monopolies. The various antitrust acts were created to keep any one corporation or group of corporations in our domestic market from creating artificial shortfalls and raising prices.

An important reason for dealing with such practices here is not that such a practice is good or bad but rather that it marks a change in government economic policy. The continuing history of our economic system is one of greater governmental action and control. The advent of the federal income tax marked an increase of this trend. In fact, this antitrust trend that began in the late 1800s may lead to even bigger things on the part of the government. In time, our society may see large-scale attempts to control various private industries. It would be no surprise if the government declared certain industries "public utilities" and regulated them as it has regulated the electric companies.

The large oil companies are prime targets for such action at present. Government control of some public utilities already allows the public to set the rate of profit and the cost of service. In some quarters, the feeling that the oil companies have gone too far in their control of the world's energy supply appears to be growing. The size of the largest of these corporate giants reflects the fact that its profit exceeds the budgets of most of the world's countries. The issue at hand is not whether to charter, regulate, or nationalize these industries. The point here is that our public and our government have begun to consider these actions seriously. This shows a sharp change in attitude toward government control of the economic sector of our nation.

Reaction to the Stock Market Crash

Our government's intervention in the economy began early in a small way as we have noted, and continued to increase slowly. This trend may seem strong, even radical, compared to the earlier lack of much government participation, yet the truly major shift in attitude came with the Great Depression of the 1930s.[4] In response to the stock market crash, the Securities Act, followed by the Securities and Exchange Act, put the government in a new position of making and enforcing rules of stock market activity.

STOCK MARKET: A place where buyers and sellers meet to trade securities.

One of the factors leading to the market crash and nationwide Depression can be offered as an example of the activities common before government regulation began. There is in the stock market a practice known as buying on margin. In effect, an investor buys common stock on credit. Before the Depression, the required margin investment averaged 10 percent of the purchase price of the common stock. In other words, a person buying stock valued at $1,000 actually paid $100 and borrowed the remainder. As long as that stock retained a value of $1,000 or more, the investor was secure. If the market value of that stock dropped below $1,000, the investor had to make up the difference in cash.

Investors with available funds to pay their debts were secure, but when the market began to fall on a broad front, many investors lacked the money to make good on their debts. This encouraged the market to drop still lower.

Several factors basic to the market in those days further complicated the issue. First, little attention was paid to the earnings of the companies whose common stock was purchased. Interest was focused on the upward movement of the stock's value. An investor in the stock market makes money in two basic ways: from the dividend the company pays based on profits, or from rises in the market value of the stock. The value of a common stock rises when more people want to buy than to sell. In many instances there is no sound reason why a stock climbs in value.

The stock market has been referred to as an irrational creature beset by fears of the unknown. This statement seems accurate when one observes stock market activities. If a presidential adviser makes an offhand statement about future good times, the stock market will rise. Conversely, a frown on the face of the Secretary of the Treasury can cause millions in paper losses from a stock market decline. It makes little difference to panic-stricken investors that the frown might have been caused by a hangover. Each day major radio stations broadcast an analysis of stock market conditions as seen by the experts. For every expert predicting good times, another predicts doom and destruction.

Only the amount that people are willing to pay determines the value of the typical share of common stock. Price should relate to the financial condition of the company and its return to the investor in the form of dividends derived from profits. Too often either hopes for future benefit or emotions push the stocks up in value.

Prior to the market crash of 1929, many people were buying stock and hoping that it would increase in market value, rather than buying for the profit derived from dividends. They made large investments with only the required 10 percent margin payment in companies that merely held blocks of shares in other companies. In turn, many of the secondary companies had holdings composed of blocks of stock in still other companies. What occurred was a large paper investment in nothing.

CREDIT: An exchange of goods and services for a promise of future payment; consumer credit usually takes the form of charge accounts, installment accounts, and personal loans.

Skill Reinforcer 18-1 *

Create an invalid syllogism from this minor premise: The Secretary of the Treasury never frowns.

---

* Answers to the Skill Reinforcers appear at the end of the chapter.

An individual would apply $1,000 and receive $10,000 in common stock in a company whose prime asset was common stock in a second company rather than production of a salable item. The company purchased this common stock using the same margin requirements demanded of the individual investor. The second company, as the first, consisted of paper investments in a third company. What had happened was an economic construction of large amounts of paper based on tiny amounts of real goods and services.

The investor at all levels intended to recover profits through capturing a higher market value of the common stock held rather than from production through dividends. When the economy began to falter and stock market values fell, margin requirements were called in, and the entire paper structure collapsed like a house of cards. While the typical American was not a market investor, nearly everyone was hurt by the crash. The increasing lack of confidence in the economic system as it had been operated affected all Americans.

The economic depression that resulted caused the passage of the Securities and Exchange Act. This act answered the clamor for government control of stock market activities. Under the new federal guidelines and regulations it became far more difficult to take the investor's money in the name of what is called management costs. The government's use of such regulatory powers and the rapidly expanding Internal Revenue Service increased.

GOVERNMENT REACTION SINCE THE GREAT DEPRESSION

The stock market crash of 1929 led not only to economic collapse but also to social problems. An entire generation of Americans was scarred by those results, and the goals and actions of our government changed. The government reacted to the economic and subsequent social crisis referred to as the Great Depression by entering into many new sectors of the economy.[5] The "alphabet-soup" agencies created by the government were intended to be temporary. Still, the flavor and philosophy developed during this period of stress lingers.

The nation faced widespread unemployment and a stagnant economy. The government reacted by employing citizens in building public works on a massive scale. In addition, it took positive action toward stimulating the arts and other segments of the economy that had ceased to operate. In areas such as the Tennessee Valley Authority, the government entered into the production and marketing of energy.

Quite possibly the government's grand entry into the economic and social lives of the people caused a growing expectation of more to come. If not, at least the people showed no sign of giving up that to which they had been accustomed. The Americans expected government to meet the needs of the people.

President Franklin D. Roosevelt, in his "fireside chat" of April 1938, described some of his proposals for meeting this challenge.

Franklin Delano Roosevelt (1882–1945) speaking to the American public during one of his famous "fireside chats."

He requested a continuance of funds for relief and other programs, and additional bank reserves. The following is his proposal to add to the nation's purchasing power.

First, to enable the United States Housing Authority to undertake the immediate construction of about three hundred million dollars of additional slum clearance projects.

Second, to renew a public works program by starting as quickly as possible about one billion dollars worth of needed permanent public improvements in states, counties and cities.

Third, to add one hundred million dollars to the estimate for federal aid highways in excess of the amount I recommended in January.

Fourth, to add thirty-seven million dollars over and above the former estimate of sixty-three million dollars for flood control and reclamation.

Fifth, to add twenty-five million dollars additional for federal building in various parts of the country.

Roosevelt was asking for a dramatic change. Compare his proposals with the earlier role of the government in economic affairs. He enlarged the government's area of concerns from matters such as patents and tariffs to include nearly every part of the economy. This would mean an about-face in the space of just a few years. The government would now deal with such things as employment levels, the money supply, and consumer protection. These matters will be explored here.

Efforts Toward Full Employment

In 1946 Congress passed the Full Employment Act. With the passage of this act, the government recognized and assumed permanent responsibility for ensuring the employment of as many people as possible. It established the Council of Economic Advisors to perform the task. This council aimed to counter the cyclical nature of the economic system.

When we refer to the cyclical nature of our economic system, we mean the recurrence of good times and bad times on a regular basis.[6] Individuals and businesses in America had come to expect, but not to enjoy, the eventual economic downtrends that were called depressions, panics, and recessions. During these periods, savings were wiped out, businesses went bankrupt, and large numbers of persons became unemployed.

Frequently, a downtrend of this nature allowed a small segment of the population to get rich at the expense of others. If money in the form of hard currency or gold were available, its buying power increased dramatically. For example, people or corporations wealthy enough to keep large amounts of hard currency or gold in a liquid form, uninvested, could purchase much more in a period of deflation than they could with an inflated dollar.

Suppose, prior to the stock market crash of 1929, a person maintained a safe deposit box in the bank with $10,000 in gold or silver. Before the Depression, the average price for a house may

Skill Reinforcer 18-2
Is $10,000 in this example the median, mode, or mean?

have been $10,000. But after the Depression had progressed and money became scarce, the same house had a market value of only $1,500. In this case, it is clear that the actual value of the money had increased. During the Depression foresighted people and groups had maintained liquid assets for just this reason.

The Great Depression seriously threatened the very fabric of our society and economic system. It became clear that the government had to take steps which, at that time, were considered temporary means of correcting a temporary problem. Long-term exposure to these temporary means tended to change the government's temporary policies into a whole new approach. This new approach resulted in the Full Employment Act.

The best means to ensure full employment for the nation was difficult to determine. Economic theories abound, and until they are actually tried, they remain only theory. The classical economic view of recurring depressions assumed that the natural law of supply and demand would operate and the economy would reach a point of natural equilibrium.[7] In short, where overproduction occurred, people would not buy. Plants would close, and everything would settle back to normal. Normal, in this sense, meant that thousands of people would be unemployed. They would lose their life's savings and have to begin from scratch until demand once more grew to a level required by Adam Smith's "invisible hand."

The new economics, however, used the theories of Keynes and Phillips, among others. Then, in the 1970s the basic premise of the Phillips Curve no longer applied. The theory behind the Phillips Curve derived from a study of the relationship between unemployment and inflation.[8] The theory states that there is an inverse relationship between the rate of inflation and the rate of unemployment. The more we have of one, the less we will have of the other. The jargon of the economist refers to this as a trade-off in that there is a give-and-take relationship between inflation and unemployment. We have been willing to trade some inflation for less unemployment. Since the Truman administration, the Council of Economic Advisors has generally accepted the reasoning behind the Phillips Curve.

The theories of John Maynard Keynes fit well with those of Phillips. Keynes noted that demand kept pace with supply only so long as all income was spent either in consumption or in investment.[9] Although we have developed new techniques for stimulating consumption, it tends to be stable. The major point lies in the area of investment. When money is inactive, the economy dries up. Keynes noted that government could step into the void and, through taxation and spending, influence the economy.

A major point in the Keynesian view was to remove money from inactive positions and place it in circulation. Because wealthier people and corporations tend to oversave, progressively higher taxes should be used to return that money to circulation. Poorer people living on all they earn make excellent distributors for

PHILLIPS CURVE: Curve which represents a trade-off between unemployment and inflation.

COST–PUSH INFLATION: Condition of generally rising prices caused by production costs that increase faster than productivity or efficiency.

FISCAL POLICY: That policy adopted by an administration to tax and spend in order to bring the nation's output and employment to desired levels.

John Maynard Keynes believed that money should remain in circulation.

MONEY SUPPLY: Sum of coin and currency in circulation, demand, time, and saving deposits (broadly defined).

INTEREST RATE: Price paid for use of money over a period of time.

money. Many of us would probably like to volunteer for the position of currency spreader, but with Keynes we have entered the world of spending economics. In other words, according to this theory, if spending decreases, depression, recession, or panic cannot be far behind.

The actual mathematics of the Keynesian view is far more complex than presented here. An example of an economic downturn can be used to illustrate it. During the 1960s, reinvestment in industry was high. A favorable business climate and tax incentives encouraged expanding production capacity to the point at which it was larger than product demand. As business grew alarmed over this overinvestment, it cut reinvestment. By 1973, shortages developed because of low production. In the Keynesian view, the government should have stepped in and countered the decline in industrial investment through major spending. What actually happened is interesting. Our nation was "blessed" with the unexpected rise in unemployment coupled with an increased rate of inflation. This set off on the same side of the ledger trade-offs that had an electrifying effect. Viewed in terms of the Phillips Curve, the effect was similar to applying a lighted match to gasoline and getting no reaction.

During the 1970s the Council of Economic Advisors believed that a higher level of unemployment would reduce the rate of inflation. Consequently, the public was treated to statements that called for sacrifice (translated "lose jobs") to beat inflation. To the politicians and economic theorists, this view may have been acceptable, but those people sacrificing their jobs and savings found it to be as unwelcome as ever.

The Phillips Curve made sense during the 1960s, but not during the 1970s. Why this "favorite" had suddenly become useless may be rooted in several areas. An analysis may show the nation's money supply was inadequate when compared to the goods produced by the economy. This can result in growing inflation. We have seen attempts to limit credit by increasing interest rates for borrowed money. It is easy to see that higher interest rates merely tack a higher price on items produced and contribute nothing to the actual production of goods and services. Interest rates as high as 20 percent in the early 1980s certainly dampened the ardor of new car and home buyers.

Other government actions have influenced both the nation's economy and the lives of many individuals. The government drastically cut back its spending in research and development in the aerospace industry, sending ripples through the economy. Perhaps we can chart the effect of government reduction of spending in this area. At one time it was thought that thousands of Ph.D.s were out of work in the Boston area alone as a result of this cutback. As these highly qualified people scattered to find jobs with colleges and universities, they displaced others stumbling down to smaller colleges and public schools. In time, the reduced job market reduced the number of students in the affected fields, which once more reduced the number of teachers needed. On a more basic level, contractors and subcontractors building parts and models for the research and development area went out of business in large numbers.

As the ripples continued, highly trained professionals began to displace people in lower positions. It became common to find holders of masters' degrees in positions created for graduates of two-year colleges. The people who had invested time and effort to attain lesser college degrees suddenly found no job market for their skills.

When large numbers of people cease earning, they also cease spending, and service industries begin to feel the pinch. Auto sales—a factor that affects upward of 20 percent of the entire factory work force in our nation—began to drop. This mainstay of our economy fell to the point where government action was needed to save it. Guaranteed loans and quotas for Japanese automobiles were among the actions taken.

Control of Money Supply

We might expect to find some silver lining in the cloud of unemployment just described. Sad to say, the expanding ripple of industry cutback was not relieved by a decline in price levels or a lag in inflation rate. A study of the reasons for this leads us to the government's efforts to control money supply.

Several variables in recent years have not been factors in years past. The first of these may prove to be basic; we are reaching the limits of available natural resources. Natural resources are finite in that there is an absolute limit to their quantity. On the other hand, the world population continues to grow at an alarming rate. The increased demand for products that are in turn limited not by capacity but by nature is a concept that will continue to affect our lives. This is different from our past experiences with over- and underproduction.

Holders of raw materials can now manipulate the monetary pattern of the world's economy. They need only to withhold small amounts of materials. Future demands may always exceed the supply of basic items. With such basic items as energy, food, and natural fiber in short supply, the inflationary spiral will probably continue. At the same time, unemployment will also rise as our own multinational corporations move manufacturing facilities to take advantage of cheap foreign labor.

Periods of some adjustment may occur for a time, but the long-range outcome of such a combination of factors is difficult to predict. This is especially true in light of our experience with the concept of "cost-push" inflation.[10] In the past, resources have always met or satisfied demand, and rising production always affected the envisioned labor costs. When scarce resources limit production, costs rise with no available offset.

INFLATION: A large and relatively sudden increase in the general price level, not to be confused with normal price increase such as after a depression.

Creating Money. We are accustomed to dealing with money in the form of cash, securities, bonds, real estate, gold, diamonds, debt, and credit. The question remains: how should enough money be created to provide the amount needed for the economy to grow at the proper rate?

Banks create credit by lending many times the amount deposited in cash. Each time the same money is deposited, the banks may lend out a major portion, creating far more money in circulation than in cash currency that actually exists. This is an old process. Early gold and salt depositories did the same thing as today's banks when they issued paper credits on deposits. So did early banks in our own nation when they printed money in response to a shortage of currency. They needed to create money with which to do business and also to provide homesteaders the necessary credit.

We issue personal money with our checking accounts. Each time we write a check on our account we are actually creating a form of currency that may travel through several hands before it is cashed and debited to our account. Through the ages, some people have had a tendency to issue their own money. While some of their products may have been pleasing to the eye, most governments have taken a dim view of monetary moonshine. Today the use of duplicating machines has enabled some people to pass bogus currency of the crudest kind. Large denomination forms of U.S. currency have been produced by sophisticated means in such quantities that it is difficult to get any seller abroad to take them. Governments have gone to great lengths to prevent counterfeiting as a means of creating money. Personal checks have been printed with portraits of the account owners to discourage forgery. Kiting, or depending on the passage of several days for a check to clear before depositing money to back the amount spent, is another popular but illegal method of creating surplus money. These are illicit, private means of creating money.

BUSINESS CYCLES: Recurrent fluctuations of general business and economic activity that take place over a period of years.

Returning to basic economic theory, we find that in the past the rise and fall of business cycles follow fluctuations in spending.[11] If we accept the principle that spending must be maintained in order to avoid severe economic fluctuation, we must accept government's new role as a regulatory factor in the economy.

The Federal Reserve System. A prime example of government regulation in our economy is the Federal Reserve System (a semi-independent agency). The controls wielded by the Federal Reserve Banks maintain money and credit in proportions that allow the nation continuing economic activity.[12] The realities of any situation differ sharply from purposes, intent, and theory. As a result, the Federal Reserve System attempts to maintain this balance with varying degrees of success.

The effects of Federal Reserve action involve credit ability, standard of living, and employment possibilities for our nation. The Federal Reserve is dealing with our ability to buy a car, obtain a mortgage, and keep a job. If money is in short supply, many businesses will lack operating capital, and buyers will lack the means of purchase.

MONETARY POLICY: Regulation of the money supply by the Federal Reserve System.

The Federal Reserve Board faces huge problems. There is a painful time lag between the board's actions and the result seen in the economy. The board attempts to maintain in circulation an amount of money adequate to allow business to be conducted. Too much money may result in inflation, while too little could result in depression. The board aims to strike a balance between the two economic extremes. This point of balance would be hard enough to find if all economists agreed upon what it would be. Unfortunately, there is no agreement upon this issue.

Methods of Control. The creation of money for use in our society is more complex than merely turning on a printing press or a stamping machine. The control of money is basic to our government's monetary policy. Toward this end, the government has three control methods to ensure the proper amount of money in circulation.[13]

In the first method, the Federal Reserve System in Washington adjusts—up or down—the percentage of reserve monies held. This limits possible bank money expansion. The legal reserve requirement regulates the volume of bank deposits and, indirectly, the volume of loans. Commercial bank deposits depend upon the dollar volume of reserves available and the size of the legal reserve ratio. By this method, they regulate the volume of bank deposits, thereby bank loans, and consequently the total money supply.

For example, when a bank receives money on deposit, it may loan out only a percentage of that money. This percentage is set by the limit required by the Federal Reserve Bank. The remainder of the money must be held in reserve. If a large percentage is to be held in reserve, the money available for loans is smaller. If the percentage of deposits to be retained for reserve is smaller, the amount available for loans is larger. This is the government's powerful tool for regulating the money supply, and it is used when long-range major changes are desired in the monetary supply.

The twelve individual Federal Reserve Banks use the second method of control in the form of interest adjustment on the loans each bank makes to member banks. The level of interest these largely independent Federal Reserve Banks charge directly affects the interest your bank charges you. If the regional reserve bank in your area lowers its interest rate to the point where loans become attractive to the borrowing public, more money flows into circulation.

Federal Reserve loans to member banks are of two types: discount loans and advance loans. When a bank obtains a discount loan, it simply endorses over some of its customers' paper to the Federal Reserve Bank. Advance loans are loans to the commercial banks, based on their securities and assets. In theory, this adjusts a harmful or dangerous reserve ratio requirement.

OPEN MARKET OPERATIONS: Purchases and sales of government securities by the Federal Reserve System.

The third method used to control the money supply is called open market operation.[14] The operation of this method can be compared to the fine-tuning device on a television set. It is used constantly to make minor adjustments in the supply of available money.[15] In brief, the Open Market Committee of the Federal Reserve System enters the open market and either buys or sells the government securities. In this way the Federal Reserve creates commercial bank reserves by buying government securities. In turn, when the Federal Reserve sells government securities, the opposite effect is felt: Commercial bank reserves are reduced.

What would happen if the money government prints were the only form of money available? Under those circumstances, only if the government itself spent or loaned the currency to the public could the money supply be increased. Essentially, the Open Market Committee is doing just that when it buys government securities. It is exchanging money for securities held by the public. If there is resistance, the committee merely raises the price it is willing to pay for those securities and puts even more money into circulation. To do the reverse, the committee sells securities at a good rate of interest, putting the liquid cash paid for them in the government's hands, thus out of circulation.

Why Bother to Control?   Perhaps at this point one might question the relevance of the matters discussed. It may be that neither inflation, deflation, the relative value of the dollar, nor the cost of home and automobile loans will ever affect a particular person. For such people, this discussion of money supply holds no importance. However, for those who intend to purchase a car, home, television or other credit-based items, these matters directly affect their pocketbook and standard of living.

The regulation of money has always been a difficult task for the government.[16] Some of the difficulty can be tied to the problem of locating where the supply is and knowing where it is heading. The fact that members of the governing body of the Federal Reserve System disagree on matters of philosophy complicates the situation further. Some of the members feel that inflation is good for the economy and keeps it growing. Others feel that the money supply should simply grow at a steady, predictable rate. Once Federal Reserve Bank members decide on a policy, they still face pressure from Congress and the president. Elected officials come under strong pressure from the voters when mortgage rates rise to an uncomfortable level.

Because of the shortage of mortgage money during the Vietnam War, tremendous pressure was brought to bear upon the Federal Reserve Bank. The war absorbed most of the available money from the credit markets. This in turn drove the price of money very high. The Reserve Bank was called on to put more money into circulation, which would have lowered interest rates only temporarily.

The ultimate effect of putting more money into the economy would be to raise the rate of inflation. People were discomfited by mortgage shortages and the rise of mortgage rates to 8.5 percent during the 1970s. The 1980s saw mortgage rates rise high into double digits, and home building fall to 20 percent of that of better years. An interesting side note is that while the federal discount rate fell to about 6 percent in 1986, revolving charges and credit cards in general maintained their interest rates at from 15 percent to 20 percent. The "Tax Reform Bill," signed in 1986, and to begin phasing in by 1987, deletes consumer interest from the list of deductibles. At the time of this writing, it is only possible to guess what this will mean to the buying public. Persons with equity in real property will continue to have deductibility for consumer purchases based upon Equity Loans. These loans are secured by a second mortgage on residential property, usually on, but not restricted to, the primary place of residence. Interest rates for these loans are substantially lower than credit card or revolving charge loans. Their rate is further reduced by the ability to deduct the cost of the loan from income. The wealthy will have lower cost purchases and those persons without substantial property will pay at a higher rate with no reduction for deductibility possible. With less money available due to tax reform, the average American may look forward to reduced buying power and hence a reduced standard of living.

It is interesting to note that a mortgage could be had in the 1940s for 3.5 percent. Measures taken to correct imbalances in the economy frequently return to haunt the initiator in the form of a much worse situation.

Velocity of Money Exchange.   There is another reason that control of the money supply is even more difficult than it has been in the past. Money tends to change hands more quickly today, that is, the velocity of exchange has accelerated. If money changes hands more often and with greater speed, then a smaller amount of money in circulation is needed to maintain the same level of business and production growth. It is difficult to know the amount of money needed at any particular time because of this increased velocity of monetary exchange.

CREDIT LINE: Upper limit which the bank sets on borrowing.

Increased use of credit cards and established lines of credit has sped up the exchange of money. These credit lines, both in cash areas and in purchase areas, have become widespread. They allow immediate and future use of money without negotiation. The psychological effect of having a credit line encourages the average person to maintain a lower savings balance for emergencies. The credit-card or credit-line balance can handle emergencies. Even with large item purchases, immediate purchase is possible. In the case of mortgage down payment, a person may use the credit line balance available rather than waiting for savings to grow to cover such costs. It is easy to see that if a person does not have to wait to build up a large balance of savings prior to a large purchase, money will change hands more often and more rapidly.

The Federal Reserve System has not exercised much control over debt created by credit cards. This means that the Reserve can not control the creation of a major source of consumer debt and is increasingly in the dark about the amount of such pseudo-money in circulation.[17] Its other major problem is that it cannot know the actual amount of money the economy needs under the conditions of heightened money exchange. If the Federal Reserve System could depend on an analysis of turnover rates of demand deposit levels directly showing the exchange velocity of money, it could adjust its policies accordingly. In other words, deferred payment purchases encouraged by widespread use of extended credit lines are almost impossible to check and are beyond the control of the Reserve System.

Consumer Protection

Since the Great Depression, our government has tried not only to control the market by restraining the sellers but also to protect the buyers as well. Consumer protection thus rounds out the efforts of our government to ensure a stable and fair economy.

In recent years, consumer groups have increased their efforts to compel government to regulate the activities of businesses for the welfare of the consumer.[18] The government has responded to these desires slowly but with growing effectiveness. It is interesting that far stricter controls have been placed on the contents of dog food than on the ingredients of baby food and candy.

Historically, the government had remained aloof from the problems of the consumer. The guide for the consumer has been "Let the buyer beware." Growing public concern over obvious problems has begun to supply the political pressure needed to even the relationship between business and the public. Our government still responds more to the powerful lobbies of the manufacturing and retail groups. Over time, however, we have seen the growing impact of various consumer protection laws. An example of the impact of these laws is found in the massive recalls of defective automobiles for repair. Both public attitudes and consumer attitudes have changed to the point where it is felt that sellers must take more responsibility for both product and service. Nothing continues forever without adjustments. The tide comes in but it also goes out, and each administration has its own priorities. In view of these differences of policy and opinion it is not surprising that occasional moves away from consumer protection and regulation of services occur.

The 1980s have seen a retreat by the federal government in the area of consumer protection. This has been in line with the policy of deregulation of industry. Airlines have been the most spectacular victims of the deregulation, with most of the old names dropping by the wayside. On the one hand it can be said that they failed to respond to market demands. On the other hand, service, safety, and maintenance have suffered, and many long term, experienced employees have been terminated in the name of economy. The Truth in Lending Act, which requires lenders to state the actual charges due on time purchases and loans, has been a giant step forward in this area.

Even though new agencies have been created to protect consumers, buyers remain at a disadvantage. A look at the actual services of such agencies will reveal the weaknesses built into such actions. Many state consumer protection agencies will act only on a broad front. They may take action against a company only if its violations are broad enough to allow a class action. In other words, if an oil company or an automobile manufacturer violates specified contracts, these state agencies may take action. However, in most instances apparently no funds exist for dealing with building contractors or others engaged in fraudulent business practices.

There is some protection for the consumer. In time, the presence of an ombudsman in each community may well force business to follow rules ignored in the past. The ombudsman is literally a citizen's representative in disputes with government and sometimes with business. In many regions, various businesses have created Better Business Bureaus to police their dealings with the consuming public. Unfortunately, their efforts accomplish little. In most instances, business owners are not required to be chartered or to adhere to what have been assumed to be fair business practices. The Better Business Bureau cannot enforce any rules or regulations.

The future may well see organizations composed both of businesses and of consumers empowered to regulate and settle complaints. There are already agencies that serve to settle disputes. One such group deals only with large appliances, while several of the automakers have set up similar boards. If such groups fail, the government will in time step in and regulate. Government regulation may or may not be the answer to these problems. Such regulation may involve high bonding requirements or other such demands, which might spell the end of the small businesss owner in our society. As we have seen in the other areas of government control of our economy, such control is not a solution without its own problems.

SUMMARY

This chapter traces the increasing involvement of the government in the United States economy. The stock market crash of 1929 is used as the watershed of that trend.

Before the crash, the government had little to do with economic affairs. It confined itself to such economic matters as tariffs, patents, and antitrust efforts. The stock market crash revealed that America's economy had become complex and in need of regulation. Unwise stock market policies had been allowed, which sent the nation toward the crash and the Great Depression.

After the crash, the government stepped in to assume new duties and powers. Established during the Great Depression years, this trend toward greater government control of the economy has increased over the years. The government used the theories of Keynes, Phillips, and others to try to reduce unemployment. The

Federal Reserve System has tried several methods of controlling the money supply in the United States. These methods range through reserve requirements, interest rates, and open market operations.

The government has tried to protect the consumer from unfair tactics on the part of the seller. These efforts have so far had limited effects.

SPECIAL TOPIC

Our Government and the Corporations—The Public and AT&T

In 1911, Chief Justice Edward Douglas White and the Supreme Court laid down the law regarding monopolies. In a decision against Standard Oil of New Jersey, he said that corporations could not have and use what he called the powers of monopoly. In theory and to some degree in practice, this decision broke up that massive giant.

As we have seen, a monopoly exists when a corporation or group of corporations controls the manufacture, production, or distribution of a product of relatively inelastic demand. The powers that derive from this position are (a) the power to cut prices below cost to the manufacturer, distributor, or service-offering corporation, which serves to drive off or eliminate competition, and (b) the ability to establish specific brands to forestall or fight off competition.

On the basis of a number of landmark Supreme Court decisions handed down as a result of the Sherman Antitrust Act, the standards required to prove monopolistic practices have been clarified. When such practices were proven, the courts would require that a company or corporation be broken up. We have also seen that some monopolies did tend to serve the public interest. These monopolies are called natural monopolies and include telephone and energy companies.

The usual justification for maintaining such monopolies is that the advantages of "economy of scale" are present. This occurs when greater production results in lower costs per unit produced. We now turn to discussion of the breakup of American Telephone and Telegraph,[19] or AT&T as it is affectionately called. The government and AT&T had been involved in litigation for the better part of a decade. Among the major points of this litigation is the

practice of the manufacturing arm of AT&T, Western Electric, holding a monopoly of sales to the Bell operating companies. Additional suits have been brought as either part of the major litigation or in individual actions dealing with the use of the Long Lines facilities and sale of non-Western-Electric equipment to subscribers to be used in conjunction with Bell (AT&T) Service.

AT&T has been made up of twenty-two local Bell operating subsidiaries. Western Electric, Bell Telephone Laboratories, and the Long Lines long-distance network. To put the size of this giant in proper perspective, we must realize that Western Electric alone is as big as United States Steel Company. Western, the manufacturing arm of the Bell system, had 1981 sales of $12.83 billion and profits of $697 million. These profits were derived from assets of $8.39 billion, which included twenty-one factories. In all, AT&T had 1980 revenues of $51 billion. Over half that amount was derived from its long-distance operations.

The smallest gem in the AT&T crown is the Bell Laboratories. Of its 22,500 employees, over 3,000 are Ph.D.s. The Labs consist of eighteen different research centers with an annual budget of $1.6 billion. It would be difficult to place profit or loss on a balance sheet, but consider that the Bell Labs have the following inventions among their over 19,000 patents: the transistor, the laser, sound movies, and high-fidelity phonographs. The most interesting series of Bell Laboratories research projects will result in a mini-revolution of the computer industry: In addition to developing computers that understand the spoken word, it is possible that computers will be designed to communicate with one another regardless of manufacturer.

What effects will the breakup of AT&T have on the economy? In the first instance, the twenty-two operating companies will be separated from AT&T, which will reduce the corporate revenues to about $30 billion. At first glance, the loss of revenue and spinning off of $80 billion in assets (two-thirds of the corporate assets) might seem to be a disaster. In reality, though there are losses that will be dealt with later, the breakup appears to be a golden opportunity. Over the years, AT&T has kept local telephone rates low by subsidizing them with high long-distance rates. With the local operating companies separate from the parent company, they will be allowed to raise their rates to justify a reasonable profit on their investment. The investment is figured on the assets of the company. Any public utility is guaranteed a profit. The local companies will be able to stand by themselves, making a profit in a slow-growth area.

Anyone owning a telephone has seen a rise in cost and a lowering of telephone service since the breakup. On the other hand, if you have been lucky enough to own substantial stock in AT&T, you are now well-off financially.

AT&T is now free to enter into many areas once forbidden it. The area of computers is a likely place to begin. Equipped as it is with the ability to communicate with virtually every household in the nation, and able to offer items such as the voice computer, AT&T would seem to be in a fine position to corner the home computer market. Equipped as it is with the prime research facility of the Western World—Bell Labs, one of the best manufacturing organizations in the country—Western Electric, and the highly profitable Long Lines, what could go wrong? It did go wrong for a time. The management was fat and not in a position to sell its product in a competitive market.

On the other side of the coin, the breakup has certain disadvantages for the public, and possibly for AT&T. Chief among them is the fact that the system works as it is, but will it work as it will be? In years past, when disaster struck a subsidiary, AT&T moved personnel and equipment from all parts of the nation to deal with the problem. When New York City lost an entire switching station, workers to repair it arrived by plane from California, Florida—all over the nation. What happens when New York Bell stands by itself? How much will local rates rise when Long Lines no longer picks up part of the bill?

In a more important vein, how will Western Electric survive? With its twenty-one plants and 156,000 employees, Western Electric has never had to compete in the open market. Everything it made went to one or another of the twenty-two operating companies. Western Electric did not have a sales operation and today it must compete with General Telephone & Electronics, International Telephone & Telegraph, International Business Machines, the Japanese, Rockwell International, Northern Telecon, and others.

In a nutshell, Bell Labs and Western Electric were not profit-oriented. As a Nobel prize winner at Bell Labs said, "As long as you work, they leave you alone." In other words, do something—any-thing—but do something.

The largest corporation in the world is going to change emphasis and direction. It will be interesting to see what happens.

We must now ask ourselves two basic questions. First, why force a breakup when AT&T was doing its job well? And second, what benefit is derived from a breakup of AT&T? Hundreds of thousands of workers will be more than discomfited if it all goes down the tube. Consumer rates are certainly higher and service is no better, if not worse. Answer these questions today, and once more in twenty years, when we will know how things turned out.

SELF-TEST QUESTIONS

1. True or false: The entry of the government into the economy has usually been a response to disaster.
2. What event marked the beginning of large-scale government involvement in the U.S. economy?
   a. Civil War
   b. World War I
   c. Stock market crash of 1929
   d. World War II

3. True or false: The use of protective tariffs began in the United States after the Vietnam War.

4. An example of early government control in the economy is:
   a. control of money supply
   b. consumer protection
   c. reduction of unemployment
   d. issuing patents

5. A major reason for the stock market crash of 1929 was:
   a. buying on the margin
   b. governmental control of money supply
   c. government restrictions on stock transfers

6. According to the Phillips Curve:
   a. the more unemployment, the more inflation
   b. tariffs are directly related to inflation
   c. unemployment causes growth of government
   d. the more unemployment, the less inflation.

7. According to Keynes, too little _____ will cause economic depression.

8. The government agency that controls the money supply is the
   _____.

9. How does the government control the money in circulation?
   a. by buying or selling government securities
   b. by setting banks' reserve requirements
   c. by adjusting interest rates

10. True or false: Money tends to change hands more quickly today.

11. True or false: Sellers today are no longer expected to take responsibility for product or service.

ANSWERS TO SELF-TEST QUESTIONS

1. true
2. c
3. false
4. d
5. a
6. d

7. spending
8. Federal Reserve System
9. a, b, c
10. true
11. false

ANSWERS TO SKILL REINFORCERS

18–1. An invalid syllogism would be:
   1. If the Secretary of the Treasury frowns, the stock market will decline.
   2. The Secretary of the Treasury never frowns.
   3. Therefore the stock market will never decline. The conclusion is invalid because it ignores the possibility that other factors may cause a stock market decline. Besides, the major premise may well go too far in weighing the importance of that person's frown. So not only is the logic invalid, but the major premise is shaky as well.

18–2. "Average" is another word for "mean." A mean house price would be determined by adding together the prices of all the houses being considered, then dividing that sum by the number of houses considered.

NOTES

1. Robert Lekachman, *Greed Is Not Enough* (New York: Pantheon, 1982).
2. John W. Evans, *U.S. Trade Policy* (New York: Worth Publishers, 1971).

3. Milton H. Spencer, *Contemporary Economics* (New York: Worth Publishers, 1971).

4. David A. Shannon, ed., *Great Depression* (Englewood Cliffs, N.J.: Prentice-Hall, 1960).

5. Broadus Mitchell, *Depression Decade: From New Era Through New Deal 1929–1941* (New York: Harper & Row, 1969).

6. Benjamin Stolberg and Warren Jay Vinton, *Economic Consequences of the New Deal* (New York: Harcourt, Brace & World, 1935).

7. Adam Smith, *The Wealth of Nations* (New York: E.P. Dutton, 1910).

8. Spencer, *Contemporary Economics*.

9. John Maynard Keynes, *General Theory of Employment, Interest, and Money* (New York: Harcourt Brace Jovanovitch, 1936).

10. Richard G. Lipsey and Peter O. Steiner, *Economics* (New York: Harper & Row, 1966).

11. Louis A. Dow, *Business Fluctuations in a Domestic Economy* (Columbus, Ohio: Charles E. Merrill, 1968).

12. Milton Friedman and A.J. Schwartz, *A Monetary History of the United States, 1867–1960* (Princeton: Princeton University Press, 1963).

13. E.W. Kemmerer and D.L. Kemmerer, *The A.B.C. of the Federal Reserve System*, 12th ed. (New York: Harper & Row, 1950).

14. Board of Governors of the Federal Reserve System, *The Federal Reserve System: Purposes and Function* (Washington, D.C., 1961); and *The Federal Reserve Act as Amended to December 31, 1956* (Washington, D.C., 1957).

15. Robert V. Roosa, *Federal Reserve Operation in the Money and Government Securities Market* (Federal Reserve Bank of New York, 1956).

16. Board of Governors of the Federal Reserve System, *Annual Reports, 1962, 1964*. See also "Is the Fed a 500 Billion Dollar Weakling?" *New York Times*, February 17, 1974.

17. Milton Friedman and David Meiselman, "The Relative Stability of Monetary Velocity and the Investment Multiplier in the United States," in *Stabilization Policies* (Englewood Cliffs, N.J.: Prentice-Hall, 1963).

18. Ralph M. Gaedeke and Warren W. Etcheson, eds., *Consumerism: Viewpoints from Business, Government and the Public Interest* (San Francisco: Canfield Press, 1972).

19. "Breaking Up AT&T," *U.S. News and World Report,* January 25, 1982.

SUGGESTED READINGS

Conklin, Paul K., *The New Deal.* New York: Thomas Y. Crowell, 1967.

Friedman, Milton, *An Economist's Protest.* Glen Ridge, N.J.: Thomas Horton and Daughters, 1975.

Galbraith, John K. *The Affluent Society.* Boston: Houghton Mifflin, 1958.

George, Victor. *Social Security and Society.* Boston: Routledge and Kagan, 1976.

Gordon, Margaret S., ed. *Poverty in America.* San Francisco: Chandler, 1965.

Mills, C. Wright. *The Power Elite.* New York: Oxford University Press, 1956.

Morris, Richard B. *Government and Labor in Early America.* Boston: N.E. University Press, 1981.

19 THE ECONOMICS OF MONEY AND BANKING

Credit Cards and Beyond

The nature of money has changed over the centuries. Is there any reason to think this will not continue? The use of "plastic money" has become more common recently, and the near future should see more of this. A system based entirely on the use of credit cards and bank cash cards might be something like this:

You awaken, dress, and head for your car. There is plenty of time this morning, because you don't have to report to work until noon. On your way downtown you stop to have your car serviced and its gas tank filled. The bill is $47.50, which you pay by presenting your card. While waiting for work on the car to be completed, you breakfast at the local diner and also pay by card. When you arrive at the shopping center, you place your car in the all-day parking area, gaining entrance by inserting your card into an automatic gate. The central computer charges the toll against your account. This process repeats itself when you purchase your needs for the week. When you drop your mail at the post office, you pay various bills such as telephone, electric, heating oil, cable television, and gasoline by check, or you have automatically charged them to your account. As you spend, most of the credits are deducted automatically from your balance. As you pass the bank, you may insert your card in a slot and receive an up-to-date statement of your cash balance.

Some major changes must be dealt with when living in a system of up-to-the-second, computer accessed electronic balances. Each time you spend or use your card, the central computer notes the location and amount of your purchase. In this manner your movements may be easily traced. In the event that the government is looking for you, you may be notified immediately by a mere cancellation of your line. At this point, you have the choice of starving to death or giving yourself up.

If you are thinking about escaping by stealing someone else's card, you had better do it soon. In the near future, this turn of events will be forestalled by eliminating cards. Account numbers would be keyed to individual voiceprints and typing patterns. Voiceprints are far more accurate and easier to record than fingerprints. Each person has an individual voiceprint that is impossible to disguise. Perhaps all door locks and building entrances will soon be keyed to central computers with a complete set of voiceprints on file. On entering a bus, store, bank, or parking lot, you will only have to speak to be identified, and your account will be charged. In addition to voiceprints, the year 1986 saw the beginning of the computer-identified typing pattern. Research on this method began in an effort to forestall entry into computer information banks by identifying the typing pattern of those with authority to use entry codes. Speed, pressure, pattern of entry, and forms of mistakes of authorized persons are analyzed and used as much as a form of recognition by the computer as are the entry codes themselves.

If you become a fugitive, a minor adjustment will add your name to a list of no-credit, no-balance individuals. This would close you out of your apartment, car, all restaurants, stores, buildings, and charge accounts in general and force you to give yourself up to the authorities.

Can you foresee any major difficulties living in a system where the government can keep tabs on every move you make? You would have less opportunity to break society's rules, but what if you did not care to live by rules that seemed not to conform to your particular value pattern?

When we reach into our purse or pocket and feel the crinkled bills and jingle the coins, we are in contact with an important aspect of economics: money. The last three chapters have been based on theory and principles. Such abstract topics are important for a well-rounded view of economics, but it is much easier to relate to this chapter's topic. Here we will explore the uses of money, both within one society and among nations. Then the subject of debt, an increasingly important concept, will be explored, followed by a study of other items of value.

MONEY AND BANKING: BASIC ECONOMIC TOOLS

Money is the most important economic tool in the life of the average person. Closely tied to this tool is the bank, which is used by many people but understood by few. Here the nature and uses of both these tools will be explored.

The Functions of Money

All of us have contact with money, and we all know that if we earn five dollars every hour we are really earning so much milk or butter or so many eggs per hour. We may equate twenty hours of work to the price of a bicycle. How many hours must we work to pay for a car?

What is money? Money represents goods and services. Money makes living easier, because we can translate work and products, which are goods and services, into paper. This paper can be traded easily for other goods and services. Money, then, is a medium of exchange.[1]

This convenient medium of exchange makes our modern economy possible. As the chapter preview suggests, the use of money—in new forms—may become much more convenient in the near future. If we lived in a moneyless world, that world would also be without the complex society we enjoy. Money makes it possible for the increased specialization of labor that enables us to engage in various fields that do not produce whole or easily marketable items. Money is this easily transferable form, the friendly five- or ten-dollar bill, permits us to purchase countless items that our industry produces, as well as other citizens' services. With money this system is convenient. Without money, the purchasing of services and such goods would be impractical or impossible.

To see how much our way of life is based on money, picture spending a typical day in a moneyless world. Imagine how you would meet your everyday needs. For example, if you were a fisherman, you will have enough to eat as long as you do not tire of eating fish. But you have other problems, one of which is your need for a new house for your growing family. To build the house you need lumber, nails, hardware, and carpenters. On visiting the lumberman, you find that your supplies will cost 650 pounds of fish. While he likes fish, he does not like it that much. At this point, the haggling begins. The lumberman will accept three cows and 50 pounds of fish, and it becomes your problem to convert the remaining 600 pounds of fish into three cows. This may require exchanging smaller amounts of fish for goats and chickens and trading them for cows. Each transaction you make will be as complicated as your arrangement with the lumberman.

We may try a simpler problem involving smaller amounts of fish. Imagine, the difficulty involved in taking a date to the movies and paying in fish. The price may be two and a half fish for your tickets. What do you do with the other half fish during the show? It would be best to pick a date with a lot of understanding or a bad cold.

In societies lacking money as we know it, the relationships of items of value to other items or services become somewhat standardized. For example, so many beads might be recognized as worth a certain number of pigs. Once these items have a relative value established, trade becomes easier. Still, it is by no means as easy as trade in a society that has a monetary system.

Looking back to the days when money was either not in use or in very short supply, we find examples of people trading almost any item for food and services. Perhaps you have heard the phrase "He is not worth his salt." This has its origins in the use of salt as a medium of exchange. In the ancient world, salt was accepted as a substitute for coinage and currency. Our word, "salary," is derived from the Latin word for salt because, for a time, Roman soldiers were paid in salt.

It is easy to understand why salt was chosen as a means of exchange. Salt is desired by people everywhere and is easily divisible. While salt would have little value in an area with an overabundance, most human groups need it. In some important ways, however, money is better than salt as a medium of exchange. Consider the greater bulk of salt and the need for dry storage of salt. It would be easy to sympathize with the salt-laden traveler caught in a rainstorm, watching his fortune melt away.

Obviously, items such as salt could serve for simple transactions, either firsthand or over long distances. Other items used as mediums of exchange include gold, silver, diamonds, pearls, shells, and tobacco. Unfortunately, there has never been enough gold or silver to allow its exclusive use, and these metals had drawbacks that precluded their use for any great amount of exchange. Anyone who has carried a hundred silver dollars in his pocket can testify to the inconvenience. Gold has been valued at a rate higher than silver, yet this metal is impractical for large transactions. A shopping trip with gold valued at $400 an ounce might be practical. The purchase of a $100,000 home, however, involves over 20 troy pounds of gold. Obviously, a single check or pile of paper money is far easier to handle than the dead weight of silver or gold.

Other factors besides the weight problem must also be considered. Precious stones, pearls, and metals valuable in themselves must be watched, guarded, and transferred to complete a purchase. They are in constant danger of theft and loss. We face the prospect of hiding the loot in a mattress, burying it in the yard, or carrying it to the point of transfer at great risk of loss. We are familiar with the problems pirates had in this regard, and with their propensity to bury treasure. A traveler's check, or one of the normal checking-account type, becomes valid only when signed. It represents a transfer of actual funds held by a bank to another account in the same or another bank. Without abstract money representing value, we must maintain and protect the actual metal or item of value.

All these factors contrast sharply with the picture in the chapter preview. This contrast goes to show how far we have come in making the use of money convenient.

The Development of Banking

Keeping money has been a problem for thousands of years. A solution in this area began with entrusting items of value to specific people for safekeeping. Since the original purpose of watching valuables was a service, the keeper (or banker) charged a fee.

Under certain circumstances there are still charges for the safekeeping of money and valuables. There is an annual charge for the convenience of a safe-deposit box in a bank. A Swiss bank account for safekeeping carries a yearly charge. When the bank can use money on deposit, it can also make a profit on it. As a result banks pay depositors in the form of interest for the use of such monies, while charging a higher rate of interest for making loans.

We must assume that the process of depositing money with individuals for safekeeping began on a personal basis, either with relatives or trusted friends serving as keepers. In time, individuals specialized in serving the needs of groups and communities. They acted as full-time guards and kept formal accounts in their depositories. The depositories were a step toward the development of the modern banking system.[2] Traveling back in time to the days of the private banker, and creating a situation where we must find someone to care for our valuables, might be something like this:

In the sixteenth century, alone and new to the city of London, you must find a relatively safe place to live right away. Even though your own safety is of great concern, you have another pressing urgency: finding a safe depository for your gold. You are alone and friendless in London because your father has died, and you have no further reason to remain in your native town. Your older brother has inherited the house and property, leaving you homeless. You will receive an annual allowance for the duration of your lifetime from the proceeds of the family estate. You also possess several hundred guineas in gold, which represent the first distribution of this estate. This is enough to live comfortably for more than a year, but you cannot keep this amount of money on your person or leave it in your lodgings. In either case, it would be stolen, which could cause immediate poverty, injury, or death. Fortunately, you have the name of a reputable private banker/ moneylender recommended by the banker who served your family in your hometown. You quickly make your way to his residence. After presenting your letter of introduction, you are admitted to the interior of a home that is well built and very secure. During your interview with the banker, you establish a schedule for monthly cash payments for living expenses and a method of allowing your creditors, such as tailors and grocers, to be paid at regular intervals. You arrange to transfer future payments from your estate directly from your hometown banker to your current banker in London, so you will not need to transport the gold personally. Without the services of the banker, who will charge a nominal fee for his work, you might have lost your money or spent most of your time watching and caring for it.

Other services a banker performs include issuing paper promissory notes, which are useful for purchasing objects requiring more gold than you wish to carry on your person. The seller will consider such a note as payment for the object purchased. Your banker will transfer the amount specified from your account to the seller's. If the seller has another banker, a paper transfer will be arranged to represent the transfer of monies.

This method of banking operated and served its purpose only as long as both parties dealing with him and other bankers knew and trusted the banker. It could not work when the banker was unknown or the distances were too great to allow eventual access to the gold itself. Bankers overcame this shortcoming by forming alliances, both locally and in distant lands. While these alliances allowed the bankers to maintain paper credits for a time, outstanding debts had to be settled eventually in terms of items of real value. This called for the actual transfer of gold and silver from one place to another.

From these beginnings, we can trace the development of the banking industry. The bank became more central to the use of money over the years:

1. Bankers merely guaranteed the safety of gold or other valuables on deposit.
2. On behalf of their clients, they attended to the details of actual transfer of valuables from one area to another.
3. Bankers found that several clients, either their own or those of members of their local alliance, sent and received monies from the same distant places. A method of paper credit made it possible to wipe out the debts of all clients without the actual transfer of valuables.

For example, imagine that George in London owed one hundred dollars to Fred in Birmingham, and that Fred in Birmingham owed the same amount to a man in London. A banker in London and a banker in Birmingham would arrange to pay their local clients without actually moving one hundred dollars in gold back and forth from London to Birmingham. Paper I.O.U.'s, then, replaced the actual gold. This simple example of a complex business illustrates the practice. When trust between bankers developed, the I.O.U.'s could be kept for a long time against the day a transfer would be required in an opposite direction or to another city.

Today this practice continues. If we could gain entrance to the gold storage rooms of the Federal Reserve Bank of New York, we would find a fair part of the world's gold in neat stacks. When an international transaction takes place, the gold is not shipped out to country A or B. It is merely moved from A's stack to B's stack. The gold itself may never leave the vault.

The Worth of Modern Money

Most modern money has no worth in itself, but it represents an implied value. The use of objects with value in themselves, such as gold and silver, has progressed to the use of scrip, or paper money. Scrip does not represent a hard or real item of value.

In the United States, this transition was not completed until the 1960s. Until the 1930s in this nation, gold coins were still in circulation, and paper money could be taken to a bank and exchanged for its face value in gold. During the 1930s, the government called in all gold coinage in the United States; however, paper currency could still be redeemed for its value in silver coinage or in bars. Silver coinage continued in use until the 1960s, when the government replaced it with the sandwich coinage made of nonprecious metals. The guarantee to pay silver on demand was removed from paper scrip money, which left the scrip itself, with no metal backing, as the abstract exchange item for goods and services. The transition has been paper for gold, then paper for silver, and now paper for more paper or coins made of nonprecious metal. The United States issued new gold coins in 1986 with stated face values. However, exchange of these coins will be made not in terms of the face value, but in terms of the market value of gold at the time of exchange.

There are numerous reasons for this change in our old system of the direct use of coinage based on precious metals. One of the most obvious is that gold and silver used in coinage is too often worth more than the value claimed by the coin. It costs more to mine and mint a dollar's worth of silver than the value claimed by the silver dollar. In 1973 a standing offer of $3.00 and more for a silver dollar, regardless of its date, became a permanent feature in most newspaper want ads. The daily financial news now carries the market price of silver coinage quoted on $1,000 bags. The average price (1982) quoted is in the neighborhood of $6,000 for $1,000 in coinage. In recent years, the value of silver has fluctuated from a high of $50 per ounce and $29,000 per 1,000 bags of silver coins, to lows in the range of $4.00 to $5.50 an ounce in 1986.

The count and review process at the U.S. Denver Mint. This is the final process in the production of coin. The coins are reviewed, inspected, counted, and bagged. They are then weighed and stored prior to shipping to Federal Reserve banks.

If the metal from which coins are minted can be sold for more than their face value, it would of course be foolish not to sell those coins for their worth and get a greater amount of paper money. When this situation occurred, silver coinage disappeared from circulation. None of the laws of the land could prevent people from melting coins and selling them as bulk metal for industrial use or for jewelry. The shortage of coins meant that business based upon coinage suffered. Vending machine operators, bus companies, and dozens of other change-oriented businesses could not operate.

Other reasons also led to suspending the use of precious metals in coinage. The population has grown by leaps and bounds, but the supply of precious metals remains limited by the actual amount present as a natural resource. In view of this, we must look at how use and supply are related. A natural resource has limits. When its limits are exhausted, the material can no longer be used. The development of our photographic and electronic industries has created a use for silver. A point had been reached demanding the choice of continuing to use silver in industry or wasting this vital resource on something as useless as coinage.

Coinage is useless? This sounds absurd to the person who is not aware of the impact of economic issues. The term "economic issues" refers not only to the positions taken by industry, business, and government but also to one's personal economic position. In addition to easing pressure on vending-machine and other metal-based industries, the taxpayer has benefited. The government no longer has to bid for coinage metal in an overpriced market, for which it provides a commodity (coin) that costs more than it is worth.

While today, we do not use money made of precious metal, we exchange it for goods and services of real value. We can buy all the manufactured items we can pay for and contract for all the services we need. People need no gold to survive, because they can do no more with gold than they can with a currency that is honored for all purchases.

We have moved from money backed by precious metals to money with no real value in itself. This transition was made without destroying the economy. Still, some emotional impact has been noted. People have a feeling about precious metals that is hard to define.

The Eisenhower silver dollar that the government minted as a form of memorial is a good example of the emotional tie to silver and gold. There was no small concern that a cheap alloy dollar lacking the silver content of the old dollars would insult the memory of the president. Gambling interests in the West worried about the lack of silver dollars, which they needed at the tables and in machines. The changeover to base metal also greatly disturbed coin collectors, and many people did not collect the new coinage. The government was relatively happy about this turn of events, because it helped to keep coins in circulation. We have to remember the need for ensuring an adequate supply of money for transaction purposes.

Another, more recent case of this new kind of money is the Susan B. Anthony dollar. This small base-metal coin has not been accepted by the American public. Surely emotional attitudes had something to do with the coin's failure.

Private mints are responding to the absence of precious metals in coins. These mints are manufacturing coinage and metal art of gold, silver, and platinum for collectors and investors. The coins are expensive, and the number minted is limited. An artificially created shortage creates a great demand for the product. It also guarantees a rise in its cost in paper money as greater numbers of people bid for the limited pieces available.

INTERNATIONAL MONEY

On the international level, money is not such a familiar topic. It is not just a matter of the stuff jingling in our pocket. The nature of money among nations with different currencies is a bit exotic. It may seem at this point like some strange, silly game played by a few rich people. That may be partly so, but that game affects our standard of living in important ways. It is worth exploring for this reason alone.

Traditionally, gold has served as the major form of international money. The reason for this is easy to explain. Intense national pride and each nation's basic distrust of other nations make each reluctant to put any faith in another nation's currency.

There are solid reasons for such attitudes of distrust. Imagine this as a possible national exchange: The United States has completed a sale of wheat to the Soviet Union. The price agreed upon was $3.00 a bushel. After the sale was completed, the Soviets revalued their currency to a higher relative level. This enabled them to equate their currency to more dollars per ruble than at the time of the sale. The United States would then receive fewer than the estimated rubles per bushel of wheat. After such an exchange, the United States might well feel that it had been cheated. The value of the American dollar is not what it used to be. In 1986 and 1987 the value of the dollar relative to the Japanese yen and other world currency fell to unusual lows. The government felt that a weaker dollar would allow the United States to compete with other nations in the export wars. We may sell more abroad, because our prices are now cheaper, but since other currency is more valuable, our real property becomes a good buy for foreign investors. As our dollar falls, we find that imported goods cost more and may now be out of reach. In addition, because our goods have become a good buy for the holders of other currency, we will find that we must pay higher prices for domestic goods. In brief, our standard of living will fall. One benefit that may come home because of a weakening dollar is that the national debt, borrowed when dollars were expensive, can now be paid back with a cheaper version. If all of the dollars floating around the world, serving as an international trading currency, are suddenly sent back to us in the form of claims for goods and services, we could be in real trouble.

INFLATION: A very large and relatively sudden increase in the general price level; this is not to be confused with normal price increases or adjustments after a depression.

DEVALUATION: Refers to the decrease in the value of a currency relative to other currencies.

A long period of chronic imbalance of payments brought on not by the private sector, which as a rule sustained a profitable balance of trade, but by government expenditures forced the dollar into a weak position.[3] In plain terms, the United States was spending far more abroad than it was receiving in payments. Thus the dollar became a currency that countries and people began to distrust. Their faith was shaken.

Trading in currency has been a popular and profitable pastime for numerous brokers and investors. The time had arrived when the dollar could be bought and sold for profit, and holders of great amounts of dollars began to sell for gold or other currencies. The sale of dollars forced the price of gold up and the price of dollars down.

Trust in the dollar as a currency has not returned to its previous level, and what the trading money of the future will be is anyone's guess. There are advantages to issuing the world's trading money, foremost of which is that other nations' continued use of the currency prevents it from being returned to the countries that created it for goods and services. Perhaps the following story will clarify the way money is traded among nations:

A well-known and powerful gangland figure passed away, either from natural causes or from the rigors of his profession. Just prior to sealing his coffin, his four most trusted aides gathered around him to show their sorrow and to give their final tribute to a dead leader. In tribute, the story goes, the aides put a large sum of money into the coffin to be buried with the body. Each aide went forth, stood silently for a moment, and then stuffed an envelope into the pocket of the corpse. The coffin was then sealed, taken to the cemetery and buried. After the service the four men met to toast their fallen leader. Their conversation came around to the amount each had placed in the coffin. The first three men stated that they had given $5,000 each. The fourth smiled gently and noted that he had indeed matched the total of the three by leaving $15,000. After the party had ended the fourth man's wife, quite shaken, asked how he could afford such a large sum of money. "Easily," he answered, "I took their fifteen thousand in cash from his pocket and left my check for $30,000."

The point of this story is that the check issued by the fourth man will never be cashed, and thus never be charged against the account of the writer. Trade money acts in much the same manner. Once it is spent, it lives its life in trade, rarely returning to the nation of its issue as a claim against goods and services.

In other words, the United States issues a dollar and spends it for goods or services abroad. The people in the United States who paid for the goods and services have the use of them. Meanwhile, the nation or person who received the dollar for goods or services spends the dollar in a third nation which, in turn, spends the dollar again. Since the dollar has value as a worldwide trading currency, it may never return to the United States as a claim against goods or services.

Black Thursday, October 24, 1929, hit the stock market with a $40 billion loss that was only the beginning of America's economic fall. Here citizens wait in line to withdraw their money from a bank. Such "bank runs" were numerous during the Great Depression.

If there were a sudden loss of faith in the currency, all the dollars might return at once to claim goods and services. Then the nation would be in the same position as a bank exposed to a run. As stated earlier, banks do not keep all their currency locked away; they expect only so many withdrawals and invest the rest of their deposits in income-producing ventures. If all depositors want to withdraw their money at the same time, the bank will be caught short. Similarly, the nation faced with a sudden demand to make good on all its outstanding currency is in for a bad time. It will either have to borrow from other nations to honor its obligations or devalue its currency.

Any nation that trades or borrows money from other nations must deal with the problem of exchanging its money for foreign money. Under normal conditions, the free market will set the exchange rates for the various national monies. In other words, the value of one currency in relation to another is set by what each can buy and by the amount that people in the money-exchange business will trade for one currency in terms of the other. The relative values of currencies are in this way set one against the other. The English pound may be worth $1.75 American, while the U.S. dollar, for years, equalled 12.5 Mexican pesos. Recent devaluations, however, have resulted in a dollar buying up to 680 pesos (Aug. 1986). Other currencies around the world are similarly weighed and valued.

As stated, the free or open market sets the relative values of the various currencies. The currencies are worth only as much as someone is willing to pay for them. Sometimes nations will not accept the market valuation of their currency. In such cases, the nation forbids trade in that currency at any rate below valuation placed by the government. An action of this sort is an attempt to retain the gold reserves at home. It leads to less foreign trade and the growth of a black market in the currency. If the government in question continues to spend abroad without selling goods and services themselves, its reserves will disappear. To maintain gold reserves and to be able to purchase things from other countries, a nation must be able to produce and sell goods and services at competitive prices. If not, there will be no customers for the products. If the prices are to be competitive, the value of the currency must be in line with its true purchasing power.

INTERNATIONAL MONETARY FUND: A fund supported by many nations that seeks to stabilize international exchange and promote balanced, orderly trade.

In all, it is safe to say that governments should not attempt to set exchange rates.[4] Still, many governments have feared or mistrusted the free-market valuations of currency. They have attempted to set the value of their currency in relation to other currencies. Groups of governments have tried to control currency changes by such means as the International Monetary Fund. Through the use of this agency, exchange rates could at least be made predictable.[5] The various governments agree to inform one another of intended revaluation of currency. Also, other nations must permit the exchange rates to be adjusted to more than a small percentage. Still, internal inflation or deflation causes immense internal pressure within nations. This has led some nations to change their valuations without waiting to consult others. This type of action weakens the International Monetary Fund and creates distrust of trading currencies. The United States has devalued its dollar in an attempt to improve its position in international trade. This was done by removing the long-term guarantee to sell gold at a rate of $35.00 per troy ounce.

This discussion of international money may be getting abstract, but it is not without importance. To see how such money matters affect us personally, we must look at the big picture. We begin by pointing to the fact that much of what we consume in this nation is made in other countries or made here from imported raw materials. Since the 1950s, the United States has been importing more raw materials than it has produced at home. Even copra, which is used as a form of animal feed, is imported, to say nothing of vast amounts of other materials necessary to our factories.

When the price of the dollar falls, the price of these raw materials rises, because the dollar has become equal to lower amounts of foreign currency. If these prices rise, then objects made from these materials also rise in price. Naturally, the price of objects produced abroad rises when the dollar is devalued. Foreign cars, television sets, stereos, and other imports have all reflected the fall of the dollar.

In addition to the price rise of foreign-made objects and commodities, some items produced in the United States have risen drastically at home. Farm products, which are in short supply worldwide, may suddenly become hard to get and expensive at home. The reason is obvious. These items are for sale to the highest bidder. If our dollar is worth less, we face the prospect of bidding against foreign buyers with a more valuable currency. They can now exchange their currency for more dollars than before. Thus when foreign buyers come to our markets to bid for fixed amounts of farm products, the price of these products will rise, forcing us to pay more for our own corn, wheat, rice, and meat. The meat price rises as feed grains leave the nation or rise in price to meet foreign demand. American properties suddenly become attractive to foreign investors. Their prices, unless they rise to meet the international rates, will be bargains which holders of currencies that have gained value in relation to the dollar cannot overlook.

A currency devaluation results in one major result for average citizens: It lowers their standard of living. It must cost more to buy less. If salaries are not pushed upward to adjust to the devaluation, we have less purchasing power. If we combine a devaluation with a high rate of inflation, we will find ourselves in a serious situation in a very short time.[6] As a result, we would face an altered diet due to higher food prices. We would face smaller and less convenient residence forms, caused by higher building and material costs. We would also have fewer convenience items, less energy for our use, and less money for any luxury enjoyed prior to devaluation.

SKILL BOX

Distinguishing Fact from Opinion

"The future may hold . . ." "We may feel . . ." "We may assume . . " These phrases from the two paragraphs above might
have alerted a reader that the author was mixing opinion with
facts. After all, when speaking of the future, stating opinion is not
uncommon.

While opinion can be of real value, it is important to watch for
this when reading anything. After all, we do not want to accept
something as fact when it is only opinion. The ability to tell the
difference between fact and opinion can help us evaluate statements before we accept them.

An opinion is a belief or judgment. It is more than just an impression, but it is not a fact. An opinion might be based on facts;
if so, it goes beyond facts, and is thus something of which we can
be less certain. A fact is something considered to be truth. It is
something agreed to be an accurate description of reality, rather
than one's judgment of reality. A fact is what is according to actual observation; an opinion is a belief concerning some truth.

It is important to remember that a fact is something that is
agreed only for the time being to be truth. This agreement can
collapse when new facts are discovered. Facts can gain or lose
support as science presses onward.

It is usually easy to spot opinions. Look for such "opinion
words" as "seems," "could," "appears," "might," and "probably." When authors or speakers use such words, it may be a cue
that they are offering opinion, not fact. Of course, even if people
say "it is" rather than "it may be," they may be wrong. That is,
"it" may not be so at all. We must decide whether or not to trust
an author to separate fact from opinion.

Opinions are not useless. They can offer food for thought. And
sometimes the facts are not known or cannot be known. Then we
must decide which opinions are of value. Opinions of well-
informed people should carry the most weight. (But that is only
the authors' opinion.)

Examples of devaluation occur around the world. In February
1982 the Mexican government announced that it would no longer
support the peso.[7] The policy had been to maintain a fixed value
for the peso relative to the dollar and other foreign currencies. The
result of this move will be initially to devalue the peso relative to
the dollar. The U.S. tourist will be able to buy more, and Mexican
products will be easier to sell abroad at a lower price.

These examples show the importance of international money
matters for our own American life-style. Changes in the value of
the dollar in relation to other currencies can result in a lower standard of living. When the standard of living falls, people suddenly
find that services once taken for granted, such as medical treatment, are unavailable or available only at great sacrifice.

In time, inflation and devaluation will make certain treatment
available only to the very wealthy. Even today a serious illness can

suddenly wipe out life savings. The cost of specialized machinery, such as heart/lung or kidney machines, has become so high that it forces many people to await a certain death rather than use the treatment. In our society, we have not had to face this sort of crisis in the past when medical treatment for specific ills was known and available. Other, poorer societies have lived and died with this situation throughout history.

The future may hold a move toward an international money. The European Common Market has plans for a European money at present, and worldwide currency will become more possible once the Common Market experiment proves a success.

Most of the effects of a worldwide money on the United States as a nation and on us as individuals can only be guessed at this point. A prime effect of becoming more of a part of the world economy would be the relaxing of national control of our economy. Recently, in deference to our huge gold reserves, the world followed our lead in being somewhat dependent on the dollar as a trade currency. At present, neither condition exists. Our gold reserves have shrunk, the dollar is shaky, and we are a net importer of natural resources. We may feel the effect of natural resources depletion, increased needs based on population growth, and new energy requirements in the growing cycle of fuel shortages. We may assume that the fuel crunch is merely a sign of future shortages and economic readjustments leading to a redistribution of the world's wealth. The fact that the world's standard of living will tend to even out means not that we as a nation will do better but rather that we will lose ground and our standard of living will drop.

COMMON MARKET: An association of European countries for the purpose of eventual abolition of tariff barriers and their borders, common import duties for outside goods, and pursuing economic policies to benefit members.

MONEY AND DEBT

It is possible to think of money as debt. If we purchase a bottle of whisky for ten dollars, we may pay for it in cash. In a real sense, until we spent the money, society was in our debt. The ten-dollar bill is really an I.O.U. issued by society. When we spend the money, we and the rest of society are obligated to the holder of the money. As long as we hold money, we are extending society a loan, payable on demand.

The I.O.U. has value only so long as the society recognizes the value assigned to that I.O.U. If the currency of any country loses credibility, the entire system falls apart. This can occur as the result of the government's overproduction of money. Indeed, people can lose faith or confidence in currency quite easily when the government produces either too much or too little money.

It is easy to see that if the government needs more money without being required to back its printed money with precious metals, merely printing another batch can solve its problem. This practice of "watering" the currency can continue unnoticed by all but the experts for a long time. Surely it is a simpler way of raising government funds than taxing citizens.

Coping with Inflation   In reality the effects of inflation and taxation are the same. Each week we are exposed to the statements the government has made rating inflation of the period just passed as this percentage or that, based upon the dollar value at some point in the past.

It may be interesting to consider how this affects the average person. Extreme cases of runaway inflation occurred in Germany after World War I and in Brazil during the early 1960s. Imagine a situation where people have just received their weekly paychecks, which they must quickly take to the bank and exchange for cash. The currency they receive has been subjected to such a fantastic rise in the inflationary spiral that they must carry it in a shopping bag. What has happened is that the value of money has declined. The term "inflation" refers to the condition of the currency: It is inflated, less solid, or watered. As the people leave the bank with a shopping bag filled with almost valueless currency, they can see inflation in the economy that surrounds them. They rush to stores to buy needed items before their value increases and the value of the currency decreases.

Our society has not yet been exposed to an inflation at this extreme. We expect yearly increases in prices and in the value of basic goods. If we purchase a home this year, we expect that the same house will be worth more in ten years than the dollar amount we paid. The question we must face is whether the actual value of the house has increased or whether the purchase of the same house merely requires more money of less value. The typical reaction to a change of this sort is that one has made a good invest- ment and that the house actually has increased in value since the time of purchase. This may well be the case, but in most cases in- flation has decreased the value of the money. An added factor to consider is the relationship between the interest rate and the infla- tion rate. If the rate of inflation is greater than the rate of interest on your mortgage, you may well have seen a profit over the years. You have borrowed expensive money and paid back cheap money. You have also paid for the use of that money at a rate that did not keep pace with its devaluation. If your interest payments were tax deductible, your actual rate of interest was even lower. The vari- able mortgage of the eighties, together with very high interest rates, has seen the end of these favorable consumer investments.

In everyday life, we can see the increase in the price of bacon. In the latter half of 1982 a pound of bacon sold for more than twice its 1975 price. The bacon weighed the same both years; it tasted the same, but it took more money to buy it in 1982 than it did in 1975. The value change occurred not in the bacon but in the currency used to purchase the bacon. If during the period that ba- con had doubled in price salaries also doubled, the bacon would be neither more expensive nor less expensive in real terms. No raise, or only a 5 percent raise, in salary would mean that the price of bacon had risen and that we face an actual devaluation of the earned dollar. The effect of inflation becomes clear when we must

Social Security is the economic mainstay of an increasingly large portion of our population.

work longer this year than last to earn enough to purchase the same item.

For some people a common response to uncontrolled inflation is a movement back to a barter system. Bartering is an exchange of property or services for another's property or services. This is a move to avoid using an untrustworthy currency. Still, under the law, one must include in income the fair market value, at the time received, of property or services one receives in bartering. If one receives the services of another in return for one's services, and you both have agreed ahead of time on the value of the services, that value will be accepted as fair market value unless the value can be shown to be otherwise, thus reducing one's taxable income.

Continuing erosion of a currency's value in itself represents a form of taxation. This plus higher rates of tax for higher incomes of lesser monetary value frequently bring about various forms of barter. A brief discussion of the sliding rates collected by our federal income tax may clarify this point.

The percentage of taxable income to be paid to the government is lower for an income of $10,000 per year than for an income of $20,000 per year. Income sometimes rises enough to make up for some of the effects of a devalued currency. When this happens, we will find ourselves paying the government far more in taxes from a larger income which purchases less. In plainer terms, the percentage of income that must be paid to the government in taxes rises as income rises to adjust to the devalued currency. We are in effect left after taxes with far less real purchasing power than we had enjoyed with a lower income. What effect the condensed tax rates of the 1986 tax reform measure will bring remains to be seen. One thing is certain—if you have large amounts of capital or income, this bill is a godsend. It has not been too many years since the high end of the income tax rate scale stood at 90% of the last dollar earned. This, in turn, fell to 50%, and will as a result of the aforementioned bill fall to 28% as a high for everyone.

During periods of runaway inflation, people tend to hoard large amounts of items purchased at today's prices for use tomorrow, to avoid buying at higher prices. Hoarding causes shortages that drive prices above the levels set by the inflation.

Coping with Depression

Why doesn't the government return to a money system limited by the amount of gold, silver, or salt available? Unfortunately this simple solution of a return to precious metals will not work. People owning gold or silver mines would find themselves in a strong situation, but the rest of the economy would be in trouble. Nature cannot supply enough silver to meet the demands of modern economy. Our government must maintain in circulation enough currency to match the economy's level of production. If too little money is available for the society's economic needs, a situation similar to what we experienced during the Great Depression of the 1930s arises.

A depression is the opposite of an inflationary period. The scarcity of money raises its value. For example, interest rates for money borrowed would rise when the supply was insufficient to meet the demands of the economy. It is also possible to have rising interest rates during a period of inflation. This would occur when lenders feel that the continuing devaluation of the currency involved would eat up their money. The lenders then charge higher rates to protect their money. To understand this, imagine that the inflationary rate is 5 percent and the interest rate charged is only 4 percent. Lenders suffer a real 1 percent per year loss on their money.

While the theory behind many economic concepts and trends is often far too complex for the average student, the impact of inflation or depression is real and immediate to all involved. The effects of the Great Depression of the 1930s left social and psychological scars on the people who lived through the period. Besides the way it touched people directly, the collapse of our major institutions radically changed the social structure of the entire country.

Many of the differences that crop up between father and son or mother and daughter today have their roots in the period of economic insecurity known as the Depression. Having grown up in boom times, people born after World War II will be less than understanding when considering their parents' desires for economic security. Parents, having lived through a period of widespread unemployment and in many cases actual hunger, find it difficult to comprehend their children's wish to take off a year from college to wander around the countryside. Children often find their parents too concerned with making a dollar and having material possessions. They tend to ignore the fact that in recent years few people have had to do without or plan far ahead to purchase even the most trivial of luxury items. Today many people do not worry about getting a job; they worry about getting the right job. There is much difference in the point of view held by people in each of these positions. People may tell themselves that they have had trouble getting a job, but have they really had any difficulty finding work?

Younger Americans have several factors complicating their lives at this time. First, as we have mentioned, our economy is under intense pressure from imports. Second, a combination of tax cuts and budget expansion has resulted in a record deficit. This will inflate our currency as it devalues abroad and as the government borrows to meet its obligations. Third, the entry of 50 percent of the population into the job market has caused a dislocation of jobs. The number of women entering the labor pool grows each year, increasing competition for work. Fortunately, this rise in females in the labor pool has been coupled with a fall-off in births, starting in 1964, and ending with a rise in the birth curve in 1980.

Still, attitudes toward jobs are not what they were in the past. Many menial or undesirable jobs available neither carry much chance of future advancement nor pay what are considered living wages. Many Americans have arrived at the point where jobs on this level no longer appeal to them. The relative affluence of most of our society makes people feel that they cannot even consider such work. During the Depression, many Americans were satisfied to find any work, regardless of its type or pay. To understand the attitude of people during this period, we will try to reconstruct conditions as they occurred.

To set this scene, we must first think about the close relationship of money and credit. The nature of credit (or debt money) emerges when the creditor surrenders value (or lends) in return for the debtor's promise of future payment. To go further, if money and credit are related, so are money, credit, and debt. Without enough money, credit, and debt, which equal modern money in circulation, the economy will not produce at its fullest. Turning off an economy's money supply is like turning off a fire's air supply. First the fire dims, then it goes out.

Now let us return to the Great Depression and compare turning off a money supply to smothering a fire. At the time, people wanted to and could work, but there was no work. There were many factories, businesses, or services that should have had employees, but they were closed or dying for lack of customers and money. One basic reason, though by no means the only reason for the Depression, was panic born of lack of trust in currency, banks, and the monetary system itself.[8]

Most people experience panic in one form or another during their lives. When panic occurs in an economic system, that system may fall like a house of cards. As panic begins to spread, credit dries up. Suppliers will no longer extend manufacturers credit for basic materials used in their factories. Wholesale warehouses begin to demand cash on delivery for items sold to stores. Consumer credit is curtailed, and the flow of business slows. Lack of air, which in this case is credit, is smothering the fire of the economy. Businesses that are slowing down begin to lay off employees.

The stock market, which is an emotional creation at best, begins to slide. The business slowdown is reflected in the dropping value of stocks in the market. To keep losses at a minimum, stock market investors begin to sell. More investors sell and few buy the stock put up for sale. Stock market prices sag and begin to fail more rapidly. Many investors have purchased stock on what are called marginal accounts. This is a form of credit. As long as the value of the stock remains higher than the amount borrowed, the investor has no trouble. If the price of stocks falls and the value computed is less than the amount borrowed, the investor must pay the difference in cash.

Banks begin to feel pressure from many different directions. Workers need money because they have been laid off. Business owners need it because their credit has been cut. Investors need it because they had to pay off their loans on marginal accounts. People begin to withdraw savings from their banks. Banks keep little in the way of liquid assets in the form of cash sitting in their vaults. A bank's business is borrowing money from depositors and lending the same money at a higher rate of interest. The bank lends the money of its depositors to mortgage homes, to build factories, and to buy cars, swimming pools, and anything else people feel they need. When depositors who need cash begin rushing to the banks for the savings, banks are forced to call upon their debtors to repay borrowed money. Needless to say, most debtors would not have borrowed from the banks if they had had cash on hand. Very soon the money supply runs out. The values of properties and businesses are only as high as the demand for them, which depends on the availability of money and credit. As the pressure mounts from depositors seeking savings, some banks unable to meet the growing demand for cash close their doors.

As the first banks close, panic spreads. Many people try to withdraw savings from other banks, either for safety or merely to see if they can still get their money. The gold and currencies available during the Depression were not enough to cover monetary needs. Money ceased to circulate. If prices were dropping, why not wait until tomorrow to buy and find prices still lower? People hoarded whatever money they salvaged and did not spend it until the bottom had been reached.

Imagine yourself as a young person living during the Depression. You might find yourself unemployed, or perhaps your income was suddenly cut drastically. If you were a salesperson, you could sell very little because your customers suffered a shortage of money and credit. Your inventory of items for sale dropped because manufacturers could no longer get enough credit to produce. Your food supply dwindled because farmers could not borrow the money needed to plant their fields. Many of the farm products harvested rotted because consumers could not pay for them.

Your mortgage payment, due each month, now represented a value much higher than either your house or your salary. When you built your house a year ago, it was worth $10,000. If it had been possible to sell it at the height of the depression, it might have brought $2,000. While the actual value of the house had decreased, you still owed the bank $9,000 on your original purchase. Your monthly mortgage payment now exceeded your monthly salary. In a short time the bank would be forced to foreclose, and you would lose all the money invested in the house.

You had $2,500 on deposit at a building and loan association for emergencies. The emergency arrived. But a massive defaulting on mortgages had bankrupted your building and loan association, and your $2,500 disappeared with the falling value of real estate.

While driving home from work, you missed a red light and crashed into another car. Although you had paid your automobile insurance premium, when you called your agent, you found that the insurance company had gone into bankruptcy. As a result, you were personally liable for the damage and injury the accident caused. Your personal economic system had begun to crumble along with the nation's economy. Taxes collected by cities and states were no longer enough to meet their payrolls. Churches, hospitals, and charitable institutions disappeared into the murk of a stagnant economy.

Suddenly you were out of work and left without a home, car, savings, or investments. Each day you looked for any kind of work. You washed cars, mowed lawns, and dug ditches if you could get the work. In time, you found the soles of your shoes had holes, and you could not afford a new pair. On occasion, your children went to bed hungry. For the most part, you ate simple food with little variety. Depending on where you lived, you may have had beans, potatoes, or rice as a staple. Large numbers of people became almost permanent residents in the city parks. Shanty-towns were springing up in some of the cities' outer zones, and hobo camps abounded. You began to see how the economic collapse could displace people.

WORKS PROJECTS ADMINIS-TRATION: Various of the federally initiated projects funded in response to the Great Depression of the 1930s.

CIVILIAN CONSERVATION CORPS: From 1933 to 1942, a national agency to provide work for youths ages 17 to 25 in restoring and conserving the nation's natural resources.

TENNESSEE VALLEY AUTHORI-TY: Chartered by the government in 1933 to build dams along the Tennessee River, to produce cheap electrical power, and generally to revitalize the region.

FEDERAL DEPOSIT INSURANCE CORPORATION: A method by which savings accounts are insured by the government against bank failure.

Eventually the government attempted to revitalize the economy by pouring money into vast projects. The Works Projects Administration (WPA), the Civilian Conservation Corps (CCC), the Tennessee Valley Authority (TVA)—all began as attempts to combat the Depression. Although salaries in such programs were low, money once more began to flow. The government established welfare programs and stricter rules for the operation of the stock market and banks. The Federal Deposit Insurance Corporation (FDIC) was created. All individual deposits in banks covered by FDIC were government insured to specific limits. By insuring deposits, the government restored the people's trust in the banking system and the currency. You could make a deposit in a bank and feel assured that, despite bank robbery, embezzlement, and depression, your money was safe. As a result of this government-backed confidence, runs on banks ceased; depositors no longer withdrew their money to test the bank or to protect their savings. The banks also restored confidence because depositors knew that panic withdrawals would not wipe out their cash on hand and force them to call in loans made to responsible borrowers. When confidence was established, the economy could function at its fullest potential because money, credit, and debt circulation were sufficient to serve the needs of the economy.

On a personal level, lack of investment credit may well have limited your future earnings. You might never have reached your full potential, because you could not get credit to finance the training you needed for higher earnings in the future. In a real sense, you might have been deprived of the opportunity to invest future earnings in a manner that would increase them.

The following are examples of the manner in which our credit rating and, as a result, our present and future income depend on the economic policies and programs of the government. The funds available for potential college students depend upon governmental programs. Funds for faculty jobs, public colleges, and various research-based university positions are all largely secured from the federal government. The availability of funds secured from the government for student loans and college support is in danger. The government helped establish and support the land-grant colleges early in our national history. These colleges made it possible for middle- and lower-class people to receive higher education at public expense. In the past years, the impetus of the G.I. bill and the large numbers of veterans seeking college training has strengthened this trend. As the demand for higher education has grown, it has often met increased credit guaranteed by the government in the form of student loans. Several universities have allowed students to borrow their tuition at a rate based on a percentage of their future earnings. In other words, a student's rate of repayment is based solely on the amount of money that he or she can be expected to earn after graduation.

In the area of small business, federal and state-backed business loans have been made available to people who otherwise would never have received them. The government changed its policy from its early position of isolation from matters of personal credit to one of guaranteeing credit lines to individuals. These programs affect the individual and the economy in general by allowing an increase in potential earning capacity, thus keeping a substantial amount of money in circulation. The increased supply of money within the economy stimulates enough credit-debt to meet the needs of the economy and to allow the development of the economy's potential.

CREDIT LINE: Upper limit set on a firm's borrowing.

During the eighties we have seen curtailment of guaranteed student loans, restriction of grants, reduction of aid to colleges, a change in the deduction rules for gifts, and a host of other rule changes acting to tighten money in the college area.

CATALOG OF ITEMS OF VALUE

As the chapter preview showed, economists consider many items as money. Plastic cards, as well as gold coins, may be used as items of value in making purchases. Here we will study the range of items of value, in order to explore more fully the subject of money, credit, and debt.

We can create a rule-of-thumb listing of types of money everyone possesses in terms of their availability for use. The most usable money is the money in our pocket. It exists in a liquid form ready for immediate use on any occasion. Money kept in a checking or a credit card account can be spent less easily because of the need to allow for check-cashing. The use of automated tellers has allowed easier access to checking accounts. Various forms of savings accounts act to limit access to money. The hours of bank business limit access to our own money. We cannot withdraw money on weekends or holidays, which add up to more than 115 days of

The automatic teller provides 24-hour, seven days per week access to your money. You may use credit cards or bank cards and use the machines of other banks from coast to coast to get your money or borrow their money.

BOND: A written promise to pay a certain sum of money by a specified date; issued by corporations, states, localities, and governments.

COMMON STOCK: A shareholder's portion of ownership in a corporation.

the year. In all, exclusive of holidays, most banks keep us away from our money in specific categories of deposit, 128 hours of each 168–hour week. This may mean that money in savings accounts is not very liquid. Many savings accounts are in the form of term notes; we may withdraw money only after a period of six months, a year, or more. Admittedly, we do receive a higher rate of interest on the money, but access is limited further. Many banks require a waiting period of thirty days or more for the withdrawal of money in any substantial amount. This rule is rarely enforced, but it exists in many areas and does limit our access to our money. Money Market Funds have acted to draw the saving public out of the banks. High interest rates and ease of withdrawal, usually by check with no interest penalty, have made such funds a new factor in this area.

The difference between hard cash in pocket, checks, and money in a savings account is easy to see. Cash in hand can be spent at once. As we work down the list, more and more qualifications and restrictions are placed between us and our money.[9] Money can be defined as any instrument that can meet any obligation in "general." If this refers to a state of 100 percent readiness for immediate use, in some respects, then, a hundred dollar bill does not meet this standard when it cannot be spent.

Many people convert cash into stocks and bonds. In buying these items, we allow money to work while we are holding it. Bonds pay interest at a preset rate. They may appreciate in value to a degree dependent on the prevailing interest rate available. In other words, the bond has a bottom limit to its value in that we may always cash it in for a set price. The bond pays a preset interest at regular intervals that do not depend on the condition of business in general or on the income of the company which issued it. If the interest rate offered for money at large falls below the rate paid by a bond, the value of the bond will increase. This is because the bond guarantees an interest rate higher than that currently available. If the current rate of interest rises above the level the bond pays, the market value of the bond decreases to about the limit guaranteed by the company that issued it. A bond is a safe investment in that its face value is guaranteed and interest is always forthcoming. (Bonds are a safer hedge against depression, but will not keep pace with runaway inflation.)

The common-stock field is a little more complex. The value of the typical share of common stock will fluctuate broadly. Often this change up or down in price has little bearing on the economic situation in general or on the profits of the particular company. The daily stock market analysis on the evening newscast shows how a presidential heart attack can depress the market and cause more in the way of dollar loss on individual shares than a poor earnings report. We hear phrases like "the glamor issues rose or fell." This refers to a group of companies which for some reason has caught the eye and enthusiasm of people buying stock. Perhaps there is a general feeling that companies involved in innovations will reap large profits in years to come. Perhaps a group of companies has given the market the impression of great future growth in its areas. Under such circumstances, large-scale public buying of that issue for future gain may increase the value of the stock. As people buy the stock, its offered price increases, and the price gain has nothing to do with the company's actual earnings. The buyers feel that the company will do well in the future. Someone buying such a share for $25 and finding that the price rose to $50 would have the option of holding the stock against possible future gain or selling it and realizing a capital gain of $25.

There are, then, two ways to make or lose money in the stock market.[10] The market price of stock can rise or fall. People do not actually make or lose money until they sell the issue. On the other hand, an investor can make money from the interest or dividends paid by the company that issued the stock if the rate if payment is adequate. It has to represent a rate as high or higher, on the basis of the investment, as one receives from a guaranteed source such as a savings account. The use of programmed buy and sell actions have further complicated market analysis. On the basis of computer analysis, groups of market traders will buy or sell large blocks of shares in the final minutes of a trading day. The activity will cause large fluctuations in stock values in a very short time. This is much like betting on a horse, but with features of bribing a jockey or two. People in the market for the long term should pay little attention to these daily swings. The 1986 Tax Reform Bill may act to dampen activity of this nature with the exclusion of capital gains as a separate category of income.

A marked difference exists between the accessibility of money held in the market and that held in cash or savings accounts. People may not wish to sell a stock at a lower price than they consider realistic. A pattern of buying and selling in the market reflects large numbers of people taking short-term profits at the end of a small market rise. This selling can depress the value of stock for a few days and oblige the owner to wait until the stock's price recovers enough to bring an adequate payment. The stock might, however, fool the stockholders and continue down, leaving them in more of a financial bind than they had anticipated. There has been a trend toward twenty-four-hour-a-day market trading that will allow the investor faster access to his or her investment. After having completed a sales order, several days will elapse before the payment will be funneled from the buyer to broker to owner. Actual access to money is considerably more limited than if the owner had maintained the investment in cash in a mattress or in the bank.

Money can also be invested in the form of real estate, jewelry, and art objects, to give a partial list. All these items have value in themselves which may fluctuate, and the owner may find their quick conversion to hard cash difficult. The fluctuating values of these items can be disturbing. Objects do not always appreciate, and frequently they depreciate. Painting in vogue or accepted as great art by one generation rapidly loses value as tastes change. Besides the changes of taste, many forgeries of valued works of art appear and are palmed off as the genuine article. As a result, investments of millions of dollars have been lost.

Some form of art has been a satisfactory investment for many people because of the dual role it plays in our complex tax situation. A person having money of a questionable nature may do well to hide it in paintings or sculpture. Many people earn sizable sums that they do not declare, to avoid paying income tax. Others in the position of having a large tax bill search for legal deductions. Works of art, because of the rapidly changing value, become a handy deductible item.

People who have engaged in a pattern of investment in recent years have gone either to Europe or to local art centers and purchased paintings of questionable reputation for relatively low prices. After holding the painting for a time, the purchaser will try to get, and usually receives, a high estimate of its value from an appraiser. Since many appraisers work on a percentage of the value of the object appraised, it is not too difficult to get a high appraisal. The purchaser may have to try several appraisers before getting stated value desired, but once that occurs, he or she can donate the paintings to a museum. Since all museums will not accept just any painting, the owner of a painting may have to prime the pump with an excellent work with foolproof credentials in order to have several doubtful works accepted. The doubtful works, with their high assessments, are deducted at the high rate from income tax paid the government. While this does take place and is difficult to trace, the majority of art gifts to museums and universities are probably originals of great value. In many cases, the value of the work has undoubtedly reached a point where it is cheaper to give it away than to sell it and pay the tax on the profit.

Perhaps an illustration of a perfectly legal but ethically questionable method of obtaining deductions can lead us to understand why the rules for deducting donations of art works was singled out in the 1986 tax bill. An individual or group would contract with a well-known and respected artist for the creation of a print or series of prints. Perhaps the contract price was $10,000 for the lot of 100. After delivery, two of the prints are put up for public sale at $5,000 each, thus setting the commercial price of the work. The remaining 98 are given to as many museums as are naturally eager to gain a free gift of a work by a noted artist. The real value of the gifts are 98 x $5,000 or $490,000. At the pre–1986 tax rate high of 50%, this is an after-deduction tax advantage of $240,000. (Remember that the sale of the initial two prints paid for the investment.)

Real estate may well appreciate in value, and holding it has additional tax advantages if it is income-producing property. Rental property can gain a far higher rate of depreciation than the actual value the property represents. As with paintings and other works of art, the market for real estate changes, and it is difficult to get rid of property quickly. The problems of title search, mortgage money, lawyers, and finding a buyer willing to meet the asking price all complicate the conversion to cash. A real-estate sale commonly takes many months to complete, even after both parties agree on price and stipulations. Consequently, holdings in real estate and expensive works of art are difficult to convert quickly into cash.

Jewelry is another form of investment made in lieu of maintaining hard cash. The old saying "Diamonds are a girl's best friend" has a basis in fact. Some forms of jewelry have been good investments, appreciating over the years. Diamonds are especially good stones to own in an inflationary period. There is considerable argument over what type cut a stone should be given for the best investment or return or, for that matter, whether the stones should even be cut. Some cuts are dated and tend to reduce the lasting value of the stone. Jewels are probably easier to convert than real estate or most paintings and sculptures, yet they are not as safe to keep. Works of art are frequently registered and normally known by the people in the field. Real estate is registered, and a title is provided, but individual stones, although they may be insured, are not normally registered. The work of art and real estate cannot be altered and resold; a precious stone may be stolen, recut, and peddled without being recognized.

One must take these major considerations into account when dealing with noncurrency forms of money or value:

1. What is the risk of loss involved in the ownership of the particular investment considered?
2. What are the advantages of ownership?
3. How quickly can the particular form considered be converted into ready cash?
4. Is there a reasonable chance for actual financial gain in the investment?
5. Is the chance of gain sufficient to make the risk involved worthwhile?
6. Can you afford to take any chance with your investment?

COLLATERAL: Property or evidence thereof deposited with a creditor to guarantee payment of a loan.

There is an old saying "If you cannot afford to lose, you cannot afford to win or even to play." In determining a person's credit rating, all the forms of money listed are taken into account. The amount of collateral or objects of value people possess set the limits for the types of loans they may receive.

SUMMARY

Money as an abstract representation of labor and the products of labor has enabled modern society to attain its present economic and social complexity. To operate, modern business demands a proper amount of money in all its forms. As our economy and population outgrew the finite limits of precious metals, the truly abstract nature of modern money expressed in goods and services became vitally apparent. Without this tool of economics, the possibility of complex technological, social, and economic development would have been sorely limited. The evolution of monetary forms and institutions from the levels of salt, precious metals, and other hard representatives of value, to paper money, credit cards, and international money has reflected the growth of human culture itself.

Banks function in a number of ways to act as safe repositories for money and to allow money not needed for immediate use to earn interest for the holder and to serve as capital for other ventures.

The value of today's base metal coinage and currency, which lacks precious metal backing, is based on trust. Without trust and faith in this abstract representation of goods and services, there is no value.

The U.S. dollar, once tied to the gold standard, has lost the trust it once enjoyed as the international currency. The international valuing of money can directly affect our standard of living. As governments set the rates of their currencies, rather than letting the open market set the rates, the value of our dollar is affected.

Inflation makes our dollar worth less. For those who have no means of adjusting their income, inflation can cause a severe drop in their standard of living.

In periods of depression, money is worth more, but it is scarce. Jobs and credit are also in short supply in such a situation. Those who lived through the Great Depression of the 1930s may well have a very different attitude toward money and security than do their children.

Items of value can be listed in order of how readily usable they are. Cash is the easiest to convert to goods and services. Other forms less easily converted may reap higher investment return for the owner, but they may also have a higher risk factor.

SPECIAL TOPIC

The Lost Nest Egg

Where has our nest egg gone?

In the past, people saved for their retirement. This was their nest egg, savings they would use to live out their retirement years. Money and other items of value continued more or less with the same value with perhaps a little appreciation. Today, however, there are ups and downs in the world of value. As we face decades of inflation, we become convinced of the need to invest in stocks and collectable precious metals, among other items of real value, in order to keep up with inflation. Examples of the inflationary effect were seen in the area of housing. We saw our parents buy homes for $8,000 to $12,000 in the

1940s and 1950s. Interest rates were 3 to 5 percent, and money was easy to borrow. In time we announced with pride that our house was worth $40,000 or $50,000. As years passed, the same house suddenly sold at over $100,000.

In the 1950s, yearly raises were measured in terms of several hundreds of dollars. By the mid–1960s, raises of 10 percent and more were common. This shows inflation, and as long as interest rates were low and the rate of inflation was moderate, most people saw it as advantageous. It was pleasant to borrow large sums of expensive money and pay it back with cheap dollars. Because the amount of money involved in the loan was fixed, and the dollars became worth less, it was less painful to repay. The dollar value of the house increased as dollars came to be worth less. This pattern of investing had affected almost all levels of American society.

As our population increased, many things that once were of little value became more expensive. The number of items created in 1910 for a population of 100 million could not possibly be enough for a population of 225 million people. The natural attrition of items makes them less numerous as the years pass. An example would be Tiffany glass. Only so much was made for the market of its day. Over the years, when it had less value, much of it was broken or discarded. The demand generated by a population of 225 million will put pressure on the market. The value of such glass would rise, and as it rose competition for such pieces pushed the prices higher.

A similar situation occurred many years ago in Holland. People started collecting tulip bulbs, and as they bid against one another for rare bulbs the prices reached astronomical heights. One day the bottom fell out of the bulb market and all the invested money was lost.

In addition to works of art, houses, guns, toy soldiers, antiques, and other items collected by people as a hedge against inflation, we have the precious metals. Gold and silver are the most common metals for investment. For many years the United States guaranteed the price of gold at about $35 per troy ounce. When we allowed the dollar to float, gold became a marketable commodity. Silver was the base of our coinage until 1964, when its value as a metal was higher than the value of the dollar it represented. The coins disappeared from the marketplace as if by magic, proving the old saying "Bad money drives out good."

Ordinary citizens have placed their faith in many items of value, including diamonds. We have grown up convinced that "diamonds are a girl's best friend" and that "diamonds are forever." When we become engaged or get married, we give diamonds, believing that we are giving an item of value for future use in an emergency. In early 1982, it suddenly became apparent that while diamonds were easy to buy, they were difficult to sell.

DeBeers Consolidated Mines of South Africa markets approximately 85 percent of the world's diamonds. Over the years, skillful ad-

vertising convinced the public that the law of supply and demand did not apply to diamonds. The public was so convinced of this that diamonds began to be treated as a commodity. All went well until interest rates rose to a point exceeding the rate of inflation. Diamonds, gold, silver, and so on, maintain value in the face of inflation, but they do not pay interest. Investers who had been buying diamonds began to sell. They invested in money market funds and high-interest paper. Some rates approached 20 percent, which allowed a safe principal and a profit.[11]

Buying precious metals, diamonds, and other collectables was an effort to maintain the value of one's savings. In addition, there would be some growth in the capital investment. In other words, if you invested $10,000, you could expect the value of your investment to rise with inflation and to exceed the rate of inflation, if you were lucky. With high interest rates, the element of luck was removed and your investments remained liquid.

The word "liquid" is very important. Diamonds are not liquid. With vast amounts of investor money piling into government bonds and notes, together with the various money market funds, the base of the diamond's value disappeared. If there are many people wishing to sell, and few people wishing to buy diamonds, the prices offered will be lower.

We can follow the rise and fall of diamond value. From 1975 to 1980, the value of what are called investment-grade diamonds doubled in value. From 1980 to 1982, the value of such an investment fell from about 40 percent to 60 percent. This is actually worse than it sounds, because buyers usually paid 25 percent above market value when they purchased stones. The New York Times (February 14, 1982) gave this example: A $15,000 stone would cost an investor $18,750. If the market value fell 50 percent, the stone would bring ± $7500. This is a financial disaster.

When many investors purchased diamonds, their brokers offered a guaranteed buy-back plan. The usual plan called for repurchase guarantee of 10 percent less than market value. While an item may have a recognized market value, it may well have no ready and apparent buyer. An example of this would be with housing. You have a house with a value set at $100,000. This value may be set by a realtor or taxing agency. Perhaps houses similar to yours in your neighborhood have recently sold for that amount. You place your house on the market and ask $100,000. The house is worth $100,000 only if you can sell it for that price. The problem with most nonliquid investments is that, while they have value, you cannot be sure of recovering that value when you need it. In the depressed real estate market of the early 1980s, homes would sit on the market for years. If you needed the value in cash, you would probably have to reduce your price. That means that you have had to reduce value in order to achieve liquidity.

Gold and silver have been exposed to wide fluctuations of value. As we have noted, gold had a value guaranteed by the United States government of $35 per troy ounce. When gold was allowed to float with the market, it rose to ± $1,000 per troy ounce. Silver rose to almost $50, and the value of silver coins rose from a par value of $1 to $1 to plus or minus $30 for $1 in silver. During the period of rising prices, investors were convinced that the prices would never fall. Small investors flocked into the precious metal market thinking to protect their nest eggs against the deflating dollar. In 1986, gold flirted with $450 and silver with $5.

Nest eggs that had come out of the stock market and gone into precious metals took a major beating before their owners could get them into high-interest commercial paper. These people would, of course, miss the stock market skyrocket that would come out of the recession of the early 1980s, and hover around 1900 in 1986.

The care and feeding of nest eggs and savings in general requires foresight, nerves of iron, and luck. Investment would be easier if inflation, depression, or changing interest rates were not factors to be considered.

SELF-TEST QUESTIONS

1. Our modern society, with its specialized production, is made possible by:
   a. items of value
   b. barter
   c. money
   d. inflation

2. True or false: The first bankers were simply trusted individuals who guaranteed the safety of valuables on deposit.

3. True or false: Our coins are made mostly of precious metal.

4. The value of a nation's currency is usually set by _____.

5. When the dollar is devalued, the price of imported goods for Americans:
   a. falls
   b. rises
   c. is not affected

6. Inflation:
   a. involves a raised value of money
   b. sometimes leads to a barter system
   c. hits hardest those people whose income is not fixed

7. In a depression there is (are):
   a. too much money in circulation
   b. too many jobs available
   c. too little money in circulation
   d. too much credit available

8. True or false: Banks closed in the Great Depression because too many people tried to withdraw their money at the same time.

9. Of the following, which is the most readily used item of value?
   a. stocks
   b. real estate
   c. savings account funds
   d. art objects

ANSWERS TO
SELF-TEST
QUESTIONS

1. c
2. true
3. false
4. the open or free market
5. b

6. b
7. c
8. true
9. c

ANSWER TO SKILL
REINFORCER

19–1. An invalid syllogism from that premise might be:
1. If there is a shortage of an item, its price will be high.
2. The price of corn is high.
3. Therefore there must be a shortage of corn.
This logic is invalid, so the conclusion may be false even if the premises are accurate. The problem with the reasoning here is that there may be other causes for the high price of corn.

NOTES

1. Harold Barger, *Money, Banking, and Public Policy* (Chicago: Rand McNally, 1962).
2. Thomas H. Goddard, *General History of Banking Institutions in the United States and Europe* (New York: H.C. Sleight, 1931).
3. David P. Calleo and Benjamin M. Rowland, *America and the World Political Economy* (Bloomington: Indiana University Press, 1973).
4. Milton Friedman, "The Case for Freely Fluctuating Exchange Rates," in *Essays in Positive Economics* (Chicago: University of Chicago Press, 1953).
5. Brian Tew, "The International Monetary Fund: Its Present Role and Future Prospects," *Essays on International Finance*, no. 36 (Princeton: Princeton University, International Finance Section, 1961).
6. H.J. Witteveen, "Inflation and the International Monetary Situation," *The American Economic Review, Papers and Proceedings*, May 1975.
7. UPI, Feb. 18, 1982, "Mexican Government No Longer Supports Peso."
8. Robert Sobel, *Panic on Wall Street: A History of America's Financial Disasters* (New York: Macmillan Co., 1972).
9. Dennis H. Robertson, *Money* (Chicago: University of Chicago Press, 1959).
10. Claude N. Rosenberg, Jr., *Stock Market Primer*, rev. ed. (New York: Paperback Library, 1970).
11. *The New York Times*, March 10, 1982.

SUGGESTED
READINGS

Friedman, Milton. *An Economist's Protest.* Glen Ridge, N.J.: Thomas Horton and Daughters, 1975.

Sampson, Anthony. *The Money Lenders, Bankers, and a World in Turmoil.* New York: Viking, 1982.

Smith, Adam. *The Wealth of Nations.* New York: E.P. Dutton, 1910.

Smith, Jerome F. *The Coming Currency Collapse and What to Do About It.* New Books in Focus, 1981.

20 GOVERNMENT AND POLITICS

A Quickie of a Bill

In the late fall of 1981, a bill was passed quickly by both Houses of Congress and signed just as quickly by President Ronald Reagan. This was not unusual, except that there were a few loud cries of "Foul!" from both Democrats and Republicans of both Houses. However, the bill was passed quickly with the support of Senators and Representatives who barely spoke to one another under normal circumstances.

What force pulled all these factions together? What interest could be common for people with views so far apart?

The issue was the financing of the natural gas pipeline from the Alaskan fields to the rest of the United States. Several years earlier, when the pipeline was proposed, the rules of operation and participation were agreed upon. The privilege of building the pipeline was exchanged for various requirements of responsibility and financing. Now, after everything was settled, the prime mover in the pipeline operation wanted government funding for the project, up front. In other words, the builder wanted the citizens of the United States to pay for the construction of a pipeline. The builder and operators would then use this publicly financed project for personal profit.

Several questions come to mind. First, Why were the conditions of the agreement changed so quickly? Second, Why should a pipeline built with public funds provide private profit at the expense of the taxpayer? Third, Why would our elected representatives vote so quickly to change an agreement that had taken so long to work out? The answers to most of these questions, and specifically the third question, lie in the name of the game—*politics*.

The oil and gas industries have contributed to the election funds of a great many politicians. Over the years, many of these same politicians have received large sums of money in the form of honorariums and expenses from this industry. This was one of the times that debts were called in.

As we saw in Chapter 1, political science is the study of government and politics. Each of us comes into daily contact with elements of both these activities. Still, many average citizens are unfamiliar with the workings of our government and its political processes. In spite of this, however, they are aware that all nations have governments and that all nations experience some measure of political activity. This chapter can deepen awareness and increase understanding of these matters, so that we can become more than just average citizens.

We need look only to the word's nations for examples of government and politics. Even the simplest societies deal in the symbols of these forms. The basis of both government and politics lies in the retention and use of power, authority, and influence. The government of any group of people consists of interwoven organizations and institutions that regulate and control the actions of members of that society.

POLITICS: That part of political science dealing with policy-making. It concerns itself with the agencies and instrumentalities that establish policy, including the legislature and all but the purely administrative functions of the executive, with the electorate, political parties, and so on. It is also concerned with the results that flow from this stage of government activity.

We come into contact with these organizations and institutions in our everyday lives. As we listen to the radio or watch television, government agencies regulate the licensing of the broadcasting stations. The laws of our government dealing with libel, advertising volume, dress codes, and other restrictions affect the material that is broadcast. If we want to drive a car, we face a series of laws administered by the Department of Transportation. Before driving, we must meet tests of age and health. Then we are subjected to regulations concerning liability and other insurance coverage. We are tested on our ability to operate a car, motorcycle, or truck under differing road conditions. If we pass all tests, we must comply with the law of the land regarding regulations of speed, parking, and driving patterns.

Now we turn to the study of this government and politics which surround us. First, some terms must be defined. Government consists of all organizations and institutions of any group of people who regulate and control the actions of society. What then is meant by politics? When we speak of politics, we refer to the specific process of wielding the forces of power and authority. Politicians use the political system to create public policy by influencing the sources of power and authority.

THE DEVELOPMENT OF GOVERNMENT

GOVERNMENT: The body of people, and the institutions they form, which regulates and controls the society.

Where did all this begin—at what point did a strong father, grandfather, or uncle give way to an elected, inherited, appointed, or anointed arbiter and ruler? No accurate answer or point in time can be noted and remembered. We cannot single out a particular instance that marked the beginning of formal government. Certain fragments of history or data recovered by archaeologists indicate the existence of forms of government at various times and places, but these are mere bits of the very long history of human beings. We can only view the possibilities and hope that an educated guess may change them into probabilities.

Why Do We Need Government?

First, we might ask why a government is needed at all. The answers to this question are many and diverse. On one hand, Thomas Hobbes (1588–1679) felt that without a form of government, people would be constantly in conflict.[1] Hobbes viewed humans as basically selfish. In this view, humans cannot see beyond "looking out for number one." On the other hand, John Locke (1632–1704) held a higher view of human nature. Locke believed that, with government, people could live in some degree of harmony.[2] Even so, occasional conflict would still arise among humans even in Locke's natural world. These conflicts could arise out of biased perception of issues and rights. Unless humans established clear principles, or laws, for settling these disputes, they might well find themselves in trouble. So even in Locke's picture of people in their natural state, government was needed.

Hobbes and Locke did not agree on the basic nature of humans, but both agreed that government was needed to ensure peaceful social life. But any reader of history knows that government does not always ensure peace. In fact, governments themselves have often caused turmoil and strife. While government is necessary, it does not always fulfill its function of ensuring peace.

There was a time, however, when there was no need for formal governmental structure among humans. Hundreds of thousands of years ago, our ancestors walked the earth in family groups. In such groups, a leader was recognized by virtue of age, strength, or kinship. Probably because the inefficient nature of hunting and gathering required traveling in small groups, government was not a problem. No doubt arguments then were settled much as they are today in similar situations. In such circumstances, little benefit would result from controlling or ruling large numbers of people. Such groups would be little more than additional mouths to feed. It is true that basic rules of behavior existed even then to regulate the relationships of members of the group. The rules were informal, and the sanctions also informal. Informal, in this sense, refers to the unwritten, uncodified nature of the rules of life. The group might know the rules, but the penalties for breaking them are neither mandatory nor clearly defined.

The need for formal rules and their enforcement comes after the production of a surplus. Only when a surplus is produced to support the specialists of a society does the need arise for a formal governing body. Of course, the surplus is only the beginning. With a surplus, we can earn a profit by working at jobs other than food gathering and production. When a portion of society is free to engage in the production of materials other than food, we suddenly see the possibility of acquiring something that others may lack. The process of allocation begins, and with this process we see an immediate difference between those who have more and those who have less. The strong, the bright, or the lucky begin to tell the weak, the dull, or the unlucky how to behave. When this process is formalized and workings are recognized by all members of a

Skill Reinforcer 20-1 *

Create an invalid syllogism from this major premise: If a surplus is produced, a government will be established.

* Answers to the Skill Reinforcers appear at the end of the chapter.

society, that society is on the road to governmental development. As we have said, the first forms of government have been lost in the past. We do not know whether those first formal governments were based on the power of religion or on the power of force. However, some early examples of governmental form will give a view of what occurred in several areas.

Early Forms of Government

In Egypt the monuments of the past show the existence of some form of government. If this statement seems to be unjustified, consider the planning and organization needed to build a large structure. Some person or group of people must decide to build the structure. This action in itself requires a form of centralized power. Next, someone must design the structure. During the design period, other people must supply the designer with materials and support. The allocation of goods and labor from a prime producer to a specialist also requires centralized power. The actual construction of the structure requires that the many laborers have freedom from food production. Any of the large Egyptian pyramids involved thousands of laborers. Residential cities were established near the construction site, raw materials were transported, and tools were made. These activities required not only a large surplus but also a setting of priorities. The person or group making up the ruling body had to agree on the priorities. They included assigning people to certain tasks. Should we build a burial vault, grain storage bin, or declare war? All these examples should provide a base for the assumption that a governmental form existed among cultures that we know only by ruins in the dust.

Two thousand years before Christ, a major event occurred in the formation of government. At that time, the Babylonian king Hammurabi caused a written set of laws to be adopted. This was a major event, for written rules with stated punishments were for the first time organized into a working code. This code could then be applied, instead of depending upon the chance feelings of a ruler.

Skill Reinforcer 20-2
Create an invalid syllogism from this major premise: If a country builds pyramids, there exists in that country a government.

God and the King.   There is historical evidence that many early forms of government were autocratic. There is little in autocracy that limits the will of the governing body. In the hands of the ruler lies all power, including that of determining life or death. The whim of the ruler is law.

Frequently, an autocracy is reinforced by its close ties with the religion of the people. For example, the pharaohs of Egypt were thought to be gods. Later, although the power of the autocrats may have been limited, still their godhood was proclaimed. The Roman emperors were thought to be divine, as were the Japanese emperors. Later, European kings assumed their rule through divine right. This belief has been so ingrained among many people that some thought the movement of an emperor's arm could cause an earthquake or a storm. Cnut, the Danish king of England, once or-

AUTOCRATIC: Characteristic of a monarch or another person ruling with unlimited authority.

AUTOCRACY: A state in which one person possesses unlimited political power.

Hammurabi, great king of the first Babylonian dynasty, receives the law from Sun God Shamash.

dered the tide to recede, and much to the surprise of many gathered to watch the spectacle, the sea disobeyed.

Citizen Participation. Ancient civilizations produced far more than the absolute power of an autocratic king. Among the ancient gifts that survive is the foundation of our present form of democracy. The Athenian idea is that of direct democracy. While giving the people final authority in matters of government seems fine at first glance, there are inconsistencies. "People" was translated to mean "citizens," thereby excluding more than half the residents of the city who fell into the slave category. Even so, the government itself was probably more democratic than any other known example. Small marginal groups living in isolation settled their own problems and devised what may or may not have been democratic forms, but the Athenian experiment was on a larger scale, that of a city-state. The Athenian model provided a rotating membership of one thousand citizens chosen from the citizenry at large to serve on the Supreme Court. Thus all citizens eventually became members of the lawmaking body. This system, however, can work only if the people participate and if it is small enough to allow all the qualified citizens a voice.

Plato (427?–347 B.C.) opposed the principle of Athenian democracy. He saw all citizens beginning life on an equal plane, allowing the wisest and best qualified to rise to rule as philosopher-kings.[3] We would like to say that the Republic as presented by Plato had solved the problems of finding the best-qualified people for government, but unfortunately, several thousand years later, the problem remains in our own society. Plato recognized the importance of law as a means of maintaining social order and stability.

DIRECT DEMOCRACY: A form of government in which the supreme power is invested in the people and exercised by them directly.

Modern Forms of Government

ABSOLUTE MONARCHY: A government in which a ruler or monarch has unlimited and arbitrary power over people and property.

TOTALITARIAN STATE: A state with a dictatorial or authoritarian form of government to which constitutional law and usage ascribe power without limit over all areas of human organization and activity.

Here we have seen several early governmental forms: the democracy of Athens and the absolute rule of the autocratic king or god-king. The absolute authority of the king continues through our own culture in history with tempering periods of broader representation. The Roman government, during its existence, touched all bases from clans to absolute monarchy, to legislative Republic, and to absolute rule under an emperor.

In more modern times, the concept of the god-king and divine right has eroded, but other forms of equally absolute rule have evolved to replace it. We may substitute the dictator for the king and find little difference in the power assumed. Certainly Joseph Stalin or Adolf Hitler wielded as much personal power as Attila the Hun or Ivan the Terrible.

The totalitarian state, controlled by a single-interest party and excluding all other political parties, resembles older systems comprised of king and nobles. Both forms allow a single, vertical column of power. All people interested in, or allowed participation in, such systems had to rise within that line of authority. The major difference seems to lie in the broader base of participation in

SKILL BOX

Begging the Question—Circular Reasoning

1. If the United States is a democracy, then its people should have ultimate power.
2. The United States is a democracy.
3. Therefore the people in the United States should have ultimate power.

This chain of logic may seem a bit suspicious; it may seem that the argument simply goes in a circle. Indeed, that is just the case.

Begging the question is one of the most common kinds of reasoning errors. It occurs when reasoners use as a premise the very conclusion they intend to reach. It is as though the people went begging in search of support for the conclusion they had already formed concerning the question at hand. Instead of actually begging for support, the people simply assume that what they believe is true, then use this assumption as a basis for an argument to prove what they assume. It is a circular argument, because if we follow it, we end up at the same place we began.

A simple example is: "Most parents don't treat their children with love, so most children grow up feeling unloved." The conclusion is simply a restatement of that belief. We end up where we started.

A more complex example shows how the reasoner accepts or assumes B and uses it as the basis for A, which is then used to support the conclusion, which is simply the assumption, B.

A. "If parents wouldn't spank their children so much, then the children would grow up to be happier adults."
B. "Therefore parents should not spank their children so much."

The argument is based on the belief that parents spank too much. This belief or assumption is also the conclusion. This shows the circular path of begging the question.

Sometimes begging the question is not so obvious. Here is an example of this subtle begging of the question:

1. Atheists have no sense of humor.
2. Jim has no sense of humor.
3. Therefore Jim is an atheist.

In this example, the major premise is probably a question-begging device. While the logic is valid enough in its form, its intention is probably just to support the "conclusion" by accepting a convenient major premise. It is simply a more respectable way of saying, "Jim is an atheist because he has no sense of humor." Of course, it is possible that the speaker ran a survey and discovered that atheists do indeed have no sense of humor. That seems highly unlikely in this situation, and we can fairly enough suspect begging of the question in this argument.

the totalitarian forms. Also, unlike the older systems, totalitarian forms may not be based on inherited position and rigid class systems.

It is possible that some day our own government will become something of a limited dictatorship. This change in our form of government would require only a reduction of the powers of Congress and the Supreme Court with a lengthening of the presidential term. We must grant that many subtle and several blatant changes must also occur prior to our embracing a totalitarian form of government.

We are taught that we live in a democracy, but it is not the democracy of Athens nor the democracy of the New England town meeting, in which forms all citizens may speak and vote on all issues. It is obvious that a nation of over 200 million citizens cannot gather together to vote on every issue. Nevertheless, if we do not live by these forms of democracy, what form of government do we have in America?

In today's world, even the most arbitrary and autocratic regimes refer to themselves as the "People's Democratic Republic of Thus and So." A semantic shift has occurred here, since many governments so described are neither people's democracies nor republics. If their forms were true democracies, all their people would have the right of direct representation, which occurs when all people vote directly for or against various proposals. As population growth expands, however, direct representation becomes impossible. Imagine the appalling spectacle of football stadiums across the nation holding hundreds of thousands of voting citizens screaming to be heard at the same time.

REPRESENTATIVE DEMOCRACY: A government in which there is an independent legislature composed of representatives freely elected by a large body of the people and given legislative and fiscal powers.

Until only recently, it was very difficult to move people or messages within a large and widespread population such as the United States. Before the communications revolution, such a population had to use representative democracy. This form of representation calls for groups of people to elect a specific person to represent their views in a central forum. The town councilperson, the state legislator, the governor, representatives, senators, and the President—all our government officials, in theory, represent the majority views of the voting public.

TODAY'S POLITICAL SYSTEM

From the form of government, we now move to the functioning of government. First, we will look at the workings of politics—the processes by which power and authority are managed. From politics we will then move into the topic of government.

The Mechanics of Politics: America as an Example

Politics makes for fascinating study. It involves humans acting in ways both noble and corrupt. Justice and greed, high ideals and lies—all are the substance of politics. Here we will examine a few of the factors that make politics what it is.

INTEREST GROUPS: People who, whether closely organized or not, have a common interest in molding public opinion or in the passage of certain types of legislation.

Interest Groups.   Besides the stars of politics—the elected politicians—there are many other players in the game. These include the groups of people who have much to say about who will be elected.

A group involved in political action.

Those groups whose power may form the base of political power are called interest groups. They are made up of people who share common needs or desires, and they are created when those people seek special treatment or legislation.

The manner in which these groups seek or attain such treatment creates subgroups: pressure groups and voting blocs. A typical pressure group may be an organization that employs lobbyists, public-relations firms, or other techniques, designed to influence both public opinion and political figures. The pressure group's organization may have relatively few members but may wield more actual influence than the members of voting blocs. Voting blocs can merely threaten to withhold or redirect their votes.

Political history cites many examples of varying voting blocs. The "Solid South" referred to a major group of southern states which, until recently, shared a political allegiance. These states made up a voting bloc that consistently supported any Democratic party candidate on the ballot. The consistency of the Solid South's voting pattern usually made it possible for the Democratic party to settle primary elections on the state level. Thus, the various office seekers in southern states ran only against other Democrats. A Republican candidate did not stand a chance. On the national level, in elections determining the presidency, Democrats depended on the Solid South as a stable base on which to build an election victory. But a price was paid for this voting solidarity. The Solid South demanded legislation favorable to the voting bloc. Only when the party proposed or adapted various bill or platform positions unfavorable to the South did the Solid South shift its support to the Republican party or to a third-party candidate.

PRESSURE GROUP: A group which exerts pressure upon public officials in order to achieve its aims or goals.

VOTING BLOCS: All voters or potential voters constituting a group, usually with some common and identifying characteristics or desires.

LOBBY: The people, collectively, who appear before a legislative body or any of its committees or seek to influence individual members to accomplish the passage or defeat of bills.

PRIMARY ELECTION: A preliminary election for the nomination of candidates for office; primary elections are classified as closed or open, depending on whether tests of party affiliation are required for participation.

Political Trading. In reviewing the political history of the United States, examples of political trading by voting blocs are obvious. In 1876, no presidential candidate had sufficient electoral votes to win. The southern group of Democratic congressmen voted in favor of the Republican candidate. In return for crossing the party lines, the South was to receive: (1) the removal of the last Union occupation troops, (2) a free hand in racial matters, (3) substantial federal funding in such areas as railroad improvement. Such political moves could only strengthen the power base of the politician involved. Obviously, since the southern white voters favored these moves, they would continue to support politicians whose actions satisfied their wishes.

The farm block also maintains strong political pressure through active lobbying. Farm lobbyists apply pressure to various legislators, often contributing to election campaigns. The 1972 election resulted in later disclosures of many illegal contributions from various lobby groups to the presidential campaign fund. The obvious intent of the contributors—the dairy industry, petroleum interests, air transport interests, and others—was to curry legislative favor with the prospective officeholder. As the number of farm voters decreases, we can see less support for their economic position on the part of their political representatives.

Our recent election campaigns had various single-interest groups busily raising funds. The interest groups spent the funds in support of their candidate. In spending their own money, these organizations were able to get around federal election laws dealing with contributions.

The senators and representatives receiving the benefit of such funds often have a great deal of power to control, stimulate, or retard business in the relevant sectors. As a result, we find that money as well as votes can be counted as part of a politician's power base. From their power base, politicians acquire authority over the various institutions of government. From this we can see the effect of political trading, an important tactic in the game of politics.

Political Plums. Let us take a closer look at the things elected officials can use in this political trading. Politicians strengthen their position by wisely giving out jobs, contracts, and services to people, businesses, and communities. Jobs available for political distribution depend upon the level and responsibility of the politician's office. It is understandable that the presidency has access to such "political plums" as federal judgeships, cabinet posts, commission posts, and many assistantships. In addition to the salary involved, we may add the benefits of honor and status, to say nothing of generous expense accounts. By giving out political jobs, successful politicians can secure cadres of people dedicated to keeping them in office.

CADRE: A group of trained personnel capable of assuming control and training others.

The use of political plums is just as important on the state level. As on the national level, the governor has cabinet posts to fill, along with numerous smaller positions ranging from state college president to forest ranger. This widespread practice of political job allocation is referred to as patronage. With regularity, political figures billed as reform candidates are elected on the premise of reducing patronage. Yet after their election, many of these politicians find that they must literally pay off supporters, workers, and other politicians who "gracefully withdrew" from the competition.

PATRONAGE: The practice of elected officials paying off political debts at the public's expense. Examples of the practice are jobs given to the party faithful.

This action usually follows a simple pattern. Two or more members of the same political party will vie for nomination to the same office. In the weeks before the party primary, which serves to select the party's candidate, certain candidates will announce to the public that for one reason or another they have chosen to withdraw their names. Typical excuses are the candidate's health, money problems, his wife's health, or the need to spend more time with children. In reality, the candidates withdrawing have read the handwriting on the wall, that is, they have realized that they cannot win. Even a bitterly contested primary battle may end with the winner and losers embracing and uttering vows of undying friendship and loyalty. The endorsement either of the losers or of those who withdrew from competition may result in their obtaining jobs within the government—if the survivor wins the general election. Each election year the public is treated to the

GENERAL ELECTION: An election held in the state at large.

spectacle of archenemies, each representing opposing views on the public good, changing their tune and endorsing their opponents' views. An even more interesting practice is that of the winning politician providing safe haven for members of an outgoing or losing administration.

What You Give, and What You Get.   As we have just seen, political power is maintained through patronage offered to people who control, or are thought to control, blocs of voters. Another way politicians maintain power is through the income they receive. Enough income is received to finance elections and maintain a style of living believed to be appropriate to the particular office. The acceptance of political contributions usually places the politician in a compromising position. We realize that money is needed to prime the elective pump, and that the salaries of most elective positions do not begin to meet expenses incurred by most officeholders. In the fall of 1986, several million dollars were expended by the two senatorial candidates in California. U.S. ambassadors to major nations are known to receive an expense allowance equal only to the money spent every year for the annual Fourth of July party. The remainder of the entertainment expense is normally out of pocket. This means that an ambassador to a major nation must be both rich and talented. Take, for example, a man who has plenty of money but no evident knowledge or skill. The prospect of becoming an ambassador may be so attractive that the man will contribute heavily to some friendly candidate's campaign. Funds from such hopeful contributors can loom large in the eyes and in the budget of a candidate faced with a tough campaign.

HONORARIUM: A payment to a professional for services for which no fee is set or legally obtainable.

On a day-to-day basis, many of our legislators may receive nominal sums of money paid as nontaxable honorariums. Such money may come from large corporations, associations, and other pressure groups. Once or twice a year, legislators may be invited to speak to clarify their stands on issues or to discuss problems affecting a certain group. In exchange, not for the time and expertise of the speaker but for expenses, a legislator may be awarded as much as $5,000. Various major newspapers have published lists of the recipients of such favors. One might argue that a Representative or Senator has a duty to the nation's taxpayers to speak and serve. In reality, the receipt of nontaxable honorariums over a period of years cannot help but influence the voting record of the receiving politician.

Imagine being in the position of having received $5,000 per year for the past ten years from the Allied Kumquat Processors. You have come to expect the little "bonus"; in fact, you have sent two children to college with that money. One day, a bill is proposed in Congress that would remove government subsidies from kumquat processors. If you vote for the bill, thereby hurting the kumquat industry, you may expect no further invitations to speak. If you vote against the bill, you may depend upon continued speaking engagements. Each day many of our legislators find themselves having to choose between representing either the majority of their electorate or the good of special-interest groups.

The question that tends to disturb people is whether the politician has been elected to serve the needs of the masses or to represent the needs of special-interest groups. It may be easy for us to forget that the politician's salary, paid by the public, is often supplemented by substantial funds from interest groups. If politicians feel they need the extra money, they cannot afford to ignore the wishes of the interest groups.

The Public Does Not Remember.   When the subject of political power is analyzed, an interesting feature emerges. Politicians pay more attention to the desires of organized groups than to the occasional interests of the public at large. To a great extent, this is because they know that groups have memories and their votes tend to be based upon those memories. To the politician, the public at large seems to remember for no longer than a few weeks at a time. As a result, legislation for the good of the public is usually passed in the months prior to election. Legislation distasteful to the public is dealt with in off-years. The 1986 Clean Water Bill, passed by both houses of Congress before the November elections, was vetoed by the president days after the election.

During a press conference, former President Richard M. Nixon made a statement in response to a question dealing with advice to Republican candidates concerning his removal or impeachment. The question implied "Do you think that Republican candidates for Congress will be hurt by association with the present administration scandal?" (This interpretation is, of course, the author's and can in no way be construed to represent the text of the question or Nixon's answer.) Nixon's response (and here we excerpt from the entire answer) was, "It is that nine months before an election no one can predict what can happen in this country. What will affect the election in the year 1974 is what always affects elections—peace and prosperity." Here Richard Nixon appeared to be saying that the American electorate has no memory. The statement also implies that the voting American is concerned more with today than with yesterday or tomorrow.

Why Enter Politics?   While dealing with the basis of political power, it is appropriate to deal also with the why of political power. Indeed, one may wonder why people enter politics (as well as why others do not). One major point must be made clear: Political action occurs in other places other than just government. Even brief exposure to the politics found within a college faculty, a fraternal club, or a corporation will show you how true this is. The political aims and actions of such nongovernmental participants are much the same as those of the governmental politicians.

If we were to analyze the contents of speeches most politicians have made regarding their aims in the political arena, our analyses

Skill Reinforcer 20-3
Where in this paragraph is an opinion expressed?

might reveal the following motives. Candidates may want to help the people, to make reforms, to aid consumers, or to cleanse the environment. They may hope to do away with corruption, to bring world peace, to stimulate the nation's economy. They may want to help the old, to help the young, to help the middle-aged. Or they may plan to build better highways and to ensure our children a better education—all at a cheaper price. People might get into politics because it appeared to be a way in which their individual views could be expressed. The professional planners, lawyers, sociologists, or economists might seek, through political participation, the chance to solve the problems of society.

Active political participation usually means belonging to a political party and taking part in its work or function. On the more sedentary side, participation may include merely keeping abreast of pertinent issues. The one avenue of political expression open to most Americans is the voting process. Unfortunately, too few of us extend ourselves enough even to cast our ballots.

People also throw their hats into the political arena simply because they want to go into politics. Almost all politicians enjoy the action, or they would not play the game. There are the ego boosts that come from winning an election, and the sweet sense of power. Also, public office offers many fringe benefits.

Consider the substantial benfits enjoyed by representatives, for example. Aside from their salary, they may join in a very liberal retirement plan that pays benefits after as little as five years' service. This period translates into one term as a senator or three terms as a representative. A senator may employ as many as seventy people, though senators from smaller states usually have fewer employees. At times, a legislator has been known to give these positions to a spouse and various other members of the family. Other fringe benefits include office space both at home and in Washington, private subways between some office buildings and the capitol, long-distance telephone and telegraph privileges, special income tax deductions for dual homes, franking privileges, travel and parking expenses, steam rooms, swimming pools, private dining room, medical care at a greatly reduced rate, and often reimbursement for haircuts or flowers.

FRANKING PRIVILEGES: The privilege of sending mail relating strictly to official business, or consisting of excerpts from the Congressional Record, free of charge, enjoyed by members of Congress and officers and agencies of the national government.

Once exposed to such benefits, people may forget their primary motives for attaining office. They may find political life itself more enjoyable than pursuit of political goals. Too often, the politician's sole motivation becomes that of remaining in office. To be sure, some elected officials have sacrificed their offices for principle. This has been so rare, however, that such instances have inspired authors to write novels.

Whatever originally motivates politicians to seek public office is subjected to great pressure from personal benefits enjoyed during their terms. They derive even greater ego satisfaction from the sense of power they get through participation in the political process. A government official can control and allocate services, resources, jobs, houses, parks, garbage collection, road-building, highway construction, and tax repayments to communities and states. Such rewards may cause officials to forget the reasons they first entered politics.

How Governments Work

We shift now from the underlying tactics of politics to some basic mechanics of government. These will include decision-making, the use of force, and change. With this knowledge, perhaps the sometimes strange actions of our government will be somewhat easier to understand.

Decision-making in Government. In a day-to-day survey of politics, we may observe decisions made on issues of vital interest to particular communities. A national energy crisis prompted a flurry of political activity during the winter of 1973–74. The government acted to allocate fair shares of available fuel to the various states and created the position of an "energy czar." The resulting allocation of energy, however, became a political game with the general public on the losing team. For reasons unknown at this time, various states received sufficient fuel while others suffered major shortages. In very plain terms, the variations in fuel allocations might be interpreted as a thinly disguised political power play.

The Reagan administration has downgraded the importance and function of the Department of Energy. This is thought to be due to oil-industry ties. In addition, far less effort has been targeted for the production of oil substitutes. Here too we may be able to see the working of the mechanics of politics in the decision-making of the government.

Decisions such as these affect each of us to a degree. Which ward receives a new park? Which state receives federal money for a national park? Which section of a city is designated to receive a low-cost housing development? In the last case, repercussions are felt firsthand. Property is condemned, causing some owners to be hurt by a reduction in property values and others to profit.

We must ask ourselves what benefits are to be derived from government's political decisions. In a real sense, these vital decisions are needed to resolve community conflicts. Who other than the government can make such decisions? We must consider, then, that government, with its associated political system, does not merely provide services in the form of protection, sewage, and water in return for the tax dollar. Government is obliged to allocate consumer goods that may be in short supply and settle disputes common to a community, state, or nation.[4]

Governments are limited in their decision-making by their citizens' acceptance or rejection of proposed decisions. The people may accept such decisions because they recognize the need for government intervention in an area of conflict. For example, if our government began food rationing, most people would be unhappy. But the majority would realize that the government was merely formalizing the fair distribution of existing food supplies.

Whatever their feeling, a substantial number of citizens would look for methods by which to beat the system. On the other hand, if a local board of adjustment ruled to allow a variance in land use, the majority of that community's citizens might object. They could appeal the decision, but, if higher levels of government upheld it, eventually they would live with it. In essence, it is accepted that the government has, within bounds of law and reason, a legitimate right to make decisions, rulings, and settlements.

Power and Force.   In watching governments work, we must always remember the presence of another decision-making factor: force. The only "legal" use of force, or violence, is that initiated by government. The government has a monopoly on the use of legitimate force and violence. In a gunfight between the police, the militia, or armed forces and any individual or group of individuals, only one side deserves public support. Even though the use of force or violence may occur outside the limits of the law, we are generally forbidden to fight back. All matters concerning undue violence by governmental agencies must be settled by the arm of government called the court. If we fight back, we almost always lose.

Yet, governments do not, as a rule, remain in power solely through the use of force. Even the most absolute of dictatorships attempts to appeal to its constituency under a guise of legitimacy. Some of the conciliatory measures proposed are economic reform or other popular arguments presented via the mass media. Under normal circumstances, a government that exceeds the authority granted by its citizens will fall—or change.

CONSTITUENCY: A body of citizens entitled to elect representatives to a legislative or other public body.

Governments and Change.   History shows us that, sooner or later, change will occur in any government. In summary:

1. Governments exist to settle conflicts and to allocate materials and benefits.
2. Politics is the tool that accomplishes governmental purposes.
3. Conditioned to inertia, we find it more difficult to change than to continue along established lines of behavior.
4. We usually prefer to go along with a bad government that is familiar and understood rather than undergo sudden or violent change for an unknown government that might be better.

To support this last statement, we may refer to historic examples. The European estate system, predominant during the Middle Ages, illustrates a situation where many people were not accorded equal rights. The serfs at the bottom of the political and social heap were not permitted to leave the land. Forced to work for the landowner, they could be deprived of their home, their spouse or sweetheart, and even their freedom. On a whim, serfs' limbs could be severed or their eyes blinded; they could even be killed. Such actions were considered acceptable during that period. In times of cruel masters, which can be translated to mean government, peo-

Ivan the Terrible.

ple hoped that each successor might be a better ruler. Any change, however, would occur within the established system. The names of various rulers describe how subjects perceived their ruler and his government: Ivan the Terrible, John Lackland, Peter the Great, Charles the Wise, Edward the Confessor, Louis the Pious, Charles the Simple, Charles the Fat, German Georgie, Merry Monarch, Ethelred the Unready, Louis the Stammerer, Louis the Sluggard, Louis the Headstrong, Louis the Cruel, Juana the Mad.

The following excerpt of a statement made by James I of England illustrates his position on the rights of kings.

> The state of monarchy is the supremest thing upon earth; for kings are not only God's lieutenants upon earth, and sit upon God's throne, but even by God himself they are called gods. There be three principle similitudes that illustrate the state of monarchy: one taken out of the word of God; and the two others out of the grounds of policy and philosophy. In the scriptures kings are called gods, and so their power after a certain relation compared to the divine power. Kings are also compared to fathers of families; for a king is truly Parens patriae, the political father of his people. And lastly, kings are compared to the head of this microcosm of the body of man.[5]

PARENS PATRIAE: The father of the country constituted in law by the state (as in the United States) or by the sovereign (as in Great Britain).

MICROCOSM: A little world, miniature universe, community, institution, or other unity believed to be an epitome of a larger unity (as of a nation or the world).

We may not agree with that view on kings, but perhaps we can agree with the earlier point about change and inertia. The principle of inertia applies clearly to political change. A body in motion tends to remain in motion, or a body at rest tends to remain at rest. Government aims to have the people remain at rest. Essentially, this is because we can deal more easily with the known than the unknown. With this in mind, it is to the advantage of even the most high-handed government to maintain at least a semblance of service to the people.

SUMMARY

Government is the organizations and institutions of people who regulate and control a society. Governments are necessary in modern societies, though the reasons for that need are the subject of debate, summarized by the differing views of Locke and Hobbes. Governments range from autocracy (rule of one person) to democracy (rule by the people). In a democracy, power is either directly in the hands of the people or in the hands of representatives chosen by the people. While government by an all-powerful king or queen is rare today, totalitarian governments are now the form of total governmental power.

Interest groups are created by people joining together to seek special treatment from the government. By voting in blocs, such groups can exert great pressure. The trading of political favors and the giving of political plums are other ways of getting and keeping political power in America. Indeed, the receipt of gifts and support can make an officeholder indebted to special interests rather than to the general voting public. In any case, the fact that the public rarely remembers what an officeholder does gives him or her some degree of freedom to ignore the public's wishes. Moreover, once officeholders begin to enjoy the many benefits of office, they may forget duty to the public and focus instead on the next election.

Few governments remain in power only through the use of force. Indeed, governments are limited in their power by the citizens' sense of what is legitimate. Within that limit, governments try to resist major change in most cases.

SPECIAL TOPIC

The Keeping of the Ex-Presidents[6]

THE RICH AFTERLIFE OF THE POLITICIAN

Washington (UPI)—American taxpayers fork out more money on their ex-presidents, some of them long dead, than they do to operate the White House.

The annual cost of about $27 million a year goes to run eight shrine-like presidential libraries and to provide staffs, offices and $86,200 pensions for Richard Nixon, Gerald Ford and Jimmy Carter.

This money, about $2 million more than this year's White House budget, also covers around-the-clock protection by the Secret Service for Ford and Carter, their wives, and Lyndon Johnson's widow, Lady Bird.

Nixon voluntarily gave up his federal security a year ago, giving a push to long-stalled legislation to curb what Sen. Lawton Chiles, D–Fla., calls "the era of the Imperial Former Presidency."

"Things have gotten out of hand," said Chiles, noting the cost of supporting ex-presidents in the style to which they have grown accustomed has soared four-fold since 1965. Back in 1955, when Harry Truman and Herbert Hoover were the living ex-presidents, these expenses totaled just $63,745.

"It is right that we ensure the dignity of the office and those who have held it, along with their safety, but we have no responsibility to make them richer or to provide imperial lifestyles," Chiles said.

This summer, after eight years of studies, hearings and wrangling with both Democratic and Republican administrations, Congress passed a bill initiated by Chiles to start to restrict presidential libraries.

The measure, the first of two aimed at ex-presidents, limits the size of new presidential libraries to 70,000 square feet and requires a private endowment to defray operating and maintenance costs.

The eight existing libraries, built with private funds but operated with about $15 million a year in taxpayer money, average 80,000 square feet, 50 percent bigger than a football field.

They house the presidential papers and memorabilia of Herbert Hoover, Harry Truman, Franklin Roosevelt, Dwight Eisenhower, John F. Kennedy, Johnson, Ford and Carter.

Although initially justified as research facilities, a congressional study found that upwards of 97 percent of visitors to the libraries are there merely to sight-see.

President Reagan, who made budget-cutting a theme of his administration, did sign the library bill, but only after backroom haggling with Congress to exempt his own yet-to-be-built library from the restrictions.

He opposes a Senate-passed bill sponsored by Chiles that would limit Secret Service protection for ex-presidents to five years and for their wives to two years. The protection could be extended at the discretion of the treasury secretary, who oversees the Secret Service, and Congress.

Ex-presidents and their spouses get protection for life, and children to age 16. A widowed spouse who remarries, as Jacqueline Kennedy Onassis did, loses the federal security as well as her pension, now $20,000 a year.

Since 1981, public expenses associated with ex-presidents have topped the annual budget of The Office of the White House, which includes utilities, maintenance, entertainment, security and salaries. White House Secret Service protection is separate and costs about $50 million.

As former chief executives, Nixon, Ford and Carter are in demand for television appearances, writing books and giving speeches, activities that provide substantial income. They have no public powers and hold no public office.

Yet, they spend an average of about $300,000 a year each in public money to rent offices, pay staffs, go on trips and plan activities.

Nixon's 3,758–square-foot office at a federal building in lower Manhattan is described as ''relatively modest'' by Helen Shuldinger, a budget director at the New York office of the General Services Administration.

The furniture is the same that Nixon bought years ago with public funds for his ''Western White House'' in San Clemente, Calif.

Ford's 4,135–square-foot office is in a building owned by the University of Southern California near Palm Beach, Calif.

Carter initially had an office at a federal building in Atlanta. This fall, he moved to a 4,000–square-foot office at the new Carter Presidential Center. The government covers his office rent.

Carter's office furnishings include an oriental rug, leather chairs and handcrafted bookcases bought with public funds.

Ford spent $1,069 on glassware and a silver coffee set. A few years ago, he charged the public $50 a month to maintain a swimming pool, $2,242 for 22 office plants and another $50 a month to have the plants watered.

The Senate-passed bill would limit offices to 4,000 square feet, require that they be in federal buildings and impose yearly staff and office allowances—initially $300,000, dropping to $200,000 in 9 years. It would also ban public funds for political or income-producing activities such as writing memoirs.

Ross Biatek, a GSA budget officer in San Francisco who helps keep tabs on Ford's account, said of former presidents and their public expenses:

''There is no abuse in the way they run their offices. The problem is when the leave the White House and set up an office. All the law says is that a former president is 'entitled to have a suitable office appropriately furnished.' ''

''What exactly does that mean?'' said Biatek. ''Is it appropriate for Jimmy Carter to have an oriental rug?''

When Truman left the White House in 1953, he returned to his Missouri home—without a pension, a staff or even Secret Service agents. He answered his own mail and paid out of his own pocket for stamps and pens.

But in 1955, Congress started to give former presidents financial homage.

First, it passed the Presidential Libraries Act to help cover the cost of preserving presidential papers. Three years later, it passed the Former President's Act, providing ex-presidents with pensions, mailing privileges and staff and office allowances. In 1965, it gave them Secret Service protection.

Truman didn't want bodyguards. In a letter to James Rowley, then head of the Secret Service, he wrote:

''Dear Jim, I phoned you this morning and told you there was no reason for the protection you've been providing for me and Mrs. Truman. I have been 13 years without it and have had no trouble. I will appreciate it very much if you will relieve me of this protection.''

Rowley refused.

After Truman died, Secret Service agents protected his wife, Bess. In the fall of 1982, when the 97–year-old former first lady slipped into a comatose state shortly before dying, the agents still guarded her.

''They were going bonkers,'' said Chiles. ''Here you had men trained to kill with either hand and suddenly they are doing absolutely nothing, except looking through (binoculars) across this way to her room.

''For what? A terrorist attack?''

The senator said Mamie Eisenhower was in similar condition in her final days and had the same type of costly Secret Service protection.

Chiles said there was never a threat against Mrs. Truman, Mrs. Eisenhower or any other former first lady. And, he said, there's never been an attack on an ex-president.

Of the three living former presidents, Nixon, who left office in the shame of Watergate, has kept the lowest public profile.

In March 1985, Nixon relinquished his federal protection, saving the government about $3 million per year.

"President Nixon believes that former presidents in conducting their affairs should place the least possible burden upon the public purse," John Taylor, a Nixon spokesman, wrote in a letter he sent to Congress last spring.

Said Chiles, "If President Nixon doesn't need coverage, who needs coverage?"

Ford entered office with little money, but has reaped a bonanza since leaving. According to the financial newspaper "Barrons," Ford received more than $1.7 million last year—much of it from speeches and serving on corporate boards of directors.

A target of two attempted assassinations while president, Ford has said publicly he appreciates the protection provided by his team of $34,000–a-year Secret Service agents. Officials won't say how many, citing security reasons.

On occasion, however, Ford has seemed to use the agents more as high-priced valets. In his travels they have been seen carrying his luggage and opening doors for him.

Carter, in an interview with CBS's ("60 Minutes") this fall, said he values the agents more for protecting his privacy than his safety.

"If a former president wants to play at all an active life, being frequently exposed to the public . . . it's not a matter of protection from assassination or injury, but it's a matter of providing some degree of privacy."

Snapped back former Treasury Secretary William Simon, a critic of the amount of security provided to former presidents, "Well, then I suggest he buy a fence."

Bob Barrett, a Ford spokesman, acknowledged that Ford is "a little sensitive" about the criticism. "Mr. Ford chooses to participate in the free entreprenurial system," he said. "It is not illegal or immoral. I feel if a person served as president, and did so honorably, we should give them protection for the rest of their lives."

Barrett said Ford believes, however, that the level of Secret Service protection might be modified or reduced, based on yearly risk assessments and the activity level of the former president.

The Secret Service says little publicly on the issue.

"By law, we are directed to protect former presidents and that's what we do," said Bill Corbett, a Secret Service spokesman.

In Stonewall, Texas, where Lady Bird Johnson resides, a few aging and somewhat paunchy Secret Service agents provide protection for the former first lady, who will celebrate her 74th birthday in December.

Mrs. Johnson, in a 1979 letter to Chiles, wrote "on the matter of Secret Service protection:

"Although I have welcomed and been very deeply grateful for the outstanding protection Congress has afforded me through this fine organization (as when they awakened me in the middle of the night a few weeks ago to evacuate my apartment because of a fire in the building) if Congress wishes to change it, I will abide by their decision."

Betty Tilson, a spokeswoman for the 73–year-old former first lady, said this fall, "That statement still stands."

SELF-TEST QUESTIONS

Determine whether each of the following statements is either true or false.

1. Government consists of the organizations and institutions that regulate and control society.
2. Politics is the control of government.
3. The United States is a true democracy.
4. Hammurabi is credited with being responsible for the first written laws.
5. All residents of Athens were represented in the Athenian democracy.
6. Thomas Hobbes felt that people could live without government.
7. John Locke felt that people could (with government) live in harmony.
8. Plato believed in the principle of Athenian democracy.
9. A representative democracy is one in which a region or area is represented by a small number of elected officials.

10. Interest groups belong only to the banking community.

11. Single interest groups are usually interested in a particular idea or piece of legislation.

12. Our politicians usually have the good of the majority of people in mind when they accept honoraria and contributions from interest groups, pressure groups and political action groups.

13. The only legal use of force is by arms of government.

14. People put up with bad government because it is easier to live with something bad but familiar than face the unknown of change.

ANSWERS TO SELF-TEST QUESTIONS

1. true	8. false
2. true	9. true
3. false	10. false
4. true	11. true
5. false	12. false
6. false	13. true
7. true	14. true

ANSWERS TO SKILL REINFORCERS

20–1. The invalid syllogism could take this form:
1. If A is so, then B will happen.
2. B has happened.
3. Therefore A is so.

Starting with the given major premise, we have:
1. If a surplus is produced, a government will be established.
2. There is a government in this country.
3. Therefore, this country is producing a surplus.

This logic is not valid. The conclusion ignores the possibility that a government might be established as a result of factors other than the production of a surplus.

20–2. The invalid syllogism here could take this form:
1. If A is so, then B is so.
2. A is not so.
3. Therefore B is not so.

With the given major premise, we have:
1. If a country builds pyramids, there exists in that country a government.
2. This country has no pyramids.
3. Therefore this country has no government.

The premises simply do not force the conclusion. That is, B may be so even if A is not. Clearly, a government might exist that chooses to build no pyramids.

20–3. The word "appeared" is a signal that the author believes but cannot prove what he says. It is a matter of belief, not fact. Still, you are free to agree with the author's interpretation.

NOTES

1. Thomas Hobbes, *Leviathan* (London: Oxford University Press, 1965).
2. John Locke, *An Essay Concerning Human Understanding* (New York: E.P. Dutton, 1973).
3. Plato, *Republic* (New York: Scribners, 1956).

4. Harold Lasswell, *Politics: Who Gets What, When, How* (New York: McGraw-Hill, 1938).

5. C.H. McIlwain, ed., *The Political Works of James I* (New York: Russell & Russell, 1918).

6. Thomas, Ferraro—U.P.I. Nov. 9, 1986.

SUGGESTED READINGS

Bentham, Jeremy. *An Introduction to the Principles of Morals and Legislation.* London: Clarendon Press, 1907.

Bernstein, Richard. *The Search for the Truth About China.* Boston: Little, Brown, 1982.

Dahl, Robert A. *Modern Political Analysis.* Englewood Cliffs, N.J.: Prentice-Hall, 1963.

Hobbes, Thomas. *The Leviathan.* New York: E.P. Dutton, 1950.

Holy Bible. Revised Standard Version.

Kennedy, John F. *Profiles in Courage.* New York: Harper & Row, 1964.

Lipset, Seymour Martin. *Political Man.* Garden City, N.Y.: Doubleday & Co., 1960.

Locke, John. *Of Civil Government.* New York: E.P. Dutton, 1924.

Machiavelli, Niccolo. *The Prince.* Edited by Mark Musa. New York: St. Martin's Press, 1964.

21 THE NATION, THE STATE, AND THE CONSTITUTION

What Good Is a Constitution?

You are awakened one night by the sound of people smashing down your front door. They wear no uniforms, offer no identification, and say little. They are heavily armed and would not hesitate to use their weapons. You are taken from your home. Your family is beaten when they protest. You are thrown handcuffed into a waiting car. There has been a lot of noise, yet no neighbors have come to your aid. No one is looking out of nearby windows. No lights turn on. You have not been kidnapped by the Mafia. Your captors are employed by the government. You are not taken to a police station to be booked and arraigned. You are not taken to a judge, nor are you offered bail. You have not been arrested. You have been taken to an unofficial prison. Over the next several years you will be beaten and exposed to electric shock and various tortures. There are other prisoners; some stay, some go. You hear that many prisoners have been taken far out to sea by plane, drugged, and thrown out. You are released and exiled from your country.

In another instance, you are rich and own thousands of acres. Then one day you find that the land records have been changed and you own nothing.

In another instance, you are a young girl and are taken to an unofficial prison where you have been raped by many different men over a period of several years. You can think of no crime you may have committed. You are just one of thousands of people who have dropped from sight.

These are not stories of Idi Amin's Uganda. While the savagery of that nation was almost unique, there was no attempt to portray its government as a government of the people.

The stories we have listed are merely composites of many noted by Jacobo Timmerman in his account of his years in Argentina.[1] Argentina is a civilized country with a formal constitution and court system. Many nations have well-conceived constitutions. A constitution lists the rights and obligations of government and its citizens. It is a contract. Argentina has a fine constitution, but it was not enforced. The constitution of any nation is only as good as the intent of government and citizens to live by their contract.

In our nation the constitution has at times been ignored. The rights of people have been violated. Fortunately our courts have had the power to protect our citizens in most cases. During the nineteenth century, the Supreme Court of the United States found that the rights of Cherokee Indians were being violated. The President of the United States, Andrew Jackson, said that since the Court had made its decision the Court should enforce it. We have had other serious attacks on our Constitution, but they have usually been beaten back.

It would be interesting to create a situation where the FBI, the CIA, or the military decided that it should assume control of government. How would they do that? And how would the people act to preserve their rights?

In this chapter we will explore the framework of government that protects us from real-life horror stories like those just described. This protection is not perfect, but the more we know about how it is supposed to work, the better we will be able to notice signs that it is not working as it should. In this way, the chapter will make us better watchdogs of our government.

Each day we go through life controlled in specific ways by rules, laws, and institutions. These controls are what we call our government. The newspapers, radio, television, and magazines advise us that we are lucky to live as free people in a free society, and on and on. People in other lands, we are told, are not so lucky as we because they are not free. They do not live in an independent society, and they are not blessed with our form of government. The obvious but usually unasked question is, "What kind of government do we have?"

Even if we answer this question, we may be unable to define our answer. In other words, many people have been conditioned to respond to specific questions with specific sets of words with vague meanings. Thus, a typical response to the question asked would be: Our government is a democracy.

As we pointed out in Chapter 20, there are different meanings of the word "democracy." Nations whose governments allow little or no representation by the people may call themselves democracies, while nations that maintain only a figurehead royalty refer to themselves as limited or representational monarchies. These monarchies may allow a great deal of democratic expression on the part of their citizens.

In the United States, we have established a varied framework of governmental forms. These forms range from absolute control exercised by an individual or small group to pure democracies. Within this framework, we will isolate the form of government that concerns us most, our own.

The form of our government should concern us. The chapter preview showed us what can happen in other forms, so we should know our government's form well. We should know what it is supposed to look like and how it should work.

THE CREATION OF OUR CONSTITUTION

At the base of our system is a document that is, in effect, a contract between the governed and the government. We refer to this contract as our Constitution. A constitution represents the basic law of a people; it establishes the basic structure and outlines the functions of our system of government. Our government was created by and continues to be bound by the rules set forth in the Constitution.

CONSTITUTION: The basic law or principles upon which a state is organized, which delegates responsibilities, rights, and power.

The Constitution of the United States did not spring full-blown from under Plymouth Rock or as the result of a thunderclap in concert with the ringing of the Liberty Bell. As with all patterns of culture, politics, and human behavior, the Constitution's roots are deep in the past. It was developed in response to changes in the cultural heritage of Western civilization and movements abroad and at home.

The Background of Our Constitution

There were many threads that, when woven together, produced our Constitution. Here we will look at the major ones. Our search for the background of our government centers on Great Britain.

John Locke. We have certain rights simply because we are human.

IMPEACHMENT: A formal written accusation by the lower house of a legislature to the upper house for the purpose of removing a civil officer (other than a member of the legislature) for treason, bribery, or other high crimes and misdemeanors.

BILL OF RIGHTS: A brief summation of certain fundamental rights and privileges guaranteed to the people against infringement by any part of the government; the first ten amendments to the Constitution of the United States are popularly called the Bill of Rights.

The Ideas of John Locke (1632–1704). John Locke was an English scholar and philosopher. In his writings are found many ideas that we take for granted today. Locke put forth the idea that such privileges as natural rights not only existed but were of vital importance. This idea can be translated into the phrase "God-given and inalienable rights." That is, Locke felt that there were certain rights to which we are entitled simply because we are human. He also referred to the concept that government exists as a contract between the leaders of any group and the people to be governed. If the contract is broken because the leaders exert more power than the contract gives them, they should be overthrown or otherwise removed. This is a radical idea. This viewpoint clearly puts the ultimate power in the hands of the people, not the leaders.

The Constitution of the United States provides several methods of removing offensive leaders without resorting to overthrow, the first and most widely used being voting them out of office. The second method specified by law deals with the impeachment of public officials for misdeeds while in office. In various local governments the procedure for removing unwanted leaders is similar, but it is referred to as a recall. Thus, although the methods of displacing government officials may differ, provisions for such removal are built into our system.

These two ideas of Locke, natural rights and giving the governed the means of removing leaders from office, are basic to our form of government.

Our English Heritage. Though we are a mixture of ethnic backgrounds, we must look to England for our government's roots. The first colonies were established mainly by English people. The English ideas of those first settlers laid the groundwork for what is now our American government.

The English heritage of the original colonies carried with it a trend of expanding popular government. We can trace the growing rights of the governed in contrast to the diminishing rights and power of royalty in England. The progression of more power being granted to the governed can be noted in the Magna Charta (1215), the Habeas Corpus Act (1679), and the English Bill of Rights (1689).

These concessions won from the royalty by the people of England had a huge effect. The result was a parliament that truly represents the people. There still exists in England a pseudo-monarchy,[2] which consists of a symbolic figurehead, seemingly preserved much as a museum piece for tourists.

A New England in North America. This English heritage of power in the hands of the governed took hold right away in the colonies of North America. While traveling to the New World the English colonists adopted the Mayflower Compact, which set the structure for the government of the colony at Plymouth. The

Massachusetts Bay Colony adopted the first written constitution. The colony established at Jamestown formed the first representative assembly in North America.

The ocean had something to do with the building of the government. The Atlantic Ocean offered isolation and forced independent action. The colonists' ability to accomplish as much as they did was probably based upon physical separation from the governing body of their homeland. Communications being what they were in those days, a group had to make decisions immediately or face harsh consequences.

The new steps taken in the colonies were neither pristine nor uncriticized; they only appeared to be so compared to earlier governmental forms. In truth, the colonial democracy was one of religious suppression. For example, in some colonies only members of the Puritan church were allowed a voice in the government. Puritans wanted religious freedom only for themselves. In these and other colonies, only white males who owned minimum amounts of property were allowed to vote. Women, blacks, and Indians must have wondered at the talk of democracy. Still, compared with what had gone before, the colonies took huge steps toward giving power to the governed rather than to those governing.

Despite these problems, American colonists did not have to worry about treatment like that described in the chapter preview. Indeed, compared with other places, Americans have always enjoyed great protection from their leaders.

ARTICLES OF CONFEDERATION: A framework for a national union approved by Congress in 1777, in effect until 1787; many of these provisions were later incorporated in the Constitution.

The Articles of Confederation. With the end of the American Revolution, the original colonies suddenly found themselves in the position of being recognized as a nation. The Articles of Confederation attempted to tie the semi-independent colonies to one another to form a nation in fact, not just in name. While the Articles served as the basis for governmental function for a time, they had many shortcomings. These faults were finally set right with the drafting of the Constitution.

The states under the Articles of Confederation did not comprise the tight, federally centralized unit we know today. In reality, the Articles created a loose confederation of the thirteen former colonies. They made no provision for a single executive (president). Instead, there were five executive departments. The central government had no legislative or coercive power over individuals.

Furthermore, the legislative portion of the government was extremely weak and uneven. Each state had one vote, and the large states, with large populations, resented this. They felt they deserved more power than the smaller states. The legal limitations placed upon Congress during this period prevented it from demanding revenue from the states. The central government could ask for taxes only from the states. Some states gave none, others a fraction of what was asked of them. Because of this, the national government was usually handcuffed by a lack of funds.

SOVEREIGNTY: Supreme and independent political authority; supreme power over citizens and subjects unrestrained by laws.

The Articles of Confederation had created a very weak governmental body. The power and sovereignty of each of the states were jealously guarded. In fact, states levied import and export tariffs upon trade between states. The situation grew worse until 1786, when the nation was seized by a major economic depression. Under such conditions, it became clear that the Articles of Confederation would have to be revised or discarded. In 1787 a convention of the states was called in Philadelphia to deal with the problem. Out of this convention was born the Constitution of the United States.[3]

Framing the Constitution

The framers of this vital document had to face a number of basic problems. These problems involved power. The central concern was who was to get how much power and how that power was to be controlled.

How Much Power to the States?   One power question involved that to be given the states. On one hand, the states recognized the need for a strong central government. On the other hand, various states feared the power of a strong, central government. In order to specify and maintain areas of responsibility, an attempt was made to achieve a balance of power between the central government and the states. However, this problem was not solved to everyone's satisfaction.

In the 1860s a bloody civil war occurred between the states of the North and South. The major point in dispute at the time was states' rights. But even as late as the 1950s, this question was argued on the floor of the Louisiana legislature. The Louisiana argument debated the rights of the states versus the rights of the federal government as they concerned civil rights activity. At one point during the proceedings, a representative excused himself from the discussion with a statement something like, "Gentlemen, it may have slipped your minds that we fought a war concerning this very matter less than one hundred years ago. I beg to point out to you that we lost that war."

STATES' RIGHTS: A generic term applied to various theories of various construction and interpretation of the Constitution ranging from state sovereignty to present-day opposition to concentration of power in the national government.

At the time of the Constitutional Convention, the feelings and issues of the states' rights argument were not nearly as sharply defined as they are today. Yet even today, considerable feeling is expressed regarding the rights of the states in relation to the central government.

Recent decades have seen the federal government exert control over new areas. Federal highway monies have been withheld until states conform to drinking age laws, highway speed laws, and tandem trailer rulings. These are only a few examples of how the central government can control the activity of the various states.

How Much Power to the People?   The second power question facing the founders was how much would be given to the people. A problem here is that of maintaining governmental stability in a nation where the people would share power in government. Alex-

The signing of the Constitution. Our constitution is a contract between the people and the government. Has our government been looking for an escape clause?

ander Hamilton has been quoted as saying, "The people are turbulent and changing; they seldom judge or determine right." Elbridge Gerry of Massachusetts expressed a similar view on this matter when he said, "The evils we experience flow from the excess of democracy."

Viewing the positions taken by these men and others who shared their views, we can see that the struggle for power existed in spheres other than those between state and federal government. This controversy was of course the struggle for power between the masses of the people and the upper-class elite. Those people who owned property or held high social and economic positions in the new nation wanted to retain their political power. We can appreciate their attitudes, but we can also understand that the mass of people who neither owned property nor controlled wealth or power might wish to attain the same goals.

We are familiar with similar concepts and desires today. Those who have power want to keep it, and those who lack power desire it. In a sense, we can say that those individuals who want to maintain things as they are can be classed as conservatives, while those who want to modify the old order are frequently referred to as liberals.

The Framers. These questions of power were only part of the huge task faced by the writers of the Constitution. Not only must these problems be solved, but the solutions must be fitted into the political heritage of the people. The framers rose to the task.

The fifty-five men who gathered to improve the Articles of Confederation quickly took it upon themselves to write a new constitution. These men have been called "an assembly of demigods." Indeed, this group had its full share of learning and foresight. Over half of these men had studied in college. Forty-two had been involved before in national politics. Most of them were middle-aged and men of means. Among them were wealthy planters, merchants, and lawyers. They were an elite.

As impressive as these men were in their learning and wealth, their real glory is based on the product of their assembly. Remembering the horrors described in the chapter preview of a government gone wrong, we can be grateful that fifty-five men happened to gather together when they did to create what they did. Now we will examine the results of their efforts.

PRINCIPLES OF OUR CONSTITUTION

Our government is limited. The Constitution sets boundaries on the power of the elected leaders' actions. This principle of limited government is the basis of the protections and liberties we enjoy.

Other principles of our Constitution are not so clear. They deal with the way power is distributed within the nation and within the central government.

A Good Constitution?

What makes a constitution a good one? Ours may well contain some flaws, some shortcomings. We might rightly want to know what is good, not just what ours includes. Here are some elements a good constitution should include:

First, a good constitution should be brief. A long document is bound to be complex, and if it is too complex, it will not be understood by many citizens. If the people do not understand the constitution, it is of little use to them.

Second, a good constitution needs balance. Its provisions should strike a balance between the powers given to the government and the freedom given to the citizens.

Third, a good constitution should be flexible. It must be able to deal with most, if not all, problems that arise after the creation of the document.[4]

The U.S. Constitution has been flexible enough to deal with the regulation of almost everything from labor-management relations to food inspection under the provisions of the Interstate Commerce Clause.

This flexibility is also shown by the great array of items that come under the First Amendment. This amendment states that Congress shall make no law abridging the freedom of speech. Under this umbrella statement, the Constitution has been called on to deal with freedom of all forms of communication. These have included such diverse topics as political dissent, long hair, pornography, and flag-burning.

The flexibility of our Constitution has served us well. Such a flexible document can remain relevant because it can deal with a broad spectrum of issues. And such a flexible constitution offers a long-lasting contract. Under that contract, the government can continue to exist without disruption.

How good a constitution is ours? Most scholars are impressed with it. In fact, some view the document as being almost sacred.

SKILL BOX

False Dilemma

"Is our Constitution perfect, or should it be replaced?" This is an example of a tactic that might be used during a political campaign. This Skill Box explores this tactic.

"Your money or your life." A dilemma offers only two choices, and neither is a pleasant prospect. Sometimes a person poses a dilemma in order to force us into a certain choice and would rather we did not consider any alternatives. This tactic is called the false dilemma, because there exist more than the choices it offers.

The false dilemma ploy is a bullying tactic. It is used not only by the robber but also by politicians, advertisers, and other persuaders. Those who use this ploy want to block our view of other options. By limiting our view, they try to force us to accept their own idea or product.

There are examples all around us. "Either you buy this smoke detector or your child will probably burn to death—so buy!" Such an emotion-packed appeal may blind us to alternatives. Or we might reply to the salesperson: "I will not buy your product, and I do not believe my child is threatened by a fire in this house." Or, if we feel threatened enough by the chance of a fire in our house, we have the option of buying some other smoke detector. There are more than the two choices of buying or burning: the "dilemma" is thus a false one.

Not only products but also ideas are sometimes sold by using the false dilemma. "Are you a Communist or a Fascist?" (There are plenty of other labels besides these two.) "We must either increase taxes or do without welfare for the poor." (How about a different program, or a smaller one?) "Are you for or against the building of nuclear power plants?" (Neither. They should be studied more before a decision is made.)

All the Skill Boxes that are concerned with errors in reasoning have a common thread. That thread is the need to be skeptical, which is part of the scientific attitude. Though scientists should have an open mind, they will not accept an idea without good reason. Concerning reasoning errors, we must require that arguments be based on valid logic. The false dilemma does not qualify.

Perhaps it is an amazing document. It has, after all, stood strong for over two hundred years. It has guided us through many crises. The principles of our amazing Constitution may not be sacred, but they are sound and amazingly sensible. This good sense can be captured in just a few pages, where we will look at these principles.

Governmental Transition

Among the many processes put forth in the Constitution is the manner in which leadership is changed. In many nations of the world, the transition from one government to another or from one leader to another is a process left to chance—or force. This process often results in a large-scale disruption of an entire system, often involving bloody battles, executions, civil wars, and general disasters.

We can look to Cuba for an example of such a disruptive transition from one leader to another. When Fidel Castro took control of that government from President Batista, no provision had been made for a peaceful transition of leadership. Though Cuba had a constitution, its provisions had been subverted to allow virtually a one-man rule. Castro's revolution resulted in a major disruption of the social and economic life of the nation. Yet there is no clear-cut policy that might allow Castro's successor to assume power peacefully.

There are worse examples of disruptive transition. Problems of succession have been part of the history of nations for thousands of years. In Roman times, Caesar's death created a vacuum that resulted in war. Alexander the Great died, and his empire was splintered. Lenin died in Russia, and Stalin's ensuing power-play resulted in Trotsky's exile to Mexico. At the death of France's President Georges Pompidou, a financial crisis arose. The price of gold on the French commodity market shot up to record levels, indicating the French people's lack of faith in the transitional methods. Gold was being hoarded by rich and poor alike in an attempt to maintain an economic guarantee against an uncertain future.

Even more recent examples of bloody transitions are not hard to find. A prime example occurred in Iran with the overthrow of the Shah. The power struggle for the control of that country began well before the anticipated demise of the Ayatollah Ruholla Khomeini. After the murder of Egypt's President Sadat, only the pressure of the United States and other interested parties allowed an orderly transition of power.

These examples are hardly a complete or in-depth picture of the traumatic effects of governmental succession in the world. Still, they allow us to compare the peaceful, bland manner in which our governments come and go, in contrast to those of other nations. Other nations do indeed have their own constitutions which, in a great many instances, prescribe the manner in which power is passed from government to succeeding government.

There is little panic in the United States during our regular governmental changes. The workings of our government are built not around the eventual changes to be experienced but on the certainty that these changes will occur regularly. Every four years a general election is held to elect a president and vice-president for the ensuing four years. Our Constitution has mandated these elections, and they have occurred, regardless of political, social, or economic conditions prevailing in our nation at the time.

We have held elections during critical periods in our nation. The Constitution mandates those elections, and the framework of our government provides machinery for them. Elections have been held prior to and during the Civil War, before World War I, and before and during World War II. In more recent imes, presidents were elected during the Korean War and the Vietnam War.

Elections have been held during depressions, recessions, panics, and droughts. In addition to the presidential elections, members of the Congress, the legislative branch of the government, which includes the House of Representatives and the Senate, are elected regularly.

*Skill Reinforcer 21–1**
Where in this paragraph is an opinion expressed?

The power of the Constitution in the United States can be seen in light of these elections during periods of extreme stress. Some critics feel that it would be far easier to postpone elections rather than allow the transfer of governmental powers during a crisis. But the fact that the elections have never been postponed points to the real and symbolic power of the document. It exists as a symbol of and for the nation. We have no royal family as a focal point, but we have the Constitution. The apparent ease with which our government allowed the transfer of presidential powers following the assassination of President Kennedy amazed the heads of other nations. Also, Vice-President Agnew resigned and was replaced without a ripple in the waters of governmental function.

PRESIDENTIAL SUCCESSION: The order in which officials succeed to the presidency in case of the removal, resignation, death, or physical disability of the president; the vice-president is next in line, followed by the Speaker of the House and the president pro tempore of the Senate, and then certain members of the cabinet.

In 1973 and 1974, the subject of President Nixon's impeachment disturbed many Americans. Presidential succession was clouded until Representative Gerald Ford was confirmed as vice-president and then president without benefit of election to those posts. The Constitution cites the order of succession to the presidency. Four or five successive presidents might die, be impeached, or otherwise be found unfit for office. Still, the position would be filled in an orderly, legal manner. Each new president would remain in office until the next regularly scheduled elections.

Balance of Power Checks and Balances

A good constitution provides a balance of power among the various parts of the government. If one part had too much power, abuses might result. In our government, the units within the national government are balanced by the Constitution. This balance is not perfect—shifts and abuses have occurred—but we have managed fairly well with it thus far.

Balance Within Congress. One place within the national government where balance is needed is in the Congress. Two bodies of elected officials make up the Congress of the United States. One of these chambers, the Senate, is composed of two elected members, or senators, for each state in the union. Originally, the Senate was even more clearly allied with the power blocs of the nation than it is today. While senators are elected in general elections by the people today, the first senators were chosen by their respective state legislatures. Not until 1913 was direct election of senators by the people mandated by constitutional amendment. In other words, prior to that amendment, senators depended for their election upon a limited group of people who controlled their state legislatures.

DIRECT ELECTION: Candidate elected directly by the people; not appointed.

The members of the House of Representatives can be called the real voice of the people. Here each seat is based on a percentage of the actual population, with a minimum of one representative per state. An interesting comparison can be made between the representatives of people in various states. If we live in one of the more densely populated areas of the country, we will find that our representative in the House may be elected from an area measured in city blocks. By the same token, our state may well have 20 million people represented by only two senators. In more sparsely settled areas of the nation, a state may have a population equal to that of an urban county, but will still have two senators and one or more representatives as its spokespeople in the government.

We can see from this that we are guaranteed a bit of power in Congress. We get a couple of senators to serve our needs, no matter how small our state. Also, no matter how urban or rural our neighborhood, we get about the same amount of representation in the House as any other citizen. Of course, the quality of that representation will not be uniform, but each citizen is counted as a member of a standard bloc of voters. Each bloc in the nation consists of about one-half million citizens. No matter where we live, our bloc gets one representative in the House. *That* is balance.

Balance Among Three Branches.   The balancing act, however, is far more complex than merely that involved in the legislature. Of the three branches of government, Congress is only one. The executive branch is headed by the president. Judicial power is vested in the court system, topped by the Supreme Court. These round out the three-way scale.

The relationship of one branch to the other is maintained by a system of checks and balances found in the Constitution. These checks and balances exist to control the power of government. They prevent the power from becoming concentrated in any individual or any branch of government. This system was established because of the fear of the framers that one person or one state or one group of states would get too much power.[5] The fears were well founded, but the system worked.

The system of checks and balances is quit simple. Each of the three branches has a check—a limit or control—over another, creating a balance. There are many examples. While Congress has the power to make laws, the president has the power to block, or veto, bills passed by Congress. But to check the president's veto power, Congress has the power to override a veto. Besides this, the Supreme Court has the power to declare a law void, even though the other two branches approved it. In fact, the Supreme Court can declare any action of the other two branches (or of the states) to be unconstitutional. These checks make it unlikely that one person or one small group will gain control over the vital lawmaking process of our country.

There are other examples. The president can appoint judges, ambassadors, and other high officials. The president can make treaties. But the Senate must approve such actions. The president is commander in chief of the armed forces. What power! But the president must ask Congress for the money and soldiers needed.

LEGISLATURE: A body of people invested with power to make, revise, and repeal statutes and other ordinary laws.

EXECUTIVE BRANCH: The branch of government responsible for executing the laws, supervising the civil and military administration, and managing foreign relations.

JUDICIAL POWER: The power to hear and decide cases and controversies in accordance with the forms and procedures prescribed by the law of the land to render judgment consistent with the provisions of law.

CHECKS AND BALANCES: Separate branches of American government are given legal powers by which they can check one another and thereby maintain a balance in which no branch can consistently override another.

TREATY: A solemn agreement or compact between two or more sovereign states for the purpose of creating, altering, or extinguishing mutual rights and reciprocal obligations; in the United States, treaties are negotiated under the direction of the president and must be ratified by a two-thirds vote of the Senate.

The Supreme Court Building in Washington, D.C. The inscription on the front of the building reads "Equal Justice Under Law."

REAPPORTIONMENT: A new apportionment, i.e., the determination by law of the number of representatives which a state, county, or other subdivision may send to a legislative body; the Constitution provides for a census every ten years, on the basis of which Congress apportions representatives according to popultion, but each state must have one representative.

And the commander cannot declare war; only Congress can do that. These and many other checks serve to balance the power of the three branches of our government. The Constitution even works within one branch, Congress, to balance the power of the large states and the small states. It was written with the intent of giving power to more populous states through the House of Representatives. Assigning two senators from each state regardless of size protected states having smaller populations.

The 1960s saw a series of Supreme Court decisions affecting the balance of power in the nation. The case of *Baker v. Carr* (1962)[6] and later *Reynolds v. Sims* (1964),[7] provided that both houses of state legislatures be based substantially on population. In other words, "one man, one vote." According to this reasoning, one group of people will have no more representation than any other. This aims to provide balance among voting districts.

An example used in the *Baker v. Carr* suit shows the need for such balancing among voting districts. Prior to this time rural areas around the nation had been given more than their fair share of representation. The smallest legislative district of the lower house in Tennessee had a population of 3,400, while the largest district had 79,000 people. This gave each of the 79,000 people a much smaller piece of the representative power than any member of the 3,400–person district. While this was an extreme case, in 1960 the largest district of every state in the union had at least twice the population of its smallest.

The same problem was found in congressional districts. Some districts had much more representation than others. A rural district in Georgia included 272,000 people, an urban one had 823,000. The Supreme Court's job was to balance the strength of these districts. The Court ruled (*Wesberry v. Sanders*) that the sizes of these Georgia districts were in violation of the Constitution.

These and other Supreme Court decisions have had a big impact on the legislative branch. Because of those decisions, voting districts have been reapportioned. That is, the boundary lines of voting districts have been redrawn to balance the districts' weights. This has been done for congressional districts as well as for state legislatures.

There have been other effects of these court decisions on the state level. Some states had used two legislative houses. One house was supposed to be based on population, the other on territory or a political basis. The Court decisions required a change in the representation of both houses in such states. New Jersey has a two-house system in which the senate, or upper house, was in the past based on county representation. Today, as a result of the one-man-one-vote decisions, the senate of that state is still elected by counties, but the number of senators from each county reflects its population.

The U.S. Senate remains untouched by these decisions, and it will probably not be affected by them in the future. The reason for this is that the Constitution fixes the Senate's representation, and it is difficult to see how the Supreme Court could find the Constitution unconstitutional. An amendment to the Constitution changing the base of senatorial representation is unlikely because senators from less populous states could block such a move.

The Electoral College: Does It Help Balance?   The framers of the Constitution intended that the power of the presidency be strictly limited. They wanted to make sure that some very strong politician did not win the office and dominate the other branches with personal and political power. To help prevent this, the president must gain office through a popular election. That is, the popular vote would check the power of the presidency by selecting and rejecting candidates every four years.

POPULAR VOTE: The vote of the qualified voters as distinguished from that of the electoral college.

Many of the framers had little trust in the voting public. It was feared that the public would make unwise choices and allow a scoundrel to win the presidency, perhaps upsetting the balance of power among the three branches. How could the people control the presidency, yet be controlled themselves in their decision-making?

The framers' answer was the electoral college. In practice, the voters select the electors, who vote as the voters wish. Yet, in theory and in fact, the electors in the electoral college could well elect a president who lost the popular election.

ELECTORAL COLLEGE: Any body of electors, limited in number, meeting in one place to choose a public official; the Constitution provides for fifty-one presidential electoral colleges, or one in each state and one in the District of Columbia; each electoral college (whose members are popularly chosen) meets in its respective state capital and votes separately for president and vice-president.

In an attempt to provide direct election of the president, the House passed a proposed constitutional amendment to do away with the electoral college in September 1969. Due to a filibuster in the Senate, that house was prevented from voting on the measure. The possibility of someone's being named president without gaining a majority of popular votes remains as long as the electoral college procedure is part of our elective process.

FILIBUSTER: A means of delaying action on a bill in the Senate by time-consuming speeches in the attempt to prevent passage of the bill.

Perhaps today the framers would trust the voting public to choose its presidents wisely, without electors. After all, we are better educated, and the mass media keep us well informed. Electronic inventions have made direct elections feasible. This could prevent any truly drastic change of the electoral college.

Federalism

The framers of the Constitution grappled with the difficult task of balancing the power within the national government, and they created several ways of solving the problem. But they faced still another balancing problem, this one involving the states and the central, national government.

FEDERALISM: A type of political organization which allows independent states to combine under a central government while maintaining their identity and some power.

The States Versus Washington.   Two centers of power evolved: the state—to deal with and control matters of an essentially local nature; and the federal—to deal with matters of national concern.

The powers delegated to Congress are listed in Article I, Section VIII, of the Constitution. At this point we are able to see where the power of the nation really lies. Only Congress had the power to tax, borrow, coin money, regulate foreign and interstate commerce, protect the coinage and currency from counterfeiters,

DELEGATION OF POWER: The transfer of authority by some organ or branch of government in which such authority constitutionally reposes in some other organ or branch or in an administrative agency.

IMPLIED POWERS: Powers not granted in express terms but existing because they are necessary and proper to carry into effect some expressly granted power.

establish uniform rules of bankruptcy, and to insure copyrights and patents. The powers mentioned thus far are all clearly economic. Many observers see the prime intent of the Constitution as being an economic regulator.[8] Other powers delegated for Congress lie in the right to establish post offices and post roads, regulate naturalization of citizens, constitute federal courts (inferior to the Supreme Court), declare war, support armies, punish piracy, maintain a navy, arm, organize, discipline, and call out the militia for internal strife and invasion, and control the District of Columbia. The Congress is charged also with the creation of all laws needed to execute all powers vested by the Constitution in the government of the United States.

Section VIII has been interpreted in various ways in recent years. It should be noted that while Congress alone can declare war, some presidents have engaged our armed forces in conflicts without a declaration of war. Examples of these actions which remain fresh in our minds are the Korean conflict or police action, the Lebanese ventures, the Dominican crisis, and the Cuban fiasco. Our troops did not land in Cuba, but our government was involved in training, equipping, and transporting the invasion force. (U.S. Marines were present in transport ships offshore.) In numerous other instances our troops have been stationed in what is called an "advisory capacity." By not declaring war and by referring to a war with such euphemisms as a "police action," the executive branch of the government has ignored the intentions of the Constitution.

Section IX deals with the various powers denied Congress with regard to the states. Congress was forbidden to levy taxes or duties on exports or to give preferential treatment to the parts of one state over another.

Article I, Section X, of the Constitution expressly limits the powers of individual states in their relationships to the central government and with foreign governments. The states are forbidden to enter into treaties, alliances, or confederations. They may not engage in any independent act of war, nor may they issue their own money. They may not create import and export duties or maintain naval units or troops. This section of the Constitution places the states in a position subordinate to the central government.

In addition to those powers clearly granted to the federal government, many other powers are judged to be "implied." Implied power derives from the phrase "deemed necessary and proper" for the execution of the delegated powers. Federal power has grown tremendously through the interpretation of implied powers. For example, federal power over labor-management relations was judged to be implied from the powers awarded to "regulate commerce among the several states." The right of the federal government to charter national banks was implied from the delegated monetary powers. Indeed, the entire complex of federal aid programs has been considered to be implied from the powers of Congress to spend for the "general welfare of the United States." It would be wrong to assume that no one has opposed this use of implied powers. Many of the states have criticized this means of increasing the power of the federal government.[9] Some representatives of such states worry that the Constitution makes so little mention of the states' powers that the states will not be able to protect their interests. Various states have taken issue with federal government activities in the mid-eighties. Already mentioned, the forcing of the drinking age to 21, and maintenance of the 55 mph speed limit by threat of withholding federal highway funds are two such issues. An issue of greater import has brought the question of states' rights to center stage. National Guard troops have been considered state militia. As state troops, they are, except in time of war or other emergency, under the control of the various states and their governors. In recent years, and specifically 1986, National Guard units have been sent, as part of their active training period, to serve in Central America. The nation is not at war and the Guard has not been federalized, yet these units have been serving in a war zone in combat situations. The complaint of the governors of those states whose units have been involved is that the federal government has no right to use state militia in this manner without federalization of the troops.

While the powers of the federal government are either clearly stated or implied in the Constitution, the states' powers are given in a negative manner. The Tenth Amendment to the Constitution says: "The powers not delegated to the United States by the Constitution, nor prohibited by it to the states, are reserved to the states respectively, or to the people." It is clear that the larger the body of implied power becomes, the smaller the power reserved to the states.

The increasing power of the central government at the expense of the states has been accomplished largely through the decisions of the Supreme Court. This erosion of power has been encouraged by the interpretation of the "Supremacy Clause." This clause states that federal power is supreme over state power when the federal government is using its delegated or implied powers. The U.S. Constitution is, of course, superior to the state constitutions, and federal laws to state laws.

The present relationship of the states to the federal government is certainly a far cry from the past. At the time of the nation's birth, each of the states was indeed an individual and sovereign unit unto itself. The Constitution of the United States worked to change thirteen small separate and distinct sovereignties into one nation having one law and one government. This was done through the framework called federalism.

Advantages and Disadvantages of Federalism. In many cases, the advantages and disadvantages of federalism are the same. This concept is not too difficult if viewed through the example of an old pun. A bachelor asked his friend, a married man, to list the advantages and disadvantages of marriage. The married man answered that the prime advantage was that he came home every evening to the same loving wife. The prime disadvantage, he mentioned, was that he came home every evening to the *same* loving wife.

In this manner, we may say that the advantages of federalism are also its disadvantages, often for the same reasons. The presence of both central and local governments allows the states to slow or impede federal power. In some instances this duality may be good; in other instances it can be bad.

The value of this duality depends entirely upon the viewpoint from which one regards the issue in question. The states impeded the progress of civil rights legislation. This action would be considered wrong by a civil rights advocate, but someone on the other side of the argument would applaud it. Frequently, some states are more liberal than the central government, and we may find ourselves on the other side of state/central government issue.

In federalism, the two sets of governments act as checks and balances on one another. For example, some state governments were more progressive than the central government concerning the election of senators. Twenty-nine states allowed the popular election of senators even before the Constitution was changed to require such actions. There are other examples of this kind of thing. Women were allowed to vote in some states before the Constitution was changed to order it in all states. And many states had abolished slavery prior to federal action on that matter.

Also, it is good to have separate sets of laws in the states. States can copy a good law adopted by another state. There is room for inventing new laws. The adoption of certain laws by most states might also force the central government to act in areas that it had neglected. On the other hand, if a state maintains or passes laws that are repressive or disliked by its people, they have the option of moving elsewhere.

Here we may consider various marriage laws that concern most people. Certain states had in the past not allowed the following:

1. Marriage between races
2. Abortion
3. Divorce (in this case, divorce procedures were such that divorce was almost impossible in many states)

The rules concerning marriage between the races have been overturned by the federal government. The laws against abortion were first changed in individual states, and then federal action was demanded. Divorce procedures remain the province of the individual states. Citizens of certain states have often traveled to more liberal states for their divorces. For many years Nevada was a favorite resort area used for this purpose. Young couples are always aware of the nearest state allowing marriage of people considered underage in their home state. These differing marriage laws remain, because of our federal system of government.

Differences among states have their good and bad points. A bad point is that reforms needed across the nation can sometimes be blocked by the states. A prime example of this is the attempts by the federal government to change state laws concerning the use of child labor. The states involved wished to continue using child labor without restrictions. After all, it was good for their economies. Goods produced using child labor were cheaper than goods produced by adults. By restricting the flow of goods produced by child labor across state lines, the Congress attempted to enforce the child-labor ban. Congress argued that once across state lines the products became subject to regulation under the interstate commerce clause of the Constitution. At first, this argument was struck down by the Supreme Court. Later it was reinterpreted. The uncontrolled use of child labor continues in the agricultural industry of the nation, because politicians find it difficult to ignore the farm vote and economic realities.

Increasing Federal Power.   Several basic needs have recently increased federal power. More and more, these needs have required resources beyond those of any one state. The states have had to turn to the federal government for solutions.

The Great Depression, which began in 1929, showed the states' weakness in dealing with such mammoth economic and social problems. In all fairness, it can be pointed out that the general attitude of government prior to this disaster was one of "grin and bear it." The federal government gained the power to tax income on a grand scale with Constitutional Amendment XVI, in 1913. This action left little real money available to the states that faced immediate and new needs. The tax systems available to most states are regressive in nature, and they do not produce enough money to solve their problems.

The states have faced urban decay and population growth. They have felt strain on their welfare agencies due to uncontrolled internal movements of people. Urban centers have spread across state lines. Water resources, which reach across several states, must be controlled and conserved. These are only a few of the problems that states face. These ugly realities have become monstrous problems. The states often have too little power or money to solve such problems. Their programs have folded under the pressure in many cases, leaving it to the federal government to take over.

Federal control has also grown with the central government's power to tax the citizens of the states and to distribute such money. To receive this money, states are bound by any requirement demanded by the central government. These requirements may differ entirely from those otherwise used in the receiving states. In the area of civil rights, a state may be forced to conform to patterns of hiring in conflict with local custom. The states have a clear-cut choice: They may conform to government regulations or forego the money.

Because most states depend entirely upon federal money to remain solvent, they are usually forced to follow regulations contrary to those they practice. The states are even bound to federal regulations for the distribution of money collected in tax revenues from their own citizens. On top of that, many states receive amounts lower than those collected.

The use of revenue-sharing was an attempt to reverse this flow of state power to federal jurisdiction. This plan allowed federal funds to flow to the states with no strings attached. This plan was not without problems, but most of them were centered in the states themselves. The states gave more political weight to the sparsely populated rural areas than to the urban ones. Because of this, federal guidelines that had been important in recent years would no longer carry any import. This could have led to a period of regressive action in areas of interstate commerce and civil rights.

With the shrinking of revenue sharing, the states seem in even worse financial situation because the total amount of federal dollars returned to the states has been effectively reduced.

In conclusion, we have a dual system of government: federal and state. The areas of control and power have tended to shift toward federal control, with some attempts to stay this tendency. Both good points and bad points are involved in the parallel existence of the two levels, and most of what is considered good or bad is a matter of personal or regional opinion.[10]

AMENDMENTS TO THE CONSTITUTION

Many people have been impressed by the wisdom and good sense found in the Constitution. It was and still is an admirable document. But it was written over two hundred years ago. While it is indeed flexible, it was found at times to fall short of the nation's needs. Fortunately the framers saw that there would be times when the document would need amendments, or additions.

Skill Reinforcer 21-2
What possible author bias is there here?

Article V of the Constitution outlines the methods for passing amendments. In essence, it requires that two-thirds of both houses propose an amendment. Then three-fourths of the states, or conventions in three-fourths of the states, must ratify the proposed amendment within a certain time period to allow it to become part of the Constitution. An alternative course allows the legislatures of two-thirds of the states to request that Congress call a constitutional convention for the purpose of proposing amendments to the Constitution. When three-fourths of the states' legislatures ratify the proposed amendment, it becomes part of the Constitution. This latter course has never been used (the state of South Carolina called a convention in relation to its Civil War difficulties.) It is dangerous for politicians in general and for the status quo in particular to open a constitutional convention that might let loose all the surprises of a Pandora's box.

The Bill of Rights

The first ten amendments to the United States Constitution are known as the Bill of Rights. Although our amendments deal with the rights of citizens, the citizens most often refer to the first ten, which they know best. While these rights have been considered basic to the freedoms enjoyed by Americans, they have been changed by interpretation and implication.

The Bill of Rights was added as part of a political trade-off. This was needed because the battle for the acceptance of the Constitution was uphill. In fact, its promoters had reason to fear that it would never be approved by enough of the states. To make matters worse, another political faction feared that the Constitution created a government so strong that it would trample the rights of the people. Because of these pressures, the promoters of the Constitution promised to pass a Bill of Rights later. This document would guarantee in writing the rights everyone seemed to assume were due the people.

The first ten amendments were proposed by Congress to the states in 1789. They were approved by three-fourths (the required number) of the states by December 15, 1791, fully three and a half years after the Constitution had passed the same test.

When people claim a "right" to something, they usually, if asked about the basis of the claim, refer to one of the first ten amendments. But do people indeed have that right? Here is the bill or statement of the rights to which people so often refer. It defines which rights may be legally claimed in our nation.

1. Congress shall make no law respecting an establishment of religion, or prohibiting the free exercise thereof; or abridging the freedom of speech, or of the press; or the right of the people peaceably to assemble, and to petition the Government for a redress of grievances.
2. A well-regulated militia being necessary to the security of a free State, the right of the people to keep and bear arms shall not be infringed.
3. No soldier shall, in time of peace, be quartered in any house, without the consent of the owner, nor in time of war, but in a manner to be prescribed by law.
4. The right of the people to be secure in their persons, houses, papers, and effects, against unreasonable searches and seizures, shall not be violated, and no warrants shall issue, but upon probable cause, supported by oath or affirmation, and particularly describing the place to be searched, and the persons or things to be seized.
5. No person shall be held to answer for a capital or other infamous crime, unless on a presentment or indictment of a Grand Jury, except in cases arising in the land or naval forces, or in the militia, when in actual service in time of war or public danger; nor shall any person be subject for the same offense to be twice put in jeopardy of life or limb; nor shall be compelled in any criminal case to be a witness against himself, nor be deprived of life, liberty, or property, without due process of law; nor shall private property be taken for public use without just compensation.

GRAND JURY: A body of from twelve to twenty-three people who are summoned to a court to hear witnesses presented on behalf of the state and, after deliberating in secret and by a majority vote, to return indictments or make presentments against all people whom they find just cause to hold for trial.

DUE PROCESS: Legal restrictions confining the government "within the limits of those fundamental principles of liberty and justice which lie at the base of all our civil and democratic institutions."

6. In all criminal prosecutions, the accused shall enjoy the right to a speedy and public trial, by an impartial jury of the State and district wherein the crime shall have been previously ascertained by law, and to be informed of the nature and cause of the accusation; to be confronted with the witnesses against him; to have compulsory process for obtaining witnesses in his favor, and to have the assistance of counsel for his defense.

7. In suits at common law, where the value in controversy shall exceed twenty dollars, the right of trial by jury shall be preserved, and no fact tried by a jury shall be otherwise reexamined in any court of the United States than according to the rules of the common law.

8. Excessive bail shall not be required, nor excessive fines imposed, nor cruel and unusual punishments inflicted.

9. The enumeration in the Constitution of certain rights shall not be construed to deny or disparage others retained by the people.

10. The powers not delegated to the United States by the Constitution, nor prohibited by it to the States, are reserved to the States respectively, or to the people.

The First Amendment mandates freedom of religion, the press, speech, assembly, and petition. Each of the rights guaranteed by the First Amendment has come under fire in recent years. The pressures governmental agencies apply to the press are examples of these attacks. In the early 1970s, reporters were jailed for protecting sources, and comedians were pressured off the air. Also rulings dealt with equal time provisions to be applied against editorial comment. The press has been denounced publicly by the executive branch in a manner that strikes a reader of the First Amendment as shocking. The right of free and peaceful assembly has also come under fire in numerous instances. These issues arose in relation to antiwar and civil-rights protests.

The Second Amendment gives the people the right to keep and bear arms. This freedom has been abridged in many states. There are two opposing views concerning these laws. The various bills to limit and/or control the ownership of guns deal with the right to life, liberty, and the pursuit of happiness. The many millions of guns floating around in the United States deprive many people of the right to life each year. The other side of the argument cites even the registration of guns as an attack on the constitutional right to keep and bear arms. It is clear that if we do not want our citizens bearing side arms in order to walk the streets at night, some control over the sale and ownership of firearms is needed.

The Third Amendment is concerned with lodging soldiers in private homes. This was a sore point in colonial times, when British troops were forced on frontier households. We are no longer threatened by such action.

The Fourth Amendment has been the subject of many court cases. Many of the rulings have weakened the effect of this amendment. It clearly guarantees freedom from unreasonable searches. Automobiles are stopped at checkpoints, without probable cause, to test the drivers for intoxication. Other vehicles are stopped for drug searches and we are threatened with the dreaded specimen bottle. Good, bad, right, wrong, for safety, or for what is perceived as the public good, these searches and invasions of our rights are not in keeping with the intent of the amendment. Such activities may have been illegal in the eyes of the framers of the Constitution.

The Fifth Amendment is probably the best known of all the amendments because of its use at television trials and hearings. Its most important aspects are the protections given to people accused of crime. The "due process clause" is responsible for many cases brought to the Supreme Court. In fact, this clause may well be the most important of the guarantees provided by the Constitution. It states that a person cannot be deprived of life, liberty, or property without due process of law. We are also protected by this amendment from self-indictment, that is, people need not testify against themselves. The Fifth Amendment protects citizens from being tried twice for the same offense. We cannot be tried or jailed without charge by a grand jury, though people are now jailed for refusing to testify while before a grand jury.

The Sixth Amendment is supportive of the Fifth. It describes the process we are due when accused of a crime. It outlines the way in which charges must be processed. This amendment guarantees us a speedy and public trial. But lawyers often use delay tactics, and the courts are clogged with cases. Many people, innocent or guilty, sit for months in jail awaiting trial. Indeed, it is possible for a person to sit in jail for a year, then go at last to trial and be declared innocent.

The Seventh Amendment also mandates trial by jury and adherence to common law by the federal courts of the nation.

The Eighth Amendment forbids the use of excessive bail, fines, or cruel and unusual punishments. But who is to say what is excessive or cruel? This is a matter of opinion of the officials involved. Bail set at $500,000 may be excessive for you, but not for a wealthy drug dealer. Also, there are endless arguments on whether the death penalty is cruel and unusual. Both sides of this question are hotly debated. A basic issue is respect for human life. But which life? One side would protect the life of the person convicted. The other would confirm the value of the victim's life by taking that of the killer. Besides this issue, there is the one concerning deterrence. The death penalty has not been proven to deter murder, says one side. The other side responds that, even if this is so, it prevents the murderer from ever striking again, even inside prison. These arguments over this part of the Eighth Amendment show how the Constitution can bend in response to social attitudes as they change over time.

The Ninth and Tenth Amendments deal with rights retained by the people and the states. The Ninth Amendment makes the point that rights enjoyed by the people shall not be limited only to those spelled out in the Constitution. The Tenth Amendment states that powers not given to the federal government or prohibited by the Constitution are reserved for the states and the people. This was needed to maintain the position and powers of the states when the Constitution was written.

Other Amendments

After the addition of the first ten amendments guaranteeing the people's basic rights, other issues arose. Some were merely technical changes that had become necessary. Others involved rights that were established by the changing values of the nation.

Amendments Eleven (1798) and *Twelve* (1804) were corrections made to allow the fluid operation of the Constitution. Amendment Eleven changed Article II, Section II, and placed suits against states in the states' own courts. Amendment Twelve replaced Article II, Section I, dealing with the election of the president. This amendment states that electors voting for the president and vice-president must specify who is to receive a vote, and for which office.

No amendments to the Constitution were made between the years 1804 and 1865. The end of the Civil War brought *Amendments Thirteen, Fourteen,* and *Fifteen* in response to the conditions of the day. *Amendment Thirteen* (1865) prohibited slavery. *Amendment Fourteen* (1868) was directed against the states and people fighting in the Civil War on the side of the Confederacy. *Amendment Fifteen* (1870) awarded the right to vote to citizens regardless of race, color, or previous condition of servitude (slavery). This amendment did *not* give women the right to vote.

There were no further amendments until 1913, when they began occurring with some regularity. *Amendment Sixteen* (1913) is important to all citizens of the United States. It gives Congress the right to direct taxation. Direct taxation is in plain terms the federal income tax. This power has allowed the federal government to supplant the states decisively in their seesaw battle for control of the nation.

Although twenty-nine states had already allowed the direct popular election of senators, the *Seventeenth Amendment* (1913) was added to the Constitution to provide that such elections be the law of the land. Prior to this time, state legislatures were empowered to appoint U.S. senators without popular election. This amendment was a major step away from elitism and political abuse.

The Eighteenth (1919) and *Twenty-first* (1933) *Amendments* may be considered together since they deal, with, first, the prohibition of intoxicating liquors and, later, the repeal of this prohibition. Prohibition is a good example of a law that failed because the vast majority of people felt that it interfered with their personal freedom.

The Nineteenth Amendment (1920) awarded women the right to vote. Prior to this time only nine states allowed women this right.

The Equal Rights Amendment, if it had been ratified by the required number of states, would have given women equal rights in all matters. That would have provided an interesting period for

PROHIBITION (1919–1933) (Const. Amends. 18 and 21): The public policy of entirely forbidding, by national or state law or constitutional amendment, the manufacture, transportation, or sale of intoxicating beverages except for medicinal or scientific purposes.

our nation. We could have faced issues such as drafting women, giving equal child-custody rights after a divorce, and denying rights to alimony, among other equalities.

The Twentieth (1933) and *Twenty-second* (1951) *Amendments* deal with dates of taking office and length of presidential terms.

The Twentieth Amendment (1933) shortens the "lame duck" period after elections and before the new Congress is sworn in, while the *Twenty-second Amendment* (1951) limits presidential tenure to two full terms. If a vice-president assumed the office of President and served more than two years of an unexpired term, he cannot run for a second term on his own. A limit of ten years is thus set for a person holding the office of President.

The Twenty-third Amendment (1961) gives the residents of Washington, D.C., the right to vote in presidential elections.

The Twenty-fourth Amendment (1964) allows citizens to vote even though they have failed to pay their taxes. This mandate is somewhat more complex and far-reaching than it might appear. Many states maintained a system of poll taxes. By denying people the right to pay those taxes, the state in effect prevented them from voting. In many cases, the presence of the tax itself was enough to bar many people from exercising their right to vote.

The Twenty-fifth Amendment (1967) allows a president the right to step aside temporarily without resigning, for health or other reasons. It also provides for the temporary removal of a disabled president, with or without presidential approval. The lines of presidential succession are more clearly drawn. The president may nominate a replacement for the vice-president, who shall take that office after receiving a majority vote of both houses of Congress.[11]

This wide-ranging amendment may have serious consequences at some future date. The ability to remove a president by means other than impeachment (as provided within the body of the Constitution) could haunt the nation. The reason for the amendment is clear. In recent years, assassinations and severe illnesses have plagued the presidency. The specter of a president felled by a stroke, yet remaining in office while incapable of fulfilling presidential duties, has given cause for alarm. During the presidency of Woodrow Wilson, this actually occurred, leaving the Executive Office unofficially in the hands of Mrs. Wilson. While the intent of the amendment is clear, the possibility of misuse also exists. This potential could result in the removal of an honest, healthy, qualified president through a political power play.

The Twenty-sixth Amendment (1971) acted to lower the voting age from twenty-one to eighteen years. This action was a response to the demand of those who were being drafted to fight in Vietnam but not allowed to vote. The issue was summed up in the saying "If I'm old enough to fight, I'm old enough to vote." In a period of political activism this logic was effective.

The Reagan Administration's Domestic Policy Council noted the eroding of states' rights in favor of federal power, and may recommend a constitutional amendment designed to return power to the various states. The report was an attack on *Baker v. Carr* and *Roe v. Wade* (1973, overturning abortion laws), and on the concept of judicial policy making. This is a broad attack on civil rights, wage controls, and other federal guidelines and regulations.[12]

This brief picture of the Constitution shows how its relationship to the individual, the state, and the nation is ever-changing. Still, the document has helped keep those relationships somewhat stable. The flexibility of the document in response to changing social conditions of the present as well as the future remains to be seen.

Having a constitution protects us, but it can sometimes get in the way when action is needed, and amendments usually come slowly. Not too many years ago, a United Nations call for a worldwide treaty against genocide was not signed by the United States. We did not sign, because the treaty allowed an outside authority to enforce the agreement. Our Constitution, however, is the "supreme law of the land" and allows no higher authority over its people. President Jimmy Carter was at the time the most recent in a long line of presidents to recommend that our nation sign this treaty. The Constitution must be amended further if we are to participate actively in any meaningful form of world government.

Perhaps the Constitution, like Robert's Rules of Order, was meant to delay hasty action. It may be that the delay provisions built into the Constitution are there to allow second and third thoughts concerning actions that could do more harm than good. For the present, the document is flexible enough to deal with most situations that will occur. The reinterpretations will continue and, like the Argus, they may reach through amendment a point where no part of the original meaning remains.

SUMMARY

A Constitution serves as a contract between the government and the people of a nation. The possession of such a contract means little if the parties to that agreement fail to uphold the terms of the agreement. In the United States we are fortunate to have a contract that guarantees essential liberties to the people, and doubly fortunate that the terms of the contract are upheld.

The roots of our Constitution lie in Great Britain. John Locke put forth the ideas of natural rights and power to the people. This, together with the English heritage brought here by the first settlers, laid the foundation of our form of government. The Articles of Confederation failed because they produced a government that was too weak. They were replaced by the Constitution.

The framers of the Constitution had to decide on how much power would be held by the states (versus the central government) and by the masses (versus the elite). To accomplish these ends, the document had to be flexible and had to balance power wisely. It also provided stable governmental transition, something rarely found elsewhere.

The Constitution contains means of balancing power within Congress and among the three branches of the government. In the latter case, the main means is a system of checks and balances. The electoral college was intended as a device through which the decisions of the masses would be filtered. Though it has outlived its usefulness, there is little chance that it will be changed.

Federalism balances the power between the states and the central government. This system works, though not without a good bit of friction. One source of friction is the increase in the power of the central government.

Our Constitution is not static. It provides change through considered amendment. Nor is the Constitution so easy to change that its terms have become meaningless.

SPECIAL TOPIC

The Constitution As It Is Affected by Our Supreme Court

The makeup and philosophy of the majority of the Supreme Court of the United States have a tremendous influence on each of us. We can look back through the history of the nation and point to several Courts that have served as pivotal points.

The Marshall Court (1801–1835) gave us nationalism, which was reaffirmed by the Civil War. Prior to the Civil War, the first ten amendments to the Constitution of the United States were considered federal law, which meant that the individual states did not have to honor these provisions. The Civil War should have settled the question of the autonomy of the individual states in relation to the national government. In fact, for over one hundred years most Americans thought the question was a dead issue.

In recent years, the Burger Court, with William Rehnquist as its spokesperson, has sought to reestablish the rights of the individual states. If the Warren Court (1953–1969) was thought to espouse equality, the "Rehnquist" Court can be considered to promote states' rights and property rights.

The March 10, 1982, issue of *The New Republic* contained an article entitled "The Rehnquist Court," written by Owen Fiss, professor of law at the Yale Law School, and Charles Krauthammer, senior editor of *The New Republic*. The authors outline the manner in which the Supreme Court is moving in a recognizable direction. As we have mentioned, other courts in other times have changed the direction of our life in the United States.

Let us turn our attention to the present and try to forecast our future. This future is really an extention of the present in that the tone for the 1980s Court would seem to be increasingly conservative. The newer justices are young and conservative, and the five older justices, while more liberal, are in their mid-seventies. We are not talking about the conservatism of former Justice John Harlan, or what has been termed "strict constructionism." There would appear to be a tendency away from the incorporation doctrine.

Prior to the Civil War, the Bill of Rights limited only the action of the national government, but the amendments to the Constitution associated with the Civil War changed our nation's legal direction. Fiss points directly to the Fourteenth Amendment as placing far-reaching restrictions on the states. He points to the section that forbade states to "abridge the privilege and immunities of citizens of the United States" or to "deprive any person of life, liberty, or property, without due process of law or to deny to any person within its jurisdiction the equal protection of the laws." These statements have been interpreted as incorporating most of the protections of the Bill of Rights and making them directly applicable to the various states. In other words, the Fourteenth Amendment specifically pointed the way around the legal objections to the application of the Bill of Rights on a state level. Fiss notes that Rehnquist generally acknowledges "that the states are formed by the generalities of the Fourteenth Amendment." Rehnquist feels that "the Bill of Rights is not to be used as a measure of compliance."

This is not a matter to be taken lightly. As Americans we have become accustomed to the protection offered us by our Constitution and the Bill of Rights. Many Americans are young enough to have experienced only the liberal interpretations of the Constitution, like those of the Warren Court. The movement over the years has been away from protection of property in favor of the protection of individual rights.

Fiss points to a 1976 action of the Supreme Court as a turning point. In that year a suit charging a pattern of police abuse of minorities in Philadelphia was dismissed. This case, *Rizzo v. Goode,* also sought structural reform and an internal disciplinary system to reduce the chance of future abuses. The precedent for hearing this case, and for the expected decision was *Brown v. Board of Education* (1954), which set the pattern for federal intervention in school segregation cases and said that the federal courts are the primary guardian of federal constitutional rights.

The Rehnquist action in *Rizzo v. Goode* was dismissal. The opinion stated that no federal court should oversee the operation of a state agency—in effect a reversal of *Brown v. Board of Education.* By dismissing this case, the Supreme Court turned its back to the state courts. There is quite a difference between the detachment of the Supreme Court of the United States, where justices are appointed for life, and the political necessities of state court justices, who are dependent on reappointment, reelection, or approval of the local legal community. The dismissal of *Rizzo v. Goode* was another move in the direction of state autonomy.

In other areas, the power of Congress was trimmed. The case of *Pennhurst State School v. Aulderman* dealt with a 1975 congressional statute that gave money to the state for the mentally retarded and codified the rights of the institutionalized mentally retarded. This bill of rights for the mentally retarded had no legal force, said Rhenquist, because Congress had not specifically invoked the power of Section V of the Fourteenth Amendment, which allows Congress to enforce its provisions by legislation. Rehnquist interprets Section V as an infringement on the states' autonomy. Even though it has been accepted that Congress exercises all its power under the Constitution, in a real way the power of Congress has been diminished with respect to the judicial and executive branches of government. Fiss further states that the power of Congress to regulate

gained from the "spending clause" has been diminished by the Rehnquist decision. Under the spending clause it has been assumed that if Congress allocated money it would have the power to impose regulations guiding the spending of that money. Rehnquist has stated that Congress had the power to offer the states a contract. If the states voluntarily and willingly accept the terms of the contract, then they would be liable to the terms. It is unlikely that congressional statutes could set forth each small detail of a contract.

Another bastion of congressional power has been the "commerce clause," which gives the power to regulate interstate commerce. Fiss notes that the Civil Rights Act of 1964 was successful because it prohibited racial discrimination in accommodations using goods that moved in interstate commerce. The Rehnquist decision in *National League of Cities v. Usery* [*] found that the federal statute mandating minimum wages and maximum hours for state and local employees was invalid, because it did not involve interstate commerce.

In summarizing his arguments, Fiss finds that Rehnquist is neither a conservative nor a strict constructionist. He is a "revisionist of a particular ideological bent." Rehnquist is pictured as attempting to look back to 1787 and trying to interpret what was in the minds of the drafters of the Constitution. Fiss notes that Rehnquist may honor the Constitution of 1787 but that he does not honor the legal interpretation and judicial precedents that have occurred since that early date. Fiss goes on to speculate on Rehnquist's inability to distinguish between the Constitution and the Articles of Confederation.

There is a general feeling that the federal government has become too strong and that perhaps its power should be diluted. It should be emphasized, however, that it has been the individual states, rather than the national government, that have over the years been more likely to infringe on the liberties of the individual. In plain terms, the national government has acted to protect our safety in the workplace, our freedom of speech, our right to be secure in our homes, and so forth. With the lessening of the power of individual states, we may once more see a house divided against itself.

* *National League of Cities v. Usery*—reversed by *Garcia v. San Antonio Metropolitan Transit Authority* (1985).

SELF-TEST
QUESTIONS

1. John Locke put forth the ideas of:
   a. natural rights
   b. a life-long presidential term
   c. the people's right to replace a government with a better one
   d. absolute authority of the government
2. The roots of our political heritage lie mostly in:
   a. India
   b. Egypt
   c. England
   d. Israel
3. True or false: The type of government established by the colonists was influenced by the presence of the Atlantic Ocean.
4. True or false: The government created by the Articles of Confederation had to be replaced because it was too strong.
5. The problems facing the framers of the Constitution included:
   a. immigration policy
   b. balancing power between the states and the central government
   c. deciding how much power to give the masses
   d. the issue of whether women should be given the right to vote
6. The framers of the Constitution were, in general:
   a. well-educated
   b. experienced in political affairs
   c. wealthy
   d. all the above
7. A good constitution should be:
   a. flexible
   b. unwritten
   c. long
   d. complex
8. True or false: Peaceful governmental transition is and has always been common.
9. True or false: Each member of the House of Representatives represents about the same number of citizens.
10. The system by which power is balanced among the three branches of our government is called _____.
11. True or false: The electoral college was intended as a filter for the decision-making of the masses in choosing a president.
12. The power of the state is balanced with that of the central government because of the system called _____.
13. In the last few decades, more power has shifted to the:
    a. state governments
    b. county governments
    c. national governments
14. An amendment to the U.S. Constitution can be proposed by:
    a. a majority of the state legislatures
    b. two-thirds of both houses of Congress
    c. a convention called by two-thirds of the states
    d. two-thirds of the voters in a national referendum
15. The first ten amendments to our Constitution are called the _____.

ANSWERS TO
SELF-TEST
QUESTIONS

1. a, c
2. b
3. true
4. false
5. b, c
6. d
7. a
8. false
9. true
10. checks and balances
11. true
12. federalism
13. c
14. b or c
15. Bill of Rights

ANSWERS TO SKILL REINFORCERS

21–1. The opinion is found in the statement "If one part had too much power, abuses might result." The key word is "might." That word makes the sentence a judgment of reality, a belief, rather than an observation of what does happen or has happened. To be a factual statement, the sentence would have to say something like ". . . Abuses have occurred in the past."

21–2. In the first two sentences, the author's tone and words show a very positive feeling toward the Constitution. The word "wisdom," for example, is not an objective one. After all, how is wisdom measured or proved?

NOTES

1. Jacobo Timmerman, *Prisoner Without a Name, Cell Without a Number* (New York: Alfred Knopf, 1981).
2. Gwendolen M. Carter and John H. Herz, *Major Foreign Powers,* 6th ed. (New York: Harcourt Brace Jovanovich, 1972).
3. Andrew C. McLaughlin, *The Confederation and the Constitution* (New York: Collier-Macmillan, 1967).
4. Andrew Gyorgy and George D. Blackwood, *Ideologies in World Affairs* (London: Blaisdell, 1967).
5. McLaughlin, *The Confederation and the Constitution.*
6. *Baker v. Carr,* 369 U.S. 186 (1962).
7. *Reynolds v. Sims,* 377 U.S. 533 (1964).
8. See Charles Beard, *An Economic Interpretation of the United States Constitution* (New York: Macmillan Co., 1935).
9. See *McCulloch v. Maryland,* 4 Wheat. 316 (1819).
10. Daniel J. Eleazar, *American Federalism: A View from the State* (New York: Thomas Y. Crowell, 1972).
11. Milton C. Cummings, Jr., and David Wise, *Democracy Under Pressure,* 2d (New York: Harcourt Brace Jovanovich, 1974).
12. Charles Cooper, *President's Domestic Policy Council Report,* Government Printing Office, 1986.

SUGGESTED READINGS

Beard, Charles. *An Economic Interpretation of the United States Constitution.* New York: Macmillan Co., 1935.

Eleazar, Daniel J. *American Federalism. A View from the States.* New York: Thomas Y. Crowell, 1966.

Hamilton, Alexander; Madison, James; and Jay, John. *The Federalist Papers.* Edited by Clinton Rossiter. New York: New American Library, 1961.

Jensen, Merrill. *The Making of the American Constitution.* New York: Van Nostrand-Reinhold, 1964.

Leach, Richard H. *American Federalism.* New York: W.W. Norton, 1970.

Murphy, Paul L. *Constitution in Crisis Times. 1918–1969.* New York: Harper & Row, 1972.

Timmerman, Jacobo. *Prisoner Without a Name, Cell Without a Number.* New York: Alfred Knopf, 1981.

White, Theodore H. *America in Search of Itself.* New York: Harper & Row, 1982.

22 POLITICAL POWER IN AMERICA

PREVIEW

"To Siberia, March!!!"

You are a member of an elite guard unit. You have been in the army for fifteen years and are known for your loyalty. Through hard work and blind obedience you have been chosen, one of only hundreds, from one of the largest armies in Europe. Your duty as a member of a guard regiment is to serve and protect the life of the czar and his family. To do this, you have trained and served.

Today your unit will be reviewed by the czar himself. This is a great honor. That the father of all the Russians should spend his time on your unit is honor itself. You and your comrades have polished and practiced for this day.

Ivan the Terrible has found fault with your unit—a dirty button, rifle, or man has displeased the czar. The ruler, the Czar Ivan the Terrible, calls your unit to attention. He then says: "To Siberia, forward, march!" The unit is last seen walking east to Siberia in the middle of winter. It is assumed that the unit marched into the Russian winter without provisions or equipment and died. The czar was an absolute monarch. Absolute monarchs have life-and-death power over their subjects. In the words of an unknown sage, "When the king says jump, his subjects ask only, 'How far?' "

In recent years we have seen some Americans question the actions of government. They have the right to question and the right to disobey an order if that order violates the law. Indeed, disobeying an illegal order is mandated by law. This is a far cry from the power of an absolute monarch.

Throughout history men and women in all societies have sought power. There are people in every city who seek power with all their might. There may well be people in our classroom or our families who want power more than they want anything else in life. Some people hunger for power, lust after it more than they do wealth. They seek power for reasons both noble and frightening. What is this thing desired so much by some people?

Power is easy enough to define. It is the element that causes someone to conform to the wishes or orders of someone else.[1]

It is also easy to see who has power. Attila the Hun had power. The chief or witch doctor of any of a thousand Stone Age tribes had power. The kings of the Middle Ages had power. In our own time generals, dictators, and religious and political leaders have power.

In some cases, power has been absolute. The powerful hold life and death for others in their hands. "Off with his head, hand, or ear," is an order that must be obeyed when the ruler has absolute power. In most cases power is limited, however. These limits are set forth in agreements between a people and the rulers. But those rulers who are given limited power often try to go beyond those limits. When this results in a state of crisis, it tests the strength of modern democratic political forms.[2]

What does all this say about our own leaders' power? What are the limits of that power, and how are they maintained? We saw in Chapter 21 that we live under a system that restricts the personal use of power. The system must correct any abuses of power. The system is established in the form of the Constitution, which acts as a contract between the governed and the governing. Remember also that this system balances the power among the levels of government and within those levels.

In this chapter we will explore power centers of our system. Only one of these centers is part of the government: the bureaucracy. The others are part of the overall system but not the government. The chapter will also describe the patterns of power in our system.

POWER: The ability to get other people to do what one wishes, regardless of the other peoples' wishes.

DICTATORSHIP: a. absolute power vested in one or two people for a strictly limited period during a crisis.
b. absolute power over a state granted to, or seized by, a leader without constitutional limitation.

ABSOLUTE POWER: Power that is unlimited and that may be exercised in an arbitrary manner.

HOLDERS OF POWER IN THE AMERICAN SYSTEM

The President of the United States has power over us. So do members of Congress and the courts. Our governor and our mayor can give us orders too. But the government is only one part of the overall American system of power; there are also the voters, the government bureaucracy, and interest groups.

The Voter

In theory, we the people tell the president and the mayor what we want them to do. That is, in a democracy, the ultimate power rests in the hands of the people. The power of our government leaders flows from the voters. We may give our power to those we elect, and we may also take it away from them. We the people command our leaders. In theory.

THE "BRAINS"

That achieved the Tammany Victory at the Rochester Democratic Convention.

Times have not changed for either party.

Skill Reinforcer 22-1 *

Put this paragraph into a syllogism that begs the question.

Here we will take a closer look at how this "power to the people" system works. What role does the voter play in fact, not just in theory?

Who Votes?   Not all Americans have the right to vote. The right is denied to people who have been convicted of certain criminal offenses. Until recently the voting rights of American Indians and the residents of the District of Columbia were somewhat restricted. Other Americans, including women and persons under specific age requirements, have been denied the right to vote by local custom or rules. In the past, black Americans found many hurdles between themselves and the voting booth. These hurdles have included the poll tax,[3] economic reprisal, literacy tests, and physical abuse. Yet Americans who have had unrestricted voting privileges have not been noted for their use of that privilege. As a result relatively small numbers of actual voters make up "the people" in whom the power is supposed to rest. These voters do not represent the will of the majority of "the people." This pattern of small voter turnout in American elections is referred to as "voter apathy."

This apathy may be based on the feeling that we really have little say in choosing candidates. At times, citizens do get angry about something, demand reform, and support a candidate of their own choosing, but most office seekers are supported by one or the other major political party.

Usually a party's nominee is selected by one of two methods: The party bosses handpick the candidate, or several people compete in a primary election to be the party's candidate. In the first instance, there is little if any input from the members. The powerful members of the party organization decide who their candidate will be. The decision may or may not take place in the famous smoke-filled room, but the method is the same. The second method, the primary election, appears to be more democratic. One problem with this method, however, is that the nominees themselves are chosen by factions of regular party members. Another problem is that, while voting in the general election is light, voting in a primary is even lighter.

Because so few people vote, the masses have allowed a small group to assume great power. It has been said that these elections, as in so many others, the American public faced the choice "Which candidate do I like *least?*" Many Americans vote by choosing what they consider to be the lesser of two evils.

How Voters Choose.   Walking into the voting booth, we face serious choices. Who will we choose as president for the next four years? Who will we choose for senators, representatives, governors, state legislators, or county, township, city, and village officials? What will be our bases for these decisions?

---

* Answers to the Skill Reinforcers appear at the end of the chapter.

SKILL BOX

> ### Propaganda Tricks, Part 1
>
> The ability to detect propaganda devices is a skill that is needed more and more in today's world. Propaganda is communication aimed at persuading people by appealing to the emotions, not to reason. As propaganda methods have become more refined and as more people are reached by mass media, propaganda has become a more powerful tool in swaying the public's attitudes.
>
> Part of the purpose of this book is to equip the readers with thinking skills so they can plot their own course and not be swayed too much by others. Toward this aim, two Skill Boxes will focus on the seven tricks of the propagandist, as described by Alfred McClung Lee and Elizabeth Briant Lee in *The Fine Art of Propaganda* (New York: Octagon Books, 1972). Some of these methods are obvious and easy to spot. Others are quite subtle. All appeal to emotions rather than reason, and we need to learn them so that we will be less likely to be caught unaware by such a method. This Skill Box will deal with three propaganda methods.
>
> One obvious propaganda trick is to attach to some idea or person a bad name or label. By calling something "communist," "misguided," or "racist," for example, a speaker hopes we will reject it without examining its merits. If the label has enough emotion attached to it for us, we may not be able to look past it in order to see the real worth of the person or idea to which the label was applied.
>
> A second propaganda trick is to link something with a positive word. If we are not careful, we might accept some idea simply because it is associated with things such as motherhood, science, or democracy. The propagandist tries to get us to lean in favor of the idea by tying it to such positive words. But remember, to avoid being pushed into accepting something, we must look past such positive words to the worth of the idea itself. We do not want to accept something just because someone calls it "patriotic" or "Christian."
>
> A third propaganda device is to transfer the feelings we have for one thing to some other thing so that we will be more likely to accept the latter. For example, a speaker may display a Bible, or use a giant American flag as a backdrop, in order to transfer our feelings for religion or nation to his or her ideas. The trick is to play on our feelings, to soften us up. As with the first two methods, the aim is to play on our emotions, not our reason. Rather than meeting us fairly and reasonably, the propagandist tries to trick us, to divert us, and, in the end, to persuade us while our mind is not watching.

Most Americans are unable to explain clearly or logically why they have selected one candidate over another. For many people, the candidate's looks are important, or perhaps his or her family is impressive, or a candidate may speak well. Even more mundane reasons can be found. A candidate is black, or not black. A candidate may be Italian, Chinese, Japanese, Jewish, Polish, Afghan, American Indian, Spanish. He is a man, or she is a woman. Equally important to many voters is age, eye color, hair, length of hair, and accent. Such things have nothing to do with the candidates' political value systems, but they may affect the way people vote.

Those who help decide who will run for office know something about how we choose who to vote for. A typical "slate" put forth by a political party will attempt to satisfy the largest blocs of its voting public by race, ethnic group, and region. The Democratic convention in the state of New York will do just that. The party needs an Italian, a WASP, a Jew, a Catholic, and upstate and downstate representation. We are left to wonder if a candidate's values matter at all.

The bland assertions by party leaders that their candidate is feeling around for a new "image" is an indictment of the voting public. Any group of people who will vote for the creation of a public relations firm should devote itself to the more important aspects of daily life, such as choosing an adequate mouthwash or breakfast cereal.

The major issue is whether the public is even looking for able legislators. If it is, does it know enough to choose a qualified person who will represent its views? Our major political parties depend upon the broad-based support of the masses. Unfortunately, it seems that in order to gain this support, they must cloud major issues.

Campaign Tactics.   Obviously no candidate would ever be elected on a program of tight money for the masses. Yet if what is really a program of tight money is called "fiscal responsibility" or "anti-inflationary," the public is likely to buy the candidate. The choice of 5 percent or 20 percent mortgages is rarely mentioned, and candidates who propose 20 percent mortgages in campaign speeches are never heard of after the election. The masses have voted for people who proposed to control inflation by enlarging the pool of the unemployed. They have seen mortgage interest rates rise to double figures in the name of fiscal responsibility.

The choices of the voters are also influenced by privilege awarded to those already in office. These advantages make it far easier to remain in office. Incumbents have cadres of workers ready to help them. These people are dedicated because of "patronage." If an officeholder awards a job to us, we will work to keep that job. People whose jobs are based on the whims of an officeholder do their best to hang on to those jobs. Many political jobholders perform no duties whatsoever. Their positions are referred to as "no show" jobs. Their salaries are paid on time with all the fringe benefits, but the "employee" is never visible. Such people are free to hold other jobs while enjoying the fruits of their political labor.

Incumbent politicians have the power to reward specific blocs of voters. These rewards can include legislative action as well as other help. In return, the voter bloc will give both money and votes to the officeholder.

SLATE: A list of candidates informally agreed on in advance of a primary election, convention, or general election.

FISCAL: Pertaining to finance, especially to problems of public revenue, expenditure, and debt.

INCUMBENT: The holder of an office.

PATRONAGE: The power to make appointments to office, especially when not governed by civil service laws or rules; also the power to grant contracts and various special favors.

Also, if their actions are newsworthy, officeholders remain in the public eye. Such constant public exposure makes the officeholder's name a household word. Most voters are prepared to vote for that which is known.

The fringe benefits some political figures are allowed (at public expense) enable them to better their odds of being reelected. One such privilege is "franking." Franking allows postage-free mail which, in many cases, is used to better an officeholder's image. A letter from a representative conveys a personal relationship to a citizen. When the average citizen finds in the mailbox an official government letter from a representative addressed to him or her personally, the receiver is inflated by the recognition, even though the letter may not say much. There is a good chance that that person will vote for the representative who acknowledged his or her existence, even though it was recognized at public expense.

The Power of the Government's Bureaucracy

Remember how the system is supposed to work? Picture the voters standing at the top of the power system, commanding the government to serve them. Remember that the government's levels and branches are kept in line by the Constitution. The central government and the powers of the states are balanced and limited. Congress, the courts, and the president watch one another to make sure no one branch gains too much power. The government in turn restricts and orders the voters.

One part of this picture for the most part escapes control: the government's bureaucracy. This part of the power system in the United States stands somewhat to the side. Established to carry out the wishes of the voters, the bureaucracy is supposed to put into practice the policies of the officials who are elected by the voters. It is supposed to do most of the actual work of governing. That is, it is supposed to be the servant of the voters. Yet the bureaucracy has itself become a power base, which while not outside the law of the land seems able to rise above the law at times.

While elected officials form a policy, the action on that policy is in the hands of the bureaucrat. Imagine a directive issued by a policy-making level of government. Once the directive disappears into the mass of offices, it may well be lost, sit forever upon a desk, or merely be filed. For inaction of this nature one would expect wholesale firings or reprimands, but this is rarely the case. One of the most difficult things is to fire an entrenched bureaucrat or dismantle an established agency. In bureaucratic circles, it is not unusual for an agency's function to disappear while the agency continues in existence for years beyond that point.

Our federal bureaucracy consists of cabinet departments, agencies, boards, and commissions created by government. Examples are the Federal Trade Commission, Federal Power Commission, Securities and Exchange Commission, Civil Aeronautics Board, Atomic Energy Commission, and the Departments of Defense, State, Treasury, Justice, Agriculture, Health and Welfare, Commerce, Labor, Transportation, Housing and Urban Develop-

The ability to bring large scale construction projects to one's district builds the power base of politicians and public servants.

ment, and Education. This is but a partial listing of federal departments, commissions and agencies. A complete listing would require a large directory.

It is said that somewhere in Washington is the Uniform Screw Thread Commission, created prior to our entry into World War I. The proposed life expectancy of this agency was no more than a year, yet it is still there, complete with budget, offices, and employees. It would not be out of line to suspect that many such agencies continue to exist all over the United States on the state and local levels, as well.

The important point concerning bureaucracy is that there is little control over its day-to-day activities. Many agencies are relatively independent of political control. The Internal Revenue Service has refused to provide its budgetary figures to Congress or the General Accounting Office. It is also interesting to note that while the American judicial system requires the state to prove guilt, the Internal Revenue Service requires citizens to prove their innocence. We have elsewhere discussed the relationship of various regulating agencies to the industry supposedly regulated. Indeed, it seems that the majority of such agencies are unresponsive to the needs of the voters.

There is more wrong with the government bureaucracy than only being unresponsive to the voters. There have been many incidents that give the impression that the rights guaranteed by our Constitution are not considered exactly sacred. Documented actions by the Central Intelligence Agency and the Federal Bureau of Investigation show violations of such rights as privacy and free speech. It should be noted that the people involved in these violations felt they were doing their job and working for the good of the nation. While this attitude is understandable, the activities were in violation of the law and the basic rights guaranteed by the Constitution. The appalling aspect of the situation is that the bodies that supposedly control these and other agencies have had little success in gleaning facts concerning those activities, let alone controlling them.

It must be noted that as of May 1973 there were in existence at least 1,439 federal commissions. Any attempt on the part of Congress to control this large number of commissions is bound to fail. Such a task would require more paid workers than Congress can support. As bureaucracy grows larger and larger, there seems to be a lessening of concern for groups that are supposed to be served. When we deal with a large bureaucracy, we may sometimes get the feeling that it is not serving us, merely putting up with us. There is in some bureaucracies a detachment that becomes, in the last analysis, self-serving. In fact, too often the initial purpose of the agency—serving the people—seems to be forgotten.

The Role of Interest Groups

The door opens to the smoke-filled room. The politicians inside look up to see who would enter. They nod and make room for another power broker: the interest group. This is perhaps how many

INTEREST GROUP: An alliance of people based on their common political aims; a pressure group.

voters see the interest group, as a sinister force working behind the scenes and against the people. But this is one part of the American power system in which voters can have their greatest impact. And interest groups serve a vital function in our political system.[4]

Why Interest Groups Have Power. In most cases, the purposes of the interest group are based on the wants and aims of a small segment of the population. If well organized, such a small, activist group can bring to bear a great deal of pressure on politicians. In fact, such small groups can apply much more pressure than much larger numbers of individuals. The strength of interest groups thus helps prevent the "tyranny of the majority" that might be found in a democracy. By joining interest groups, citizens can be heard loud and clear, even if the majority would have them silent.

The politician is likely to believe that members of interest groups are more likely to remember than other citizens. This belief makes possible the success of interest groups. A bloc of written letters from an organized group of activists carries the weight of a bloc vote in the upcoming election. Examples of such groups are the various teachers' associations, the Sierra Club, and the Moral Majority. A typical eastern state teachers' association lists more than 75,000 members. If this number is multiplied by spouses, parents, and voting-age children, a politician is faced with a bloc vote that could decide an election.

Though groups of this nature are small, their bloc voting habits make politicians wary of causing offense. Emotional issues, such as danger to the environment or consumer protection, have created several nationwide groups whose power is out of proportion to the actual numbers of their members. The members, however, are highly vocal and active. Their applied pressures and carefully placed statements in the public media can stir the masses to action, brief as it may be. Since the politician avoids such mass thought and action, the interest group works to influence elected officials by these practices and also by lobbying.

LOBBYING: The attempt by a pressure group to persuade elected government officials to act in ways that will best benefit the aims of the pressure group.

The Art of Lobbying. The term "lobbying" can be defined as influencing public officials by supplying information or campaign donations and/or by outright bribery.[5] Some recent examples of lobbying carried to extremes have been associated with the oil industry, the national health plan, the highway trust fund, mining safety regulations, and the International Telephone & Telegraph case publicized prior to and during the Watergate investigation.

A typical interest group, the American Medical Association (AMA), has been able to block a national health plan through wise use of the public media, donations of large sums of money, and other means. Obviously, it would not be in the best interest of that group's members to have a government agency set medical fees or otherwise regulate medical services.

It may be easier to found a new religion than to create a new medical school.

Through a well-conceived public relations plan, the AMA has convinced the public that it would be easier to build one of the great pyramids than to create a new medical school. Limiting the number of medical schools appears to have one purpose: limiting the number of trained doctors. Such action guarantees a higher income for doctors through increased demand for services from a limited number of doctors. This is the old game of supply and demand played with deadly consequences. The AMA defends its actions by stating that it is guaranteeing standards. It is difficult however, to explain why the percentage of today's population qualified to train for the medical profession is lower than the percentage thirty years ago. When one considers women's entrance into the professional marketplace, the AMA case becomes even weaker.

The AMA is an interest group that is skilled in playing on the fears of the public. Television programs depicting idealized versions of the medical profession are geared to reinforce the public's confidence and to strengthen the concept of the paternal, all-knowing "family doctor." The public has placed doctors on a pedestal. The medical profession has succeeded in promoting its interests. After all, it has (1) gained a position of public respect for the profession, (2) ensured an income out of proportion to training and skills, and (3) become the inspector, policymaker, and judge of medical activities.

Professional lobbyists of a dozen similar interest groups are always at work influencing politicians and the opinions of the masses.[6] The masses are caught somewhat in the middle, since their interests are usually not in line with any interest group.

The activities of mining groups are another example of effective lobbying. The opinion that mine safety is fine for the miner, rough on mine owners, and results in high prices for the public is subject to debate. Morally, there is no question that mine-safety acts were needed. It was the job of the mine union's lobby to sway the public and the politicians. There is still work needed on effective enforcement procedures. Further confusion in this area is seen in the fact that the original mine-safety regulations did not require mine owners to allow government inspectors access to their mines. Nor was failure to comply with safety regulations penalized. In some cases the professional lobby group saw no real advantage to mine-safety regulations. From the point of view of mining lobbyists, regulations would result only in mine closings and loss of income to the unions. Thus, mine workers' groups had to fight their own lobby which, in concert with mine owners, attempted to water down the safety codes.[7]

Examples of other measures passed without regard to public safety can be cited. The enforcement of a water pollution law caused one of the largest producers of pig iron to close. Since this action would hurt the nation's economy, however, the court order was reversed. As a result, Lake Superior continued to receive huge amounts of poisons. Although the loss of Lake Superior as a clean, living lake is against the public interest, the pollution continued. In the court case against this producer/polluter, evidence pointed to actual human deaths from waste material. Still, a final decision on this issue has taken much more time and pressure.

On the reverse side of the coin, the enforcement of anti-air-pollution devices has resulted in some unexpected situations. The anti-pollution device tends to remove acid-neutralizing material. As a result, rain has been found to contain many times more acid than it did in the days before anti-pollution. The acid-laden rain has decreased forest growth, and it may have disastrous effects upon the general public.

As each interest group pushes for its own advantage, other interest groups counterbalance the efforts. The result is usually a balance on any issue. In those cases where diverse interest groups work for the same end, the masses often stand to lose. The example of both the mine owners and the leaders of mine unions working to defeat mine-safety regulations is such an instance.

Skill Reinforcer 22-2
Is this a false dilemma?

PATTERNS OF POLITICAL POWER IN AMERICA

As we make our way through the power system in America, what are the patterns to be seen around us? Is there one group whose grasp we cannot escape, or are there several groups who are so busy competing with one another that we may make our moves with a good deal of freedom? One view is comforting, the other is not. But which is accurate? The experts find it difficult to give us a clear answer on this question. The main problem is that power is so hard to study. Those who study power disagree on where the power lies and who has it.

Here we will study two models of political power, the elitist and the pluralist. They are quite different from each other, but each has supporters. This in itself shows that the concept of power is not easy to study.

ELITE: A relatively small group of people who own a relatively large proportion of the available resources of a society.

Some of the first work done on the concept of a "power elite" is by C. Wright Mills in his *The Power Elite.*[8] A later study of elitist power can be found in Floyd Hunter's study of the power system in Atlanta, Georgia.[9] Hunter tried to find out "who runs the city." He questioned community leaders and businesspeople and concluded that a business elite held power in that city.

The pluralist position is represented by Robert Dahl in his study of the power structure in New Haven, Connecticut.[10] He said that Hunter's results were based on faulty methods of research and claimed that Hunter found an elite simply because he questioned members who had a large part of the power. Dahl's study of New Haven deals with a number of key issues faced by the city. He found only one person, the mayor, to be a central figure in all the decisions. As such, Dahl concluded that the pressure various interest groups exerted upon elected officials overwhelmed the power of those officials.

A further study by Bachrach and Baratz noted problems in both models, elitist and pluralist.[11] They contended that some unknown group filtered the problem areas that would be considered. In this way such a group controlled which decisions would be made and which would never come up for consideration.

The Elitist Concept   The elitist model or picture of power patterns is not comforting. Any reader of this book is not likely to be part of the small group of people holding power. Instead we are part of the masses. That is not a pleasant position in which to find oneself. The masses have little power, and feel frustration because of it. Still, if this model is accurate, we would do well to learn something about the elite's membership and sources, and how it maintains and uses its power.

A Description of the Elite. A study of the elite [12] as a group shows that the members get the giant share of what is considered good or of value in a society. In plain terms, elitists can get more goods and services than the majority of people. Their larger incomes may buy them advantages. Also, we can see that elitist members of society are treated quite differently from the public at large.

We see many examples of "special" treatment. In airports there are V.I.P. lounges. In cities there are special parking areas. On highways special license plates identify the limousines of the elite, and they tend to excuse the owners from observing traffic laws or other regulations. In legal matters, the elite are treated with deference. Their crimes or misdemeanors are often washed out of the courts prior to trial. They receive light sentences if they are ever convicted for crimes that would net harsh treatment for the masses. Enjoying a superior life-style, elitists are secure in the knowledge that their residences are carefully guarded by special police or private security.

We have come to expect public servants to protect the elite in a manner denied the masses. Compare the deaths of skid row bums, which are barely noted by law enforcement agencies, to chance physical assaults upon the person or even the property of the elite. A bicycle stolen from a young member of the elite in New York's Central Park elicits more concern among the public safety directors than the rapes and murders of hundreds of citizens at the lowest socioeconomic level. Those who receive the most in the way of goods and services, safety, and special treatment may then be included in the power-wielding elitist group. Those who do not enjoy these advantages are included in the powerless groups of the masses.

History of Elites. In the West, the formal division of social groups into the elite and the masses goes well back into history. We can follow the new elites arising just after the collapse of the Roman Empire.

In its beginnings, this elite system was called the estate system. It came about as a result of a broken contract. While the Romans had ruled, the contract between the governed and the government was clear. But when the government of the Romans withdrew, a void was left. Into this void stepped the protectors who became the governors. In return for protection, the masses pledged work and loyalty.

The invention of the gun tended to make all people equal and reduced dependence upon a warrior governing class. The great plagues reduced the population of Europe to the point where people were more important than land. The Americas offered land to all, and from Spain's looting came the capital needed for the rest of Europe to develop industry and a group to vie with the elite.

Even though the changing social and political patterns called for the end of the estate system, it continues today in some areas. For example, approximately 2,500 people owned 50 million acres in Chile.[13] This leaves only 7 million acres that are owned by the rest of the people. Other nations, prior to the upheavals of World War II, had similar patterns of landownership. In these nations, most of the privately owned land was in the form of huge estates owned by a tiny portion of the population.

In our own society, there has been a change from one form of elitist power base to another. In the United States, landholdings have never really been as important as they have been in other nations, mainly because, until recently, a surplus of American land has been available for the taking. The United States has had a tradition of going west for cheap land. In Europe, the power base was land, and all land was owned. If all land was titled and always inherited, a landless person had no way to acquire land. Such a system offered little chance for social mobility. The vast areas of land in the west kept the United States from developing a power base of this nature.

The large pre-Civil War estates or plantations in the southern United States were somewhat like the estate system in Europe. Labor for these plantations took the form of slavery and, later, a form of land bondage.

How America's Elitist System Works.   Power in America has its base in economics. This is the same base upon which the estate system rested, but the difference is that the holders of power now deal in a more fluid economic power base—money.

Money is well suited to our society. Money is easy to transfer. No emotional ties are created by the possession of the substance. Even though some families have maintained large amounts of money, there are no social or legal reasons why the poor cannot also obtain large amounts.

Power in American society is based in the holding and distribution of economic benefits.[14] In the past, very wealthy people have controlled these benefits. The benefits may be in the form of

Theodore Roosevelt (1858–1919), a Republican, during his first term as president, in 1903. Franklin D. Roosevelt, a Democrat, also became president.

actual cash payments, income-producing jobs, and/or contracts to provide goods or services. In recent years, the trend has been to remove such power from the hands of individuals. They are being replaced by corporations and power blocs.

The elitist concept focuses on a small group. This group of powerful people forms a stable elite. These few people, rather than the nation as a whole, make the important decisions. There is an important point to be noted here. The goals and desires of the elite differ from those of the masses. This elitist concept also points to the importance of elected officials. These officials are often in a position to carry out the decisions made by the elite. In fact, those officials are sometimes members of the elite.[15]

It is not difficult to pick out the names of various government leaders who have come from this extremely wealthy and powerful group. At one time the Rockefeller family produced the governors of New York and Arkansas. A third member of the family is now a political power in West Virginia. He is married to the daughter of another powerful figure former Senator Charles Percy of Illinois. These figures are not restricted to any single political party or region, however. Although both were members of the elite, the two Roosevelts were in opposite camps.

In the political arena, wealthy political figures have distinct advantages. For one, they can afford to finance their own campaigns. As such, the members of the elite represent their own views. Politicians who must depend upon contributions from the elite to pay for their campaigns may well find themselves representing the views of the elite. The elitists thus have access, through their representatives, to the fruits of office. Among these are the "plums" that ensure continued power and support.

These plums can take many forms. There are high-paying jobs for supporters. There are policymaking jobs for those who hope to join the elite. There are also honorary positions, such as that of ambassador, to say nothing of the pork barrel benefits.

The central policy making positions tend to be dear to the heart of the elite. Such positions include being Secretary of Labor, Agriculture, or Treasury, for example. The regulatory agencies for the stock exchanges, the Federal Communications Commission, the directors of the Federal Reserve Banks, and the Federal Power Commission, among others, are also important to the holders of power. The reasons are obvious. Imports and exports, balance of trade, evaluation and flow of currency, interest rates, and stock market regulations are only part of the picture. This is an enormous picture that affects the pocketbooks of the elite, and the masses must be regulated.

It is also obvious that individuals, corporations, and large interest groups use their power to maintain the climate of this large picture. They can arrange the picture to benefit themselves as much as possible. Along this line, we can point to the use of our armed forces to protect U.S. corporate properties in other nations.

And we have heard of the State Department's intervention in the internal affairs of other nations on behalf of American business interests.

On a different level, federal subsidies have been paid to American export companies to ensure profit. This profit had been denied to the *producers* of those exported products. Indeed, the American/Soviet grain deals ensured large profits for the exporters and suppliers by restricting news of the negotiations to several large companies. The sale brought about shortages of all food and feed products, which forced a tremendous rise in prices. The crowning blow was that the same American taxpayer who financed the export subsidies for these products was forced to pay doubly at the grocery store. Obviously the public and the farmer suffered from this action.

In theory, the elected representatives of "the people" should represent the voters—the people. The elitist concept shows a different point of view. It sees the representatives elected by the people but approving decisions actually made by a very small group of people. The elitist view points to the concentration of power in the hands of a few and creates only an illusion in the hands of the masses. A favorite reference is President Dwight D. Eisenhower's warning about the power of what he called the "military-industrial complex." [16] In real terms, then, the power of the nation would appear to be in the hands of the large contributors to elected officals and those wealthy members of elected officialdom who do not require such backing—the elite.

There is some justification for an elite. After all, decisions must be made and power must be lodged somewhere. This applies to universities, corporations, and other institutions as well as government. When Charles E. Wilson said, "What's good for G.M. is good for the nation," he meant that the interests of the General Motors Corporation and the nation were the same. Furthermore, he meant that the interests of the business community were the interests of the nation. This meant that the members of the elite decided not only what was good for their own business interests but also what was good for the entire nation. This shows clearly the long reach of the elite.

From time to time, large newspapers print a list of gifts members of Congress receive. Fees paid to senators and representatives for talks or discussions vary from very small to much more than any speech is worth. There are reports of campaign donations from interest groups that range into the millions of dollars. The 1972 presidential election saw wholesale contributions by large corporations in violation of existing laws. Although many of the contributors have been prosecuted for their actions, the fines were lower than the levels of the contributions. These funds, however, were sometimes forced from the corporate elite by the political elite. In recent elections, PACS, or Political Action Committees, have filled the void created by new election laws.

The corporate and political elitist groups appear to have combined forces to further their interests. The corporate elite managed to place or maintain certain members of the political elite in power. This action ensured favorable treatment in many areas of governmental control. The treatment by the executive branch, such as in the Justice Department and other agencies already mentioned, are examples. The political elite wished to maintain its positions of power for obvious reasons, such as deference in sentences given for breaking federal law.

PERJURY: Violation of an oath; falsely swearing.

An attorney general pleads guilty to what can only be called perjury—sentence: one month, suspended. A vice-president is forced to resign but is not forced to serve a jail term for his offenses. Other members of the executive branch staff are found guilty of various crimes but receive only symbolic sentences. A former president is given a wholesale pardon—prior to indictment. The prime concern of their associates and the public appeared to be whether the sentences imposed would cause them to be disbarred or otherwise cast out of "public life," thereby losing their livelihood.

The activity of the political elite bears some discussion. Each election year the public is presented with politicians running for office. These candidates are judged for the most part on (1) personal appearance, (2) public-speaking ability, and (3) the backing of an interest group or party. None of the qualifications mentioned has any relation to the offices they are running for. Too often, people experienced in little more than "political" affairs are placed in charge of complex government departments. One eastern governor appointed a woman to head the state's motor vehicle department. Her sole work experience had been several years as a secretary. City councilpersons have had spouses appointed to fill their remaining terms of office. A governor of a large southern state was succeeded in office by his wife while he finished his prison term. A person appointed as an ambassador was being questioned by the Senate. He could not even pronounce the name of the prime minister of the country to which he was being assigned. On losing an election, a veteran politician can count on being handed one political plum after another. In most cases, these jobs pay more than those in which civil servants work for the greater part of their lives.

This is all part of our power system, from the elitist point of view. By taking care of their supporters, the elite take care of themselves.

The Pluralist Concept

Perhaps we are not controlled by simply a few members of an elite and their hired hands. While our power system makes sense from the elitist viewpoint, there is also support for another view. Indeed, some students of our power system claim that the pluralistic concept better explains how the system works.

The Case for the Pluralist Concept. Rather than one small group of powerful people controlling our nation, it may be that several such groups trade power on major issues, keeping everything on an even keel. Pluralist power is viewed as being spread widely among many competing groups. No single group is seen to be so very powerful in more than a few key issue areas. In such a situation, the give-and-take among groups, which is needed to accomplish anything, would prevent overall control by a single interest group.[17]

The pluralist believes that power is highly decentralized. That means that rather small groups are able to pressure the government enough to satisfy their wants. It is through such interest groups that the average citizen is able to exert power. The variety of these many groups and their diverse desires are the leveling agent in the American political system.

In the pluralist model, both the elected official and the voter have political power. The politician represents a regional or local interest group. Examples are the midwestern wheat farmers, the New York liberals, the Southwest oil interests, and the industrial Northeast. The voters in each region expect the region's elected official to attend to the concerns of that region. In this view, all voters have their own power centers looking out for their political interests.

The Case for a Pluralist-Elitist Picture. Both concepts make sense. Both seem to explain how the power system in our nation works. Rather than choosing only one of the concepts, we can combine them to build a complete picture of the patterns of power.

We have an elite; evidence for this is abundant and clear. Its form varies both in makeup and through time. The elite is composed in part of the (1) long-term wealthy, (2) long-term politicians, (3) corporate representatives, and (4) established group representatives. The pluralist concept is also present; it is seen in the attention the elite gives to various diverse interest groups. The give-and-take among interest groups would tend to maintain a middle-of-the-road course of government action.

Then what interests do these various groups share? In other words, does the business interest group, if it largely controls government, act solely to further its own interests? Do the various business interests have enough in common to steer the government away from the public good?

Over a period of a century, the labor interests appear to have developed an elite. The children and grandchildren of labor leaders have appeared in the leadership of the various national unions. The power of labor has grown and become concentrated.

In this light, we can envision a situation in which labor and business elites defend shared interests. "What's good for General Motors is good not only for business but also for labor, and so is good for the country." This might indicate that at one time or another business and labor elitists would see the advantages of maintaining a strong position for the manufacturing sector.

SUMMARY

Power is the ability of someone to control the actions of other people. The power system in our nation includes, besides the elected officials, at least three other power bases. In theory, the voter is at the top of the system, commanding government workers and officials. But many citizens do not vote. Those who do often base their choices on things unrelated to the candidate's ability to serve the needs of the voters. In fact, campaigns are often based on the belief that voters do not really care so much about the candidate's promised action. Besides, the voters are likely to forget the promises anyway.

The government's bureaucracy is another power base, though it is supposed to be merely the workhorse of the voter.

Interest groups function because they are clearly activist, and politicans know such groups can support them with bloc votes and money. Lobbying is central to this success.

There is a good deal of debate among political scientists about the patterns of power. One viewpoint claims that the power system is controlled by a small group, an elite. This elite is pictured as being stable and very powerful. The members get government officials and workers to serve the needs of the elite by offering them various resources as rewards. The pluralistic viewpoint sees various interest groups and regions choosing their own representatives, who compete on a national level. This competition maintains a balance in the power system. A combination of both concepts presents a fuller picture of that system.

SPECIAL TOPIC

A Case of Power in America

In 1974, a book entitled *The Power Broker: Robert Moses and the Fall of New York* appeared in U.S. bookstores.[18] The author, Robert A. Caro, would win the Pulitzer Prize for his in-depth study of power. The power in question was wielded by Robert Moses, a man who was never elected to public office but who held actual power.[19]

After graduating from Yale and earning a doctorate, Robert Moses fought Tammany Hall (the name for the Democratic political machine in New York City). He made such a nuisance of himself that Tammany Hall decided to crush him. It did so with great efficiency, leaving him with no job in 1918.

Why would an organization like Tammany Hall take notice of a thirty-year-old Ph.D.? Tammany Hall held power in New York at that time, power that came from its ability to control voters and hand out vast numbers of patronage positions to loyal supporters. Moses, in his idealism, had suggested a practice that was unheard of in New York City political circles because it would have taken away the base of Tammany Hall's power.

What was this heresay? Robert Moses put forth a plan that would have introduced the *merit* system to city hall. Moses had come into city government with the administration of a *reform* mayor, John Purroy, in 1914. While serving, he devised a numerical grading system that treated every aspect of a city employee's job performance. You can understand that Robert Moses was not the most popular person in the city administration. City employees who owed their jobs to the *machine* rather than to their ability lived in fear of this man and expressed their hate.

Today many watchdog agencies try to protect the people from such abuses by political machines, yet these abuses are rampant. Many jobs in state and local governments across the nation are known as "no show" positions, jobs for which people are paid but are not expected to come to work. You can imagine what abuses took place before some form of control was in place. Moses was on the scene too early with too much idealism and too little power.

Caro points out that when Robert Moses returned to city politics, he came without his idealism. When Moses returned, he held power in varying degrees from 1924 to 1968—forty-four years. At one point he held fourteen public positions at the same time.

The story of Robert Moses is the story of grasping, wielding, and maintaining power without benefit of elected position. Moses never held elected office, yet he was able to control those who did. Moses served under the New York governorships of Smith, Roosevelt, Lehman, Dewey, Harriman, and Rockefeller. In the city of New York he served Mayors La Guardia, O'Dwyer, Impelliteri, Wagner, and Lindsay. His story is one of maintaining control through Republicans and Democrats—friends and enemies.

An example of Moses' power occurred when Robert Wagner was being sworn in as mayor of New York City. After Wagner took the oath, he administered oaths and handed official appointment blanks to appointees. As usual, Moses was sworn in as City Park Commissioner and City Construction Coordinator. He did not receive the usual appointment to the City Planning Commission. For years Moses had been proposing construction under one hat, approving it under the hat of the Planning Commission, and constructing it as City Construction Coordinator, but many organizations had been trying to deprive Moses of at least one of the interlocking positions. Among the organizations were The Citizen's Union, the City Club, and liberal elements of the labor movement.

After the ceremony, Moses, enraged, picked up a blank appointment form, filled it out, followed the mayor into his office, and had him sign the appointment to the Planning Commission.

This may sound like small potatoes, but let us now enter the world of power and understand how power feeds itself and grows healthy. The most interesting point to be made was that Robert Moses' power was not in the public view. His empire consisted of a confederation of four public authorities plus the New York City Park Department and the Long Island State Park Commission. According to Caro, these separate entities were ruled as a tightly administered monarchy, consisting of fleets of yachts, cars, trucks, and armed uniformed workers—"bridge and tunnel officers and Long Island Parkway police." The agencies were above and aside from city, state, or federal governments; they had their own bond resolutions, their own laws, and, most important, their own source of income. The empire controlled over 103,071 acres of land, made up of parks and highways of New York and Long Island and areas around the upstate power dams.

Caro points out that the yearly budget of the Long Island State Park Commission and the City Park Department ran as high as $213 million. The Triborough Bridge and Tunnel Authority (one of the four public authorities controlled by Moses) ran a profit, after expenses, of $30 million a year. Other monies available to Moses came from urban renewal sources. Between 1949 and 1957, some $267 million was spent in New York City.

The legal control of these vast amounts of money made Robert Moses a powerful man. With the legal power and authority to build the Verrazano Narrows Bridge, he extended his power to the Port Authority of New York and New Jersey. That organization had the money to build the bridge, but not the authority to do so.

The personal power of Robert Moses was enlarged in other ways. He hired detectives to build files on large numbers of city and state officials. His surplus allowed him to maintain a large public relations staff, and if someone did not see the light as perceived by Moses, that person's career could be destroyed through the media. Caro points to the 1938 and 1958 communist witch-hunts in New York City, both of which were said to have relied upon information, innuendo, and falsehood supplied by Moses.

Caro points out that Moses had a secret veto by the New York State Department of Public Works over the awarding of all New York metropolitan area public works. It is said that no engineer who openly disagreed with Moses ever received one of the contracts. The ability to dole out retainer contracts, fees, and com-

missions in large numbers and amounts created a loyal constituency. The following groups, aside from politicians, had an interest in maintaining Moses in power: banks, labor unions, bond underwriters, insurance firms, retail stores, and real-estate manipulators. Add to these the vast work force of the various authorities, and you have a constituency that maintained Moses in power for over forty years.

SELF-TEST QUESTIONS

1. The ability to make others conform to one's wishes, regardless of the wishes of others, is called _____.

2. True or false: According to this chapter, the voters play a commanding role in America's political system.

3. According to this chapter, which influences the way we vote?
   a. patronage
   b. franking
   c. candidate's speaking ability

4. _____ is supposed to carry out the policies drawn up by elected officials.

5. True or false: Our government bureaucracy is responsive to the voters' wishes.

6. An interest group is:
   a. always large
   b. a pressure group
   c. well organized and activist
   d. rarely effective

7. The success of an interest group depends on its:
   a. lobbying
   b. bloc voting
   c. money

8. Which concept assumes that the power system is controlled by one group?
   a. elitist
   b. pluralistic
   c. democratic
   d. autocratic

9. True or false: A ruling elite is a recent development in Western society.

10. True or false: In the pluralistic model, there is still some concentration of power.

ANSWERS TO SELF-TEST QUESTIONS

1. power
2. false
3. a, b, c
4. the government bureaucracy
5. false
6. b, c
7. a, b, c
8. a
9. false
10. true

ANSWERS TO SKILL REINFORCERS

22–1. 1. In a democracy, the people rule.
2. We live in a democracy here in the United States.
3. Therefore we the people rule here in the United States.

The danger here is in the second statement. Do we indeed live in what may be truly defined as a democracy? If the United States does not fully fit the definition of democracy, then the conclusion is not true.

22–2. Yes. As you see later in the chapter, there is a third possible viewpoint, a combination of the pluralistic and elitist concepts. The author proposes only these two (at first) in order to focus your attention on the two major, generally studied options. There is no evil intent here, but still you should be aware of and on guard against this sort of thing.

NOTES

1. Bertrand Russell, *Power* (New York: W.W. Norton, 1938).
2. Bertrand de Jourvenal, *On Power* (New York: Viking Press, 1946).
3. The Twenty-Fourth Amendment restricts the use of a poll tax to bar voting in federal elections or primaries leading to those elections.
4. Graham Wooton, *Interest Groups* (Englewood Cliffs, N.J.: Prentice-Hall, 1970).
5. Abraham Holtzman, *Interest Groups and Lobbying* (New York: Macmillan Co., 1966).
6. Lester W. Milbrath, *The Washington Lobbyists* (Chicago: Rand McNally, 1963).
7. J. DeMuth, "Mine Safety: Less Is More?" *America* 126 (1972).
8. C. Wright Mills, *The Power Elite* (New York: Oxford University Press, 1956).
9. Floyd Hunter, *Community Power Structure: A Study of Decision Makers* (Chapel Hill: University of North Carolina Press, 1953).
10. Robert Dahl, "Power in New Haven: The Pluralist Thesis," in *Power in Postwar America,* ed. Richard Gillam (Boston: Little, Brown, 1971).
11. Peter Bachrach and Morton S. Baratz, "Two Faces of Power," *American Political Science Review* 58 (1962).
12. Mills, *The Power Elite.*
13. George Borgstrom, *The Hungry Planet* (New York: Collier, 1967).
14. David Ricardo, *The Principles of Political Economy and Taxation* (New York: E.P. Dutton, 1911).
15. Harold Lasswell, *Politics: Who Gets What, When, How* (New York: Whittlesey House, 1936).
16. Mills, *The Power Elite.*
17. Robert A. Dahl, *Who Governs?* (New Haven: Yale University Press, 1961).
18. Robert Caro, *The Power Broker: Robert Moses and the Fall of New York* (New York: Alfred Knopf, 1974).
19. Caro wrote a second study of power, *The Years of Lyndon Johnson* (New York: Alfred Knopf, 1982).

SUGGESTED READINGS

Caro, Robert A. *The Power Broker: Robert Moses and the Fall of New York.* New York: Alfred Knopf, 1974.

———— *The Years of Lyndon Johnson.* New York: Alfred Knopf, 1982.

Horowitz, Irving L., ed. *Power, Politics, and People: The Collected Essays of C. Wright Mills.* New York: Oxford University Press, 1963.

Lederer, William J. *The Ugly American.* New York: W.W. Norton, 1958.

Peter, Laurence J., and Hull, Raymond. *Peter Principle: Why Things Always Go Wrong.* New York: William Morrow & Co., 1969.

23 AMERICAN POLITICAL PARTIES

PREVIEW

Party Politics or Justice?

The last scenes of what may have been the ultimate in political infighting took place in 1982. Abscam had earlier burst upon the American scene. What occurred was a confidence operation set up and sprung on certain congressmen and one senator. The nation, usually blasé about gigantic favors, rip-offs, and assorted other dealings was upset with the nature of the Abscam dealings.

In retrospect, questions can be directed toward the how and the why of the operations and convictions. Why could be linked to the fact that the scam took place prior to the 1980 primary elections. Many of those entrapped in the Abscam mesh were openly opposed to the renomination of President Carter. Win or lose, in the trials that followed, the participants lost all political credibility.

The last act of this melodrama began when Senator Harrison Williams of New Jersey was forced to resign his seat in the Senate.[1] If Senator Williams had resigned prior to January 1, 1982, a Democratic governor of New Jersey could have appointed another Democrat to replace him. If the Senate hearings had been held prior to January 1, 1982, a Democratic majority would have heard the case. If the Democrats had won the 1980 elections for the presidency and the Senate, would the outcome have been different? Was there ever a chance that Senator Williams could have been found innocent, regardless of the evidence for or against him? Did Senator Williams do anything more in dealing with the FBI than other elected officials do in taking large amounts of money from religious organizations, the AMA, the energy consortium, the military industrial complex, and others?

"Government and Politics" is an interesting game. It can be comfortable, and it can be dangerous.

"I am a Democrat." "I am a Republican." "He is a conservative."
"Vote for me." "Vote for her." "This is the party representing you."
Every two years, we hear the same statements as the congressional
races begin. Every four years, we are exposed to a more intense
form of political propaganda as the presidential elections approach. Political contests on the local level suffer from similar
pressure.

Most Americans think of themselves as members of one of the
national parties. Few Americans are aware of why they have taken
such a position. Even fewer Americans are aware of the actual
purpose or reason for the existence of political parties in our
system.

To enhance awareness about our party system, some of the
system's aspects will be explored in this chapter. How does our
party system compare to those in other nations and those in our
past? Who are the participants in our party system? What are the
mechanics of our system? Such knowledge will help make one a
player in our political system, not just a pawn.

PARTY: A body of voters organized for the purpose of influencing or controlling the policies and
conduct of government through
the nomination, and, if possible,
the election of its candidates to
office.

POLITICAL PARTIES IN PERSPECTIVE

In order to understand something, it is helpful to stand back and
get a broad view of it. To see a thing's true shape, its importance,
and its place in the larger scheme of things, an arms-length study
is needed. This section offers such a perspective. First, we will
back off and view our party system as part of a development over
time. Next, we will look at other systems, in other nations.

The Development of America's Party System

In our nation's early history, there were no political parties.
During colonial times, interest groups would form concerning
some policy of the governors and then fade. Political parties were
not required in the Constitution. In fact, they are not even mentioned. The framers feared the jealousies and divisions that parties
would cause. It was hoped that the electoral college would make
parties unnecessary. Indeed, our first president, George Washington, and the members of the first Congress gained their posts
without party aid. Washington even attacked parties in his famous
Farewell Address.

Skill Reinforcer 23-1*

What is a syllogism that could
lead to the conclusion "Political
parties are unconstitutional"?

REPUBLICAN PARTY: A major
party that arose in 1854; in the
main it has been a sectional party
supported by business interests
and by farmers in the West.

Skill Reinforcer 23-2

What thinking error is found in
this sentence: The alliance of Jefferson and Burr caused the disappearance of the Federalists?

Our Earliest Political Leaders.   It was not long before the members of the first Congress began to form groups based upon different political viewpoints. The leaders of the two major groups were
Alexander Hamilton and Thomas Jefferson. The viewpoints of the
first parties, which grew from those two groups, have not
changed. Hamilton organized the Federalists, who were backed by
commercial and banking interests, as are the Republicans of today.
The Federalists stood for a strong central government. The Democratic-Republicans were formed by Jefferson's supporters. They
represented the interests of the frontier, small farmers, and southern planters. An alliance was formed between Jefferson and Aaron
Burr, whose political organization controlled New York City. This

* Answers to the Skill Reinforcers
appear at the end of the chapter.

Thomas Jefferson, leader of the Democratic-Republicans.

COALITION: A combination, union, or alliance of parties.

DEMOCRATIC PARTY: A major party that traces its origin from the Republican party of Jefferson; generally speaking, it has been inclined more than the Republicans to favor the average person and disposed less toward the promotion of business interests.

FACTIONS: Groups of people with common interests, usually in opposition to the majority.

Types of Party Systems

broadened the political base of the Democratic-Republicans and resulted in a coalition of rural and urban dwellers. This is the same power base enjoyed by the modern Democrats.

The Era of Good Feelings. With the election of Jefferson to the presidency in 1800, the Federalists lost power and support. In time they would disappear from the American political scene. Serious squabbles occurred within the Democratic-Republican party but this period, called the "Era of Good Feelings," was for the most part free of competitive party politics until the beginning of Andrew Jackson's administration in 1828.

The Jacksonian Era. An opening up of the political process and the party system occurred in the Jacksonian era. During this period, the practice of holding nominating conventions got its start. It also marked the beginning of direct election of members of the electoral college by popular vote. People with broad popular support took over the leadership of political parties from the elite. At this point, the base of some power shifted to the lower classes and grass-roots political organization.

In 1834 the two-party system returned with the formation of the Whig party. The Whigs consisted of anti-Jackson factions. The Whigs gave way to the Republicans, who emerged in the 1850s.

Following the Civil War, the United States grew greatly in size and saw a new economic structure formed. The parties adapted to this. The Republican party increasingly reflected the viewpoint of the conservative, moneyed interests. Conversely, the Democrats appealed to the common people and had greater support among the new urban masses.

The United States has what is called a two-party political system. Political systems can indeed be classified by the number of parties they possess. By looking at some of the other types, we can see more clearly the strengths and weaknesses of our own system.

Many nations have a single-party system, and others have multi-party systems. Single-party examples are easily found in a totalitarian setting. Multi-party systems are usually associated with parliamentary systems.

Political parties in the United States may be considered to be broad-based, in contrast to those typically found in nations that use a parliamentary system. Broad-based, in this sense, refers to the widespread support needed to elect any official in the United States.

Our system has a winner-take-all element, which tends to limit representation of minority views. The winner of even a one-vote victory controls the position to which he or she has been elected for a specific period of time. Many people who voted for the losers have no representation of their views. For this reason, each of the major political parties must appeal to the broadest possible group of people.

Andrew Jackson ended the "Era of Good Feelings."

PARLIAMENTARY SYSTEM: A government such as that of Great Britain or Canada, among others, in which the executive, consisting of a prime minister and ministerial colleagues in a cabinet, directs the administration and exercises political leadership on condition that it shall at all times command the support of a majority of the legislature or parliament.

PLANK: A section of a party platform referring to a distinct subject.

CANDIDATE: A person who seeks public office through the established procedures of nomination and election.

PROPORTIONAL REPRESENTATION: A device (more common in Europe than in America) for electing the members of a legislative body in a way that reflects all groups or factions in proportion to their strength.

VOTE OF NO CONFIDENCE: In parliamentary governments, a formal expression of the withdrawal of political support of the ministry by the legislative majority.

WHO'S WHO IN AMERICA'S PARTY SYSTEM

This attempt to win mass approval presents to the public planks that do not seem to differ greatly from candidate to candidate or from party to party. If either party were to endorse a radical point of view or purpose, only a minority of voters would approve. The party that did so would probably lose the election. Both the major parties must stress that their candidates stand for issues important to the majority of American voters.

The Parliamentary System. Many parliamentary systems ensure that minority views will be represented. This is accomplished through proportional representation.

Consider this hypothetical example of proportional representation at work. First, assume that you live in a town with 1,000 voters. After the vote has been counted, it is found that one party has received 500 votes and two other parties have received 250 votes each. Under the American system, the candidate of the party receiving the most votes would win. Under a system of proportional representation the sum of the two minor parties would equal the representation of the major vote-getter.

Politics in the United States also differs in that offices are filled for specific periods of time. The system at work in other nations allows the ruling party to remain in power only as long as it retains control of the assembly. The rules concerning the seating of minority parties frequently prevent the party receiving the most seats from exercising rule without the help of one or more of the minority parties. These minority parties contribute voting members to the government. If the needs of the minority parties are not met, they can withdraw their support of the government and force a new election.

Lack of Confidence. Anyone following international news will have read of the fall of the Italian, French, or English government. This change occurs whenever the ruling party cannot pass legislation for lack of voting support in its assemblies. This lack of support is referred to as a loss of confidence. Once the appointed leader of the ruling or governing body loses support through a vote of no confidence, he or she must go before the president, queen, or other figurehead of state and resign. Votes of confidence allow the control of majority party action to be tempered both by public opinion and by minority-party aims.

If people do not want to be pushed around in our political system, they must be participants. As when playing in any game, it helps to know something about the other players and the rules governing their actions. So if we want some control over the political forces acting on us, we will want to learn about our system's participants. This section can help, by describing the people and the groupings involved in our political party system.

The Makeup of American Political Parties

What kinds of people can we expect to find in our political parties? A simplified view is that the Democratic party is composed of such types as city dwellers, minority groups, the poor, and the laborers. The Republican party draws its support mainly from the rich, small-town dwellers, suburbanites, business groups, and members of the old families. By "old families" we mean those that arrived before the great immigrations of the late 1800s and early 1900s.

Recent elections saw some change in these long-held views. Single-issue religious groups held to the Republicans. Though Jews stayed with the Democrats, many shifted. Many union members and well-established ethnic groups overestimated their net worth and voted Republican.

The values expressed by these national political parties attract people typically associated with the groups mentioned. The Democratic philosophy features the use of government for change. Republican philosophy at the most basic level will stand for individual accomplishment as opposed to governmental intervention. In the Democratic view, the government was designed to affect the lifestyle of the citizenry directly. It cannot be denied that this has occurred. The structure of the New Deal, the War on Poverty, and other major projects is typical of Democratic programs.

The British Parliament Building.

The many government agencies that have been formed since the Great Depression of the 1930s have had both economic and social effects on our nation. This impact is the crux of the issue. Presented with the same set of facts and figures, either political camp will see good or bad in what has occurred as a result of governmental intervention. This intervention has entered into what had been the private sector. Many people will look with some displeasure at areas of our society that have been exposed to government regulation. No clear dividing line has been drawn between the positions taken by members of either major party.

This lack of definite separation is due to the nature of our political system, a system that demands broad-based support from all segments of society. In such a system, right-wing Republicans must make themselves appealing to the liberal voter. The liberals must also try to please the more conservative members of their voting public. Each party must try to capture votes from groups normally associated with the other, or there is little hope for political victory.

The Politician and the Party System

The prime goal of a party is to gain control of the machinery of government. To do this, the party attempts to place a person of its choice into an office. This person then gets the attention, the limelight. He or she is the star of the show. But what does the "star" do once in an office? What are the goals of the politician?

Politicians have some good reasons for using the party system to get elected. Of course there is the reward that comes from

SKILL BOX

Propaganda Tricks, Part 2

In the heat of a campaign certain tactics may be used to influence votes. If we are to avoid being pushed into emotional decisions, we need to be able to recognize attempts to persuade us through appeals to our emotions. Such attempts called propaganda, are found not only in the words of some politicians, but also in those of advertisers and other persuaders. Even some scientists, whom we should expect would avoid emotional appeals, rather than use them, sometimes use propaganda methods. (This is explained by the fact that some scientists are not as objective as they should be.) This all goes to show that we need to be on guard whenever ideas, people, or products are being pushed at us. Three propaganda methods were described in the Skill Box of Chapter 22. Here four more propaganda methods will be examined, based on the descriptions in *The Fine Art of Propaganda* by Alfred McClung Lee and Elizabeth Briant Lee (New York Octagon Books, 1972).

The Band Wagon Method tries to make us follow the crowd, to jump on the bandwagon. "Everyone is buying this product—so should you! After all, you don't want to be left out of the crowd." The urge to conform is perhaps within all of us to some degree, but to resist this propaganda trick we must examine on its own merits whatever is being pushed on us.

The testimonial tries to persuade us on the basis of what a special person says. An admired (or hated) person will promote (or attack) something, and we are expected to accept or reject that something on that basis. In the testimonial we are told what some hero, star, or bum said. As with other propaganda methods, it is hoped that we will allow ourselves to be led by the nose rather than think for ourselves.

In the Plain Folks Method, the speaker hopes the ideas will be accepted because he or she is "just one of the people" or "just plain folks," like one of our neighbors. Since "the people" are good, we are to accept the ideas of a person who is one of the people. Like other propaganda methods, this one tries to get us leaning toward accepting something without bothering to examine its merits. After all, we can trust our "neighbor," can't we?

In Card stacking, propagandists arrange their argument solely to persuade, not to inform. They select only certain facts and ignore others. They offer incomplete facts, irrelevant facts, or falsehoods to sell an idea. While we all try to present our arguments in as favorable a light as possible, our arguments can usually be challenged or questioned by listeners. It is in the mass media that we must watch most of all for card-stacking, because we cannot challenge those statements. For example, when we hear "three out of four doctors approve," we cannot find out how those doctors were chosen. Perhaps fifty doctors were asked, only three approved, and thus 46 were ignored in the report. We can rarely get answers to our questions of "How do you know?" or "Is that really true?" Because of this, we must beware of card-stacking in the mass media, because there it is hardest to spot.

helping to shape the social and economic life of the nation, but legislation can also give more personal rewards. It can produce personal gain for politicians or gains for groups friendly to politicians or to which they belong. Also politicians can receive patronage with which to reward supporters, friends, and relatives. Politicians may also be in the position to make administrative decisions for personal or group gains.

There are also more direct rewards. Political positions pay well for the amount of work involved. The fringe benefits usually equal in untaxable income the salaries received by career workers. Elected officials of stature receive cars to use, with maintenance and insurance included, and frequently drivers are provided. Provision is made for the official's residence, or he or she may receive an allowance for household expenses. Household help is sometimes provided, although the payroll classification for such jobs may be hidden among secretarial or other labels. Many politicians accept as a matter of course the indirect benefits of landscaping and maintenance of privately owned property and possessions. This is true even though this use of publicly paid labor and materials is illegal.

Throughout their elected terms, the prime concern of many politicians appears to be getting reelected and thereby retaining the many benefits that come with their office. Also, many people awarded patronage positions contribute a percentage of their publicly paid incomes to the support of their sponsors' political careers. People receiving jobs through patronage are sometimes expected to make cash payments or to campaign for the reelection of their patron.

CAMPAIGN: The contest of rival nominees for a particular office and of their respective political organizations to win the support of voters at the polls.

On February 1, 1976, the General Services Administration (GSA) released a list of 311 representatives and members of the executive branch directing job referrals to that agency. Based upon the data GSA accumulated, the Civil Service Commission found that many government officials had violated the merit system by hiring political favorites rather than promoting career employees. This report cited as an example the 196 referrals made by Harry S. Flemming, described as a White House talent scout during the Nixon administration. Flemming was quoted as stating that political loyalty was in his mind a leading criterion for job selection in the Nixon administration. In 1970 Mr. Flemming was still saying that his job application form "was designed to discover party registration, campaign experience, Congressional sponsorship and former government jobs" and "that it was devised to exclude not only Democrats but also persons who had worked for Democrats." [2]

Interested Parties

Besides the politicians and "the people," there are some very important participants in our party system. In fact, it may be said that the system is controlled by these participants: interest groups and political activists.

Interest Groups and Political Parties. Political parties supply the basis for satisfying desires of interest groups. Interest groups need party organizations to get what they want. Conversely, political parties need various interest groups to win elections. Interest groups provide a solid voting bloc upon which the political parties can depend. With support from sufficient numbers of interest groups, a party need only attract a minimal number of "undecided" voters. The voting record of interest groups exceeds the rather apathetic record of the general public. On any given issue, a highly organized group can produce far more votes than it has members, while such things as bad weather may well discourage the general public from voting.

The parties may be viewed as power brokers who respond to the wants, claims, and desires of the more powerful and organized interest groups. The weaker, more apathetic interest groups are ignored. It can be said, then, that "all power is organization."

Political Activists. Average citizens usually find that the vote is their only method of political expression. Surprisingly few people registered to vote do in fact vote. A local school board, city, or town council election may draw less than 20 percent of the registered voters. Rarely is the total of 50 percent participation reached in local elections.[3] Even in contests of high voter interest, such as presidential elections, total voter participation may run only as high as 75 percent and as low as 53.5 percent (1976).[4]

The average citizen contrasts sharply with the political activist. An activist is a person who works for, contributes to, and otherwise engages in some aspect of decision-making in the political process.

If we note the small number of voters, it should come as no surprise to find that political activists represent an even smaller percentage of the public. Statistics show that as few as 28 percent of the public is interested enough in political activity to bother to try to persuade others to vote in one manner or another. An even lower percentage of the voting public (19 percent) bothers to attend political rallies. These functions appear to have little meaning, since the overwhelming majority of people who attend have already made up their minds so far as their voting patterns are concerned. Perhaps the sight of many people attending a rally helps to convince the committed further that it is on the right side of the battle lines.

Somewhere between 2 percent[5] and 20 percent[6] of the voting public have actually expressed interest in political clubs and organizations to the extent of actually becoming members. Some 31 percent[7] belong to associations that will occasionally take a stand on housing or school affairs.

Activists show even more clearly their involvement in the money they give to their causes. Only 424 people donated 25 percent of the $48.1 million reported by both parties to have been spent on the 1968 elections. This shows that relatively small numbers of people actually contribute large amounts to political groups.[8] The Republican party spent the years leading up to the 1980 election developing small rather than large contributions. The experiment paid off handsomely.

Some people, organizations, and businesses contribute to both political parties. This old technique was practiced during the various religious and political wars that have beset Europe through history. Many powerful families would assign one son to support each side or religion. This made it possible to maintain lands and power during troubled times.

Skill Reinforcer 23-3
Do you spot any stereotyping in this paragraph?

It might be useful here to build a mental image of political activists. We can assume that they are better educated than the average citizen.[9] Activists also belong to a higher social class level than the average citizen; few members of minority groups are activists. One might easily expect that such people would be more likely to attempt to control political machinery. From their point of view they have much at stake, and so want to control political decisions as much as they can.

Activists do not always come from the higher social levels. From time to time various ethnic groups respond to their special social and economic problems. They have banded together, and in the cities have formed powerful political groups. In recent years, as a result of the passage of the Voting Rights Act of the 1960s, the black population has developed a political awareness. The passage of the act itself would not have created the black voting blocs that now exist. Political organizers and activists worked to mold these new voters into a powerful pressure group.

PRESSURE GROUP: An organization that promotes specific economic, moral, or other causes by employing paid agents or lobbyists to influence legislators and public officials by endorsing candidates nominated by political parties or by conducting systematic education or propaganda campaigns among the general public.

Nationally, public feeling about politicians and political parties appears to be a widespread conviction that the system is unresponsive to the needs and desires of the public.[10] The prevailing opinion is that any participation in politics is a waste of time. This keeps the public on the sidelines in large numbers. We have seen the furor over Watergate, Abscam and the Iranian arms shipments. Before, after, and in between these events we have had numerous small and large examples of the abuse of the public trust. We have even heard officials stating that it is better to cover up some misconduct than cause the public to lose the faith.

The question that we find in the minds of politicians and public alike is: How much corruption, power-grabbing, self-seeking, and general dishonesty can we accept, and when should we blow the whistle? Should an arbitrary figure, like that set for the difference between grand larceny and petty larceny, be written into the Constitution to mark the limits to which honest politicians may act in their own interest? The only answer to these questions lies in the active participation of all citizens in the political process. Cheating and dishonesty will remain, but perhaps they will become more evenly distributed.

HOW AMERICA'S PARTY SYSTEM WORKS

Equipped with some knowledge about our political party system and its participants, we are ready to turn to the mechanics of the system. We have explored the structure and identified who is involved; now we ask how the system works. This section explores what parties try to do, how they are organized, and how much power they have.

Functions of Political Parties

Thousands of citizens are actively involved in political parties, and one might wonder what good comes from all that human energy. As we will see here, the parties work in ways that are both good and not so good for the voting public.

One of the prime functions of political parties is the recruitment, selection, and training of "leaders." To maintain control, the party must faithfully sponsor people with public appeal. The selection of General Eisenhower for the presidential nomination after World War II is a good example of the search for a prime candidate. The man was a national hero, honest, reasonably intelligent, and a father figure to most of the nation. Both major parties tried to persuade him to head their ticket. The Republicans eventually succeeded, and after Eisenhower's election to the presidency, they controlled the government for eight years.

Other examples of this nature are easy to find in local and state elections across the nation. Often with disregard for actual ability, party leaders have selected astronauts, actors, civil rights leaders, and reactionary leaders to run for specific posts. These people are often chosen because of their popularity with the public. Once candidates are known publicly, the party that sponsors them works to secure the desired office. The party works for the candidates' election or possibly appointment to a visible post as a prelude to running for elective office. After serving an apprenticeship in an appointed post in the public eye, the potential candidate may enter a race for elective office.

This identification process serves a public function. After all, if the nation's voters were presented with candidates about whom nothing was known, the right to vote would have little meaning. That is, the voter's decision must be an informed one, in theory.

In reality, the public knows or cares little about the real abilities or shortcomings of most seekers of public office. The public seems interested only in such points as appearance (of candidate, wife, and children), diction, voice, pastimes, social connections, and the candidate's made-to-order image.[11] This was made quite clear by the Knight-Ridder survey of voter concerns in the 1977 national election. Economic, social, and political issues were seen as far less important to the voter than the personal image the candidate projected. The public is expected to vote for or against a candidate on the basis of information the party and candidate have presented prior to election. It is not surprising that the public sees the cliché of campaign promises as a smoke screen behind which most politicians hide.

The public interest seems best served in the period just prior to election. The less popular activities, such as tax bills and President Reagan's veto of the Clean Water Bill, appear just after elections. After all, politicians know that this period will fade from memory by the time the next campaign arrives. The public is left with a choice between voting for the party that is "in" or the party that is "out." Party labels and aims may be inconsistent and misleading, but the public can at least punish an offending party by voting it out of office.

While the view of party activity presented here has been cynical, there are some functions that actually seem to benefit the public. An agenda for discussion is presented for the public. Issues are brought to light even though compromise between political and private interest groups will water down solutions to problems. We might well ask if the Watergate scandal would have been made public at all without the existence of conflicting political parties and views. Burt Lance in the Carter administration and Richard Allen in the Reagan administration are other examples of political highlighting.

Party Organization

A political party in America is comprised of many groups and people of diverse interests. It is clear that such an organization cannot function at only the national level. Several levels are needed to give all members some chance to affect the organization. American political parties therefore function at many levels. Some of these levels come into focus only during presidential or state-wide elections. We know already that power lies in political organization; the question here is, where are the bases of the parties' organization?

First, we can look at the regional level of party functioning. Regional differences can be important, as seen in the answer to this question. "Is an eastern Democrat the same as a southern Democrat?" After looking into the matter, we might find that eastern Republicans and Democrats have more in common with each other than with members of their own parties elected from other regions of the country.

The base of political party power, however, lies in the lowest governmental levels. That is not to say that political parties operate at a low level but rather that the state and local segments of political parties choose their candidates and have been known actually to elect them. Yet a candidate who has *only* state and local backing stands little chance of competing in or winning a national election.

We can really say that each of the national parties is composed of fifty separate party systems, one for each state. Some state parties even stand opposed to the aims and direction of their national party. The national parties cannot act too strongly in opposition to state and local parties if they care to maintain any representation at all in a particular state. At times, entire regions will revolt against the dictates or positions of national parties. When this

Party power comes from the grass roots.

occurs, as it did to the Democrats in the South on several occasions, presidential candidates are in trouble. The national party has the job of nominating and electing the president. Only if the party accomplishes that task is it possible to put basic programs into effect. This means that the national party cannot elect a president without the work, cooperation, and agreement of the state parties.

Aside from the president and vice-president, all elected officials have their base in state and local politics. Senators may have offices in Washington and be a national power, but their power base is at home. Home may be any of several key counties or cities in their states. Representatives may sit in judgment of the nation's taxes, educational funding, arms allocations, and legislation of worldwide import. Yet with all this they are dependent not on the support of the state, the nation, or the world but on the residents of their congressional districts. Representatives may be a power in Washington, but if they neglect the issues vital to their farmer, suburban, and city supporters, they can be removed and sent back to their law practices. The support of local interests is far more important to a representative than the sympathy of the national party or the president.

The national party is an organization that appears in time for presidential elections but has little substance at other times. In the last analysis, state and local parties place politicians in the position of being elected. The state and local party structure gets out the vote and works for the candidates. That state and local structure maintains or rejects the national politician, for without a base in a supportive area a politician is out of business.

Limits on Parties' Power

We have devoted this chapter to America's political parties because they are important parts of our political system. Political parties are powerful, but their power has clear limits.

The separation of powers granted to the three major branches of the American government balances the power of the branches themselves. This separation also limits the power of each political party. While one party may control the White House through the presidency, the other might control one or both houses of Congress. The two-year term for all congressional representatives allows displeased public and interest groups to alter the party representation in the House of Representatives dramatically. Every two years, one-third of the members of the Senate stand for election. This allows a more moderate shift in political representation in that house. Presidential power lasts for a maximum of only eight years, and serious misconduct would result in nonreelection after the first four-year term. The Supreme Court stands as a major hedge between the White House and overwhelming political control of both houses of Congress. In the judiciary branch a judge, once appointed, can remain secure for life. The freedom of action brought about by such a secure position allows the members of the Supreme Court to follow their personal principles rather than those of the electorate. A corrupt Supreme Court brings more disaster to our system of political power balance than corruption in any other branch of the federal government.

The nature of the American electoral system itself further limits the political power of parties. Many states and cities hold elections on dates different from those on which national elections take place. In this manner, the local interests are separated from national interests. The cumulative effect of thousands of such elections tremendously affects the actual power base of political parties. Local issues, then, can be the pivot of national power.

On the state and local level, another factor tends to influence the basic structure. Primary elections offer the masses the opportunity to cut the control of party bosses. These elections make it possible for a person without organization backing actually to win the nomination of that party and, in turn, to be elected to office under the party banner.

Sometimes a person who wins public confidence and support without any connection to either of the party organizations appears on the political scene. When this happens, a nonpartisan election may occur. In this instance, the parties realize that it would be useless to oppose such a person, and all political factions give him or her nominal support. The public may well come out ahead in such a situation, but the parties suffer through loss of control. Even a nonpartisan candidate is often preferred by most party bosses to a nasty primary fight between factions of the same organization. A bitter primary fight can leave a party so shattered that for years to come it will have too little unity to win an election.

The final control of overstrong political parties is part of the nature of our nation. There are great differences among the various regions and political parties, on a nationwide basis. This ensures the existence of broad-based, vaguely defined, poorly organized, undisciplined, disconnected collections of state and local political groups. These collections are not strongly linked to concerns of local importance. In this light, such issues as busing, zoning regulations, or a school board fight over teacher tenure may rock and eventually sink the political ship of the national party. The base of power on the local level can change over such issues and affect the complexion of state government.

As the state party organization nominates national figures, the entire delicate balance can shift. If an issue such as a statewide sales or income tax is at the crux of debate, local affairs will certainly have national implications.

PRIMARY ELECTION: A preliminary election for the nomination of candidates for office; primary elections are classified as closed or open depending on whether tests of party affiliation are required; as mandatory or optionally depending on whether the state law requires a primary or leaves to each party the choice to adopt it or not and merely provides machinery for its operation.

NONPARTISAN ELECTION: An election, usually for local or state judicial offices, which excludes the nominees of national political parties by law.

SUMMARY

A political party is an organization that tries to gain control over the government by electing appropriate candidates to office.

There were no parties at our nation's beginning, but the two major parties began soon and evolved over the next seventy years.

The Federalists were replaced by the Whigs, who were followed by the Republicans. The Democratic-Republicans developed into the Democratic party that we know today.

Unlike some others, ours is a two-party system. Our system is a broad-based, winner-take-all type, which makes for few differences between the major parties' offerings. In contrast, parliamentary systems allow more minority representation but less stable governments.

Our two major parties attract different kinds of people. City dwellers, minority groups, the poor, and labor are most often Democrats. The rich, business people, and those in small towns and suburbs most often vote Republican. Democrats stand for government being used as a tool for change. Republicans favor less governmental action.

Politicians participate in the party system in order to win elections and the many rewards of public office. Reelection often becomes a prime concern for the politician, who wants to retain those rewards.

Interest groups and political activists are important participants in the party system. In fact, they make the system run.

The main function of political parties is to present candidates to the voters. The selection of these candidates is not always in the best interests of the voting public, however. Broad appeal, rather than ability, is too often the basis of this selection.

American political parties function at several levels. The most basic is the local level. A politician depends on local support more than any other level of support.

While political parties in the United States are important and powerful, they have limits to their powers. The major way this power is limited is through the separation of power of our government's branches. The way elections are scheduled allows one party's politician to be replaced by another's rather frequently. Also, some people win so much popular support that they do not need party support. And because of the great differences among the regions of our country, local issues have great influence over state and national party policies. This prevents a national party from wielding too much power.

SPECIAL TOPIC

PACs and Parties

We have recently been treated to a new wrinkle in the field of political action: the Political Action Committee (PAC). Such organizations act as the terrorist gangs of politics. They work apart from formal affiliation with a candidate, but for a candidate's benefit.

The terrorist organizations may do the work of government, but the government will still be able to say that it has no connection with political murder or other devastation.

In the world of PACs we have groups that operate with no restriction on money or activity. While formal candidates operate within a system developed over the years, and under restrictions placed on spending, the PACs can do what they wish.

In many instances, the PAC will act to defeat candidates rather than to elect a candidate. Character assassination and dirty tricks are standard operating procedure. The result of their underhanded actions can be denied, deplored, and ignored. Each denial brings the subject back to the public eye.

In the following article by Jane Stone, entitled "Have Calumny, Will Travel," which appeared in *The Nation*, October 10, 1981, the question of whether elections are for sale is discussed.

HAVE CALUMNY, WILL TRAVEL[12]

Just a few days after the November elections, the National Conservative Political Action Committee (N.C.P.A.C., commonly known as "Nickpack") held a news conference to announce its hit list for 1982. It was a brassy, audacious gesture that rubbed the Democrats' noses in the enormousness of what they had lost on November 4.

That so many people came to listen was testimony not only to the emergence of the New Right as a hot political story but also to N.C.P.A.C.'s sudden prominence on the national political scene. Almost unknown until the 1980 elections, its bitter, and largely negative, campaign—that is, one directed against, not for, a specific candidate—made it, if not a household word, at least a name not to be taken lightly in the House or in the Senate.

In 1980, N.C.P.A.C. targeted with its dollars President Jimmy Carter and six Democratic Senators—Birch Bayh of Indiana, Frank Church of Idaho, Alan Cranston of California, John Culver of Iowa, George McGovern of South Dakota and Thomas Eagleton of Missouri. With the exception of Cranston and Eagleton, all were defeated. For 1982, N.C.P.A.C. has marked, among others, Edward Kennedy of Massachusetts, Howard Metzenbaum of Ohio, Donald Riegle Jr. of Michigan and Paul Sarbanes of Maryland.

The activities of N.C.P.A.C. have been heralded as the opening shots in a new era of the electoral battle: the rise of the ideological political action committee unaffiliated with either of the major parties. Only it is not the PACs

that are independent—it is their expenditures. An independent political action committee's expenditures are considered independent because the committee is not aligned with any one candidate or party; its financial outlays must be made without the candidate's (or his authorized committee's) knowledge or approval. Beyond this requirement, there is no limit on the amount a PAC can spend on any candidate; nor do its expenditures count against the $29.4 million limit imposed on Presidential candidates who accept public financing.

N.C.P.A.C. is not the only independent political action committee. It was not even the biggest spender in 1980. That distinction fell to the Congressional Club, a North-Carolina-based group whose honorary chairman is Republican Senator Jesse Helms. The Congressional Club spent $4.6 million during the last election, with virtually all the money going to Ronald Reagan's Presidential campaign. (It has raised $2.4 million during the first six months of 1981.) N.C.P.A.C. was the second largest spender, disbursing almost $3.3 million.

The total expenditures of independent PACs in the 1980 elections were $16.1 million. That is twenty times the amount recorded in the 1976 elections, when independent campaign spending first came into wide use. While the most recent reports on PAC spending come from Federal Election Commission (F.E.C.) data on PAC contributions to campaign treasuries, this is the first analysis of the money these PACs have spent independently.

My analysis of the F.E.C. figures shows that 81 percent—or $13.4 million—of the $16.1 million handed out in the 1980 elections was disbursed by the ideologically conservative PACs. Liberal PACs spent less than 1 percent of the total; labor PACs, 0.4 percent; corporate PACs, 0.3 percent; trade association PACs, 10.4 percent and individuals, 6.4 percent [for the major spenders, see listing on page 600]. Independent PACs spent $6 million for Reagan, as compared with $18,500 for Carter. Even though it is unclear what their effect will be on upcoming elections—and how much they had to do with the conservative victories of 1980, for that matter—the conservative PACs are here to stay. "History has shown that it is never possible to separate the power of money from the power of politics," said a lobbyist for the Christian Voice Moral Government Fund. "Election laws just don't work."

But even the most ardent conservative candidates accept the embraces of the New Right PACs somewhat sheepishly. Not that they are unappreciative of the PACs' efforts; they are, however, reluctant to be too closely identified with groups that run television ads featuring dead fetuses and label opponents "baby killers." Consequently, the recipients of conservative PAC money try to downplay its effects. This is exemplified by the remarks of Senator Charles Grassley, who was the beneficiary of the commercials described above in his race against liberal incumbent John Culver in Iowa. N.C.P.A.C., Grassley told the press after his election, "had a somewhat negative impact" on his election bid because of the "flamboyant" and "negative" campaign the group ran against Culver. To which a spokesman for the Christian Voice Moral Government Fund commented: "That's O.K. He probably had no other political choice but to berate us. We just wanted him in office, and if deriding us will help him stay in office, that's O.K. by us."

N.C.P.A.C.'s efforts in the Grassley-Culver race were a textbook case of independent conservative political action committee strategy: hit 'em, hit 'em often and hit 'em anywhere you can. Independent PACs are the shock troops of the New Right. "We're not interested in respectability," says John Terrence Dolan, the committee's chairman. "We're going to beat [them] and send a shiver down the spines of . . . senators and congressmen."

"Images are important, not issues," Dolan explains. "We start early and use repetition and it's bound to have an impact. Start with an image like George McGovern doesn't represent South Dakota. Keep hitting away. That's more effective than George McGovern did or didn't do X, Y or Z for South Dakota."

Dolan said his organization would attack a targeted senator with a barrage of radio commercials running as often as seventy-two times per day and television commercials as frequently as 200 times per week. "By November," Dolan boasted, "there will be people voting against [him] without remembering why." Dolan asserted that these tactics could elect Mickey Mouse to the United States Senate.

"We were in the league with N.C.P.A.C. and other groups in using an attack philosophy," said Mark Longabaugh, research director of the Fund for a Conservative Majority. "Trade associations and other business groups don't do that as often, because they are more concerned with buying access [to candidates]."

The independent committees scorn the latter approach. Rather than winning the ears of

TOP 15 INDEPENDENT PACs (1980)

1. Congressional Club		$4,633,467.92
2. National Conservative Political Action Committee		$3,287,490.67
3. Fund for a Conservative Majority		$2,008,761.88
A Washington, D.C.-based lobby and political action committee, this group advocates a conservative social and fiscal legislative agenda. It spent its funds in support of candidates sympathetic to its causes, particularly Ronald Reagan.		
4. Americans for an Effective President		$1,272,047.07
Created by former White House assistant Peter M. Flanigan and former Air Force Secretary Thomas C. Reed, it spent the bulk of its funds in support of candidates sympathetic to its causes, particularly Ronald Reagan.		
5. Americans for Change		$707,884.28
Headed by Senator Harrison (Jack) Schmitt (R-New Mexico), the group supported Ronald Reagan and other conservative candidates.		
6. Cecil R. Haden		$600,528.00
A Texas industrialist who spent the bulk of his funds in support of John Connally's primary race for President, then for Ronald Reagan.		
7. National Rifle Association		$444,799.42
8. Christian Voice Moral Government Fund		$401,887.89
This group is strongly anti-homosexual rights, antiabortion and pro-prayer in schools. It spent money in support of candidates sympathetic to its position.		
9. 1980 Republican Presidential Campaign Committee for Ronald Reagan		$314,690.00
10. American Medical Association		$172,439.91
11. Stewart Rawlings Mott		$144,146.00
An individual who donates to liberal causes.		
12. Gun Owners of America		$120,000.00
A PAC founded by State Senator Bill Richardson of California to promote the right to keep and bear arms. It opposes candidates and legislation which favor gun control.		
13. Americans for Life		$119,115.25
A national group supporting antiabortion measures.		
14. Norman Lear		$108,000.00
15. League of Conservation Voters		$102,842.00
A group that works to protect the environment.		

a hundred candidates, they prefer to defeat a carefully selected half dozen. In 1980, they concentrated on races "where we felt we could make a difference," as a staffer at the National Rifle Association put it.

Such relentless pressure by the PACs can cause a backlash against their own candidates. Many PACs focus on emotional, polarizing issues—issues that the candidate might prefer to downplay in the interest of coalition-building. Independent expenditures can also disrupt the efforts of the candidate and his staff to retain control over the campaign. If you can't, by law, even be aware of a PAC's activities, there is theoretically no way to monitor them.

"Independent spending is not a reason for glee by the candidate," said Mark Green, an unsuccessful liberal Democratic candidate for Congress from New York City. Green suggested that there would be "an inevitable tension between a campaign staff planning its own strategy and an outside group trying to influence a campaign. Running a campaign is a delicate operation, and you select those few things that maximize your assets and minimize your opponent's. Quite likely an outside group coming in to do things for your campaign that are out of your jurisdiction would be inconsistent with your strategies and, therefore, counterproductive."

In practice, candidates and the independent PACs have found imaginative ways to circumvent the problem. "It was easy for us to communicate through the press," said an official for the Christian Voice Moral Government Fund. "We would tell the press what we were going to do and they would print it. If the candidate didn't like it, he could tell the press and chances are they would print it. Then the PAC would find out and change its strategy."

But how much are all these plans, ads, strategems and independent dollars really worth to a candidate? The 1980 elections provided few clear answers. One political observer commented: "N.C.P.A.C. is like a rooster who takes credit for the dawn. There were definitely other forces which led to the defeat of liberal Democratic senators."

A postelection analysis published by *Congressional Quarterly* came to a similar conclusion: "Republican officials and many of the candidates who ousted liberal Democrats said the New Right's role was minimal, and in some cases, harmful to their campaigns. They attrib-

uted the victory to a list of more familiar factors: fresh, but experienced candidates, generous doses of party financing, a popular Presidential candidate atop the ticket and a throw-the-bums-out mood. On one point, the analysts were much in agreement: Whatever role the New Right played was due in large part to the press's fascination with the phenomenon."

The power of the new independent PACs should not, however, be underestimated. Lance Tarrance, a Houston pollster who was hired by Grassley, discovered a significant N.C.P.A.C. effect very early in the Iowa race that could be attributed to an anti-Culver advertising blitz. Because of the blitz, the incumbent was weakened before a challenger had even been chosen.

"In 1979, it was not altogether clear to people where Culver was ideologically," Tarrance said. "He was seen as slightly liberal . . .. By the summer of 1980, Culver was perceived to be very, very liberal. That was not the result of Grassley's campaign. He was busy getting the nomination."

Public-interest groups have challenged independent spending on the ground that it is a way to skirt the campaign finance laws. Common Cause, which helped push through the 1974 election financing law, has filed suit against Americans for Change, a conservative group headed by Senator Harrison (Jack) Schmitt, a New Mexico Republican. The suit, which failed in the lower courts, is now pending in the Supreme Court. Common Cause argues that unlimited independent spending will destroy the entire system set up in 1974 to regulate campaign financing and set spending limits.

Thus far, the courts have ruled that restraints on independent campaign contributions impair freedom of speech. In 1976, the Supreme Court ruled in *Buckley v. Valeo* that supporters of Federal candidates may spend unrestricted amounts in elections as long as they do not coordinate their spending with the official campaign. Dissenting, Justice Byron White expressed the fear that independent spending would result in "transparent and widespread invasion of the contributions limit."

As a result of the unsuccessful attempts to stop independent spending, many progressive groups have decided that if you can't beat them, join them. "Independent spending is effective, deplorable and probably not preventable," according to Mark Green. "The only constitutional antidote to right-wing spending, however, is left-wing spending."

In this spirit, a number of progressive groups have begun raising money to act as a counterweight to the influx of conservative spending. Groups such as McGovern's Americans for Common Sense, former lobbyist Victor Kamber's Pro–PAC, Norman Lear's People for an American Way, Kennedy's Fund for a Democratic Majority and Independent Action have set up research operations and, in some cases, will be forming independent PACs.

"The New Right has demonstrated that there is a market for PAC activity. We will be a small PAC, but hopefully we can work with other liberal PACs to counter some of the New Right gains in the last election," noted Wally Chal-

mers, the executive director of the Fund for a Democratic Majority. "There are many approaches a PAC can use when disbursing its funds. N.C.P.A.C. and the rest showed that there is plenty of room for innovation in spending." Kamber's Pro–PAC hopes to be the left's answer to N.C.P.A.C. It will spend the major part of the money it raises in direct-mail solicitations in carefully chosen races.

What will this influx of money do to already high campaign costs? It appears that if the courts don't step in, there is nowhere to go but up. Only about 110 PACs of the more than 2,000 in existence spent independently in the last election. And only twenty individuals made use of this provision in the campaign financing laws. As independent spending gains wider acceptance in the political community, however, many more will make use of the loophole.

SELF-TEST QUESTIONS

1. Republican support comes mainly from groups described as _____ .
2. Parliamentary systems allow for _____ representation.
3. Our system of elections can be described as _____ .
4. Urban centers have been known as strongholds of the _____ party.
5. True or false: Tax bills are usually passed just after elections.
6. Politicians pay more attention to
   a. minority groups
   b. the average voter
   c. interest groups
7. Corruption is most dangerous in the _____ branch of government.
8. American voters are known for their _____ level of participation.
9. Most politicians' primary interest is _____ .

ANSWERS TO SELF-TEST QUESTIONS

1. conservative, rural, well-to-do, etc.
2. minority
3. winner-take-all
4. Democratic
5. true
6. interest groups (c)
7. judicial
8. low
9. reelection

ANSWERS TO SKILL REINFORCERS

23–1. 1. The Constitution established our form of government.
   2. Political parties are not established by the Constitution.
   3. Therefore political parties are not constitutional.
   The conclusion clearly is not accurate. Political parties are a legitimate part of our political system. The problem with this syllogism, which leads to a wrong conclusion, lies in the major premise. The Constitution established the formal system of government, but not the entire political system.

23–2. False cause. The alliance of Jefferson and Burr came before the disappearance of the Federalists, but there is nothing in the text to suggest that the earlier event caused the later one.

23–3. Probably not. First, the footnote refers you to some research on which the picture of the political activist is based. A few traits are assumed to be true of a large number of people, but there seem to be good grounds for the assumptions. Also, stereotyping involves exaggeration and often judging. The general statements here do not fit the mold of the stereotype.

NOTES

1. "End of a Sleazy Affair," *Newsweek,* March 22, 1982; and "The Senate's Search for Integrity," *America,* March 20, 1982.
2. Ernest Holsendolph, "Influence Peddling Is Hinted in Job Referrals," *New York Times,* February 2, 1976.
3. John C. Bollems, ed., *Metropolitan Challenge* (Dayton, Ohio: Metropolitan Community Studies, 1959).
4. Federal Election Commission, *Study of American Electorate,* Government Printing Office, Washington D.C. 1984.
5. Robert E. Lane, *Political Life* (New York: Free Press, 1959).
6. Morris Axelrod, "Urban Structure and Social Participation," *American Sociological Review* 21 (February 1956).
7. Lane, *Political Life.*
8. Herbert Alexander, *Financing the 1968 Election* (Lexington, Mass.: D.C. Heath, 1971).
9. Mark Benny and Phyllis Geiss, "Social Class and Politics in Greenwich," *British Journal of Sociology,* December 1950, and Angus Campbell, "The Passive Citizen," *Acta Sociologica* 6 (fasc. 1–2, 1962).
10. W.D. Burnham, "The Changing Shape of the American Political Universe," *American Political Science Review,* March 1968.
11. Knight-Ridder Newspapers Personal Opinion Poll: A National Survey, January 19–23, 1976.
12. Reprinted from Jane Stone, "Have Calumny, Will Travel," *The Nation,* October 10, 1981, with permission of The Nation Magazine, The Nation Associates, Inc. Copyright © 1981 by Nation Enterprises/Nation Associates, Inc.

SUGGESTED READINGS

Binkley, Wilfred F. *American Political Parties,* 4th ed. New York: Alfred Knopf, 1963.

Gatlin, D.S. "Party Identification, Status, and Race in the South: 1952–1972." *Public Opinion Quarterly* 39 (Spring 1975): 39–51.

Greenstein, Fred I. *The American Party System and the American People.* Englewood Cliffs, N.J.: Prentice-Hall, 1970.

Hapgood, David. *The Purge That Failed: Tammany vs. Powell.* New Brunswick, N.J.: Eagleton Institute, 1958.

Sheed, Wilfred. *Clare Booth Luce.* New York: E.P. Dutton, 1982.

Taubman, William. *Stalin's American Policy.* New York: W.W. Norton, 1982.

Wills, Garry. *The Kennedy Imprisonment.* Boston: Little, Brown, 1982.

24 INTERNATIONAL RELATIONS

International What?

The concept of international relations has been with us from the earliest days of written history and as far back in time as the first instance of two groups of hunter-gatherers meeting to talk or fight about fishing rights or possession of a particularly fine berry bush. Certainly we can see the idea of nationality or self in the biblical references to the land of the people of Israel and the people of Canaan or the land of the Pharaohs, the city of Jericho and the minions of Babylon.

In those days population was small and resources short, yet people of different groups either sought to protect what they had from other groups or tried to figure a way to gain control of what other groups owned. Talk or fight, steal or trade, when one distinct group deals with another, we have the beginnings of international relations.

Over the years, the size of the groups involved has increased from wandering bands to tribes to city states to nations as we know them today. Seminational combinations of a number of nations also exist along with our attempts at world government. Perhaps the basis of nationality lies in a commonality of interest and identification. As the group grows or encompasses different peoples, the important factor would be one of self-identification, the feeling of "we" as opposed to "them." At what point do Walloons and Flemings think of themselves as Belgians? When will the two major camps of Irish think of themselves as Irish? Will the inhabitants of Israel ever think of themselves as Israeli as opposed to Arab and Jew? The United States has integrated its many pieces into a whole. Canada, on the other hand, still has a significant portion of its people wishing to be separated as a French-speaking entity. A modern nation can exist confortably when subgroups see themselves first as citizens of that nation and only secondarily or ritually as part of separate, identifiable groups. When a people can get beyond the point of mandating specific representation for specific groups, they are on the way to nation or state status.

Many nations existing today, and, for that matter, in the past, are composed of groups that, given their choice, would exist as independent nations. Examples are easily found and include Nigeria, recent host to the attempted Ibo independence movement. This resulted in the Biafran war. The various portions of the British, Austrian, and Ottoman Empires have become independent. On the other hand, there are numerous examples of groups that wish independence, not the least of which are Puerto Rico, Scotland, and the Baltic States.

People operate to settle disputes, meet needs, or build compromises within the framework of their own society. We can examine those operations in terms of the processes we dealt with in earlier chapters on government and politics. These operations can be called domestic relations. But, in relationships *between* nations there are no constitutions, binding laws, or common norms to set forth the rights and obligations of the parties. Interest groups and political parties of domestic relations are replaced in international relations by nations and blocs of nations. International relations are complex and differ substantially from domestic relations; this chapter looks at some of those differences and the ways nations deal with one another.

Relations between nations are complicated by economic, political and ideological factors not ordinarily found within any one country. Different nations have special resources and products; some have valuable resources to exploit and others have little to offer the world. Ideally, although all countries contribute to the world economy, some are enormously rich and others are pathetically poor. Also, trade barriers such as tariffs interfere, and different media of exchange complicate matters. Further, economic alliances within which no tariffs are allowed place themselves in positions of advantage. International economic relations are also complicated by the sometimes rather self-seeking economic decisions various nations make due to their fear of dependence on other nations in time of need. In an effort to insure self-sufficiency in case of war, a nation may maintain unprofitable industries such as an aging steel industry, even when the products could be purchased more cheaply from foreign producers. International relations clearly offer a different set of problems and require different solutions than do domestic relations.

Without either formal or informal relations between any of the approximately 140 nations of the world, there are only two choices of interaction—avoidance or war. There must be mechanisms for settling disputes, meeting needs, and compromising because different peoples have different needs, internal norms, and laws. Thus, when differing peoples come into contact, conflicts will arise and war will result unless such mechanisms are available. The mechanisms employed to settle disputes between nations, adjust trade, regulate travel, and put forth articles of worldwide agreement all come under the heading International Relations.

FACTORS AFFECTING A NATION'S STATUS AMONG OTHER NATIONS

As we saw earlier in Chapter 7, individual humans usually arrange themselves within a prestige hierarchy (social stratification), much as chickens establish a barnyard "pecking order." Similarly, nations of people are concerned with their status within the pecking order of the other nations with whom they must deal. Each nation's position in that pecking order depends on its power which is measured by the degree it can affect the behavior of other nations and their goals and power.

Power A nation's ability to exert its will internationally depends on several factors, some psychological and some physical. On the psychological side, a people with a strong sense of their own superiority and morality give their nation strength. A nation's power is based on how strongly people identify with the nation and its culture and how ready they are to make sacrifices for the nation. Strong leadership is another psychological factor affecting a nation's power.

A nation's ability to take risks for the sake of progress is another important factor. A population with some degree of material security can afford to take risks in trying new technologies. On the other hand, people whose bellies are empty are unlikely to try a new system of crop rotation or a new seed, because poor results could mean starvation.

Physical factors influencing a nation's power include geography and population. Although substantial regional differences can affect domestic relations, such differences are more common and more dramatic on the international scene. In the following examples, we can see how differences in such physical factors as geography and population affect international relations.

Throughout history, favorable geographical condition allowed continued independence and strength for some nations and constant war and/or domination of others. The mountains of Switzerland have allowed a defense so easy that conquest was not worth the cost to other nations. Conversely, the relatively featureless landscape of Poland has invited invasion over the centuries. Easily navigable internal rivers have allowed easy access to some nations by invading forces, while being located upon an island gives both the protection of isolation and the open seacoast for attack. Ancient Egypt prospered from having the Nile as a central corridor of communication and the surrounding deserts as a protective buffer.

Another important geographical feature is the fertility of the land. Some countries find food production difficult because of their ecology. There may be too much rain or too little. The soil may be poor in nutrients and be useful only for growing low-protein crops.

The possession of fertile land does not guarantee a surplus of food production to those without the technical ability to work the soil. American Indians lived upon the Great Plains for thousands of years without the ability to break the soil with a plow. Other natural resources may be present, but without the technology or capital to take advantage of these resources, they are valueless.

Population is another physical factor affecting a nation's power. It is difficult to say a country is overpopulated—or underpopulated—without taking into consideration such factors as the available food supply, general economic condition, and technological sophistication of the people. A population may be huge, but the people may be unproductive and lacking in helpful technologies. Poor sanitation, inadequate medical care, and poor food storage and transportation can all sap the strength of the people.

Clearly, a large population composed of untrained, uneducated, and underproductive citizens will reduce a nation's ability to respond adequately to an aggressive neighbor. The People's Republic of China has been weighed down by excessive population and has attempted to deal with that situation. Many of the methods employed by the Chinese government were draconian, but the very size of its population seemed to call for drastic action. In response to these attempts to control the population aspect and improve its overall economic outlook, The Agency for International Development withheld $25 million from the United Nations Fund for Population Activities.[1]

The example just cited was the use of an international agency either to impose specific ideological values upon another nation or to hinder the attempts of that nation to improve its power position relative to other nations by getting a handle on its own population problem.

In a totally opposite situation, an announcement making the news from Singapore[2] indicated that the government there, worried about the lagging birth rate of educated couples, has offered the equivalent of a $10,000 tax deduction for children born to selected couples. The government felt that because the birth rate for educated couples was so low, replacement population would not be available in the future.

These examples of government population programs indicate the importance of population in determining a nation's position in the world's hierarchy.

Goals   International relations are complicated not only by geography and population differences among countries but by the different goals each of those countries is trying to attain. All nations aim to survive, but some can also afford to aim for more prestige or to protect or spread a system of ideas.

Survival.   The most important national goal is the maintenance of the nation's entity. This is a fundamental goal but one which some countries have not fulfilled. We have seen the countries of Latvia, Lithuania, Estonia, and others incorporated into the Soviet Union. Tibet has become part of China. Serbia and Montenegro disappeared after World War I due to a general rearrangement of Europe's map. As the result of Roman conquest, Carthage not only lost its population to death and slavery, but its land was plowed under and laced with salt. Foreign policy, which is simply a nation's plan for pursuing its own self interest, naturally has as its basic objective the survival and security of the state.

The Queen of England and her consort in royal procession.

Prestige.   This goal concerns nonmaterial aspects of a nation's existence. The concept of prestige is one with which we are all quite familiar. In our own country we seem overly concerned with the image we exude at any given moment and seem to be gauging our prestige level in the world community with a thermometer.

The real side of prestige or respect is power, both perceived and imagined. As an example, the Falkland Island War shows the importance of power in achieving prestige. This war between England and Argentina was disaster for both countries. The government of Argentina was seen as having bungled the entire matter, and as a result was replaced. The British won the war but lost much of their prestige. Britain's difficulty in defeating a third-class military power was seen as a major military problem. The problem was not one of inefficiency, which can be overlooked after the weight of a great military power is brought to bear. It was one of having to muster the home fleet for an effort that was not only expensive, but strained the resources of Britain's armed services to the limit. Prestige is always lost by the defeated, but in the Falkland War even the winner suffered loss because it barely had enough power to win what should have been a fairly easy victory.

An example in the other direction was the United States' overwhelming of Grenada. It is possible the number of U.S. military in place for that operation was more than the total population, including medical students, on the island. There should be no prize awarded for military efficiency, but the impression given was one of great military power and no reluctance to use that power. The Soviet Union's military reaction in Hungary (1956) and Israel's use of a club in reaction to flea bites give the same impression, one of real power.

The Iranian revolution reclaims the symbols in its rush toward revitalization through reinstitution of real or imagined elements from its past.

Ideology.   An ideology is a body of beliefs or ideas; it is the basis for the way an individual or group thinks. Ideology can be the basis for an economic system, a social order, a form of government, or a religion. The maintenance or spread of ideology is a major part of the foreign policy of many nations today as in the past. The efforts of the Hundred Years' War, the various Crusades, and the spreading of the word of Allah all have their base in religious fervor no less than the fundamentalist revival of today's Shiites in Iran and elsewhere. Capitalism and socialism each have their advocates, and we are certainly familiar with the wars fought in their behalf. In the past, countries fought to maintain the rights of Kings. In fact, the army of the United States of America joined with the soldiers of the Republic of France to fight in Russia (after World War I) in an attempt to regain the throne of Russia for the czar. Britain and Japan were among other nations represented in Russia at that time.

NATION VERSUS NATION

Nations are not always opposed to one another, as the "versus" in our title implies. Nations sometimes cooperate and recognize common needs. But often a conflict of interests arises between countries, and here we examine two forms that conflict has taken for several centuries: colonization and imperialism. To understand these two forms is to understand much of today's international relations.

Colonialism and Imperialism

Colonialism and imperialism are important concepts and practices that have been used to better the position of an initiating nation, usually at the expense of other nations.

COLONIALISM: The means by which a nation will resettle its own population in a sparsely populated area or an area depopulated for the purpose of that settlement and control.

Colonialism.   In the case of colonialism, a nation would establish its own citizens in an underdeveloped region or perhaps a region with few inhabitants. In some important instances, such as the British Colonies of North America, substantial native populations resided in the lands chosen for settlement, yet the natives were not considered humans. In other cases the form of land ownership was not recognized by the laws of the colonizing nation and hence did not qualify for consideration—the nation simply took the land it wanted. If either of these statements seem too strong, let us point to the hunting of Australian Aborigines by the colonial British in lieu of foxes. Lest we feel too superior, we may also point to the fact that a bounty was once offered for American Indian scalps in New Mexico.[3] Colonizing nations sometimes make whatever rules they wish.

The major reasons for colonial ventures are usually economic and military, but we cannot ignore the fact that some nations feel the need to spread their ideologies. The need for raw materials, and the eventual presence of a market for the manufacturers created by those raw materials, lies at the base of the economic motive. Our own original colonies were examples of economic colonization.

Military considerations in the past fell into the category of coaling stations and naval bases. The British maintained control of Gilbraltar in order to control entry to the Mediterranean Sea, while our Panama Canal Zone came close to qualifying as a colony. The Germans planned to settle their excess population in lands occupied by Slavs. The simple way to make these lands available was to depopulate them. In this case the desire was expansion rather than actual colonization.

IMPERIALISM: One nation taking control of the area and population of another nation or region.

Imperialism.   Imperialism is the extension of a nation's control over the land and population of what had been another political entity. The British takeover of the various nations or nation states that composed India is one example of imperialism. Other examples are the race to control Africa with the Belgian king owning the Congo, Portugal controlling Angola, the British controlling a north-south line of entities from Egypt to South Africa, the French controlling most of North Africa, the Germans establishing control and giving up that control over African regions as the result of World War I. Let us not forget about Portugal in Brazil, and Spain in the remainder of South and Central America. Our experience in Vietnam was based on an attempt to somehow hold on to what had been French Indochina.

The imperialist experience usually results in the indigenous population being cast in the role of second-class citizen. We have evidence in our films and literature to support this claim. Most Americans have seen or read "Gunga Din," "Elephant Walk," or any of a series of Bengal Lancer pictures. If we can sit back and analyze what is being said, we will see that the European, regardless of rank, is seen as superior to even the most highly educated and wealthy "native." In recent years a television series based upon "The Raj Quartet" (four books), written by Paul Scott,[4] and entitled "The Jewel in the Crown" appeared on public channels. A major subplot of the series centered on a young man educated in the best schools in England, speaking only English and living the life of English gentry while in England. When his father lost his fortune, the young man had no choice but to return to India, the home of his family. As an Indian who spoke no Hindi, educated as an upper-class Englishman and with all the cultural attributes of that group save appearance, he was faced with the prospect of being an outcaste isolated from both groups. He was seen by the English as only an Indian, and by the Indians as almost, but not quite, an Englishman. The interesting point in this example is that regardless of how well the Indian performs, how much wealth is accumulated, and how well he is educated, the person remains an Indian and is not considered the equal of a poor, uneducated Englishman.

NATIONALISM: A form of political ethnocentrism. Setting the loyalty and devotion to a political or cultural entity or state above consideration of all else.

As colonies achieve economic stability, they often seek political independence, as did the prosperous North American British Colonies. Imperial possessions seek independence when national-

The USS Stark, hit by Iraq, caused bluster and posturing at the Iranians.

ism—a sense of patriotism and devotion to the nation state—develops.

The U.S. versus the U.S.S.R. versus the Third World

The international community has been divided into three "worlds." The United States is part of the First World, which includes non-communist, developed or industrialized nations. The First World is mostly found in the northern half of the globe, and includes such countries as the U.S., Canada, Western Europe, Japan, Israel, plus the southern countries of Australia, New Zealand, the Union of South Africa, and probably Argentina. The Second World includes communist countries, industrialized or not: the U.S.S.R., the People's Republic of China, Eastern Europe, and smaller countries such as Vietnam and Cuba. The Third World is simply everyone else. Because it contains so many diverse nations, the Third World is sometimes subdivided into the Third, Fourth, and Fifth Worlds.

The Fifth World is those nations with so few resources that they can not feed their own people. The Fifth World nations comprise the welfare roll of the world; they will always require outside help. Members of this category are Niger, Chad, Ethiopia, and Bangladesh.

The Fourth World nations require time, loans, and technical assistance, but they have the potential for economic development. With such help, such countries can probably become strong enough to compete in the world market system and to provide their people with a relatively good standard of living. They can become paying customers as well as sellers in the world market. Fourth World countries possess some resources such as oil, tin, rubber, timber, or potential agricultural production. Fourth World nations have potential, but need help to make good use of it. Examples of Fourth World nations are Ecuador, Peru, Sudan, and India.

With the Fourth and Fifth Worlds set aside, the Third World can be defined as developing noncommunist nations. They are on the way to economic development; they need time, not handouts. Third World countries have begun to build roads, capitalize on resources, and train people. Many of these nations are formidable competitiors in at least one part of the world market. This category includes such nations as Brazil, South Korea, Taiwan, Mexico, Libya, Saudi Arabia, and Iran. Some of these countries may be considered part of the First World, depending on how economic development is measured within the classification scheme. The Third World most commonly refers to the Third, Fourth, and Fifth Worlds, and we will use the term in that inclusive fashion in the rest of our discussion. We will explore the relations between the First World nation of the United States, the Second World nation of the U.S.S.R., and the entire Third World.

The aim of the United States in regard to the Soviet Union is one that was inherited from the French and British. In brief, the aim has been to keep Russia bottled up, keep her from warm water, and minimize her contact with Asia, the Pacific, Central and South America, Africa, and India. In other words, our intent is to keep Russia out of the race for control of raw materials and people. We are not talking about Communism, because there have been concerted efforts to isolate Russia even prior to Napoleon. Ideology is not as important in this instance as competition.

The Soviet Union and the United States have too much in common to ever get along without some sparks flying. We are both large countries in terms of area and both have diverse geographical areas. Both countries have significant minority populations, and both have the frontier complex. We had our Wild West and Alaska and they have Siberia and the Cossacks, etc. Russian literature of the last century points to various instances of contact by Great Russians with frontiersmen and the attempts by the Russians to emulate their wilder countrymen. The American literature citing the mountain men and their relationships with the Indians, or Natty Bumpo in "The Last of the Mohicans," is comparable.

We compete with the Soviets in trade, space, military, control of smaller nations, athletics, the arts, and almost every conceivable cultural area. It is a foregone conclusion that these two nations, even if they shared economic, religious, educational, linguistic, and political institutions, would still be competitors. If we then consider that each of these systems is quite different, it is not surprising that we face each other as opponents.

The Soviet Union has accomplished many of the aims of the czars. It controls Eastern Europe well into Germany, and has regained its lost territory from Japan. Mongolia is controlled, China is lost, and India seems well-situated in the Third World. While the Soviets have not regained Alaska, they have strong footholds in Cuba and Nicaragua.

In looking at the United States, the Soviets see a nation with an alien political system. They see an economic system that they equate with the bad old days of the czar. They remember the invasion of their territory by the United States and other Western nations after World War I, in support of the czar.

While all of this is true, there are considerations that bear expressing. The Russian government under the czars was cruel and inhuman. The Soviet government under Stalin and his followers has been at least as cruel and inhuman. Travelling in Russia in the 1870s, a police pass was needed to go from one town to the next. Crossing the border into Prussia was frequently done at night, slipping between armed guards. Travel and residence in the Soviet Union is still controlled. People leaving the Soviet Union have been forced to do the same in modern days. The Iron Curtain is not new, but the fabric is different. We have cultural expectations and traits that are different from those of the Soviets, so it is natural that we distrust each other and view one another through the rose-colored glasses of ethnocentrism.

Prospects for the Third World seem grim at best. Poverty is rampant, as are unemployment, malnutrition, and population

A street in Calcutta, India, a city of over 10 million. The Third World has major problems today and monumental problems looming in the near future.

growth. Twenty percent of children surviving birth in the Third World die of malnutrition before their first birthdays. From ten to twenty million adults die each year from starvation in these regions. Possibly a billion Third World residents are illiterate.

Political problems are many in the Third World. Religious fanaticism and nationalism seem to thrive by giving hope, to some, of improving their situation. It is probable that a growing series of nationalist or nativistic movements with political, religious, and/or cultural bases will continue to flourish in Third World countries.

Pressures from the Third World may possibly cause some strange alliances in the future. The United States is coming under pressure today on its southern border, with many thousands of people from all over the world lining up to try to cross into what is perceived as an area of hope and stability. Gaining less notice are those highly trained, or at least not so culturally dissimilar, people who each year meld into the fabric of our society, with or without the proper passports, green cards, or other permissions. The opportunities available in a complex economy and society are too desirable for most trained people to ignore. What chance has a high tech professional in a land with no high tech industry? Medical doctors educated at great expense in the United States by their government suddenly become aware of the differences in opportunities offered in their homeland compared to opportunities available by remaining here. The reality is that the brain drain has continued.

NATIVISTIC MOVEMENT: An irrational return to specified traits associated with a society's happier past in order to create the base for a more satisfying life-style.

THIRD WORLD: Those nations unaligned with either the United States camp or the Soviet camp. In some instances Third World has become another word for underdeveloped.

METHODS OF INTERNATIONAL PROBLEM MANAGEMENT

During the past several decades, Third World nations have begun to demand changes in the world order. Spokespersons for these nations have claimed that their countries' economic problems have been largely caused by exploitation by the First World, in the form of colonization and imperialism. The Second World is rarely accused of these same actions—the Soviet Union's control of Eastern Europe and invasion of Afghanistan are somehow not considered imperialism. Some Third World spokespersons insist that the First World exploited South America, Africa, and Southern Asia, and have now rigged the world market in order to keep the Third World nations in a suppressed condition. To right this wrong, help is demanded of the First World. Such help would take several forms, including soft loans, technical assistance, and cash grants.

First and Second World nations do give help to the Third World. The First World's motive seems to be the creation of markets around the globe and to prevent domination by the Second World. A desperately poor country provides a poor market and is a danger to capital investments. The businesses of the First World want paying customers, and as the Third World develops, their citizens will be able to buy more consumer goods. Various Third World nations are now providing a cheap manufacturing base for First World industrialists. The Second World's motive seems to be political and economic control.

A major form of help given to the Third World is financial in nature. Loans help the Third World nations develop their economies, create jobs, and thus create consumers. When Third World nations conclude they cannot repay the loans due to high interest rates and fluctuating prices for natural resources, they ask for extensions or modified terms or they may default. Several large debtors in default could cause the collapse of the U.S. banking system, and this spectre has hovered over the economic community for several years. Ironically, the Third World's debts have given those nations some leverage in international relations.

With all the conflicting demands and interests just described, it seems that war would be continuous. But there have been substantial periods of relative peace. Several methods are available to resolve conflicts without resorting to war: diplomacy, international organizations, international law, and terrorism.

Diplomacy

DIPLOMACY: The method by which the representatives of one nation work to attain that which is in their nation's best interest by compromise, threat, bargain, trade, or reason. Not infrequently, falsehood, theft, bribery, blackmail, and espionage are utilized in an attempt to achieve desired ends.

In Central America, before the Spanish conquest, there were many city states. A fair number of these city states were at war with one another at any given time. One of the goals set by most of these societies was to capture large numbers of other people to sacrifice to the gods. Almost anyone would do and, as a result, travel was not safe. There was, however, a group of people who traveled freely from city to city without fear of bodily harm. They were traders and were protected by agreement understood by all cities. These people performed services for their various homelands and for the people they visited. Trade was important, but so was contact between groups, as well as the information gathered by observation. In their own way, these early traders, gleaners of information and conveyors of messages, were early diplomats.

Today, world diplomatic representatives are held safe from disaster and law. They receive no speeding tickets, cannot be arrested for even the most serious of crimes, and seem to be above death and retaliation in most cases. They live by and are protected by ritual forms of behavior. They are usually civil and polite to each other when the rest of the world is at each other's throats. Every now and again the code of behavior is broken, such as was the case in Iran with the holding of our diplomatic staff. When this happens, the rest of the world is shaken, because there is no precedent. To put this in the proper light, we must realize that Japanese and American diplomats were safely returned to their homelands after the Pearl Harbor attack. Most nations of the world maintain representatives in every other nation of diplomatic consequence. Even Germany under Hitler played by the rules governing treatment of diplomats.

Unofficial Diplomacy. Problems have arisen in recent years when various nations utilized representatives not associated with their nation to achieve goals and perform actions not recognized as legitimate by the rules of diplomatic agreement. The Iranian situation saw an element of that nation, portrayed as not being under the control of the government proper, holding our foreign service people. There was an attempt on the part of the established Iranian diplomatic service to adhere to formalities by holding senior members of our staff under a modified house arrest and attempting to refer to the action by other terms.

A similar situation was found to exist in the United States when, contrary to the policy set by law, arms were sold to Iran, profits were sent to support the Nicaraguan Contra movement, and private donations were solicited by government agencies. The original arms sale was made in order to obtain the release of American hostages held in Lebanon by Shiite groups backed unofficially by Iran.

In addition to the internal private donations directed to the Contras, there is evidence that the Sultan of Brunei and the King of Saudi Arabia contributed heavily to the Contra cause. It is difficult to find a reason for these donations being linked to the national interests of these nations, except that the giving would improve relations between their governments and the current administration in the United States.

Embassies and consular offices abound in nations of any size or wealth. The duties of the officials are to serve the citizens of their countries while abroad. Trade, travel, immigration, and like duties are the superficial functions most obviously noted. Military attaches keep an eye on military developments. Other officials keep their eyes on economic trends, political movements, and social conditions.

At the highest levels, treaties are negotiated and national desires satisfied, within the ability of the diplomats to do so. Negotiations are at the very heart of diplomacy, and it is the aim of each diplomat to achieve as many of his nation's basic goals and desires as possible. This should be accomplished by giving away as little as possible to the other side.

Diplomacy and Power.   The diplomat is aided or hindered by his nation's real or imagined power. Not only is the actual power important, but so is the realization that a nation is willing to employ that power to achieve its desires. The United States has been perceived as a nation with power, but with a reluctance to use that power to achieve its aims. During and before the 1950s and '60s, it was not uncommon or unexpected for the United States to sponsor revolution and to back aims with troops. We did not hesitate to put troops ashore in Korea, Lebanon, and Santo Domingo. Other less publicized affairs led to uprising in Guatemala, and to war on the Costa Rican border. The overthrow of the governments of Chile and South Vietnam were par for the course in those days. The turning point in a policy that had put troops into Nicaragua, Mexico, Russia, and other countries in this century seems to have been the Cuban invasion. Our troops and planes were ready and on station, but we did not use them. We sat offshore and watched while the invading Cubans were wiped out by Castro's forces. Several things may well have occurred, not the least of which could have been a threat by the Soviets to enter the conflict, using their power. We used the same threat during the Cuban missile crisis. The major mistake made during this affair was not landing the "Free Cuban Troops" in Oriente province where they could have set up a government and been recognized and openly aided by the United States. The area is so wild that the new government could have been in residence for several weeks before Castro's forces could even face them. This would have met the test of legitimacy.

Thus far we have dealt with power, employed by nations with perceived ability to use governmental force, to punctuate a diplomatic point. What other options are at hand for those nations not wishing to face a confrontation with a stronger nation? What options are at hand in those instances where two nations of equal power do not wish a confrontation? In these instances, it becomes easier and safer for a nation to employ a third party to fight in their own name, but for the benefit of the sponsoring nation. It was to the benefit of China and the Soviet Union that the United States pour men and materiel into Vietnam. Until her own borders were threatened, it was to the advantage of China to allow the North Koreans to fight and die for her objectives. The United States could not be better served than by the civil war in Afghanistan, which has cost the Soviet Union dearly in men and materiel. These activities are rather "up-front" with the sponsors known to all. The next level of activity is somewhat less controlled and operates outside the usual agreements and limitations placed upon participants in a formal war.

International Organizations

Another method of resolving problems on the international scene is the use of international organizations. Members of an organization can talk to one another; this talk may prevent misunderstandings, provide channels for negotiation and compromise, and thus prevent war.

The United Nations is a world organization and a step toward world government in the real sense

LEAGUE OF NATIONS: Formed after World War I as part of the peace settlement. Never had the membership of all of the world's powers at the same time. The United States never joined. Formal ending in 1946 when personnel and property were transferred to United Nations.[5]

UNITED NATIONS: A world organization of states, based on the wartime meetings between the Allied leaders (London Declaration, January 1941, Atlantic Charter 1942, Moscow Conference 1943, Teheran Conference 1943, Dumbarton Oaks Conference 1944, and Yalta Conference 1945.) Differed from League of Nations in that all the leading nations are members. Still not a true legislative body.

Alliances between groups are as old as human social life. Alliances on an international scale are a more recent development. The League of Nations, formed after World War I, was the first attempt at world government. The League met with little success. The United States refused to commit itself to such an entangling alliance in which all members were pledged to enter into military defense of any one of the members.

Near the end of World War II, the United Nations was established as the second major attempt at an international organization. The United Nations has never become a true legislative body with the power to decide and enforce its decisions. In the end, the Security Council still has the prospect of the veto of any of its decisions by any of the "Big Five."

The United Nations does have fourteen agencies, both leftovers from the League of Nations and those born of World War II, that deal with everything from labor to postal problems, weather, trade, money, health, etc. While the United Nations has been criticized by many for being a forum for talk and not much else, it has provided the base for military intervention and peace-keeping forces. The very presence of the forum allows contact between even those governments that do not maintain formal relations.

International Law

BIG FIVE: The most powerful allied winners of World War II (the United States, the Soviet Union, England, France, and China).

When diplomacy fails and international organizations prove inadequate, there are alternatives to war if the nations involved in a dispute agree to abide by the decisions of international courts. The United States and Iran agreed to abide by the decision of a tribunal of this type in the dispute over assets of the Iranian government frozen in the United States after the fall of the Shah. The 1987 decision was that the United States should return the money. There are clear rules for the obligations of newly formed states regarding the debts owed by former states, and if a state is subdivided, what portion of the debt will go with each new entity.

Though many trade disputes can be settled in this manner, international law usually deals with matters such as the right of free passage at sea. The agreement provides that a nation's boundary be extended—first three and then twelve miles, and now up to two hundred miles at sea. Disputes arise over both mineral and fishing rights when these lines overlap between nations. Concern over the rights of nations when dealing with the bottom of the open sea have presented new areas of litigation not covered by precedent and custom.

International law represents custom and agreement in the manner in which a nation can gain and lose territory. The final act in territorial loss is by war. Warfare had, prior to the World Wars, abided by a detailed list of what was forbidden and what was accepted. Indiscriminate killing of noncombatants was, for quite some time, considered a violation of international law, as was the use of poison gas, dum dum or exploding bullets, and mistreatment of captives. Most of these agreements have passed into disuse. Diplomats are usually safe in time of war, but even that practice is not uniform in its observance.

The American Vietnam War Memorial in Washington, D.C. stands as a mute reminder of the cost of international relations gone sour. War is afterall the mark of a failure of diplomacy.

Terrorism If a group or nation finds that it is unable to meet conventional power threats or inspire fear through threat of the use of power, terror remains. While we have seen growing use of this technique in recent years, we must not presume that its philosophy is new. Even an old favorite such as Robin Hood could be classed as a terrorist. Did his band not live hidden away, with their aim being the downfall of the government? Did they not break the law of the land, robbing and pillaging as they saw fit? Forget for a moment that most readers are sympathetic to Robin and find Prince John to be a tyrant. The fact remains that the Merry Men in Sherwood Forest were, in a sense, terrorists bent upon the downfall of their government. William Tell and other fighters against inequity find themselves in the same category. Today's bombers and kidnappers may find little sympathy among those being bombed and kidnapped, but they are seen as heroes and fighters among their own people.

Various nations do not perceive themselves as having enough power to confront major powers, so they enlist either mercenaries or ideological fanatics to further their aims. These actions are taken with an anonymity that mitigates against retaliation. The sponsoring nation decries the inhumanity of the act, but denies any responsibility or connection. Meanwhile, money, training facilities, and safe haven are provided. The terrorists are not bound by conventional rules and rituals that protect the typical diplomat. The diplomatic world is shocked when agreements are broken and consulates are bombed. The order of diplomacy is broken when representatives are themselves kidnapped, as was the case of the Church of England's envoy Terry Waite in Lebanon. This action was more troubling than most in that Mr. Waite was acting as an unofficial go-between for the release of hostages. In such a position, he was thought to be immune and above intimidation or danger. The question arises as to the safety and validity of any

SKILL BOX

Classifying Problems

Problem-solving is a necessary task of life. Sometimes it is a burdensome chore, but other times it is something of a game, a challenge. In either case, this Skill Box can help you, not necessarily by making problem solving more enjoyable, but by making it more effective. This Box can show how to avoid wasting time looking for the wrong kind of solution or using the wrong thinking strategy. The idea here is that by simply pausing for a moment to decide what kind of problem we are facing, we can more effectively solve it.

We can classify problems into basically two types. Each one requires a different strategy and different expectations. Each type of problem can be labeled by the kind of thinking system on which it is based: closed or open.[6] Some problems do not fit clearly into only one category, but in general, mathematical and formal logic problems are usefully approached by the closed thinking system, and more everyday problems by the open system.

In the closed system, the thinking leads us to a definite, easily recognized answer or solution. An example would be our search for the answer to the question, "What will happen if I add this chemical to that one?" In such a problem we know exactly what kind of answer we are searching for, and are likely to know when we have found it by reasoning from established laws to a specific answer. This kind of problem requires deduction, which was explained in Chapter 3.

Social scientists are often faced with problems based on an open thinking system, which requires inductive reasoning, explained in Chapter 2. This is unfortunate for those problem-solvers, because answers are more elusive and vague in an open system. Such answers are harder to find and to recognize with certainty. Sociologists are often faced with questions such as, "What is the best way to decrease drug abuse?" or "What can be done about child abuse?" Such open-system questions may have no certain answer, or several answers. Researchers trying to solve such problems can rarely ever be certain that a "correct" or worthwhile answer has been found.

Working within a closed system is an advantage natural scientists often have over social scientists. Chemists, mathematicians, and physicists can often use deduction, working from established laws toward clear, definite answers. Social scientists must more often reason inductively, from an incomplete set of available evidence toward a general rule, or a generalization. Any generalization in an open system is tentative, because new evidence often arises and disrupts the induced conclusion.

All problem-solvers, whether scientists or not, need to identify the problem and the thinking system in which it is based. By identifying the thinking system needed, the chances become greater that the appropriate thinking strategy will be chosen at the beginning of the problem-solving process. Also, this identification makes it easier to understand the kind of solution to expect from one's problem-solving efforts.

Terrorism at work—a Shiite Moslem hijacker points his pistol toward an ABC American television crew at the Beirut International Airport after the hijackers took control of the jet and held passengers hostage.

agreement made with groups acting outside of accepted convention.

There are also terrorists acting in their own behalf. These groups are in the shadows and are difficult to identify. There will be no settlement of grievance because there is no grievance put forth other than broad ideological demands which call for a government to dissolve itself. In many instances the attempts of these groups to disrupt travel, trade, and institution maintenance result in the indiscriminate slaughter of uninvolved citizenry. In a real sense, they attempt to spread terror. Airliners are bombed, travel terminals are bombed, shopping areas are bombed, automobiles and trucks are loaded with explosives and set off in crowded streets, killing friend and foe alike. Places of worship are invaded and the congregants killed, all to the purpose of creating a sense of unease and dissatisfaction with the government in power.

The governments involved may react in several ways. They may try to cope with the situation without changing the style of their law enforcement. If they are able to control the situation in this manner, they (the government) will win. If the government response is too heavy, the people will find its manner repressive and the terrorists may gain followers.

SUMMARY

International relations deals with interaction between nations or states sharing no common law or constitution or, in most cases, values. National groups often grow larger in size due to population growth, or for economic reasons such as colonialism or imperialism, or for political reasons. World organizations such as the League of Nations and the United Nations have not become true world governments because of their lack of actual power. Regional alliances, both military and economic, seem to be the base for future national entities.

Nations have expectations or goals, prime among which is survival, followed by prestige among nations, and maintenance of a particular ideology. The relative position of nations is largely determined by the variables of geography, wealth, and demography.

Major groups of nations have particular points of view. At present the attitudes of the United States and the Soviet Union are of utmost importance. We seem to be in a period of change, with a growing liberalism in the Soviet area and a corresponding conservatism in the United States. These attitude changes are only relative to former positions, and both nations would have to change considerably if they are in any way to mirror each other. The Third World presents a problem for both the Soviet and American camps. There is little that can be done to alter the situation of poverty that exists in these areas. The threats of fanaticism and nativism will manifest themselves in the near future.

Nations deal with each other through diplomatic means, and when that fails we may have war. Diplomacy and war, along with trade and communication, are understood conventions that exist between nations. These customs are called international law. International law exists only at the whim of the participating states. As such, power may make law. The law exists only if the states agree that it exists.

SPECIAL TOPIC

The Recent Middle East:
Some Lessons in International Relations

In the late fall of 1986, the United States was treated to the beginnings of Irangate. In effect, contrary to established policy and the will of Congress, the Reagan administration transferred military equipment to Iran for a sum in excess of cost, with the difference being forwarded to the Contras fighting the Nicaraguan government. This last transfer was also in violation of the law of the land. The violations of United States law, if they occurred, are not the subject of this discussion. Instead we will focus on the aims of the activities and benefits sought for the involved nations.

A brief background look will show that it has been policy for Western countries over the years to keep the Soviet Union from gaining a warm-water port. This is a term not heard in recent years, but when sea power was more important to the nations of the world, it appeared with regularity in history books and diplomatic pouches. The Panama Canal was built after a Colombian revolution and the formation of a country (Panama) by the United States. The Suez Canal was built and controlled by the French, with English involvement. The need to control various islands as coaling stations also led to national action and reaction.

The need to keep Russia bottled up had the French and the English backing the Turks in the Crimean War ("Charge of the Light Brigade," Florence Nightingale, etc.). The English split Afghanistan off from Iran in the last century to provide a buffer between Russia and India. The English assumed nominal control of Iran when the defeat of Turkey in World War I left a power vacuum. England controlled the Iranian oil fields and access to the Persian Gulf until the United States replaced them well after World War II. For a time, the Soviets controlled

a portion of Iran, and local nationalists made things sticky, but eventually the Shah was in place and things settled down for a time.

Meanwhile, in Asia, the British saw to it that the Japanese navy was ready to blast the Russians in the Russo-Japanese War (1904–5). As a result of this war, the Russians lost Port Arthur, Korea, and the southern half of Sakhalin Island. The Japanese lost these and more when the Soviets moved in at the end of World War II.

Back to the present in the middle east: the cast of nations includes Israel, still in a state of war with most of the Arab world (and a good many Muslim non-Arab states) and having suffered the loss of her chief friend in the area with the fall of the Shah of Iran. The present regime has been decidedly unfriendly toward Israel. Iran is at war with Iraq and has been under an arms embargo by most Western states including the United States. The Iran-Iraq war has been going on for years with little hint of an ending. From time to time one side or the other gains an advantage, but this is neutralized by outside action. When Iraq was on the verge of producing atomic weapons, the Israelis were somehow able to bomb the installation out of existence. It is difficult to imagine this raid taking place without the help of the Saudis and Jordan, both of which have been aiding Iraq in opposition to Iran, and both of whom have been at war with Israel since 1948.

The United States has been currying favor with Iraq, yet shipped parts and missiles to Iran. We do not want to force Iran to seek help from the Soviet Union. Yet these were the same people that held our diplomats prisoner in violation of international law. These were also the people who had been involved in the killing of servicemen in Lebanon, and held other Western civilians, including a number of Americans, hostage for long periods of time. The shipping of arms to Iran involved the Saudis, Israelis, Spanish, and the United States, each for their own reasons.

The ongoing war between Iraq and Iran is keeping large amounts of oil off the world market, and, as such, keeps the price of oil from falling to new depths. The same war keeps both Iran and Iraq from concentrating their attentions upon Israel. Saudi Arabia and other relatively weak countries are spared the attention of the fundamentalist Shiites, and the strong military power built by the Shah is no longer a threat to upset the power balance of the region.

Meanwhile, in Afghanistan, originally part of Iran, the Soviet Union is involved in a bloody, expensive, and futile war of attrition. China and the United States, among others, have been supplying war materials, while Pakistan offers a safe base of operations. The United States would prefer that this war continue and act as a thorn in the side of the Soviet Union, breeding the same discontent there as did our long-term problem in Vietnam. The war provides the United States with an opportunity to shine in the eyes of the Third World by supplying arms. On the other side, the Soviets suffer the indignity of not being able to win, as well as taking on the mantle of international heavy by leaning on the citizens of Afghanistan.

Israel, now at peace with Egypt, can share the bounty of tourism with that nation. On her northern border sit a pair of problems, Syria and Lebanon. At this point there seems little chance that the near future will bring peace between Syria and Israel. At least this relationship seems clear. Within Lebanon, relationships are somewhat muddled. Israel and the Lebanese Christians have had a close military relationship. When Syria shifted its support to the Shiite Muslims, they (the Shiites) fought the Christians, Israelis, and, most recently, the Palestine Liberation Organization. The mortal enemy of the P.L.O. is, of course, Israel. The Lebanese Christians began aiding the P.L.O. in their fight against the Shiites (in return for money). From the Christian point of view, it is better to have the P.L.O. and the Shiites fighting each other, rather than fighting the Christians. The Israelis were somewhat put out about this shift at the time of this writing, but it is not inconceivable that the P.L.O. and the Israelis could find a common ground against the Shiites.

Meanwhile, Jordan and Israel, though still technically at war, have had a relatively open trade policy over the Jordan River. The two countries share administration of some facets of the occupied West Bank government.

The picture is further complicated by the presence of United Nations troops at various points, outgunned and outmanned, to keep the peace.

We will not deal with the trouble between Libya and Egypt, Libya and Chad, or the Sudan, Ethiopia, the Suez Canal, or the various areas that the Western nations feel must be free for navigation, or any of the many other wars, famines, disputes, or other difficulties in the area. Let us simply state that this is an area that utilizes much of what international relations has to offer.

SELF-TEST QUESTIONS

Determine whether each of the following statements is either true or false.

1. Nations must be of a recognized size before other nations see them as independent.
2. International relations are codified and the terms of these relationships are binding on all participating nations.
3. Nativism is a term that refers to native or underdeveloped nations.
4. The United Nations was once called the League of Nations.
5. The United Nations is a true world government.
6. Survival is a basic national goal.
7. Third World nations are usually poor, underdeveloped, and overpopulated.

8. The United States once landed troops in Russia to help the czar against the Reds.
9. International law has only the force that the participating nations allow.
10. War is a tool of International relations.

ANSWERS TO SELF-TEST QUESTIONS

1. false
2. false
3. false
4. false
5. false

6. true
7. true
8. true
9. true
10. true

NOTES

1. A.P., Washington, Aug. 28, 1986.
2. A.B.C. News, May 14, 1987.
3. Deming, New Mexico, Oct. 11, 1885.
4. Paul Scott, *The Jewel in the Crown* (New York: Avon Books, 1979).
5. Charles O. Learsche, Jr. and Abdul A. Said, *Concepts of International Politics*, 2d ed. (Englewood Cliffs, N.J.: Prentice-Hall 1970).
6. Eric R. Emmet, *Handbook of Logic* (Totowa, N.J.: Littlefield, Adams, 1967).

SUGGESTED READINGS

Aron, Raymond. *Peace and War.* Garden City, N.Y.: Doubleday, 1977.

Barney, Gerald O. *The Global 2000 Report to the President of the U.S.* Elmsford, N.Y.: Pergamon Press, 1980.

George, Susan. *How the Other Half Dies.* Harmondsworth, England: Penguin Books, 1975.

Herz, John. *International Politics in the Atomic Age.* New York: Columbia University Press, 1959.

Kennan, George F. *Russia and the West Under Lenin and Stalin.* Boston: Little Brown, 1960.

Appendix: THE CONSTITUTION OF THE UNITED STATES OF AMERICA

Preamble

We the People of the United States, in Order to form a more perfect Union, establish Justice, insure domestic Tranquility, provide for the common defense, promote the general Welfare, and secure the Blessings of Liberty to ourselves and our Posterity, do ordain and establish this Constitution for the United States of America.

Article I

Section 1. All legislative Powers herein granted shall be vested in a Congress of the United States, which shall consist of a Senate and House of Representatives.

Section 2. (1) The House of Representatives shall be composed of Members chosen every second Year by the People of the several States, and the Electors in each State shall have the Qualifications requisite for Electors of the most numerous Branch of the State Legislature.

(2) No Person shall be a Representative who shall not have attained to the Age of twenty five Years, and been seven Years a Citizen of the United States, and who shall not, when elected, be an Inhabitant of that State in which he shall be chosen.

(3) Representatives and direct Taxes shall be apportioned among the several States which may be included within this Union, according to their respective Numbers, which shall be determined by adding to the whole Number of free Persons, including those bound to Service for a Term of Years, and excluding Indians not taxed, three fifths of all other Persons. The actual Enumeration shall be made within three Years after the first Meeting of the Congress of the United States, and within every subsequent Term of ten Years, in such Manner as they shall by Law direct. The Number of Representatives shall not exceed one for every thirty Thousand, but each State shall have at Least one Representative; and until such enumeration shall be made, the State of New Hampshire shall be entitled to chuse three, Massachusetts eight, Rhode Island and Providence Plantations one, Connecticut five, New York six, New Jersey four, Pennsylvania eight, Delaware one, Maryland six, Virginia ten, North Carolina five, South Carolina five, and Georgia three.

(4) When vacancies happen in the Representation from any State, the Executive Authority thereof shall issue Writs of Election to fill such Vacancies.

(5) The House of Representatives shall chuse their Speaker and other Officers; and shall have the sole Power of Impeachment.

Section 3. (1) The Senate of the United States shall be composed of two Senators from each State, chosen by the Legislature thereof, for six Years; and each Senator shall have one Vote.

(2) Immediately after they shall be assembled in Consequence of the first Election, they shall be divided as equally as may be into three Classes. The Seats of the Senators of the first Class shall be vacated at the Expiration of the Second Year, of the second Class at the Expiration of the fourth Year, and of the third Class at the Expiration of the sixth Year, so that one third may be chosen every second Year; and if Vacancies happen by Resignation, or otherwise, during the Recess of the Legislature of any State, the Executive thereof may make temporary Appointments until the next Meeting of the Legislature, which shall then fill such Vacancies.

(3) No Person shall be a Senator who shall not have attained to the Age of thirty Years, and been nine Years a Citizen of the United States, and who shall not, when elected, be an Inhabitant of that State for which he shall be chosen.

(4) The Vice President of the United States shall be President of the Senate, but shall have no Vote, unless they be equally divided.

(5) The Senate shall chuse their other Officers, and also a President pro tempore, in the Absence of the Vice President, or when he shall exercise the Office of President of the United States.

(6) The Senate shall have the sole Power to try all Impeachments. When sitting for that Purpose, they shall be on Oath or Affirmation. When the President of the United States is tried, the Chief Justice shall preside: And no Person shall be convicted without the Concurrence of two thirds of the Members present.

(7) Judgment in Cases of Impeachment shall not extend further than to removal from Office, and disqualification to hold and enjoy any Office of honor, Trust, or Profit under the United States: but the Party convicted shall nevertheless be liable and subject to Indictment, Trial, Judgment, and Punishment, according to Law.

Section 4. (1) The Times, Places and Manner of holding Elections for Senators and Representatives, shall be prescribed in each State by the Legislature thereof; but the Congress may at any time by Law make or alter such Regulations, except as to the Places of chusing Senators.

(2) The Congress shall assemble at least once in every Year, and such Meeting shall be on the first Monday in December, unless they shall by Law appoint a different Day.

Section 5. (1) Each House shall be the Judge of the Elections, Returns, and Qualifications of its own Members, and a Majority of each shall constitute a Quorum to do Business; but a smaller Number may adjourn from day to day, and may be authorized to compel the Attendance of absent Members, in such Manner, and under such Penalties as each House may provide.

(2) Each House may determine the Rules of its Proceedings, punish its Members for disorderly Behavior, and, with the Concurrence of two thirds, expel a Member.

(3) Each House shall keep a Journal of its Proceedings, and from time to time publish the same, excepting such Parts as may in their Judgment require Secrecy; and the Yeas and Nays of the Members of either House on any question shall, at the Desire of one fifth of those Present, be entered on the Journal.

(4) Neither House, during the Session of Congress, shall, without the Consent of the other, adjourn for more than three days, nor to any other Place than that in which the two Houses shall be sitting.

Section 6. (1) The Senators and Representatives shall receive a Compensation for their Services, to be ascertained by Law, and paid out of the Treasury of the United States. They shall in all Cases, except Treason, Felony and Breach of the Peace, be privileged from Arrest during their Attendance at the Session of their respective Houses, and in going to and returning from the same; and for any Speech or Debate in either House, they shall not be questioned in any other Place.

(2) No Senator or Representative shall, during the Time for which he was elected, be appointed to any civil Office under the Authority of the United States, which shall have been created, or the Emoluments whereof shall have been increased during such time; and no Person holding any Office under the United States, shall be a Member of either House during his Continuance in Office.

Section 7. (1) All Bills for raising Revenue shall originate in the House of Representatives; but the Senate may propose or concur with Amendments as on other Bills.

(2) Every Bill which shall have passed the House of Representatives and the Senate, shall, before it become a Law, be presented to the President of the United States; If he approve he shall sign it, but if not he shall return it, with his Objections to the House in which it shall have originated, who shall enter the Objections at large on their Journal, and proceed to reconsider it. If after such Reconsideration two thirds of that House shall agree to pass the Bill, it shall be sent together with the Objections, to the other House, by which it shall likewise be reconsidered, and if approved by two thirds of that House, it shall become a Law. But in all such Cases the Votes of both Houses shall be determined by yeas and Nays, and the Names of the Persons voting for and against the Bill shall be entered on the Journal of each House respectively. If any Bill shall not be returned by the President within ten Days (Sundays excepted) after it shall have been presented to him, the Same shall be a Law, in like Manner as if he had signed it, unless the Congress by their Adjournment prevent its Return in which Case it shall not be a Law.

(3) Every Order, Resolution, or Vote, to Which the Concurrence of the Senate and House of Representatives may be necessary (except on a question of Adjournment) shall be presented to the President of the United States; and before the Same shall take

Effect, shall be approved by him, or being disapproved by him, shall be repassed by two thirds of the Senate and House of Representatives, according to the Rules and Limitations prescribed in the Case of a Bill.

Section 8. (1) The Congress shall have Power To lay and collect Taxes, Duties, Imposts and Excises, to pay the Debts and provide for the common Defense and general Welfare of the United States; but all Duties, Imposts and Excises shall be uniform throughout the United States;

(2) To borrow money on the credit of the United States;

(3) To regulate Commerce with foreign Nations, and among the several States, and with the Indian Tribes;

(4) To establish an uniform Rule of Naturalization, and uniform Laws on the subject of Bankruptcies throughout the United States;

(5) To coin Money, regulate the Value thereof, and of foreign Coin, and fix the Standard of Weights and Measures;

(6) To provide for the Punishment of counterfeiting the Securities and current Coin of the United States;

(7) To Establish Post Offices and Post Roads;

(8) To promote the Progress of Science and useful Arts, by securing for limited Times to Authors and Inventors the exclusive Right to their respective Writings and Discoveries;

(9) To constitute Tribunals inferior to the supreme Court;

(10) To define and punish Piracies and Felonies committed on the high Seas, and Offenses against the Law of Nations;

(11) To declare War, grant Letters of Marque and Reprisal, and make Rules concerning Captures on Land and Water;

(12) To raise and support Armies, but no Appropriation of Money to that Use shall be for a longer Term than two Years;

(13) To provide and maintain a Navy;

(14) To make Rules for the Government and Regulation of the land and naval Forces;

(15) To provide for calling forth the Militia to execute the Laws of the Union, suppress Insurrections and repel Invasions;

(16) To provide for organizing, arming, and disciplining, the Militia, and for governing such Part of them as may be employed in the Service of the United States, reserving to the States respectively, the Appointment of the Officers, and the Authority of training the Militia according to the discipline prescribed by Congress;

(17) To exercise exclusive Legislation in all Cases whatsoever, over such District (not exceeding ten Miles square) as may, by Cession of particular States, and the Acceptance of Congress, become the Seat of the Government of the United States, and to exercise like Authority over all Places purchased by the Consent of the Legislature of the State in which the Same shall be, for the Erection of Forts, Magazines, Arsenals, dock-Yards, and other needful Buildings;—And

(18) To make all Laws which shall be necessary and proper for carrying into Execution the foregoing Powers, and all other Powers vested by this Constitution in the Government of the United States, or in any Department or Officer thereof.

Section 9.   (1) The Migration or Importation of Such Persons as any of the States now existing shall think proper to admit, shall not be prohibited by the Congress prior to the Year one thousand eight hundred and eight, but a Tax or duty may be imposed on such Importation, not exceeding ten dollars for each Person.

(2) The privilege of the Writ of Habeas Corpus shall not be suspended, unless when in Cases of Rebellion or Invasion the public Safety may require it.

(3) No Bill of Attainder or ex post facto Law shall be passed.

(4) No Capitation, or other direct, Tax shall be laid, unless in Proportion to the Census or Enumeration herein before directed to be taken.

(5) No Tax or Duty shall be laid on Articles exported from any State.

(6) No Preference shall be given by any Regulation of Commerce or Revenue to the Ports of one State over those of another: nor shall Vessels bound to, or from, one State be obliged to enter, clear, or pay Duties in another.

(7) No money shall be drawn from the Treasury, but in Consequence of Appropriations made by Law; and a regular Statement and Account of the Receipts and Expenditures of all public Money shall be published from time to time.

(8) No Title of Nobility shall be granted by the United States: And no Person holding any Office of Profit or Trust under them, shall, without the Consent of the Congress, accept of any present, Emolument, Office, or Title, of any kind whatever, from any King, Prince, or foreign State.

Section 10.   (1) No State shall enter into any Treaty, Alliance, or Confederation; grant Letters of Marque and Reprisal; coin Money; emit Bills of Credit; make any Thing but gold and silver Coin a Tender in Payment of Debts; pass any Bill of Attainder, ex post facto Law, or Law impairing the Obligation of Contracts, or grant any Title of Nobility.

(2) No State shall, without the Consent of the Congress, lay any Imposts or Duties on Imports or Exports, except what may be absolutely necessary for executing it's inspection Laws: and the net Produce of all Duties and Imposts, laid by any State on Imports or Exports, shall be for the Use of the Treasury of the United States; and all such Laws shall be subject to the Revision and Controul of the Congress.

(3) No State shall, without the Consent of Congress, lay any Duty of Tonnage, keep Troops, or Ships of War in time of Peace, enter into any Agreement or Compact with another State, or with

a foreign Power, or engage in War, unless actually invaded, or in such imminent Danger as will not admit of delay.

Article II   **Section 1.**   (1) The executive Power shall be vested in a President of the United States of America. He shall hold his Office during the Term of four Years, and, together with the Vice President, chosen for the same Term, be elected, as follows:

(2) Each State shall appoint, in such Manner as the Legislature thereof may direct, a Number of Electors, equal to the whole Number of Senators and Representatives to which the State may be entitled in the Congress; but no Senator or Representative, or Person holding an Office of Trust or Profit under the United States, shall be appointed an Elector.

(3) The Electors shall meet in their respective States, and vote by Ballot for two Persons, of whom one at least shall not be an Inhabitant of the same State with themselves. And they shall make a List of all the Persons voted for, and of the Number of Votes for each; which List they shall sign and certify, and transmit sealed to the Seat of the Government of the United States, directed to the President of the Senate. The President of the Senate shall, in the Presence of the Senate and House of Representatives, open all the Certificates, and the Votes shall then be counted. The Person having the greatest Number of Votes shall be the President, if such Number be a Majority of the whole Number of Electors appointed; and if there be more than one who have such Majority, and have an equal Number of Votes, then the House of Representatives shall immediately chuse by Ballot one of them for President; and if no Person have a Majority, then from the five highest on the List the said House shall in like Manner chuse the President. But in chusing the President, the Votes shall be taken by States the Representation from each State having one Vote; A quorum for this Purpose shall consist of a Member or Members from two thirds of the States, and a Majority of all the States shall be necessary to a Choice. In every Case, after the Choice of the President, the Person having the greater Number of Votes of the Electors shall be the Vice President. But if there should remain two or more who have equal Votes, the Senate shall chuse from them by Ballot the Vice President.

(4) The Congress may determine the Time of chusing the Electors, and the Day on which they shall give their Votes; which Day shall be the same throughout the United States.

(5) No person except a natural born Citizen, or a Citizen of the United States, at the time of the Adoption of this Constitution, shall be eligible to the Office of President; neither shall any Person be eligible to that Office who shall not have attained to the Age of thirty five Years, and been fourteen Years a Resident within the United States.

(6) In case of the removal of the President from Office, or of his Death, Resignation or Inability to discharge the Powers and Duties

of the said Office, the Same shall devolve on the Vice President, and the Congress may by Law provide for the Case of Removal, Death, Resignation or Inability, both of the President and Vice President, declaring what Officer shall then act as President, and such Officer shall act accordingly, until the Disability be removed, or a President shall be elected.

(7) The President shall, at stated Times, receive for his Services, a Compensation, which shall neither be increased nor diminished during the Period for which he shall have been elected, and he shall not receive within that Period any other Emolument from the United States, or any of them.

(8) Before he enter on the Execution of his Office, he shall take the following Oath or Affirmation: "I do solemnly swear (or affirm) that I will faithfully execute the Office of President of the United States, and will to the best of my Ability, preserve, protect and defend the Constitution of the United States."

Section 2. (1) The President shall be Commander in Chief of the Army and Navy of the United States, and of the militia of the several States, when called into the actual Service of the United States; he may require the Opinion, in writing, of the principal Officer in each of the Executive Departments, upon any Subject relating to the Duties of their respective Offices, and he shall have Power to grant Reprieves and Pardons for Offenses against the United States, except in Cases of Impeachment.

(2) He shall have Power, by and with the Advice and Consent of the Senate to make Treaties, provided two thirds of the Senators present concur; and he shall nominate, and by and with the Advice and Consent of the Senate, shall appoint Ambassadors, other public Ministers and Consuls, Judges of the supreme Court, and all other Officers of the United States, whose Appointments are not herein otherwise provided for, and which shall be established by Law; but the Congress may by Law vest the Appointment of such inferior Officers, as they think proper, in the President alone, in the Courts of Law, or in the Heads of Departments.

(3) The President shall have Power to fill up all Vacancies that may happen during the Recess of the Senate, by granting Commissions which shall expire at the End of their next Session.

Section 3. He shall from time to time give to the Congress Information of the State of the Union, and recommend to their Consideration such Measures as he shall judge necessary and expedient; he may, on extraordinary Occasions, convene both Houses, or either of them, and in Case of Disagreement between them, with Respect to the Time of Adjournment, he may adjourn them to such Time as he shall think proper; he shall receive Ambassadors and other public Ministers; he shall take Care that the Laws be faithfully executed, and shall Commission all the Officers of the United States.

Section 4.   The President, Vice President and all civil Officers of the United States, shall be removed from Office on Impeachment for, and Conviction of, Treason, Bribery, or other high Crimes and Misdemeanors.

Article III   **Section 1.**   The judicial Power of the United States, shall be vested in one supreme Court, and in such inferior Courts as the Congress may from time to time ordain and establish. The Judges, both of the supreme and inferior Courts, shall hold their Offices during good Behaviour, and shall, at stated Times, receive for their Services a Compensation, which shall not be diminished during their Continuance in Office.

Section 2.   (1) The judicial Power shall extend to all Cases, in Law and Equity, arising under this Constitution, the Laws of the United States, and Treaties made, or which shall be made, under their Authority;—to all Cases affecting Ambassadors, other public Ministers and Consuls;—to all Cases of admiralty and maritime Jurisdiction;—to Controversies to which the United States shall be a Party;—to Controversies between two or more States;—between a State and Citizens of another State;—between Citizens of different States;—between Citizens of the same State claiming Lands under the Grants of different States, and between a State, or the Citizens thereof, and foreign States, Citizens or Subjects.

(2) In all Cases affecting Ambassadors, other public Ministers and Consuls, and those in which a State shall be a Party, the supreme Court shall have original Jurisdiction. In all the other Cases before mentioned, the supreme Court shall have appellate Jurisdiction, both as to Law and Fact, with such Exceptions, and under such Regulations as the Congress shall make.

(3) The trial of all Crimes, except in Cases of Impeachment, shall be by Jury; and such Trial shall be held in the State where the said Crimes shall have been committed; but when not committed within any State, the Trial shall be at such Place or Places as the Congress may by Law have directed.

Section 3.   (1) Treason against the United States, shall consist only in levying War against them, or, in adhering to their Enemies, giving them Aid and Comfort. No Person shall be convicted of Treason unless on the Testimony of two Witnesses to the same overt Act, or on Confession in open Court.

(2) The Congress shall have Power to declare the Punishment of Treason, but no Attainder of Treason shall work Corruption of Blood, or Forfeiture except during the Life of the Person attained.

Article IV   **Section 1.**   Full Faith and Credit shall be given in each State to the public Acts, Records, and judicial Proceedings of every other State. And the Congress may by general Laws prescribe the Manner in which such Acts, Records and Proceedings shall be proved, and the Effect thereof.

Section 2. (1) The Citizens of each State shall be entitled to all Privileges and Immunities of Citizens in the several States.

(2) A Person charged in any State with Treason, Felony, or other Crime, who shall flee from Justice, and be found in another State, shall on demand of the executive Authority of the State from which he fled, be delivered up, to be removed to the State having Jurisdiction of the Crime.

(3) No Person held to Service or Labour in one State, under the Laws thereof, escaping into another, shall, in Consequence of any Law or Regulation therein, be discharged from such Service or Labour, but shall be delivered up on Claim of the Party to whom such Service or Labour may be due.

Section 3. (1) New States may be admitted by the Congress into this Union; but no new State shall be formed or erected within the Jurisdiction of any other State; nor any State be formed by the Junction of two or more States, or Parts of States, without the Consent of the Legislatures of the States concerned as well as of the Congress.

(2) The Congress shall have Power to dispose of and make all needful Rules and Regulations respecting the Territory or other Property belonging to the United States; and nothing in this Constitution shall be so construed as to Prejudice any Claims of the United States, or of any particular State.

Section 4. The United States shall guarantee to every State in this Union a Republican Form of Government, and shall protect each of them against Invasion; and on Application of the Legislature, or of the Executive (when the Legislature cannot be convened) against domestic Violence.

Article V The Congress, whenever two thirds of both Houses shall deem it necessary, shall propose Amendments to this Constitution, or, on the Application of the Legislatures of two thirds of the several States, shall call a Convention for proposing Amendments, which, in either Case, shall be valid to all Intents and Purposes, as part of this Constitution, when ratified by the Legislatures of three fourths of the several States, or by Conventions in three fourths thereof, as the one or the other Mode of Ratification may be proposed by the Congress; Provided that no Amendment which may be made prior to the Year One thousand eight hundred and eight shall in any Manner affect the first and fourth Clauses in the Ninth Section of the First Article, and that no State, without its Consent, shall be deprived of its equal Suffrage in the Senate.

Article VI (1) All Debts contracted and Engagements entered into, before the Adoption of this Constitution shall be as valid against the United States under this Constitution, as under the Confederation.

(2) This Constitution, and the Laws of the United States which shall be made in Pursuance thereof; and all Treaties made, or

which shall be made, under the Authority of the United States, shall be the supreme Law of the Land; and the Judges in every State shall be bound thereby, any Thing in the Constitution or Laws of any State to the Contrary notwithstanding.

(3) The Senators and Representatives before mentioned, and the Members of the several State Legislatures, and all executive and judicial Officers, both of the United States and of the several States, shall be bound by Oath or Affirmation, to support this Constitution; but no religious Test shall ever be required as a Qualification to any Office or public Trust under the United states.

Article VII   The Ratification of the Conventions of nine States shall be sufficient for the Establishment of this Constitution between the States so ratifying the Same.

ADDITIONAL ARTICLES AND AMENDMENTS

Articles in addition to, and amendment of, the Constitution of the United States of America, proposed by Congress, and ratified by the legislatures of the several states pursuant to the fifth article of the original Constitution.

Amendment I (1791)   Congress shall make no law respecting an establishment of religion, or prohibiting the free exercise thereof; or abridging the freedom of speech, or of the press; or the right of the people peaceably to assemble, and to petition the Government for a redress of grievances.

Amendment II (1791)   A well regulated Militia, being necessary to the security of a free State, the right of the people to keep and bear Arms, shall not be infringed.

Amendment III (1791)   No Soldier shall, in time of peace be quartered in any house, without the consent of the Owner, nor in time of war, but in a manner to be prescribed by law.

Amendment IV (1791)   The right of the people to be secure in their persons, houses, papers, and effects, against unreasonable searches and seizures, shall not be violated, and no Warrants shall issue, but upon probable cause, supported by Oath or affirmation, and particularly describing the place to be searched, and the persons or things to be seized.

Amendment V (1791)   No person shall be held to answer for a capital, or otherwise infamous crime, unless on a presentment or indictment of a Grand Jury, except in cases arising in the land or naval forces, or in the Militia, when in actual service in time of War or public danger; nor shall any person be subject for the same offence to be twice put in jeopardy of life or limb; nor shall be compelled in any criminal case to be a witness against himself, nor be deprived of life, liberty, or property, without due process of law; nor shall private property be taken for public use, without just compensation.

Amendment VI (1791) In all criminal prosecutions, the accused shall enjoy the right to a speedy and public trial, by an impartial jury of the State and district wherein the crime shall have been committed, which district shall have been previously ascertained by law, and to be informed of the nature and cause of the accusation; to be confronted with the witnesses against him; to have compulsory process for obtaining witnesses in his favor, and to have the Assistance of Counsel for his defence.

Amendment VII (1791) In Suits at common law, where the value in controversy shall exceed twenty dollars, the right of trial by jury shall be preserved, and no fact tried by jury, shall be otherwise re-examined in any Court of the United States, than according to the rules of the common law.

Amendment VIII (1791) Excessive bail shall not be required, nor excessive fines imposed, nor cruel and unusual punishments inflicted.

Amendment IX (1791) The enumeration in the Constitution, of certain rights, shall not be construed to deny or disparage others retained by the people.

Amendment X (1791) The powers not delegated to the United States by the Constitution, nor prohibited by it to the States, are reserved to the States respectively, or to the people.

Amendment XI (1798) The Judicial power of the United States shall not be construed to extend to any suit in law or equity, commenced or prosecuted against one of the United States by Citizens of another State, or by Citizens or Subjects of any Foreign State.

Amendment XII (1804) The Electors shall meet in their respective states and vote by ballot for President and Vice-President, one of whom, at least, shall not be an inhabitant of the same state with themselves; they shall name in their ballots the person voted for as President, and in distinct ballots the person voted for as Vice-President, and they shall make distinct lists of all persons voted for as President, and of all persons voted for as Vice-President, and of the number of votes for each, which lists they shall sign and certify, and transmit sealed to the seat of the government of the United States, directed to the President of the Senate;—The President of the Senate shall, in the presence of the Senate and House of Representatives, open all the certificates and the votes shall then be counted;—The person having the greatest number of votes for President, shall be the President, if such number be a majority of the whole number of Electors appointed; and if no person have such majority, then from the persons having the highest numbers not exceeding three on the list of those voted for as President, the House of Representatives shall choose immediately, by ballot, the President. But in choosing the President, the votes shall be taken by states, the representation from each state having one vote; a quorum for this purpose shall consist of a member or members from two-thirds of the states, and a majority of all the states shall be necessary to a choice. And if the House of Representatives shall not choose a President whenever the right of choice shall devolve upon them before the fourth day of March next following, then the Vice-President shall act as President, as in the case of the death or other constitutional disability of the President.—The person having the greatest number of votes as Vice-President, shall be the Vice-President, if such number be a majority of the whole number of Electors appointed, and if no person have a majority, then from the two highest numbers on the list, the Senate shall choose the Vice-President; a quorum for the purpose shall consist of two-thirds of the whole number of Senators, and a majority of the whole number shall be necessary to a choice. But no person constitutionally ineligible to the office of President shall be eligible to that of Vice-President of the United States.

Amendment XIII (1865)

Section 1. Neither slavery nor involuntary servitude, except as a punishment for crime whereof the party shall have been duly convicted, shall exist within the United States, or any place subject to their jurisdiction.

Section 2. Congress shall have power to enforce this article by appropriate legislation.

Amendment XIV (1868)

Section 1. All persons born or naturalized in the United States, and subject to the jurisdiction thereof, are citizens of the United States and of the State wherein they reside. No State shall make or enforce any law which shall abridge the privileges or immunities of citizens of the United States; nor shall any State deprive any person of life, liberty, or property, without due process of law; nor deny to any person within its jurisdiction the equal protection of the laws.

Section 2. Representatives shall be apportioned among the several States according to their respective numbers, counting the whole number of persons in each State, excluding Indians not taxed. But when the right to vote at any election for the choice of electors for President and Vice President of the United States, Representatives in Congress, the Executive and Judicial officers of a state, or the members of the Legislature thereof, is denied to any of the male inhabitants of such State, being twenty-one years of age, and citizens of the United States, or in any way abridged, except for participation in rebellion, or other crime, the basis of representation therein shall be reduced in the proportion which the number of such male citizens shall bear to the whole number of male citizens twenty-one years of age in such State.

Section 3. No person shall be a Senator or Representative in Congress, or elector of President and Vice President, or hold any office, civil or military, under the United States, or under any State, who having previously taken an oath, as a member of Congress, or as an officer of the United States, or as a member of any State legislature, or as an executive or judicial officer of any State, to support the Constitution of the United States, shall have engaged in insurrection or rebellion against the same, or given aid or comfort to the enemies thereof. But Congress may by a vote of two-thirds of each House, remove such disability.

Section 4. The validity of the public debt of the United States, authorized by law, including debts incurred for payment of pensions and bounties for services in suppressing insurrection or rebellion, shall not be questioned. But neither the United States nor any State shall assume or pay any debt or obligation incurred in aid of insurrection or rebellion against the United States, or any claim for the loss or emancipation of any slave; but all such debts, obligations and claims shall be held illegal and void.

Section 5. The Congress shall have power to enforce, by appropriate legislation, the provisions of this article.

Amendment XV (1870) **Section 1.** The right of citizens of the United States to vote shall not be denied or abridged by the United States or by any State on account of race, color, or previous condition of servitude.

Section 2. The Congress shall have power to enforce this article by appropriate legislation.

Amendment XVI (1913) The Congress shall have power to lay and collect taxes on incomes, from whatever source derived, without apportionment among the several States, and without regard to any census or enumeration.

Amendment XVII (1913) (1) The Senate of the United States shall be composed of two Senators from each State, elected by the people thereof, for six years; and each Senator shall have one vote. The electors in each State shall have the qualifications requisite for electors of the most numerous branch of the State legislatures.

(2) When vacancies happen in the representation of any State in the Senate, the executive authority of such State shall issue writs of election to fill such vacancies: Provided, That the legislature of any State may empower the executive thereof to make temporary appointments until the people fill the vacancies by election as the legislature may direct.

(3) This amendment shall not be so construed as to affect the election or term of any Senator chosen before it becomes valid as part of the Constitution.

Amendment XVIII (1919) **Section 1.** After one year from the ratification of this article the manufacture, sale, or transportation of intoxicating liquors within, the importation thereof into, or the exportation thereof from the United States and all territory subject to the jurisdiction thereof for beverage purposes is hereby prohibited.

Section 2.   The Congress and the several States shall have concurrent power to enforce this article by appropriate legislation.

Section 3.   This article shall be inoperative unless it shall have been ratified as an amendment to the Constitution by the legislatures of the several States, as provided in the Constitution, within seven years from the date of the submission hereof to the States by the Congress.

Amendment XIX (1920)   (1) The right of citizens of the United States to vote shall not be denied or abridged by the United States or by any State on account of sex.

(2) Congress shall have power to enforce this article by appropriate legislation.

Amendment XX (1933)   **Section 1.**   The terms of the President and Vice President shall end at noon on the 20th day of January, and the terms of Senators and Representatives at noon on the 3rd day of January, of the years in which such terms would have ended if this article had not been ratified; and the terms of their successors shall then begin.

Section 2.   The Congress shall assemble at least once in every year, and such meeting shall begin at noon on the 3rd day of January, unless they shall by law appoint a different day.

Section 3.   If, at the time fixed for the beginning of the term of the President, the President elect shall have died, the Vice President elect shall become President. If the President shall not have been chosen before the time fixed for the beginning of his term, or if the President elect shall have failed to qualify, then the Vice President elect shall act as President until a President shall have qualified; and the Congress may by law provide for the case wherein neither a President elect nor a Vice President elect shall have qualified, declaring who shall then act as President, or the manner in which one who is to act shall be selected, and such person shall act accordingly until a President or Vice President shall have qualified.

Section 4.   The Congress may by law provide for the case of the death of any of the persons from whom the House of Representatives may choose a President whenever the right of choice shall have devolved upon them, and for the case of the death of any of the persons from whom the Senate may choose a Vice President whenever the right of choice shall have devolved upon them.

Section 5.   Sections 1 and 2 shall take effect on the 15th day of October following the ratification of this article.

Section 6.   This article shall be inoperative unless it shall have been ratified as an amendment to the Constitution by the legislatures of three-fourths of the several States within seven years from the date of its submission.

Amendment XXI (1933)   **Section 1.**   The eighteenth article of amendment to the Constitution of the United States is hereby repealed.

Section 2.   The transportation or importation into any State, Territory, or possession of the United States for delivery or use therein of intoxicating liquors, in violation of the laws thereof, is hereby prohibited.

Section 3.   This article shall be inoperative unless it shall have been ratified as an amendment to the Constitution by conventions in the several States, as provided in the Constitution, within seven years from the date of the submission hereof to the States by the Congress.

Amendment XXII (1951)   **Section 1.**   No person shall be elected to the office of the President more than twice, and no person who has held the office of President, or acted as President, for more than two years of a term to which some other person was elected President shall be elected to the office of President more than once. But this Article shall not apply to any person holding the office of President when this Article was proposed by the Congress, and shall not prevent any person who may be holding the office of President, or acting as President, during the term within which this Article becomes operative from holding the office of President or acting as President during the remainder of such term.

Section 2.   This article shall be inoperative unless it shall have been ratified as an amendment to the Constitution by the legislatures of three-fourths of the several States within seven years from the date of its submission to the States by the Congress.

Amendment XXIII (1961)   **Section 1.**   The District constituting the seat of Government of the United States shall appoint in such manner as the Congress may direct:
A number of electors of President and Vice President equal to the whole number of Senators and Representatives in Congress to which the District would be entitled if it were a State, but in no event more than the least populous state; they shall be in addition to those appointed by the states, but they shall be considered, for the purposes of the election of President and Vice President, to be electors appointed by a state; and they shall meet in the District and perform such duties as provided by the twelfth article of amendment.

Section 2.   The Congress shall have power to enforce this article by appropriate legislation.

Amendment XXIV (1964)

Section 1. The right of citizens of the United States to vote in any primary or other election for President or Vice President, for electors for President or Vice President, or for Senator or Representative in Congress, shall not be denied or abridged by the United States or any State by reason of failure to pay any poll tax or other tax.

Section 2. The Congress shall have power to enforce this article by appropriate legislation.

Amendment XXV (1967)

Section 1. In case of the removal of the President from office or of his death or resignation, the Vice President shall become President.

Section 2. Whenever there is a vacancy in the office of the Vice President, the President shall nominate a Vice President who shall take office upon confirmation by a majority vote of both Houses of Congress.

Section 3. Whenever the President transmits to the President pro tempore of the Senate and the Speaker of the House of Representatives his written declaration that he is unable to discharge the powers and duties of his office, and until he transmits to them a written declaration to the contrary, such powers and duties shall be discharged by the Vice President as Acting President.

Section 4. Whenever the Vice President and a majority of either the principal officers of the executive departments or of such other body as Congress may by law provide, transmit to the President pro tempore of the Senate and the Speaker of the House of Representatives their written declaration that the President is unable to discharge the powers and duties of his office, the Vice President shall immediately assume the powers and duties of the office as acting President.

Thereafter, when the President transmits to the President pro tempore of the Senate and the Speaker of the House of Representatives his written declaration that no inability exists, he shall resume the powers and duties of his office unless the Vice President and a majority of either the principal officers of the executive department or of such other body as Congress may by law provide, transmit within four days to the President pro tempore of the Senate and the Speaker of the House of Representatives their written declaration and the President is unable to discharge the powers and duties of his office. Thereupon Congress shall decide the issue, assembling within forty-eight hours for that purpose if not in session. If the Congress, within twenty-one days after receipt of the latter written declaration, or, if Congress is not in session, within twenty-one days after Congress is required to assemble, determines by two-thirds vote of both Houses that the President is unable to discharge the powers and duties of his office, the Vice President shall continue to discharge the same as Acting President; otherwise, the President shall resume the powers and duties of his office.

Amendment XXVI (1971)

Section 1. The right of citizens of the United States, who are eighteen years of age or older, to vote shall not be denied or abridged by the United States or by any State on account of age.

Section 2. The Congress shall have power to enforce this article by appropriate legislation.

INDEX